ABOUT THE LAW
sourcebook

LEGAL RESEARCH,

Second Edition

Wesley Gilmer, Jr.

WRITING & ADVOCACY
a sourcebook

anderson publishing co. / law-related studies
cincinnati

Library of Congress Cataloging-in-Publication Data

Gilmer, Wesley.
Legal research, writing & advocacy.

(About the law sourcebook)
Bibliography: p.
Includes index.
1. Legal research—United States. 2. Legal composition. 3. Trial practice—United States. I. Title. II. Title: Legal research, writing, and advocacy. III. Series.
KF240.G53 1986 340'.072073 86-24967
ISBN 0-87084-646-9

Third Printing—June, 1990

CONTENTS

FOREWORD

But, my son, be warned: there is no end of opinions ready to be expressed. Studying them can go on forever, and become very exhausting!

Ecclesiastes 12:12 (The Living Bible).

THE AUTHOR

Wesley Gilmer, Jr., M.S.L.S., J.D., is a member of the Kentucky, Ohio and federal bars, and a professional librarian. From 1952-1967 he practiced law at Danville, Kentucky. At the University of Cincinnati College of Law, where he was the assistant law librarian (1967-1976), he taught Legal Research, Writing and Appellate Advocacy and served as the moot court adviser. Currently he is the Kentucky state law librarian in the Administrative Office of the Courts at Frankfort (since 1976).

He has served as a member of the part-time faculties of Midway College in Midway, Kentucky, where he taught Legal Research and other courses in the legal assistant ("paralegal") program (1977-1980), Eastern Kentucky University, where he taught Legal Research & Writing (1980-1981), and The Institute for Paralegal Studies, Sullivan Centre, Louisville (1981), where he taught Legal Research. He served as a member of the Paralegal Advisory Committee (1981-1983) at the Institute for Paralegal Studies.

Mr. Gilmer is the author of *Guide to Kentucky Legal Research,* 1979, and *Guide to Kentucky Legal Research 2d,* 1985, the reviser of *The Law Dictionary (Cochran's Law Lexicon,* 5th ed., 1973 and 6th ed., 1986), *Anderson's Manual for Notaries Public,* 5th ed. 1976 and supplements, *Forms for Commercial Transactions (Kentucky Legal Forms* v. 1), is the author of numerous legal periodical articles, and a former member of the Editorial Board of *The Journal of Legal Medicine* (1975-1977).

PREFACE

LEGAL RESEARCH, WRITING & ADVOCACY, Second Edition, is designed to answer the most-frequently-asked legal research and writing questions of persons studying law or studying about the law. The identity of these kinds of questions is based on the day-to-day experience of the author in answering questions over a period of many years. The book is addressed principally to beginning students. It should be useful, however, to junior and senior students, lawyers, paralegals, and the many college students who are studying law-related courses such as criminal justice, corrections, constitutional law, business law, and political science, and to nonlegal educators who are preparing themselves for the teaching of law-related courses in general education.

This book is not designed to furnish all the answers that one might pose about legal literature or legal research and writing, nor is it designed to describe all the materials that one might possibly encounter in a law library. There are other books available that can do much of that for persons who need that much and that kind of information. Such books are listed in CHAPTER 5 at the Classified Subject Bibliography under "Legal Research," "Legal Writing," and "Reports of Cases." Instead, this book is intended to be a useful sourcebook or outline which will answer contemporary legal-research questions for persons working on contemporary problems. It is designed to aid the reader to do legal research as a practicing lawyer or paralegal would, and cope with the kinds of problems that are usually encountered in day-to-day law practice. It is intended to be useful both in a course of study, and as a permanent reference book.

Contrary to the format of other books in this field, LEGAL RESEARCH, WRITING & ADVOCACY, Second Edition, has an early chapter, CHAPTER 2, concerning the *Uniform System of Citation* which furnishes useful examples of citation forms for each state and the District of Columbia, and the United States courts and statutes, in a typewriter typeface. The theory of this is that: (a) it familiarizes the reader with the language of legal research and writing before he or she starts to learn about law books in detail, and (b) it serves as a useful overview of the various law books that he or she will encounter when studying the details of legal research and writing.

The book explains how legally-trained people think about a problem before they select books for their research and consult them. It supplies a useful way to accomplish legal research, mapping for the reader a course of travel through the legal-research maze, including some ideas concerning the points of beginning. A more detailed description of legal research sources follows. It includes a classified subject bibliography intended to help answer the frequently asked question, "Where can I look for . . ."

In the belief that legal research is not an end in itself, but a means for the generation and expression of ideas, this work goes beyond the topic of legal research and deals with vehicles in which legal research is used. The chapters on legal research memoranda, brief writing, and oral argument are intended to be helpful to students and other persons who must use their legal research for such purposes as legal-memorandum writing, brief writing, appellate advocacy, and moot court.

This book also treats an important topic which is infrequently covered in some programs of study. A bibliographic essay concerning medical books is furnished in CHAPTER 14 for persons who need this kind of information in advocacy courses, medical-law courses, or employment. For the student intending to enter the practice of law or become a paralegal, it will be a useful guide during the period of study and afterward.

The book has evolved over a period of about 18 years. During that time a number of students, teachers, library colleagues, lawyers, and paralegals contributed ideas for this work. The author is very grateful for their aid, and of course assumes the responsiblity for what is contained herein.

The author would be grateful if readers who have suggestions to offer concerning the improvement of LEGAL RESEARCH, WRITING & ADVOCACY, Second Edition, would communicate those suggestions to him or the publisher. It is their intention that this be a useful book, and readers can aid in making it so by offering suggestions for its future improvement.

W. G.
April 30, 1987

ACKNOWLEDGMENTS

The author gratefully acknowledges the permissions of the following copyright owners to republish the various quotations and illustrative pages.

American Bar Association Journal, Chicago, Illinois.

Banks-Baldwin Law Publishing Co., Cleveland, Ohio.

The Belknap Press of Harvard University Press, Cambridge, Massachusetts.

Cincinnati Chapter of the Federal Bar Association, Cincinnati, Ohio.

Columbia Law Review, New York, N.Y.

Columbia University Press, New York, N.Y.

The Harrison Company, Norcross, Georgia.

Holt, Rinehart and Winston, Inc., New York, N.Y.

Jurimetrics Journal.

The Lawyers Co-Operative Publishing Co., Rochester, New York.

Maine Law Review, Portland, Maine.

McGraw-Hill Book Company, New York, N.Y.

Memphis State University Law Review, Memphis, Tennessee.

Stevens & Sons Ltd., London, England.

The University of Chicago Law Review, Chicago, Illinois.

West Publishing Co., St. Paul, Minnesota.

INTRODUCTION

The Importance of Legal Research and Writing to Law Students and Paralegal Students

When you went to high school and college, perhaps ten percent or maybe as little as five percent of the buildings and floor space on your campus was devoted to the library. You probably granted the library a similar proportion of importance. It is, of course, a matter of speculation whether your decision to afford to the library some particular proportion of importance depended upon the amount of floor space allocated to it, or your time consumed in using it, or perhaps other factors such as your individual interest in books and literature.

At many law schools, approximately fifty percent of the floor space and building is devoted to the law library. This represents approximately five to ten times the pro rata dedication of buildings and floor space to library purposes on many high school and college campuses. This difference in the pro rata space allocated to the library indicates the relative importance of libraries and legal research in the study of law and paralegalism.

Many people go through college giving a minimum amount of attention to the university's library. You cannot do that in law school or paralegal school and be successful, however. Your proficiency in using legal literature, and in knowing how to research the intricate legal problems which you will encounter, is likely to be a direct index to your overall success.

Each of you will learn a large amount of substantive law during the time that you are students. What you learn in the casebooks and the classrooms, however, will be only a vague guide for your activities as a practicing lawyer or paralegal. In order to apply what you learn in the casebooks and the classrooms, it will be necessary for you to have a strong understanding of how to utilize law books.

There are many reasons for this claim. One of the important reasons is that it is a physical impossibility for teachers to cover all of the precedent cases, statutes, and varied fact situations which you are likely to encounter when you leave school, in the relatively few months that you will be students. Another reason supporting this determination is the fact that annually in the United States there are tens of thousands of new statutes enacted by the various legislatures and over 50,000 new decisions published by the various courts. You of course will be fortunate if you can keep up with your course assignments, let alone familiarize yourself with the new statutes and new, published decisions.

The building blocks of a successful legal or paralegal career are precedent cases, statutes, administrative regulations and articles concerning law in books and periodicals. Much of your building material, including these building blocks mentioned, is discovered through the use of secondary sources such as legal textbooks and treatises, legal encyclopedias, article indexes, and law digests. If you fail to recognize the importance of this material in all its various forms, and do not know how to use it competently, you will be in the same position as an engineer who does not understand how to read blueprints.

American law libraries contain large and diverse collections of legal literature, which are in large part collections of judicial decisions organized only according to the time sequence in which they occurred. Their importance is based upon the doctrine that we call *stare decisis,* which in the main is the idea that when a court has once laid down a principle of law which is applicable to a particular state of facts, the court will tend to follow that principle and apply it to all future cases in which the facts are substantially the same. Accordingly, the business of discovering the decisions of previous cases, which constitute precedents, is a large portion of a practicing attorney's preparation for the decision-making and the advocacy that is his or her life's work and the support furnished by a valuable paralegal. In America, the dual jurisdictions of the federal government and the fifty states, some of which have been reporting decisions since late in the eighteenth century, contribute to the size of the legal collections with which we must cope.

With regard to statutes and precedent cases, and to a lesser extent, administrative regulations and articles in books and law journals, lawyers, paralegals, and students involve themselves to a great degree in a process of searching for authorities. They are usually looking for authorities that are more or less applicable to a particular fact problem. The size of the mass of the various authorities, and the variety among them, call for an organized study of legal literature in legal and paralegal education. If legal and paralegal education were to be reduced to a bare minimum of what we must have, one of the things that would necessarily remain in the curriculum would be a course concerning legal research. Even in a few years after a graduate leaves school, the law will significantly change in particular respects. You have observed this yourself in recent years. Recall that there have been recent changes in the age of majority from 21 to 18, and there have been the advents of no-fault divorce and no-fault accident insurance. A look at today's, next week's, and next month's newspapers will likely reveal other changes in the law. This phenomenon, which is perpetually with us, makes it absolutely necessary that we have a very strong understanding of legal literature and how to use it.

Legal research should not be divorced from legal writing. One of the most severe criticisms that practicing lawyers receive from the judges before whom they practice is the failure to come to court well-prepared. This includes not only the failure to come to court with a knowledge of the precedents and statutes that bear upon the case which they are litigating, but also the failure to file an adequate trial memorandum of law in a case which is being tried or an adequate appellate brief in a case on appeal. To a large extent, your success depends upon your ability to find, and then apply through various kinds of writings, the statutes and precedent cases which bear on a problem and which in litigation are used for the purpose of persuading the judge that your client's position is the better one.

This is not simply "pie in the sky," which relates to the distant time when you graduate. It has an immediate urgency for you, because early in your studies you will likely be preparing research memoranda which will require the skills mentioned, and writing adversary briefs which will call upon you to utilize these skills even more intensely. Later, a law student may be on Law Review or Moot Court, or write a paper under the supervision of a member of the Faculty. These projects require extensive legal research and writing skills. Aside from the curriculum, many students obtain employment as legal clerks with law firms while they are studying. Most of the time their work assignments at those law firms require intensive application of legal research and writing skills.

You will find legal research and legal writing intellectually stimulating. It is a vital part of the lawyer's and paralegal's world.

COLLATERAL REFERENCES

Complimentary copies of the following publishers' material for students and instructors are available from the publishers indicated:

How to Use Shepard's Citations, 1980. Shepard's/McGraw-Hill, P.O. Box 1235, Colorado Springs, Colorado 80901.

Learning Lexis: A Handbook for Modern Legal Research, 1986. Mead Data Central, 9393 Springboro Pike, P.O. Box 933, Dayton, Ohio 45401.

The Living Law: A Guide to Modern Legal Research, 1984. Lawyers Co-Operative Publishing Co., Rochester, New York 14603 and Bancroft-Whitney Co., San Francisco, California 94107.

West's Law Finder: A Legal Research Manual, 1982. College and Law School Department, West Publishing Co., St. Paul, Minnesota 55102.

This material is informative and useful. It is recommended for the purpose of supplementing this book.

LEGAL RESEARCH, WRITING & ADVOCACY

Second Edition

1. LAWYERS AND PARALEGALS: COMPLEMENTS TO EACH OTHER

Legal research, legal writing, and advocacy are activities in which both lawyers and paralegals participate. This book is directed to both law students and paralegal students. Some persons study for the professional practice of law, aspiring to become members of the bar with J.D. degrees; other persons study for a shorter period of time but learn the same kinds of things as the J.D. candidate and aspire to become paralegals.

Lawyers must recognize the competence of paralegals, and learn to rely upon their very useful skills in order to lighten the lawyer's work load and make the delivery of legal services economical and prompt. Paralegals must understand that they are not licensed to practice law but possess important knowledge and skills that are also possessed by lawyers. Paralegals can profitably use those skills to make the lawyer more efficient.

THE COMPETENCE OF PARALEGALS

Many paralegals have a detailed understanding of narrow fields of the law and their intricacies; in some instances the paralegal's knowledge is better than that of the generalist lawyer who must spread his attention over a broad spectrum of legal concepts. Lawyers must learn to rely upon paralegals so as not to consume the time needed to reinvent the wheel every time a problem within the expertise of the paralegal comes into the office.

Lawyers do not have a corner on legal research and writing. Frequently paralegals have had more training in legal research than the lawyers. A thoughtful, painstaking, thorough paralegal, whose responsibilities are fewer than the lawyer's, can often capably perform legal research that the lawyer wishes to accomplish but has little time to do. Lawyers can take advantage of these persons' skills by selecting the issues needing to be researched and suggesting the kinds of literature that should be consulted. Lawyers can select leading cases that need further scrutiny and ask a paralegal to use the citators, look for law review articles concerning them, and check the digests for references to similar cases. Lawyers can ask a paralegal to scan the current law-review indexes and select some articles for the lawyer to read. Lawyers can ask the paralegal to furnish him or her a draft of, among other things, a memorandum of law, a trial brief, an appellate brief, or an oral argument. When they are submitted for the lawyer's revision, the lawyer can point out parts that need reinforcement, edit the draft, restate it, and the like, calling upon the paralegal to make appropriate changes. All of these things, and many others, will lighten the work load of the lawyer and simultaneously improve the quality and economy of the lawyer's work.

In some instances a paralegal may do a better job than a lawyer. The paralegal may be better at English composition or grammar than the lawyer, better at spelling, better at using indexes, better at organizing files, and the like. A paralegal may have useful, nonlegal skills and knowledge that the lawyer does not possess, *e.g.*, accounting, anatomy, biology, or library science skills. Frequently success in profitably employing the services of a paralegal is limited only by the following two factors:

- What the employing lawyer is willing to allow the paralegal to do, and
- What the paralegal can in fact do well.

Just as we cannot unify the capabilities of lawyers, likewise we cannot unify the skills of paralegals or what they are likely to be able to do when they are employed. A resourceful lawyer will use his or her imagination to fully utilize the services of paralegals.

It is particularly important for newly-admitted lawyers to learn about paralegals. Although as law students they spent several years studying the law, in many instances they learned a lot of theory and obtained a broad overview of many parts of the law, but did not learn much concrete law, or how to accomplish particular objectives. A paralegal can be of great assistance to the new lawyer, because the paralegal will likely have a familiarity with many details that the law-school graduate never learned. The member of the bar, on the other hand, has a broader and deeper understanding of many things that the paralegal only touched on briefly in the paralegal program.

THE IMPORTANCE OF PARALEGALS

The paralegal profession has a growing importance for the legal profession. The legal assistant concept is not a new one, because many persons have long performed paralegal functions in law offices, government employment, and corporations. The word "paralegal" has come into vogue only in recent years, however. Delivery of legal services has become more far-reaching in recent years, and lawyers are learning that they can perform their duties better if they delegate some of their work to other persons they can trust to do it well. Legal insurance, low-cost legal ciinics, and legal-aid societies have extended legal services to many segments of American society that previously did not receive them.

The employment of paralegals has grown rapidly since the mid-1970's. The U.S. Bureau of Labor Statistics estimates that there will be more than 65,000 paralegals by 1990. Approximately 32,000 paralegal students are enrolled in 350 training programs in the United States.

The American Bar Association has a Standing Committee on Legal Assistants which approves programs of paralegal instruction. Paralegals are trained to work under the general supervision of a member of the bar and perform tasks which in former years were performed by attorneys. The paralegal performs professional tasks, as distinguished from clerical duties. The professional tasks performed by paralegals include helping to interview clients and witnesses, researching legal issues, investigating facts, drafting documents, assisting in litigation, keeping a calendar of due dates, drafting interrogatories, preparing tax returns, and managing the law office. In contrast, the member of the bar leads the interviewing of clients and witnesses, determines legal rights and responsibilities, checks the documents drafted by the paralegal, decides on discovery measures, analyzes the file, takes depositions, conducts trials, and otherwise appears in court.

THE ETHICS OF PARALEGALISM

The utilization of paralegals is not without limits, however. There are ethical obligations placed upon the lawyer and consequent limitations on the activities of the paralegal. Paralegals must perform their work under the direction of a member of the bar. This is a two-way street because (a) the lawyer must in fact supervise and direct the paralegal, and (b) the paralegal must abide by the supervision and direction of the lawyer and not stray into illegal, unauthorized practice of law.

One court has said:[1]

> "The reason for prohibiting the practice of law by those who have not been examined and found qualified to practice is frequently misunderstood. It is not done to aid or protect the members of the legal profession either in creating or maintaining a monopoly or closed shop. It is done to protect the public from being advised and represented in legal matters by unqualified persons over whom the judicial department can exercise little, if any, control in the matter of infractions of the code of conduct which, in the public interest, lawyers are bound to observe."

In a case in which an operator of a secretarial service who was not a member of the bar was enjoined and ordered to stop various activities, the court said:[2]

> " * * * We hold that Ms. Brumbaugh, and others in similar situations, may sell printed material purporting to explain legal practice and procedure to the public in general and she may sell sample legal forms.
>
> * * *

---

[1]State v. Sperry, 140 So.2d 587, 595 (Fla. 1962).

[2]Florida Bar v. Brumbaugh, 335 So.2d 1186, 1194 (Fla. 1978).

> Further, we hold that it is not improper for Marilyn Brumbaugh to engage in a secretarial service, typing such forms for her clients, provided that she only copy the information given her in writing by her clients. In addition, Ms. Brumbaugh may advertise her business activities of providing secretarial and notary services and selling legal forms and general printed information. However, Marilyn Brumbaugh must not, in conjunction with her business, engage in advising clients as to the various remedies available to them, or otherwise assist them in preparing those forms necessary for a dissolution proceeding. More specifically, Marilyn Brumbaugh may not make inquiries nor answer questions from her clients as to the particular forms which might be necessary, how best to fill out such forms, where to properly file such forms, and how to present necessary evidence at the court hearings. Our specific holding with regard to the dissolution of marriage also applies to other unauthorized legal assistance such as the preparation of wills or real estate transaction documents. While Marilyn Brumbaugh may legally sell forms in these areas, and type up instruments which have been completed by clients, she must not engage in personal legal assistance in conjunction with her business activities, including the correction of errors and omissions."

A later, highly-publicized case concerned similar activities which were found to constitute the practice of law by a person who was not a member of the bar. The defendant was permanently enjoined from further unauthorized practice of law.[3] According to the court, she sold do-it-yourself divorce kits, obtained facts from customers by oral questions and answers, and wrote the information on an intake sheet. The court said that she prepared papers that she considered necessary for filing and securing dissolution of marriages, she held conferences with her customers and asked questions in connection with them, she furnished detailed instructions as to how the papers should be filed, service of process secured, and hearings set, and she held briefing sessions concerning questions and answers to be offered at the trial. The court said that she followed the progress of the case, and furnished a diagram of the court chambers and where to find the judge to whom the case had been assigned.

After the unauthorized-practice case was decided in the state Supreme Court, the U.S. Supreme Court dismissed her appeal for want of a substantial federal question.[4]

She was later charged in the state court with contempt of court for violating the injunction. In the later case, the court held (1) she was not entitled to a jury trial because she was not sentenced to more than six months and no fine was imposed, and (2) she was in contempt of the previous court order. She was sentenced to county jail for a 120-day term; 90 days was suspended if she did not violate the injunction for two years.[5] Less than 24 hours before she was to report to the jail, the Governor and his cabinet granted her clemency.

---

[3]Florida Bar v. Furman, 376 So.2d 378 (Fla. 1979).

[4]Furman v. Florida Bar, 444 U.S. 1061, 100 S.Ct. 1001, 62 L.Ed.2d 744 (1980).

[5]Florida Bar v. Furman, 451 So.2d 808 (Fla. 1984).

Each state has jurisdiction to determine its own rules of ethics concerning paralegalism. For that reason, the cases discussed above may or not be totally in point in other states. They are probably representative of American law, however.

There are some written precepts which offer ethical guidance to the lawyer and the paralegal. Two different codes or sets of rules must be considered. Although each state is free to determine its own rule of ethics, nearly all of the states have in force the *Code of Professional Responsibility,* adopted by the American Bar Association in 1969. This *Code* may soon be displaced, however, by the new *Model Rules of Professional Conduct,* adopted by the American Bar Association in 1983, but not adopted as yet by many states.

Under the present *Code* the following provisions are pertinent:

> **EC 3-5** It is neither necessary nor desirable to attempt the formulation of a single, specific definition of what constitutes the practice of law.* Functionally, the practice of law relates to the rendition of services for others that call for the professional judgment of a lawyer. The essence of the professional judgment of the lawyer is his educated ability to relate the general body and philosophy of law to a specific legal problem of a client; and thus, the public interest will be better served if only lawyers are permitted to act in matters involving professional judgment. Where this professional judgment is not involved, non-lawyers, such as court clerks, police officers, abstracters, and many governmental employees, may engage in occupations that require a special knowledge of law in certain areas. But the services of a lawyer are essential in the public interest whenever the exercise of professional legal judgment is required.
>
> **EC 3-6** A lawyer often delegates tasks to clerks, secretaries, and other lay persons. Such delegation is proper if the lawyer maintains a direct relationship with his client, supervises the delegated work, and has complete professional responsibility for the work product.** This delegation enables a lawyer to render legal service more economically and efficiently.

Under the proposed *Model Rules* the following provisions are pertinent:

---

*"What constitutes unauthorized practice of the law in a particular jurisdiction is a matter for determination by the courts of that jurisdiction." *ABA Opinion* 198 (1939).

"In the light of the historical development of the lawyer's functions, it is impossible to lay down an exhaustive definition of the 'practice of law' by attempting to enumerate every conceivable act performed by lawyers in the normal course of their work." State Bar of Arizona v. Arizona Land Title & Trust Co., 90 Ariz. 76, 87, 336 P.2d 1, 8-9 (1961), *modified,* 91 Ariz. 293, 371 P.2d 1020 (1962).

**"A lawyer can employ lay secretaries, lay investigators, lay detectives, lay researchers, accountants, lay scriveners, nonlawyer draftsmen or nonlawyer researchers. In fact, he may employ nonlawyers to do any task for him except counsel clients about law matters, engage directly in the practice of law, appear in court or appear in formal proceedings a part of the judicial process, so long as it is he who takes the work and vouches for it to the client and becomes responsible to the client." *ABA Opinion* 316 (1967).

* * *

RULE 5.3 Responsibilities Regarding Non-lawyer Assistants

With respect to a nonlawyer employed or retained by or associated with a lawyer:

(a) a partner in a law firm shall make reasonable efforts to ensure that the firm has in effect measures giving reasonable assurance that the person's conduct is compatible with the professional obligations of the lawyer;

(b) a lawyer having direct supervisory authority over the nonlawyer shall make reasonable efforts to ensure that the person's conduct is compatible with the professional obligations of the lawyer; and

(c) a lawyer shall be responsible for conduct of such a person that would be a violation of the rules of professional conduct if engaged in by a lawyer if:

(1) the lawyer orders or, with the knowledge of the specific conduct, ratifies the conduct involved; or

(2) the lawyer is a partner in the law firm in which the person is employed, or has direct supervisory authority over the person, and knows of the conduct at a time when its consequences can be avoided or mitigated but fails to take reasonable remedial action.

COMMENT:

Lawyers generally employ assistants in their practice, including secretaries, investigators, law student interns, and paraprofessionals. Such assistants, whether employees or independent contractors, act for the lawyer in rendition of the lawyer's professional services. A lawyer should give such assistants appropriate instruction and supervision concerning the ethical aspects of their employment, particularly regarding the obligation not to disclose the information relating to representation of the client, and should be responsible for their work product. The measures employed in supervising nonlawyers should take account of the fact that they do not have legal training and are not subject to professional discipline.

RULE 5.5 Unauthorized Practice of Law

A lawyer shall not:

(a) practice law in a jurisdiction where doing so violates the regulation of the legal profession in that jurisdiction; or

(b) assist a person who is not a member of the bar in the performance of activity that constitutes the unauthorized practice of law.

COMMENT:

The definition of the practice of law is established by law and varies from one jurisdiction to another. Whatever the definition, limiting the practice of law to members of the bar protects the public against rendition of legal services by unqualified persons. Paragraph (b) does not prohibit a lawyer from employing the services of paraprofessionals and delegating functions to them, so long as the lawyer supervises the delegated work and retains responsibility for their work. See Rule 5.3. Likewise, it does not prohibit lawyers from providing professional advice and instruction to nonlawyers whose employment requires knowledge of law; for example, claims adjusters, employees of financial or commercial institutions, social workers, accountants and persons employed in government agencies. In addition, a lawyer may counsel nonlawyers who wish to proceed pro se.

2.
THE CRYPTOGRAPHY OF THE LEGAL PROFESSION: A UNIFORM SYSTEM OF CITATION

A thorough working knowledge of the forms of citation prescribed by *A Uniform System of Citation*[1] is indispensable to the judge, lawyer, paralegal, and student, because they communicate with each other in court opinions, briefs, legal memoranda, law-review articles, treatises, and correspondence via the cryptic notations explained in the *Uniform System*. Rules of court and local custom will cause members of the profession to make minor variations in this otherwise nearly universal method of noting references to legal and nonlegal literature; this may occur especially with regard to citations of local-state statutes and court rules. In the main, however, *A Uniform System of Citation* is the lawyer's, paralegal's, and student's handbook. He must constantly keep it available to interpret the symbols contained in legal references, so that he will understand the symbols used, and thereby be able to identify, locate, and to some extent evaluate, the materials to which he finds references in legal literature.

The importance of this small book is underscored by the following remarks by an Associate Justice of the Supreme Judicial Court of Maine:

> Webber, *Appellate Advocacy with Maine Flavor,* 18 MAINE L. REV. 59, 61-62 (1966):
>
> * * *
>
> The well-prepared brief serves its next and most useful purpose when the opinion writer begins his task of research. Here again he has occasion to be grateful to the advocate who furnishes him with quick and accurate references to the pages of the record. Even after he has perused the record in its entirety he will rely if he can upon the brief to aid him as he returns to the record for selected bits and pieces necessary to his opinion. He is often grateful for the table of citations used in the brief — citations which are complete and in the form they will take if they are used in the opinion. Such a citation would include the year the case was decided and references to both the official and unofficial reports. There is good reason for emphasizing these elementary rules of citation since they have been too often ignored. When one takes into account the physical limitations of many of the county law libraries in which we are compelled to do our work, he is immediately aware of the practical advantages to be gained from proper citation. Presumably the attorney cites a case because he hopes it will be read, and yet his careless disregard of approved citation methods does nothing to promote that worthy objective. No brief writer should be without a small paperback captioned "A Uniform System of Citation."

---

[1]At present, 14th edition, 1986. Published and distributed by The Harvard Law Review Association, Gannett House, Cambridge, Massachusetts 02138.

* * *

The following schedule is offered for the purpose of providing examples of the commonly-used forms prescribed by *A Uniform System of Citation*. The examples are not exhaustive, but merely illustrative. They are perhaps illustrative of the citations that are used in 90% or more of everyday legal writing, however. For specific applications of the rules to concrete problems, reference should always be made to the wealth of information contained in *A Uniform System of Citation*.

The examples are supplied in typewritten characters. The *Uniform System* offers one set of rules for briefs and memoranda, which are usually typewritten, and another set for law-review footnotes, which are usually set in type and printed. Since the work of lawyers, paralegals, and students is usually prepared on typewriters and submitted in typewritten form, only the former set of rules will be dealt with here.

For an explanation of abbreviations see the appendix of abbreviations, post.

CITING CASES

Basic Form

The case name such as *Smith v. Green,* the volume number of the report(er), the abbreviation for the name of the report(er), page number, and year of decision in parenthesis. When citing a case in the text of a memorandum or a brief, the name of the case, including the *v.*, must be underlined.

The citation must always identify the court which decided the case. Often the name of the report(er) will do this. As examples, citations to *U.S.*, *S. Ct.*, *L.Ed.*, *Ohio St.*, *Iowa*, *Tenn.*, *Ill.*, *Ind.*, and *N.Y.* identify the court because those report(er)s report cases from only one court. In other instances, the identity of the court which decided the case will not be apparent because cases from several different courts are published in some of the report(er)s, such as *F.2d*, *F. Supp.*, *Ohio Op. 2d*, *Ohio L. Abs.*, *N.J. Misc.*, *Pa. D.&C.*, *S.W.2d*, and *P.2d*. In the latter instances, the parenthesis in which the year of decision is stated must also include an identification of the court, *e.g.*, (11th Cir. 1984) or (Ky. 1978).

Case Names

• Spell out the first named party's last name on each side of the case:

Smith v. Green

Not

Charles Smith and Mary Smith, his wife v. Robert Green, Betty Green, his wife, and The Happy Home Finance Co.

• Do not omit any portion of a partnership name, however; nor may you omit an identification of the first relator:

Gilmer & Pennington

Ohio ex. rel. Johnson

• Although some courts, especially trial courts, tend to designate additional parties on each side of the case with *et ux.*, *et al.*, or the like, omit them:

Smith v. Green
Not
Smith et ux. v. Green et al.

• Omit the given names and initials of individuals, but not of business firms:

Block Not Henry Block
H. & R. Block for the firm
G. & C. Merriam Co. for a firm

• If the name clearly indicates that a party is a business firm, then omit Inc., Ltd., and the like. The use of R.R., Co., Bros., and Association would be examples of such an indication.

Southern Railway System
Not
Southern Railway System, Inc.

• Omit words which describe parties who are named:

Jones
Not
Jones, Administrator
Bank of Springfield
Not
Bank of Springfield, Executor

• Ordinarily, never abbreviate the first word of a party's name, but if widely recognized initials identify the party, you may use them:

ABC, CBS, EPA, ILGWU, NAACP, NBC, NLRB, UAW
Not
U.S. or U.S.A.

• Abbreviate *Ass'n.*, *Co.*, *Corp.*, *Inc.*, *Ltd.*, *Mfg.*, *&*, and *No.* (number).

• In state-court cases, omit the name of the state:

State not State of Arizona
Commonwealth not Commonwealth of Pennsylvania
People not People of the State of California

• In federal-court cases, use only the name of the state; omit "State of," "Commonwealth of," and "People of the State of:"

Arizona not State of Arizona
Pennsylvania not Commonwealth of Pennsylvania
California not People of the State of California

• Use *ex rel.* instead of

on the relation of
for the use of
on behalf of, and the like.

• Use *In re* instead of:

In the matter of
Petition of, and the like.

Federal Courts

United States Supreme Court

Cite to official reports (*U.S.*) when possible. The *Uniform System* says not to give parallel citations for United States Supreme Court cases, but this is an unrealistic rule. Some judges want the unofficial citations, too; local state court rules may or may not specify how to handle this matter. It is likely that only a minority of the courthouses, judges' offices, and law offices in the United States have the official reports (*U.S.*). For these reasons, parallel citations to the unofficial reports, *S.Ct.* and *L.Ed.*, are recommended, contrary to the rule in the *Uniform System*. Many judges and lawyers prefer to use *L.Ed.* because it contains, in addition to the reports of cases, annotations concerning selected cases and abstracts of the briefs of counsel; others prefer *S.Ct.* because it supplies West Publishing Co.'s key numbers in addition to the report of the case.

(a) As recommended by *A Uniform System of Citation:*

Edwards v. Arizona, 451 U.S. 477 (1981)
Sandstrom v. Montana, 442 U.S. 510 (1979)

(b) As suggested by experience and preferred by many judges:

Edwards v. Arizona, 451 U.S. 477, 101 S. Ct. 1880, 68 L.Ed.2d 378 (1981)
Sandstrom v. Montana, 442 U.S. 510, 99 S. Ct. 2450, 61 L.Ed.2d 39 (1979)

(c) When the report has not appeared in any advance parts to bound reports of cases, *e.g.*, *U.S.*, *S. Ct.*, or *L.Ed.*:

Koehler v. Engle, 52 U.S.L.W. 4383 (U.S. Mar. 26, 1984)
Torjsen v. Smith, 52 U.S.L.W. 3598 (U.S. Feb. 21, 1984)

(d) Recent cases that have appeared in *S. Ct.* but not in *U.S.*:

Train v. City of New York, 95 S. Ct. 839 (1975)
Illinois v. Gates, 103 S. Ct. 2317 (1983)

(e) Older cases reported in v. 1-90 *U.S.* The first 90 volumes of the *United States Reports* were originally published as the reports of named individuals; they were known by those names. Later they were reorganized into the *United States Reports* and renumbered chronologically. When citing those cases, give both the *U.S.* volume number and the nominative report volume number:

Hayburn's Case, 2 U.S. (2 Dall.) 409 (1792)
Massie v. Watts, 10 U.S. (6 Cranch) 148 (1810)

If you choose to furnish in addition the citations to the unofficial reporters, as described above in (b), citation may be made only to *L.Ed.* The nominative reports covered only the years 1790-1874; *S. Ct.* did not begin until 1882:

Home Insurance Co. v. Morse, 87 U.S. (20 Wall.) 445, 22 L.Ed. 365 (1874)

Table of Nominative Reports

1 U.S. to 4 U.S.	1 Dall. to 4 Dall.
5 U.S. to 13 U.S.	1 Cranch to 9 Cranch
14 U.S. to 25 U.S.	1 Wheat. to 12 Wheat.
26 U.S. to 41 U.S.	1 Pet. to 16 Pet.
42 U.S. to 65 U.S.	1 How. to 24 How.
66 U.S. to 67 U.S.	1 Black to 2 Black
68 U.S. to 90 U.S.	1 Wall. to 23 Wall.

United States Courts of Appeals

There is no official report of these cases; they usually appear only in *F.2d.* Occasionally they will also appear in some selective, specialized reporter.

Engle v. Koehler, 707 F.2d 241 (6th Cir. 1983)
Hughes v. Whitmer, 714 F.2d 1407 (8th Cir. 1983)

United States Court of Claims

Jones Bros. Bakery v. United States, 411 F.2d 1282 (Ct. Cl. 1969)

United States District Courts

There is no official report of these cases; they usually appear only in *F. Supp.* Occasionally they will also appear in some selective, specialized reporter.

Holtzman v. Schlesinger, 361 F. Supp. 553 (E.D.N.Y. 1973)
Eisen v. Carlisle & Jacquelin, 50 F.R.D. 471 (S.D.N.Y. 1970)

Bankruptcy Courts

Cases decided since 1979 should be cited to West's *Bankruptcy Reporter.*

In re Garcia, 42 Bankr. 33 (Bankr. D. Colo. 1984)

Older Federal Cases

Jackson Co. v. Gardiner Inv. Co., 200 F. 113 (1st Cir. 1912)
United States v. Burr, 25 F. Cas. 30 (C.C.D.Va. 1807) (No. 14,692d)

Unpublished Reports of Cases

Furnish the name of the case, its file number, and in parenthesis a designation of the court and full calendar date of the decision.

United States v. Touchstone, Nos. 82-114, 82-1241 (6th Cir. Jan. 31, 1984)
Zurich Insurance Co. v. Raymark Industries, No. 78-L-8760 (Cook County, Ill., Cir. Ct. Sep. 23, 1983)
Crown Cork & Seal Co. v. Aetna Casualty & Surety Co., No. 1292 (Philadelphia County, Pa., C.P. Aug. 2, 1983)

State Courts

Most state cases are found in, and must be cited to, at least two report(er)s, the official state report and the unofficial West Publishing Company (hereinafter called "West") reporter. In some instances, particularly New York Court of Appeals (the highest New York court) cases and California Supreme Court cases, the more recent cases must also be cited to a third reporter.

• Cite to both the official report and the West regional reporter. Give the official citation first and the West citation last.

• Cases decided before the initiation of the West regional reporters *(A., N.E., N.W., P., S.E., So., S.W.)*, which occurred somewhere between 1879 and 1887 depending upon the particular region in question, need only be cited to the official report. There were certain earlier unofficial reports such as *Am. Dec.*, *Am. R.*, and *Am. St. R.* which reprinted selected cases of general interest, and because of the occasional difficulty in finding the older reports of cases it is helpful to the reader to give a parallel citation to those reports if there is no West report and if the case has in fact been reported in the earlier unofficial report.

American Decisions (1770-1869) — Trudo v. Anderson, 10 Mich. 357, 81 Am. Dec. 795 (1862).
American Reports (1870-1887) — Peters v. Siders, 126 Mass. 195, 30 Am. R. 671 (1879).

• In some states, after certain dates, there are no official state reports. When citing cases from those states which are not published in official reports, cite the West reporter and indicate the court of decision in the date parenthetical. The highest court of a state, regardless of what it may be called, is indicated by merely furnishing the abbreviation for the state, *e.g.*, (Alaska 1980), (Del. 1981), and (Fla. 1982). Lower court cases are indicated with more information. See the concrete examples shown below.

• Maryland, New York, and Virginia call their highest court the Court of Appeals, or some variation thereof, while the other states usually call their highest court the Supreme Court. Prior to January 1, 1976, Kentucky called its highest court the Court of Appeals; now its highest court is called the Supreme Court. Some states, including Kentucky after January 1, 1976, have an intermediate court called a Court of Appeals. In New York the trial-level court of general jurisdiction is called the Supreme Court and the intermediate appellate court is called Appellate Division.

Finding the Other Citations

Commonly the initial discovery of a precedent case in an annotated statute book, a legal encyclopedia, a digest, a periodical article, or a textbook or treatise will reveal all of the citations to the case. In that instance the researcher must merely make complete notes, including the citations.

In other instances the researcher may initially find only the official citation, or only the West or other unofficial citation. In the latter instances, he will need the other citations. These are available from several sources.

Perhaps the most commonly used source is the entry in parenthesis shown in *Shepard's Citations, e.g.,* (79SE564). When the researcher uses *Shepard's* for other purposes, he can obtain the parallel citation at the same time. Other quick sources of this information include the "Table of Cases" of the appropriate law digest, and the "Blue Book[s]" published by West. The "Blue Book[s]" take you in only one direction, however. They are tables showing the volume and page of the West reporter for cases cited to the official reports. There are various kinds of "Blue Book[s]" available for this purpose, e.g., the *National Reporter Blue Book* and the *Kentucky Blue Book.* Frequently the official citation may be found at the beginning of the unofficial publication of the case in the West reporters.

Alabama

Mazer v. Jackson Insurance Agency, 340 So. 2d 770 (Ala. 1976)
Horne v. Patton, 291 Ala. 701, 287 So. 2d 824 (1973)
Metropolitan Life Insurance Co. v. Kenneghy, 71 So. 2d 292 (Ala. Ct. App. 1954)

The official *Alabama Reports* and *Alabama Appellate Court Reports* are no longer published. Citations to cases after 295 *Ala.* (1976) and 57 *Ala. App.* (1976) should be made to *So.2d.* Reprints of the Alabama cases in *So.2d* are published under the title *Alabama Reporter.*

Alaska

Davis v. State, 499 P.2d 1025 (Alaska 1972)

The official *Alaska Reports* are no longer published. Citations to cases after 17 *Alaska* (1958) should be made to *P.2d.* Reprints of the Alaska cases in *P.2d* are published under the title *Alaska Reporter.*

Arizona

State v. Watson, 120 Ariz. 441, 586 P.2d 1253 (1978)
Christy v. Hoke, 127 Ariz. 169, 618 P.2d 1095 (Ct. App. 1980)
Kitchell Corp. v. Hermansen, 8 Ariz. App. 424, 446 P.2d 934 (1968)

Arkansas

Meeks v. State, 80 Ark. 579, 98 S.W. 378 (1906)
Sanders v. Arkansas-Missouri Power Co., 267 Ark. 1009, 593 S.W.2d 56 (Ct. App. 1980)

Reprints of the Arkansas cases in *S.W.2d* are published under the title *Arkansas Cases*.

California

Ramirez v. Brown, 9 Cal. 3d 199, 507 P.2d 1345, 107 Cal. Rptr. 137 (1973)
People v. Lovercamp, 43 Cal. App. 3d 823, 118 Cal. Rptr. 110 (1974)

California Supreme Court cases after 53 *Cal. 2d* 187 (1959) must be cited to three reports, *Cal. 2d* or *Cal. 3d, P.2d,* and *Cal. Rptr.*

Colorado

People v. Leahy, 173 Colo. 339, 484 P.2d 778 (1970)
Gomogda v. Prudential Ins. Co. of America, 31 Colo. App. 154, 501 P.2d 756 (1972)
Hunter v. Hayes, 533 P.2d 952 (Colo. Ct. App. 1975)

The official *Colorado Reports* and *Colorado Court of Appeals Reports* are no longer published. Citations to cases after 200 *Colo.* (1980) and 44 *Colo. App.* (1980) should be made to *P.2d.* Reprints of the Colorado cases in *P.2d* are published under the title *Colorado Reporter.*

Connecticut

Corrigan v. Antupit, 131 Conn. 71, 37 A.2d 697 (1944)
Coffin v. Faggella, 5 Conn. Cir. Ct. 85, 242 A.2d 792 (App. Div. 1967)
Potter v. Ridge Realty Corp., 28 Conn. Supp. 304, 259 A.2d 758 (Fairfield County Super. Ct. 1969)

Reprints of the Connecticut cases in *A.2d* are published under the title *Connecticut Reporter.*

Delaware

Johnson v. State, 379 A.2d 1129 (Del. 1977)
American Hardware Corp. v. Savage Arms Corp., 37 Del. Ch. 59, 136 A.2d 690 (Sup. Ct. 1957)
Air Mod Corp. v. Newton, 59 Del. 148, 215 A.2d 434 (1965)
In re Estate of Morrow, 59 Del. 262, 219 A.2d 137 (New Castle County Orphans Ct. 1966)

Wagner v. Olmedo, 323 A.2d 603 (Del. Super. Ct. 1974)

The official *Delaware Reports* and *Delaware Chancery Reports* are no longer published. Citations to cases after 59 *Del.* (1966) and 43 *Del. Ch.* (1968) should be made to *A.2d.* Reprints of the Delaware cases in *A.2d* are published under the title *Delaware Reporter.*

District of Columbia

United States v. Simmons, 302 A.2d 728 (D.C. 1973)
Allen v. Morton, 495 F.2d 65 (D.C. Cir. 1973)
Broadcasting Publications, Inc. v. District of Columbia, 114 U.S. App. D.C. 163 (1962)
Murray v. United States, 288 F. 1008 (D.C. Cir. 1923)

The District of Columbia Court of Appeals, formerly known as the District of Columbia Municipal Court of Appeals, reports its cases in *A.2d.*

The U.S. Court of Appeals for the D.C. Circuit reports its cases, and its predecessor courts reported their cases, in *F.2d* and *U.S. App. D.C.* Previously D.C. appellate cases were published in *App. D.C.* (1893-1941) and various nominative reports (1893 and prior). Citation of these cases to *F.2d* or *F.* is preferred; if they are not found in *F.2d* or *F.*, citation may be made to the other reports.

Florida

Street v. Sugerman, 202 So. 2d 749 (Fla. 1967)
In re Warner's Estate, 160 Fla. 460, 35 So. 2d 296 (1948)
Couch v. Connecticut General Life Insurance Co., 216 So. 2d 72 (Fla. Dist. Ct. App. 1968)
Strawn v. Theodore Strawn, Inc., 39 Fla. Supp. 11 (Lake County Cir. Ct. 1973)

The official *Florida Reports* are no longer published. Citations to cases after 160 *Fla.* (1948) should be made to *So. 2d.* Reprints of the Florida cases in *So. 2d* are published under the title *Florida Cases.*

Georgia

Northbrook Excess & Surplus Insurance Co. v. J.G. Wilson Corp., 250 Ga. 691, 300 S.E.2d 507 (1983)
Porter v. Lassiter, 91 Ga. App. 712, 87 S.E.2d 100 (1955)

Hawaii

McBryde Sugar Co. v Robinson, 54 Haw. 174, 504 P.2d 1330 (1973)
Cosmopolitan Finance Corp. v. Runnels, 2 Haw. App. 33, 625 P.2d 390 (1981)
Jacoby v. Kaiser Foundation Hospital, 622 P.2d 613 (Haw. Ct. App. 1981)

Idaho

Twin Falls Clinic & Hospital Building Corp. v. Hamill, 103 Idaho 19, 644 P.2d 341 (1982)

Belt v. Belt, 106 Idaho 426, 679 P.2d 1144 (Ct. App. 1984)

Beginning in 1982 the Idaho Court of Appeals cases are reported in *Idaho Reports*. Therefore, if the Court of Appeals decided the case, indicate that fact in the parenthesis containing the year. If there is no such indication, the meaning is that the Supreme Court decided the case.

Illinois

Darling v. Charleston Community Memorial Hospital, 33 Ill. 2d 326, 211 N.E.2d 263 (1965)

McGinnis v. First National Bank, 214 Ill. App. 295 (1919)

Tegtmeyer v. Tegtmeyer, 306 Ill. App. 169, 28 N.E.2d 303 (1940)

S.M. Wilson & Co. v. Prepakt Concrete Co., 23 Ill. App. 3d 137, 318 N.E.2d 722 (1974)

Indiana

Wallace v. State, 232 Ind. 700, 116 N.E.2d 100 (1954)

Lawshe v. Glen Park Lumber Co., 176 Ind. App. 344, 375 N.E.2d 275 (1978)

The official *Indiana Reports* are no longer published. Citations to cases after 1981 should be made to *N.E.2d*. The official *Indiana Court of Appeals Reports* and *Indiana Appellate Court Reports* are no longer published. Citations to cases after 1979 should be made to *N.E.2d*. Reprints of the Indiana cases in *N.E.2d* are published under the title *Indiana Cases*.

Iowa

Freese v. Lemmon, 210 N.W.2d 576 (Iowa 1973)

State v. Dodd, 346 N.W.2d 42 (Iowa Ct. App. 1984)

The official *Iowa Reports* are no longer published. Citations to cases after 261 *Iowa* (1968) and all citations of Iowa Court of Appeals cases (since 1977) should be made to *N.W.2d*. Reprints of the Iowa cases in *N.W.2d* are published under the title *Iowa Reports*.

Kansas

Kirkpatrick v. Seneca National Bank, 213 Kan. 61, 515 P.2d 781 (1973)

Smith v. Vanguard Products Corp., 9 Kan. App. 2d 585, 682 P.2d 1313 (1984)

Kentucky

Griffith v. St. Walburg Monastery, 427 S.W.2d 802 (Ky. 1968)

Searcy v. Fayette Home Telephone, 143 Ky. 811, 137 S.W. 777 (1911)
Powell v. Winchester Bank, 551 S.W.2d 820 (Ky. Ct. App. 1977)

The official *Kentucky Reports* are no longer published. Citations to cases after 314 *Ky.* (1951) should be made to *S.W.2d.* Reprints of the Kentucky cases in *S.W.2d* are published under the title *Kentucky Decisions.*

Prior to January 1, 1976, the highest court in Kentucky was called the Court of Appeals. In the parenthesis containing the year, that court should be indicated by *Ky.*, not *Ky. Ct. App.* After January 1, 1976, the highest court is called the Supreme Court and should be indicated by *Ky.* in the parenthesis.

In August, 1976, a new Kentucky Court of Appeals was implemented. When citing cases from that court, the indication in the parenthesis should be *Ky. Ct. App.*

Louisiana

State v. Boleyn, 328 So. 2d 95 (La. 1976)
W.T. Grant Co. v. Mitchell, 263 La. 627, 269 So. 2d 186 (1972)
In re Richardson, 284 So. 2d 185 (La. Ct. App. 1973)

The official *Louisiana Reports* are no longer published. Citations to cases after 263 *La.* (1972) should be made to *So. 2d.* Reprints of the Louisiana cases in *So. 2d* are published under the title *Louisiana Cases.*

Maine

Cranston v. Commercial Chem. Corp., 324 A.2d 301 (Me. 1974)
Cole v. Lord, 160 Me. 223, 202 A.2d 560 (1964)

The official *Maine Reports* are no longer published. Citations to cases after 161 *Me.* (1965) should be made to *A.2d.* Reprints of the Maine cases in *A.2d* are published under the title *Maine Reporter.*

Maryland

State ex. rel. Oldham v. Sherman, 234 Md. 179, 198 A.2d 71 (1964)
Dishman v. Dishman, 59 Md. App. 435, 476 A.2d 213 (1984)

Massachusetts

Commonwealth v. Klein, 372 Mass. 823, 363 N.E.2d 1313 (1977)
Cellucci v. Sun Oil Co., 2 Mass. App. Ct. 722, 320 N.E.2d 919 (1974)
Arrow Paper Corp. v. Boylston Foods, Inc., 48 Mass. App. Dec. 46 (Boston Mun. Ct. 1972)

Reprints of the Massachusetts cases in *N.E.2d* are published under the title *Massachusetts Decisions.*

Michigan

O'Neill v. Morse, 385 Mich. 130, 188 N.W.2d 785 (1971)
People v. Hocquard, 64 Mich. App. 331, 236 N.W.2d 72 (1975)

Minnesota

Calder v. City of Crystal, 318 N.W.2d 838 (Minn. 1982)
Constructors Supply Co. v. Bostrom Sheet Metal Works, 291 Minn. 113, 190 N.W.2d 71 (1971)
State v. Anderson. 388 N.W.2d 784 (Minn. Ct. App. 1986)

The official *Minnesota Reports* are no longer published. Citations to cases after 312 *Minn.* (1977) should be made to *N.W.2d.* Reprints of the Minnesota cases in *N.W.2d* are published under the title *Minnesota Reporter.*

Mississippi

Derden v. Morris, 247 So. 2d 838 (Miss. 1971)
West Bros. v. Illinois Central Railroad, 222 Miss. 335, 75 So. 2d 723 (1954)

The official *Mississippi Reports* are no longer published. Citations to cases after 254 *Miss.* (1966) should be made to *So. 2d.* Reprints of the Mississippi cases in *So. 2d* are published under the title *Mississippi Cases.*

Missouri

Gustafson v. Benda, 661 S.W.2d 11 (Mo. 1983)
State ex. rel. Ferguson v. Donnell, 349 Mo. 975, 163 S.W.2d 940 (1942)
Trogdon v. Strumberg, 514 S.W.2d 25 (Mo. Ct. App. 1974)
Butler v. Equitable Life Insurance Society, 233 Mo. App. 94, 93 S.W.2d 1019 (1936)

The official *Missouri Reports* and *Missouri Appeal Reports* are no longer published. Citations to cases after 365 *Mo.* (1956) and 241 *Mo. App.* (1955) should be made to *S.W.2d.* Reprints of the Missouri cases in *S.W.2d* are published under the title *Missouri Cases.*

Montana

Roundup Cattle Feeders v. Horpestad, 184 Mont. 480, 603 P.2d 1044 (1979)

Nebraska

Magruder v. Magruder, 190 Neb. 573, 209 N.W.2d 585 (1973)

Nevada

Wheeler v. Twin Lakes Riding Stable, Inc., 88 Nev. 485, 500 P.2d 572 (1972)

New Hampshire

Poliquin v. MacDonald, 101 N.H. 104, 135 A.2d 249 (1957)

New Jersey

Kirsch Holding Co. v. Borough of Manasquan, 59 N.J. 241, 281 A.2d 513 (1971)

Malaker Corp. v. First Jersey National Bank, 163 N.J. Super. 463, 395 A.2d 222 (App. Div. 1978)

State Farm Mutual Automobile Insurance Co. v. Toro, 127 N.J. Super. 316 A.2d 745 (Super. Ct. L. Div. 1974)

State v. Carney, 69 N.J.L. 478, 55 A. 44 (Sup. Ct. 1903)

Coven v. First Savings & Loan Association, 141 N.J.Eq. 1, 55 A.2d 244 (Ch. 1947)

Prall v. United States Leather Co., 6 N.J. Misc. 967, 143 A. 382 (Sup. Ct. 1928)

New Mexico

O'Cheskey v. Hunt, 85 N.M. 388, 512 P.2d 961 (1973)

Romero v. Prince, 85 N.M. 474, 513 P.2d 717 (Ct. App. 1973)

The *New Mexico Reports* contain cases from both the Supreme Court and the Court of Appeals. Therefore, if the Court of Appeals decided the case, indicate that fact in the parenthesis containing the year. If there is no such indication, the meaning is that the Supreme Court decided the case.

New York

Garcia v. Iserson, 33 N.Y.2d 421, 309 N.E.2d 420, 353 N.Y.S.2d 955 (1974)

Karpinski v. Ingrasci, 34 A.D.2d 403, 312 N.Y.S. 2d 473 (1970)

Wojcik v. Aluminum Co. of America, 18 Misc. 2d 740, 183 N.Y.S.2d 351 (Erie County Sup. Ct. 1959)

Cain v. Cain, 28 Abb. N. Cas. 423, 20 N.Y.S. 45 (Sup. Ct. N.Y. County 1892)

Mitchell v. Bunch, 2 Paige Ch. 606, 22 Am. Dec. 669 (N.Y. Ch. 1831)

The highest court in New York is called the Court of Appeals; its cases are published in *N.Y.2d, N.E.2d,* and *N.Y.S.2d.* New York Court of Appeals cases after 1 *N.Y.2d* 1 (1956) must be cited to all three reports.

The trial-level court of general jurisdiction is called the Supreme Court; its cases are published in *Misc.2d* and *N.Y.S.2d.* The intermediate appellate court is called the Appellate Division; its cases are published in *A.D.2d* and *N.Y.S.2d.*

North Carolina

Crockett v. First Federal Savings & Loan Association, 289 N.C. 620, 224 S.E.2d 580 (1976)

Revco Southeast Drug Centers, Inc. v. North Carolina Board of Pharmacy, 21 N.C. App. 156, 204 S.E.2d 38 (1974)

Reprints of the North Carolina cases in *S.E.2d* are published under the title *North Carolina Reporter.*

North Dakota

Oakes Farming Association v. Martinson Brothers, 318 N.W.2d 897 (N.D. 1982)

Magee v. Equitable Life Assurance Society, 62 N.D. 614, 244 N.W. 518 (1932)

The former *North Dakota Reports* are no longer published. Citations to cases after 79 *N.D.* (1953) should be made to *N.W.2d*. Reprints of the North Dakota cases in *N.W.2d* are published under the title *North Dakota Reports*.

Ohio

State v. Chaney, 11 Ohio St. 3d 208, 465 N.E.2d 53 (1984)

State v. Cross, 58 Ohio St. 2d 482, 391 N.E.2d 319 (1979)

Ramsey v. Riley, 13 Ohio 157 (1844)

Woyma v. Ciolek, 11 Ohio App. 3d 288, 465 N.E.2d 486 (1983)

W.F.I., Inc. v. Hebert Business Furniture Co., 12 Ohio Misc. 2d, 465 N.E.2d 1360 (Cleveland Mun. Ct. 1983)

Ward v. Edy, 14 Ohio Op. 487 (Lucas County C.P. 1938)

Daly v. Tucker, 9 Ohio Dec. Reprint 255, 11 Ohio L. Bull. 320 (Hamilton County Dist. Ct. 1884)

MacBride v. Gould, 16 Ohio Dec. 241, 3 Ohio N.P. (n.s.) 462 (Franklin County C.P. 1905)

Providence Washington Insurance Co. v. Garretsville, 67 Ohio L. Abs. 370, 120 N.E.2d 501 (Franklin County C.P. 1953)

Rose v. Toledo, 14 Ohio Cir. Dec. 540, 1 Ohio C.C. (n.s.) 321 (Lucas County Cir. Ct. 1903)

Parson v. Curl, 11 Ohio L. Abs. 503, 36 Ohio L. Rptr. 126 (Morrow County Ct. App. 1931)

State ex rel. Pansing v. Lightner, 32 Ohio N.P. (n.s.) 376 (Montgomery County C.P. 1934)

Griffith v. County Commissioners, 1 Ohio Dec. Reprint, 457 (Wyandot County Dist. Ct. 1852)

The first 20 volumes of the reports of cases from the Ohio Supreme Court (1821-1852) are cited *Ohio*. Thereafter they are cited *Ohio St.* (1852-1964), *Ohio St. 2d* (1964-1982), and *Ohio St. 3d* (since 1982). The intermediate appellate court reports are cited *Ohio App.* (1913-1964), *Ohio App. 2d* (1964-1982), and *Ohio App. 3d (since 1982).*

Ohio St. 3d, Ohio App. 3d, and *Ohio Misc. 2d* are published together in a single volume under the title *Ohio Official Reports* (since 1982).

Reprints of the Ohio cases in *N.E.2d* are published under the title *Ohio Cases*.

Oklahoma

In re Estate of Flemings, 542 P.2d 517 (Okla. 1975)
Lawson v. State, 484 P.2d 1337 (Okla. Crim. App. 1971)
Tanner v. Western Publishing Co., 682 P.2d 239 (Okla. Ct. App. 1984)

The official *Oklahoma Reports* and *Oklahoma Criminal Reports* are no longer published. Citations to cases after 208 *Okla.* (1953) and 97 *Okla. Crim.* (1953) should be made to *P.2d.* Reprints of the Oklahoma cases in *P.2d* are published under the title *Oklahoma Decisions.*

Oregon

Pallus v. Yorkbrough, 219 Or. 611, 347 P.2d 620 (1960)
Bixler v. First National Bank, 49 Or. App. 195, 619 P.2d 895 (1980)

Pennsylvania

Commonwealth v. Chermansky, 430 Pa. 170, 242 A.2d 237 (1968)
Commonwealth v. Stanley, 265 Pa. Super. 194, 401 A.2d 1166 (1979)
Szychulski v. Commonwealth, Unemployment Compensation Board of Review, 12 Pa. Commw. 68, 317 A.2d 54 (1974)
Rudolph, Palitz & Co. v. Premium Food Co., 24 Pa. D. & C.2d 357 (Philadelphia County C.P. 1961)
In re Digrius, 45 Del. Co. R. 209, 8 Pa. Fiduc. 264 (Orphans' Ct. 1958)

When citing cases in *Pa. D. & C., Pa. D. & C.2d,* or *Pa. D. & C.3d,* also furnish a citation to the legal reporter for the county, if it is available.

Rhode Island

Leonard v. Mattos, 509 A.2d 992 (R.I. 1986)
Jeffrey v. American Screw Co., 98 R.I. 286, 201 A.2d 146 (1964)

The official *Rhode Island Reports* are no longer published. Citations to cases after 1980 should be made to *A.2d.*

South Carolina

Graham v. Graham, 253 S.C. 486, 171 S.E.2d 704 (1970)
McDonald v. State Farm Mut. Auto. Ins. Co., 287 S.C. 40, 336 S.E.2d (Ct. App. 1985)

The *South Carolina Reports* contain cases from both the Supreme Court and the Court of Appeals. Therefore, if the Court of Appeals decided the case, indicate that fact in the parenthesis containing the year. If there is no such indication, the meaning is that the Supreme Court decided the case.

South Dakota

City of Rapid City v. Kahler, 334 N.W.2d 510 (S.D. 1983)
Holt v. Holt, 84 S.D. 671, 176 N.W.2d 51 (1970)

The former *South Dakota Reports* are no longer published. Citations to cases after 90 *S.D.* (1976) should be made to *N.W.2d*. Reprints of the South Dakota cases in *N.W.2d* are published under the title *South Dakota Reports*.

Tennessee

Mitchell Engineering Co. v. Melton, 478 S.W.2d 888 (Tenn. 1972)
Lancaster v. Montesi, 216 Tenn. 50, 390 S.W.2d 217 (1965)
Waddell v. Davis, 571 S.W.2d 844 (Tenn. Ct. App. 1978)
Goodner v. State, 484 S.W.2d 364 (Tenn. Crim. App. 1972)

The official *Tennessee Reports, Tennessee Appeals,* and *Tennessee Criminal Appeals Reports* are no longer published. Citations to cases after 225 *Tenn.* (1971), 63 *Tenn. App.* (1971), and 4 *Tenn. Crim. App.* (1971) should be made to *S.W.2d*. Reprints of the Tennessee cases in *S.W.2d* are published under the title *Tennessee Decisions*.

Texas

Gracia v. RC Cola-7-Up Bottling Co., 667 S.W.2d 516 (Tex. 1984)
Baumler v. Hazelwood, 162 Tex. 361, 347 S.W.2d 560 (1961)
Sherrill v. Estate of Plumley, 514 S.W.2d 286 (Tex. Civ. App. 1974)
Toombs v. State, 514 S.W.2d 259 (Tex. Crim. App. 1974)
Bean v. State, 17 Tex. Crim. 60 (1884)

The official *Texas Reports, Texas Civil Appeals Reports,* and *Texas Criminal Appeals* reports are no longer published. Citations to cases after 163 *Tex.* (1962), 63 *Tex. Civ. App.* (1911), and 172 *Tex. Crim.* (1963) should be made to *S.W.* or *S.W.2d*. Reprints of the Texas cases in *S.W.2d* are published under the title *Texas Decisions*.

Utah

State v. Kennedy, 616 P.2d 594 (Utah 1980)
Parker v. Rampton, 28 Utah 2d 36, 497 P.2d 848 (1972)
Salt Lake County v. Salt Lake City, 42 Utah 548, 134 P. 560 (1913)

The official *Utah Reports* are no longer published. Citations to cases after 30 *Utah 2d* (1974) should be made to *P.2d*. Reprints of the Utah cases in *P.2d* are published under the title *Utah Reporter*.

Vermont

White v. Hubbard, 131 Vt. 423, 306 A.2d 707 (1973)

Virginia

Walker v. Commonwealth, 225 Va. 5, 301 S.E.2d 28 (1983)
Brinkley v. Brinkley, 1 Va. App. 222, 336 S.E.2d 901 (1985)

Washington

DeFunis v. Odegaard, 82 Wash. 2d 11, 507 P.2d 1169 (1973)

Hellbaum v. Burwell & Morford, 1 Wash. App. 694, 463 P.2d 225 (1969)

Reprints of the Washington cases in *P.2d* are published under the title *Washington Reporter.*

West Virginia

Wheeling Dollar Savings & Trust Co. v. Singer, 250 S.E.2d 369 (W. Va. 1978)

Baldwin v. Butcher, 155 W. Va. 431, 184 S.E.2d 428 (1971)

The official *West Virginia Reports* are no longer published. Citations to cases after 157 W. Va. (1973) should be made to *S.E.2d.*

Wisconsin

Kramer v. Alpine Valley Resort, 108 Wis. 2d 417, 321 N.W.2d 293 (1981)

State v. Beaudry, 119 Wis. 2d 96, 349 N.W.2d 106 (Ct. App. 1984)

The *Wisconsin Reports 2d* contain cases from both the Supreme Court and the Court of Appeals. Therefore, if the Court of Appeals decided the case, indicate that fact in the parenthesis containing the year. If there is no such indication, the meaning is that the Supreme Court decided the case.

Wyoming

Condict v. Hewitt, 369 P.2d 278 (Wyo. 1962)

Morris v. Jackson, 66 Wyo. 369, 212 P.2d 78 (1949)

The official *Wyoming Reports* are no longer published. Citations to cases after 89 *Wyo.* (1959) should be made to *P.2d.* Reprints of the Wyoming cases in *P.2d* are published under the title *Wyoming Reporter.*

CITING CONSTITUTIONS[2]

Constitutions are ordinarily cited without an indication of year. The year of adoption and year of repeal are added in parenthesis if the provision cited is no longer in force. Former constitutions that have been superseded are indicated by adding the year of adoption in parenthesis.

U.S. Const. art. III, § 2
U.S. Const. amend. XVI
Ky. Const. § 109 (1891-1975)
Ky. Const. art. IV, § 1 (1850)

---

[2] Virtually all forms of citations for statutes and ordinances, and some forms of citation for constitutions, call for the use of the § symbol, which only a few typewriters have. Some typists improvise by making two small letters s, the first placed one-half line above the other: § . Other typists make the § symbol with a pencil or pen. A third improvisation consists of typing Sec. in lieu of the § symbol. Any one of these alternatives is acceptable for legal memoranda or briefs.

Mont. Const. art. II, § 18
N.D. Const. art. I, § 9
N.M. Const. art. II, § 12
Ohio Const. art. I, § 16

CITING STATUTORY MATERIAL[3]

Federal Statutes including Internal Revenue Code

Citations to federal statutes should ordinarily be to the *United States Code* (U.S.C.). The *United States Code Annotated* (U.S.C.A.) or the *United States Code Service* (U.S.C.S.) may be cited when the U.S.C. does not contain the material.

Inclusive numbers must be furnished when citing consecutive sections or subsections; *"et seq."* may not be used:

Truth in Lending Act, 15 U.S.C. §§ 1601-1613 (1982)
Sherman Anti-Trust Act, 15 U.S.C. § 1 (1982)
Soldiers' & Sailors' Civil Relief Act of 1940, 50 U.S.C. app. § 501 (1982)
28 U.S.C. § 454 (1982)
44 U.S.C. § 906 (Supp. V 1981)
50 U.S.C.A. § 23 (West 1951)
16 U.S.C.S. § 228a (Law. Co-op. 1978)

The Internal Revenue Code, which is tit. 26 U.S.C., is cited differently:

I.R.C. § 2001 (1982)
I.R.C. § 62 (West 1984)
I.R.C. § 70 (Law. Co-op. 1984)

State Statutes

Definitive answers to concrete questions regarding citations to the statutes of the various states may be found in *A Uniform System of Citation.*

The following examples are supplied in typewritten characters because most written legal work, such as school memoranda, law-office memoranda, court briefs, and the like are prepared on typewriters and submitted in typewritten form.

In some instances, there are official and privately-published unofficial editions of the state statutes. In many instances the courts and law offices prefer the privately-published editions because they are published more promptly and have better editorial work.

---

[3] *Id.*

Alabama

Ala. Code § 6-5-482 (1975)
Ala. Code § 13A-5-40 (Supp. 1984)

Alaska

Alaska Stat. § 09.10.055 (1983)
Alaska Stat. § 41.35.045 (Supp. 1984)

Arizona

Ariz. Rev. Stat. Ann. § 12-564 (1976)
Ariz. Rev. Stat. Ann. § 13-703(E) (Supp. 1980).

Arkansas

Ark. Stat. Ann § 61-153 (1971)
Ark. Stat. Ann. § 34-2616 (Supp. 1983)

California

Cal. Civ. Code § 43.6 (West 1981)
Cal. Civ. Code § 1942 (West Supp. 1984)
Cal. Civ. Proc. Code § 340.5 (West 1975)
Cal. Lab. Code § 1102 (West 1971)
Cal. Prob. Code § 1050 (West 1981)
Cal. Prob. Code § 6409(a) (West Supp. 1984)

The California statutes are organized into approximately 29 named "codes" such as Civil Code, Health & Safety Code, Vehicle Code, Welfare & Institutions Code, and others. The citation should identify the particular code by name, furnish the section number, and include the name of the publisher, *i.e.*, Deering or West, in the parenthesis with the year of publication.

Colorado

Colo. Rev. Stat. § 13-80-105 (1973)
Colo. Rev. Stat. § 13-80-127 (Supp. 1982)

Connecticut

Conn. Gen. Stat. § 45-274(a) (1983)
Conn. Gen. Stat. Ann. § 45-67 (West 1981)
Conn. Gen. Stat. Ann. § 52-584 (West Supp. 1983)

Delaware

Del. Code Ann. tit. 10, § 8127 (1974)
Del. Code Ann. tit. 18, § 6856 (Supp. 1982)

District of Columbia

D.C. Code Ann. § 19-319 (1981)
D.C. Code Ann. § 22-1504 (Supp. 1984)

Florida

Fla. Stat. § 733.806 (1981)
Fla. Stat. § 921.141(3) (Supp. 1982)
Fla. Stat. Ann. § 95.11(4)(b) (West 1982)
Fla. Stat. Ann. § 63.062 (West Supp. 1983)

Georgia

Ga. Code Ann. § 27-2534.1(7) (Harrison 1983)
Ga. Code Ann. § 3-1102 (Harrison Supp. 1982)

The *Official Code of Georgia Annotated* is published by Michie; citations to it need not identify the publisher. Citations to the *Code of Georgia Annotated* must identify the publisher, Harrison, in the parenthesis.

Hawaii

Haw. Rev. Stat. § 560:2-110 (1976)
Haw. Rev. Stat. § 657-7.3 (Supp. 1982)

Idaho

Idaho Code § 5-219(4) (1979)
Idaho Code § 25-2808 (Supp. 1984)

Illinois

Ill. Rev. Stat. ch. 110½, § 2-5(a) (1983)
Ill. Ann. Stat. ch. 110, § 13-212 (Smith-Hurd 1982)
Ill. Ann. Stat. ch. 110, § 13-214 (Smith-Hurd Supp. 1983)

Indiana

Ind. Code § 29-1-2-10 (1982)
Ind. Code Ann. § 34-4-20-2 (Burns 1973)
Ind. Code Ann. § 34-4-20-2 (Burns Supp. 1983)

Iowa

Iowa Code § 633.224 (1983)
Iowa Code Ann. § 614.1(9) (West 1983)
Iowa Code Ann. § 902.1 (West Supp. 1984-85)

Kansas

Kan. Stat. Ann. § 60-513 (1976)
Kan. Stat. Ann. § 20-2603 (Supp. 1983)

Kan. U.C.C. Ann. § 84-2-208 (Vernon 1983)
Kan. Civ. Proc. Code Ann. § 60-401 (Vernon 1983)
Kan. Crim. Code Ann. § 21-4113 (Vernon 1981)
Kan. Crim. Proc. Code Ann. § 22-2903 (Vernon 1981)
Kan. Corp. Code Ann. § 17-2711 (Vernon 1981)

Kentucky

Ky. Rev. Stat. Ann. § 413.135 (Baldwin 1981)
Ky. Rev. Stat. Ann. § 27A.210 (Baldwin Supp. 1984)
Ky. Rev. Stat. Ann. § 391.140(1) (Michie/Bobbs-Merrill 1972)
Ky. Rev. Stat. Ann. § 413.140(2) (Michie/Bobbs-Merrill Supp. 1982)

The citation should include the name of the publisher, *i.e.*, Baldwin or Michie/Bobbs-Merrill, in the parenthesis with the year of publication.

Louisiana

La. Civ. Code Ann. art. 1240 (West 1952)
La. Civ. Code Ann. art. 2432 (West Supp. 1984)
La. Rev. Stat. Ann. § 9.2772 (West Supp. 1983)

Maine

Me. Rev. Stat. Ann. tit. 14, § 752-A (1964)
Me. Rev. Stat. Ann. tit. 15, § 101 (Supp. 1984-85)

Maryland

Md. Ann. Code art. 16, § 78(c) (1981)
Md. Cts. & Jud. Proc. Code Ann. § 5-109 (1980)
Md. Cts. & Jud. Proc. Code Ann. § 5-108 (Supp. 1983)
Md. Est. & Trusts Code Ann. § 3-105(c) (1974)

The Maryland statutes are, in part, organized into approximately 30 named "codes" such as Agriculture Code, Elections Code, Public Safety Code, Transportation Code, and others. The citation should identify the particular code by name, and furnish the section number. In some instances, however, the citation will be to material in the *Annotated Code of Maryland* (Md. Ann. Code).

Massachusetts

Mass. Ann. Laws ch. 260, § 2B (Law. Co-op. 1980)
Mass. Gen. Laws Ann. ch. 196, § 7 (West 1958)
Mass. Gen. Laws Ann. ch. 197, § 25A (West Supp. 1984-85)

The citation should include the name of the publisher, *i.e.*, Law. Co-op. or West, in the parenthesis with the year of publication.

Michigan

Mich. Comp. Laws § 700.139 (1979)
Mich. Comp. Laws Ann. § 710.13 (West 1968)
Mich. Comp. Laws Ann. § 600.5838 (West Supp. 1983)
Mich. Stat. Ann. § 27A.5839 (Callaghan 1977)

Minnesota

Minn. Stat. § 524.2-110 (1982)
Minn. Stat. § 145.424 (Supp. 1983)
Minn. Stat. Ann. § 524.1-101 (West 1975)
Minn. Stat. Ann. § 541.051 (West Supp. 1983)

Mississippi

Miss. Code Ann. § 91-1-17 (1972)
Miss. Code Ann. § 15-1-36 (Supp. 1983)

Missouri

Mo. Rev. Stat. § 474.090 (1982)
Mo. Ann. Stat. § 565.005 (Vernon 1979)
Mo. Ann. Stat. § 516.105 (Vernon Supp. 1984)

Montana

Mont. Code Ann. § 2-6-205 (1983)

The Montana statutes are kept up-to-date by replacing paperback volumes. For that reason, no supplement examples are provided.

Nebraska

Neb. Rev. Stat. § 25-223 (1979)
Neb. Rev. Stat. § 24-715 (Supp. 1984)

Nevada

Nev. Rev. Stat. § 268.012 (1983)

The Nevada statutes are kept up-to-date by looseleaf supplementation; the replacement pages are dated. For that reason, no supplement examples are provided. If citation is made to *Nevada Revised Statutes Annotated*, the publisher, Michie, must be identified in the parenthesis.

New Hampshire

N.H. Rev. Stat. Ann. § 507-C:4 (1983)
N.H. Rev. Stat. Ann. § 477:44 (Supp. 1983)

New Jersey

N.J. Stat. Ann. § 3B:5-13 (West 1983)
N.J. Stat. Ann. § 2A:14-1.1 (West Supp. 1983)

New Mexico

N.M. Stat. Ann. § 38-1-16 (1978)
N.M. Stat. Ann. § 30-20-13(C) (Supp. 1982)

New York

N.Y. Dom. Rel. Law § 114 (McKinney 1977)
N.Y. Civ. Prac. L. & R. 214:6 (McKinney Supp. 1983)
N.Y. Est. Powers & Trusts Law § 2-1.5 (McKinney 1981)
N.Y. Real Prop. Law § 235-a(1) (McKinney Supp. 1983)
N.Y. Soc. Serv. Law § 374(2) (McKinney 1983)

The New York statutes are organized into approximately 90 named consolidated "laws," such as Business Corporation Law, Domestic Relations Law, Penal Law, Vehicle & Traffic Law, and others, and approximately 8 uncompiled laws, such as the Code of Criminal Procedure, Family Court Act, Uniform District Court Act, and others. The citation should identify the particular law by name, furnish the section number, and include the name of the publisher, *i.e.*, McKinney or Consol., in the parenthesis with the year of publication.

North Carolina

N.C. Gen. Stat. § 1-15(c) (1983)
N.C. Gen. Stat. § 7A-144 (Supp. 1983)

North Dakota

N.D. Cent. Code § 47-19-41 (1978)
N.D. Cent. Code § 28-01-18(3) (Supp. 1983)

Ohio

Ohio Rev. Code Ann. § 2105.051 (Anderson 1976)
Ohio Rev. Code Ann. § 2305.11(B) (Anderson Supp. 1983)
Ohio Rev. Code Ann. § 2305.131 (Baldwin 1975)
Ohio Rev. Code Ann. § 2903.01 (Baldwin Supp. 1982)

The citation should include the name of the publisher, *i.e.*, Anderson or Baldwin, in the parenthesis with the year of publication.

Oklahoma

Okla. Stat. tit. 84, § 185 (1981)
Okla. Stat. Ann. tit. 10, § 60.23 (West 1981)
Okla. Stat. Ann. tit. 76, § 18 (West Supp. 1983)

Oregon

Or. Rev. Stat. § 12.110(4) (1981)
Or. Rev. Stat. § 12.135 (Supp. 1981)

Pennsylvania

18 Pa. Cons. Stat. Ann. § 7321(a) (Purdon 1983)
20 Pa. Cons. Stat. Ann. § 2109.1 (Purdon Supp. 1983)
Pa. Stat. Ann. tit. 42, § 5536 (Purdon 1981)
Pa. Stat. Ann. tit. 23, § 2711 (Purdon Supp. 1983-1984)

Rhode Island

R.I. Gen. Laws § 33-1-11 (1969)
R.I. Gen. Laws § 9-1-14.1 (Supp. 1983)

South Carolina

S.C. Code Ann. § 15-3-640 (Law. Co-op. 1976)
S.C. Code Ann. § 15-3-545 (Law. Co-op. Supp. 1982)

South Dakota

S.D. Codified Laws Ann. § 57A-2-317 (1980)
S.D. Codified Laws Ann. § 21-55-1 (Supp. 1983)

Tennessee

Tenn. Code Ann. § 29-26-116 (1980)
Tenn. Code Ann. § 2-7-104 (Supp. 1984)

Texas

Tex. Fam. Code Ann. § 16.08 (Vernon 1975)
Tex. Prob. Code Ann. § 44 (Vernon 1980)
Tex. Rev. Civ. Stat. Ann. art. 5227 (Vernon 1962)
Tex. Rev. Civ. Stat. Ann. art. 5536a (Vernon Supp. 1982)

The Texas statutes are, in part, organized into approximately 28 named "codes" such as Family Code, Penal Code, Probate Code, Vehicles Code, and others. The citation should identify the particular code by name, and furnish the section number. In some instances, however, the citation will be to material in the *Revised Civil Statutes of the State of Texas* (Tex. Rev. Civ. Stat. Ann.) which is organized into articles, analogous to sections; citations to Tex. Rev. Civ. Stat. Ann. should be made to the articles in the ordinary way that most statutes are cited to sections.

Utah

Utah Code Ann. § 78-14-4 (1977)

Utah Code Ann. § 78-11-23 (Supp. 1983)

Vermont

Vt. Stat. Ann. tit. 13, § 4816(c) (1974)
Vt. Stat. Ann. tit. 12, § 521 (Supp. 1983)

Virginia

Va. Code Ann. § 64.1-17 (1980)
Va. Code Ann. § 55-248.25 (Supp. 1983)

Washington

Wash. Rev. Code § 11.04.041 (1983)
Wash. Rev. Code Ann. § 11.04.085 (1979)
Wash. Rev. Code Ann. § 4.16.350 (Supp. 1983)

West Virginia

W. Va. Code § 55-2-12 (1981)
W. Va. Code § 16-2-6 (Supp. 1984)

Wisconsin

Wis. Stat. § 853.19 (1981-82)
Wis. Stat. Ann. § 893.55 (West 1983)
Wis. Stat. Ann. § 809.50 (West Supp. 1984-85)

Wyoming

Wyo. Stat. § 1-3-111 (1983)
Wyo. Stat. § 15-1-113(d) (Supp. 1984)

Session Laws

Furnish the official name or a popular name of the act, or both, and the public law or chapter number. If it has no such name, call it "Act of . . ." followed by the full calendar date of its enactment, approval, or effective date. Precede the title of the session-law book with the abbreviated name of the state, regardless of whether it appears in the official title of the book. Add in parenthesis the year in which the act was passed, unless it appears in the name of the act or session-law book. Privately edited or compiled session laws should be identified with the name of the editor or compiler, *e.g.*, Anderson, Baldwin, Deering, or West, in parenthesis.

Tax Reduction and Simplification Act of 1977, Pub. L. No. 95-30, 91 Stat. 126

Probate Law & Procedure Act, ch. 842, § 44, 1983 Cal. Legis. Serv. 4491 (West)

Act of Mar. 30, 1984, ch. 165, 1984 Ky. Acts 406
Montana Water Use Act, ch. 452, 1973 Mont. Laws 1121
Act of Mar. 11, 1959, ch. 334, § 4, 1959 N.D. Laws 624
Act of Mar. 16, 1917, ch. 156, § 33, 1917 Wash. Laws 651

Legislative History

Citations to United States legislative history material, except for debates, must (a) identify the house (Senate or House of Representatives) from which it came, (b) furnish the number and session of the Congress, and (c) provide the year of publication. Frequently the material is reprinted in *United States Code Congressional and Administrative News*; in many instances this is the most readily accessible source of the information. It is therefore very helpful to the reader to provide a parallel citation to that source:

H. R. Rep. No. 1549, 91st Cong., 2d Sess. (1970), reprinted in 1970 U.S. Code Cong. & Admin. News 4007, 4022

City and County Ordinances

Ordinances are cited similarly to statutes. Furnish the name of the enacting city or county, the abbreviation for the state, the name of the code of ordinances, the section or other subdivision of the code, and the year of the volume. If the ordinance is not codified, furnish its number or name and the full calendar date of its adoption.

Cincinnati, Ohio, Municipal Code § 506-85 (1971)
Cincinnati, Ohio, Administrative Code art. 7, § 2 (1971)
Danville, Ky., Ordinance 418 (Jan. 12, 1960)
Newport, Ky., Code of Ordinances § 130.03 (1970)

Uniform and Model Acts, Codes, and Rules

Code of Judicial Conduct Canon 2 (1972)
Code of Professional Responsibility EC 3-6 (1969)
Model Penal Code § 2.08 (Proposed Official Draft 1962)
Model Rules of Professional Conduct Rule 1.4 (1983)
Model Rules of Professional Conduct Rule 1.4 Comment (1983)
U.C.C. § 2-208, Comment 2 (1966)
U.C.C. § 9-503 (1972)
Unif. Anatomical Gift Act § 2(a) (1968)
Unif. Probate Code § 2-110 Comments (1977)

Rules of Evidence and Procedure

Fed. R. Civ. P. 29
Fed. R. Crim. P. 10
Fed. R. Evid. 803(18)

6th Cir. R. 17(1)
Ariz. R. Civ. P. 28(a)
D.C. Super. Ct. R. Civ. P. 28
Ind. Trial R. 28
Ky. R. Crim. P. 7.26(1)
Mont. R. Evid. 301(b)(2)
Nev. Justices' Ct. R. Civ. P. 1
N.J. R. Civ. Prac. 4:12-1
N.M. R. Civ. P. 26(B)(1)
N.D. R. Civ. P. 56(c)
Tenn. R. Civ. P. 19.01
Vt. R. Crim. P. 32(a)(1)

Current rules are cited without a date. Former rules should be cited to an official source wherein they are published with a date in parenthesis.

ADMINISTRATIVE CASES

The names by which administrative cases are cited consist of the full name of the first-mentioned private party or the official subject title. No adverse party should be listed, except for Tax Court and Board of Tax Appeals decisions, which are cited naming adverse parties, as in court cases.

Captioning for the Deaf, 63 F.C.C.2d 378 (1976)
WGN of Colorado, Inc., 31 F.C.C.2d 413 (1971)
Jerry Roth Chevrolet, Inc., 194 N.L.R.B. 352 (1971)
Houston-New Orleans Local-Service Investigation, 44 C.A.B. 206 (1966)
Chicago & Eastern Illinois Railroad-Stock, 338 I.C.C. 282 (1970)
Tennessee Telephone Co., 4 Pub. Util. Rep. (PUR) 4th 68 (Tenn. Pub. Serv. Comm'n 1974)
Mariani v. Commissioner, 54 T.C. 135 (1970)

ATTORNEY GENERAL OPINIONS

Federal

43 Op. Att'y Gen. 2 (1977)

State

1984 Op. Att'y Gen. (Ky.) 84-535

ADMINISTRATIVE REGULATIONS

Administrative regulations are cited in a form analogous to the forms for citing statutes. Federal administrative regulations are codified in the annual *Code of*

Federal Regulations (C.F.R.) to which the citation should ordinarily be made, except for *Treasury Regulations,* which are cited to a separate codification. The name of the regulation is required. If the material does not appear in C.F.R., the *Federal Register* (Fed. Reg.) should be cited.

If the *Federal Register* states where the regulation will appear in the *Code of Federal Regulations*, furnish that information in parenthesis.

Distinct from the usual practice concerning the citation of statutes and regulations, *Treasury Regulations* (Treas. Reg.) citations do not include the year of the codification in the parenthesis. If the regulation cited has never been amended, furnish in the parenthesis the year that it was promulgated. If it has been amended, furnish the year of the last amendment.

The various state administrative regulations are treated similarly.

Truth in Lending, 12 C.F.R. § 226.1 (1984)
49 Fed. Reg. 16,057 (1984)
Treas. Reg. § 1.501(c)(7)-1 (1960)
Ind. Admin. R. (40-2139)-B14 (Burns 1967)

LAW REVIEWS AND OTHER LEGAL PERIODICALS

See also, Appendix of Abbreviations.

Articles

Furnish the last name of the author without the author's initial, except for student work. The author of student work is not designated. Underline the article's title. Furnish the volume number, the abbreviation for the periodical, and page number. Add in parenthesis the year of the article's publication.

Nodiff, Copyrightability of Works of the Federal and State Governments under the 1976 Act, 29 St. Louis U. L.J. 91 (1984).

Wiebusch, New Hampshire Civil Practice and Procedure: Default, 25 N.H.B.J. 277 (1984).

Rutter, A Jurisprudence of Lawyers' Operations, 13 J. Legal Educ. 301 (1961).

Frankel, Lawlessness in Sentencing, 41 U. Cin. L. Rev. 1 (1972).

Younger, A Judge's View of Unconscionability, 5 U.C.C. L.J. 348, 350-351 (1973).

When reference is made to an article generally, cite the first page of the article. When reference is made to specific pages in the article, cite the first page and add the numbers of the specific pages about which you are writing, as in the last example.

Students' Articles

Omit the name of the student author; in place of the author's name, furnish the designation which the periodical gives to the article, *e.g.*, "Student Note,"

"Comment," "Note," or the like. Student authors' full names may be furnished at the end in parenthesis, however.

Student Note, The Contempt Statutes: At Odds with Domestic Enforcement, 29 S.D.L. Rev. 164 (1983).

Comment, Antenuptial Agreements and Divorce in Georgia: Scherer v. Scherer, 17 Ga. L. Rev. 231 (1982).

Notes and Comments, Smokless Tobacco: Defective Marketing Creates a New Toxic Tort, 21 Tulsa L.J. 499 (1986) (authored by Michael F. McNamara).

Note, Regional Approach to Planning, 50 Iowa L. Rev. 582 (1965).

Comment, Durational Residency Requirements for Divorce, 123 U. Pa. L. Rev. 187 (1974).

If the periodical does not have such a designation for the article, merely furnish the title:

Tideland Ownership — Time for Reform, 36 U. Cin. L. Rev. 121 (1967).

Branzburg v. Hayes: A Need for Statutory Protection of News Sources, 61 Ky. L.J. 551 (1972-73).

Short student-comments concerning recent cases, recent statutes, and the like may be cited by designation alone.

Recent Case, 46 Temp. L.Q. 146 (1972).

No Volume Number

If the periodical has no volume number, use the year of publication as a volume number and omit the year of publication which would otherwise be added in parenthesis.

Swift, Restraints on Defense Publicity in Criminal Jury Cases, 1984 Utah L. Rev. 45.

Strong, Questions Affecting the Admissibility of Scientific Evidence, 1970 U. Ill. L.F. 1.

Nonconsecutive Pagination

When the periodical does not have consecutive pagination throughout the volume, but begins the pagination of each issue with page 1, as is the case with many bar association and other journals, cite it by the date or publication period of the issue, and omit the parenthetical reference to the year:

Fullin, The Insanity Defense: Ready for Reform ?, Wis. B. Bull., Dec., 1982, at 13.

Miike, Public Policy Directions in Medical Malpractice, 4 J. Legal Med., April, 1976, at 9.

Benthall-Nietzel, Staff Attorneys and Kentucky Courts in Transition, 41 Ky. Bench & B., Jan., 1977, at 27.

TEXTS AND TREATISES

Basic Form

The volume number (if more than one); author and first initial; title of book underlined; section number or paragraph number if so organized, otherwise the page number; edition (if more than one); year of publication.

F. Cohen, Handbook of Federal Indian Law 349-57 (1982).
1 A. Corbin, Contracts § 38 (1950, Supp. 1984).
E. Farnsworth, Contracts 814-815 (1982).
J. Hall, Search and Seizure § 7:1 (1982).
1 W. Holdsworth, History of English Law 317 (1903).
H. Kalven & H. Zeisel, The American Jury 14 (1966).
4 J. Kent, Commentaries on American Law 444 (9th ed. 1888).
K. Llewellyn, The Bramble Bush 78 (1930).
F. Maitland, The Forms of Action at Common Law 2 (1962).
4 J. Moore, W. Taggert & J. Wicker, Moore's Federal Practice Par. 26.64 (2d ed. 1983).
G. Palmer, The Law of Restitution § 7.5 (1978).
J. White & R. Summers, Uniform Commercial Code 353 (2d ed. 1980).
12 S. Williston, A Treatise on the Law of Contracts § 1473 (1970).
C. Wright & A. Miller, Federal Practice and Procedure §§ 2021-2028 (1970).

Exception

An unusual form is prescribed for books which have an editor instead of an author:

3 American Law of Property § 15.6 (A. Casner ed. 1952).
Prosser & Keeton on the Law of Torts § 76 (W. Keeton ed. 5th ed. 1984).

DICTIONARIES

Ballentine's Law Dictionary 319 (3d ed. 1969).
Black's Law Dictionary 290 (rev. 5th ed. 1979).
2 Bouvier's Law Dictionary 1947 (8th ed. 1914).
Cochran's Law Lexicon 94 (5th ed. 1973).
The Law Dictionary 240 (6th ed. 1986).

RESTATEMENTS

Restatement (Second) of Contracts § 210, Comment b (1981).
Restatement (Second) of Contracts § 302 (1981).

Restatement (Second) of Judgments § 26(1)(b) (1982).
Restatement (Second) of Trusts § 170 (1959).

LEGAL ENCYCLOPEDIAS

Cite legal encyclopedias by volume number, abbreviation for the encyclopedia, the topic or title underlined, section number, and year of the volume's publication in parenthesis.

When writing memoranda of law and briefs, avoid significant reliance on the text of legal encyclopedias. In the main, they are useful overviews of the topic and valuable case-finding devices, but are seldom sources of persuasive textual statements of law.

20 Am. Jur. 2d Courts § 4 (1965).
52 C.J.S. Landlord & Tenant § 431 (1968).

Local state legal encyclopedias, *e.g., California Jurisprudence 3d, Florida Jurisprudence 2d, New York Jurisprudence 2d, Ohio Jurisprudence 3d, Tennessee Jurisprudence, Texas Jurisprudence 3d,* and the like, are cited similarly.

ANNOTATIONS

Annotation, Medical Malpractice: Res Ipsa Loquitur in Negligent Anesthesia Cases, 49 A.L.R.4th 63 (1986)
Annotation, Supreme Court's Views as to Civil Liability of Judges, 55 L.Ed.2d 850 (1979)

U.C.C. REPORTING SERVICE

Occasionally there will be cases reported in this service that are not published any other place. Usually this service is a useful parallel reference that furnishes a third source at which the reader may find cases dealing with the Uniform Commercial Code. A reference to this service is especially useful to readers who practice a large amount of Uniform Commercial Code law; many of them are unlikely to have ready-access to the official reports of all the states or the National Reporter System, but are likely to have this service in their offices.

Every citation to a service, except U.S.L.W., must indicate the publisher in parenthesis.

The *Uniform System of Citation* does not require a parallel citation to this service, however.

Ford Motor Co. v. Reid, 8 U.C.C. Rep. Serv. (Callaghan) 985 (Ark. 1971).
Hempstead Bank v. O'Dee Equipment Sales Corp., 11 U.C.C. Rep. Serv. (Callaghan) 222 (Nassau County, N.Y., Sup. Ct. 1972).

LOOSELEAF SERVICES[4]

Furnish the volume number, abbreviation for the title of the service, publisher in parenthesis, subdivision, and date. If the looseleaf material is expected to be bound, the name of the bound reporter should be furnished in parenthesis, if it is different from the looseleaf reporter's name. If possible, furnish the volume number of the expected bound reporter.

Hayes v. United States, [1969] Stand. Fed. Tax Rep. (CCH) (69-1 U.S. Tax Cas.) Par. 9204 (5th Cir. 1968).

Coal Conversion: Federal Incentives Seen Needed to Encourage Commerical Production of Coal Processes, [1975] Energy Users Rep. (BNA) (No. 86) A-17.

Status of Highway Safety Funds, [1968] 3 Urb. Aff. Rep. (CCH) Par. 17,709 at 9957.

SIGNALS

If a case is cited, the meaning of the citation is that the case directly supports the statement for which the citation is made.

If the citation is for a different purpose, that fact should be indicated to the reader by the following signals:

Accord	The authority cited directly supports the statement but differs from the problem, *e.g.*, concerning the facts or in another jurisdiction.
Cf.	The authority cited supports a different proposition, but lends support by analogy. An explanation of the relevance of the authority cited is frequently needed.
Contra	The authority cited is contrary to the statement.
E.g.,	The authority cited is one among several that supports the statement.
See	The authority cited does not state the proposition, but supports it because the authority has a result that is consistent with it.
See also	The authority cited is additional support for the statement. An explanation of the relevance of the authority cited is frequently needed.

[4] Most typewriters do not have square brackets. Some typists improvise by leaving space and then marking in the square brackets with a pencil or pen: [ ] . Others merely use parenthesis: ( ). Either alternative is acceptable for legal memoranda or briefs.

SHORTENED FORMS OF CASE CITATIONS

When an authority has been fully cited previously within the same general discussion, subsequent citations of it may be shortened. When the subsequent citation appears within a different subheading, however, clarity and convenience to the reader usually require that the case be cited in full the first time it is cited within the new subheading.

Beer v. United States, 425 U.S. at 138.
Beer, 425 U.S. at 138.
425 U.S. at 138.

SHORTENED FORM OF CASE NAME

A case that has been cited in full in the same general discussion may be called by a readily apparent party's name, without any citation. The use for this purpose of a governmental party's name is inappropriate, however.

Stokes v. Brennan, 476 F.2d 699 (5th Cir. 1973), may be called Stokes.
Tidewater Oil Co. v. United States, 409 U.S. 151 (1972), may be called Tidewater Oil Co.

3.
PROBLEM ANALYSIS

WHY ARE WE RESEARCHING?

Ordinarily, the object of legal research is to analyze a factual event or transaction for the purpose of trying to determine various rights and duties incident to it. As an example, a particular sale of an automobile (a) may be contemplated for the future, (b) may be presently taking place, or (c) may have already occurred. In any event, the label "sale of an automobile" masks a large number of unique and crucial facts.

Whether any one fact is relevant to the research mainly depends on our reason for analyzing the event or transaction. If our purpose is to consider the buyer's recourse, if any, for the early deterioration of the paint, then the color of the automobile may be relevant, because by their nature certain paints tend to be unstable and deteriorate more rapidly than other colors. On the other hand, in most of the situations where legal research is done, the color of the automobile is irrelevant. At times, other facts will be irrelevant, depending upon our objective for doing legal research.

If the object of our research were a determination of the seller's liability, if any, for defects in the brakes of the automobile 3 months and 4,000 miles after its sale, the color of the automobile would be inconsequential. If the brakes failed and the automobile injured someone, certain other facts would be irrelevant to the question of the seller's liability, *e.g.*, whether the automobile was bought on credit, whether the rate of interest on the buyer's loan was higher than the legal limit for loan interest, or whether the buyer had a liability insurance policy. Nevertheless, for other purposes, those facts can be relevant.

What we are pointing to is that when we prepare ourselves for legal research we must first determine the purpose of that research. We decide: (1) What is the area of conflict or disagreement?, and (2) What facts bear on that area of conflict? Stated differently: (1) We determine what lawyers call the question or issue; and (2) Determine which specific facts in the cluster of facts comprising the event are material to the resolution of that particular question or issue.

MATERIAL FACTS

Considering the same sale of the automobile, but departing from the problems of the deteriorating paint and failing brakes, let us recognize some of the potential material facts and areas of law relating to this single sales transaction.

(a) There might be an advertisement in a newspaper that attracts the customer, Mr. Ay, to the dealer, Bee Co., because of the advertisement's representations, *e.g.*, "1981 Ecksmobile, used, 4-door, radio, heater, air conditioning, no down payment, 10% interest." Mr. Ay might try out the automobile, find that it is noisy in the drive train, and tell the salesman, Mr. Seay, about the noise. The salesman's response is, "I don't think there is anything to worry about. A lot of late-model Ecksmobiles do that. Our mechanic checked it over and didn't find anything wrong." Mr. Ay showed the automobile to his wife and she liked it. Jointly they decided that they would buy it and that, among other personal uses, she would use it going to her job. Mr. Ay told Mr. Seay that he and his wife would buy it. Mr. Seay wrote up an order form. Mr. Ay signed the form and Mr. Seay took it to Mr. Bee, the president of Bee Co., his employer, for his approval. Mr. Bee signed it, and Mr. and Mrs. Ay subsequently signed financing papers, *e.g.*, a promissory note and a security agreement, with Dee Finance Co., whereby they obligated themselves to pay 30 monthly installments of $300. The automobile was delivered to Mr. Ay and he took it home.

(b) There could be a large variety of reasons for the analysis of this sale. For example, if the automobile needed major repairs to the drive train while the Ay's were away from home on a trip, the cost of which they want to recoup from the seller, Bee Co., the oral statements of the salesman, Mr. Seay, and the specific terms of the order form which Mr. Ay and Mr. Bee signed might be relevant. In most states, the law bearing on the facts of this problem would, in large part, come from Article 2 of the *Uniform Commercial Code* (U.C.C.), which has been adopted with a few variations by the legislatures of 49 states, the District of Columbia and the Virgin Islands, and from the reported court precedent cases which have been decided under it. Access to that material comes via numerous books, and we will explore those avenues later. Ordinary contract law might bear on the problem. Such law is found, among other places, in precedent cases. The problem might also be affected, in the alternative, by the nonstatutory law or common law of strict liability or deceit.

(c) As another example, if an impasse were to occur between the seller, Bee Co., and the buyer, Mr. Ay, concerning recoupment of the cost of the repairs, resulting in a claimed breach of contract by Bee Co., and the Ays' refused to make the payments to Dee Finance Co., the specific words of the financing papers and any intimacy of Bee Co. with Dee Finance Co., if such existed, would be relevant. The law bearing on this problem would in large part come from Article 3 of the U.C.C. and the precedent cases decided under it.

(d) This problem would also be influenced by Article 9 of the U.C.C. and the precedent cases decided under it, because Dee Finance Co. had a security agreement, *e.g.*, a chattel mortgage, on the 1981 Ecksmobile. Mr. Ay might have a disagreement directly with Dee Finance Co. Assume that the advertised 10% interest actually amounted to a 20% effective rate, because it was add-on interest, and Mr. & Mrs. Ay did not understand that fact when they signed the order form with Bee Co. and the financing papers with Dee Finance Co. The words of representation in the newspaper advertisement, the words of disclosure in the order form to Bee Co., and the words of disclosure in the financing papers with Dee Finance Co. would become relevant. The law bearing on those facts, *i.e.*, the rights and remedies of the Ay's and the duties of Dee Finance Co., would in large part be found in the *Truth-in-Lending Act,* as published in the *United States Code* and in the adminstrative regulations promulgated under that act by the Federal Reserve Board, known as *Regulation Z,* and published in the *Code of Federal Regulations.* If the question of usury under the same facts were to be a part of this dispute, that law would largely be found in the appropriate state statutes, which are compiled into codes, as they relate to the financing transaction between Mr. & Mrs. Ay and Dee Finance Co. In all instances, the precedent cases decided under those acts, regulations, and statutes would be a part of the law which must be considered and applied.

(e) As another example, assume that Mr. and Mrs. Ay later have irreconcilable differences between them and engage in a lawsuit for dissolution of marriage or divorce. Among the questions that are apt to be in need of resolution in that lawsuit are: (1) Who will get possession and ownership of the 1981 Ecksmobile? and (2) Who will make the payments for the Ecksmobile to Dee Finance Co.? Among the facts which will bear upon these questions are the transportation needs of the respective parties, the relative incomes and financial needs of the respective parties, and the financial net worths of the respective parties. In the main, the law to be applied in resolving these questions will be found in the appropriate state dissolution of marriage or divorce statutes, which in some respects vary greatly from state to state. As in all of the other examples, the precedent cases which were previously decided under the state statutes would be a part of the law which must be applied.

TRIAL AND ERROR

How does a legal researcher identify and select the specific facts which are relevant to these various disputes? How does he know where to look for law which he can apply?

To a large extent, the experience of legal education or paralegal education gives the researcher sufficient knowledge to tentatively recognize the topics of law which are applicable, and the facts which are apt to be relevant. Please note the use of the words, "tentatively" and "apt." A physician makes a tentative diagnosis of what is apt to be his patient's illness, after an examination of the facts which appear to him. He makes a physical examination, obtains the results of laboratory tests, and asks questions of the patient; after considering the facts thus gleaned within the framework of the tentative diagnosis, and studying the problem, he reaches some kind of final diagnosis. A legal researcher performs in a similar way when analyzing a legal problem.

We work by a kind of trial and error method. We tentatively identify issues and facts which appear to be central to the problem, based initially on our education and experience. We revise the tentative identifications, based upon substantial subsequent research in legal literature and thoughtful consideration. Often, we will discover that in the first interview with the client or witness, we failed to inquire as to certain facts, because only after the subsequent legal research regarding the specific problem, did we determine that those particular facts were relevant, perhaps even crucial. Often, we will discover that the first theory regarding the resolution of the dispute was inaccurate. We may select alternative theories, or even discard earlier theories, all based upon the results of the research which we undertook relative to the unique problem case.

As an example of this method of analysis, consider the above-mentioned problems regarding the repairs to the 1981 Ecksmobile's drive train, and the potential theories of recovery by Mr. & Mrs. Ay against Bee Co., previously mentioned, *i.e.*, U.C.C., ordinary contract law, and common-law theories of strict liability or deceit. If our research were to reveal that strict liability of the seller for harm caused by a defective product would not be applicable unless personal injuries or death had resulted, we would have to discard that theory, because the claim is only for a repair bill to the Ecksmobile. If our research were to reveal that the oral statements of the salesman, Mr. Seay, were not admissible into evidence for the purpose of contradicting the express and unambiguous words of the written order form, we would probably have to abandon the use of those particular spoken words, and look solely to the express written terms of the order form. These are illustrations of the consequences of legal research, and why it is vital to your work.

WRITE UP A LIST OF WORDS WHICH IDENTIFY THE PROBLEM

A leading publisher of law books advocates analysis of fact problems along the lines of the words which describe the facts and legal questions which are apparent. The publisher says that this will generally prove to be most satisfactory, and that it should always be used first, unless the legal researcher knows the name of a case in point, or the specific topic relating to the point(s) of law.[1]

It is a workable method of analysis. When you use this method, write the words on a list. The words which the publisher suggests that you use tend to be classifiable as follows. The examples given below relate to the various hypothetical problems mentioned above.

---

[1] See WEST'S LAW FINDER 21-23 (1982).

Classification	**Examples**
PARTIES	Finance Companies
	Husband and Wife
	Salesmen
	Used Car Dealers[2]
PLACES; THINGS	Advertisement
	Automobiles
	Brakes
	Chattel Mortgages
	Negotiable Instruments
	Paint
	Purchase Order
	Secured Transactions
BASIS OF ACTION; ISSUE	Breach of Contract
	Divorce
	Fraud
	Lending
	Negligence
	Parol or Extrinsic Evidence
	Products Liability
	Sales
	Strict Liability
	Truth in Lending
	Warranty
DEFENSES	Parol Evidence
	Puffing
	Usury
RELIEF SOUGHT	Damages
	Divorce
	Property Settlement

Using these words, and perhaps other words, the legal researcher looks into the general index of various law books and follows the most appropriate references which he finds. Some of the words in these examples may sound foreign to the beginning student, and some which sound familiar may be found to have a different meaning in a legal sense. A portion of your early difficulties in law school, paralegal school, or law-related education will involve understanding the nomenclature of law. The experience of your education will make most of them household words for you, however.

---

[2] "Buyer" and "Seller" might seem to be logical headings, but they will not be found in the indexes to the digests. If you consult a legal-encyclopedia index for these words, you will find that they are subheadings of such categories as "Sales" or "Markets and Marketing."

Although the analysis mentioned above is particularly recommended for digests, it is suitable for most other works, *e.g.*, statutes, legal encyclopedias, annotated case series, legal textbooks, and legal treatises.

SELECT AN APPROPRIATE TOPIC

An alternate approach to legal literature is to refer to the topic subdivisions of legal encyclopedias, digests, law library card catalogs, or published bibliographies. In a legal encyclopedia or digest, several hundred topics are arranged alphabetically. This is analogous to the arrangement of the ordinary general encyclopedia that you used in college or high school. The topics are also sometimes called "titles" and in library card catalogs are usually called "subject headings." When selecting a topic in a legal encyclopedia or digest, it is important to examine the scope note at the beginning of the topic, in order to determine whether your particular problem appears to be that subject. As an example, if you were dealing with a case involving illegal sales of whiskey, you might think of "Criminal Law" as the topic, or of "Prohibition" as perhaps a better topic. Neither would be correct, however, and you would discover that fact by using the scope note. "Intoxicating Liquors" would be the most appropriate topic. A significant familiarity with the topics is necessary for the reader to bypass the general index.[3]

Once the appropriate topic has been selected, there are two ways to sort the contents of the topic. (1) Nearly every legal encyclopedia has a title index at the back of the volume containing the topic, or if the topic spans two or more volumes, the index will usually be in the last such volume. (2) Nearly every legal encyclopedia and digest has an outline of the contents of each title at the beginning of that title.[4] Via these routes, you can frequently bypass the general index, if you have been fortunate enough to select the correct topic. This is not the recommended approach for beginners, however. The use of the words which describe the facts of the problem and the general index, as described above, is the recommended route.

There are numerous other ways to accomplish legal research. Mainly we have discussed legal encyclopedias and digests. All of the sources cannot be explained in this short introduction, because they need to be examined in detail in order to make them understandable. Perhaps it is worthwhile, however, to note some of the other sources. Via legal textbooks, legal treatises, annotated case series, statute books, citators, and in other ways, you will obtain your references to statute and precedent cases. The word-analysis method mentioned above is a good way to look at factual problems, and factual problems are your primary, if not sole, springboard for legal research.

---

[3] For various examples of scope notes, see Appendix A: Pages from Other Books.

[4] For various examples of outlines of contents (occasionally called an "analysis") see Appendix A: Pages from Other Books.

4. A RESEARCH METHOD

When dealing with the complex topic of legal research, it is difficult to decide whether to discuss specific parts of it before discussing the sum of those parts, or conversely, to view it in its entirety before we look at its components. The theory of this chapter is that we can understand our journey better, and hopefully navigate it more easily, if we look at our entire course of travel on a road map before actually setting out on it. Therefore we will examine the wilderness before looking at the trees.

There is no universally best way to do legal research. To a large extent, the best way depends upon the nature of the problem to be researched, and the legal researcher's individual preferences. If you have a concrete label for the nature of your problem, *e.g.*, contract, tort, or crime, and you are reasonably certain of that determination, you should select a specific book from the smorgasbord of law books as classified in the subsequent bibliographic essay, or from a law library catalog, or you can work from the commonly-used legal encyclopedias, annotated case series, and digests.

Often you will not have a clear, concrete label. Much legal research will begin from the ground up. When you are unable to otherwise select a specific law book, as suggested above, you will need to follow a course designed to comprehend all of the legal literature likely to be in point, and simultaneously to shorten your travels through the wilderness as much as possible. One such procedure which has been successful is summarized below in consecutive steps.

THE CONCEPT OF AUTHORITY

Within the various spheres of American law, *i.e.*, the federal jurisdictional sphere, and the respective fifty states' jurisdictional spheres, there are a few primary publications, called "authority," and a much larger number of secondary publications, which are also called "authority."

Primary Authority

- Constitutions.
- Statutes.
- Administrative regulations, if (a) they are authorized by statute, and (b) they have been adopted in the manner authorized by statute.
- Reports of cases from a higher court within the jurisdiction.

Secondary Authority

- Reports of cases from (a) outside the jurisdiction, or (b) a lower court within the jurisdiction, or (c) a coequal court within the jurisdiction.
- Annotations in statute books.
- Reports of cases' headnote's, reporter's additions, and editorial additions.
- Legal textbooks; legal treatises.
- Law reviews; bar journals.
- Law dictionaries.
- Form books.
- Attorney General opinions.
- Legal encyclopedias.
- Digests.
- Annotations in selected case series.
- Restatements.
- Citators.

All primary authority is frequently called "the law" and described as "mandatory," but there is a hierarchy within primary authority. Constitutions are supreme, and in most instances statutes are second in predominance. Administrative regulations, if they are consistent with the constitutions and statutes, also rank high as primary authority.

Reports of cases are the part of the law which furnishes the concrete application of the abstract generalizations stated in constitutions, statutes, and administrative regulations to real facts. Whether there is a conflict between constitutions and statutes, between constitutions or statutes and administrative regulations, and what the consequence of such conflicts shall be, are also the province of the reports of cases. There is a third kind of application of reports of cases, and that is the common law, or unwritten traditional law, that has grown up over the centuries without the influence of relevant constitutions, statutes, or administrative regulations.

It is not so easy to describe a hierarchy in the realm of secondary authority. Some secondary authority rises almost to the level of primary authority; this is mainly because it is logical, scholarly, thoughtful, and persuasive. Other secondary authority is merely descriptive and may be fairly called a finding device. Still other secondary material is principally bibliographic; its purpose is to locate, and point the legal researcher toward, primary authority.

CONSECUTIVE STEPS

• Annotated Statutes and Rules of Procedure

Ordinarily, begin your legal research in the appropriate or most likely statute book. If your problem is procedural, use the appropriate or most likely rules of civil or criminal procedure book. As with most reference books, open the general index. Using words selected according to the process of analysis previously described, try several of them for references to specific sections of the statutes which bear on your problem. You are apt to find a relevant statute. Its annotations, *i.e.*, the editorial work appended below the words of the legislature, will often lead you swiftly to precedent cases, law review articles, and essays in annotated cases series such as *A.L.R.* or *L.Ed.2d,* which relate to that aspect of your problem. As an example, in a lawsuit involving an automobile wreck, you are likely to find a relevant traffic statute which defines the duties of the parties when turning, overtaking, or driving on residential streets, the breach of which would be negligence. The statute's annotations would refer you to precedent cases, essays in annotated case series, and law review articles concerning the statute. If the statutes of a particular state are not annotated, the statutes volume or section of *Shepard's Citations* for that state will provide similar, but cryptic, references which will aid you in expanding your research, once you have found a statute that applies to your problem.

If the index to the statute book does not help, and you exhaust the apparent possibilities, do not count this as a loss. The determination that there are no relevant statutes is a very important determination in itself. Having so determined, you can confidently concentrate on nonstatute law, *i.e.*, precedent cases. Otherwise, you would always be wondering whether there is a controlling statute lurking in the books, which you have overlooked and which seriously affects your case.

There is, of course, the problem of determining which statute or procedural rules book to consult. To a large extent, this feel for a case is gradually developed over the entire period of study and experience, which will continue for a lifetime, particularly regarding the distinction between state statutes and federal statutes. To another extent, some of it is fairly apparent. If for instance, Mr. and Mrs. Ay are engaged in divorce litigation in the courts of the State of Illinois, or if their disputes with Bee Co. and with Dee Finance Co. arose from a transaction in

Illinois, it is reasonably apparent that the Illinois statutes and rules of procedure are the relevant ones for the cases, even though Mr. & Mrs. Ay may have been married in Missouri and have their bank account in Indiana.

More difficult is the determination of how far you should go into the various codified laws or statutes. How do you know that some of the difficulties between Mr. & Mrs. Ay and the Dee Finance Co. are severely influenced by *Regulation Z* of the Federal Reserve Board, as set forth in the *Code of Federal Regulations*? In other words, how do you know even to consult that source? On first examination, the dispute seems to be a matter regulated by state law, as codified by state statutes and interpreted and applied by state courts in reported precedent cases.

It is no easy thing to induce the idea that superimposed upon state law there are sometimes particular federal laws or regulations, *e.g., Regulation Z* or the payroll withholding provisions of the *Internal Revenue Code (I.R.C.).* Although *Regulation Z* may sound foreign to you, you were probably not surprised by the mention of the payroll withholding provisions of the *I.R.C.* This lack of surprise occurs because you live in contemporary America and have read about, and probably experienced, payroll withholding. This is perhaps a clue to how you could know about *Regulation Z.* It is part of contemporary life in America and you could have read about it in the newspaper. You have perhaps seen the forms used by credit-card issuers in disclosing information about the finance charges for late payments, and when payment must be made in order to avoid a finance charge. Perhaps in obtaining a loan of money from a bank, or in buying an item of goods on credit, you encountered similar disclosures. Those disclosures, and others, are a product of *Regulation Z.*

The understanding to be gleaned from this is that, to a large extent, legal researchers must be knowledgeable concerning the world about them, and must have some idea of the types of literature and sources of law that exist. They need to have a good idea of what they are looking for before their search begins or the problem occurs. They must satisfy this advance need by regularly reading, *e.g., United States Law Week, National Law Journal,* law-review articles, bar association journals, and sources of news.

• Law Review Articles

One of the collateral references to which annotated statutes can lead you is law-review articles. They were also noted as one of the kinds of reading which legal researchers should regularly use to keep up with contemporary affairs.

If during your research you find references to law-review articles which might aid you, promptly turn to them. They are often the product of long hours and intensive, uncompensated study by knowledgeable persons. In those articles, you will frequently find that a large amount of your work has been done for you. They often survey timely topics of law and collect the precedents in their footnotes.

Law-review articles are usually your best source of new ideas and ingenious arguments, and much of law practice requires the creation, finding, and application of new ideas and ingenious arguments. The most disappointing fact concerning law-review literature is that you cannot expect to find a relevant article for a large number of problems. As an estimate, you can probably expect to find a helpful article for only about 10% of your work.

As the legal researcher follows the successive steps outlined in this chapter, he or she is likely to pick up references to law-review articles in a great many places. In addition to the likelihood that the annotated statutes will provide such references, they will also appear in some digests, many legal textbooks and legal treatises, and in the footnotes of other law-review articles. *Shepard's Citations* will cite you to law-review articles. Often the most recent law-review articles will cite you to earlier law-review articles on the same subject. Collateral references to selected law-review articles are found in *A.L.R. (American Law Reports Annotated)*

The main storehouses of references to law-review articles are *Current Law Index,* which began in 1980, and *Index to Legal Periodicals* which goes back much further. These indexes should be consulted some time in your research.

• Legal Encyclopedias

The commonly-used national legal encyclopedias, *American Jurisprudence 2d (Am. Jur. 2d)* and *Corpus Juris Secundum (C.J.S.),* and the legal encyclopedias which are published especially for specific states, *e.g.*, *California Jurisprudence 3d, Florida Jurisprudence 2d, New York Jurisprudence 2d, Ohio Jurisprudence 3d, Tennessee Jurisprudence,* and the like, are often valuable sources of references to precedent cases.

As an early step in your legal research, following the use of the statute book and whatever references you may have obtained via its annotations, or if the statute has no annotations, via *Shepard's Citations,* the legal encyclopedia that you choose will usually provide a major number of references to precedent cases. Legal encyclopedias are especially useful to obtain an overview of an unfamiliar area. Access to the contents of the legal encyclopedias is gained via their general indexes, the title indexes, the scope notes, and the topical outlines.

Although the publishers of legal encyclopedias suggest that you can cite and rely on their text statements as being authoritative, and courts and lawyers often do so, the best use of legal encyclopedias is to use them as case-finding devices, and not as sources of textual statements of the law. *Am. Jur. 2d* is supplemented by the five series of *American Law Reports Annotated (A.L.R.)* to which it offers copious references. *C.J.S.* is supplemented by the footnotes in its predecessor, *Corpus Juris (C.J.),* to which it makes constant reference. Each of them is kept up-to-date with annual pocket parts and occasional replacement volumes. Either of these mammoth sets should ordinarily be the legal researcher's primary source of nonstatutory law, *i.e.*, precedent cases.

There will be no attempt here to suggest relative evaluations of the various legal encyclopedias. The quality of the articles, titles, and chapters within each of them varies. It is often wise to use two or more legal encyclopedias, because they serve as a check against each other. In most instances, the national encyclopedias and their related titles will serve as complete sources of local-state case law, and simultaneously place the local-state case law in a national perspective.

• Annotated Case Series

A.L.R., previously mentioned, *United States Supreme Court Reports Lawyers' Edition (L.Ed), Negligence & Compensation Cases Annotated (Negl. & Comp. Cas. Ann.),* and *Uniform Commercial Code Reporting Service (U.C.C. Rep. Ser.),* fit into this general classification of materials. They are collections of selected precedent cases supplemented with various amounts of editorial additions, usually centered around a timely topic.

A.L.R. is the most comprehensive of the four. It tends to treat portions of all of the various topics in law. References to *A.L.R.* are likely to be found in the annotations to the statutes, *Shepard's Citations,* and *Am. Jur. 2d. A.L.R.* annotations are also available to you directly, via digests especially designed for that job, via word indexes, and via handy *Quick Indexes.* Viewed in a context of the universe of American legal literature, *A.L.R.* is probably the best indexed and most accessible set of law-finding devices.[1]

A.L.R. consists of nearly 500 large volumes of selected precedent cases and extensive essays concerning narrow points of law of editorial selection. It is not a work designed to cope with every possible point of law. Rather, it is designed to exhaustively treat the most notable topics. As is the case concerning law-review articles, if you are fortunate enough to find an *A.L.R.* annotation relative to your problem, you will often find that a large amount of your work has been done for you. Because *A.L.R.* treats selected topics and is not an omnibus work, it cannot be expected to be of assistance in more than approximately 10% of your work. Along with the legal encyclopedias, *A.L.R.* is an indispensable resource.

An analogous publication exclusively devoted to cases decided by the United States Supreme Court is *L.Ed.* This publication, now in its second series *(L.Ed.2d),* reports the cases and other proceedings from the United States Supreme Court, and furnishes annotations of editorial selection concerning topics dealt with in the Supreme Court cases. These annotations are accessible to legal researchers, among other avenues, via the *L.Ed. Index to Annotations* and the *U.S. Supreme Court Digest L.Ed.*

Although offered by a different publisher, *Negligence [and] Compensation Cases Annotated (Negl. & Comp. Cas. Ann.)* tends to do much of the same thing that *A.L.R.* does, except that *Negl. & Comp. Cas. Ann.'s* coverage is restricted to tort law. It has its own indexes which to a large extent utilize the factual aspects of cases. If you are dealing with a tort problem, you can often gain valuable time by consulting this work early through its indexes. It is particularly valuable for the discovery of precedents involving unusual fact situations. *E.g.*, if you have a

---

[1]*See Chapter 5: Studying Law on Your Own* at the chart concerning Use of A.L.R. Series. See also Appendix A: Book Illustrations.

client whose toes were traumatically amputated when a pool table with a defective leg fell on his foot, you can look up "pool table" in the Common Sense Index to *Negl. & Comp. Cas. Ann., 4th series,* and find that just such a case has been litigated.

Both *A.L.R.* and *Negl. & Comp. Cas. Ann.* have a second feature which adds to their utility, particularly for the legal researcher whose office law-book collection must necessarily be limited in size. There are few law firms which can or will collect and house the vast number of published precedent cases from all of the states and the United States courts, but from time to time those cases are significant to all lawyers. *A.L.R.* and *Negl. & Comp. Cas. Ann.* make it their objective to republish in full from all the jurisdictions what their editors believe to be significant leading cases of national interest.

This function of republishing selected precedent cases from all jurisdictions is the main characteristic and value of *Uniform Commercial Code Reporting Service (U.C.C. Rep. Ser.).* In a relatively small but valuable way, *U.C.C. Rep. Ser.* also supplies editorial comments. It has an index and a multivolume digest which are organized around the section numbers of the *U.C.C.*, and which provide further analysis within each section number. These features of the index and digest make the cases directly accessible to the legal researcher after he or she discovers the relevant section numbers of the *U.C.C.*, either via the local state statutes or the publisher's companion edition of the *U.C.C.* The work's coverage is limited to matters pertinent to the *U.C.C.* If you are dealing with a commercial problem involving the *U.C.C.*, *e.g.*, sale of goods, commercial paper, banking, or secured transactions, you can often save much time by promptly consulting *U.C.C. Rep. Serv.* for verbatim reports of precedent cases from all of the state and federal courts, with occasional editorial remarks.

• Digests

Digests have certain valuable and unique characteristics, but in ordinary legal research operations the use of them can often be postponed until near the end of the search, in the hope that the other searches in the annotated statutes, law review articles, legal encyclopedias, annotated case series, and *Shepard's Citations* will minimize or obviate the need to consult a digest.

To many persons, digests are often a slow avenue of legal research. In digests, the succeeding paragraphs which abstract similar precedent cases tend to be repetitive. At times, digests also tend to be difficult to comprehend, because their authors often express each point of law in one sentence, regardless of its length or the intrinsic difficulty of communicating an entire complex thought in one sentence.[2] In comparison with a national encyclopedia or other national work, *e.g.*, a national textbook, treatise, or *A.L.R.*, digests for particular states tend to leave

---

[2]Long sentences are not exclusively characteristic of digests, however. Other legal publications, *e.g.*, *A.L.R.*, often have them too.

a vacuum in your research when no precedent case exists in that state regarding the point of law which you are seeking.

The few indispensable functions performed by digests make them uniquely valuable. Notable among the features of a digest are the table of cases and the defendant-plaintiff table. If you know the name of a pertinent precedent case, *e.g.*, *Brown v. Board of Education of Topeka,* a digest can soon find that case for you, and references to all similar cases, via its table of cases. That table will give you citations to the places where the case is reported in full, and references to the places in the digest where it and other similar cases are abstracted.

If your citation to a case is garbled, *e.g.*, you know only that the case is someone against Green, you can use the defendant-plaintiff table to find the names of all the cases in which the last named party was Green, and the names of their opponents, along with the citations of the places where those cases are reported in full. The two national legal encylopedias do not have such tables. *A.L.R.*, *Negl. & Comp. Cas. Ann.*, and *U.C.C. Rep. Ser.,* provide tables of the cases republished in those sets, however.

When using a table of cases in a digest to find a particular precedent case, it is necessary that the reader have enough information about the particular case that he can isolate the specific digest in which it should be abstracted. Because of the limited coverage of the various digests, it is important that the reader know, *e.g.*, whether the case for which he is searching is a Kansas case, a Texas case, a case from the United States courts, or that it was decided during a particular range of years covered by a particular *Decennial Digest* or *General Digest*. Without that much information, several or many digests would have to be consulted. As an example, if you were to desire to find the report of *Plessy v. Ferguson* or *Brown v. Board of Education of Topeka* via the table of cases of a digest, you should also know that the case was decided in the United States Supreme Court, or the approximate year in which it was decided, *i.e.*, 1896 and 1954 respectively, or both.

Another valuable use of digests which can be accomplished via other works, but which is probably accomplished best via a digest, is the discovery of recent cases. Some digests, *e.g.*, *West's General Digest,* will quickly provide references to recent cases concerning a particular point of law or topic; it will promptly disclose relatively recent cases from all jurisdictions. This is no small benefit if your quest is to update your legal research of two years ago which was done in preparation for a trial, so that you can be current for an oral argument next week on an appeal in the same case.

Digests are especially good for the discovery of cases which are similar to other known cases. By using West Publishing Co.'s Key Number System, a case which you have located in any West Publishing Co. digest or reporter can be traced to all other similar cases abstracted in any other West Publishing Co. digest. The Key Numbers serve as constant labels for the pigeon-holes where all similar cases are abstracted in the various West Publishing Co. state, federal, regional, and national digests.

Law digests are designed to be self-contained legal-research devices, by which the abstracts of pertinent precedent cases and their citations in the various reports and reporters are located via the descriptive word index of each digest.

• Textbooks, Treatises, and Restatements

To a large extent, the bibliography hereafter[3] treats this subject in detail, but a few points should be made in this summary. Do not overlook the legal textbooks, legal treatises, and *Restatements*. They are useful sources of descriptive material and criticism. The smaller textbooks, sometimes called hornbooks, are especially useful for the purpose of obtaining a scholarly overview of an unfamiliar area of law. Many textbooks and treatises are regularly consulted and cited by the courts in supporting, and even leading roles. If the courts read them and cite them in their opinions, even though they are secondary authority, they should also be used by the lawyers practicing in those courts and their paralegal assistants. The footnotes of the textbooks and treatises are usually invaluable sources of case references, law review articles, and *A.L.R.* annotations.

The *Restatements of the Law,* many of which are in their second edition, were published after many years of intensive study by the American Law Institute. They are but secondary authority, but many of them are highly respected by the courts.

• Citators

All of the applicable precedent cases and law-review articles which have been located by the methods summarized in the foregoing steps must be subjected to the unique scrutiny of a citator.

While there are a few other kinds of citators, *e.g.*, for federal tax materials, the front-runner is *Shepard's Citations.* The crucial and sensitive role of the citator makes the failure to use it for all of your cases and law-review articles tantamount to playing Russian roulette.

Shepard's Citations, via citation symbols akin to those prescribed by *A Uniform System of Citation,* but which must be verified from a table in the front of each *Shepard's* volume, provides parallel citations, references to prior history of precedent cases, and important references to subsequent treatment of your chosen cases and articles. Among other things, it will lead you to the answer to such pivotal questions as whether the precedent has been subsequently affirmed, distinguished, explained, modified, criticized, reversed, or overruled. It will refer you to *A.L.R.* annotations and law review articles concerning the precedent.

Shepard's will also accomplish other things for you. Among them, you can look up your selected law-review articles in *Shepard's* and find references to

[3] See *Chapter 5: Studying Law on Your Own* at Classified Subject Bibliography.

subsequent precedent cases and subsequent law-review articles that commented upon them. *Shepard's* is indispensable.

• Computer-Assisted Legal Research

The leading computer-assisted legal research services are Auto-Cite, Lexis, and Westlaw. They are innovative devices that constitute different kinds of avenues into legal literature.

Auto-Cite does the kind of things that *Shepard's Citations* does. It verifies the citation that you already have, furnishes parallel citations in the other report(er)s, tells you whether the case is still good law, and tells you whether the case has been discussed in an *A.L.R.* annotation, or *L.Ed. 2d* annotation. Auto-Cite furnishes the citation and title of the annotation if the case has been discussed.

If the press of time does not permit you to use *Shepard's Citations,* Auto-Cite is a useful substitute. It will not furnish as much information about the subsequent treatment of your chosen precedent case, however. It is wise to use both Auto-Cite and *Shepard's Citations* because occasionally the information obtained from one will be different from the information obtained from the other. As is the case concerning various law books, Auto-Cite and *Shepard's Citations* can serve as checks against each other.

Lexis is a giant group of libraries containing cases, statutes, *Code of Federal Regulations, Federal Register,* attorney general opinions, briefs, and other legal material in full text. Lexis contains such libraries of various depths for each of the 50 states and the United States. In addition, Lexis has full-text libraries of selected law reviews; the *National Law Journal, Legal Times,* and various nonlegal periodicals and news services are available in its related library, Nexis. The libraries in Lexis and the features which Lexis offers grow daily, and any attempt here to describe or list them all would be futile; the enumeration would be out of date in a few months. The Lexis sales representative is the best source of such up-to-date information.

Lexis is not indexed. Its major characteristic is the ability to, in effect, rapidly scan every word of every sentence of every paragraph of every case, or other analogous items in its library, for the occurrence of particular words, numbers, phrases, or combinations of words, numbers, and phrases. This is something that we humans cannot do with our eyes, but the computer can do electronically and rapidly. This kind of research requires the legal researcher to be imaginative, and to think out his own search patterns. He must recognize that the computer does mechanical research, and does it well, but does not think for itself. Because Lexis can search for words, numbers, phrases, and combinations of any of them, it

(1) can serve as a finder of cases that mention particular topics, and in particular contexts,

(2) can exclude the mention of the topic in other unwanted contexts, and

(3) can search for numbers and names, such as citations of cases, law-review and bar-journal articles, statute numbers, and administrative regulation numbers.

Westlaw does virtually the same thing with its data bases, which tend to be similar to the libraries in Lexis. All states and the United States material are available on Westlaw. Frequently the choice of whether to use Westlaw or Lexis is greatly influenced by the variety and depth of the data bases or libraries that each may have available, *e.g.*, whether particular material is in the data base or library, or how far back a particular data base or library goes.

Exclusive features of Westlaw are the ability to use the West Key Number System in finding cases and the ability to examine editorially-prepared synopses and abstracts called headnotes. Lexis does not have either.

Both Lexis and Westlaw have the recent parts of *Shepard's Citations* in their libraries or data bases. Both of them have various copyrighted books in their libraries. Both of them put cases in their libraries or data bases that are not yet available in print; they are excellent sources of unpublished slip opinions. As is the case with Lexis, the data bases in Westlaw and the features which Westlaw offers grow daily, and any attempt to describe or list them here would be futile because the enumeration would be out of date soon thereafter. The Westlaw sales representative is the best source of such up-to-date information.

There are two principal difficulties with computer-assisted legal research. First, there is a resistance among some book-oriented persons to using a typewriter-like keyboard, a video-display terminal, and an optional printer for hard copy, connected by telephone lines to a distant computer. This is foreign to some legal researchers. In addition, the user of computer-assisted legal research is confined during the time that he or she must operate the keyboard and read from the display terminal; one cannot go to their desk and chair to do the work unless the terminal is located there.

Second, the cost of computer-assisted legal research is considerable. Installation costs, initial equipment charges or monthly equipment-rental fees, and the cost of online computer time are substantial.

Ideally, computer-assisted legal research is a step that the legal researcher should not ignore. There are some times when the computer can greatly shorten research time or do things for the legal researcher that cannot be done by books.

Occasionally you can begin your legal research via the computer, particularly if you are knowledgeable concerning the subject you are researching and know the kind of language that would likely appear in the cases for which you are looking. Most of the time, however, legal research should be begun in law books as outlined in this chapter, and the computer should be used to refine your work.

5.
STUDYING LAW ON YOUR OWN: A BIBLIOGRAPHIC ESSAY

"Mounting evidence from educational psychology confirms that the basic function of the educational process is to enable a student to learn how to learn; by now it is abundantly clear that the effective lawyer faces the necessity for lifetime learning."[1]

A significant portion of a law student's and paralegal student's education consists of using legal literature, and thereby learning how to learn from it. Upon first encountering legal education or paralegal education, the fledgling student is apt to conceive of legal literature as a formidable wilderness with no easily discoverable guideposts. It is the purpose of this essay to furnish some guideposts which will be of assistance to students in their study, and incidentally to practicing lawyers and paralegals following such study.

Unlike a large portion of contemporary education, particularly the sciences, history, and mathematics, which are reasonably definable and tangible, law is nothing more than a large collection of ideas. Stated otherwise, law is only ideas in the minds of people, which are set down on paper.

Because law is ideas, and ideas are not always fully and firmly formed, it is important to recognize at the outset that to a significant extent law is flexible, and that at best, law is imprecisely stated in print. Often a decision in a lawsuit is a choice of the better of two or more good arguments. Not infrequently there is disagreement concerning that choice; therefore there are majority court opinions and dissenting court opinions.

---

[1] Strong, *Pedagogic Training of a Law Faculty*, 25 J. Legal Educ. 226, 238 (1973).

SOURCES OF LAW[2]

The basic framework of American law is the constitutions of the various states and of the United States. Supplementing this framework are statutes or acts of legislatures, whose purpose is to add detail or to implement the provisions of the constitutions. In addition, on many occasions administrative agencies enact rules or regulations which are authorized by the statutes for the purpose of adding details and implementation to the statutes.

On top of these sources of law, the specific and detailed statements of American law come from court decisions. Reports of cases apply the constitutions, the statutes, and the administrative regulations, and supply the implementation and construction of them.

No written piece of paper is self-executing, nor is it apt to be complete. A homely analogy is a grocery list which dictates that the purchaser should buy bread, meat, and potatoes. It leaves numerous details unspecified; as an example, should the bread be whole-wheat, rye or white? Should the potatoes be fresh, frozen, or dehydrated? Should the meat be steak, ground beef, or hot dogs? Similarly, the constitutions, statutes, and administrative regulations leave many unanswered questions, when it comes to applying their written precepts to the facts of each problem case. No draftsman of an abstract rule which is drawn for prospective application, such as a constitution, statute, or administrative regulation, can possibly foresee and deal with all future realities.

The reports of cases are records of the ways in which the abstract statements of law in constitutions, statutes, and administrative regulations have been applied to the concrete facts of genuine factual disputes. They record the court decisions which fit the concepts of the constitutions, statutes, and administrative regulations to the facts of reality.

In a large number of lawsuits, there are either no well-known, written provisions of law which can be fairly described as uniquely applicable to the problem before the court, or else there are vague, general, conflicting principles which simultaneously indicate different solutions. In such instances, the courts must resolve disputes, and the attorneys for the parties must create their own arguments or advice. Often, the principal guidance which attorneys and judges receive comes from previous court decisions, or perhaps from a farsighted article or book.

Constitutions and Statutes

The various constitutions of the United States and the states are usually published in the statute books of the respective jurisdictions to which they per-

---

[2]Concerning the various theories of law, see the Classified Bibliography at "Philosophy of Law," page 110.

tain. When statutes are first enacted by the United States Congress or by a state legislature, they are collected and published in a book of legislative acts which were enacted at that particular session of the legislature. For the United States government, those books are the *United States Statutes at Large.* For the various states, the books have different names, but the generic term for such books is session laws.

The legislative acts are later blended with older legislative acts that are still in effect into a compilation called a code, which reflects the combined status of all the statute law that was ever passed, amended, or repealed, as of some particualr date. For the United States Government, this is the *United States Code.* For the various state governments, this material would take on such names as *Arizona Revised Statutes, Kentucky Revised Statutes, Pennsylvania Consolidated Statutes,* or *Tennessee Code.*

These few examples are only representative of what may be anticipated from the fifty states and the District of Columbia. The official codes, which are commonly organized and promulgated by a public officer in each jurisdiction, are often republished by commercial publishers with important unofficial editorial work added. In a few instances, there are no official publications of the codes, and commercial publishers do the entire project; in other instances there are no commercial publications of the codes and the only available edition is the official edition.

The commercial editions, *e.g., United States Code Annotated* or *United States Code Service* for the federal statutes, or *Mississippi Code Annotated, Vernon's Annotated Missouri Statutes,* or *Utah Code Annotated,* are more commonly consulted by lawyers because of the editorial work or references, called annotations, which are in them. The annotations amount to expansions of the statutes by directing the reader to reports of cases, law review articles, *A.L.R.* annotations, attorney general opinions, and the like which bear upon the statutes.

Users of statute books can expect to find one or more codes for the United States, each of the fifty states, and the District of Columbia. The large variety of state codes and the space consumed in listing them would make it largely inappropriate to furnish a complete bibliography of them here.[3] They are usually identified by the name of the state to which they pertain and by the word "statutes" or "code".

Codes are organized into titles and chapters for the purpose of collecting in one place all of the statutes that are in effect and relate to a particular topic. The usual avenue to specific statutes is the index portion of the multivolume set. Often cross-references between different statutes will assist the reader, if he has found the wrong statute.

---

[3]For a catalog of state statutes, see Chapter 2: The Cryptography of the Legal Profession at "Citing Statutory Material — State Statutes," page 27, and *A Uniform System of Citation* 177-216 (14th ed. 1981).

Uniform Laws Annotated

Students studying the law of the various states, and lawyers and paralegals practicing in the various states, will find useful as an accessory to their local-state code or statute books the varous volumes of *Uniform Laws Annotated* which contain and discuss the various uniform acts that have been enacted by the legislatures of the states or adopted by the local-state courts.

Uniform Laws Annotated consists of 20 volumes supplemented by annual pocket parts and paperback pamphlets; it contains material concerning over 125 uniform acts drafted by the National Conference of Commissioners on Uniform State Laws and recommended for adoption by the states. It is not until they are adopted in the state legislatures, however, that they become local-state statute law.

In addition to the official words of the uniform acts as recommended by the National Conference of Commissioners on Uniform State Laws, *Uniform Laws Annotated* furnishes official comments of the draftsmen, official explanations, official reasons for changes, variations in the jurisdictions that adopted the act, collateral references to law-review commentaries, collateral references to West Publishing Co. key-number digests and *Corpus Juris Secundum,* and abstracts of state- and federal-court decisions from the various jurisdictions that adopted the act. It supplies the local-state citations to the uniform acts and to the local-state session laws, and date of adoption, for each jurisdiction in which the act has been adopted.

An annual pamphlet furnished with the set organizes the *Uniform Laws Annotated* material by furnishing:

(a) Alphabetically arranged pages for each state, the District of Columbia, Puerto Rico, and the Virgin Islands, whereon are listed in alphabetical order the uniform acts adopted in those respective jurisdictions with the volume and page where each begins;

(b) A Directory of Acts which lists alphabetically all of the uniform acts in the set, with the volume and page where each begins; and

(c) A unified, topical index to all the acts in the set.

Because of the official comments, explanations, reasons, and the like, and the many collateral references which *Uniform Laws Annotated* furnishes, it is frequently more useful to research the local-state law concerning a uniform act in *Uniform Laws Annotated* than in the local-state code or statute books. When researching in *Uniform Laws Annotated* in this manner, however, it is important to verify the information concerning the local-state law found in *Uniform Laws Annotated* by consulting the local-state code or statutes and local-state practice books, to see whether there is inconsistent local-state authority.

Administrative Regulations

An increasingly significant portion of federal law, and to some extent state law, which affects our daily lives is contained not in the constitutions or the statutes, but in the administrative regulations which are adopted by the various governmental agencies charged with the carrying-out and enforcement of the directives contained in the statutes. As an example, the details of what the Federal Reserve Board regulates are set forth, not in the acts of Congress, but in the administrative regulations which the Federal Reserve Board has adopted. The regulations of the Board, *e.g.*, *Regulation Z*, are published in the *Code of Federal Regulations*. In order to discover those regulations, the user of the *Code of Federal Regulations* must consult its index. Similarly, regulations are adopted by the administrative agencies of the state governments and some of them are codified in published books or codes of regulations.[4]

Reports of Cases; Headnotes

The classified bibliography that follows furnishes a list of references wherein bibliographic information concerning the various reports of cases may be found.[5] Little, if anything, would be gained by furnishing such information in this book. It is sufficient to note that there are hundreds of different series of reports of cases, which either continue to grow in number of volumes each year or have been discontinued for various reasons.

The cases which are reported in the tens of thousands of volumes of reports of cases are no better organized in relation to each other, or in relation to similar cases that have been reported over the years, than would be the articles in a 200-year collection of daily newspapers. They are compiled only according to the chronological order of their announcement. They are not accessible without some auxiliary source for finding the specific cases needed; a large proportion of legal literature is devoted to that purpose. The various finding devices which are mentioned below, and the other references which the legal researcher obtains from annotated statutes or codes, textbooks, treatises, periodicals, and elsewhere, are the channels of access to the cases.

Via these sources, a legal researcher will discover references to specific cases which bear on particular points of law and which must be related to the problem case by way of their facts and outcomes. It is through them that you must ordinarily approach the precedent cases.

When the legal researcher finds the precedent cases, they will almost always be embellished with editorial work, *i.e.*, editorial summaries and headnotes. It is important that the researcher recognize a separation of the reports of cases as written by the courts from the editorial work, because the cases are primary materials of the law but the editorial work is not. The editorial work is at best secondary.[6]

---

[4] See Using the Code of Federal Regulations, Federal Register, and List of Code of Federal Regulations Sections Affected, page 130, this chapter.

[5] See the Classified Bibliography at Reports of Cases, page 113, this chapter.

[6] See Slip Opinion from U.S. Supreme Court, Slip Opinion from Court Clerk, and Analysis of a Report of a Case, page 131, this chapter.

Justice Robert Lukowsky of the Kentucky Supreme Court put it well when he stated:

> We hasten to remind both bench and bar that headnotes are not the work of the court and do not state its decision. They are simply the work of commercial publishers and give their understanding of the decision, which may or may not be correct. They are prepared for the convenience of the profession so that its members may find potentially applicable opinions through the digest system. Each member of the profession is still required to determine the meaning of each opinion for himself.[7]

Similarly, the slip opinions of the United States Supreme Court, before they are published in *Lawyers' Edition, Supreme Court Reporter,* or elsewhere, with editorial additions, bear the following note:

> NOTE: Where it is feasible, a syllabus (headnote) will be released, as is being done in connection with this case, at the time the opinion is issued. The syllabus constitutes no part of the opinion of the Court but has been prepared by the Reporter of Decisions for the convenience of the reader. See *United States v. Detroit Lumber Co.*, 200 U.S. 321,337.

This is not to say that the headnotes and editorial work are not useful. They help the legal researcher find and analyze the court's opinion. Rather, they are not official statements of the law and should not be relied upon by the legal researcher as categorical statements of the law.

Headnotes are the principal content of one of the finding devices described below, *i.e.*, digests. This caveat concerning the headnotes in the reports of cases applies equally to the headnotes found in the digests.

FINDING DEVICES

Usually, the most formidable problem in legal research is to find the appropriate precedent cases in the vast wilderness of precedent cases which are in print. The precedent cases are as varied in facts and subject matter as are all of the news items in all of the nation's newspapers published since the early history of America, *e.g.*, 1789, the effective date of the United States Constitution.

The number of such cases which are reported in the United States increases at an approximate annual rate of more than 50,000 per year. One important reporter, *Federal Reporter 2d,* grows at the rate of one large volume every two weeks.

---

[7] Board of Adjustments v. Flood, 581 S.W.2d 1, 3 (Ky. 1979). The rule in Ohio, however, is that the precedent in each case is to be found in the official syllabus rather than in the text of the opinion. Cassidy v. Glossip, 12 Ohio St. 2d 17, 231 N.E.2d 64 (1967).

Each precedent case is unique. If for no other reason, the precedent cases will differ according to place and time, and in American law that distinction can be significant. No precedent case is subject to an exact classification, or to a classification which is likely to be acceptable to every person's mind. The avenues to the precedent cases are of necessity numerous, and a major portion of legal literature is devoted to serving as devices for the discovery of the cases.

Digests

Digests are classified collections of editorially-prepared headnotes or abstracts which are designed to summarize, often in one sentence, a particular point of law for which a precedent case is said to stand. The material found in digests is not the law; it is only a collection of the headnotes described above from the reports of cases. Such digests are similar to abstracting devices which you may have encountered previously, *e.g.*, *Chemical Abstracts, Dissertation Abstracts,* or *Education Abstracts.*

Legal researchers use digests for the purpose of discovering precedent cases; after the cases are discovered via the digest, they must be read by the legal researcher to determine whether they are supportive of the point for which they are cited, in the context of the problem at hand. Digests analyze the pages of the reports of cases according to the subject matter and the decision rendered, along lines which the editors of the digest believe to be significant.

The objective of a digest is to pull together references to all of the precedent cases within a given period of time, or within a given jurisdiction, or within a given court system, which stand for the same point or related points of law. Access to the contents of digests is via their general indexes, or at the option of the researcher, via the analytical tables that precede each of the more than 400 alphabetically arranged digest topics.[8]

The coverage of digests varies. Some of them have been prepared for single states, *e.g.*, California, Florida, Michigan, or New York; some for groups of neighboring states, *e.g.*, Virginia and West Virginia combined or the *Pacific Reporter* states; some for single courts, *e.g.*, U.S. Supreme Court, or court systems, *e.g.*, *West's Federal Practice Digest 3d.* The *Decennial Digests* cover all American courts during particular periods of time. There is little, if anything, that would be gained here by furnishing a definitive list of the various digests in use in the United States.

The *American Digest* undertakes the giant task of abstracting and organizing the American reports of cases from 1658 to date. It is divided into various units confined to some particular span of years, *e.g.*, a digest for 1658-1896 called the *Century Digest,* and subsequent 10-year digests called *Decennial Digests.* The

---

[8]See List of Digest Topics, pages 122-127, this chapter.

current era, *i.e.*, 1976 to date, is covered by the *Ninth Decennial Digest Part 1* (1976-1981) and a series of temporary, bound volumes called the *General Digest* (1981-date). Their purpose is to abstract and organize recent decisions. In the future, the *Ninth Decennial Digest Part 1* and the *General Digest* (1981-1986) will likely be recompiled into a *Decennial Digest* for the years 1976-1986.

In large part, lawyers and paralegals who use digests do not frequently use the *American Digest*. Mainly, they are seeking the law of one specific state or federal law. They will therefore use the smaller digests, *e.g., Arkansas Digest, Idaho Digest, Maine Digest, Oregon Digest,* or *West's Federal Practice Digest 3d.* Depending, however, upon the object of their research and their personal preferences, among other things, some legal researchers may use other legal literature as their finding devices to the almost total exclusion of digests.

Digests evidence the common characteristic of legal publishers, which is the constant effort to make certain that law books are up-to-date. Digests accomplish this objective by supplementation and eventual replacement of the volumes containing topics which have been the subject of change and growth. Although a particular digest or some other law book may have been published in some specific earlier year, it is usually kept up-to-date with pocket part supplements, pamphlet supplements, permanent bound supplements, or replacement volumes which cumulate the previous bound volume and its supplements. Not infrequently, when new volumes are published, the organizational framework of the topic is modified to accommodate new concepts that have developed in the law since the original publications of the digest or volume.

Martindale-Hubbell Law Digests

One unusual digest deserves special recognition. Although it is not characteristic of the digests above-mentioned, a large and valuable collection of legal information and beginning references is available in the Law Digests volume of *Martindale-Hubbell Law Directory.*[9] The Law Digests volume consists of the following parts:

- Separate digests of the laws of each of the fifty states, the District of Columbia, Puerto Rico, and the Virgin Islands. It includes information regarding state courts and United States District Courts sitting in those states and other jurisdictions under the topic, *Courts*.
- A digest of the copyright, patent, and trademark laws of the United States.
- Digests of the laws of the federal government of Canada and each of Canada's ten provinces.
- Digests of the law of over fifty other foreign countries, including the laws of the commonwealth and the states of Australia.

---

[9]Currently, v. 7, 116th ed., 1985. For bibliographic information, see the Classified Bibliography at "Directories," page 93.

• Information regarding the United States Courts. Information concerning the United States District Courts is included in the topic, *Courts,* in the digests of state laws mentioned above.

• The complete text of numerous uniform and model acts.

• An American Bar Association section which contains, among other things, a directory of ABA officials, the Model Rules of Professional Conduct and the Code of Judicial Conduct.

If a lawyer has available the first mentioned digests, legal encyclopedias, statute books, and reports of cases for the various jurisdictions, as is often the case in an academic, large bar association, or large court library, the digests volume of *Martindale-Hubbell Law Directory* is not a frequently-used device. The best purpose which the Law Digests volume can accomplish is to aid a legal researcher in gaining a toehold on the law of another state, discovering information about an unfamiliar court, or in discovering other information which otherwise would be unavailable to him in the limited resources of most law offices. If you are in a small-town law office in Maine, and you need information concerning the law of Arizona, the Law Digests volume is an excellent source of that information. It is revised and replaced annually.

Martindale-Hubbell Law Directory is not ordinarily the first wave of attack on legal problems, but when there is nothing more adequate at hand, it is an excellent point of beginning.

Encyclopedias and Annotated Case Series

Other devices are designed to accomplish the same object as digests. Perhaps most notable among them are the legal encyclopedias and the annotated case series. Legal encyclopedias take on many of the characteristics of ordinary general encyclopedias, *e.g., Encyclopaedia Britannica* or *World Book Encyclopedia.* They are alphabetically organized into topics, with sections within each topic, and like *Encyclopaedia Britannica,* are most effectively used via their general indexes.

Legal encyclopedias provide a text statement of law and significant footnotes which refer to precedent cases offered as support for the statements of law contained in the text portion of the encyclopedias. By the use of legal encyclopedias, readers may obtain a summary of the editors' opinions of the status of the case law, together with references to precedent cases which the editors suggest support those summaries.

Users of legal encyclopedias must read the cases for themselves and determine whether they support the points for which they are cited, within the context of the facts of the case on which the legal researcher is working. Some lawyers and judges rely on the text of legal encyclopedias as an authoritative statement of the law. The best use of a legal encyclopedia, however, is to use it for the same purpose that a digest is used, *i.e.,* as a finding device for the discovery of precedent cases.

Encyclopedias and annotated case series are usually prepared for a national readership. There are some instances in which legal encylopedias are designed to relate the law of individual states alone. Perhaps economics determine whether such state-oriented legal encyclopedias are published.

The national legal encyclopedias are *American Jurisprudence 2d* and *Corpus Juris Secundum*; they undertake to describe the law in a national perspective. They concentrate on case law. They are not recommended for use concerning local variations in national viewpoints which are created by local-state statutes or state constitutions, unless those variations have been applied in reported cases. There are usually state practice books which are mentioned below and which should be used to discover those variations. If there are local-state statutes analogous to statutes in other states, *e.g.*, statutes concerning licensing of motor vehicles, recording of deeds, or the *U.C.C.*, the national legal encyclopedias will usually discuss and cite the local state-court decisions concerning such topics, regardless of the state from which they come.

Annotated case series, *e.g.*, *A.L.R. (American Law Reports Annotated),* complement encylopedias and to some extent compete with them. Their purpose is commonly to reprint a selected recent case concerning a timely topic and to follow it with an extensive essay concerning a topic with which the case dealt. Those essays are supported with references to the precedent cases on which the authors of the essays rely for their statements. In this respect, the essays are similar to the texts of legal encyclopedias. The legal encyclopedias and the essays in the annotated case series are supplemented at least annually by cumulative pocket parts, or as in the case of some of the annotated case series, by permanent bound supplements and cumulative paperback supplements.

The contents of annotated case series are chronologically organized, and similar to the reports of cases, cannot be efficiently used except via a comprehensive general index. While frequent references are obtained to the annotated case series via other sources, *e.g.*, annotated statutes, citators, textbooks, treatises, and legal encyclopedias, ordinarily the general indexes which are components of each series are the main avenues of access.

Most notably, *A.L.R.* is perhaps the best indexed of all the legal finding devices. It is frequently consulted via the footnotes of the closely associated legal encyclopedia, *American Jurisprudence 2d,* but it has several other finding devices which are useful to legal researchers, depending upon whether the quest is for a general topic or for a narrow topic. If the quest is for a general topic, *ALR Quick Index* is preferable. If the quest is for more narrow topics or for better descriptions of the specific problems with which the annotation deals, *ALR Word Index* and *ALR Digest* are preferred.[10]

---

[10] See chart styled "Use of A.L.R. Series," pages 128-129, this chapter.

LEGAL PERIODICALS, TEXTBOOKS, AND TREATISES

The library materials described above are very important for a conventional search of ordinary legal authority. They are not usually the best sources of criticism or innovative thought. The legal encyclopedias, annotated case series, digests, and annotated statutes perform a vital function which is largely unparalleled in nonlegal literature.

The critical and analytical literature on which legal researchers rely for new ideas and resourceful arguments is usually in other sources. Specifically, law-review articles, legal textbooks, and legal treatises are the most valuable sources of material of this nature.

Law-review articles are found in legal periodicals which are analogous to the professional periodicals in other disciplines, *e.g.*, accounting, economics, engineering, medicine, psychology, and sociology. They are frequently written by judges, practicing lawyers, and law teachers. Their purpose is to discuss new ideas and treat subjects which cannot immediately get into book form, or which are not sufficiently long to justify the extensive treatment which would be characteristic of a book. Commentary and analysis of recently-reported precedent cases is a significant function of legal periodicals; such articles are often written by law students.

There are several hundred legal periodicals, the count of which depends to some extent upon the definition of a legal periodical. The most significant legal periodicals are ordinarily indexed in *Current Law Index,* since 1980, and the *Index to Legal Periodicals* which goes back many years earlier. The number of periodicals so indexed varies from time to time. Presently about 700 legal periodicals are indexed in *Current Law Index* and 400 are indexed in *Index to Legal Periodicals*. The periodicals indexed in each include law-school reviews, commercially-published periodicals, and a number of bar-association journals.

Most notable among the legal periodicals not indexed are the local, legal newspapers which report courthouse business, and some bar association publications. Even if particular periodicals are identified as being indexed in the *Index to Legal Periodicals,* that is no assurance that all of the articles in that periodical are so included, because certain short pieces are omitted from it.

Current Law Index and the *Index to Legal Periodicals* are the legal researcher's main avenues to legal periodical literature. Another index, the *Index to Periodical Articles Related to Law,* provides access to selected articles of legal significance which appear in nonlegal periodicals, and in some legal periodicals which are not otherwise indexed. In certain special areas there are other indexes, *e.g., Anderson's Index,* which analyzes and organizes tort and trial literature in the *Journal of the American Trial Lawyers Association (A.T.L. L.J.).*

From time to time, nearly every periodical publishes its own cumulative index, which may or may not suit the needs of a particular reader. If the legal researcher is interested in only one or two journals, *e.g.*, a particular state-bar journal, or a particular law-school review, he or she may find that the indexes for those individual periodicals will suit their needs, perhaps even better than *Current Law Index* or the *Index to Legal Periodicals*. In some instances, the various indexes to the individual periodicals may provide a more thorough analysis of the contents of the periodicals.[11]

In some disciplines the professional periodicals are subject to being classified into specialties within that discipline. Most notable, perhaps, are the specialty classifications which can be assigned to medical journals. In law, such classifications are generally inappropriate. For the most part, articles dealing with various legal subjects are apt to be found in almost any legal publication, because most legal publications are general in scope. It is true that in a relatively few instances there are some legal publications which tend to confine their coverage to narrow areas; they are the exception, however.

Most American law schools publish one or more law reviews in approximately four to eight issues per year. Some bar associations, *e.g.*, American Bar Association, Association of Trial Lawyers of America, the Association of the Bar of the City of New York, and many state bar assocations, publish quality periodicals. A number of commercial publishers provide the legal profession with specialized journals which otherwise would not be available to persons practicing in special fields.

Legal textbooks and treatises are a significant source of information, criticism, and innovation. The following classified bibliography describes a large number of them. Most textbooks and treatises are directed toward relatively narrow areas of law, and are therefore readily adaptable to the classifications of a subject bibliography. They frequently can serve the legal researcher as a good beginning point for research in that subject. They furnish extensive footnotes with collateral references to precedent cases, *A.L.R.* annotations, and law-review articles. They are usually kept up-to-date with supplements and replacement volumes. Their authors are frequently leading authorities on the subject.

FORMS AND JURY INSTRUCTIONS

The classified bibliography which follows includes two classifications that should be specially noted. They are "Forms" and "Jury Instructions." The forms are divided into "Litigative" forms and "Transactional" forms.

In the application of abstract principles of law to the unique realities of life, *i.e.*, the practice of law, there is a constant need for paper work. Virtually everything that the practitioner does with his or her legal knowledge requires some kind of written work. The transactions in which people engage require that a memorial of the transaction be written and we therefore need transactional forms. The litigation in which people are involved requires writings, *e.g.*, complaints, answers, motions, notices, orders, judgments, and the like; we therefore need litigative forms.

---

[11] See Classified Bibliography at "Periodicals," pages 109-110, this chapter.

When a lawsuit is finally wound down to the crucial stage, *i.e.*, submission to the jury, we need jury instructions; they are the court's statement to the jury of the law applicable to the case under submission. The lawyers prepare these for the judges.

These kinds of writings represent the apex of a lawyer's and paralegal's work; they are the culminations of all their efforts. For that reason, some persons say that the place to begin your work on a transaction is the form books, and the place to begin your preparation for a lawsuit is the jury instructions. The form books and jury-instructions books frequently have footnotes, annotations, and collateral references in them which can speed you to the law relevant to your transaction or lawsuit. Experienced persons suggest that if you know what the final statement of the transaction or the law of the case will likely be, you can then work backward through the lower stages of the problem and ably support the apex. For that reason, in an appropriate case, you may wish to begin at the form books or jury instructions, discover what you need to cap off your work, and then build your transaction or lawsuit to fit the mold so selected.

A note of caution concerning the use of form books and published jury instructions is appropriate, however. The forms and jury instructions are only valuable to you if your transaction or lawsuit fits them. The forms and jury instructions should be used only by draftsmen who are knowledgeable concerning the facts of the transaction or event for which they are used, and the state and federal law applicable to the facts. At their best, form and jury-instruction books constitute only a guide or a checklist; they are sources of ideas. The user of form books and published jury instructions must sort out the ideas which are inappropriate for the intended use. Do not adopt the first form or jury instruction that seems to fit, without considering each provision in it to determine whether the particular provision is as fitting as the form or instruction first appeared to be. Consider alternatives, make an intelligent choice, and tailor the final selection to fit the particular facts and law of the transaction or lawsuit before you.

CURRENT AWARENESS

Law changes every day. Legal researchers are responsible for keeping abreast of the enormous number of new legal developments which occur each year, and generally legal literature does a very good job of helping them do this. Only by having an understanding of legal literature, however, may they find the latest information when they need it.

Numerous devices are used for these purposes. Notable among them are the pocket part supplements and cumulative bound supplements which have already been mentioned in connection with digests, legal encyclopedias, and annotated case series. Those supplements, in one or more various forms, are characteristic of nearly all legal literature.

A substantial part of the titles in the following bibliography are described as looseleaf. With regard to some legal topics, there has been a demand for the reporting of information on a frequent basis which has not been satisfactorily served by the six-month or annual frequency which is the ordinary characteristic of statute books, digests, legal encyclopedias and the annotated case series. Such demands have occurred in numerous fields, notably federal taxation, state taxation, labor law, family law, legal and judicial ethics, criminal law, and environmental law. The result of this demand has been the appearance of weekly, and sometimes less frequent, supplementation of topical law books through the process of substitution of new pages for old pages to reflect changes, and the addition of other pages to reflect completely new developments.

Such material is obtained on a subscription basis and costs relatively much per year. This type of material is often called a looseleaf service or looseleaf reporter. It is used by persons who desire and are willing to pay for rapid reporting of changes and new developments. Looseleaf reporters have their own indexes which are frequently brought up to date. Some of the looseleaf reporters are not only supplemented on a weekly basis, but are completely replaced annually, *e.g.*, those treating federal income taxation.

Paperback advance parts of reports of cases are published weekly for all jurisdictions. They are cumulated into bound volumes, and the weekly paperback editions are then destroyed. The texts and treatises are usually supplemented, but are not always supplemented on as regular or predictable schedules as are the other legal materials. Generally the commercial publishers of the annotated statutes are very dependable to deliver all new legislation to their subscribers at or before its effective date, and to supplement it no less frequently than annually.

There are two publications which are worthy of special mention as sources of very up-to-date legal information. They are both published weekly in looseleaf form.

- *United States Law Week* reports the full opinions and other proceedings of the United States Supreme Court as soon as they are released. It also supplies a general-law section in which selected current decisions from state and federal courts are promptly summarized and classified.
- *Current Index to Legal Periodicals* is furnished in mimeographed or xeroxed 8½″ x 11″ sheets, classified by topic. It is intended for eventual destruction when the regular, bound periodical indexes come out in printed form. It serves the valuable purpose of furnishing classified references to legal periodical literature concurrent with the publication of the periodical, and considerably in advance of the appearance of the advance parts to the regular, bound periodical indexes.

The citators, mainly *Shepard's Citations,* must not be overlooked. There are similar devices in use in the scientific disciplines, *e.g.*, *Science Citation Index,* but for the most part, legal citators are highly unusual bibliographic tools.

The purpose of a legal citator is to supplement a bare precedent case, statute, or periodical article with references which will cast light on the current value of the precedent case, statute, or periodical article and inform the reader as to the weight which he should give it. A citator gives a legal researcher references to reports of cases, essays in annotated case series, and periodical articles which reflect subsequent judgments of the courts and legal writers concerning particular cases, statutes, or articles.

Attention is called to the important fact that citators furnish only references to subsequent material which specifically mentions the earlier material. If the subsequent material is in accord, or takes a contrary view, but does not mention the earlier material, a citator will not reveal the subsequent material for you. Legal citators are used via a unique system of abbreviations consisting of letters and arabic numerals, which takes on some of the characteristics of the *Uniform System of Citation*. However, the user of *Shepard's Citations* must be conscious that the key to the references is in the front of the volume, and that the symbols are apt to vary in meaning from set to set.

Let us take a hypothetical case which you have found and upon which you intend to rely, called *Smith v. Green*. If it were decided five years ago, fifty years ago, or more or less time ago and held a particular point of law, that case can and must be evaluated by way of a citator. The citator will give the legal researcher references to later cases which, among other things, may have followed it, explained it, criticized it, reversed it, or overruled it. The user may find periodical literature references concerning the case, or he may find where it has been discussed in an essay in an annotated case series. The legal citator is indispensable to a legal researcher.

Citators are supplemented and cumulated, and like digests, are available for a great number of separate states, the United States Supreme Court, the lower United States courts, and the National Reporter System. There are citators for other legal publications too, *e.g.*, the *Restatements*, the *Code of Federal Regulations*, and legal periodicals. The large number of different citators makes it inappropriate to publish a comprehensive list of them here. It is doubtful whether a representative list of them would be of significance. More than 75 such works are published by Shepard's/McGraw-Hill.[12]

LOCAL-STATE PRACTICE BOOKS

This book is not directed toward the practice of law in any particular state or jurisdiction. For that reason, there are no local-state references provided in the classified bibliography. It is important, however, that the legal researcher understand that there is a high probability that in any one state there will be a large number of special books which practicing lawyers and paralegals frequently use and rely upon with reference to the concrete problems before them. In many instances, such books are their first wave of attack on particular local-state research problems.

---

[12] See *How to Use Shepard's Citations* (1980), Colorado Springs, Shepard's/McGraw-Hill.

They have the purpose of bringing together statutes, references to precedent cases, model forms, and comments regarding local-state law practice. Such local-practice books are published by national and nonnational publishers for sale within the local states.

As one example which is not representative of the fifty states, there are state-oriented legal encyclopedias, *e.g.*, *California Jurisprudence 3d, Florida Jurisprudence 2d,* and *Texas Jurisprudence 3d*; most states do not have local state legal encyclopedias. Most states have numerous other local-practice books concerning various subjects, however. As additional examples, there are often local-state practice books consisting of one or more volumes, treating appellate practice, collections, corporate law and practice, criminal practice, eminent domain, family law, forms for commercial transactions, forms for litigation, jury instructions, mechanics' lien law, municipal law, probate law, procedure, real estate, school law, taxation, traffic law, trial evidence, wills, and worker's compensation.

Local-practice books are concerned with important details, and how to accomplish particular concrete objectives. They are indispensable to the practicing lawyer and paralegal, but from the standpoint of an overview of legal literature, which is the purpose of this book, there is little that would be gained by adding descriptive lists of such publications for one state or for all states, which would be commensurate with the space required to do so. The student must just remember that such aids are not to be overlooked when practicing law or dealing with law in any particular state.

CLASSIFIED BIBLIOGRAPHY

The following bibliography is classified mainly by subject. Many of the subjects in the classified bibliography can also be expected to be treated in the legal encyclopedias, the annotated case series, and the digests. Some of the books are short; some of them are long. Some of the books are descriptive; some of them are critical. The particular books listed in the classifications may or may not assist the reader, depending upon his or her need. In the main, all of the books are good beginning points for legal research. The list within each classification has been intentionally kept small, so that readers will not be overwhelmed.

Classifications of law are only artificial creations of people's minds, just as is law itself. For this reason, it is important that the legal researcher take notice of the cross-references which are listed in many of the classifications, and further recognize that there are possible topics under which an area of inquiry might reasonably be labeled, other than the one which is selected. In large part, the topics or classifications have been selected according to the courses of instruction in American law schools and paralegal schools. They are relatively few, however, in comparison to the number of topics or subject headings in the legal encyclopedias, digests, annotated case series, and law-library catalogs.[13]

Accounting

American Institute of Certified Public Accountants, *AICPA Audit and Accounting Manual*, 1984. Chicago, Commerce Clearing House, 752 p.

American Institute of Certified Public Accountants, *AICPA Codification of Statements on Auditing Standards Nos. 1-47*, 1984. Chicago, Commerce Clearing House, 816 p.

American Institute of Certified Public Accountants, *AICPA Professional Standards*, 1984. Chicago, Commerce Clearing House, 2 v.

SEC Accounting Guide, 1984. Chicago, Commerce Clearing House, 1112 p.

Administrative Law

Frank E. Cooper, *State Administrative Law*, 1965. Indianapolis, Bobbs-Merrill Co., 2 v. No supp. published.

Kenneth Culp Davis, *Administrative Law Text*, 3d ed. 1972. St. Paul, West Pub. Co., xvi, 617 p.

Kenneth Culp Davis, *Administrative Law Treatise*, 2d ed. 1978- . San Diego, K.C. Davis Pub. Co., 4 v.

Charles H. Koch, Jr., *Administrative Law and Practice*, 1985- . St. Paul, West Pub. Co., 2 v.

Bernard Schwartz, *Administrative Law*, 1976. Boston, Little, Brown & Co., xiv, 730 p.

Admiralty

admiralty, the jurisdiction exercised by United States courts over maritime contracts, torts, injuries and seizures, including cases arising on the navigable lakes and rivers. U.S. Const. Art. III, Sec. 2. In England, this jurisdiction is exercised by the Probate, Divorce and Admiralty Division of the High Court of Justice, and is confined to cases arising on the high seas and those portions of rivers and sounds in which the tides rise and fall.

Grant Gilmore & Charles L. Black, Jr., *The Law of Admiralty*, 2d ed. 1975. Mineola, N.Y., Foundation Press, xxi, 1101 p.

Elijah E. Jhirad, Alexander Sann & Bari Chase, *Benedict on Admiralty*, 7th ed. 1983- . N.Y., Matthew Bender, 22 v.

---

[13] The definitions for the legal classifications published herein are from *The Law Dictionary*, 6th edition, 1986, by Wesley Gilmer, Jr., and used by permission.

Alex L. Parks, *The Law of Tug, Tow, and Pilotage*, 2d ed. 1982. Centreville, Md., Cornell Maritime Press, cxxvi, 1228 p.

Advocacy — *See* "Appellate Advocacy" and "Trial Advocacy."

Agency

agent, a person authorized by another (the principal), to do an act or transact business for him, and to bind the principal within the limits of that authority. An agent may be general, to do all business of a particular kind; or special, to do one particular act. The agent's power to bind the principal is according to the scope of his authority.

Harold Gill Reuschlein & William A. Gregory, *Handbook on the Law of Agency and Partnership*, 1979. St. Paul, West Pub. Co., xxxv, 625 p. Part 1 Agency, p. 1-245.

W. Edward Sell, *Agency*, 1975. Mineola, N.Y., Foundation Press, xix, 226 p.

American Legal History

Charles M. Cook, *The American Codification Movement*, 1981. Westport, Conn., Greenwood Press, xi, 234 p.

William Winslow Crosskey & William Jeffrey, Jr., *Politics and the Constitution in the History of the United States*, 1953, 1980. Chicago, Univ. of Chicago Press, 3 v.

Max Farrand, *The Framing of the Constitution of the United States*, 1913. New Haven, Conn., Yale Univ. Press, ix, 281 p.

Max Farrand, ed., *The Records of the Federal Convention of 1787*, rev. ed. 1937. New Haven, Conn., Yale Univ. Press, 4 v.

Lawrence M. Friedman, *A History of American Law*, 1973. N.Y., Simon & Schuster, 655 p.

Alexander Hamilton, *The Federalist: A Commentary on the Constitution of the United States*, John C. Hamilton, ed. 1869. Philadelphia, Lippincott, clxv, 659 p., vi.

James Willard Hurst, *Law and Economic Growth*, 1964. Cambridge, Mass., Belknap Press of Harvard Univ. Press, xx, 946 p.

James Willard Hurst, *Law and Social Process in United States History*, 1960. Ann Arbor, Univ. of Mich. Law School, 361 p.

James Willard Hurst, *The Growth of American Law: The Law Makers*, 1950. Boston, Little, Brown, xiii, 502 p.

Wilfred J. Ritz, *American Judicial Proceedings First Printed Before 1801: An Analytical Bibliography*, 1984. Westport, Conn., Greenwood Press, xlviii, 364 p.

See also "Constitutional Law."

Annotated Case Series

American Law Reports Annotated (A.L.R.):
[1st Series], v. 1-175, 1919-1948;
2d Series, v. 1-100, 1948-1965;
3d Series, v. 1-100, 1965-1980;
4th Series, v. 1- , 1980- ;
Federal, v. 1- , 1969- .

Rochester and San Francisco, Lawyers Co-Op. Pub. Co. and Bancroft-Whitney.

There are digests, word indexes, and *Quick Indexes* for use with the *A.L.R.* series.

See also "Commercial Transactions," *Uniform Commercial Code Reporting Service,* and "Torts," *Negligence [and] Compensation Cases Annotated.*

Antitrust

anti-trust acts or **antitrust acts,** various federal and state statutes intended to protect trade and commerce from unlawful restraints and monopolies.

American Bar Association, Section of Antitrust Law, *Antitrust Civil Jury Instructions*, 1980. Chicago, ABA, xii, 208 p.

Phillip Areeda & Donald F. Turner, *Antitrust Law*, 1978- . Boston, Little, Brown, 6 v.

Attorney General's National Committee to Study the Antitrust Laws, *Report*, Stanley N. Barnes & S. Chesterfield Oppenheim, Chmn., 1955. Washington, U.S. Gov't Printing Office, xiii, 393 p. paperback. Reprinted, 1981, by Wm. S. Hein & Co., Buffalo, N.Y.

Earl W. Kintner, *Federal Antitrust Law*, 1980- . Cincinnati, Anderson Pub. Co., 9 v.

William T. Lifland, *State Antitrust Law*, 1984- . N.Y., Law Journal Seminars-Press, 1 v. looseleaf.

Julian O. Von Kalinowski, *Antitrust Laws and Trade Regulation,* 1969- . N.Y., Matthew Bender, 16 v., looseleaf. Monthly antitrust report.

See also "Franchising" and "Unfair Competition."

Appellate Advocacy

advocate, an attorney who speaks or writes, or both, in support of his client's cause.

Norman Brand & John O. White, *Legal Writing: The Strategy of Persuasion*, 1976. N.Y., St. Martin's Press, xvi, 205 p.

Brief for Appellants, *Brown v. Board of Education*, [347 U.S. 483 (1954)]. N.Y., NAACP Legal Defense and Educ'l Fund, xxxii, 235 p.

Leon Friedman, ed., *Argument: The Oral Argument Before the Supreme Court in Brown v. Board of Education of Topeka, 1952-55*, 1969. N.Y., Chelsea House, *l*, 601 p.

Girvan Peck, *Writing Persuasive Briefs*, 1984. Boston, Little, Brown, 312 p.

Edward D. Re, *Brief Writing and Oral Argument*, 5th rev. ed. 1983. Dobbs Ferry, N.Y., Oceana, xxii, 484 p.

Robert L. Stern, *Appellate Practice in the United States*, 1981. Washington, Bureau of National Affairs, 568 p.

Robert L. Stern & Eugene Gressman, *Supreme Court Practice*, 5th ed. 1978. Washington, Bureau of National Affairs, xlix, 1255 p.

Frederick Bernays Weiner, *Briefing and Arguing Federal Appeals*, 1967. Washington, Bureau of National Affairs, xvi, 527 p.

See also "Legal Writing."

Arbitration

arbitration, the voluntary submission of a matter in dispute to the non-judicial judgment of one, two, or more disinterested persons, called arbitrators, whose decision, called an award, is binding upon the parties.

Martin Domke, *The Law and Practice of Commercial Arbitration*, 1968-1984, Gabriel M. Wilner ed. Wilmette, Ill., Callaghan & Co., 1 v. looseleaf.

George Goldberg, *A Lawyer's Guide to Commercial Arbitration*, 2d ed. 1983. Philadelphia, ALI-ABA Committee on Contin. Prof. Educ., xv, 167 p.

Marvin Hill, Jr. & Anthony V. Sinicropi, *Evidence in Arbitration*, 1980. Washington, Bureau of National Affairs, 212 p.

Id., Remedies in Arbitration, 1981. Washington, Bureau of National Affairs, 372 p.

Edwin R. Teple & Robert B. Moberly, *Arbitration and Conflict Resolution*, 1979. Washington, Bureau of National Affairs, 614 p.

Bankruptcy — *See* "Debtor-Creditor Relations."

Bibliographies

Columbia Univ., *Dictionary Catalog of the Columbia University Law Library*, 1969- . Boston, G.K. Hall & Co. 28 v., First [1974] supp. 7 v., Second [1977] supp. 4 v.

Law Books 1876-1981, 1981. N.Y., R.R. Bowker Co., 4 v. Supplemented by *Law Information*, 1982- .

Julius J. Marke & Edward J. Bander, *Deans' List of Recommended Reading for Prelaw and Law Students*, 2d ed. 1984. N.Y., Oceana Pubs., xxi, 387 p.

See also "Legal Research," "Periodical Indexes," and "Reports of Cases."

Bills & Notes — *See* "Commercial Paper."

Biography

Ass'n of American Law Schools, *Directory of Law Teachers*, 1983-1984. St. Paul and Mineola, N.Y., West Pub. Co. and Foundation Press, 920 p. paperback. Annual.

Leon Friedman & Fred L. Israel, ed., *The Justices of the United States Supreme Court 1789-1969*, 4 v. 1969, v. 5 "The Burger Court 1969-1978," 1978. N.Y., R.R. Bowker Co.

Allen Johnson, ed., *Dictionary of American Biography, 1927-1936*, 1944 Supp. 1, 1958 Supp. 2, N.Y., Charles Scribner's Sons, 22 v.

Judges of the United States, 2d ed. 1983. Published under the auspices of the Bicentennial Committee of the Judicial Conference of the U.S., Washington, Superintendent of Documents, U.S. Government Printing Office, xix, 681 p.

William Draper Lewis, ed., *Great American Lawyers*, 1907-1909, Philadelphia, John C. Winston Co., 8 v.

Who's Who in American Law, 3d ed. 1983. Chicago, Marquis Who's Who, xvi, 863 p. Annual.

See also "Directories."

Business Law

See "Business Organizations," "Commercial Transactions," and "Contracts."

Business Organizations

business, every trade, occupation, or profession. Uniform Partnership Act § 2.

organization, a corporation, government, or governmental subdivision or agency, business trust, estate, trust, partnership, or association, two or more persons having a joint or common interest, or any other legal or commercial entity. U.C.C. § 1-201(28). Accord, Uniform Probate Code §§ 1-201(27), 5-103(12).

American Bar Foundation, *Model Business Corporation Act Annotated*, Committee on Corporate Laws, ed., Willard P. Scott Chmn., 2d ed. 1971- . St. Paul, West Pub. Co. for American Bar Foundation, 5 v.

Alan R. Bromberg, *Crane and Bromberg on Partnership*, 1968. St. Paul. West Pub. Co., xviii, 695 p.

Commerce Clearing House, *Professional Corporations Handbook*, 1973- . Chicago, Commerce Clearing House, 2 v. looseleaf.

William Meade Fletcher, *Corporation Forms Annotated*, Stephen M. Flanagan 4th ed. 1981- . Wilmette, Ill. Callaghan & Co., 15 v.

William Meade Fletcher, *Cyclopedia of the Law of Private Corporations*, 1983- rev. Cynthia Van Swearingen. Wilmette, Ill., Callaghan & Co., 34 v.

Harry G. Henn & John R. Alexander, *Laws of Corporations and Other Business Enterprises*, 3d ed. 1983. St. Paul, West Pub. Co., xli, 1371 p.

Harold Gill Reuschlein & William A. Gregory, *Handbook on the Law of Agency and Partnership*, 1979. St. Paul, West Pub. Co., xxxv, 625 p. Part 2 Partnership and Other Unincorporated Business Units, p. 246-503.

Uniform Laws Annotated, v. 6, *Uniform Partnership Act and Uniform Limited Partnership Act*, 1969- . St. Paul, West Pub. Co., viii, 631 p.

See also "Agency."

Civil Liberties and Civil Rights

civil rights, the rights of citizens of the United States guaranteed by the Constitution of the United States, particularly Amendments I, XIII, XIV and XV. (2) The rights of a citizen.

liberty, a broad and flexible term for freedom, absence of restraint, or self-determination. (2) Authority to do something.

Chester James Antieau, *Federal Civil Rights Acts: Civil Practice 2d*, 1980. Rochester, Lawyers Co-Op. Pub. Co., 2 v.

Joseph G. Cook & John L. Sobieski, *Civil Rights Actions*, 1983- . N.Y., Matthew Bender, 5 v. looseleaf. 6 v. projected.

Norman Dorsen, Paul Bender & Burt Neuborne, *Emerson, Haber & Dorsen's Political and Civil Rights in the United States*, 4th ed. 1976. Boston, Little, Brown & Co., 2 v. and supps.

Sheldon Nahmod, *Civil Rights and Civil Liberties Litigation: A Guide to Section 1983*, 1979- . Colorado Springs, Shepard's/McGraw-Hill, 400 p.

See also "Constitutional Law" and "Employment Discrimination."

Commercial Paper

commercial paper, negotiable instruments *(q.v.), e.g.,* checks and promissory notes.

Henry J. Bailey, *Brady on Bank Checks*, 5th ed. 1979 and supp. Boston, Warren, Gorham & Lamont, various pagination, 1 v.

Barkley Clark, *The Law of Bank Deposits, Collections and Credit Cards*, rev'd ed. 1981. Boston, Warren, Gorham & Lamont, various pagination, 1 v. and supp.

John J. Clarke, Henry J. Bailey III & Robert Young, Jr., *Bank Deposits and Collections*, 4th ed. 1972. Philadelphia, Joint Comm. on Contin. Legal Educ. of ALI and ABA, 285 p., paperback.

Ralph C. Clontz, Jr. & Terry D. Rice, *Truth-in-Lending Manual*, 5th ed. 1982 and supp. Boston, Warren, Gorham & Lamont, 2 v. and supp.

Henry Harfield, *Letters of Credit*, 1979. Philadelphia, ALI-ABA Comm. on Contin. Prof. Educ., xvii, 167 p. paperback.

Frederick M. Hart & William F. Willier, *Commercial Paper Under the Uniform Commercial Code* (2 & 2A *Bender's Uniform Commercial Code Service*), 1972- . N.Y., Matthew Bender, 2 v.

William D. Hawkland, *Commercial Paper*, 2d ed. 1979. Philadelphia, ALI-ABA Committee on Contin. Prof. Educ., xiv, 154 p. paperback.

Norman Penney & Donald I. Baker, *The Law of Electronic Fund Transfer Systems*, 1980 and supp. Boston, Warren, Gorham & Lamont, various pagination, 1 v. and supp.

W.M. Willson, J.H. Vaughan & R.F. Thiele, eds., *Michie on Banks and Banking*, perm. ed. rev'd and enlarged 1973- . Charlottesville, Va., Michie Co., 12 v.

See also "Commercial Transactions" and "Consumer Protection."

Commercial Transactions

commercial law, that branch of the law which concerns the relationships of persons engaged in business or doing business.

Richard M. Alderman & Richard F. Dole, *A Transactional Guide to the Uniform Commercial Code*, 2d ed. 1983. Philadelphia, Joint Committee on Continuing Legal Educ. of the ALI and ABA, 2 v.

Ronald A. Anderson, *Anderson on the Uniform Commercial Code*, 2d ed. 1970- . Rochester, N.Y., Lawyers Co-Op. Pub. Co., 5 v. and forms 2 v.

Bender's Uniform Commercial Code Service, Peter F. Coogan, William F. Hogan, Detlev F. Vagts, et al., 1965- . N.Y., Matthew Bender, 22 v., looseleaf.

Peter J. Betsos, *Modern UCC Litigation Forms*, 1978- . rev. Howard A. Benick. (v. 4, 4A *Bender's Uniform Commercial Code Service*), N.Y., Matthew Bender, 2 v. looseleaf.

Robert Braucher & Robert A. Riegert, *Introduction to Commercial Transactions*, 1977. Mineola, N.Y., Foundation Press, 551 p.

Uniform Commercial Code Reporting Service, 1965- . Chicago, Callaghan & Co., [37 v.], looseleaf advance parts, state correlation and code index, "Findex" volume. *Case Digest* [13 v.].

Uniform Laws Annotated, v. 1, 1A, 2, 2A, 3, 3A, *Uniform Commercial Code*, 1968- . Mineola, N.Y., and St. Paul, Edward Thompson Co. and West Pub. Co. v. 4-5 Forms.

James J. White & Robert S. Summers, *Handbook of the Law Under the Uniform Commercial Code*, 2d ed. 1980. St. Paul, West Pub. Co., xx, 635 p.

See also "Commercial Paper," "Consumer Protection," "Contracts," "Mortages," "Sales of Personal Property," and "Secured Transactions."

Bibliography

Mitchel J. Ezer, *Uniform Commercial Code Bibliography*, 1972- . Philadelphia, Joint Committee on Contin. Legal Educ. of ALI and ABA, xxx, 539 p. and supps.

Comparative Negligence

comparative negligence or **comparative fault,** a doctrine in tort law which allows proportionate recovery if both the plaintiff and defendant were negligent and thereby contributed to the cause of an injury. This doctrine is in effect in 42 states, Puerto Rico, and the Virgin Islands.

Carroll R. Heft & C. James Heft, *Comparative Negligence Manual*, 1971- . Mundelein, Ill., Callaghan & Co., 1 v. looseleaf.

Joseph W. Little, Edward Martin, Dean F. Davis, et al., *Comparative Negligence*, 1984- . N.Y., Matthew Bender, 3 v. looseleaf.

Victor E. Schwartz, *Comparative Negligence*, 1974- . Indianapolis, Allen Smith, 434 p.

Henry Woods, *The Negligence Case: Comparative Fault*, 1978- . Rochester, N.Y., Lawyers Co-Op. Pub. Co. 628 p.

Conflict of Laws

conflict of laws, the variance between the laws of two states or countries relating to the subject matter of a suit brought in one of them, when the parties to the suit, or some of them, or the subject matter, belong to the other.

American Law Institute, *Restatement of the Law, Second: Conflict of Laws, 2d*, 1971-1980. St. Paul, American Law Institute Pubs., 4 v.

Robert A. Leflar, *American Conflicts Law*, 3d ed. 1977. Indianapolis, and Charlottesville, Va., Bobbs-Merrill Co., xiv, 688 p.

Eugene F. Scoles & Peter Hay, *Conflict of Laws*, 1984. St. Paul, West Pub. Co., xxxi, 1233 p.

Russell J. Weintraub, *Commentary on the Conflict of Laws*, 2d ed. 1980. Mineola, N.Y., Foundation Press, xx, 635 p.

Constitutional Law

constitution, the fundamental and basic law of a state or nation which establishes the form and limitations of government and secures the rights of the citizens. (2) The Constitution of the United States was adopted in a convention of representatives of the people, at Philadelphia, September 17, 1787, and became the law of the land on the first Wednesday in March, 1789. 1 Stat. 10 (1861). (3) Each of the states composing the United States has a constitution of its own.

Alexander M. Bickel, *The Supreme Court and the Idea of Progress*, 1978. New Haven, Conn., Yale Univ. Press, xvi, 210 p.

Congressional Research Service, Library of Congress, *The Constitution of the United States of America*, Lester S. Jayson, *et. al.*, eds., 1973 and 1978 supp. Washington, U.S. Gov't Printing Office, xliv, 1961 p.

Harvard Law Review, Cambridge, Mass., Harvard Law Review Ass'n. Annual November issue No. 1.

Philip B. Kurland, ed., *Supreme Court Review*, 1960- . Chicago, Univ. of Chicago Press. Annual. Indexed in *Current Law Index* and *Index to Legal Periodicals.*

John E. Nowak, Ronald D. Rotunda & J. Nelson Young, *Constitutional Law*, 2d ed. 1983. St. Paul, West Pub. Co. xxix, 1317 p.

Bernard Schwartz, *Constitutional Law*, 1979. N.Y., Macmillan Pub. Co., xvii, 525 p.

Laurence H. Tribe, *American Constitutional Law*, 1978. Mineola, N.Y., Foundation Press, 1204 p.

Charles Warren, *The Supreme Court in United States History,* new and rev. ed. 1926. Boston, Little, Brown, 2 v. 1924 ed. 3 v.; 1937 ed. 2 v.

See also "American Legal History," "Civil Liberties and Civil Rights," and "Criminal Procedure," William A. Grimes and Charles H. Whitebread.

Consumer Protection

Consumer Protection Act, various state laws dealing with unfair, unconscionable, false, misleading, or deceptive actions or practices in the conduct of trade or commerce. Among other things, they tend to deal with contracts, combinations, and conspiracies in restraint of trade, provide for investigation and enforcement by the state attorney general, and for restoration of property.

Bureau of National Affairs, *Product Safety & Liability Reporter*, 1973- . Washington, Bureau of National Affairs, weekly looseleaf.

Commerce Clearing House, *Consumer Credit Guide*, 1969- . Chicago, Commerce Clearing House, 5 v. looseleaf.

Commerce Clearing House, *Consumer Product Safety Guide*, 19 - . Chicago, Commerce Clearing House, 3 v. looseleaf.

Earl W. Kintner, *A Primer on the Law of Deceptive Practices*, 2d ed. 1978. N.Y., Macmillan Pub. Co., xx, 706 p.

National Consumer Law Center, *Consumer Credit and Sales Legal Practice Series*, 1982. Boston, National Consumer Law Center, 10 v., supps., and *NCLC Reports*. Volumes titled: *Consumer Bankruptcy Law and Practice, Consumer Usury and Credit Overcharges, Debt Collection Harassment, Equal Credit Opportunity Act, Fair Credit Reporting Act, Odometer Law, Repossessions, Sales of Goods and Services, Truth in Lending in Transition,* and *Unfair and Deceptive Acts and Practices.*

See also "Commercial Paper," Ralph C. Clontz, Jr., & Terry D. Rice, and "Product Liability."

Contracts

contract, an agreement between competent parties, upon a legal consideration, to do or to abstain from doing some act. It is usually applied to simple or parol contracts, including written as well as verbal ones.*** (2) The total legal obligation which results from the parties' agreement as affected by the U.C.C. and any other applicable rules of law. U.C.C. § 1-201(11). (3) A promise or a set of promises for the breach of which the law gives a remedy, or the performance of which the law in some way recognizes as a duty. Restatement (Second) of Contracts. § 1.

American Law Institute, *Restatement of the Law Second: Contracts*, 1981-1982. St. Paul, American Law Institute Pubs., 6 v.

John D.Calamari & Joseph M. Perillo, *The Law of Contracts*, 2d ed. 1977. St. Paul, West Pub. Co., 878 p.

Arthur Linton Corbin, *Corbin on Contracts*, 1963- . St. Paul, West Pub. Co., 12 v., 1984 paperback supps. 2 v.

E. Allen Farnsworth, *Contracts*, 1982. Boston, Little, Brown & Co., xxiii, 984 p.

Samuel Williston, *A Treatise on the Law of Contracts*, Walter H. E. Jaeger 3d ed. 1957- . Mt. Kisco, N.Y., and Rochester, N.Y., Baker, Voorhis & Co. and Lawyers Co-Op. Pub. Co., 22 v.

See also "Commercial Transactions."

Copyright

copyright, subject to various limitations provided for by law, the exclusive rights to do and to authorize any of the following: (a) to reproduce the copyrighted work in copies or phonorecords; (b) to prepare derivative works based upon the copyrighted work; (c) to distribute copies or phonorecords of the copyrighted work to the public by sale or other transfer of ownership, or by rental, lease, or lending; (d) in the case of literary, musical, dramatic, and choreographic works, pantomimes, and motion pictures and other audiovisual works, to perform the copyrighted work publicly; and (e) in the case of literary, musical, dramatic, and choreographic works, pantomimes, and pictorial, graphic, or sculptural works, including the individual images of a motion picture or other audiovisual work, to display the copyrighted work publicly. 17 U.S.C. § 106; 90 Stat. 2546 (1976). Generally treated in tit. 17 U.S.C., 90 Stat. 2541 (1976).

American Society of Composers, Authors and Publishers, *Copyright Law Symposium*, 1939- . N.Y., Columbia Univ. Press, annual. Indexed in *Current Law Index* and *Index to Legal Periodicals.*

Harry G. Henn, *Copyright Primer*, 1979. N.Y., Practising Law Institute, xxvii, 785 p.

Melville B. Nimmer, *Nimmer on Copyright,* 1963- . N.Y., Matthew Bender, 4 v. looseleaf.

Henry P. Tseng, *New Copyright U.S.A.*, 1979. Columbus, Ohio, AMCO Int'l, xviii, 434 p. paperback.

Corporations — *See* "Business Organizations."

Corrections

correction, punishment.

Neil P. Cohen & James J. Gobert, *The Law of Probation and Parole*, 1983- . Colorado Springs, Shepard's/McGraw-Hill, xxii, 837 p.

Joseph G. Cook, *Constitutional Rights of the Accused: Post-Trial Rights*, 1976- . Rochester, N.Y., Lawyers Co-Op. Pub. Co., ix, 471 p.

John W. Palmer, *Constitutional Rights of Prisoners*, 3d ed. 1985. Cincinnati, Anderson Pub. Co., xiv, 1004 p. Text and footnotes p. 1-245; judicial decisions (cases) p. 247-843. Appendices, table of cases, index.

Larry W. Yackle, *Postconviction Remedies*, 1981- . Rochester, N.Y., and San Francisco, Lawyers Co-Op. Pub. Co. and Bancroft-Whitney, xxi, 776 p.

See also "Habeas Corpus."

Creditors' Rights — *See* "Debtor-Creditor Relations."

Crimes

crime, a flexible term for violations of law which are punished by the state or nation because of their effect on the public.

F. Lee Bailey & Henry B. Rothblatt, *Complete Manual of Criminal Forms: Federal and State*, 2d ed. 1974- . Rochester, N.Y., and San Francisco, Lawyers Co-Op. Pub. Co. and Bancroft-Whitney, 2 v.

Id., *Defending Business and White Collar Crimes: Federal and State*, 1969- . Rochester, N.Y., Lawyers Co-Op. Pub. Co., xxviii, 740 p.

Id., *Handling Misdemeanor Cases*, 1976- . Rochester, N.Y., and San Francisco, Lawyers Co-Op. Pub. Co. and Bancroft-Whitney, xxx, 545 p.

David Bernheim, *Defense of Narcotics Cases*, 1972- . N.Y., Matthew Bender, 2 v. looseleaf.

Criminal Law Reporter, 1967- . Washington, Bureau of National Affairs, weekly looseleaf.

Richard E. Erwin, Marilyn Kroll Minzer, *et. al., Defense of Drunk Driving Cases: Criminal — Civil*, 3d ed. 1984- . N.Y., Matthew Bender, 3 v. looseleaf.

John P. McCahey, ed. dir., James Farragher Campbell, P. David Fisher & David A. Mansfield, *Defense of Speeding, Reckless Driving & Vehicular Homicide Cases*, 1984- . N.Y., Matthew Bender, 1 v. looseleaf, various pagination.

B. Anthony Morosco, *Prosecution and Defense of Sex Crimes*, 1976- . N.Y., Matthew Bender, 1 v., looseleaf.

Rollin M. Perkins & Ronald N. Boyce, *Criminal Law*, 3d ed. 1982. Mineola, N.Y., Foundation Press, xxxv, 1269 p.

Charles E. Torcia, *Wharton's Criminal Law*, 14th ed. 1978- . Rochester and San Francisco, Lawyers Co-Op. Pub. Co. and Bancroft-Whitney, 4 v.

Criminal Procedure

procedure, the manner in which litigants proceed in the adversary conduct of a lawsuit, including the various steps by which the parties go about the litigation process. Occasionally called practice. Usually codified by rules or in codes, *e.g.,* *** Federal Rules of Criminal Procedure, analogous state rules of procedure, and various state codes of practice.

American Bar Ass'n, *Standards for Criminal Justice*, 2d ed. 1980- . Boston, Little, Brown. 4 v. looseleaf.

F. Lee Bailey & Henry B. Rothblatt, *Complete Manual of Criminal Forms, Federal and State*, 2d ed. 1974- . Rochester, N.Y., Lawyers Co-Op. Pub. Co., 2 v.

Joseph G. Cook, *Consitutional Rights of the Accused: Pre-Trial Rights*, 1972- Rochester, N.Y., and San Francisco, Lawyers Co-Op. Pub. Co. and Bancroft-Whitney, ix, 572 p.

Id., *Constitutional Rights of the Accused: Trial Rights*, 1974- . Rochester, N.Y., and San Francisco, Lawyers Co-Op. Pub. Co. and Bancroft-Whitney, ix, 426 p.

William A. Grimes, *Criminal Law Outline*, annual. Reno, National Judicial College, paperback. Useful as a quick reference.

Wayne R. LaFave & Jerold H. Israel, *Criminal Procedure*, 1984- . St. Paul, West Pub. Co., 3 v.

Wayne R. LaFave & Jerold H. Israel, *Criminal Procedure*, 1985. St. Paul, West Pub. Co., xlvii, 1142 p. Abridgement of 3 v. treatise above.

Richard B. McNamara, *Constitutional Limitations on Criminal Procedure*, 1982- . Colorado Springs, Shepard's/McGraw-Hill, xxviii, 419 p.

Charles E. Torcia, *Wharton's Criminal Procedure*, 12th ed. 1974- . Rochester, N.Y. Lawyers Co-Op. Pub. Co., 4 v.

Charles H. Whitebread, *Constitutional Criminal Procedure*, 1978- . Washington, American Academy of Judicial Education, xiv, 434 p.

Charles H. Whitebread, *Criminal Procedure*, 1980- . Mineola, N.Y., Foundation Press, xxii, 622 p.

See also "Corrections" and "Habeas Corpus."

Damages

damage, an injury to person, property, or reputation, occasioned by the wrongful act or negligence of another, or by accident. It may occur as a result of tort or breach of contract.

damages, a flexible term for the reparation in money which is allowed by law on account of damage *(q.v.)*. Accord, Restatement (Second) of Torts § 12A. They may be general, such as necessarily and by implication of law arise from the act complained of; special, such as under the peculiar circumstances of the case arise from the act complained of, but are not implied by law; compensatory, sufficient in amount to cover the loss actually sustained; exemplary, punitive, or vindictive, when in excess of the loss sustained and allowed as a punishment for torts committed with fraud, actual malice, or violence; nominal, when the act was wrong, but the loss sustained was trifling; substantial, when the loss was serious. Accord, Restatement (Second) of Torts §§ 902-908.

Charles T. McCormick, *Damages*, 1935. St. Paul, West Pub. Co., 811 p.

Kenneth R. Redden, *Punitive Damages*, 1980- . Charlottesville, Va., Michie Co., xvii, 1009 p.

Jacob A. Stein, *Damages and Recovery: Personal Injury and Death Actions*, 1972- . Rochester, N.Y., and San Francisco, Lawyers Co-Op. Pub. Co. and Bancroft-Whitney, xiv, 670 p.

See also "Equity," Dan B. Dobbs.

Debtor-Creditor Relations

bankruptcy, jurisdiction exercised by United States courts and created by federal statute. It concerns the affairs of insolvent debtors and includes voluntary petitions of natural persons, wage earner plans, and corporate reorganizations. Bankruptcy existed in Roman law and in English law. Congress is empowered to establish uniform laws on the subject of bankruptcies. U.S. Const. Art. I, Sec. 8. (2) Occasionally, insolvency.

Bankruptcy Service, Lawyers' Edition, 1979- . Rochester, N.Y., and San Francisco, Lawyers Co-Op. Pub. Co. and Bancroft-Whitney, 13 v. looseleaf.

Lawrence P. King, ed., *Collier on Bankruptcy*, 15th ed. 1979- . N.Y., Matthew Bender, 7 v., appendix 3 v., index 1 v., looseleaf.

Shepard's Bankruptcy Citations, 1980- . Colorado Springs, Shepard's/McGraw-Hill. 1 v. and supp.

West's Bankruptcy Digest, 1979- . St. Paul, West Pub. Co. [11 v. paperback].

Decedents' Estates

decedent, a deceased person. ***

estate, the condition and circumstance in which a person stands with regard to those around him and his property. *** (3) Includes the property of a decedent, trust, or person whose affairs are subject to the Uniform Probate Code, as originally constituted and as it exists from time to time during administration. Uniform Probate Code § 1-201(11).

William Herbert Page, *Page on the Law of Wills*, William J. Bowe & Douglas H. Parker rev. 1960- . Cincinnati, Anderson Pub. Co., 11 v. *Page Wills Manual*, abridgment, forthcoming.

Uniform Laws Annotated, *Uniform Probate Code*, 1983- . (v. *8 U.L.A.*), St. Paul, West Pub. Co., xii, 804 p.

See also "Estate Planning," "Taxation, *Federal Estate & Gift*," and "Trusts."

Dictionaries

Ballentine's Law Dictionary, William S. Anderson 3d ed., 1969. Rochester and San Francisco, Lawyers Co-Op. Pub. Co. and Bancroft-Whitney Co., ix, 1429 p.

Black's Law Dictionary, Michael J. Connolly & Joseph R. Nolan 5th ed. 1979. St. Paul, West Pub. Co., 1455 p.

Bouvier's Law Dictionary and Concise Encyclopedia, 1914, 3d revision, 8th ed., by Francis Rawle. Kansas City, Mo., and St. Paul, Vernon Law

Book Co. and West Pub. Co. 2 v. Reprinted 1984, Buffalo, N.Y., Wm. S. Hein & Co.

Bouvier's Law Dictionary, Baldwin's Century ed. 1934, William Edward Baldwin, ed. Cleveland, Banks-Baldwin Law Pub. Co., 1245 p.; 1934 supp. 86 p.

The *Bouvier's* dictionaries are especially useful to find definitions and collateral references concerning traditional legal concepts. They will frequently refer the reader to the origins of various legal concepts.

The Law Dictionary, Wesley Gilmer, Jr., rev., 6th ed. 1986. Cincinnati, Anderson Pub. Co., xiv, 426 p.

Words and Phrases, St. Paul, West Pub. Co., 90 v.

Digests

digest, a methodically arranged and indexed compilation of abstracts of decisions, intended to aid a legal researcher in finding precedent cases which are relevant to his or her problem cases. (2) Formerly, a textbook concerning the law.

A pamphlet furnished by a large publisher of digests lists 59 different national, federal, regional, state, and court digests which it publishes. *West's Law Finder*, 1982, St. Paul, West Pub. Co., p. 14-15. There are also other publishers of digests.

See also "Directories," *Martindale-Hubbell Law Directory*, v. 7, and text.

Directories

American Association of Law Libraries, Kamla J. King & Anne H. Butler, eds., *Directory of Law Libraries*, 1984 ed. Chicago, Commerce Clearing House, xxv, 168 p., paperback.

Association of American Law Schools, *Directory of Law Teachers*. St. Paul, and Mineola, N.Y., West Pub. Co. and Foundation Press, annual paperback.

Congressional Directory, 1983-1984, 98th Congress. Washington, U.S. Government Printing Office, xxxii, 1177 p. paperback.

Congressional Staff Directory, Charles B. Brownson, ed., 1982. Mt. Vernon, Va., Congressional Staff Directory, xiv, 1184 p.

Martindale-Hubbell Law Directory, annual, Summit, N.J., Martindale-Hubbell, 7 v. Annual directory of lawyers, organized by states, and cities within the states, contained in v. 1-6. The "Law Digests" are in v. 7.

United States Court Directory, 1984. Washington, Administrative Office of the U.S. Courts, 302 p., 8½" x 11" paperback.

United States Government Manual, 1984/85. Washington, Office of the Federal Register, vii, 913 p.

Want's Federal-State Court Directory, annual. Washington, Want Pub. Co., 1985 ed. 130 p., 8½″ x 11″.

Domestic Relations —*See* "Family Law."

Drafting

draftsman, a person who composes or authors a legal instrument.

Reed Dickerson, *The Fundamentals of Legal Drafting*, 1965. Boston, Little, Brown, xx, 203 p.

Rudolf Flesch, *How to Write Plain English: A Book for Lawyers and Consumers*, 1979. N.Y., Harper & Row Pubs. xiii, 126 p.

Richard C. Wydick, *Plain English for Lawyers*, 1979. Durham, N.C., Carolina Academic Press, 91 p.

See also "Forms, *Litigative*," "Forms, *Transactional*," and "Legal Writing."

Education Law

E. Gordon Gee & David J. Sperry, *Education Law and the Public Schools: A Compendium*, 1978. Boston, Allyn & Bacon, various pagination, 1 v. looseleaf.

H.C. Hudgins, Jr. & Richard S. Vacca, *Law and Education: Contemporary Issues and Court Decisions*, 1979. Charlottesville, Va., Michie Co., x, 364 p.

William A. Kaplin, *The Law of Higher Education*, 1978. San Francisco and Washington, Jossey-Bass Pubs., xxvii, 500 p.

Lawrence Kotin & William F. Aikman, *Legal Foundations of Compulsory School Attendance*, 1980. Port Washington, N.Y., 441 p.

Robert C. O'Reilly & Edward T. Green, *School Law for the Practitioner*, 1983. Westport, Conn., Greenwood Press, xiv, 314 p.

Leroy J. Peterson, Richard A. Rossmiller, & Marlin M. Volz, *The Law and Public School Operation*, 2d ed. 1978. N.Y., Hagerstown & San Francisco, Harper & Row Pubs., x, 528 p.

James A. Rapp, ed. & auth., *Education Law*, 1984- . N.Y., Matthew Bender, 3 v. looseleaf.

William D. Valente, *Law in the Schools*, 1980. Columbus, Ohio, Charles E. Merrill Pub. Co., xvii, 556 p.

Martha L. Ware & Madaline Kinter Remmlein, *School Law*, 4th ed. 1979. Danville, Ill., Interstate Printers & Pubs., xxxvi, 583 p.

Periodical

Journal of Law & Education, v. 1- , 1972- . Cincinnati, Jefferson Law Book Co. Indexed in *Current Law Index* and *Index to Legal Periodicals*.

Employment Discrimination

Commerce Clearing House, *EEOC Compliance Manual*, 1 v. looseleaf.

William L. Diedrich, Jr. & William Gaus, *Defense of Equal Employment Claims*, 1981- . Colorado Springs, Shepard's/McGraw-Hill, 500 p.

Howard C. Eglit, *Age Discrimination*, 1982- . Colorado Springs, Shepard's/ McGraw-Hill, 500 p.

Arthur Larson, *Employment Discrimination*, 1975- . N.Y., Matthew Bender, 4 v. looseleaf.

Mary Green Miner & John B. Miner, *Employee Selection Within the Law*, 1979. Washington, Bureau of National Affairs, 590 p. Supplemented by *Uniform Guidelines on Employee Selection Procedures*, rev'd ed. 1980, 80 p. paperback.

Lee Modjeska, *Handling Employment Discrimination Cases*, 1980- . Rochester, N.Y. and San Francisco, Lawyers Co-Op. Pub. Co. and Bancroft-Whitney, 559 p.

Barbara Lindemann Schlei & Paul Grossman, *Employment Discrimination Law*, 2d ed. 1983- . Washington, Bureau of National Affairs, 1720 p.

Encyclopedias

American Jurisprudence 2d, v. 1- , 1962- . Rochester and San Francisco, Lawyers Co-Op. Pub. Co. and Bancroft-Whitney, [107 v.].

American Jurisprudence [1st], v. 1- , 1936- . San Francisco and Rochester, Bancroft-Whitney and Lawyers Co-Op. Pub. Co., 66 v. Superseded by *American Jurisprudence 2d.*

Corpus Juris, v. 1-72, 1914-1937. Brooklyn and London, American Law Book Co. and Butterworth & Co. Partially superseded by *Corpus Juris Secundum,* which uses the footnotes of *Corpus Juris* as additional supporting references.

Corpus Juris Secundum, v. 1- , 1936- . Brooklyn and St. Paul, American Law Book Co. and West Pub. Co. [137 v.].

There are various other, earlier legal encyclopedias; they are seldom consulted.

English Law

The English and Empire Digest, 1919- , 1979- reissue. London, Butterworth & Co. [74 v.].

Earl of Halsbury, *The Laws of England*, 1973- . 4th ed. by Lord Hailsham of St. Marylebone. London, Butterworth & Co., [56 v.].

Bibliography

A.G. Chloros, ed., *A Bibliographical Guide to the Law of the United Kingdom, the Channel Islands and the Isle of Man*, 2d ed. 1973. London, Univ. of London, xvii, 301 p.

Environmental Law

environmental law, the resolution of disputes, usually between the national or state government and someone whom it accuses of violating its laws, concerning the conditions surrounding mankind and affecting his comfort and well-being, *e.g.*, air pollution, water pollution, heat pollution, noise pollution, solid waste disposal, and weather modification.

Ray J. Davis & Lewis O. Grant, *Weather Modification Technology and Law*, 1978. Boulder, Colo., Westview Press, xviii, 124 p.

Environment Reporter, v. 1- , John D. Stewart, ed., 1970- . Washington, Bureau of National Affairs, looseleaf.

Frank P. Grad, *Treatise on Environmental Law*, 1973- . N.Y., Matthew Bender, 5 v. looseleaf.

Harold P. Green, ed., *Energy Law Service*, 1978- . Wilmette, Ill., Callaghan & Co., 3 v. Treats environmental regulation.

Gail Boyer Hayes, *Solar Access Law*, 1979. Cambridge, Mass., Ballinger Pub. Co., xix, 303 p.

Sandy F. Kraemer, *Solar Law*, 1978- . Colorado Springs, Shepard's, ix, 364 p.

John H. Minan & William H. Lawrence, eds., *Legal Aspects of Solar Energy*, 1981. Lexington, Mass., Lexington Books, xiii, 231 p.

William H. Rodgers, Jr., *Handbook on Environmental Law*, 1977. St. Paul, West Pub. Co., 908 p.

Frank P. Skillern, *Environmental Protection*, 1981- . Colorado Springs, Shepard's/McGraw-Hill, xxii, 384 p.

William A. Thomas, ed., *Legal and Scientific Uncertainties of Weather Modification*, 1977. Durham, Duke Univ. Press, viii, 155 p.

V. J. Yannacone, Jr., Bernard S. Cohen & Steven G. Davison, *Environmental Rights and Remedies,* 1972- . Rochester, Lawyers Co-Op. Pub. Co., 3 v.

Equity

equity, fairness. (2) A type of justice that developed separately from the common law, and which tends to complement it. The current meaning is to classify disputes and remedies according to their historical relationship and development. Under modern rules of civil procedure, law and equity have been unified. Fed. R. Civ. P. 2. (3) Historically, the courts of equity had a power of framing and adapting new remedies to particular cases, which the common-law courts did not possess. In doing so, they allowed themselves latitude of construction and assumed, in certain matters such as trusts, a power of enforcing moral obligations which the courts of law did not admit or recognize.***

William Q. DeFuniak, *Handbook of Modern Equity*, 2d ed. 1956. Boston, Little, Brown, xii, 269 p.

Dan B. Dobbs, *Handbook on the Law of Remedies: Damages, Equity, Restitution*, 1973. St. Paul, West Pub. Co., xxiii, 1067 p.

Graham Douthwaite, *Attorney's Guide to Restitution*, 1977- . Indianapolis, Allen Smith Co., vii, 580 p.

Henry Lacey McClintock, *Handbook of the Principles of Equity*, 2d ed. 1948. St. Paul, West Pub. Co., xxxii, 643 p.

George E. Palmer, *The Law of Restitution*, 1978- . Boston, Little, Brown. 4 v.

John Norton Pomeroy, *A Treatise on Equity Jurisprudence*, Spencer W. Symons 5th ed. 1941. San Francisco and Rochester, N.Y., Bancroft-Whitney and Lawyers Co-Op. Pub. Co. 5 v.

Estate Planning

estate, the condition and circumstance in which a person stands with regard to those around him and his property. *** (3) Includes the property of a decedent, trust, or person whose affairs are subject to the Uniform Probate Code, as originally constituted and as it exists from time to time during administration. Uniform Probate Code § 1-201(11).

A. James Casner, *Estate Planning*, 5th ed. 1984- . Boston, Little, Brown, 6 v., v. 1, 5 looseleaf, and 1984 bound supp.

Commerce Clearing House, *Financial & Estate Planning*, 19 - . Chicago, Commerce Clearing House, 4 v. looseleaf.

James F. Farr & Jackson W. Wright, Jr., *An Estate Planner's Handbook*, 1979- . Boston, Little, Brown, 720 p.

E. Fiore, M. Friedlich, T. McInerney & A. Chevat, *Modern Estate Planning*, 1981- . N.Y., Matthew Bender, 6 v. looseleaf.

William Parsons, *Lifetime and Testamentary Estate Planning*, 9th ed. 1983. Philadelphia, ALI-ABA Committee on Continuing Prof. Educ., xvi, 228 p.

John R. Price, *Contemporary Estate Planning*, 1983- . Boston, Little, Brown, 896 p.

Jeffrey A. Schoenblum, *Multistate and Multinational Estate Planning*, 1982- . Boston, Little, Brown, 2 v.

Harold Weinstock, *Planning an Estate, 2/e*, 1982- . Colorado Springs, Shepard's/McGraw-Hill, 425 p.

See also "Taxation, *Federal Estate & Gift*."

Estates — *See* "Decedents' Estates."

Evidence

evidence, proof, either written or unwritten, of allegations at issue between parties. It may be (a) direct or indirect, which latter includes circumstantial evidence; (b) substantive, *i.e.,* directed to proof of a distinct fact, or corroborative, *i.e.,* in support of previous evidence; (c) intrinsic, *i.e.,* internal, or extrinsic, *i.e.,* not derived from anything to be found in the document itself; (d) original or derivative, *i.e.,* which passes through some channel, *e.g.,* parol, as opposed to original documents or evidence.***

American Jurisprudence Proof of Facts Annotated, 1959- , and *American Jurisprudence Proof of Facts 2d*, 1974- . San Francisco and Rochester, N.Y., Bancroft-Whitney Co., Lawyers Co-Op. Pub. Co., 30 v. and 41 v., Fact Book, Quick Index.

E. Gardner Brownlee, *Objections to Evidence*, 1974. Reno, National Judicial College, 175 p. looseleaf.

Edward W. Cleary, gen. ed., *McCormick on Evidence*, 3d ed. 1984. St. Paul, West Pub. Co., xxix, 1372 p.

Federal Rules of Evidence Service, 1979- . Wilmette, Ill., Callaghan & Co. [15 v.], *Digest* [5 v.], "Rules of Evidence & Finding Aids," "Current Volume," looseleaf advance parts.

Burr W. Jones, *Jones on Evidence*, 6th Spencer A. Gard ed. 1972- . Rochester, N.Y., and San Francisco, Lawyers Co-Op. Pub. Co. and Bancroft-Whitney, 4 v.

David W. Louisell & Christopher B. Mueller, *Federal Evidence*, 1977- . Rochester, N.Y., and San Francisco, Lawyers Co-Op. Pub. Co. and Bancroft-Whitney, 5 v.

Stephen A. Saltzburg & Kenneth R. Redden, *Federal Rules of Evidence Manual*, 3d ed. 1982 and supp. Charlottesville, Va., Michie Co., xxxii, 907 p.

John H. Wigmore, *Evidence in Trials at Common Law*, P. Tillers rev. 1983 and supp. Boston, Little, Brown, 12 v. and supp.

See also "Trial Advocacy."

Family Law

Family Law Reporter, weekly looseleaf. Washington, Bureau of National Affairs.

Leander J. Foley & Theodore McMillian, *Family Law*, 1976. Reno, National College of the State Judiciary, vii, 309 p., paperback.

Ann M. Haralambie, *Handling Child Custody Cases*, 1983- . Colorado Springs, Shepard's/McGraw-Hill, xxiii, 621 p.

Patricia M. Hoff, Joanne Schulman, Adrienne E. Volenik & Jean E. O'Daniel, *Interstate Child Custody Disputes and Parental Kidnapping: Policy,*

Practice & Law, 1982. Washington and Chicago, Legal Services Corp. and ABA, 1 v. paperback, various pagination.

Harry D. Krause, *Child Support in America: The Legal Perspective*, 1981. Charlottesville, Va., Michie Co., xv, 700 p.

Alexander Lindley, *Separation Agreements and Ante-Nuptial Contracts*, rev'd ed. 1967- . N.Y., Matthew Bender, 2 v. looseleaf.

John P. McCahey, Martin Kaufman & Celeste Kraut, *Child Custody & Visitation Law and Practice*, 1984- , Alan D. Scheinkman rev. N.Y., Matthew Bender, 4 v. looseleaf.

National Council of Juvenile & Family Court Judges, *Child Support Enforcement Judicial Benchbook*, 1981. Reno, National Council of Juvenile & Family Court Judges, 1 v., 8½" x 11" looseleaf, various pagination. organized by dividers.

Sidney B. Schatkin, *Disputed Paternity Proceedings*, rev'd 4th ed. 1975- . N.Y., Matthew Bender, 2 v., looseleaf.

See also "Juvenile Law."

Federal Courts and Jurisdiction

American Law Institute, *Study of the Division of Jurisdiction Between State and Federal Courts*, 1969. Philadelphia, American Law Institute, xix, 587 p.

Henry J. Friendly, *Federal Jurisdiction: A General View*, 1973. N.Y., Columbia Univ. Press, 199 p.

Henry M. Hart, Jr. & Herbert Wechsler, *The Federal Courts and the Federal System*, 2d ed. 1973 and supp. Mineola, N.Y., Foundation Press, lxxxviii, 1657 p. Law-school casebook.

Martin H. Redish, *Federal Jurisdiction: Tensions in the Allocation of Judicial Power*, 1980. Indianapolis and Charlottesville, Va., Michie Co. and Bobbs-Merrill Co., xiii, 361 p.

Charles Alan Wright, *The Law of Federal Courts*, 4th ed. 1983. St. Paul, West Pub. Co., xiv, 1098 p.

Forms

form, *** A model to aid a person in drawing up an instrument, pleading, order, judgment, or other legal document.

Litigative

American Jurisprudence Pleading and Practice Forms Annotated, rev'd 1967- . San Francisco and Rochester, N.Y., Lawyers Co-Op. Pub. Co. and Bancroft-Whitney, 32 v.

Louis R. Frumer & Marvin Waxner, *Bender's Federal Practice Forms*, 1951- . N.Y., Matthew Bender, 16 v. looseleaf.

James Wm. Moore & Louis R. Frumer, *Moore's Manual: Federal Practice Forms*, 1964- . N.Y., Matthew Bender, 4 v. looseleaf.

West's Federal Forms, 3d ed. 1982- . St. Paul, West Pub. Co., 12 v.

See also "Crimes," F. Lee Bailey & Henry Rothblatt, and "Jury Instructions."

Transactional

American Jurisprudence Legal Forms, 2d ed. 1971- . Rochester, Lawyers Co-Op. Pub. Co., 28 v.

Saul Gordon & Stephen Kurzman, *Gordon's Modern Annotated Forms of Agreement*, rev'd 1970. Englewood Cliffs, N.J., Prentice-Hall, xi, 2093 p.

Marvin Hyman, *Basic Legal Forms With Commentary*, 1981- . Boston, Warren, Gorham & Lamont, 1 v. looseleaf.

Nichols Cyclopedia of Legal Forms Annotated, rev'd 1974- . Chicago, Callaghan & Co., 23 v.

Jacob Rabkin & Mark H. Johnson, *Current Legal Forms with Tax Analysis*, 1948- . Albany, Matthew Bender, 22 v. looseleaf.

Franchising

franchise, *** The privilege of marketing the products and using the trade name, trademarks, and capitalizing on the good will of a manufacturer, merchant, or other business concern. It is usually conferred for a consideration.

ABA Section of Antitrust Law, *Franchise Law Bibliography*, 1984. Chicago, American Bar Ass'n, vii, 120 p., paperback.

Harold Brown, *Franchising Realities & Remedies*, 1982- . New York, Law Journal Seminars-Press, 1 v. looseleaf, various pagination.

Gladys Glickman, *Franchising*, 1969- . N.Y., Matthew Bender, 4 v. looseleaf.

Philip F. Zeidman, ed., *Legal Aspects of Selling & Buying*, 1983- . Colorado Springs, Shepard's/McGraw-Hill, xlv, 555 p.

See also "Antitrust."

Governmental Liability

Shepard's Ed. Staff, *Civil Actions Against State Government, Its Divisions, Agencies and Officers*, 1982- . Colorado Springs, Shepard's/McGraw-Hill, xxxiv, 939 p.

Shepard's Ed. Staff, *Civil Actions Against the United States, Its Agencies, Officers and Employees*, 1982- . Colorado Springs, Shepard's/McGraw-Hill, xii, 544 p.

Habeas Corpus

ha'beas cor'pus, *l.* (that you have the body), words used in various writs, commanding one who detains another to have, or bring, him before the court issuing the same. See also, *habeas corpus ad subjiciendum.*

ha'beas cor'pus ad subjicien'dum, the celebrated prerogative writ of American and English law, which is the usual remedy for a person deprived of his liberty. Its purpose is to test the legality of the restraints on a person's liberty, *i.e.,* whether he is restrained of his liberty by due process of law, not whether he is guilty or innocent. It is addressed to him who detains another in custody, and commands him to produce the body of the person in custody, with the day and cause of his caption and detention, and to do, submit to, and receive whatever the court shall think fit. This writ is guaranteed by U.S. Const. Art. I, Sec. 9, and by the state constitutions. 28 U.S.C. §§ 2241-2255.

Joseph G. Cook, *Constitutional Rights of the Accused: Post-Trial Rights*, 1976- . Rochester, N.Y., Lawyers Co-Op. Pub. Co. Ch. 4, Habeas Corpus §§ 86-126 (118 p.) and appendix.

William F. Duker, *A Constitutional History of Habeas Corpus*, 1980. Westport, Conn., Greenwood Press, ix, 349 p.

Wayne R. LaFave & Jerold H. Israel, *Criminal Procedure*, 1984- . St. Paul, West Pub. Co. Federal Habeas Corpus §§ 27.2-27.9 (107 p.).

United States Code Annotated, tit. 28, §§ 2241-2255, St. Paul, West Pub. Co. Contains copious case notes in 3 books.

United States Code Service, tit. 28, §§ 2241-2255, Rochester, N.Y., Lawyers Co-Op. Pub. Co. Contains case notes and collateral references in 2 books.

Donald E. Wilkes, Jr., *Federal and State Postconviction Remedies and Relief*, 1983- . Norcross, Ga., Harrison Co., xiii, 318 p.

Larry W. Yackle, *Postconviction Remedies*, 1981- . Rochester, N.Y., and San Francisco, Lawyers Co-Op. Pub. Co. and Bancroft-Whitney, xxi, 776 p.

Insurance

insurance, the act of providing against a possible loss, by entering into a contract with a licensed corporation that is willing to bind itself to make good such loss, should it occur. The instrument by which the contract is made is called a policy; the consideration paid to the insurer, who is sometimes called an underwriter, is called a premium. Fire and marine insurance is usually by way of indemnity, *i.e.,* only such sum is paid by the insurer as is actually lost, and, on making such payment, he is entitled to stand in the place of the assured. (2) In the case of life or accident insurance, the insurer undertakes, in consideration of a premium, to pay a certain sum to the insured, or his legal representatives, on his death or injury by an accident. (3) There are many various types of insurance, each of which are defined by the respective policies which evidence the agreements between the parties, *e.g.*, automobile insurance, creditor life insurance, homeowner insurance, owner, landlord, and tenant insurance, and worker's compensation insurance.

John Alan Appleman & Jean Appleman, *Insurance Law and Practice with Forms*, 1941- . Kansas City and St. Paul, Vernon Law Book Co. and West Pub. Co., 59 v.

Olga Becker, *Index/Citator to Insurance Law*, 2d ed. 1979- . St. Louis, Index/Citator System, 2 v.

George J. Couch, *Cyclopedia of Insurance Law 2d*, Ronald A. Anderson ed. 1959- . Rochester, Lawyers Co-Op. Pub. Co., 30 v.

Robert E. Keeton, *Basic Text on Insurance Law*, 1971 and supp. St. Paul, West Pub. Co., xviii, 712 p.

Irvin E. Schermer, *Automobile Liability Insurance: No-Fault Insurance, Uninsured Motorists, Compulsory Coverage*, 2d ed. 1981, rev'd 1984. N.Y., Clark Boardman Co., 2 v. looseleaf.

International Law

international law, is either public or private. (1) The former regulates the conduct of independent nations toward each other. (2) The latter decides the tribunal before which, and the law by which, private rights shall be determined.

American Law Institute, *Restatement of the Law, Second: Foreign Relations Law of the United States*, 1965. St. Paul, American Law Institute Pubs., xxvi, 679 p.

Encyclopedia of Public International Law, 1981- . Max Planck Institute for Comparative Public Law and Int'l Law, Amsterdam and N.Y., North-Holland Pub. Co., 7 v.

Melquiades J. Gamboa, *A Dictionary of International Law and Diplomacy*, 1973. Queson City, Philippines, Central Law Books Pub. Co., x, 351 p.

Biswanath Sen, *A Diplomat's Handbook of International Law and Practice*, 2d rev. ed. 1979. Hague and Boston, Nijhoff, 529 p.

United States Treaties and Other International Agreements, v. 1- , 1950- . Washington, Department of State, serial.

Digests

In international law, digests tend to serve a purpose analogous to a legal encyclopedia or treatise.

Green Haywood Hackworth, *Digest of International Law*, 1940-1944. Washington, U.S. Gov't Printing Office, 8 v. Coverage from 1906.

John Bassett Moore, *A Digest of International Law,* 1906. Washington, U.S. Gov't Printing Office, 8 v. Pre-1906 coverage.

Arthur W. Rovine & Marian Lloyd Nash, *Digest of U.S. Practice in International Law*, 1973- . Washington, U.S. Gov't Printing Office.

Marjorie M. Whiteman, *Digest of International Law*, 1963-1973. Washington, Superintendant of Documents, Department of State. 15 v. Particularly treats period from 1943 to 1963.

Periodicals

In international law, periodicals tend to serve a purpose analogous to a legal digest, via their individual indexes.

American Journal of International Law, v. 1- . 1907- . Contains quarterly "Contemporary Practice of the U.S. Relating to International Law."

International Legal Materials, v. 1- , 1962- .

Jurisprudence — See *"Philosophy of Law."*

Jury Instructions

jury directions, or **jury instructions,** a statement given by the judge, which sets forth the law applicable to a particular lawsuit, which has been heard by a jury and is about to be decided by the jury. Fed. R. Civ. P. 51.

Edward J. Devitt & Charles B. Blackman, *Federal Jury Practice & Instructions*, 3d ed. 1977- . St. Paul, West Pub. Co., 3 v. and paperback supp.

Graham Douthwaite, *Jury Instructions on Damages in Tort Actions*, 1981- Indianapolis, Allen Smith Co., xi, 554 p.

Id., *Alexander's Jury Instructions on Medical Issues*, 2d ed. 1980- . Indianapolis, Allen Smith Co., xiv, 520 p.

Robert L. McBride, *The Art of Instructing the Jury*, 1969- . Cincinnati, W. H. Anderson Co., xviii, 545 p.

A. H. Reid, *Reid's Branson Instructions to Juries*, 1960- . Charlottesville, Va., Michie Co., 7 v. Civil actions, criminal offenses, forms.

Juvenile Law

juvenile courts, tribunals specially created by various state statutes to supervise dependent, neglected, and delinquent children, *i.e.*, persons under a specified age.

Lindsay G. Arthur, ed., *National Bench Book for Juvenile Courts*, 2d ed. 1979. St. Paul, American Caselaw Corp., xvii, 158 p., paperback.

F. Lee Bailey & Henry B. Rothblatt, *Handling Juvenile Delinquency Cases*, 1982- . Rochester, N.Y., and San Francisco, Lawyers Co-Op. Pub. Co. and Bancroft-Whitney, xviii, 527 p.

Samuel M. Davis, *Rights of Juveniles*, 2d ed. 1980- . N.Y., Clark Boardman, 1 v., various pagination, looseleaf.

Institute of Judicial Administration-ABA, *Juvenile Justice Standards*, 1980. Cambridge, Mass., Ballinger Pub. Co., 20 v.

National Council of Juvenile & Family Court Judges, *Judicial Review of Children in Placement Deskbook*, 1981. Reno, National Council of Juvenile & Family Court Judges, xii, 195 p. 8½″ x 11″ looseleaf.

See also "Family Law."

Labor Law

Gerald E. Berendt, *Collective Bargaining*, 1984- . Charlottesville, Va., Michie Co., xvi, 340 p.

Decisions and Orders of the National Labor Relations Board, 1935/36- , v. 1- . Washington, U.S. Gov't Printing Office. Serial.

Labor Cases, 1940- . Chicago, Commerce Clearing House. Serial.

Labor Law Reporter, 1965- . Chicago, Commerce Clearing House, 15 v. looseleaf. (Federal labor relations 6 v., Federal wages-hours 2 v., State laws 3 v., Employment practices 4 v.).

Labor Relations Reference Manual, 1935- . Washington, Bureau of National Affairs. Serial.

Charles J. Morris, ed., *The Developing Labor Law*, 2d ed. 1983- . Washington, Bureau of National Affairs, 2 v.

Land Planning

Robert M. Anderson, *American Law of Zoning 2d*, 1976- . Rochester, N.Y., Lawyers Co-Op. Pub. Co., 5 v.

Daniel R. Mandelker, *Land Use Law*, 1982- . Charlottesville, Va., Michie Co., xvi, 407 p.

Craig A. Peterson & Claire McCarthy, *Handling Zoning and Land Use Litigation: A Practical Guide*, 1982- . Charlottesville, Va., Michie Co., xxxi, 737 p.

Arden H. Rathkopf, *The Law of Zoning and Planning*, 4th ed. 1956- . N.Y., Clark Boardman Co., 5 v. looseleaf.

Norman Williams, Jr., *American Planning Law; Land Use and the Police Power*, 1974 and supp. Chicago, Callaghan & Co., 5 v.

Emmett C. Yokley, *Zoning Law and Practice*, 4th ed. 1978- . Charlottesville, Va., Michie Co., 8 v.

Landlord & Tenant — *See* "Property."

Law Office Management

Mary Ann Altman & Robert I. Weil, *How to Manage Your Law Office*, 1973- . N.Y., Matthew Bender, 1 v. looseleaf.

Frank Arentowicz, Jr., & Ward Bower, *Law Office Automation and Technology*, 1980- . N.Y., Matthew Bender, 1 v. looseleaf.

Sidney W. Frost & James C. Dunlap, *Automated Law Office Systems: A Survey of Today's Tools and Techniques*, 1983. St. Paul, West Pub. Co., xxiii, 422 p., paperback.

Paul S. Hoffman, ed., *Law Office Economics and Management Manual*, 1970- . Wilmette, Ill., Callaghan & Co., 2 v. looseleaf.

See also "Legal Profession and Ethics," Thomas W. Brunner, *et al.*

Legal Drafting — *See* "Drafting."

Legal Profession and Ethics

Thomas W. Brunner, Julie P. Hamre, & Joan F. McCaffrey, *Legal Assistant's Handbook*, 1982. Washington, Bureau of National Affairs, 225 p. paperback.

Code of Judicial Conduct. See *Martindale-Hubbell Law Directory* v. 7 and Wesley Gilmer, Jr., *The Law Dictionary* 417-426 (1986).

Code of Professional Responsibility. See *American Jurisprudence 2d* Desk Book (1962), 1978 Cumulative Supplement Document 91:1 (not included in 2d, 1979 ed.); Henry Campbell Black, *Black's Law Dictionary* xvii-lxvii (Rev. 4th ed. 1968, 1970) (not included in 5th, 1979, ed.); and Wesley Gilmer, Jr., rev., *Cochran's Law Lexicon (The Law Dictionary)* 370-429 (5th ed. 1973).

Donald R. Fretz, Rodney A. Peeples & Thomas C. Wicker, *Ethics for Judges*, 1982. Reno, National Judicial College, vii, 88 p., paperback.

Lawyer's Manual on Professional Conduct, 1984- . Washington, ABA and Bureau of National Affairs, 2 v., looseleaf.

Ronald E. Mallen & Victor B. Levit, *Legal Malpractice*, 1981- . St. Paul, West Pub. Co., xviii, 1055 p.

David J. Meiselman, *Attorney Malpractice: Law & Procedure*, 1980- . Rochester, N.Y., and San Francisco, Lawyers Co-Op. Pub. Co. and Bancroft-Whitney, xv, 516 p.

Model Rules of Professional Conduct. See *Martindale-Hubbell Law Directory* v. 7 and Wesley Gilmer, Jr., *The Law Dictionary* 397-415 (1986).

William P. Statsky, *Introduction to Paralegalism: Perspectives, Problems and Skills*, 2d ed. 1982. St. Paul, West Pub. Co., xii, 700 p.

See also "Law Office Management."

Legal Research

Morris L. Cohen & Robert C. Berring, *How to Find the Law*, 8th ed. 1983. St. Paul, West Pub. Co.,xxxix, 790 p.

J. Myron Jacobstein & Roy M. Mersky, *Fundamentals of Legal Research*, 2d ed. 1981. Mineola, N.Y., Foundation Press, xli, 614 p.

Miles O. Price, Harry Bitner & Shirley Raissi Bysiewicz, *Effective Legal Research*, 4th ed. 1979. Boston, Little, Brown, xix, 643 p.

See also "Bibliographies," "Directories," American Association of Law Libraries, "Quotations," "Reports of Cases," and "Statutory Construction," Gwendolyn B. Folsom.

Legal Writing

Frank E. Cooper, *Writing in Law Practice*, 2d ed. 1963. Indianapolis, Bobbs-Merrill, xix, 527 p.

David Mellinkoff, *Legal Writing: Sense and Nonsense*, 1982. N.Y., Charles Scribner's Sons, xxix, 242 p.

A Uniform System of Citation, 14th ed. 1986. Cambridge, Harvard Law Review Ass'n, xii, 255 p., paperback.

Henry Weihofen, *Legal Writing Style*, 2d ed. 1980. St. Paul, West Pub. Co., xi, 332 p.

English

The Chicago Manual of Style, 13th ed. 1982. Chicago, Univ. of Chicago Press, ix, 739 p.

J. E. Silverthorn & Devern J. Perry, *Word Division Manual*, 2d ed. 1970. Cincinnati and Chicago, South-Western Pub. Co., viii, 151 p. paperback. Deals with the 15,000 most-used words in business communication.

William Strunk, Jr. & E. B. White, *The Elements of Style*, 3d ed. 1979. N.Y., Macmillan Co., xvii, 85 p., hardbound and paperback.

Thesauri

Richard Soule, *Dictionary of English Synonyms,* George H. Howison ed. 1967. Brooklyn, P. Shalom Pubs., 488 p.

Richard Soule, *A Dictionary of English Synonyms*, Alfred Dwight Sheffield ed., 1966. Boston, Little, Brown, xxiv, 614 p.

Webster's Collegiate Thesaurus, 1976. Springfield, Mass., G. & C. Merriam Co., 32a, 944 p.

See also "Appellate Advocacy," "Drafting," and "Quotations."

Legislation — *See* "Statutory Construction."

Litigation — *See* "Jury Instructions," "Procedure," and "Trial Advocacy."

Medical Law

forensic medicine, the application of medical knowledge to the resolution of legal disputes; the influence of medical science on a lawsuit. (2) Sometimes used as a synonym for medical jurisprudence. *(q.v.)*

medical jurisprudence, the influence of law on medicine and its practice. Sometimes used as a synonym for forensic medicine *(q.v.)*

J. Brooke Aker, Arthur C. Walsh & James R. Beam, *Mental Capacity*, 1977- . Colorado Springs, Shepard's, xx, 372 p.

Mary M. Bertolet & Lee S. Goldsmith, eds., *Hospital Liability Law & Tactics*, 4th ed. 1980. N.Y., Practising Law Institute, xiii, 789 p.

William H. L. Dornette, ed., *Legal Aspects of Anesthesia*, 1972, Philadelphia, F. A. Davis Co., xiii, 599 p. Intended for physician readers but valuable to students, lawyers, and paralegals as a summary.

Leo Gelfand, Raoul D. Magana, R. R. Merliss, *et al.*, *Courtroom Medicine*, 1962- . N.Y., Matthew Bender, 33 v., looseleaf.

Frank P. Grad & Noelia Marti, *Physicians' Licensure & Discipline*, 1979. Dobbs Ferry, N.Y., Oceana Pubs., viii, 471 p.

Marshall Houts, *Lawyers' Guide to Medical Proof*, 1974- . N.Y., Matthew Bender, 3 v., looseleaf.

David W. Louisell, Harold Williams & Charles Kramer, *Medical Malpractice*, 1984- . N.Y., Matthew Bender, 3 v. looseleaf.

L. Stanley McQuade, *Medical Practice for Trial Lawyers*, 2d ed. 1985. Norcross, Ga., Harrison Co., xxix, 589 p.

Steven E. Pegalis & Harvey F. Wachsman, *American Law of Medical Malpractice*, 1980- . Rochester, N.Y. and San Francisco, Lawyers Co-Op. Pub. Co. and Bancroft-Whitney, 3 v.

Ann M. Rhodes & Robert D. Miller, *Nursing & The Law*, 4th ed. 1984. Rockville, Md., Aspen Systems Corp., ix, 345 p.

Arnold J. Rosoff, *Informed Consent*, 1981. Rockville, Md., Aspen Systems Corp., xi, 520 p.

Fay A. Rozovsky, *Consent to Treatment: A Practical Guide*, 1984. Boston, Little, Brown, xxxviii, 698 p.

Uniform Laws Annotated, *Estate, Probate and Related Laws*, 1983 and supp. (*U.L.A.* v. 8A), St. Paul, West Pub. Co. Contains and discusses, among other things, "Uniform Anatomical Gift Act."

Jon R. Waltz & Fred E. Inbau, *Medical Jurisprudence*, 1971. N.Y., Macmillan, xiv, 398 p. Intended for physician readers, but valuable to students, lawyers, and paralegals as a summary. Significant bibliographies and references to precedents.

See also CHAPTER 14, "Studying Medicine on Your Own: A Bibliographic Essay Concerning Medical Literature."

Mortgages

mortgage (môr gāg), (a dead pledge), a conveyance of real or personal property to a person called the mortgagee, to secure the payment of money by the mortgagor and to become void upon the performance of such act. At common law, such conveyances became absolute upon failure to perform the condition, but in equity, the mortgagor is permitted to redeem. The manner in which the equity of redemption may be barred is regulated by various state statutes. A legal mortgage is one created by the conveyance or assignment of the property to the mortgagee. An equitable mortgage is one in which the mortgagor does not actually convey the property, but does some act by which he manifests his intention to bind it as security. (2) Any conveyance, agreement, or arrangement in which property is used as security or collateral. Uniform Probate Code §§ 1-201 (25), 5-103 (11).

George E. Osborne, Grant S. Nelson, & Dale A. Whitman, *Real Estate Finance Law*, 1979. St. Paul, West Pub. Co., xxix, 885 p.

Patrick J. Rohan, *Real Estate Financing: Text, Forms, Tax Analysis*, 1973- . (v. 4, 4 pt. 2, 4A, 4B, 4C & 5 of *Real Estate Transactions*). N.Y., Matthew Bender, 6 v., looseleaf.

See also "Property," A. James Casner and Richard R. Powell.

Municipal Corporations

city, or **municipal corporation,** a public corporation established as a subdivision of a state for local governmental purposes, with various powers of government vested in its own officials.

Chester James Antieau, John Michael Antieau, Frederic White, *et. al., Local Government Law*, 1985- . N.Y., Matthew Bender, 7 v. looseleaf.

Rudolph W. Fischer, J. F. Corcoran, & Janette Simons, [*Shepard's*] *Ordinance Law Annotations*, 1979- . Colorado Springs, Shepard's, 12 v.

Eugene McQuillin, *The Law of Municipal Corporations*, 3d ed. rev'd, 1971- . Wilmette, Ill., Callaghan & Co., 22 v.

Thomas A. Matthews & Byron S. Matthews, *Municipal Ordinances: Text and Forms*, 2d ed. rev'd 1972- . Wilmette, Ill., Callaghan & Co., 7 v.

Osborne M. Reynolds, Jr., *Handbook of Local Government Law*, 1982. St. Paul, West Pub. Co., xxix, 860 p.

C. Dallas Sands & Michael E. Libonati, *Local Government Law*, 1981- . Wilmette, Ill., Callaghan & Co., 4 v. looseleaf.

Patents

patent, a flexible term for a grant of some privilege, property, or authority, by the government or sovereign to one or more individuals. *** (3) An instrument granting to original inventors the exclusive right for a period of years to manufacture, sell, and use the invention described therein. Congress may enact patent laws, U.S. Const. Art. I, Sec. 8.

Donald S. Chisum, *Patents*, 1978- . N.Y., Matthew Bender, 6 v. looseleaf.

Anthony W. Deller, *Walker on Patents*, 2d ed. 1964- . Mount Kisco, N.Y., Baker, Voorhis & Co., and Rochester, N.Y., Lawyers Co-Op. Pub. Co., 9 v. To be superseded by Ernest Bainbridge Lipscomb, III, below.

Lester Horwitz & Irving Seidman, *Patent Office Rules and Practice*, rev. ed. 1971- . N.Y., Matthew Bender, 8 v., looseleaf.

Ernest Bainbridge Lipscomb, III, *Walker on Patents*, 3d ed. 1984- . Rochester, N.Y. and San Francisco, Lawyers Co-Op. Pub. Co. and Bancroft-Whitney, [2 v.]. Projected to consist of 11 v. and supersede Anthony W. Deller, above.

Peter D. Rosenberg, *Patent Law Fundamentals*, 2d ed. 1984 rev.- . N.Y., Clark Boardman Co., 2 v. looseleaf.

Periodicals

The roster of legal periodicals is constantly changing. Significant bibliographies of legal periodicals are published elsewhere. See, *e.g.*, *Current Law Index*, v. 4, p. vii-xvii (1983), *Index to Legal Periodicals*, v. 22, p. xiii-xxiii (1984), and subsequent volumes and issues.

Indexes

Current Index to Legal Periodicals, Seattle, Univ. of Washington Law Library and Washington Law Rev., weekly, classified, 8½″ x 11″ sheets.

Current Law Index, 1980- , v. 1- . Belmont, Calif., Information Access Co., monthly. Eight monthly issues, three quarterly cumulations, one annual cumulation.

Index to Legal Periodicals, January, 1926- , v. 1- . New York, H. W. Wilson Co. Articles must be at least five ordinary pages or two folio pages, and case notes, bibliographies, biographies, and notes of legislation at least two ordinary pages or one folio page in order to qualify for inclusion. Earlier indexes are available.

Index to Periodical Articles Related to Law, ten-year index 1958-1968, five-year cumulation 1969-1973, five year cumulation 1974-1978, and supp. Dobbs Ferry, N.Y., Glanville Publications. 3 v. and paperbacks.

Legal Contents (formerly *Contents of Current Legal Periodicals*), 1972- . v. 1- . Wilmington, Del., Corporation Service Co. Monthly, lists complete table of contents of all major law reviews and journals. Indexes all articles, case comments, notes, and recent decisions by fields of law.

Philosophy of Law

Benjamin N. Cardozo, *The Growth of the Law*, 1924. New Haven, Conn., Yale Univ. Press, Humphrey Milford and Oxford Univ. Press, 145 p.

Benjamin N. Cardozo, *The Nature of the Judicial Process*, 1921. New Haven, Conn., Yale Univ. Press, Humphrey Milford and Oxford Univ. Press, 180 p.

Benjamin N. Cardozo, *The Paradoxes of Legal Science*, 1928. N.Y., Columbia Univ. Press, 142 p.

Morris R. Cohen & Felix S. Cohen, *Readings in Jurisprudence and Legal Philosophy*, 1951. Boston, Little, Brown, xvi, 944 p. 1979 ed. by Philip Schuchman, Boston, Little, Brown, xviii, 1099 p.

Jerome Frank, *Courts on Trial*, 1950. Princeton, N.J., Princeton Univ. Press, xii, 441 p.

Jerome Frank, *Law and the Modern Mind*, 1930. N.Y., Brentano's. Reprinted 1970, Gloucester, Mass., Peter Smith, xxxv, 404 p.

Oliver Wendell Holmes, Jr., *The Common Law*, 1881. Boston, Little, Brown, xvi, 422 p.

Karl N. Llewellyn, *The Common Law Tradition: Deciding Appeals*, 1960. Boston, Little, Brown, xii, 565 p.

Edwin W. Patterson, *Jurisprudence: Men and Ideas of the Law*, 1953. Brooklyn, Foundation Press, xiii, 649 p.

Roscoe Pound, *Jurisprudence*, 1959. St. Paul, West Pub. Co., 5 v.

Planning — *See* "Land Planning."

Probate — *See* "Decedents' Estates."

Procedure

procedure, the manner in which litigants proceed in the adversary conduct of a lawsuit, including the various steps by which the parties go about the litigation process. Occasionally called practice. Usually codified by rules or in codes, *e.g.*, Federal Rules of Civil Procedure *(q.v.)*, Federal Rules of Criminal Procedure *(q.v.)*, analogous state rules of procedure, and various state codes of practice.

Jack H. Friedenthal, Mary Kay Kane & Arthur R. Miller, *Civil Procedure*, 1985. St. Paul, West Pub. Co., 740 p.

Milton D. Green, *Basic Civil Procedure*, 2d ed. 1979. Mineola, N.Y., Foundation Press, xiv, 327 p.

David F. Herr, Roger S. Haydock & Jeffrey W. Stempel, *Motion Practice*, 1985. Boston, Little, Brown, 688 p.

Fleming James, Jr. & Geoffrey C. Hazard, Jr., *Civil Procedure*, 3d ed. 1985. Boston, Little, Brown, 736 p.

James Wm. Moore *et. al.*, *Moore's Federal Practice*, 2d ed. 1948- . N.Y., Matthew Bender, 34 v. looseleaf.

James Wm. Moore & Allan D. Vestal, *Moore's Manual: Federal Practice and Procedure*, 1962- . N.Y., Matthew Bender, 2 v. looseleaf. 4 v. forms also available.

James L. Underwood, *A Guide to Federal Discovery Rules*, 1979- . Philadelphia, ALI-ABA Committee on Continuing Prof. Educ., xv, 286 p.

Marlin M. Volz *et al.*, *West's Federal Practice Manual*, 2d ed. & rev'd 2d ed. 1970- . St. Paul, West Pub. Co., 14 v.

Charles A. Wright, Arthur R. Miller, *et al.*, *Federal Practice and Procedure*, 1969- . St. Paul, West Pub. Co., 29 v.

See also "Criminal Procedure."

Product Liability

product liability, the portion of American law which deals with the responsibility of a manufacturer or seller of merchandise to the buyer and other persons affected by the merchandise, concerning the quality of the merchandise and the consequences resulting from a lack of quality in the merchandise.

Louis R. Frumer & Melvin I. Friedman, *Products Liability*, 1984- . N.Y., Matthew Bender, 10 v. looseleaf.

Robert D. Hursh & Henry J. Bailey, *American Law of Products Liability*, 2d ed. 1974- . Rochester, N.Y., and San Francisco, Lawyers Co-Op. Pub. Co. and Bancroft-Whitney, 6 v.

William Kimble & Robert O. Lesher, *Products Liability*, 1979- . St. Paul, West Pub. Co., xviii, 441 p.

Model Uniform Product Liability Act, 44 Fed. Reg. 62,714-62,750 (1979).

Product Safety & Liability Reporter, 1973- . Washington, Bureau of National Affairs, weekly looseleaf.

Paul Sherman, *Products Liability for the General Practitioner*, 1981- . Colorado Springs, Shepard's/McGraw-Hill, xiv, 389 p.

See also "Consumer Protection."

Property

property, a very extensive and flexible term for various rights of ownership; this may be (a) general or absolute; (b) special or qualified, as in the case of a bailee for a special purpose. (2) Everything that is owned. In this sense it is (a) real, or (b) personal. (3) Anything that may be the subject of ownership. Uniform Probate Code § 1-201(33); accord, § 5-103(17).

American Law Institute, *Restatement of Property*, 1936-1944. St. Paul, American Law Institute Pubs., 5 v.

American Law Institute, *Restatement of Property (Second)*, 1977- . Landlord & Tenant §§ 1.1-21.2 (2 v.); Donative Transfers §§ 1.1-10.2 (1 v.). St. Paul, American Law Institute Pubs.

Ralph E. Boyer, *Survey of the Law of Property*, 3d ed. 1981. St. Paul, West Pub. Co., xv, 766 p.

Ray Andrews Brown, *The Law of Personal Property*, Walter B. Raushenbush 3d ed. 1975. Chicago, Callaghan & Co., xviii, 719 p.

John M. Cartwright, *Farm and Ranch Real Estate Law*, 1972- . Rochester, N.Y., and San Francisco, Lawyers Co-Op. Pub. Co. and Bancroft-Whitney, xiv, 457 p.

A. James Casner, ed., *American Law of Property*, 1952- . Boston, Little, Brown, 8 v. and 1952-1976 hardbound supp.

Roger A. Cunningham, William B. Stoebuck & Dale A. Whitman, *The Law of Property*, 1984. St. Paul, West Pub. Co., xx, 1070 p.

Milton R. Friedman, *Contracts and Conveyances of Real Property*, 3d ed. 1975- . N.Y., Practising Law Institute, xx, 923 p.

Milton R. Friedman, *Leases*, 2d ed. 1983. N.Y., Practising Law Institute, 3 v.

Richard R. Powell, *The Law of Real Property*, 1969- . Patrick J. Rohan, recomp., N.Y., Matthew Bender, 13 v.

Robert S. Schoskinski, *American Law of Landlord & Tenant*, 1980- . Rochester, N.Y., and San Francisco, Lawyers Co-Op. Pub. Co. and Bancroft-Whitney, xvii, 910 p.

See also "Mortgages" and "Secured Transactions."

Quotations

John Bartlett, *Familiar Quotations*, 14th Emily Morison Beck ed. 1968. Boston, Little, Brown, xviii, 1750 p.

Joseph R. Conlin, *The Morrow Book of Quotations in American History*, 1984. N.Y., William Morrow & Co., 352 p.

Eugene C. Gerhart, *Quote It! Memorable Legal Quotations*, 1969. N.Y. and Albany, N.Y., Clark Boardman Co. and Sage Hill Pubs., xii, 766 p.

M. Frances McNamara, *2,000 Famous Legal Quotations*, 1967. Rochester, N.Y., Aqueduct Books Div., Lawyers Co-Op. Pub. Co., xviii, 718 p.

Oxford Dictionary of Quotations, 3d ed. 1979. N.Y., Oxford University Press, xix, 907 p.

Laurence J. Peter, *Peter's Quotations: Ideas for our Time*, 1977. N.Y., William Morrow & Co., 540 p.

Real Property — *See* "Property."

Remedies — *See* "Equity."

Reports of Cases

reports, or **reports of cases,** various bound books in which are published the courts' opinions in precedent cases which have been judicially argued and determined. Occasionally called reporters. See *table of abbreviations,* post, and Chapter 2.

Mary R. Chapman, *Bibliographical Index to the State Reports Prior to the National Reporter System*, 1977. Dobbs Ferry, N.Y., Trans-Media Pub. Co., 66 p.

Miles O. Price & Harry Bitner, *Effective Legal Research*, 1953. N.Y., Prentice-Hall, xii, 633 p. Reprinted, 1969, South Hackensack, N.J., and N.Y., Rothman Reprints and Augustus M. Kelley Pubs. Appendix I "American Law Reports and Digests" p. 383-420; Appendix II "British and Canadian Material" p. 421-450.

Charles C. Soule, *The Lawyer's Reference Manual of Law Books and Citations*, 1883. Boston, Soule & Bugbee, x, 497 p.

A Uniform System of Citation, 14th ed. 1986. Cambridge, Mass., Harvard Law Review Ass'n, paperback. "H. United States Tables," "Federal" p. 173-177; "States" p. 177-217; "Other American Jurisdictions" p. 217-219; "G. Foreign Materials and Tables" p. 139-170.

Restitution— *See* "Equity."

Sales of Personal Property

sale, *** (2) The passing of title to goods from the seller to the buyer for a price. U.C.C. § 2-106(1).

sales, transactions in goods (U.C.C. § 2-102), as contradistinguished from transactions in real property.

Richard W. Duesenberg & Lawrence P. King, *Sales and Bulk Transfers Under the Uniform Commercial Code*, 1966- . (v. 3, 3A *Bender's Uniform Commercial Code Service*). N.Y., Matthew Bender, 2 v.

William D. Hawkland, *Sales & Bulk Sales*, 3d ed. 1976. Philadelphia, Joint Committee on Continuing Legal Educ. of the ALI and ABA, xvii, 232 p., paperback.

Robert J. Nordstrom, *Handbook on the Law of Sales*, 1970. St. Paul, West Pub. Co., xxii, 600 p.

Alphonse M. Squillante & John R. Fonseca, *Williston on Sales*, 4th ed., 1973- . Rochester, N.Y., and San Francisco, Lawyers Co-Op. Pub. Co. and Bancroft-Whitney, 3 v.

See also "Commercial Transactions."

Secured Transactions

secured creditor, a creditor who holds security which assures him that a debtor's promise to pay will be performed.

secured party, a lender, seller, or other person in whose favor there is a security interest, including a person to whom accounts, contract rights, or chattel paper have been sold. When the holders of obligations issued under an indenture of trust, equipment trust agreement, or the like are represented by a trustee or other person, the representative is the secured party. U.C.C. § 9-105(1)(i).

security interest, an interest in personal property or fixtures which secures payment or performance of an obligation. The term also includes any interest of a buyer of accounts, chattel paper, or contract rights. U.C.C. § 1-201(37).

Barkley Clark, *The Law of Secured Transactions under the U.C.C.*, 1980 and supp. Boston, Warren, Gorham & Lamont, various pagination, 1 v.

Peter F. Coogan, William F. Hogan & Detlev F. Vagts, *Secured Transactions under the Uniform Commercial Code*, 1963- . (v. 1, 1A, 1B, 1C *Bender's Uniform Commercial Code Service*). N.Y., Matthew Bender, 4 v. looseleaf.

William B. Davenport & Ray D. Henson, *Secured Transactions II*, 1966. Philadelphia, Joint Committee on Continuing Legal Educ. of the ALI and ABA, xii, 147 p., paperback.

William B. Davenport & Daniel R. Murray, *Secured Transactions*, 1978. Philadelphia, ALI-ABA Committee on Continuing Prof. Educ., xx, 457 p.

Ray D. Henson, *Handbook on Secured Transactions*, 2d ed. 1979. St. Paul, West Pub. Co., xxvii, 504 p.

Oscar Spivack, *Secured Transactions I*, 3d ed. 1963. Philadelphia, Joint Committee on Continuing Legal Educ. of the ALI and ABA, 157 p., paperback.

See also "Commercial Transactions."

Securities Regulation

security, *** (3) An instrument which is issued in bearer or registered form, and is of a type commonly dealt in upon securities exchanges or markets or commonly recognized in any area in which it is issued or dealt in as a medium for investment, and is either of a class or series or by its terms is divisible into a class or series of instruments, and evidences a share, participation or other interest in property, or in an enterprise or evidences an obligation of the issuer. U.C.C. § 8-102(1)(a). (4) Any note, stock, treasury stock, bond, debenture, evidence of indebtedness, certificate of interest or participation in an oil, gas or mining title or lease or in payments out of production under such a title or lease, collateral trust certificate, transferable share, voting trust certificate or, in general, any interest or instrument commonly known as a security, or any certificate of interest or participation, any temporary or interim certificate, receipt or certificate of deposit for, or any warrant or right to subscribe to or purchase, any of the foregoing. Uniform Probate Code §§ 1-201(37), 5-103(20).

Blue Sky Law Reporter, 1964- . Chicago, Commerce Clearing House, 4 v., looseleaf.

Federal Securities Law Reporter, 1969- . Chicago, Commerce Clearing House, 7 v., looseleaf.

Thomas Lee Hazen, *The Law of Securities Regulations*, 1985. St. Paul, West Pub. Co., xxx, 739 p.

Louis Loss, *Commentary on the Uniform Securities Act*, 1976. Boston, Little, Brown, xii, 203 p.

Id., *Fundamentals of Securities Regulation*, 1983- . Boston, Little, Brown, 1392 p.

Id., *Securities Regulation*, 2d ed. and supp. 1961- . Boston, Little, Brown, 6 v.

National Assocation of Securities Dealers Manual, 1975- . Chicago, Commerce Clearing House, 1 v., looseleaf.

New York Stock Exchange Listed Company Manual, 1983- . N.Y., N.Y. Stock Exchange, 1 v. looseleaf.

Securities Regulation and Law Report, 1969- . Washington, Bureau of National Affairs, 2 v. weekly looseleaf.

Sentencing

sentence, a judgment of punishment in a criminal proceeding.

James M. Burns & Joseph S. Mattina, *Sentencing*, 1978. Reno, National Judicial College, x, 404 p., paperback.

Arthur W. Campbell, *Law of Sentencing*, 1978- . Rochester, N.Y., and San Francisco, Lawyers Co-Op. Pub. Co. and Bancroft-Whitney, xiii, 560 p.

Hyman Gross & Andrew von Hirsch, eds., *Sentencing*, 1981. N.Y., Oxford Univ. Press, ix, 397 p., paperback.

J. L. Miller, Marilyn McCoy Roberts & Charlotte A. Carter, *Sentencing Reform: A Review and Annotated Bibliography*, 1981. Williamsburg, Va., National Center for State Courts, vi, 132 p., 8½″ x 11″ paperback.

See also "Criminal Procedure."

Social Security, Medicare and Medicaid

Old Age and Survivors Insurance Benefits Act, an act to establish a system of Federal old age benefits, and to enable the several States to make more adequate provision for aged persons, blind persons, dependent and crippled children, maternal and child welfare, public health, and the administration of their unemployment compensation laws; to establish a Social Security Board; to raise revenue; and for other purposes. 42 U.S.C. §§ 301 *et seq.*; 49 Stat, 620 (1935) as amended.

Health Insurance for the Aged and Disabled Act, unofficially called Medicare Act, title I of the Social Security Amendments of 1965, as subsequently amended; an act to provide a hospital insurance program for the aged under the Social Security Act with a supplemental medical benefits program, and an expanded program of medical assistance, to increase benefits under the Old-Age, Survivors, and Disability Insurance System, to improve the Federal-State public assistance programs, and for other purposes, 26 U.S.C. §§ 72 *et seq.*; 42 U.S.C. §§ 303 *et seq.*; 44 U.S.C. §§ 1395 *et seq.*; 45 U.S.C. §§ 228e *et seq.*; 79 Stat. 290 (1965), as subsequently amended.

Robert E. Francis, *Social Security Disability Claims*, 1983- . Wilmette, Ill., Callaghan & Co., 1 v. looseleaf.

Barbara E. Lybarger & Neil Onerheim, *An Advocate's Guide to Surviving the SSI System*, 1985. Boston, Mass. Poverty Law Center, 491 p. Table of cases volume also available.

Harvey L. McCormick, *Medicare and Medicaid Claims and Procedures*, 1977- . St. Paul, West Pub. Co., xiii, 921 p.

Id., *Social Security Claims and Procedures*, 3d ed. 1983. St. Paul, West Pub. Co., 2 v.

Social Security Handbook, 7th ed. 1982. Washington, U.S. Dept. of Health and Human Services, v, 457 p., paperback. Irregular serial. For sale by Superintendent of Documents.

Unemployment Insurance Reporter, Federal and Home State, 1965- . Chicago, Commerce Clearing House, v. 1, 1A. 4 v. looseleaf.

Statutory Construction

statutory construction, the act of a court in determining the meaning of a statute as it relates to a particular factual dispute before it.

Julio Cueto-Rua, *Judicial Methods of Interpretation of the Law*, 1981. Baton Rouge, Paul M. Hebert Law Center, La. State Univ., xix, 508 p.

Reed Dickerson, *The Interpretation and Application of Statutes*, 1975. Boston, Little, Brown, xx, 309 p.

Gwendolyn B. Folsom, *Legislative History: Research for the Interpretation of Laws*, 1972. Charlottesville, Va., Univ. Press of Va., viii, 136 p.

Felix Frankfurter, *Some Reflections on the Reading of Statutes*, 1947. N.Y., Ass'n of the Bar of the City of N.Y., 29 p. Authorized facsimile published 1979, Ann Arbor, Mich., Univ. Microfilms Int'l.

James Willard Hurst, *Dealing With Statutes*, 1982. N.Y., Columbia Univ. Press, vi, 140 p.

C. Dallas Sands, *Statutes and Statutory Construction*, 4th ed. 1972- . 1984 rev. by Norman J. Singer. Chicago, Callaghan & Co., 6 v. 1st (1891)-3d (1943) eds. prepared by J. G. Sutherland *et al.*

Taxation

tax, a sum of money assessed against, and collected from, a person for the support of the government. An income tax is one proportioned to the amount of his income. A poll tax is one which is assessed on all individuals alike, *i.e.*, by the head, without reference to the value of his property or the amount of his income. Indirect taxes are those levied on articles manufactured or imported, *e.g.*, excise and customs, so called because the tax is not levied on the consumer directly, but is in reality paid by him in the enhanced price of the article.***

tax avoidance, a legitimate organizing of a taxpayer's affairs so as to minimize the amount of taxes which he must pay, *e.g.*, electing to take advantage of the alternatives which are offered to a taxpayer within the framework of the revenue laws.

tax evasion, a deceit consisting of a breach of law, by which the revenue laws' application to a particular taxpayer are frustrated.

Federal Estate & Gift

Federal Estate and Gift Tax Reporter, 1971- . Weekly looseleaf, Chicago, Commerce Clearing House, 3 v.

M. Carr Ferguson, James J. Freeland & Richard B. Stephens, *Federal Income Taxation of Estates and Beneficiaries*, 1970 and 1984 supp. Boston, Little, Brown, 776 p.

David T. Link & Larry D. Soderquist, *Law of Federal Estate and Gift Taxation: Analysis*, 2 v. 1980- ; *Code Commentary*, 1 v., 1978- . Wilmette, Ill., Callaghan & Co., looseleaf.

Joseph Rasch, *Handling Federal Estate and Gift Taxes*, 4th Harris ed. 1984- . Rochester, N.Y., Lawyers Co-Op. Pub. Co., 3 v.

See also "Estate Planning" and "Taxation, *Federal Income*," Boris I. Bittker and Jacob Rabkin & Mark H. Johnson.

Federal Income

Boris I. Bittker, *Federal Taxation of Income, Estates and Gifts*, 1981- . Boston, Warren, Gorham & Lamont, 6 v.

Boris I. Bittker & James S. Eustice, *Federal Income Taxation of Corporations and Shareholders*, 4th ed. 1979- . Boston, Warren, Gorham & Lamont, various pagination.

Federal Tax Guide-Control Edition, 1962- . Chicago, Commerce Clearing House, 2 v., looseleaf.

Federal Tax Handbook. Englewood Cliffs, N.J., Prentice-Hall, 1 v. annual paperback. 1984 ed. 720 p.

Federal Taxes. Englewood Cliffs, N.J., Prentice-Hall, 11 v. annual looseleaf.

Helen E. Marmoll, *Atlas' Tax Aspects of Real Estate Transactions*, 6th ed. 1984. Washington, Bureau of National Affairs, 496 p.

Jacob Mertens, Jr., *The Law of Federal Income Taxation*, James J. Doheny ed. 1954- . Wilmette, Ill., Callaghan & Co., 57 v.

Daniel Q. Posin, Jr., *Federal Income Taxation of Individuals and Basic Concepts in the Taxation of All Entities*, 1983. St. Paul, West Pub. Co., xxxi, 491 p.

Jacob Rabkin & Mark H. Johnson, *Federal Income, Gift and Estate Taxation*, 1942- . N.Y., Matthew Bender, 15 v. looseleaf.

Standard Federal Tax Reporter. N.Y., Commerce Clearing House, 16 v. annual looseleaf.

U.S. Master Tax Guide. Chicago, Commerce Clearing House, annual paperback.

Arthur B. Willis, John S. Pennell, Philip F. Postlewaite, *Partnership Taxation*, 3d ed. 1981- . Colorado Springs, Shepard's/McGraw-Hill, 2 v. looseleaf.

Your Federal Income Tax. Department of the Treasury, Internal Rev. Serv., annual paperback.

State

All-State Sales Tax Reports, 19 - . Chicago, Commerce Clearing House, 4 v. looseleaf.

Paul J. Hartman, *Federal Limitations on State and Local Taxation*, 1981- . Rochester, N.Y. and San Francisco, Lawyers Co-Op. Pub. Co. and Bancroft-Whitney, xii, 743 p.

Jerome R. Hellerstein, *State Taxation, I. Corporate Income and Franchise Taxes*, 1983- . Boston and N.Y., Warren, Gorham & Lamont, xxvii, 706 p. Forthcoming v. II deals with sales, use, gross-receipts taxes, death, personal income, and specialized levies.

State and Local Taxes: [Various States], and *All States Unit*, 19 - . Englewood Cliffs, N.J., Prentice-Hall, 2 v. looseleaf.

State Tax Cases Reporter: All States, 1967- . Chicago, Commerce Clearing House, 1 v. looseleaf.

State Tax Guide: All States, 1967- . Chicago, Commerce Clearing House, 2 v. looseleaf.

[*Various States*] *Tax Reporter*, 19 - . Chicago, Commerce Clearing House, looseleaf. *E.g.*, Ky. 2 v., Ohio 3 v.

Tenants' Rights — *See* "Property."

Torts

tort, any one of various, legally recognized, private injuries or wrongs which do not arise as the result of a breach of contract.

American Law Institute, *Restatement of the Law, Second: Torts 2d*, 1965-1966. St. Paul, American Law Institute Pubs., 4 v. and appendix 6 v.

Graham Douthwaite, *Jury Instructions on Damages in Tort Actions*, 1981- . Indianapolis, Allen Smith Co., xi, 554 p.

W. Page Keeton, ed., *Prosser and Keeton on the Law of Torts*, 5th ed. 1984. St. Paul, West Pub. Co., xxiii, 1456 p.

Clarence Morris & C. Robert Morris, Jr., *Morris on Torts*, 2d ed. 1980. Mineola, N.Y., Foundation Press, xiv, 443 p.

Negligence [*and*] *Compensation Cases Annotated:*
[1st Series] v. 1-39, 1912-1936;
New Series, v. 1-30, 1937-1952;
3d Series, v. 1-30, 1953-1967;
4th Series, v. 1-[47], 1968-[1985].
Wilmette, Ill., Callaghan & Co.
Common Sense Index, 1 v. looseleaf.

Stuart M. Speiser, *Recovery for Wrongful Death 2d*, 2d ed. 1975- . Rochester, N.Y., Lawyers Co-Op. Pub. Co., 2 v. and *Economic Handbook.*

Stuart M. Speiser, Charles F. Krause & Alfred W. Gans, *The American Law of Torts*, 1983- . Rochester, N.Y., and San Francisco, Lawyers Co-Op. Pub. Co. and Bancroft-Whitney, v. 1 in print.

Bibliography

Anderson's Index to the A.T.L. (NACCA) Law Journal, v. 1-33 and 1978 supp. for v. 34-36, William Schwartz, Dir., 2d ed. 1971- . Cincinnati, Anderson Pub. Co., ix, 696 p.

See also "Comparative Negligence," "Governmental Liability," "Medical Law," "Product Liability," and "Trial Advocacy."

Trademarks

trademark or **trade-mark,** a distinctive mark, signature, or device, affixed to an article or to its wrapper, package, or container, to show that it is manufactured, grown, or selected by a particular person, firm, or corporation. In a case of infringement, courts will enjoin the wrongdoer from using an imitation of a trademark.

Jerome Gilson, *Trademark Protection and Practice*, 1974- . N.Y., Matthew Bender, 2 v. looseleaf.

Ethan Horwitz, *World Trademark Law and Practice*, 1982- . N.Y., Matthew Bender, 2 v. looseleaf.

J. Thomas McCarthy, *Trademarks and Unfair Competition*, 1973- . Rochester, N.Y. and San Francisco, Lawyers Co-Op. Pub. Co. and Bancroft-Whitney, 2 v.

Trademark Law Handbook, annual. N.Y., Clark Boardman Co., 1 v. paperback.

See also "Unfair Competition."

Trial Advocacy

advocate, an attorney who speaks or writes, or both, in support of his client's cause.

American Jurisprudence Trials, 1964- . San Francisco and Rochester, N.Y., Bancroft-Whitney and Lawyers Co-Op. Pub. Co., 32 v.

Bender's Forms of Discovery, 1981- . N.Y., Matthew Bender, 19 v. looseleaf.

Douglas Danner, *Pattern Interrogatories*, 1970- . Rochester, N.Y., Lawyers Co-Op. Pub. Co., 5 v.

Richard A. Givens, *Advocacy: The Art of Pleading a Cause*, 1980- . Colorado Springs, Shepard's/McGraw-Hill, xxi, 417 p.

Irving Goldstein & Fred Lane, *Goldstein Trial Technique*, 2d ed. 1969- . Fred Lane 3d ed. 1984- . Wilmette, Ill., Callaghan & Co., 3 v. 3d ed. looseleaf.

Robert E., Keeton, *Trial Tactics and Methods*, 2d ed. 1973. Boston, Little, Brown, xxi, 456 p. and *Basic Expressions* supp., 1979.

Sydney C. Schweitzer, *Cyclopedia of Trial Practice*, 2d ed. 1970- . Rochester, N.Y., Lawyers Co-Op. Pub. Co., 10 v.

Jacob A. Stein, *Closing Argument: The Art and the Law*, 1982- . Wilmette, Ill., Callaghan & Co., 1 v. looseleaf.

Trusts

trust, a right in property held by one person, called the trustee, for the benefit of another, called the beneficiary, or cestui que trust. Trusts are divided into active, where the trustee has some duty to perform, so that the legal estate must remain in him or a successor, or the trust be defeated; passive, where the trustee simply holds the title in trust for the beneficiary, and has no duties to perform; express, where it is created by express terms in a deed, will, or other instrument; implied, including precatory, constructive, and resulting trusts, where a court will presume, from the nature of the transaction, the relations of the parties and the requirements of good faith, that a trust was intended, though no express words be employed to create it.

George Gleason Bogert, *Handbook of the Law of Trusts*, 5th ed. 1973. St. Paul, West Pub. Co., xx, 528 p.

George Gleason Bogert & George Taylor Bogert, *The Law of Trusts and Trustees*, rev'd 2d ed. 1984- . St. Paul, West Pub. Co., 22 v.

Austin Wakeman Scott, *Abridgment of the Law of Trusts*, 1960. Boston, Little, Brown, xxvii, 796 p.

Austin Wakeman Scott, *The Law of Trusts*, 3d ed. 1967- . Boston, Little, Brown, 6 v.

See also "Decedents' Estates" and "Taxation, *Federal Estate & Gift*."

Unfair Competition

Rudolf Callmann, *The Law of Unfair Competition, Trademarks, and Monopolies*, 4th ed. 1981- . Louis Altman rev., Wilmette, Ill., Callaghan & Co., 9 v.

See also "Antitrust" and "Trademarks."

Uniform Commercial Code — *See* "Commercial Paper," "Commercial Transactions," "Sales of Personal Property," and "Secured Transactions."

Wills — *See* "Decedents' Estates."

Worker's Compensation

worker's, or **workmen's, compensation,** various state remedies provided for by statute, by which indemnity for injuries or death arising out of private employment is furnished to employees and their dependents. The liability of the employer is usually in a limited amount, and is determined independently of the fact of negligence or lack of negligence.

Arthur Larson, *The Law of Workmen's Compensation*, 1984- . N.Y., Matthew Bender, 10 v. looseleaf.

Arthur Larson, *Workmen's Compensation for Occupational Injuries and Death*, 1984- . N.Y., Matthew Bender, 2 v., looseleaf. Desk edition abridgment.

Zoning — *See* "Land Planning."

LIST OF DIGEST TOPICS

These topics are from West Publishing Co.'s *Ninth Decennial Digest, Part I, American Digest System, 1976-1981*, as modified through v. 33 *West's General Digest, 6th Series* (1985). Because of changes in legal concepts and the subject matter with which law deals, changes in the topics occur from time to time. The frequency of those changes and the extent of them are not greatly significant in an overview of the system, however.

With only a few minor exceptions, all of the West digests use these topics and West's *Corpus Juris Secundum* uses similar topics.

Lawyers Co-Operative Publishing Co.'s *American Jurisprudence 2d, A.L.R.*, and *Index to Legal Periodicals* use similar or analogous topics. Therefore, familiarity with this list of topics will be a major advantage when using any of the finding devices mentioned.

Abandoned and Lost Property
Abatement and Revival
Abduction
Abortion and Birth Control
Absentees
Abstracts of Title
Accession
Accord and Satisfaction
Account
Account, Action on
Account Stated
Accountants
Acknowledgment
Action
Action on the Case
Adjoining Landowners
Administrative Law and Procedure
Admiralty
Adoption
Bailment
Bankruptcy
Banks and Banking
Beneficial Associations
Bigamy
Bills and Notes
Blasphemy
Bonds
Boundaries
Bounties
Breach of Marriage Promise
Breach of the Peace
Bribery
Bridges
Brokers
Building and Loan Associations
Burglary
Canals
Cancellation of Instruments

Adulteration
Adultery
Adverse Possession
Affidavits
Affray
Agriculture
Aliens
Alteration of Instruments
Ambassadors and Consuls
Amicus Curiae
Animals
Annuities
Appeal and Error
Appearance
Arbitration
Armed Services
Arrest
Arson
Assault and Battery
Assignments
Assistance, Writ of
Associations
Assumpsit, Action of
Asylums
Attachment
Attorney and Client
Attorney General
Auctions and Auctioneers
Audita Querela
Automobiles
Aviation
Bail
Conversion
Convicts
Copyrights and Intellectual Property
Coroners
Corporations
Costs
Counterfeiting
Counties
Court Commissioners
Courts
Covenant, Action of
Covenants

Carriers
Cemeteries
Census
Certiorari
Champerty and Maintenance
Charities
Chattel Mortgages
Chemical Dependents
Children Out-Of-Wedlock
Citizens
Civil Rights
Clerks of Courts
Clubs
Colleges and Universities
Collision
Commerce
Commodity Futures Trading Regulation
Common Lands
Common Law
Common Scold
Compounding Offenses
Compromise and Settlement
Condominium
Confusion of Goods
Conspiracy
Constitutional Law
Consumer Credit
Consumer Protection
Contempt
Contracts
Contribution
Credit Reporting Agencies
Criminal Law
Crops
Customs and Usages
Customs Duties
Damages
Dead Bodies
Death
Debt, Action of
Debtor and Creditor
Declaratory Judgment
Dedication

DIGEST TOPICS—*Continued*

Deeds
Deposits and Escrows
Deposits in Court
Descent and Distribution
Detectives
Detinue
Disorderly Conduct
Disorderly House
District and Prosecuting Attorneys
District of Columbia
Disturbance of Public Assemblage
Divorce
Domicile
Dower and Curtesy
Drains
Drugs and Narcotics
Dueling
Easements
Ejectment
Election of Remedies
Elections
Electricity
Embezzlement
Embracery
Eminent Domain
Employers' Liability
Entry, Writ of
Equity
Escape
Escheat
Estates in Property
Estoppel
Evidence
Exceptions, Bill of
Exchange of Property
Exchanges
Execution
Executors and Administrators
Exemptions
Explosives
Extortion and Threats
Extradition and Detainers
Factors
False Imprisonment
False Personation
False Pretenses
Federal Civil Procedure
Federal Courts
Fences
Ferries
Fines
Fires
Fish
Fixtures
Food
Forcible Entry and Detainer
Forfeitures
Forgery
Fornication
Franchises
Fraud
Frauds, Statute of
Fraudulent Conveyances
Game
Gaming
Garnishment
Gas
Gifts
Good Will
Grand Jury
Guaranty
Guardian and Ward
Habeas Corpus
Hawkers and Peddlers
Health and Environment
Highways
Holidays
Homestead
Homicide
Hospitals
Husband and Wife
Implied and Constructive Contracts
Improvements
Incest
Indemnity
Indians
Indictment and Information
Infants

Injunction
Innkeepers
Inspection
Insurance
Insurrection and Sedition
Interest
Internal Revenue
International Law
Interpleader
Intoxicating Liquors
Joint Adventures
Joint-Stock Companies and Business Trusts
Joint Tenancy
Judges
Judgment
Judicial Sales
Jury
Justices of the Peace
Kidnapping
Labor Relations
Landlord and Tenant
Larceny
Levees and Flood Control
Lewdness
Libel and Slander
Licenses
Liens
Life Estates
Limitation of Actions
Lis Pendens
Logs and Logging
Lost Instruments
Lotteries
Malicious Mischief
Malicious Prosecution
Mandamus
Manufactures
Maritime Liens
Marriage
Master and Servant
Mayhem
Mechanics' Liens
Mental Health
Mercantile Agencies
Military Justice
Militia
Mines and Minerals
Miscegenation
Monopolies
Mortgages
Motions
Municipal Corporations
Names
Navigable Waters
Ne Exeat
Negligence
Neutrality Laws
Newspapers
New Trial
Notaries
Notice
Novation
Nuisance
Oath
Obscenity
Obstructing Justice
Officers and Public Employees
Pardon and Parole
Parent and Child
Parliamentary Law
Parties
Partition
Partnership
Party Walls
Patents
Paupers
Payment
Penalties
Pensions
Perjury
Perpetuities
Physicians and Surgeons
Pilots
Piracy
Pleading
Pledges
Poisons
Possessory Warrant
Post Office

DIGEST TOPICS—*Continued*

Powers
Pretrial Procedure
Principal and Agent
Principal and Surety
Prisons
Private Roads
Prize Fighting
Process
Products Liability
Prohibition
Property
Prostitution
Public Contracts
Public Lands
Public Utilities
Quieting Title
Quo Warranto
Railroads
Rape
Real Actions
Receivers
Receiving Stolen Goods
Recognizances
Records
Reference
Reformation of Instruments
Reformatories
Registers of Deeds
Release
Religious Societies
Remainders
Removal of Cases
Replevin
Reports
Rescue
Reversions
Review
Rewards
Riot
Robbery
Sales
Salvage
Schools
Scire Facias
Seals
Seamen
Searches and Seizures
Secured Transactions
Securities Regulation
Seduction
Sequestration
Set-Off and Counterclaim
Sheriffs and Constables
Shipping
Signatures
Slaves
Social Security and Public Welfare
Sodomy
Specific Performance
Spendthrifts
States
Statutes
Steam
Stipulations
Submission of Controversy
Subrogation
Subscriptions
Suicide
Sunday
Supersedeas
Taxation
Telecommunications
Tenancy in Common
Tender
Territories
Theaters and Shows
Time
Torts
Towage
Towns
Trade Regulation
Treason
Treaties
Trespass
Trespass to Try Title
Trial
Trover and Conversion
Trusts

Turnpikes and Toll Roads
Undertakings
United States
United States Magistrates
United States Marshals
Unlawful Assembly
Urban Railroads
Usury
Vagrancy
Vendor and Purchaser
Venue
War and National Emergency
Warehousemen
Waste
Waters and Water Courses
Weapons
Weights and Measures
Wharves
Wills
Witnesses
Woods and Forests
Workers' Compensation
Zoning and Planning

USE OF A.L.R. SERIES

SUBSTANTIVE MATERIAL	AVENUES OF ACCESS	SUPPLEMENTATION
ALR [1ST] 175 v. (1919-1948)	ALR FIRST SERIES QUICK INDEX 1 v. PERMANENT ALR [1ST] DIGEST 12 v. ALR [1ST] WORD INDEX TO ANNOTATIONS 4 v. Footnotes in *American Jurisprudence 2d,* *Shepard's Citations,* annotated statutes, treatises, and textbooks. *See also* FEDERAL QUICK INDEX that follows.	ALR [1ST] BLUE BOOK OF SUPPLEMENTAL DECISIONS 6 v. (1929-)
ALR 2D 100 v. (1948-1965)	ALR 2D QUICK INDEX 1 v. ALR 2D DIGEST 7 v. ALR 2D WORD INDEX 3 v. Footnotes in *American Jurisprudence 2d,* *Shepard's Citations,* annotated statutes, treatises, and textbooks. *See also* FEDERAL QUICK INDEX that follows.	ALR 2D LATER CASE SERVICE 23 v.; pocket parts (1954-)

SUBSTANTIVE MATERIAL	AVENUES OF ACCESS	SUPPLEMENTATION
ALR 3D 100 v. (1965-1980)	ALR 3D [&] 4TH QUICK INDEX 1 v. A.L.R. DIGEST TO 3D, 4TH, FEDERAL (1985-) 9 v. Footnotes in *American Jurisprudence 2d,* *Shepard's Citations,* annotated statutes, treatises, and textbooks. *See also* FEDERAL QUICK INDEX that follows.	Pocket parts in bound volumes.
ALR 4TH [35 v.] (1980-)	ALR 3D [&] 4TH QUICK INDEX 1 v. A.L.R. DIGEST TO 3D, 4TH, FEDERAL (1985-) 9 v. Footnotes in *American Jurisprudence 2d,* *Shepard's Citations,* annotated statutes, treatises, and textbooks.	Pocket parts in bound volumes.
ALR Fed. [71 v.] (1969-)	FEDERAL QUICK INDEX (3d ed. 1980-) 2 v. This work is an index to *A.L.R. Fed.* and, among other things, federal material in *ALR* [1st], *ALR 2d,* and *ALR 3d.* *TABLE OF CASES* *REPORTED AND LAWS &* *REGULATIONS CITED* 1 v. A.L.R. DIGEST TO 3D, 4TH, FEDERAL (1985-) 9 v. Footnotes in *American Jurisprudence 2d,* *Shepard's Citations,* annotated statutes, treatises, and textbooks.	Pocket parts in bound volumes.

USING THE CODE OF FEDERAL REGULATIONS (C.F.R.), FEDERAL REGISTER (Fed. Reg.), AND LIST OF CODE OF FEDERAL REGULATIONS SECTIONS AFFECTED (LSA).

LSA — LIST OF CFR SECTIONS AFFECTED

The LIST OF CFR SECTIONS AFFECTED is a monthly publication designed to lead users of the Code of Federal Regulations (CFR) to amendatory actions published in the Federal Register (FR). It should be shelved with current CFR volumes. Entries are by CFR title, chapter, part, and section. Proposed rules are listed at the end of appropriate titles.

HOW TO USE THIS FINDING AID

The CFR is revised annually according to the following schedule:

Titles 1-16—as of Jan. 1
17-27—as of April 1
28-41—as of July 1
42-50—as of Oct. 1

To bring these regulations up to date, consult the most recent LIST OF CFR SECTIONS AFFECTED for any changes, additions, or removals published after the revision date of the volume you are using. Then check the CUMULATIVE LIST OF PARTS AFFECTED appearing in the Reader Aids of the latest Federal Register for less detailed but timely changes published after the final date included in this publication.

Boldface page numbers under a particular title indicate that the page numbers span 2 years. **Boldface** is used to distinguish the current year from the previous year.

Cite a page reference from this publication as 49 FR for 1984 page numbers Example: Page 45872 cite as 49 FR 45872.

ISSUES TO BE SAVED

There is no single annual issue of the LIST OF CFR SECTIONS AFFECTED. Four ANNUAL ISSUES must be saved; the DECEMBER issue is the ANNUAL for Titles 1-16; the MARCH issue is the ANNUAL for Titles 17-27; the JUNE issue is the ANNUAL for Titles 28-41; the SEPTEMBER issue is the ANNUAL for Titles 42-50. ANNUAL ISSUES to be saved are clearly designated on the cover.

PARALLEL TABLE OF AUTHORITIES AND RULES

Following Title 50 is an update to Table I—Parallel Table of Authorities and Rules found in the CFR Index and Finding Aids. This table contains authority citations added to or removed from Table I as a result of documents published in the Federal Register since January 1.

TABLE OF FEDERAL REGISTER ISSUE PAGES AND DATES

A table is included at the end of this publication which identifies the inclusive page numbers and corresponding Federal Register issue dates for the period covered.

INDEXES

An INDEX to the daily Federal Register is published monthly and is cumulated for 12 months. A separate volume, the CFR Index and Finding Aids to the entire Code of Federal Regulations, is revised as of January 1 each year.

Slip Opinion from U.S. Supreme Court

(Slip Opinion)

Caveat concerning headnotes.

NOTE: Where it is feasible, a syllabus (headnote) will be released, as is being done in connection with this case, at the time the opinion is issued. The syllabus constitutes no part of the opinion of the Court but has been prepared by the Reporter of Decisions for the convenience of the reader. See *United States* v. *Detroit Lumber Co.*, 200 U. S. 321, 337.

Court of decision.

SUPREME COURT OF THE UNITED STATES

Syllabus

Style of case.

ALOHA AIRLINES, INC. *v.* DIRECTOR OF TAXATION OF HAWAII

APPEAL FROM THE SUPREME COURT OF HAWAII

File number of case; date of decision.

No. 82–585. Argued October 4, 1983—Decided November 1, 1983*

Headnote prepared by Reporter of Decisions.

A Hawaii statute imposes a tax on the annual gross income of airlines operating within the State, and declares that such tax is a means of taxing an airline's personal property. Section 7(a) of the Airport Development Acceleration Act of 1973 (ADAA) prohibits a State from levying a tax, "directly or indirectly, on persons traveling in air commerce or on the carriage of persons traveling in air commerce or on the sale of air transportation or on the gross receipts derived therefrom," but provides that property taxes are not included in this prohibition. Appellant airlines each brought an action for refund of taxes assessed under the Hawaii statute, claiming that the statute was pre-empted by § ... ...aii Tax Appeal Court rejected this pre-emption argur... Supreme Court affirmed.

...ld: Section 7(a) pre-empts the Hawaii stat...

(a) When a federal statute unambigu...

...icular kind of tax on an indust...

...es here by its plain la...

Request for corrections.

NOTICE: This opinion is subject to formal revision before publication in the preliminary print of the United States Reports. Readers are requested to notify the Reporter of Decisions, Supreme Court of the United States, Washington, D. C. 20543, of any typographical or other formal errors, in order that corrections may be made before the preliminary print goes to press.

SUPREME COURT OF THE UNITED STATES

Nos. 82–585 AND 82–586

82–585 ALOHA AIRLINES, INC., APPELLANT *v.* DIRECTOR OF TAXATION OF HAWAII

82–586 HAWAIIAN AIRLINES, INC., APPELLANT *v.* DIRECTOR OF TAXATION OF HAWAII

ON APPEALS FROM THE SUPREME COURT OF HAWAII

[Decided November 1, 1983]

Opinion of the court written by a justice.

JUSTICE MARSHALL delivered the opinion of the Court.

These appeals present the question whether 49 U. S. C. § 1513(a) preempts a Hawaii statute that imposes a tax on the gross income of airlines operating within the State. We conclude that the Hawaii tax is preempted.

I

In 1970, Congress committed the federal g... ...sting States and localities in expandi... ...n's air transportation system ...ent Act of 1970, P...

Slip Opinion from Court Clerk

RECOMMENDED FOR FULL TEXT PUBLICATION
See, Sixth Circuit Rule 24

File number of case. ——— Nos. 81-3696, 82-3560

Court of decision. ——— **UNITED STATES COURT OF APPEALS**

FOR THE SIXTH CIRCUIT

Style of case. ———

GERALDINE HARRIS, et al.,
Plaintiffs-Appellants,

v.

CITY OF CANTON, OHIO, et al.,
Defendants-Appellees.

ON APPEAL from the United States District Court for the Northern District of Ohio.

Date of decision. ——— Decided and Filed January 13, 1984.

Panel hearing case. ——— Before: KENNEDY and JONES, Circuit Judges and COHN, District Judge.*

Opinion of the court written by a judge. ——— JONES, Circuit Judge. This is a co[...] appeal in which the plaintiffs-appellants, G[...]dette Harris and Willie G. Harris, [...]is- court orders dism[...] States and Ohio Con[...]ed a pendent state claim for [...]oss of consortium. A summons and marsha[...] form were properly executed and delivered to the clerk at the time of filing. The filing fee and United States Marshal's service charge were paid immediately. The Marshal did not attempt to serve the complaint upon the defendants, however, apparently feeling free not to act since outstanding fees for other cases were still owed by plaintiffs' counsel.

Note: In this example, no syllabi are furnished. When later published in *Federal Reporter 2d*, the publisher will supply editorially-prepared synopses and abstracts called headnotes, and assign West Key Numbers.

The action was filed in the Northern District of Ohio, Eastern Division. On May 17, 1979, Judge Robert B. Krupansky filed a pretrial order requiring the plaintiffs to effect service of process within thirty days of the filing of the complaint. That order provided that absent such service the action would be dismissed *sua sponte*. On September 5, 1979, the complaint still not having been served by the U.S. Mar-

Analysis of a Report of a Case

90 SUPREME COURT, JANUARY TERM, 1984 [15 Ohio St. 3d

Statement of the Case

Style of case.

JONES ET AL., APPELLANTS, *v.* VIP DEVELOPMENT COMPANY, APPELLEE
GAINS, EXECUTRIX, APPELLANT, *v.* CITY OF PAINESVILLE, APPELLEE.
HAMLIN ET AL., APPELLANTS AND CROSS-APPELLEES, *v.*
SNOW METAL PRODUCTS, APPELLEE AND CROSS-APPELLANT.

[Cite as Jones *v.* VIP Development Co. (1984), 15 Ohio St. 3d 90.]

Headline to aid reader furnished by official reporter.

Workers' compensation—Receipt of workers' compensation benefits does not preclude action against employer for common-law intentional tort—"Intentional tort," defined—Setoff of award not permitted.

Collateral reference to state legal encyclopedia furnished by publisher.

O.Jur 2d Workmen's Compensation §§ 15, 22.

Syllabi usually furnished by official reporter after approval by judge who wrote the opinion; occasionally furnished by judge.

1. An intentional tort is an act committed with the intent to injure another, or committed with the belief that such injury is substantially certain to occur.
2. The receipt of workers' compensation benefits does not preclude an employee or his representative from pursuing a common-law action for damages against his employer for an intentional tort.
3. An employer who has been held liable for an intentional tort is not entitled to a setoff of the award in the amount of workers' compensation benefits received by the employee or his representative.

(Nos. 84-139, 84-339 and 84-409—Decided December 31, 1984.)

APPEAL from the Court of Appeals for Hamilton County.
APPEAL from the Court of Appeals for Lake County.
APPEAL and CROSS-APPEAL from the Court of Appeals for Cuyahoga County.

Statement of the case furnished by judge who wrote the case.

In case No. 84-139, plaintiffs-appellants John R. Jones and Douglas Pridemore were employed by defendant-appellee VIP Development Company. On October 8, 1980, both plaintiffs were working at a company-owned construction site, installing a sewer line. While they were guiding a manhole condui... ...ed by a hydraulic excavator, the boom ... excavato... a high voltage electric... Plai... ...plied for...

94 SUPREME COURT, JANUARY TERM, 1984 [15 Ohio St. 3d

Opinion, per C. Brown, J.

Opinion of the court written by a judge.

CLIFFORD F. BROWN, J.

I

The first issue presented by these appeals concerns the definition of the term "intentional tort." Each of the three causes under consideration today involves complaints which allege, or attempt to allege, an intentional wrongful act. Because plaintiffs are suing their employers, their success or failure in alleging and proving the requisite intent is critical to their recovery, given this court's ruling in *Blankenship* v. *Cincinnati Milacron Chemicals* (1982), 69 Ohio St. 2d 608 [23 O.O.3d 5...

In *Blankenship,* we held that neither Section 35, Arti... Constitution[1] nor R.C. 4123.74[2] precludes an emp... damages at common law against his employer f... But where the injury suffered at the work... inflicted the employee's sole avenue of re... compensation system. Our task ... for purposes of clarifyi... ...ly, we propo...

15 Ohio St. 3d] JONES *v.* VIP DEVELOPMENT 95
Opinion, per C. Brown, J.

to follow from what the actor does. * * *" *Id.* at 35. See, also, *Payne* v. *Vance* (1921), 103 Ohio St. 59, 69.

Thus, a specific intent to injure is not an essential element of an intentional tort where the actor proceeds despite a perceived threat of harm to others which is *substantially certain,* not merely likely, to occur. It is this element of substantial certainty which distinguishes a merely negligent act from intentionally tortious conduct. Where a defendant acts despite his knowledge that the risk is appreciable, his conduct is negligent. Where the risk is great, his actions may be characterized as reckless or wanton, but not intentional. The actor must know or believe that harm is a substantially certain consequence of his act before intent to injure will be inferred. The existence of this knowledge or intent on the part of the actor may be inferred from his conduct and surrounding circumstances. *Davis* v. *Tunison* (1959), 168 Ohio St. 471 [7 O.O.2d 296], paragraph two of the syllabus.

Material in square brackets, *e.g.*, citations to other reporters, furnished by publisher.

Thus, an intentional tort is an act committed with the intent to injure another, or committed with the belief that such injury is substantially certain to occur. See 1 Restatement of the Law 2d, Torts (1965) 15, Section 8A.[3] We hereby reject the proposition that a specific inte[illegible] necessary t[illegible] [illegible]nding of intentional misconduct.

W[illegible] [illegible]les in mind, we must now [illegible]
[illegible]d of the thre[illegible]

Ju[illegible]
pleas cou[illegible]

Judgments accordingly.

Other judges who voted with the judge who wrote the opinion of the court.

CELEBREZZE, C.J., SWEENEY and J. P. CELEBREZZE, JJ., concur.

LOCHER, J., concurs in part and dissents in part.

W. BROWN and HOLMES, JJ., separately dissent.

Other opinions written by other judges on the court.

LOCHER, J., concurring in part and dissenting in part. I join the dissents of Justice William B. Brown and Justice Holmes with regard to the double recovery issue, finding the language of the Ohio Constitution [illegible]recluding two compensatory awards for the same injury. [illegible]that the claimants herein are not preclude[illegible] [illegible]ies, I find it necessary

6. COMPUTER-ASSISTED LEGAL RESEARCH

The last ten years have witnessed the growth of a new concept, *i.e.*, computer-assisted legal research. In the 1960's there were several experimental systems being developed; by 1975 some of them were being marketed.Now they are being widely advertised and installed in large courts, law offices, and law libraries.

The speed of the computer, and the ability to transmit its information nationwide via telephone lines, resulting in the computer's capacity to quickly match a request with the data that it contains, count the data, manipulate it, and print it out in a subscriber's office, have created an entirely new way of accomplishing legal research.

A computer which is located centrally may be connected via telephone lines to distant subscribers' terminals, and two-way communication via an office keyboard, an office video-display terminal, and a printer serve to bring quickly to the subscriber certain kinds of information that heretofore could have been obtained only by long and tedious searching in books.

There are other such services in existence, but the ones most commonly seen in courts, law offices, and law libraries are three: (a) Auto-Cite, a service of Lawyers Co-Operative Publishing Co., (b) Lexis, a service of Mead Data Central, and (c) Westlaw, a service of West Publishing Co. Although general descriptions of each of the services are provided below, the services are constantly under development; their features and data bases are constantly being expanded. For that reason, concrete information concerning the features and data bases of each service at any particular time can best be obtained from the Auto-Cite, Lexis, and Westlaw representatives.

AUTO-CITE

Auto-Cite is a computer-assisted legal-research service with a data base of citations and notations concerning virtually all court decisions that have been published in the United States. In many areas of the law, administrative decisions are also included. The data base deals with decisions appearing in the federal, state, and regional reporters, and in major topical and looseleaf reporters covering areas such as trade, labor, patents, bankruptcy, tax, securities, and other specialized disciplines.

Auto-Cite fills three major needs. The first service provided is to give the legal researcher the ability to verify the accuracy and completeness of case citations, and to check on the currency of case information. The legal researcher requests information from Auto-Cite by typing in a volume number, a report(er) abbreviation, and a page number. The citation and case-history response is in chronological sequence, starting with the opinion requested, and moving to the current status of that case. Legal history of the case, both direct and indirect, is provided. Extraneous information such as references to cases which merely cite or mention the requested opinion is eliminated; the legal researcher can quickly determine whether later court action has affected the validity of the case.

Second, the Auto-Cite response includes parallel references to virtually all publications in which the case has been reported, without placing a restriction on the type of citation used to request the information, and without regard to who published the opinions. Thus, Auto-Cite is a fast way to locate opinions in alternative sources. This is useful to the legal researcher who does not have the National Reporter System handy, but has local or specialized report(er)s.

Parallel references are easy to identify on Auto-Cite. Auto-Cite furnishes an easy-to-read citation sentence; parallel citations appear next to each other, separated by commas, similar to the way they should appear in legal writing.

Third, Auto-Cite identifies where the requested case, or any of its history cases, may have been discussed in an essay in *A.L.R. 2d, 3d, 4th* and *Federal,* and *L.Ed.2d.* The full titles of the essays and precise references to the citing sections are furnished.

A legal researcher can conduct an electronic search of the entire annotated reports system by beginning with a single citation to a relevant case. While the initial citation must be relevant to the issue of interest, it need not be exactly on point. It can be drawn from any source, and it can be from any jurisdiction, any court, and virtually any report(er). The response to this initial citation will show every essay in which the requested case has been discussed, and all later essays that have supplemented or superseded all or a part of those essays. Possibly, the legal researcher will find in this response an essay on point. If not, the researcher can pick out the citation of the closest essay, re-enter Auto-Cite with that essay citation, and receive a list of related essays. Repeating this process helps the researcher to zero in on the legal issue or factual application desired. When the citation to an essay that covers the legal issue of interest is located, the legal researcher may turn to the book for a discussion of the cases on the issue.

Auto-Cite contains timely case information from the first available published source, often from the looseleaf or topical reporters. Annotation (essay) information is available as soon as the annotation is published.

LEXIS

Lexis is a computer-assisted legal-research service that is not indexed; it furnishes full-text searching of reports of cases and other material. It has a very large case-law and other-materials data base that varies in extent from jurisdiction to jurisdiction. A legal researcher enters the words, phrases, numbers, or combinations likely to have been used in dealing with the ideas behind the research question. After a short period of time, documents using those search terms are available for display on the video screen. A search request is frequently modified in order to narrow the inquiry and eliminate superfluous cases, however.

Lexis furnishes the information in a printed-out format chosen by the legal researcher, *i.e.*, (a) citations only, (b) key words in context with citations, (c) complete copies of opinions with citations, or (d) selected segments of the opinions with citations.

The Lexis libraries contain modern full-text case law from 50 states and the federal courts. In addition, specialized libraries which focus on particular areas of practice are available. These include federal libraries covering:

tax	bankruptcy
securities	banking
trade regulation	energy
international trade	public contracts
communications	admiralty
patents, trademarks & copyrights	military justice
	environmental law

Besides case law, the specialized libraries contain rules, regulations, administrative decisions, and other secondary-source information. Lexis also offers law review articles from major American law schools, libraries of foreign law, and material from publishers such as Matthew Bender, Commerce Clearing House, Bureau of National Affairs, and Research Institute of America. The service contains Auto-Cite, which is available separately, and the newer parts of *Shepard's Citations*.

Lexis makes it possible to do several things that are not feasible with traditional legal research methods. *E.g.*, a legal researcher can retrieve all the opinions on a certain subject that were written by a particular judge or decided in a particular court. Lexis is also useful to research unique facts and to find unpublished decisions. Lexis claims to improve the thoroughness and currentness of research results. Because materials are on-line in full text, and there are no predefined index terms, a Lexis researcher does not have to rely on an indexer or headnote editor's judgment. Therefore, a legal researcher using Lexis can frequently pinpoint ideas that, because of subtlety, newness, or an indexer or editor's concept or oversight, were not captured in an index.

Lexis research often produces more current results than traditional methods. Because Lexis gets cases directly from the courts, rather than from publishers, there is no delay for indexing, headnoting, typesetting, printing, and mailing. Therefore, cases and other materials are available sooner on Lexis than they are in books; U.S. Supreme Court cases are on-line within 48 hours of their release, and cases from other courts are often available on Lexis in slip opinion form.

In addition to the comprehensive legal materials on-line, Lexis subscribers also have access to Nexis, a large, full-text database of news and information including *New York Times, National Law Journal,* and *Legal Times*; Lexpat, which contains the full text of all U.S. patents issued since 1975; Exchange, a financial and business information service; Naars, which contains annual reports from approximately 4,000 companies; Medis, an on-line database of clinical medical publications, *i.e.,* journals, newsletters, and textbooks; and other materials useful to lawyers and paralegals.

WESTLAW

Westlaw is a computer-assisted legal research service providing print-outs of retrieved documents. It has a full-text database of modern cases which includes the full text of court opinions plus editorially-prepared summaries and headnotes. Summaries tell the researcher what the case is about; headnotes provide an abstract of each point of law in a case.

Westlaw's database includes modern portions of the *Supreme Court Reporter, Federal Reporter, Federal Supplement, West's Bankruptcy Reporter, Military Justice Reporter,* and other West Publishing Co. reporters. Full-text-plus coverage of all 50 states is provided from at least 1967 to date; many states have additional coverage extending to earlier years.

Westlaw also has specialized libraries in the following areas:

tax	government contracts
securities	copyright and trademark
insurance	communications and mass media
labor	antitrust and business regulation
admiralty	forensic services directory
patents	Black's Law Dictionary
bankruptcy	national defense
financial	national texts and periodicals
energy	American Bar Ass'n summaries

The researcher can retrieve an immediate *Shepard's* list for cases in Westlaw. This list includes the subsequent history of a case, other cases which have cited or treated the case, and notations as to how the case is treated in the citing cases.

Shepard's is complemented by Insta-Cite, West Publishing Co.'s case-history and case-validation system. Insta-Cite works as an integral function of Westlaw and permits the researcher to quickly move between Insta-Cite and Westlaw. Information is added to Insta-Cite prior to publication in advance sheets; therefore, the results obtained from Insta-Cite are very current. Insta-Cite also assists in obtaining parallel citations to other report(er)s.

Westlaw may be used to search for documents containing words or phrases relevant to the researcher's problem. *E.g.*, the researcher may require that Westlaw retrieve cases which contain the phrase, "res ipsa loquitur." It is also possible to specify the proximity relationship between search terms. Grammatical connectors on Westlaw are the fundamental units of written language: the sentence, the paragraph, and the document. In addition, numerical connectors allow search terms to be ordered within a given number of words of each other.

Alternate search terms can be added. Research can be broadened or narrowed by adding or eliminating terms or by changing the proximity commands.

A variety of techniques are available for reviewing search results. The term mode is generally the most efficient method of browsing through a case to see the context in which search terms are used. Westlaw also has a locate feature which permits the user to find specific terms within retrieved documents. The terms that the researcher wishes to locate may either be the same or different than the terms in the original inquiry.

Westlaw can be used to locate cases which are classified in the West Publishing Co. digests under a specific key number or topic. This capacity allows the researcher to retrieve court opinions based on legal concepts as well as the occurrence of particular words. Cases classified under a key number can be retrieved in Westlaw by entering the following command: (000k000). Key number searches may also be combined with word and phrase searches.

Each Westlaw document is made up of several parts or segments known as fields. Cases on Westlaw contain the following fields: citation, title, court, judge, synopsis, digest, topic, and opinion. The researcher may wish to limit searches to a specific field or combination of fields. *E.g.*, the title field would be used to retrieve a case where the name of one or both of the parties was known and the researcher wished to limit the search to only the title of cases within the data base; similarly, the citation field would be used to retrieve a case for which user knew the citation.

Information Furnished by Auto-Cite

Auto-Cite request entered by user

Note precise history phrase; Auto-Cite follows language of court

If case has "history" (later proceedings that affect its validity), response includes full information for history case, including party names, date of decision, court, and all parallel citations

```
321 fsupp 99

   Albrecht v Herald Co. (1970, ED Mo) 321 F Supp 99, 1971 CCH Trade
   Cases P 73456, affd in part and revd in part Albrecht v Herald
   Co.*1 (1971, CA8 Mo) 452 F2d 124, 1971 CCH Trade Cases P 73754, 16
   ALR Fed 1

     TO DISPLAY COLLATERAL ANNOTATIONS CITING ANY OF THE
     FOLLOWING, ENTER AN ANNOTATION CITE REQUEST.

   ANNOTATION REFERENCES

   *1    Allowance of attorneys' fees under sec. 4 of Clayton Act (15
         USCS sec. 15), authorizing award of "reasonable attorney's
         fee" as part of costs recoverable in private antitrust
         treble-damage suit. 21 ALR Fed 750, sec. 28

         Measure and elements of damages under 15 USCS sec. 15
         entitling person injured in his business or property by reason
         of anything forbidden in federal antitrust laws to recover
         treble damages. 16 ALR Fed 14, secs. 9, 17, 18, 20
```

Note also that full titles of annotations are given, along with specific selections in which case was cited

Auto-Cite request entered by user

Response includes:

Party names

Date of decision (court is indicated by official reporter citation)

Official citation and all parallel citations

The fact that response contains no history is important: It means that no later case has commented unfavorably on the requested case

```
121 vt 221
   McDonnell v Montgomery Ward & Co.*1 (1959) 121 Vt 221, 154 A2d 469,
   80 ALR2d 590

     TO DISPLAY COLLATERAL ANNOTATIONS CITING ANY OF THE
     FOLLOWING, ENTER AN ANNOTATION CITE REQUEST.

   ANNOTATION REFERENCES

   *1    Products liability: stoves, 93 ALR3d 99, secs. 3, 4.

         Manufacturer's duty to test or inspect as affecting his liability
         for product-caused injury, 6 ALR3d 91, secs. 3, 14.

         Liability of manufacturer or seller for injury caused by
         household and domestic machinery, appliances, furnishings,
         and equipment, 80 ALR2d 598, secs. 4, 7, 16, 18, 33 (secs.
         19-26 superseded by Products liability defective heating
         equipment, 1 ALR4th 748, and sec. 32 superseded by 93 ALR3d
         99, supra, and sec. 39(n) superseded by Liability of manufacturer
         or seller for personal injury or property damage caused by
         television set, 89 ALR3d 210).

         Application of res ipsa loquitur rule in case of injury or
         damages from heating unit, electrical appliance, etc.,
         installed by defendant, 3 ALR2d 1448, supp sec. 4.
```

List of all annotations that have cited case

Note that history to annotations, i.e., later annotations that have superseded all or a part of an annotation, is given

7. SOLVING PROBLEMS: PREPARATION OF A LEGAL-RESEARCH MEMORANDUM

A large portion of the work which beginning lawyers and paralegals do consists of writing memoranda of law. This is not a temporary duty, but a skill to be applied in varying amounts during entire professional careers. In large part, lawyers are society's problem solvers. They undertake to provide concrete responses to unique problems which are presented to them by their clients. Lawyers use memoranda of law for the purpose of expressing and communicating their ideas regarding the problems, guiding themselves, and recording their reasons for their specific actions in response to the problems. In large part, the legal memorandum is the lawyer's blueprint for the entire handling of a problem; stated otherwise, it is the program of action or the battle plan. As such, the memorandum of law must provide a concrete response to a problem and justify the conclusion which is reached, because it is the foundation for what the lawyer later does in regard to the problem.

At the outset, it is perhaps appropriate to say something about style and language. Each student must be himself or herself, develop his or her own style, and not try to mimic someone else. Style will develop and take care of itself. The most important goal for the writer of a memorandum of law is to clearly communicate ideas. Simple language, short sentences, and a conscious choice of precise words are hallmarks of effective communication. Do not write for the purpose of impressing the reader with your vocabulary, or your ability to construct complex sentences. Engage in writing for the purpose of communicating.

* * *

Cocke, *Do You Apprise or Tell?* 71 CASE & COMMENT 12 (Nov.-Dec., 1966):

Strength In Simplicity

I'm not saying that lawyers should adopt the one-syllable vocabulary of the first-grade student. However, simple writing can have genuine strength and dignity, and still be understandable. The Lord's Prayer and Twenty-third Psalm have endured for centuries, though they are written in language a child can understand.

Look at some of the great statements of history — phrases uttered in the heat of battle by men who wanted to communicate, not confuse:

"Don't fire until you see the whites of their eyes."

"Damn the torpedoes! Full speed ahead."

"These are the times that try men's souls."

. . . and that World War II classic of conciseness:

"Sighted sub. Sank same."

. . . or General McAuliffe, receiving a surrender or be killed mandate from a German general when his forces were surrounded in the Battle of the Bulge in 1944, sent back a one-word reply: "Nuts!"

Clarity alone may not account for the enduring quality of statements like "Don't give up the ship!" but it's doubtful that Lawrence's remark would be printed in every history book in the country if he had said, "Please be advised to retain control of this vessel until further notice."

Wasted Words Mean Wasted Time

The writer who thinks he needs big words to express a simple thought or idea is wasteful. He wastes his own time and the time of his reader who must understand and use what he's written. The habitual user of big words and fancy language, unfortunately, is more interested in impressing people than in expressing thoughts.

* * *

Students' Work

There are at least two kinds of legal memoranda submitted by students. They are described as follows:

1. A closed research memorandum, for which the precedent cases and statutes to be considered are limited, are cited, or are printed in a casebook or other materials. Such a memorandum is not realistic, but it is good initial training.

2. An exhaustive open memorandum, for which all of the authorities must be found, using knowledge concerning the resources of the law library. This is a realistic example of the kind of memorandum that a lawyer or paralegal will prepare.

Writing a Legal Research Memorandum

All legal-research memoranda concern fact problems. It is not important that the students all reach one unique conclusion concerning the fact problem, but it is most important that they reach a conclusion. How they arrive at their conclusion is also important. A quest for intellectual truth is the guideline in writing a legal-research memorandum. Be objective. Say what you believe, in view of the facts of the unique problem case, the statutes, and the precedent cases.

A legal-research memorandum is not argumentative. Without fearing that the opposition will discover the weaknesses in your case, you should candidly appraise and evaluate the facts. When you write your memorandum, your primary purpose is to determine the best advice that can be given to the client. The client's problem is very important to him, and he should not only know his case's strong points, but its weaknesses as well.

When you do your work on the legal research memoranda, constantly think in the contexts of: (a) the unique facts of the problem case, and (b) legal materials. First, become thoroughly familiar with the facts; the importance of this point cannot be overemphasized. Only when you fully understand the facts, can you select and use authorities, *i.e.*, precedent cases and statutes, which are especially pertinent to the facts. This means that you must read and re-read the facts, and constantly compare and relate the facts to the authorities.

Read the authorities. Examine their components. Distill from the precedent cases and statutes such principles and concepts as may be pertinent to the unique facts of the problem case. Distinguish dictum from holding. Apply the principles and concepts found in the authorities directly to the facts of the problem case. The authorities must be analyzed, distinguished if possible, reconciled if possible, and synthesized into something new, *i.e.*, a memorandum of law that relates to the unique facts of the problem case.

In so treating each precedent case:

(a) Recognize the material facts of the precedent case, so that its outcome has a specific meaning with regard to the facts of the problem case;

(b) Recognize the issues of law, and the principles and concepts that were generated as a by-product of the resolution of the precedent case.

Apply the principles and concepts of the precedent case to the facts of the problem case. Do this in the following ways:

(a) Demonstrate how the favorable precedent cases are factually similar to the problem case and suggest why the principles from the precedent cases which favor the interest of the client should control the outcome of the problem case.

(b) Demonstrate how the precedent cases are factually different from your problem case, when the principles generated by the precedent cases are contrary to the interests of the client.

(c) When the facts in the precedent cases are not closely parallel to those in the problem case, but there are identifiable similarities, use the principles which favor the interests of the client, by analogy, as support for a proposition favorable to the client's problem case.

(d) Anticipate the precedent cases and arguments that might be raised against you. Attempt to predict whether the unfavorable precedents and arguments will prevail against you, or whether there are facts or arguments by which the client may avoid them.

Dictum and Holding

You have been advised to distinguish dictum from holding. Dictum is a statement by a judge concerning a point of law which is not necessary for the decision of the case in which it is stated. Usually dictum is not as persuasive as its opposite, *i.e.*, holding. Holding is the principle which reasonably may be drawn from the decision which a judge actually makes in a case; it is the resolution of the unique dispute which is before the judge in a specific case.

Organization

The focal point of a legal-research memorandum is the client's factual problem. The only discussion of statutes or precedent cases that is appropriate for the memorandum is a discussion which relates them to the client's factual problem. Avoid discussion of peripheral matters which do not relate to the client's factual problem, regardless of how interesting the peripheral matters may be.

A legal-research memorandum is a lawyer's foundation for successful practice in all but the simplest cases, and on close examination you will find very few simple cases. Sometimes a case looks simple only because the lawyer erroneously believes that it is simple.

There is a large area for the writer's unique contribution when writing the memorandum. He or she must decide on the manner and order of discussion and treatment of the authorities. Although the following is addressed to student work, minor modifications will adapt the subdivisions to law practice. Major subdivision headings should be indicated as follows and presented in approximately the following order:

TO: Course and section in which submitted.

FROM: The name of the student.

DATE: The date on which the memorandum is due.

RE: A caption, such as the name of the client, or the name of a potential lawsuit.

QUESTION PRESENTED: Skillfully state the issue(s) so as to guide the reader of the memorandum to focus on the specific legal problems manifest by the facts. *See* "Pointing Out the Problem" that follows.

CONCLUSION AND RECOMMENDATION: Prepare a concise answer to the question(s) presented. You might wish to add recommendations such as action to be taken, strategy to be pursued, and suggestions for additional questions of fact to be determined.

FACTS: An accurate statement of the facts in your own words, unless this requirement is waived by your instructor. Some employers do not require this.

DISCUSSION: A candid and objective discussion of the principles and concepts harvested from the statutes and precedent cases. Demonstrate how they indicate the outcome of the problem. Use subheadings to separate the points discussed; they serve as labels and help both the writer and the reader to stay organized. Subheadings should be logical, topical, and indicate the direction of thought of the material that follows.

Procedural Steps

The approach to the preparation of your legal-research memorandum should be:

(a) Know the facts of the client's case.

(b) Read and abstract each precedent case and statute for your own reference. Be particularly aware of, and make notation of, the way that it bears on the client's problem case.

(c) Outline the intended paper for your own reference. Organize your thoughts.

(d) Draft the paper for the first time; write each point identified by a subheading separately so that their relative locations may be changed.

(e) Edit the first draft.

(f) Redraft the paper and re-edit it several times before submitting it. Many successful lawyers and judges put their written work through three or more drafts before they are willing to call it a finished product.

Managing the Precedent Cases

At the risk of oversimplifying a complex skill, let us point out that, in large part, the precedent cases will bear on the problem case in essentially the following manner. Relate the precedent cases to the problem case by demonstrating the significant factual similarities and the significant factual differences between the precedent cases and the problem case. Suggest and demonstrate that the outcome of the problem case is indicated by the outcome of the precedent case. Make use of the reasons given for the decisions reached in the precedent cases.

Avoid systematic reliance on the abstract statements of rules or principles which are used as justifications for the decisions in the precedent cases. Although it is acceptable infrequently to use such abstract statements when they suit your purposes, do not use them as substitutes for the above-described factual applications. If you insist on occasionally using abstract statements, you will usually find the best ones in scholarly legal treatises and law-review articles. When writing a legal-research memorandum, work primarily with the facts, results, and reasoning in the precedent cases.

Pointing Out the Problem

The facts which generate issues or questions of law occur in large quantities. The statements of parties and witnesses and the documents involved, or a trial record in which the facts are found, will often be voluminous and chaotic. The abilities to: (a) create a shortened statement of facts, and (b) distill the statement of facts into a drastically shortened and highly-informative statement of issues, are needed skills, the development of which are begun in legal-research and writing courses.

Factual problems are in most instances your sole reason for writing a legal-research memorandum. The convergence of various unique facts generates the problems, and the problems call for your solution. Although a problem is a product of the voluminous facts, it is susceptible of being stated in a condensed form.

This skill is of tremendous importance. It has additional purposes in the litigation process, which will be discussed elsewhere in this book, but for the present purposes of writing legal-research memoranda, we emphasize that the purpose of a statement of the issues is to aid the person with whom the writer is communicating, and the writer, to focus on the specific legal problems generated by the facts and simultaneously exclude irrelevant questions. It tells the reader to whom you are introducing the facts and legal reasoning precisely what the memorandum of law is about.

Examples of Statements of the Issues or Questions

The appellant in *Ex Parte Murry,* 455 So.2d 72, 73 (Ala. 1984) made the statement of the issue crystal clear when he stated it as follows:

> "[W]hether the offense of the murder of a police officer who is in the performance of his duty requires proof of knowledge that the victim is in fact a police officer before the offense may be elevated to a capital one."

In *Brown v. Board of Education,* 347 U.S. 483, 493 (1954), the court said that the issue was:

> Does segregation of children in public schools, solely on the basis of race, even though the physical facilities and other 'tangible' factors may be equal, deprive the children of the minority group of equal education opportunities?

If possible, the issue should be concisely stated, as was done in *Kaufman v. United States,* 394 U.S. 217, 218 (1969):

> The question here is whether the claim of a federal prisoner that he was convicted on evidence obtained in an unconstitutional search and seizure is cognizable in a post-conviction proceeding under 28 U.S.C. § 2255.

The same attributes are illustrated by the questions drafted by the Court in *Goss v. Board of Education*, 406 F.2d 1183, 1185-1186 (6th Cir. 1969):

> . . . Presented to us upon plaintiffs' appeal are the following statements of questions involved:
>
> Whether the Knoxville School System is completely desegregated in spite of the fact that the Negro schools under dual operation remain identifiable as Negro schools and are attended almost exclusively by Negro students?
>
> Whether the Knoxville School System should have been ordered to pair identifiable Negro schools which could be paired, locate new construction to help eliminate identifiable Negro schools, and take other affirmative action to disestablish segregation?

When the problem is complicated, it is necessary to state succinctly some of the material facts, and to use several sentences to compartmentalize the question. This was done in *Canales v. Baker*, 406 F.2d 685, 686 (10th Cir. 1969):

> Appellant, Rito Canales, entered a plea of guilty to a second degree murder charge in the New Mexico state court. As a result of the plea he was sentenced to a term in the state penitentiary. The petition here involved was filed pursuant to 28 U.S.C. § 2254 and denied by the Federal District Court for the District of New Mexico. The trial court denied the petition on the grounds that Canales had failed to exhaust his state remedies pursuant to 28 U.S.C. § 2254(b) and (c) and that the state court had already made a valid determination of the merits on the issues by virtue of an evidentiary hearing.
>
> * * *
>
> The two issues presented on appeal are whether Canales exhausted his state remedies and whether § 2254 requires that a state prisoner be granted an evidentiary hearing upon a petition for habeas corpus in federal court.

The compartmentalization is more graphic in the style employed in *Harris v. Wainwright*, 406 F.2d 1 (5th Cir. 1969):

> This is an appeal from the denial by the District Judge of a petition for a writ of habeas corpus. The double-barreled question presented is whether (a) Florida's arraignment procedure is such a critical stage of the criminal proceeding in a capital case that (b) the lack of counsel during arraignment establishes a *per se* violation of constitutional rights without any showing of prejudice.

Also note the form of the issue as framed by the court in *Castilleja v. Southern Pacific Co.*, 406 F.2d 669, 670 (5th Cir. 1969):

> This is an appeal from a judgment entered upon a general jury verdict in a wrongful death action. The tragedy occurred in Guadalupe County, Texas, when a train of the Southern Pacific Railway struck a truck and killed Ausencio Castilleja, a passenger in the truck. The appellants, Castilleja's widow and minor children, were the unsuccessful plaintiffs in the court below. The primary issue involved in this appeal is whether the district court erred when, in the course of charging the jury on the issue of whether Castilleja was contributorily negligent in failing to keep a lookout for trains, it failed to instruct that under Texas law Castilleja had *no* duty to act as a lookout in the absence of exceptional circumstances.

An otherwise unacceptably cryptic statement of the issue may be used, when it is joined to an explanatory statement of the relevant facts. For example, in *Duty v. Dotson,* 406 F.2d 816, 817 (6th Cir. 1969) the Court said:

> The most serious question presented on the appeal is whether the District Judge committed reversible error at the beginning of the second trial in refusing to sustain defendant's challenge for cause against the seating of two prospective jurors who at that time were plaintiffs in pending lawsuits. * * * . . . Defendant exercised his peremptory challenges of the two prospective jurors in question and they did not serve on the jury. There is no showing that defendant's use of these two peremptory challenges in this manner exhausted his supply of peremptory challenges.

The first sentence of the foregoing, standing alone, would not be acceptable because it is not informative. The addition of the subsequent sentences makes the statement useful.

The foregoing examples of statements of the issue are notable, because: (a) they stand on their own feet without making reference to undisclosed facts; and (b) they convey to the reader easily-understood information which tells the reader precisely what the case is about.

When you write your statements of the issues or questions, avoid meaningless references such as: "in the record," "under the evidence," "as stated in the complaint," "as shown by the testimony," and "under the facts and circumstances." Such references do not tell your reader anything, and they serve to make your statement vague.

Chapter 9, Stating the Issues or Questions, deals further with the topic and furnishes additional examples.

Example A: Memorandum of Law

<u>MEMORANDUM</u>

TO: Tough, Demanding & Goodpay
Attorneys at Law
ATTN: Mr. Demanding

FROM: Pat Preston

DATE: June 1, 19xx

RE: Smith v. Bank of XXXXX

Pursuant to your request, I have researched for you the legal question that appears to be relevant to this dispute. Specifically, the question is as follows:

QUESTION

Where a stop-payment order describing a check was 50¢ different from the actual amount of the check, but all other descriptive information in the stop-payment order was accurate, and obtained by the bank at its request without informing the customer that any single item of descriptive information called for on the bank's stop-payment order form was more important than the other items of information, should the stop-payment order be binding on the bank when the bank's computer was programmed to signal the stop-payment of checks solely according to the amount of the check, without reference to any other data requested of the customer by the bank?

In my opinion, the question should be determined in the affirmative, *i.e.,* in favor of the customer.

I.

THE PRECEDENT CASES INDICATE THAT RELIANCE BY A BANK UPON ONE SINGLE ITEM OF INFORMATION AS BEING THE IDENTIFIER OF A CHECK ORDERED TO BE STOPPED IS NOT A DEFENSE AGAINST A SUIT FOR VIOLATION OF THE ORDER.

Under the UCC, adopted in Kentucky, a customer may by order to his bank stop payment of any item payable for his account. The order must be received at such time and in such manner "as to afford the bank a reasonable opportunity to act on it prior to any action by the bank with respect to the item." KRS 355.4-403(1). The Official Comments concerning this section by the drafters of the UCC state that the position taken by the section is that stopping payment is a service which depositors expect and are entitled to receive from banks, notwithstanding its difficulty, inconvenience, and expense. "The inevitable occasional losses through failure to stop should be borne by the banks as a cost of the business of banking." UCC 4-403, Official Comment 2. A payment in violation of an effective direction to stop payment is an improper payment, even though it is made by mistake or inadvertence. Any agreement to the contrary is invalid, if in paying the item over the stop-payment order the bank has failed to exercise ordinary care. UCC 4-403, Official Comment 8.

A Kentucky case prior to the UCC held that a drawer could recover damages for the bank's failure to stop payment on a check, notwithstanding that the drawer gave the bank erroneous information as to the amount of the check, where the bank was given correct information concerning its date, number, and the name of the payee, was informed that the check was the only one drawn to the payee, and was told the reason for stopping payment. *Kentucky-Farmers Bank v. Staton,* 314 Ky. 313, 235 S.W.2d 767 (1951). Cases subsequent to the UCC are in accord. See *Thomas v. Marine Midland Tinkers Nat'l Bank,* 86 Misc. 2d 284, 381 N.Y.S. 2d 797, 18 UCC Rep. Serv. 1273 (N.Y. Co., N.Y., Sup. Ct. 1976) (an error of one digit in the statement of the check's number was held to be insignificant), and *Elsie Rodriguez Fashions v. Chase Manhattan Bank,* 23 UCC Rep. Serv. 133 (N.Y. Co., N.Y., Sup. Ct. 1977) (defendant's payment of a check for $1804 after confirming receipt of a stop payment order for a check in the amount of $1804.10 was held improper). These two cases appear to be the only post-UCC cases on the point.

II.

SECONDARY AUTHORITIES SAY THAT THE COMPUTERIZATION OF BANKING SHOULD, UNDER SOME CIRCUMSTANCES, AFFECT THE PRE-UCC CASES.

According to one textbook, to a certain extent the validity of a stop-payment order should depend on the procedures that the drawee uses to identify stopped checks and on the reasonableness of the procedures. As an example, it says that an incorrect check number is no cause for complaint by a bank that examines checks solely by the name of the payee, but it would be to a bank that hunts for stopped checks principally by reference to check numbers. "When the customer gives erroneous information or gives less information than the banker asks for, we urge courts to review the information given to determine whether a reasonably prudent banker with that information should have found the check." It adds, however, that unless the depositor fails to live up to his contract with respect to stop orders, "any stop order should be sufficient that would enable a reasonably prudent banker using ordinary care to find the stopped check." J. White & R. Summers, *Handbook of the Law under the Uniform Commercial Code* § 17-5 at 577 (1972).

An article in the *Kentucky Law Journal* approaches computerization a bit differently. In commenting concerning what information the stop payment order must contain, it says that when a bank uses a computer system which is programmed to stop all payments of checks of a given amount drawn on a particular account, absolute accuracy in the stop payment order will be required. It adds that no court decisions have been found under the UCC in which a stop-payment order was declared ineffective because of erroneous information, where a bank put the stop payment order on its computer. "However, courts may hold that before a stop payment order will be declared ineffective, the bank will be required to inform the customer on the stop payment order form in conspicuous bold type that absolute accuracy is required to implement the stop payment order." Lakin, *Stop Payment Order: What Hath the Uniform Commercial Code Wrought?,* 63 Ky. L.J. 299, 310-317 (1975).

III.

FAIRNESS UNDER THE FACTS TENDS TO FAVOR THE CUSTOMER.

Mr. Smith says that he called the bank, advising that he wished to stop payment on the check, and "At this time, I gave your employee the exact information as recorded in my check book. My records indicate check No. 1928 was for $3,250.50 and I feel certain that was the amount I gave on the phone. Your employee then advised that I come in and sign the Stop Payment Request." He further states that when he went to the bank to sign the stop payment order as requested, "The order had been prepared before I arrived. I reviewed and signed it."

An examination of the bank's "Stop Payment Request Form" reveals that the handwriting of the customer is different from the handwriting which filled in the descriptive information. The form calls for various items of information including the drawer, the amount, the date, the payee, and the check number. Nowhere does the form state or infer that any one item of information called for by this form furnished by the bank is more important, or the only important item. The fact that the bank's form requests the various items of information indicates to the contrary.

These facts tend to lean the decision in favor of the customer, especially under the interpretation given by Lakin in the *Kentucky Law Journal*. The comment by White & Summers is less concrete, but it boils down to a requirement that the banker be reasonably prudent and use ordinary care to find the stopped check. If the customer had been warned that the amount of the check was the crucial, pivotal, and sole information that the bank would use, that would have perhaps been more persuasive on behalf of the bank.

I hope that this analysis will assist you in making a determination of the question.

Example B: Memorandum of Law

MEMORANDUM

TO: Tough, Demanding & Goodpay
Attorneys at Law
ATTN: Ms. Tough

FROM: Pat Preston

DATE: August 22, 19xx

RE: Jack Jones v. Sarah Jones

This is in response to your request for legal research concerning the separation agreement in this case, by which the parties agreed "not to have any type of relations with members of the other sex for a period of six months * * *, due to the present living arrangements.'' If either party were to have such a relationship, he or she would ''forfeit'' a certain sum of money at the end of each year. The facts indicate that (a) the man held parties in his apartment with a female and (b) he had been seen in an automobile with a female.

The issue is the legal consequence of this state of facts in view of the separation agreement.

I do not find any similar or analogous family-law cases in point, either with the provisions of the agreement or the facts.

Counsel has cited *Matthews v. Matthews,* 162 S.E.2d 697 (N.C. 1968). The holding of the case is that if a contract is vague and uncertain with no definite meaning there is no valid contract. It also says that if a contract merely requires someone to do something that they are otherwise required by law to do, the contract is without consideration. Counsel has also cited *Swint v. Swint,* 395 P.2d 114 (Ore. 1964); I did not see that it is relevant. It says that if the parties relied on a property settlement but the divorce decree was void and the wife is now dead, equity will sever the separate property settlement and enforce it.

I.

ORDINARY RULES OF CONTRACT CONSTRUCTION ARE APPLIED TO SEPARATION AGREEMENTS.

Separation agreements should be interpreted in accordance with the principles which are invoked for construction of all types of agreements. 2 A. Lindley, *Separation Agreements and Ante-Nuptial Contracts* § 32, 3. Special Rules (1985); 42 C.J.S. *Husband and Wife* § 598 (1944); 24 Am. Jur.2d *Divorce and Separation* § 838 (1983). *Richey v. Richey,* 389 S.W.2d 914, 917 (Ky. 1965) quotes the rule concerning this point found in Am. Jur.2d.

Courts should not use their construction powers to attribute to agreements intentions which are not articulated by the parties when the agreements were made, nor add provisions to agreements which the parties did not elect to include. 2 A. Lindley, *supra,* § 32, 3. Special Rules. No Kentucky cases are cited for this proposition. Constructions are ordinarily improper if they would create onerous or unreasonable conditions. *Id.*.

II.

THE POLICY OF THE LAW IS TO COMPENSATE CONTRACTING PARTIES FOR THEIR ACTUAL DAMAGES AS A RESULT OF A BREACH; IT IS NOT TO PENALIZE PARTIES WHO DO BREACH.

There appears to be a descending order of remedies for a breach of contract:

Actual damages;
Liquidated damages;
Forfeiture;
Penalty.

The descending order stated indicates the relative favor and disfavor which the courts have for the remedies. In descending order, the courts favor actual damages, then liquidated damages, and have considerable disfavor for forfeitures and penalties. See the discussion in 5 S. Williston, *A Treatise on the Law of Contracts* 637-642, 667-672 (3d ed. 1961).

In a case concerning penalties assessed in a government contract for the delivery of dried eggs, the U.S. Supreme Court said that a particular liquidated-damages provision in a contract was included, not to make a fair estimate of damages to be suffered, but to serve only as an added spur to performance. "It is well-settled contract law that courts do not give their imprimatur to such arrangements. * * * All provisions for damages are, of course, deterrents of default. But an exaction of punishment for a breach which could produce no possible damage has long been deemed oppressive and unjust." *Priebe & Sons v. United States,* 332 U.S. 407, 413, 68 S.Ct. 123, 127, 92 L.Ed. 32 (1947) (5-4 decision).

I do not find Kentucky cases that state this point as clearly, but several are consistent with it. In *Smith v. Ward,* 256 S.W.2d 385 (Ky. 1953), the Court held that $10,000 liquidated damages was not recoverable where the actual damages proved were $1,655.28, because the liquidated damages were disproportionate. It said that liquidated damages are enforced only when damages are uncertain or difficult of reasonable ascertainment, and the amount is not too greatly disproportionate to the injury. Similarly, it is not the policy of the courts to enforce stipulated damages provisions that are far in excess of the actual damages that would naturally flow from a breach. *Uncle George Orphans Home v. Landrum,* 551 S.W.2d 582 (Ky. Ct. App. 1977)(dictum). *Accord, Fidelity & Deposit Co. v. Jones,* 256 Ky. 181, 75 S.W.2d 1057 (1934)(dictum: a party with no damages because of another's violation of contract cannot recover liquidated damages). When a party seeking a forfeiture has a remedy to recover damages by suit, the forfeiture, which amounts to a penalty only, cannot be enforced. *Lee v. Davis,* 5 Ky. Ops. 617 (1871). *Accord, Mattingly Bridge Co. v. Holloway & Son Construction Co.,* 32 Ky. L. Summary No. 8 p. 19 (Sup. Ct. June 13, 1985)(adopts *Restatement (Second) of Contracts* § 356(1) (1981), and says that the award of liquidated damages is forbidden when they are nothing more than a penalty of forfeiture).

In order for the Court to enforce a forfeiture, the grounds on which the forfeiture is allowed should be well established. *Case v. Stacey,* 283 Ky. 808, 813, 143 S.W.2d 497 (1940). The facts of this precedent case are not in point; the issue was a forfeiture of timber on account of the nonpayment of timber rent, even though payment was made to an administrator and partial heir.

III.

AN INTERPRETATION WHICH DOES NOT INVOLVE A FORFEITURE IS FAVORED.

When the intention of the parties is doubtful, a provision for forfeiture should be strictly construed against the person for whose benefit the forfeiture is suggested. This is because of the long-standing rule that forfeitures are regarded with disfavor and an interpretation which does not involve a forfeiture is favored. *Perros v. Stone's Adm'r,* 305 Ky. 142, 146-147, 202 S.W.2d 160 (1947). *Accord,* 17 Am. Jur.2d *Contracts* § 500 (1964); *Schwartz Amusement Co. v. I.O.O.F,* 278 Ky. 563, 128 S.W.2d 965 (1939)(dictum).

Courts are reluctant to declare and enforce a forfeiture if by reasonable construction it can be avoided. *Id.*

While not in point factually, *Equitable Life and Casualty Ins. Co. v. Rutledge*, 9 Ariz. App. 551, 454 P.2d 869 (1969), is instructive. It holds that contracts will be construed to avoid a forfeiture if possible. There the insurance agents had changed principals and the former principal sought to cause a forfeiture of earned commissions upon the ground that the agents had violated the contract by which they were formerly employed. The Court did not enforce the forfeiture because the agents had not actually solicited for another insurer in violation of their agreement, although they had made preparations to do so.

IV.

THE COURT MAY WISH TO TAKE ORAL TESTIMONY CONCERNING THE INTENTION OF THE PARTIES.

Although we usually think that the parol-evidence rule prevents the court from hearing testimony concerning the intention of the parties, there are some exceptions to the rule.

The parol-evidence rule does not apply when the writing is ambiguous. *Gibson v. Sellars*, 252 S.W.2d 911 (Ky. 1952), was a lawsuit to quiet title to oil and gas in place beneath particular real property. The court construed the instrument as expressly excepting coal and mineral rights, and therefore did not hold directly on this point. At 913, however, the court stated that extrinsic proof is competent and may be employed in construing language, the meaning of which is obscure or which is susceptible of two or more interpretations. It cautioned, however, that because of the inherent danger of the rule, its use is permitted only in those cases where the language to be construed is so ambiguous or obscure in meaning as to defy interpretation otherwise. The Court added that an extension of the rule would result in chaos and confusion and it would be impossible to determine the rights of the parties to a contract without viewing all of the circumstances surrounding the execution of the document in question.

Parol evidence may be used to determine the intent of a separation agreement. In *Ainsworth v. Ainsworth*, 289 S.W.2d 517 (Ky. 1956), the court held that a separation agreement was ambiguous and therefore extrinsic parol evidence was admissible to show what the parties intended. In that case, one of the parties was dead. On a second appeal, *Ainsworth v. Ainsworth,* 321 S.W.2d 33 (Ky. 1959), the widow's testimony that it was the intent of the intestate and herself in making the separation agreement that the children of both of intestate's marriages were to share equally in the estate was held to be competent.

On an appeal from an order based upon the conclusion of a trial court that the language of a particular agreement required the husband to pay all expenses of the wife to the time of dissolution of marriage, the court said that while that conclusion may prove to be correct, it could not arise from the ambiguous language of the agreement. It reversed and remanded with instructions to the trial court to conduct an evidentiary hearing to determine what the parties intended when they agreed that the husband shall continue to be obligated to pay all the obligations of the parties until the time of the dissolution. *Bacardi v. Bacardi,* 386 So.2d 1201 (Fla. Ct. App. 1980).

If you wish to consult an essay concerning the parol-evidence rule and the admissibility of extrinsic evidence, see annot., 40 A.L.R.3d 1384-1403 (1971 and supp). Subsections deal with how ambiguity is ascertained (§§ 3, 4), and how it is clarified (§§ 5, 6). The essay does not cite any Kentucky cases, however.

8. WHAT SKILL IS IMPORTANT TO AN ADVOCATE?

One of the most important applications of lawyer's skills in legal research and legal writing is in the advocacy process. Many of the skills which a lawyer uses in the advocacy process are diffused throughout trials, appellate work, and administrative agency hearings, but the discussion of advocacy in this book will generally concern appellate work. This is not to say, however, that the advocacy skills mentioned in this book are useful only in the appellate phase of litigation; they are useful in all phases of litigation.

As an advocate, a lawyer undertakes one of his most important functions, *i.e.*, writing and speaking in support of his client's case to someone with authority to act officially concerning it. The foundation for a lawyer's successful writing and speaking in advocacy is legal research and knowledge of the record in the case to be decided. The materials from which the lawyer builds his written and spoken message are ideas, words, and language. Note what some knowledgeable persons have said about these topics.

* * *

Rossman, *Better English for Lawyers as Draftsmen and Advocates,* 48 A.B.A.J. 1048, 1051 (1962):

Possibly the day has come in which we should recognize that before an applicant is permitted to hang a license upon the walls of his office signifying that he is competent to serve clients, the young man should be required to give evidence of reasonable proficiency in expressing himself with clarity and precision. If his bar examination paper is written in such poor style that, although it indicates an adequate acquaintance with the law, it denotes inability to express himself, hesitancy to admit him to the practice might go a long way to encourage law schools to see to it that each of their graduates is prepared to serve clients.

* * *

John Selden (1584-1654, English jurist), *Table Talk of John Selden* 100 (F. Pollock ed. 1927):

Syllables governe the world.

* * *

Justice Felix Frankfurther, quoted in Vodiga, *Euthanasia and the Right to Die — Moral, Ethical and Legal Perspectives,* 51 Chi.-Kent L. Rev. 1, 2 (1974):

[T]he law *is* semantics!

* * *

In the appellate process and other advocacy processes, words are instruments which engage the minds of judges. An advocate attempts to persuade the judge's mind favorably via language, and to avoid language which repels it. There is great difficulty, however, in determining what language persuades favorably, and what language repels. Some judges will be persuaded by the same words that fail to persuade other judges.

This quandary is easily illustrated by the fact that there are frequent majority and minority or dissenting opinions in some courts, after the justices have read and heard the same arguments by the same counsel.

M.Swinford, *Kentucky Lawyer* 95-96 (1963).

Colonel William Colston of the Cincinnati law firm of Harmon, Colston, Goldsmith and Hoadly, was a well known attorney in Kentucky. He was a Confederate veteran and, I am told, lost an arm in the service of the Southern cause. He was counsel for the Southern Railway System for many years. At one time when he had a case to argue before the United States Supreme Court, he took the president of the company to Washington with him. While they were waiting for their case to be heard, the client wandered about the building, inquiring of the habits and practices of the justices in the conduct of the business of the court. He found a bailiff who was glad to answer all questions and who entertained him with various stories of incidents in connection with sessions of that eminent tribunal. One thing he learned was that there was a rule of court that any attorney addressing it must wear a vest. "You see," the garrulous attache elaborated, "some of the attorneys go far beyond the rules and appeal to the vanity of the judges by dressing in formal attire, with striped trousers and cutaway coat. Your lawyer is complying with the rules by wearing a vest but has on only a plain business suit."

Several weeks later the ruling of the court came down deciding the case against the railroad. Colonel Colston immediately phoned the company and talked to the gentleman who had been with him in Washington. "Well, we lost our case," he said. "I know why," was the disgruntled response. "Why?" asked the Colonel. "Because you weren't dressed right," said the president. To which came the rejoinder from the disappointed but still belligerent Colonel Colston, "Well, by God, that's a better reason than any they gave in the opinion."

Chaffee, *The Disorderly Conduct of Words,*
41 COLUM. L. REV. 381, 382-384 (1941).

I.

The first lesson I have learned is, that language is not used solely for the communication of thought. That purpose is uppermost in our minds when we write opinions or briefs or law review articles, and hence we lawyers easily forget that words are frequently employed with quite a different object — to make somebody do something. Ogden and Richards stress this emotive function of language as distinguished from its communicative function; and illustrate this by printing Malinowski's observations on the speech of children and savages.[1] They do not employ language, he says, as a condensed piece of reflection and a record of fact or thought, as does the author of a book or inscription. With them, language functions as a link in concerted human activity, as a piece of human behavior. It is a mode of action and not an instrument of reflection. For example, among primitive people:

> A word, signifying an important utensil, is used in action, not to comment on its nature or reflect on its properties, but to make [the utensil] appear, be handed over to the speaker, or to direct another man to its proper use.

It takes only a little thought for us to realize that among civilized adults language is largely employed for the same emotive purpose. One instance will suffice — the young wife who complained, "When I ask Charles if he loves me, he acts as if I were asking for information."

What bearing has this emotive function on law? More than we like to admit. The clerk's prelude to the session of court, — "Oyez! oyez! oyez!" — aims to produce an attitude of seriousness and wrench us out of the careless moods of everyday life. The lawyer's address to a jury is only in part an attempt to organize the evidence clearly. In large measure, he seeks to evoke emotion and action, namely, a favorable verdict. Nor can we say that the emotive function is always absent from the lawyer's argument before an appellate court. When Mr. Joseph Choate told the United States Supreme Court in 1895 that a 2 percent income tax had "scattered to the winds the great fundamental principle of private property,"[2] he was not aiming to give accurate information but to create judicial hostility to the statute. Indeed, some experienced advisers consider that the main purpose of appellate argument is to make the judges want to decide your way. It is even said that the citation of authorities is a solemn pretext. My own view is quite different, but here too action is the end desired — a decision for one's client — and not merely the transmission of clear ideas.

When one gets into this vein, he discovers the emotive function operating in almost all speech and writing. The communication of facts and thoughts seems never completely separated from the desire to make somebody do something or feel somehow. Nothing appears sterilized from emo-

---

[1] Malinowski, supplement to OGDEN & RICHARDS, MEANING OF MEANING (4th ed. 1936) 309-321 *passim*.

[2] See Pollock v. Farmers' Loan & Trust Co., 157 U.S. 429, 534 (1895).

tion except a quitclaim release. Even when the informative purpose is very strong as in a law-book, the author wants to write so that a publisher will print it and lawyers will buy it. Although a law review article gets no compensation, it may produce academic promotion or esteem among the elect. Most audacious of all is the idea that a judicial opinion is more than pure thought. Does not the judge hope thereby to win over a hesitating colleague, to reconcile the losers to their fate, and perhaps to make courts in other states eager to follow his views?

Why worry? It's one of the things language is for. Probably the distinction between the communicative and emotive functions is only a matter of degree. The transmission of information and the creation of an attitude in the listener are dual purposes in most speech, though in varying proportions. Because we believe reason to be our best guide, we must exert ourselves in legal expression to make our thoughts fit things and our words fit our thoughts, to keep down the emotional element, and above all to pick and choose among possible emotions. The evocation of a sense of fairness may be within the emotive function as truly as the stimulation of hatred and greed, but it is a much more legitimate aim.

However, our major concern as lawyers is with the communicative function of language, to which my remaining observations will be devoted. My next main point is that *The Meaning of Meaning* gives us much help in understanding the true relation between a word and the object for which the word stands. (I use "object" loosely to embrace persons and abstract ideas as well as tangible things; the semanticists use instead the technical word "referent").

To start with, the word is not the same as what it points to. Obvious as this statement may seem, the contrary belief is constantly cropping up; that words have existence and power, that they are equivalent to the things and persons they denote, or nearly so. It is something like the relation assumed by primitive or superstitious minds between the god and the image. A Harvard professor fell into conversation with a peasant in the Campagna, who asserted defiantly that there was no God. "I suppose you don't believe in the Devil either." Quick as a flash the peasant crossed himself and looked behind him with terror.

Although this identification of the word with the object is avoided by more sophisticated minds, they often slip just one peg down into the deeply-rooted notion that the word inevitably and unalterably belongs to a particular thing or person. A name is like a label chained around the object by God's order, which nobody must presume to detach. "And whatsoever Adam called every living creature, that was the name thereof."

An Englishman was lunching in a Paris restaurant. He knew no French, the waiter little English. They engaged in the friendly task of giving names in their respective languages to things at which the Englishman pointed. Eventually he pointed at the bread. "Pain," said the waiter; and the

Englishman burst out laughing. "What you call it, M'sieur?" "Bread" — and the waiter laughed. At this the Englishman got angry. "M'sieur," expostulated the waiter, "you laugh when I say 'Pain,' I laugh when you say 'Bread'." Back came the Englishman, "But it *is* bread, you know."

* * *

Marshall, *The Federal Appeal,*
COUNSEL ON APPEAL 139-153[3]
(A. Charpentier ed. 1968)

(Mr. Justice Marshall, who became a member of the United States Supreme Court on September 1, 1967, formerly served as Solicitor General of the United States and as judge of the United States Court of Appeals for the Second Circuit. He took his legal training at Howard University. He was active in the advocacy of civil-rights cases while serving as special counsel for the NAACP.)

There is no one particular way of being an effective advocate, and each of us finds this out each time he appears in court. Some of you have argued as many cases as I have, if not more; therefore, I won't presume to state anything more than my own views, with no attempt to persuade you of their universal applicability.

Nor will I set forth a list of rules for the effective appellate advocate in the federal courts. Several speakers have alluded to John W. Davis's superb 1940 speech, "The Argument of an Appeal," in which are set forth ten commandments any advocate should observe. In addition, Frederick Bernays Wiener has written an *apologia pro vita sua, Briefing and Arguing Federal Appeals* — which, incidentally, he might easily have called *My Life in Court* — thoroughly covering the subject.

Hence, I think it is safe to assume that every lawyer knows that the prerequisites for effective appellate advocacy are such points as making a concise, sympathetic, yet accurate statement of the facts and phrasing an issue to capture the interest of the court both intellectually and emotionally.

I won't tell you how to win a case on appeal, though of all the answers I have thought of over the years, only one is close to being accurate. Why did I qualify my statement by saying "is close to being accurate"? I cannot forget the case of *Lyons v. Oklahoma*. In that murder case, tried in a small town in Oklahoma, my client was convicted and sentenced to life imprisonment.

---

[3] From The Association of the Bar of the City of New York, COUNSEL ON APPEAL (A. Charpentier, Editor).

After the trial, the assistant attorney general of Oklahoma and the trial judge both assured me privately that I would get a reversal on the confession point. After I had lost by 2 to 1 in the Court of Criminal Appeals of Oklahoma, I was again assured privately by the court and the assistant attorney general I would win in the Supreme Court.

By the time the case was argued in the Supreme Court of the United States all sides and everyone else in the world were in complete agreement: I was a sure winner. End of the story: The judgment was affirmed. Perhaps we should have a course entitled "How to Win the Sure Winners." Rather than that, I would pass on to you the answer I give to people who ask, "What is the most important case you have argued?" My reply has always been, "The next one."

A federal appeal, as I shall define it, is any case argued before a federal appellate court, primarily the Courts of Appeals and the Supreme Court. Thus, a state case brought to the Supreme Court is a federal appeal at least for tonight.

It is impossible to draw a clear line between a federal appeal and a state appeal. The jurisdictional boundaries we all know. Once they have been established, the advocacy in handling the particular appeal is much the same. The same is true of the lawyers preparing and arguing the appeals. For example, there is no longer even a small, recognizable Supreme Court bar. The percentage of federal appeals is growing at an accelerated rate, and the number of lawyers handling these appeals is, likewise, increasing daily. Statistics show a similar increase in appeals in state courts. Therefore, I cannot resist the temptation to make a few comments on appellate advocacy in general.

It is particularly important in an appellate court to know the tribunal. As the then Judge Cardozo said, "The great tides and currents which engulf the rest of men do not turn aside in their course and pass judges by."

Most lawyers can't help but know something of the views of the Justices of the Supreme Court and of each individual Justice thereof. But the admonition is just as true of the Courts of Appeals, although there is not nearly as much published material concerning the latter. In the Supreme Court you always know who the members of the panel are, while in some of the Courts of Appeals you discover the members of the panel only when they enter the courtroom — surprise!

I can remember my first sitting in the Court of Appeals for the Second Circuit. I sat with Justices Waterman and Smith, and those of you who know them know that the three of us are of about the same size. When the three of us walked in, one of the lawyers said, "What! The forward line of Notre Dame!"

I would not want you to infer from these remarks that the quality of justice in a Court of Appeals depends on the particular panel assigned to a case. That is far from the truth. However, an effective advocate must not be oblivious to the interests of the particular judges before whom he is arguing.

For example, a judge quite often grows fond of a particular opinion on which he has labored for weeks or months. Would you insult him by not having read his *magnum opus,* published just three days before your argument? Would you expect to discuss poetry with Robert Penn Warren, having read only his novels, or discuss art with Picasso, having seen only the paintings of his early blue period?

Indeed, knowledge of a judge's recent opinions aside, knowing the panel members, their background and interests, provides valuable clues that will enable you to answer questions in a way that will, as the late Karl Llewellyn once said, "capture the court." Of course, a judge wants to do justice, but it is the advocate's job to interest him enough to do so by deciding the case correctly — for your client, obviously.

A word of caution is in order. I do not suggest that the lawyer should pander to what he considers to be the judge's personal intuitions, real or fancied. To the contrary, I urge that you should be aware of the judge's stated views of the law involved and try to convince him that the position you assert is at least encompassed within his overall views. On the other hand, to attempt to play up to any judge's alleged personal views as contrasted with his true legal opinions is to play Russian roulette.

All the lawyers I know, especially those who have written on advocacy, stress the importance of oral argument. Most judges do, too. I suspect that those who don't have become so inured to the poor arguments that are often made that they do not appreciate the value of oral argument in general. During a few arguments in the Second Circuit, I've recalled with approval the remark in *King Henry VI,* Part II, "The first thing we do, let's kill all the lawyers."

We all know that in the Supreme Court and in many of the Courts of Appeals, votes are cast and opinion writing assigned soon after argument, usually within a week. Although those votes may later change, in most cases, I think it accurate to say, they don't. The impression you leave with the judges in the courtroom is often the impression on which they decide your case, but this is based on the prior reading of the brief as well as on the oral argument.

The volume of appeals in federal courts is steadily increasing. The number of appeals in the Courts of Appeals has increased by over 50 percent in the last four years. Too many litigants are taking literally Ambrose Bierce's definition of an appeal: "In law, to put the dice into the box for another throw."

In the last fiscal year, the number of appeals docketed in the Second Circuit, for example, increased by 20 percent. Yet you still have the same amount of time in which to argue your case. If a federal judge has less time to read the briefs and so on, must he not rely more on you personally in the courtroom to point out the key issues, the tentative resolution?

One difficulty with increasing volume is that it causes some judges to go into the courtroom completely cold.

If a judge hasn't read the briefs, at least to the extent of acquiring familiarity with the facts and knowledge of the issues, then he can't participate with counsel in a fruitful discussion, which is what a good oral argument is.

Recently I heard a Justice of the Supreme Court tell a group of judges and lawyers that when he was an advocate he assumed that after he had briefed and argued a case, the judge had no difficulty in using the brief and argument to write his opinion. He believed that nothing more was needed. However, when he reached the other side of the bench, he discovered to his surprise that he had to do considerable research and work in deciding the case.

Regardless of the panel you get, the questions you get, or the answers you give, I maintain it is the brief that does the final job, if for no other reason than that opinions are often written several weeks and sometimes months after argument. The arguments, great as they may have been, are forgotten. In the seclusion of his chambers the judge has only the briefs and the law books. At that time your brief is your only spokesman.

I suppose that the distinctive feature of a federal appeal and one that is of obvious significance to the advocate is the nature of the issues usually presented. Of course, there are many federal appeals, in diversity cases for example, that differ little from the typical appeal in a state court. However, in a number of federal appeals the issues become larger than the particular interests represented by the immediate litigants. A question of the interpretation of a federal statute decided by the Second Circuit has import far beyond the court's geographical limits. And, of course, virtually all the cases in the Supreme Court are of national significance in one way or another, for that is the very nature of Supreme Court litigation.

In the October, 1964, term of the Supreme Court there were 2,178 applications for review. Only 132 were accepted for argument. I think it clear that many of those 2,000 plus applications should not have been submitted to the Court. Thus, the advocate in the Supreme Court and, in many cases, in the Courts of Appeals must be prepared to relate his case to the law generally, to advise the court why the change urged, or the *status quo* to be preserved, is desirable, and to inform the court of the consequences of the position he advocates, because the court is looking beyond the interests of the parties immediately before it.

Did anyone doubt that the positions of the parties in *Brown v. Board of Education* portended the demise of more than just segregated schools? What about *Gideon, Mapp,* and *Escobedo*? When the Supreme Court asked if *Betts v. Brady* should be reconsidered, wasn't it clear that the Court was concerned with more than just the fate of Clarence Gideon?

In noting that, as a matter of national scope, issues in federal appeals are more likely to transcend the immediate case, I should state that it is frequently the advocate's most interesting and difficult task to convince the Supreme Court to take his case on certiorari. At the same time, all too many lawyers feel that petitioning for certiorari, regardless of the objective significance of the case, is as necessary as noting an appeal to the Court of Appeals, thus burdening the Supreme Court.

With regard to grounds for appeal to the Courts of Appeals and for petitioning to the United States Supreme Court, I think often of the lawyer whose only complaint is not yet a recognized ground for appeal or certiorari, to wit, "I am unhappy with the lower court's decision." You have got to have more.

There are many cases decided adversely to the government that the Solicitor General decides not to take to the Supreme Court because he feels that the case is not "cert-worthy." Because of that exercise of judgment, naturally, a greater percentage of government petitions are granted.

While it is true that government cases often present significant and recurring issues of the kind calling for Supreme Court review, there is still room for the skill of an effective advocate in the borderline cases.

For example, *United States v. Ventresca* did not present an issue of great importance. The issue was whether or not an affidavit in support of a search warrant was sufficient to establish probable cause.

Indeed, the government's petition began: "The Solicitor General seeks certiorari in this small and intrinsically unimportant case . . ." We felt that the Court of Appeals had read the particular affidavit in an unduly technical manner. We sought certiorari in the belief that —

> upholding the activities of law-enforcement agencies that have scrupulously observed the procedure for safeguarding constitutional rights and satisfying the substantial requirements for a search warrant is no less important than the invalidation of convictions because of disregard for individual rights or official overreaching.

Our petition was granted, and we prevailed on the Court, with the majority opinion stating 380 US at 11-112:

> This court is alert to invalidate unconstitutional searches and seizures whether with or without a warrant. ... By doing so, it vindicates individual liberties and strengthens the adminstration of justice by promoting respect for law and order. This Court is equally concerned to uphold the actions of law enforcement officers consistently following the proper constitutional course. This is no less important to the administration of justice than the invalidation of convictions because of disregard of individual rights or official overreaching.

I think the *Ventresca* case is a good example of the role played by an effective advocate. Of course, we can all think of other examples.

Supreme Court practice requires three distinct types of presentation. The petition for certiorari must be short, concise, and exemplary of John W. Davis's admonition, "Go for the jugular vein." The decision of the lower court is not only clearly wrong, it is shocking and, if allowed to stand, will disrupt the entire existing federal judicial system. It is not only worthy of review, but it is, likewise, of compelling national significance. The country simply couldn't exist without the review.

Now, if by any chance certiorari is granted, the brief on the merits must prove that point. There is where you get the problem, and it's a problem that grows. If certiorari is granted without any limitation, you are confronted with the question of which subsidiary point to brief and of how much briefing is to be done on that point and how much on the other points. How far must you go into legislative history on a minor point?

One thing is certain. You cannot approach a brief on the merits without a well-organized plan and careful appraisal. The rules themselves clearly point to the proper procedure.

Once you have carefully prepared an adequate statement of the case and a concise and convincing summary of argument, your outline should be complete. You should have the answer to the question presented. Little advice can be given on the final problem: to be short and concise without losing either a point or the flavor of a point. The solution, of course, must vary with the case and with the draftsman. It could very well be true that some briefs are too long, and, indeed, I am a witness to it. There was a brief in the school cases, the brief on the merits. It totaled 250-odd pages. The one thing I remember about that brief was that during the final printing, late one Sunday night, the printer called us and said he thought a change would have to be made on the cover. We asked what should be changed, and he said, "Very frankly, do you really want to call this book a brief?"

The final step, of course, is oral argument. Here my admonition would be that in preparing for the argument you make every effort to escape the inevitable, that is, that the best answer any of us has made to a question or questions from the bench is the one he thinks of in the cab on the way back to the hotel from the court.

You should bear that in mind in preparing your argument, and canvass thoroughly the points that are obvious and inherent in the questions. Be prepared for more questions than you get, and be sure your answers are accurate and concise and are prepared with complete candor. Nonresponsive and evasive answers merely invite the guillotine.

Finally, on this point, be sure you understand the question and its implications. Often when you hear the start of a question and it appears to be just the one you have been waiting for, you miss the rest of the question, which is what the justice is interested in. Your answer is less than satisfactory, and you give the impression of being evasive.

Much of what has been suggested for the Supreme Court, of course, is equally applicable to an appeal in the Court of Appeals. Although the federal judiciary consists of courts of limited jurisdiction, the issues run from constitutional questions to those of less widespread importance presented in, for example, diversity automobile cases.

* * *

I have not put emphasis in this talk on the appellee, or respondent, the bottom side of these cases, because practically all I have said applies to whichever side you are on. The only thing I do want to mention is that I am more and more impressed by the failure of lawyers to use a beautiful opinion by the lower court, scholarly done, busting with research. It is sad to see an appellee or respondent prepare his brief, finish his oral argument, and never once rely on the opinion of the judge below.

I mention that merely as one addition. Finally, I close with the frustration I started with. Having gone over the books and articles on federal appellate procedures and having prepared these few remarks and done the best I can, I still have the feeling that I should end as I started, with John W. Davis's "Go for the jugular vein." There is not one of you in this room who hasn't read it at some time or another. Hardly 1 out of 100 lawyers has filed a case on appeal who is not familiar with that admonition — go for the jugular vein — but when you hear the arguments and read the briefs of so many of those lawyers, you find that in aiming for the jugular vein they have put a pinprick in a small vein of the big toe.

* * *

Reference

See also Webber, *Appellate Advocacy with Maine Flavor,* 18 Maine L. Rev. 59-64 (1966).

9. STATING THE ISSUES OR QUESTIONS

One very important purpose of the statement of the issues or questions in a court brief or memorandum of law, or spoken orally to a court or judge, is to guide the person or persons with whom the writer or speaker is communicating to focus on the specific legal problems generated by the unique facts of the problem case.

When a judge or attorney reads your brief or memorandum, the statement of the issues will be the first thing, and one of the most important things, that he or she reads. It will be followed by a statement of the case, a statement of the facts, and your argument of law.

The statement of the issue tells the reader what the case is about, before he or she plunges into the particulars of the facts and legal arguments. It therefore aids the reader to exclude irrelevant matters, and to know the answer to the frequent mental inquiry, "What is this case all about?"

In the advocacy process, the statement of the issues takes on an added function. This is a result of the adversary nature of judicial proceedings, and the fact that in such proceedings the opposing lawyers will of necessity have differing partisan viewpoints. Without sacrificing accuracy or candor, an advocate will subtly season an otherwise bland statement, so that the seasoning will create a taste favoring his client. The issues as thus stated by an advocate will often indirectly suggest their own answer, *i.e.*, the answer that the advocate wants the court to accept. The conscious choice of forceful and demonstrative words, and their organization in relation to each other, is part of the process by which this is accomplished.

As an example, in *Car-Ron Asphalt Paving Co. v. Commissioner,* 758 F.2d 1132 (6th Cir. 1985), the majority said:

* * *

> EDWARDS, Circuit Judge. At issue in this case are deductions from federal corporate income tax on the part of Car-Ron Asphalt Paving Company in the amount of $87,987 in 1975 and $4,372 in 1976. These deductions were claimed because taxpayer Car-Ron had paid these sums as bribes ("kickbacks") to a vice-president of Forest City Enterprises named Nicholas Festa. ***
>
> It is petitioner's claim that he is entitled, contrary to the holding of the Tax Court, to these deductions because although these were bribes paid to

secure the contracts referred to, such bribes were not crimes under the criminal law of the State of Ohio. The government, by brief and oral argument, concedes that the payments were not illegal under Ohio law. However, these transactions were not devoid of criminal conduct.

* * *

The dissent's view of the issue was different, however:

* * *

JONES, Circuit Judge, dissenting. With due respect for the views of my esteemed colleagues, I am compelled to dissent. My views are straightforward. The issue in this case is whether legal kickback payments by Car-Ron Asphalt Paving Company are deductible under I.R.C. § 162(a) as "ordinary and necessary" business expenses. ***

The proper question is whether Car-Ron's legal kickback payments were "appropriate and helpful" for developing its business. ***

* * *

Similarily, in *In re Laminated Veneers Co.*, 471 F.2d 1124 (2d Cir. 1973), the majority said this concerning the issue:

* * *

The question here is whether Commercial's secured interest in 'equipment' gave it a lien on two Oldsmobile automobiles owned by the bankrupt. ***

* * *

The dissent, however, described the issue differently:

* * *

The majority correctly states the question here as "whether Commercial's secured interest in 'equipment' gave it a lien on two Oldsmobiles owned by the bankrupt." Essentially, this question revolves itself into two very distinct issues: 1) was it the intent of the parties, as expressed in the security agreement, that Commercial could look to these Oldsmobiles as collateral for its loan to the bankrupt; 2) if such was the expressed intent, is the term, 'equipment,' a sufficient description of the collaterial under §§ 9-110 and 9-203 of the New York Uniform Commercial Code to create valid security interest in this collateral? ***

* * *

The majority and minority opinions took differing views of the issues in *F.P.C. v. Florida Power & Light Co.,* 404 U.S. 453, 92 S.Ct. 637, 30 L.Ed.2d 600 (1972). The majority said:

* * *

We are asked to determine whether the Federal Power Commission exceeded its statutory authorization when it asserted jurisdiction over the Florida Power & Light Co. Section 201(b) of the Federal Power Act, as amended, 49 Stat. 847, 16 U.S.C. § 824(b), grants the Federal Power Commission jurisdiction over 'the transmission of electric energy in inter-

> state commerce and . . . the sale of electric energy at wholesale in interstate commerce, but . . . not [over] any other sale of electric energy. . . .' Section 201(c) defines energy transmitted in interstate commerce as energy 'transmitted from a State and consumed at any point outside thereof.'
>
> * * *
>
> We granted certiorari to determine if either of the FPC's tests provides an acceptable basis at law and a sufficient basis in fact for the establishment of jurisdiction.
>
> * * *
>
> The minority, however, did not accept this form of the question, and said:
>
> * * *
>
> There can be no doubt that Congress has constitutional power to regulate under the Commerce Clause the interstate 'commingling' of electric power involved in the instant case. * * * The question is whether it has done so.
>
> * * *
>
> Rather than the engineering battle over tracing methods, the central question ought to be whether the 'commingling' is so *de minimis* as to warrant the fastening of the federal bureaucracy on this local company.
>
> * * *

Occasionally, a court will comment upon counsel's form of the question. In *Roudebush v. Hartke,* 405 U.S. 15, 92 S.Ct. 804, 31 L. Ed.2d 1 (1972), the court did so, rejected the form of the question as submitted by counsel, and substituted its own form of the question:

> * * *
>
> We consider first the claim that these appeals are moot. This claim is based upon the proposition, as stated in the appellee Hartke's brief, that the 'basic issue' before the Court is 'whether appellee Hartke or appellant Roudebush is entitled to the office of United States Senator from Indiana.' Since the Senate has now seated Hartke, and since this Court is without power to alter the Senate's judgment, it follows, the argument goes, that the case is moot.
>
> The difficulty with this argument is that it is based on an erroneous statement of the 'basic issue.' Which candidate is entitled to be seated in the Senate is, to be sure, a nonjusticiable political question — a question that would not have been the business of this Court even before the Senate acted. The actual question before us, however, is a different one. It is whether an Indiana recount of the votes in the 1970 election is a valid exercise of the State's power, under Art. I, § 4, to prescribe the times, places, and manner of holding elections, or is a forbidden infringement upon the Senate's power under Art. I, § 5.
>
> * * *

It is important that you recognize that there is no absolutely correct statement of the issues. Rather, the issues are dependent upon your point of view. Avoid thinking about your case in terms of the true rule, or the only possible formation of the statement of the issues. Instead, recognize that how you perceive the issue determines how you argue or decide the case. Let us examine, for example, the majority opinion's statement of the issue in *Firefighters Local Union No. 1784 v. Stotts*,—U.S.—, 104 S. Ct. 2576, 81 L.Ed.2d 483 (1984). In writing it, Justice White said:

* * *

> The issue at the heart of this case is whether the District Court exceeded its powers in entering an injunction requiring white employees to be laid off, when the otherwise applicable seniority system would have called for the layoff of black employees with less seniority.

* * *

The dissent, written by Justice Blackmun, did not agree with this statement of the issue. In the dissent, Justice Blackmun said:

* * *

> After ignoring the appropriate standard of review, the Court then focuses on an issue that is not in these cases. It begins its analysis by stating that the "issue at the heart of this case" is the District Court's power to "ente[r] an injunction requiring white employees to be laid off." *** That statement, with all respect, is simply incorrect.

* * *

> *** The question in these cases remains whether the District Court's authority pursuant to the consent decree enabled it to enjoin a layoff of more than a certain number of blacks. The issue is not whether the District Court could require the city to layoff whites, or whether the District Court could abrogate contractual rights of white firefighters.

* * *

Sometimes a court's opinion will quote the divergent statements of the question as offered by opposing counsel. In *Williams v. Marion Rapid Transit, Inc.*, 152 Ohio St. 114, 116, 87 N.E.2d 334, 335 (1949), the court's opinion began by saying:

* * *

> The question of law presented to this court is stated, in the brief of the plaintiff, as follows: 'Is a viable child, injured while *en ventre sa mere,* who survives such injury, without remedy under the law of Ohio for permanent injuries suffered by reason of the negligence of another?'
>
> The defendant in its brief states the issue as follows: 'Does there exist in Ohio a right of action by an infant for alleged injuries caused by the alleged negligence of another to said infant while in its mother's womb?'

* * *

The case was one of first instance in the Ohio Supreme Court. Plaintiff shaped his question to suggest that reason and justice should mold the law of Ohio, regardless of what other states may have held in earlier cases. Predecents from other states favored the position of defendant, and defendant's statement of the question suggested that the law of Ohio was affected by the out-of-state precedents.

You will note that in each of the quoted divergent pairs of statements of the issue, the authors of the statements perceived, or chose to perceive, the facts of the case differently. What gave those facts those differences?

In advocacy, we communicate ideas via organized collections of abstractions, *i.e.,* words. The important thing about any word is how you understand it; the word is half his that speaks it and half his that hears it. This process is analogous to passing and receiving a football. The object of a football pass is that the receiver get the ball, which is analogous to a message. The success of the pass depends upon both the passer and the intended receiver. The passing and receiving of a football, and the written or oral offering and judicial acceptance of an issue of law, which is a message carrying an idea, can both be envisaged as a transmission and a reception punctuated by a long, arcing journey. The success of the offered statement of the question depends upon the way the court takes hold of the collection of words, just as the success of the pass depends upon the way the receiver of the pass takes hold of the football. In both examples, however, the success of the receiver depends to a large extent upon the skill of the originator. The originator's skill is simply a precise management of the matter at hand. For the football player it is a precise management of the ball; for the advocate it is a precise management of words.

One thing that the football passer makes certain of is to put the ball in a location where the intended receiver is likely to be able to take hold of it. Analogous to the football passer, an advocate must so design his statement of the issue that the statement is likely to be received by the court. The advocate's statement must be so framed that it is within the limits of the court's receptiveness; it must be consistent with the court's concept of justice.

The late Professor Karl N. Llewellyn of the University of Chicago illustrated this concept when he stated as follows:

Llewellyn, *A Lecture on Appellate Advocacy,*
29 U. CHI. L. REV. 627, 630, 632-635 (1962).

* * *

Of course the first thing that comes up is the issue; and the first art is the framing of the issue so that if your framing is accepted, the case comes out your way. Got that? Second, you have to capture the issue, because your opponent will be framing an issue very differently. You have got to so frame yours that it "sells the Court," to use the term of the marketplace, which I abhor — so that it "captures the field," is what I prefer, because I see this not as a matter of the marketplace but as a matter of war, once you're really into a case of appellate advocacy. And third, you have to build a technique of phrasing of your issue which not only will help you capture the Court but which will stick your capture into the Court's head so that it can't forget it.

* * *

First is a case in which an entrepreneur of the big oil operating type (an amazing fraternity; small but amazing) had put together a combine between a French syndicate and an American group, and had operated under the well-understood rule, at least in France, that when you did this kind of thing and got it all put together, you got your commission from each side because you had done your job like a decent citizen. He got his commission from the French combine and the Americans, being sweet people, told him to go to hell. (Laughter.) So he sued.

The issue turned on whether, being an agent, he had not gotten his commission from his principal. And he found in the books, or at least his counsel did, a rule of "double agency" which you will find in all books on agency. If there is a complete disclosure made to each side of all points all the way along the line, you can be entitled to a commission from each side. Thus, there was a possiblity of double agency, and his counsel, being in my opinion complete idiots, argued the case on this basis.

Now if I am right about the nature of the tribunal, and the nature of the general state of facts, as seen by tribunals, they could not have been sillier. Agency connotes to the ordinary American judge (a) loyalty and (b) diligence as duties. And you can't possibly — you can't possibly simultaneously satisfy loyalty to two people. I may quote again from a gentleman whom I have mentioned earlier this evening: "Man cannot serve two masters"; this is in the minds of American judges. And, you can't have diligence in favor of both at once.

So this case was taken up on that basis, and was of course lost.[1] I don't see how it could help but be lost. But we have sitting in our books a completely different concept, the concept of brokerage. Brokerage involves, in nobody's mind, any suggestion of loyalty and diligence. It involves only what was in the facts, to wit, complete disclosure; and the job of the broker is to bring people together into a deal that they both like, or they all like, if it happens to be a multi-party transaction. Here was the wherewithal to put the facts into a frame that would fit a body of law available and comfortable, emotionally comfortable to the Court. Being missed, the case was lost. I do not say it would have been won had it been done this way. What I do say is, instead of a scattered shot-gun setup, twenty to one against you, you had something like an even chance. And I

---

[1] Reese v. Texas Co., 292 N.Y. 583, 55 N.E.2d 48 (1943).

would have been willing, under good argument, to take the loser's half of the bet.

Let's take another: In a case known as *Jenkins against Moyse,*[2] we had two utterly dirty lice opposed to each other. I have never seen a case in which the stink was less easy to take. We had on the one hand an enterpriser who was in financial difficulty and had no character; and on the other hand we had one of the money lenders who reminds you of Shylock in his worst moments.

The situation was one in which this somewhat distressed borrower was looking for money, and the lender said, "I can't possibly give it to you unless you incorporate." And this was in New York.

Now, the New York Usury Law is quite queer in two aspects; at least it's untypical of the country. If you have a usurious transaction, New York is tougher than any law I know. You don't forfeit the interest, you don't forfeit double interest, you forfeit the whole, if it's usurious at all. And there's a special provision that says that if there's any security, that's void, too.[3] So that the equitable attempt to save at least the principle and make the debtor — what is the old phrasing? — "do equity if he is to get equity" is gone by statute in New York if it's a usurious transaction.

But there is a later New York statute that says that a business corporation cannot plead usury.[4] So what this lender did was to say, "Look, incorporate yourself, my friend, and then I will give you $25,000, against your note for $40,000, at 6 per cent on the 40." (Laughter.) And the borrower incorporated himself, and he got this deal. Then, being just as sweet smelling a skunk as the lender, he is bringing a suit to have the mortgage declared void, for usury. (Laughter.) And you know, what can you do about this? You see, you haven't got a decent citizen in striking distance. (Laughter.)

Two lower court instances decided that this was an evasion of the Usury Law.[5] And I think this is a reasonable decision. It is not the only reasonable decision; it is a reasonable decision. What interests me is what happened in the Court of Appeals. New counsel came in, and new counsel made clear to the Court that really this provision about corporations, business corporations not being allowed to plead usury, was a defense of the defenseless. That in the absence of such a provision, people who were most in need of money would be cut off from the money market completely by the Usury Law. And the legislature, with the wisdom inherent in the New York Legislature (Laughter), had chosen to open up an avenue whereby people

---

[2] Jenkins v. Moyse, 254 N.Y. 319, 172 N.E. 521 (1930).

[3] N.Y. GEN. BUS. LAW § 373. The 1960 Session of the New York legislature amended this provision so that if the lender is "a savings bank, a savings and loan association, or a federal savings and loan association" only the interest is forfeited.

[4] N.Y. GEN. BUS. LAW § 374(1).

[5] Jenkins v. Moyse, 229 App. Div. 743, 241 N.Y. Supp. 901 (1930).

in desperate need of funds, and in not too good financial condition, in business transactions, could have a wherewithal to pay whatever was needed to give them the money that they needed. And the Court looked at this and said, "This is fine."

The thing that I want you to see is that even in the construction of a set of statutes, the thing that was moving the Court was what had been brought home to them by counsel. It made sense, for the situation, "to decide my way," and so the Court selected, and the Court reversed the lower court.

But the situation has to be so diagnosed, and the issue has to be so framed, and the sense had to be made so clear that this particular possible way of handling that statute carries the Court, instead of being rejected.[6]

Let's take a further instance, and a final one, on this particular point. There was for a long time in Pennsylvania a machinery — am I boring you? (Laughter) — There was for a long time in Pennsylvania a machinery for mining anthracite coal, which moved in terms of leaving supporting pillars of coal as you went further and further into the seam. The idea was that when you finally got to the end of the seam, you would come back out, and take out the pillars, because they had to be pretty big pillars. They were economically significant pillars.

Some lawyer, somewhere along the line, got the notion that the normal right of a purchaser of surface rights to support against subsidence could be taken out of the rights of the purchaser by explicit clause in the deed. Do I make this thing clear?

Ordinarily, when we divided the law into surface rights and mineral rights, the guy that has the surface rights is supposed to have surface rights, and so he's supposed to be able to build or farm or do whatever he wants. But this shrewd lawyer — I will call him "a Philadelphia lawyer" — I don't know who he was, and nobody knows who he was — conceived the notion that you could cut out of your deed the right to have the surface stay even. So that when the time came that you wanted to mine out the pillar, and the surface dropped, the guy who had bought the rights on top had no objection. (Laughter.) And this got to be be so firmly established in the practice of Pennsylvania law that the right to support from the bottom got a name in the practice which I think exists nowhere else in the country. It was the third estate in land. There were surface rights, mineral rights, and the right to support from the bottom. (Laughter.)

Well, this moves perfectly well, and without any trouble to anybody, until the time comes that over one piece of anthracite mines population begins to really encroach and a whole chunk of the city of Scranton finds itself built on this kind of deed, you see, which was a standard deed. (You know what happens when you buy real estate, anywhere. What kind of a

[6]The opinion in the New York Court of Appeals was by Lehman, who understood both real estate and business finance. (See LLEWELLYN, THE COMMON LAW TRADITION: DECIDING APPEALS 228, n. 25 (1960).)

deed do you get? You get the kind of deed that's customary in the community. Suppose you say, "I want a different kind of deed." What happens? They say, with all respect to the ladies present, "Go to hell." And this is what you get. And you just get what you get.) (Laughter.) But it did happen, I repeat, that the city of Scranton really grew out over quite a piece of this anthracite stuff.

Then came the time when they came to the end of the seam and it began to become clear that they were going to go right back, letting the pillars come out. And what would happen to the surface, the business of the people on that surface? (Laughter.) And humanitarian elements and interested elements got together, and the Legislature passed a statute, that forbade the taking out of pillars in such fashion as to endanger life.[7] I abbreviate it very greatly.

A suit by the owner of a single residence finally came before the Supreme Court and the defense challenged the constitutionality of this statute.[8] John W. Davis was for the defendant coal company and I am excited by his posing of the issue, in the oral argument. (It isn't done nearly as well in the brief.) Tradition has it that Davis opened his argument before the Supreme Court in language substantially equivalent to what I am about to state: "This case involves the question of whether the Legislature of Pennsylvania has the constitutional power to donate the property of the Pennsylvania Coal Company to Mr. and Mrs. Patrick Mahon." (Laughter.) The case was won by Mr. Davis, Mr. Justice Holmes writing the opinion.

But look at what a posing of the issue; look at the way in which the entire body of interest, of the state, was removed from discussion by "Mr. and Mrs. Patrick Mahon." This is the kind of thing I'm talking about. And what I want to bring home to you is that it doesn't take axe murder and love nest, and it doesn't take a cause celebre, and it doesn't take anything at all in the way of extraordinary stuff, to put to the appellate advocate this type of problem.

* * *

When a court accepts a statement of the issues as posed by either side of a lawsuit, or when a court rejects all of the proffered statements and establishes its own statement of the issues, the court in effect selects from the cluster of facts in the lawsuit those particular facts which it considers to be pertinent to the merits of its resolution of the dispute. Those facts which the court selects thereby become material facts. The corollary of such a selection is that the court relegates the rest of the facts to a relatively inferior position. Accordingly, an advocate must be highly concerned that the court accept the statement of the issues that contends for his client's point of view.

---

[7] Penn. Laws 1921, pp. 1198-1200 (Kohler Act) PA. STAT. ANN. tit. 52, 661-71 (1954).

[8] Pennsylvania Coal Co. v. Mahon, 260 U.S. 393 (1922).

When the question for decision is complicated, it may be necessary to use several sentences and compartmentalize the problems, as was done by the court in *Louisville & Jefferson County Metropolitan Sewer District v. Travelers Insurance Co.*, 753 F.2d 533 (6th Cir. 1985):

* * *

> LIVELY, Chief Judge. This diversity case involves two distinct issues, one relating to insurance coverage and the other concerning the proper application of the equitable principles underlying the doctrine of unjust enrichment. The insurance question is whether property damage caused by the unlawful act of a third person having no proven animosity against the insured property owner is covered by a "vandalism and malicious mischief" provision in the owner's insurance policy. If coverage is found to exist, the remaining question is whether the property owner, who recovers part of the loss from one or more tort-feasors after the insurance company denies liability, is entitled to recoup from the insurer a proportionate part of the expenses of the recovery * * * .

Similarly, this was also done by the Court in *Moor v. County of Alameda,* 411 U.S. 693, 93 S.Ct. 1785, 36 L.Ed.2d 596 (1973):

* * *

> This case raises three distinct questions concerning the scope of federal jurisdiction. We are called upon to decide whether a federal cause of action lies against a municipality under 42 USC §§ 1983 and 1988 for the actions of its officers which violate an individual's federal civil rights where the municipality is subject to such liablity under state law. In addition, we must decide whether, in a federal civil rights suit brought against a municipality's police officers, a federal court may refuse to exercise pendent jurisdiction over a state law claim against the municipality based on a theory of vicarious liability, and whether a county of the State of California is a citizen of the State for purposes of the federal diversity jurisdiction.

* * *

It often aids in communicating your thoughts, and keeping them distinct in your reader's mind and your mind, if you number the issues which you have compartmentalized, as was done in *Thompson v. United States,* 474 F.2d 323 (9th Cir. 1973):

* * *

> Three interdependent questions are presented on appeal: (1) Whether the appellant raised the defense of improper denial of conscientious objector status; (2) if so, whether he presented a *prima facie* case for that classification to his local board; and (3) if so, whether the local board had a basis in fact for its denial of the classification.

* * *

The following example of compartmentalized statements of the issues is also informative and well organized:

Morton Salt Co. v. N.L.R.B., 472 F.2d 416 (9th Cir. 1972):

* * *

> This case involves the assessment of fines by a union against certain of its members for refusing to honor a sister union's picket line. The principal issues it presents are:
> (1) Was the imposition of any discipline whatsoever an unfair labor practice violation of a no-strike provision in the applicable labor contract; and, if not,
> (2) Is the validity of the fines affected by the reasonableness of the amounts?

* * *

The following statement of the issue was selected because of its brevity and clarity. In *Estate of Cull v. Commissioner,* 746 F.2d 1148 (6th Cir. 1984), the court said:

> *** The issue presented is whether a full-time gambler for his own account can be engaged in a "trade or business" within the meaning of 26 U.S.C. § 62(1) for the purpose of determining adjusted gross income even though he offers no goods or services to others. Petitioner-appellee contended that Dan Cull could deduct his net gambling losses for purposes of arriving at his adjusted gross income subject to tax, regardless of whether these losses exceeded his winnings. In so doing, Mr. Cull could avoid a minimum tax that would otherwise be due on excess itemized deductions pursuant to 26 U.S.C. § 56(a). ***

Examples

Examine the following statements of issues which are intended to be persuasive. Notice the generalizations which their authors chose to draw from the unique facts in the testimony. Please also notice the large amount of information that has been packed into a few sentences.

Example 1

A mental patient who was known by the State to possess suicidal tendencies was assigned by the State to State Hospital which was located adjoining Happiness Lake, and State Hospital placed her in a group of patients supposedly under the supervision of two aids. After having exhibited indecision and vacillation, this mental patient was allowed to leave the group of patients and the aids without being observed, was later seen running toward the adjoining lake in which six patients had drowned during the previous six years in the same general area, and was herself subsequently drowned in the lake. The hospital maintained an open-door policy toward this patient and other patients. The physical barriers between the patient's assigned station and the lake were such that the patient could by-pass them, go through a gate, or climb over them.

Does the administrator of the patient's estate have a cause of action against the State on account of the death of the patient, for the benefit of the patient's children and himself as her husband?

Example 2

Appellees suggest that the questions presented are as follows:

I.

When abutting property owners know of no reason to believe that the successor to a utility which installed water lines will not continue to serve them water, even though the lines are sold, does the abutting property owner have any cause of action against the seller of the water lines?

II.

Do abutting property owners, who are also the original subdividers, have any cause of action against a utility, which transfers the ownership of its water distribution system, for sums paid to the utility by the abutting property owners as a prerequisite to the utility having extended its lines to serve the properties?

Example 3

Is an attack on the efficacy and existence of a drug, the therapeutic merits of which are still under investigation, of such overriding public interest that the developers should be powerless to stop defamatory statements concerning themselves and the drug?

Avoid Statements in the Following Forms

In none of the foregoing examples is there any significant attempt to incorporate undisclosed facts, circumstances, a trial record, or history, by a cryptic reference.

In comparison, the following examples are meaningless questions:

Did the trial court err in not granting a new trial?

Was a prima facie case proven by the evidence?

Were the court's instructions to the jury correct?

The statement of the issue or question as presented by an advocate must be meaningful. It must be factual and stand on its own feet without making reference to an undisclosed group of facts in the record, in someone's testimony, or the like.

For a statement of the issues to be useful, it must meet the following test: If it were cut out of your brief and displayed on a bulletin board, it should adequately inform anyone who reads the question from the bulletin board what the case is about. Otherwise, it does not serve its purpose.

10.
THE FACTS WIN THE CASE

"[C]opious citation of generalities become platitudes that don't bring you any nearer to the concrete case. I always say that I will admit any general proposition that anyone wants to lay down and decide the case either way."

O. W. Holmes, Jr.
1 HOLMES-LASKI LETTERS
390 (M. Howe ed. 1953)

When the judges, the staff attorneys, and the law clerks read your brief, they will read the facts before they read the argument of law. In order to succeed, you must first demonstrate to the court the merits of your case on its facts, *i.e.*, you must demonstrate that a decision in your client's favor is right and fair under the facts. An accurate, candid, and persuasively-toned statement of facts is often more than half of the preparation for the arena in which advocates do their battle.

Many appellate cases could be decided either way and be soundly justified in a well-written and entirely acceptable opinion; in this regard, note Justice Holmes' remark above. What often motivates a court to decide a case in a particular way is the court's reaction to the concrete facts, as a group of persons with sense, emotion, and legal training, and subject to their individual and collective lifetime experiences.

Judges usually approach every new case with a more or less manageable familiarity with the law which is likely to bear on the problem. As the facts of the new case are unfolded before the judges, they will usually be able to recall enough legal principles to recognize the different directions in which the decision might go, and to select tentative reasons for a decision. The judges are, however, primarily interested in making a fair decision concerning the conflict revealed by the facts of the unique problem case before them. They sense a responsibilty to make a fair decision. Judges know the law reasonably well, but what they do not know are the unique facts of your case, especially as your client views them. When writing your brief, tell the facts to the court in such a way that the facts create a reaction by the court, which will be favorable to your client.

You have done similar things before, in other situations. When you tell a joke, you try to tell it in such a way that when you are finished telling it, your listener will laugh. You do not introduce your joke with a statement such as, "This is funny;" you do not conclude it with a statement such as, "Now laugh." On the contrary, you avoid all such obvious statements in the hope that your story, *i.e.*, the facts as you present them, will create a reaction in the mind of your listener which will cause him or her to think, "This is funny," and to actually laugh.

Ordinary story-telling is done in the same way. When you tell a child the story of Hansel and Gretel, or the story of Red Riding Hood, you tell the story, *i.e.*, state the facts of the case, in such a way that the listener will reach some very definite conclusions about the relative merits of the opposing sides in those stories. In the case of *Hansel et al. v. Witch,* you might want to convey the idea that Hansel and Gretel were justified in pushing the Witch into the oven. This is analogous to the objective of defense counsel in a prosecution for crime. In the case of *Red Riding Hood v. Wolf,* you might want to convey the idea that the woodsman had probable cause to cut open the wolf. Perhaps this is analogous to the objective of a prosecuting attorney who wants to uphold the actions of police officers in conducting a search.

When journalists want to persuade their audience, they do not usually state their opinions expressly. They narrate and illustrate a factual story, and try to cause the members of their audience to form their own opinions. Even though the journalist may have a particular opinion or viewpoint in mind, which he wants the members of the audience to share, he does not usually tell the audience what it is. The journalist's objective is for the audience to reach that opinion or viewpoint from the facts. If this succeeds, it becomes the audience members' opinion or viewpoint. When it has been created as theirs, they are more likely to cherish it.

This is what we must do when we write our briefs and make our oral arguments. We must marshall and emphasize our facts in such a way that the reader or listener is at first persuaded in our client's favor from the facts of the case, without arguing the law or citing authorities.

Llewellyn, *A Lecture on Appellate Advocacy,*
29 U. CHI. L. REV. 627, 637-638 (1962).

* * *

I've got first a corollary that derives from what I have been saying, and that is that the statement of facts, be it in the brief or be it oral, is the complete guts of your case. And I'm going to give you two statements of facts, one by an utter master, and another in exactly the same case, as an effort to show you how it can be done just the other way on the same facts and the same case.

The statement by the master is Cardozo in *Wood against Lady Duff-Gordon.*[1] And you will get that, as I read it to you. You must remember that Cardozo was a truly great advocate, and the fact that he became a great

---

[1] Wood v. Lucy, Lady Duff-Gordon, 222 N.Y. 88, 118 N.E. 214 (1917).

judge didn't at all change the fact that he was a great advocate. And if you will watch, in the very process of your listening to the facts, you will find two things happening. The one is that according to principle number one, you arrive at the conclusion that the case has to come out one way. And the other is, that it fits into a legal frame that says, "How comfortable it will be, to bring it out that way. No trouble at all. No trouble at all."

"The defendant styles herself" — now watch the way in which she is subtly made into a nasty person — "The defendant styles herself 'a creator of fashions.' Her favor helps a sale. Manufacturers of dresses, millinery, and like articles are glad to pay for a certificate of her approval. The things which she designs, fabrics, parasols, and what not, have a new value in the public mind when issued in her name. She employed the plaintiff to help her turn this vogue into money."[2]

Does this sound — this is an interposition — does this sound like a business deal? Does a business deal sound like a legally enforceable view? Nothing is being said about that. But watch it grow on you. And if I hadn't stopped to tell you about it, it would have grown until you just took it, without a word.

"He was to have the exclusive right" — watch this language — "exclusive right" — what wonderful legal language, to make it legally enforceable — "He was to have the exclusive right . . . to place her own designs on sale, or to license others to market them. In return, she was to have one-half of 'all profits and revenues' derived from any contracts he might make. The exclusive right was to last at least one year from April 1, 1915, and thereafter from year to year unless terminated by notice of ninety days."[3]

My heavens, isn't this legal?

"The plaintiff says that he kept the contract on his part, and that the defendant broke it. She placed her indorsement on fabrics, dresses and millinery without his knowledge, and withheld the profits. He sues her for the damages, and the case comes here on demurrer.

"The agreement of employment is signed by both parties. It has a wealth of recitals. The defendant insists, however, that it lacks the elements of a contract. She says that the plaintiff does not bind himself to anything. It is true that he does not promise in so many words that he will use reasonable efforts to place the defendant's indorsements and market her designs."[4]

Now, is there any way to bring that case out, except one? Isn't it obvious that we are going to imply a promise on the part of the plaintiff which will

---

[2] Id. at 90, 118 N.E. at 214.
[3] *Ibid.*
[4] *Ibid.*

satisfy the requirement of consideration and the decency of the situation?[5]

All right, now try this: "The plaintiff in this action rests his case upon his own carefully prepared form agreement, which has as its first essence his own omission of any expression whatsoever of any obligation of any kind on the part of this same plaintiff. We thus have the familiar situation of a venture in which one party, here the defendant, has an asset, with what is, in advance, of purely speculative value. The other party, the present plaintiff, who drew the agreement, is a marketer eager for profit, but chary of risk. The legal question presented is whether the plaintiff, while carefully avoiding all risk in the event of failure, can nevertheless claim full profit in the event that the market may prove favorable in its response. The law of consideration joins with the principles of business decency in giving the answer. And the answer is no."

Same case. Entirely the same case. But it brings me to the next fundamental point, which is that if you have an intelligent appellant, to rest upon his statement of the facts, if you are the respondent, is suicide. Did you hear me? If he is any good, you're cooked. (Laughter.) You have a positive case to make, and you can only make it by restating the facts so that they fit into your picture of what the whole thing is. And I think with that I can practically stop, can't I, because I've made the fundamental point.

No. I do have to say one thing about oral, and written, before I stop. The division between your oral argument and your brief is quite clear. Your brief has to provide the Court with the technical wherewithal to be perfectly happy in deciding your way with no qualms of legal conscience at all. And your brief ought also to provide, at some place, — Kenison is quite magnificent on this: Kenison says that at an appropriate place your brief ought to say, "A suggested rationale for this case," and thereby offer the court something that it can lift, verbatim, into the opinion taking care of all prior authority, phrasing the whole satisfactorily, and applying it to the case in hand.

* * *

Examples from the Courts

The published reports of precedent cases contain a great many examples of statements of facts which speak for one side of the case or the other. When we slowly read some of the statements of facts, we cannot help but know which way the court is going to decide the case, because the facts lead the reader to but one inescapable conclusion, if he is a person whose goal is to render a fair and just decision under the unique facts of the case.

[5] "We think, however, that such a promise is fairly to be implied. . . . A promise may be lacking, and yet the whole writing may be 'instinct with an obligation,' imperfectly expressed. . . . If that is so, there is a contract." 222 N.Y. at 91, 118 N.E. at 214.

As an example, consider whether the facts argue for or against the proposition that defendant Yaqui was entrapped:

UNITED STATES v. McLERNON, 746 F.2d 1098
(6th Cir. 1984)

* * *

In 1974, agent Charles Hamlin of the Drug Enforcement Administration traveled to Phoenix, Arizona where he befriended Yaqui. The two became very close friends and eventually engaged in an Indian "blood brother ritual." In 1977, Hamlin left Arizona for Cincinnati. Hamlin then phoned Yaqui to say that he had some drug contacts and asked Yaqui "to keep his eyes open for possible drug connections." Yaqui, however, did not pursue any such connections. In early 1982, Hamlin again called Yaqui to explain that he was in financial trouble with a Chicago syndicate group and begged him to bring about a drug transaction. Hamlin called upon his Indian "blood brother" to do anything he could to help.

Although Yaqui had no prior experience with cocaine, he tried to help Hamlin. Hamlin instructed Yaqui in cocaine transactions and continually pressured him to attain one. In March, 1982, Yaqui informed Hamlin that he had, as Hamlin desired, secured individual cocaine contacts, including Tony Langley. Hamlin spoke to these contacts and on one occasion traveled to Phoenix to try to formalize a deal. But these deals fell through. Hamlin then began to pressure Yaqui by telling him more about his syndicate debts. Hamlin described to Yaqui the people who were threatening him:

> I mean, these power people, these ain't nickle-dime, they run Atlantic City and all — I mean, they're all over the country. They're heavy. (RTT Tape No. 3, 14:8-10).

In April, 1982, Hamlin told Yaqui over the phone that he would be killed if Yaqui could not arrange a cocaine deal. Yaqui testified that he observed Hamlin carrying a gun and wearing a bullet-proof vest. He began fearing Hamlin and, thus, exaggerated his cocaine connections in order to ease the pressure.

In late 1982, Yaqui made a major cocaine contact while negotiating a business deal for distributorships. Yaqui met Valdez and the two sent $2,000 to Hamlin so he could come to Phoenix and negotiate a deal. On January 13, 1983, Yaqui and Hamlin met with Valdez and proceeded to discuss a cocaine deal. Hamlin told Valdez, through Yaqui as interpreter, that he had mob connections in the East. Hamlin insisted that any drug delivery would have to take place in Cincinnati. Valdez preferred Los Angeles and left the meeting. Hamlin returned to Cincinnati, angered at Yaqui for what appeared to be another broken deal.

Later in January, Valdez visited Yaqui at Yaqui's shop. Yaqui told Valdez that he feared Hamlin. The two agreed to go to Cincinnati to talk with Hamlin and his associates. Valdez called Hamlin and told him that they intended to make a sale of ten kilos on a trial basis and if everything went well they could sell 300 kilos. On January 25, 1983, Hamlin next met Valdez and Yaqui at the Cincinnati Airport and then introduced undercover DEA agents Stuart and Palma as drug dealers. Hamlin informed Yaqui that these men were dangerous and that one of them was a "hit man." Yaqui told Stuart that he only played an intermediary role and that Valdez controlled the cocaine. Yaqui stated that he had not seen the 300 kilos of cocaine, but knew that they were available. Agent Stuart replied that he wanted large quantities and many transactions. The parties, however, tentatively agreed to a ten kilo sale of cocaine. Valdez told the agents that the cocaine was of superior quality. On the following day, January 26, 1983, the men made a tentative delivery plan.

Yaqui and Valdez returned to Phoenix. On January 28, Agent Stuart phoned Yaqui. In order to remove himself from any further involvement in the cocaine transaction, Yaqui told Stuart that he faced an Arizona murder investigation and was advised by his attorney to "lie low" for a while. On January 29, Hamlin called Yaqui. Yaqui stated that the cocaine deal was still on but that he would not be involved. On January 31, Yaqui told Stuart that he would arrange to have Stuart talk directly with Valdez. Yaqui resisted Stuart's constant pressure to stay in the deal.

Stuart then contacted Valdez. Valdez expressed displeasure with all of the traveling required, but agreed to meet with agents Palma and Stuart. Valdez informed the agents that Yaqui was no longer involved. On February 9, 1983, the agents called Valdez at Carranza's Los Angeles apartment. Valdez told Palma that the ten kilo deal could go through as soon as he could make some arrangements. Palma, Stuart, and Valdez agreed to make the deal in Cincinnati.

On Feburary 12, 1983, Stuart and Palma met Valdez at the Cincinnati airport. Valdez told the agents that the cocaine would be delivered in a secret compartment of a car driven from the west coast by a man named Scott and a woman. Valdez also stated that he had a large cocaine operation. Palma testified at trial, over repeated objections, that Valdez had told him of his lengthy past involvement with cocaine.

On February 16, Valdez phoned the agents that the cocaine had arrived. Valdez suggested that they rent a garage in which to make the deal. They rented two garages in Fairfield, Ohio. After the couriers arrived, Stuart told Valdez that he wanted to see the cocaine before he gave him the money. Valdez agreed. He went to his hotel room to get "Scott," the courier, who was later identified as Scott McLernon. The men all traveled to the rented garage. McLernon took the packages out of a secret backseat compartment. Stuart tested the cocaine and then placed Valdez and McLernon under arrest. DEA agents subsequently arrested Carranza, who had remained in his hotel room. After his arrest, McLernon was asked by DEA agent Power about the girl with whom he had driven across the country. He agreed to take the agents back to his hotel where Sherri Farrell waited.

Once in the hotel room, the agents seized a note pad and a calendar, both of which were admitted into evidence. Farrell voluntarily accompanied the agents to their offices and was questioned extensively. After Agent Stuart finished questioning Farrell, she was placed under arrest. On the next day, Yaqui was arrested in Phoenix by federal agents.

After indictment and jury trial, Valdez was found guilty of one count of conspiracy under 21 U.S.C. § 846, twelve counts of unlawful telephone use under 21 U.S.C. § 843(b), two counts of interstate travel to promote unlawful activity under 18 U.S.C. § 1952 and one count of possession with intent to distribute cocaine under 21 U.S.C. § 841(a)(2). Carranza was found guilty of one count of conspiracy under 21 U.S.C. § 846, one count of unlawful interstate travel under 18 U.S.C. § 1952 and one count of possession with intent to distribute cocaine under 21 U.S.C. § 841(a)(1). Yaqui was found guilty of one count of conspiracy under 21 U.S.C. § 846. McLernon was found guilty of one count of conspiracy under 21 U.S.C § 846, one count of unlawful interstate travel under 18 U.S.C. § 1952, and one count of possession with intent to distribute cocaine under 21 U.S.C. § 841(a)(1). Farrell was found guilty of one count of conspiracy under 21 U.S.C. § 846, one count of unlawful interstate travel under 18 U.S.C. § 1952 and one count of possession under 21 U.S.C. § 844.

* * *

Is there more than one fair, just, and reasonable decision that could be rendered, considering the unique facts of the following case? What was the importance of precedent in the court's decision?

* * *

KETELSEN v. STILZ
184 Ind. 702, 111 N.E. 423 (1916)

* * *

LAIRY, J. — Appellant brought this action to recover damages resulting to her from an exchange of a piece of real estate for real estate owned by one McCleay, which damages were alleged to have been occasioned by the fraud of appellees. It appears from the allegations of the complaint that appellees were real estate agents and that as such they sold to appellant a piece of property assuring her at the time that in case she desired to dispose of it they would assist her without charge. Appellant afterward consulted appellees with reference to the disposition of the property and was informed that they represented McCleay who owned a desirable rental property, and they advised her to exchange her property for that owned by McCleay. Appellant alleges that she made the exchange upon the advice of appellees, the negotiations being conducted by them, and that during these negotiations they made false and fraudulent representations as to the character, condition and value of the McCleay property, which resulted in damage to appellant, and which form the basis of this action. The sufficiency of the complaint is not questioned on appeal. Appellees filed an affirmative answer to the complaint, which was held good as against a demurrer for want of facts. To this answer appellant filed an affirmative reply to which a demurrer was addressed by appellees and sustained by the court. The rulings of the court in passing upon these demurrers are assigned as error.

Only a single question is presented. From these pleadings, it appears that prior to the commencement of this action appellant sued McCleay, the owner of the real estate for which she exchanged her property, and recovered a judgment based upon fraudulent representations made by him in the same transaction with reference to the exchange of the same property. It further appears that appellant caused an execution to be issued against McCleay on this judgment, which execution was returned *nulla bona.*[6] Under the facts thus shown, appellees take the position that McCleay was a joint tortfeasor with them and that the recovery of a judgment against him for the tort for which all were jointly and severally liable and the issue of an execution thereon, operated to release the other tortfeasors from liability. By its rulings, the trial court sustained the position of appellees. Appellant takes the position that she is entitled to one satisfaction of her demand, that she has a right to sue all, either jointly or separately, and that nothing short of a satisfaction, release or discharge of her claim in favor of one of the joint tortfeasors will operate as a release to the others.

It seems to be well-settled law in England since the case of *Brown v. Wooton* (1606), 4 Croke's Rep. 73, Yelv. 67, that a judgment against one tortfeasor may be pleaded in bar of an action for the same cause brought against another as a joint tortfeasor, without averring satisfaction of the judgment. *Buckland v. Johnson* (1854), 15 C.B. 145, 80 C.L. Rep. 145; *Brimsmead v. Harrison* (1872), 7 L.R.C.P.D. 547, 41 L.J.C.P.N.S. 190.

Appellees assert that the doctrine announced in *Brown v. Wooton, supra,* was the common law of England at the time of the settlement of Jamestown, that our code adopts the common law of England at that date, as the common law of Indiana and that the courts of this State are thereby bound to follow the law as announced in that case. § 236 Burns 1914, § 236 R.S. 1881. While it is true that the section of the statute pointed out makes the common law of England the common law of Indiana, and that the case of *Brown v. Wooton, supra,* declares the law to be in accordance with the principle asserted by appellees, we can not subscribe to the proposition that we are bound to accept the rule announced by the decision relied on and the cases cited in support thereof as being a part of the common law as the term

[6] Nulla bona (no goods) is a return made by a sheriff to an execution in a civil action, or other writ commanding him to seize the goods of a person, when he finds no property to act upon. THE LAW DICTIONARY 234, 6th ed. W. Gilmer, rev., copyright 1986 by Anderson Publishing Co., Cincinnati.

"common law of England" is used in the statute referred to. It is appellees' position that by virtue of the statute all rules of the common law of England in the year 1607, are, except as otherwise provided, in full force in this State, and that in determining what such rules were we must look to the ruling decisions rendered by the English courts up to that time. Appellees misinterpret the statute in question as to the meaning of the term common law as therein used, and also as to the application of the specific period therein designated to parts of the section other than that to which it was meant to be applied. The section reads in part as follows: "The law governing this State is declared to be * * * *Fourth.* The common law of England, and statutes of the British Parliament made in aid thereof prior to the reign of James the First (excepting certain enactments) and which are of a general nature, not local to that kingdom * * *." As viewed by this court, it was not the purpose of the legislature by this section of the statute to adopt the rules of the common law as announced and applied by the courts of England prior to 1607, but that the purpose was to adopt the general principles of the common law which underlie and control all rules of decision throughout all time, as the same were affected by the acts of the British Parliament passed in aid thereof prior to the time mentioned. The statute was declaratory in its nature, Indiana being carved out of that portion of America settled by the English colonists who brought with them the common law at the time the settlement was established, and the statutes of Parliament in aid of the common law were to be distinguished from those passed in derogation of it. Such acts were to be distinguished also from the acts of the British Parliament passed after the physical separation from the mother country, after which time courts were to look particulary to American legislation and to the reports of American courts for improvements and modifications of the rules of the common law.

The common law of England was derived from the universal usage and custom of the early English people, and is a system of jurisprudence founded upon principles of justice as it was conceived and administered by the English courts of law, in contradistinction to the methods of administering justice employed by the courts of equity, and that system of jurisprudence which formed the basis of the Roman or civil law. From this common-law system, and from the usages, customs and maxims upon which it is founded, innumerable rules and principles emanated, as the courts from time to time declared what they understood to be the correct law applicable to the matter before them and such law was determined by a system of reasoning and of administering justice consistent with the universal usages, customs and institutions of the English people. The common law grew to be a system of applying to litigated instances, just, reasonable and consistent rules of decision, suitable to the genius of the people and to their social, political and economic conditions and the system once established has never changed.The rules so deduced from this system, however, were continually changing and expanding with the progress of society in the application of this system to more diversified circumstances and under more advanced periods. The common law by its own principles adapted itself to varying conditions and modified its own rules so as to serve the ends of justice as prompted by a course of reasoning which was guided by these generally accepted truths. One of its oldest maxims was that where the reason of a rule ceased, the rule also ceased, and it logically followed that when it occurred to the courts that a particular rule had never been founded upon reason, and that no reason existed in support thereof, that rule likewise ceased, and perhaps another sprang up in its place which was based upon reason and justice as then conceived. No rule of the common law could survive the reason on which it was founded. It needed no statute to change it but abrogated itself. * * *

The principles of the English common law system as its theory assumes and its history proves were not applicable or suited to one country or condition of society only, but on the contrary by reason of their properties of expansibility and flexibility their application to many became practicable. The adoption of the common law in the most general terms by the government of any country did not necessarily require or admit of an unqualified application of all its rules, without regard to local circumstances and the then present enlightened conception of reason and justice. This system of jurisprudence has been adopted by virtue of statutory enactment by most of the states of the Union, but according to the prevailing decisions, the rules as declared by the English courts at one period or another have been controlling only so far as they were suited to and in harmony with the genius, spirit and objects of American institutions. Whether so-called common law rules have been followed strictly in the several states has depended upon the extent to which they have seemed reasonable, and for this reason what are considered proper rules of the common law in one state are not necessarily so considered in another, and likewise rules considered proper dictations of the common law in the eighteenth century are not now so considered in the twentieth. Since courts have had an existence in America, they have never hesitated to take upon themselves the responsibility of saying what are the proper rules of the common law. While courts may properly refer to well-known repositories of legal learning, to ascertain and arrive at the correct rules applicable, and may look to American as well as English books, neither precedents nor opinions of judges can be said with strict propriety to be the law. Although they are to be regarded as proper exponents of the law as adopted, they are to be received merely as evidence of the law rather than as the law itself. * * *

We can not believe, then, that our legislature intended to petrify the rules of the common law as declared by judicial decisions at any one time or period, and to set them up in such unflexible form as to make them absolute rules of decision throughout all time. The theory of our adopted system is that the law consists not in the actual rules enforced by the decisions of the courts, but consists only in the principles from which these rules flow. Under the section of the statute relied on where there are no governing enactments of the legislature, the courts of this State are in all matters coming before them, to endeavor to administer justice according to the promptings of reason and common sense, which are the cardinal principles of the common law, and they are not to accept blindly the decisions of the English courts of any particular time or period without inquiring as to the reasons upon which they rest. To do so would be to adopt a practice which would be in direct violation of the theory of that common law which the statute prescribes we are to follow. *** In view of what has been said this court does not feel called upon to adopt the rule as announced in *Brown v. Wooton, supra,* and the later English cases.

Only one state, Virginia, is fully committed to the English rule. The decisions of Rhode Island and Pennsylvania at one time seemed to follow it, but the later decisions of these states on the subject are more in conformity with the American doctrine. The overwhelming weight of authority in this country is to the effect that nothing short of a full satisfaction or its equivalent can make good a plea of former judgment in tort, offered in bar of an action against a joint tortfeasor who was not a party to the first judgment. The cases from the various states are collected in a note to the case of *Blackman v. Simpson* (1899), 120 Mich. 377, 79 N.W. 573, as reported in 58 L.R.A. 410. Some cases hold that joint tortfeasors may be sued jointly or severally at the option of the plaintiff; and that, if each be sued separately such suits may be pursued to final judgment; but that having obtained judgment, plaintiff must elect as against whom he will take out an execution; and that when he takes execution against one judgment defendant, he must enter a perpetual stay of execution as to each of the other judgments. This rule seems to have been announced in the early decisions of this State. *Davis v. Scott* (1822), 1, Blackf. 169; *Allen v. Wheatly* (1834), 3, Blackf. *332; *Fleming v. McDonald* (1875), 50 Ind. 278, 19 Am. Rep. 711; *Ashcraft v. Knoblock* (1896), 146 Ind. 169, 45 N.E. 69.

The case of *Davis v. Scott, supra,* consists of only three lines in which it is stated that a plea of former recovery and execution against a joint tortfeasor is a good plea in bar to an action for assault and battery and false imprisonment. This case seems to have been followed in the other Indiana cases cited above in which the rule is more fully stated. This rule seems to be a kind of a compromise between the English rule and the rule adopted by the weight of authority in this country. It is everywhere recognized that an injury caused by the joint wrong of two or more parties gives rise to but a single cause of action and that, while each of the wrongdoers is severally liable for the whole damage, the plaintiff is entitled to only a single satisfaction. A release to one of several joint tortfeasors or the receipt of satisfaction from one, operates in favor of all, and so if a judgment taken against one is fully satisfied all are released.

The rule adopted by the majority of American courts commends itself to the judgment of this court. It seems reasonable to hold that the injured party should be entitled to one compensation and no good reason has been suggested to show why an ineffectual attempt to collect a judgment rendered against one of several joint tortfeasors should operate to bar further proceedings against another who is jointly liable. * * *

* * *

The following cases have been selected because they, like the other cases published in this chapter, contain persuasive statements of the facts.

In *Stevens v. Bordenkircher*, 746 F.2d 342 (6th Cir. 1984) the issue was whether a writ of habeas corpus should be granted by a federal court to a state prisoner on account of alleged violations of his United States constitutional rights in a state-court trial. The federal court's statement of facts was as follows; what does it indicate concerning the outcome of the case?

* * *

Crockett Stevens and his brother, Rodney, were indicted for murder by the Harlan County, Kentucky Grand Jury in May, 1974. Petitioner's trial was delayed until the government's principal witness, Robert Lynn Bennett, was returned to Kentucky from New Mexico pursuant to a material witness subpoena. Bennett, who was charged with twelve counts of fraud, was in the custody of New Mexico law enforcement officials.

According to the testimony of witnesses at petitioner's trial, Kenneth Smith disappeared on the night of July 31, 1973. Bennett, the prosecution's principal witness, testified concerning the facts of Smith's murder as allegedly related to him by his uncle, Mac Williams, and the Stevens brothers. Bennett testified that petitioner, Rodney, and Williams met Smith at Danny Ray's Drive-In in Harlan, Kentucky. Smith was persuaded to accompany the three men to a "hollow" where they consumed alcoholic beverages. Bennett stated that "by chance" Williams took a .45 automatic from Smith, forced Smith to lay down near his car, and fired five bullets into him. The body was then concealed in the woods. Bennett testified further that shortly after Smith's death, he accompanied petitioner, Rodney, Williams, and another individual to recover and rebury the body. The men picked up the body, placed the corpse in the trunk of an automobile, and drove through the winding roads of Harlan County until they arrived at a huge mound of sawdust; the corpse was buried in the sawdust pile. Finally, Bennett disclosed that he observed bullet holes in the victim's chest.

Prior to trial, petitioner's counsel attempted unsuccessfully to obtain from the prosecuting attorney information which could have been used to impeach Bennett's testimony. Without any information concerning Bennett's criminal record, the defense attempted to cross-examine Bennett, whose testimony was crucial to the Commonwealth's case. Bennett was asked to list the charges pending against him. Before the prosecution objected, Bennett had listed the charges of possession of a firearm, auto theft, and possession of marijuana. After sustaining the prosecution's objection, the trial court denied a defense request for permission to cross-examine Bennett in order to elicit evidence of bias and motive. Thus, the jury that found petitioner guilty never learned of several significant facts which would have, according to the district court, cast some doubt on Bennett's motive for testifying.

Gary Bryant, the other key witness in petitioner's trial, testified that on the night of Smith's disappearance he observed Rodney talking to an unidentified individual in a car in Cawood, Kentucky, the area from which Smith disappeared. The defense was similarly precluded from examining Bryant as to any motive or bias he may have had in testifying for the prosecution.

The other significant piece of incriminating evidence introduced at petitioner's trial was the victim's death certificate. The death certificate was introduced at trial through a witness who, according to the district court, had no knowledge of the victim's death and was not the proper custodian of the records. The district court found that "[t]he proper witness to have introduced the certificate" was the Harlan County Coroner, Dr. Begley. Although Dr. Begley had been subpoenaed and had not been released by the court from his duty to testify, the prosecutor decided, as a favor to Dr. Begley, to release him informally from the subpoena. Defense counsel objected to admission of the death certificate because the coroner's absence would deny petitioner the opportunity to cross-examine him; the judge admitted the death certificate into evidence but refused to delay trial to ensure the coroner's presence. The death certificate identified the body recovered from the sawdust pile as that of Kenneth Smith, specified that the cause of death was gunshot wounds to the thorax which were inflicted by an assailant, and noted the approximate date of death.

During the habeas corpus proceedings in 1981, the district court ordered a magistrate to conduct an evidentiary hearing. At the hearing, several significant facts which could have been elicited from Bennett at petitioner's trial, were disclosed. For example, petitioner was not permitted to demonstrate that Bennett faced charges in El Paso other than those he listed and, additionally, that Bennett asked for leniency from El Paso authorities in return for his cooperation with Kentucky officials. Furthermore, the jury was not informed that Bennett was charged with twelve counts of fraud in New Mexico only fifteen days prior to petitioner's trial and that the Commonwealth had searched for Bennett for over a year before having him returned to Kentucky pursuant to a material witness warrant. Finally, the jury never learned that Bennett was granted immunity from prosecution for Smith's murder and that Bennett was staying at the home of the Harlan County Sheriff who provided him with expenses while in Harlan for petitioner's trial. In essence, the evidence adduced at the evidentiary hearing revealed that the defense was precluded from examining Bennett concerning his motive for testifying, bias, and prejudice.

The evidentiary hearing also revealed evidence pertaining to Bryant's testimony at petitioner's trial. For example, the jury never learned that Bryant was facing a charge of auto theft in Harlan County, that his trial on this charge had been continued twice, and that at the time of petitioner's trial he was on probation for auto theft. An inmate who met Bryant in prison testified at the hearing that Bryant had perjured himself at petitioner's murder trial because the sheriff had promised him a "deal" in the pending auto theft charge in return for his testimony against the Stevens brothers. Furthermore, Bryant himself admitted lying at petitioner's trial. Bryant testified that he was threatened with a more severe sentence in his pending auto theft case if he would not testify against the Stevens brothers. In contrast, if he incriminated petitioner and Rodney, according to Bryant, he would receive a lighter sentence and be transferred to a minimum security facility. Neither the magistrate nor the district court credited Bryant's testimony.

Evidence regarding information contained in the death certificate was also elicited at the evidentiary hearing. At petitioner's trial, the death certificate purported to be a statement by the absent coroner that an autopsy revealed the identity of the body, the cause of death, and the approximate date of death. At the evidentiary hearing, however, Dr. Begley testified that when he examined the remains of the body buried in the sawdust pile, nothing was left of the corpse except fifteen pounds of bones, including a portion of the upper jaw, a few ribs, and one or more fingers. Dr. Begley indicated that he did not perform an autopsy on the remains and found no evidence of bullets or metallic fragments from an x-ray of the remains. Dr. Begley further stated that he could not determine the identity of the body, the cause of death, the date of death, whether the death occurred as a result of homicide, or whether the death resulted from one or more gunshot woulds inflicted by an alleged assailant. Moreover, the coroner disclosed that he had discussed these facts with the prosecutor prior to trial. Finally, Dr. Begley indicated that he recorded gunshot wounds as the cause of death because the police informed him that they had a witness who stated that the victim had been shot; the witness was Robert Lynn Bennett. Accordingly, the death certificate that appeared to be independent evidence corroborating Bennett's testimony was, in fact, Bennett corroborating Bennett.

* * *

In *Copley v. Richardson,* immediately below, the Court's opinion contains a verbatim copy of selected portions of the question-and-answer dialogue in the transcript of testimony. Ordinarily, it is wise to avoid such direct quotations; it is usually better to paraphrase the testimony and tell the facts in narrative form. When resorted to sparingly, however, the verbatim question-and-answer form can be effective, as *Copley v. Richardson* demonstrates:

COPLEY v. RICHARDSON

475 F.2d 772 (6th Cir. 1973)

Before EDWARDS, KENT and LIVELY, Circuit Judges.

PER CURIAM.

Plaintiff-appellant appeals from an order entered by a District Judge affirming the Secretary of Health, Education and Welfare's denial of child benefits under § 202(d)(1)(B) of the Social Security Act, 42 U.S.C. § 402(d)(1)(B) (1970), which provides benefits for a child (of an insured person) who is under a disability which began before the child attained the age of 18.

The Hearing Examiner, whose findings of fact were accepted by the appeals counsel and by the District Judge, summarized the disability record as follows:

> The record shows that this claimant has had at least eight periods of hospitalization. She was first hospitalized for a period of six months in 1941, and, thereafter, was hospitalized from January to June 1942; for a period to time in 1947; for some time in 1956; from May to August 1959; from December 1960 to April 1963; from August to December 1968; and from May to October 1969. The diagnosis submitted by the Columbus State Hospital in December 1969 was chronic brain syndrome, nonpsychotic organic brain syndrome with epilepsy. The hospital record shows that she was subject to depression and suicidal ideas, and that she was prone to outbursts of temper and hostility.
>
> The Hearing Examiner wishes to state, at this point, that this claimant has a significant problem, which had its onset prior to age 18.

Subsequent thereto, however, the Hearing Examiner found that over a period of seven years appellant had demonstrated "an ability to perform substantial gainful activity" by working part-time at a restaurant and by working as a part-time maid at the home of her employer "for all of which she is paid at the rate of $1.25 an hour and earns approximatley $30 a week."

These findings we hold to be unsupported by substantial evidence in this record. We note that appellant appeared alone before the Hearing Examiner, without benefit of legal counsel, and responded to questions which called for a description of the sorts of work she performed and the hourly rate she was paid therefor. The Hearing Examiner, however, made no inquiry as to her weekly, monthly, or yearly earnings, or the impact upon her earnings of the repeated periods of hospitalization, or the impact upon her employment of her seizures, depression, suicidal ideas and attempts, and outbursts of temper and hostility.

* * *

The employment relied upon by the Hearing Examiner as evidence of claimant's capacity for substantial gainful activity is clearly one where the employer would be required to file Social Security earning reports. Under these circumstances, we believe that Exhibit 9, which the Hearing Examiner had introduced in this record, takes on added significance. This Social Security "earnings certificate" shows that appellant earned a total of $1,943.53 between the years of 1936 and 1969. In many of these years the report shows no earnings at all. It shows 1967 to have been claimant's highest year of earnings, with $822. The next highest year was 16 years earlier, in the year 1951, when she earned $296.77.

Section 6403 of the Claims Manual of the Social Security Administration deals with substantial gainful activity (SGA). Subsection 6403(c), entitled "earnings of less than $90 per month," reads:

Where average monthly earnings are less than $90 a month, an assumption may be made that the work is not SGA in the absence of evidence to the contrary. This assumption may be made for both sheltered and non-sheltered employment.

We believe that the administrative record in this case, taken as a whole, demonstrates a lack of substantial evidence to support the findings of fact of the Secretary and impels a reversal and remand for the award of disability benefits.

Although not essential to that conclusion, the following questions and answers between the Hearing Examiner and the claimant help to illustrate the nature and extent of the underlying disability:

> Q: Well now, Miss Copley, assume that you were offered full time employment as a domestic instead of working part time, what would be your difficulty?
>
> A: Well, my main difficulty is my education in getting any regular work.
>
> Q: I'm talking about work as a domestic employee like you're doing now, except on a full time basis.
>
> A: Well, people won't hire me when they find out I'm an epileptic. You mention epileptic and they won't hire you 'cause they are afraid of you, 'cause I have a grand-mal kind of epilepsy and I pass out and foam at the mouth and jerk, and I don't remember. I sometimes come out fighting.
>
> Q: Do you still have these epileptic seizures?
>
> A: Oh yes.
>
> Q: How often do you have them?
>
> A: Now, I've only had two in four years, but that's because the state hospital changed my medicine.
>
> Q: So it's pretty well controlled?
>
> A: It's getting that way but the doctor thinks that I'm in a change of life, but they think that I might go mentally insane by the time I go through the change of life.

> Q: Is this what they told you?
>
> A: Uh huh, if I didn't keep active, and since my family won't have nothing to do with me, I raise birds.
>
> Q: Why won't your family have anything to do with you?
>
> A: Well, they have been ashamed of me all my life. I've had one brother tried to choke me twice.
>
> Q: What kind of birds do you raise?
>
> A: I've got a canary, paul parrot, finch, and a parakeet.
>
> Q: You like raising birds?
>
> A: Yes.
>
> Q: Do you train them?
>
> A: No, I just feed them and just love to hear them holler, because I don't have anyone to talk to, and in the summer I'd take out walks in the woods, just to see the animals because people won't have nothing to do with me.

The judgment of the District Court is reversed. The case is remanded to the District Court for the entry of an order awarding disability benefits claimed in this proceeding.

* * *

Judging from the statement of facts, as they appear in the courts' opinions, what were the outcomes of the following cases?

UNITED STATES v. ESCAMILLA

467 F.2d 341, 343-344 (4th Cir. 1972)

Before HAYNSWORTH, Chief Judge, and WINTER, CRAVEN, BUTZNER, RUSSELL and FIELD, Circuit Judges, sitting in banc.

WINTER, Circuit Judge:

Defendant, Mario Jaime Escamilla, was convicted of involuntary manslaughter, in violation of 18 U.S.C.A. § 1112, perpetrated on Fletcher's Ice Island T-3, an unclaimed island of ice in the Arctic Ocean, and sentenced to imprisonment for three years.

* * *

I

T-3 is an island of glacial ice, composed of approximately 99% ice and less than 1% land matter, which meanders slowly about the general area of the Arctic Ocean. First sighted by an American in 1947, T-3 has been occupied since 1952 under the auspices of the United States Government, particularly the Departments of the Air Force and Navy, except for part of the years 1961-1962 when the island was grounded on the coastline of Alaska near Point Barrow. T-3 is used as a research station — a platform for scientific study, and it is particularly well suited for this purpose because of its controlled environment and its unique stability. The research operations on T-3 are supported by the Naval Arctic Research Laboratory, funded by the Office of Naval Research, under contract to the United States Government. The laboratory supplies equipment and materials and designates a person to be the station manager of the group of men on the island. Personnel from several entities man the island — United States Geological Survey, Lamont Geological Laboratories, University of Washington, University of California, and the General Motors Defense Research Laboratory.

Discipline and order on the island depend upon cooperation of all of the men and the effectiveness of the group leader, particularly in the summer months when it is virtually impossible to remove any wrongdoer from the ice. There are no medical facilities on the island, no doctor and, indeed, during the summer of 1970, no person trained in any aspect of medical science.

In May of 1970, a group of men arrived on T-3 expecting to remain there until late September or early October. Included were (a) the deceased, Bennie Lightsey, an employee of the United States Weather Bureau, who had been designated as station manager by the Arctic Research Laboratory, (b) the defendant, an employee of General Motors Defense Research Laboratory, (c) Donald Leavitt, who was an employee of the Arctic Research Laboratory, and whose nickname was "Porky," and (d) sixteen others. During the summer an acute problem arose from Porky's excessive drinking and resultant uncontrolled behavior. Prior to July 16, 1970, the date on which Lightsey was killed, Porky, at least three times, attacked various personnel at the station, including defendant, with butcher cleavers, mainly in an effort to obtain access to alcoholic beverages.

On July 16, while defendant was working at the General Motors camp, approximately one mile from the main camp where he lived in a trailer, he received a telephone call from his roommate, Charles Parodi, who told him that Porky was drunk and had taken some wine from their trailer. It should be noted that locked doors on T-3 were unknown because of potential fire hazard. Parodi pleaded with defendant to return to the trailer and defendant undertook to do so. He took with him a rifle selected from the common store to protect himself from the drunken Porky when he arrived back at the camp and later he loaded it. When defendant returned to the trailer he left his rifle and went to the next trailer to warn Porky to stay away from the raisin wine which was stored in defendant's trailer. Defendant found Porky and the station manager, Lightsey, consuming 190 proof Ethyl alcohol cut with grape juice and home made raisin wine. Defendant then returned to his trailer and soon thereafter heard footsteps approaching. Believing that it was Porky, he raised the rifle, put the safety off, opened the bolt, and assuring himself that the rifle was loaded, returned the bolt to the firing position and pointed the gun at the door. It was not Porky, but Lightsey, who entered the trailer.

A discussion of increasing intensity then ensued between the two over whether or not Porky should be allowed some of defendant's raisin wine. Parodi was present for part of the discussion, but after he left defendant ordered Lightsey out of the trailer, waving the gun back and forth at him. The gun discharged and Lightsey was hit. Lightsey died a short time after the wound, despite the efforts of members of the camp, including defendant, to save him. There was no witness to the actual shooting, except the two participants, but there was evidence, on which the defense heavily relied, that the rifle was defective in an unforeseeable but most deadly way, *i.e.*, it could be discharged without pulling the trigger by banging it, by dropping it, by putting the safety on and off, by ramming the bolt handle down, and by applying slight pressure to the bolt handle when holding it.

* * *

BROWN v. RICHARD H. WACHOLZ, INC.
467 F.2d 18, 19 (10th Cir. 1972)

Before BREITENSTEIN, SETH and DOYLE, Circuit Judges.

WILLIAM E. DOYLE, Circuit Judge.

In this diversity action for personal injuries the plaintiff-appellant recovered a verdict in the amount of $1,705.00, which was the exact dollar amount of his out of pocket expenses for hospital and medical. He seeks a reversal, contending that the trial court erred in refusing to grant a new trial because of the inadequacy of the award.

The injury was the result of plaintiff-appellant's slip and fall on the sidewalk in front of defendant's place of business. The fall was on ice which had formed on the sidewalk below a drain spout from defendant's building. This occurred as plaintiff was leaving the defendant's restaurant after having eaten dinner there. He was walking with the aid of canes when the fall occurred. The evidence showed that plaintiff-appellant had a pre-existing condition. He had had poliomyelitis some years before and this left him with deterioration of his thigh muscles on the right leg. When he fell his right femur was broken at a point about six to eight inches above the knee joint. This injury necessitated an internal reduction operation which was performed by an orthopedic surgeon in a hospital in Dallas, Texas.

After the injury, and following the taking of x-rays in a hospital in Leadville, plaintiff's companions transported him by automobile (camper) to Texas for treatment by an orthopedic surgeon who had previously adminstered to him. There the open reduction operation was performed and a six-inch stainless steel plate with screws was installed. Plaintiff remained in the hospital for about 11 days, but was confined to a wheelchair for a period in excess of three months thereafter, or until February 1, 1970. After that, he continued in a cast or splint for an additional two months.

The medical testimony described the operation in some detail and was to the effect that both healthy muscle tissue and that which had been affected by the disease which plaintiff had previously suffered was removed. Thus, it is contended that the injury and the surgical procedure produced additional scarring of the remaining healthy tissue, and that he has permanent disability in the function of the right leg. The testimony of the orthopedic surgeon who performed the operation was that plaintiff suffered a 20 percent impairment of the leg which resulted in inability to control the inward rotation of the affected leg and foot, resulting in impairment of plaintiff's ability to walk, drive a car and perform other functions. Following the return of a verdict for the amount of actual out of pocket medical and hospital expenses, plaintiff moved for a new trial based on the alleged inadequacy of the damages. This motion was denied.

The primary question before us is whether the action of the trial court in denying the motion for a new trial was an abuse of discretion which requires a new trial.

* * *

BOYCE v. PI KAPPA ALPHA HOLDING CORP.
476 F.2d 447, 448-450 (5th Cir. 1973)

Before JOHN R. BROWN, Chief Judge, MOORE and RONEY, Circuit Judges.

MOORE, Circuit Judge:

This is an appeal from a Florida common law negligence action which was removed from the Florida State court to Federal District Court on grounds of diversity jurisdiction. The complaint alleged that plaintiff-appellee Jonathan Boyce on July 20, 1970, was an invitee at the Pi Kappa Alpha Fraternity House on the University of Miami campus (hereinafter "Pike House"), premises owned by defendant-appellant Pi Kappa Alpha Holding Corporation, and that as a result of defendent's negligence, plaintiff was caused to dive into an empty swimming pool and to sustain paralytic injuries. The cause came on for trial by jury on October 13, 1971. After several days of testimony special interrogatories were submitted to the jury which required them to determine the status of the plaintiff on defendant's property, the negligence of the defendant, and the degree of negligence, if any. The jury determined that plaintiff's status had been that of an invitee, that defendant had been negligent, and that defendant's conduct constituted willful and wanton negligence, the latter determination precluding a jury finding on the question of plaintiff's contributory negligence. The plaintiff was awarded damages in the amount of $850,000.

On appeal from that verdict, and judgment thereon, the defendant-appellant here asserts numerous points of error. Resolution of this appeal must necessarily commence with a recitation of the facts surrounding this most unfortunate event.

On July 20, 1970, plaintiff-appellee Boyce was a student at the University of Miami in Coral Gables, Florida, and a member of the Phi Delta Theta social fraternity. Then 23 years old, he was attending the university's summer session. At approximately 2:00 P.M. on that date plaintiff, his fraternity roommate Charles Parker, and several others went to the Varsity

Inn, a student beer parlor which they frequented, on the average, once or twice weekly. The small group remained at the Inn until 5:30-6:00 P.M., socializing and drinking beer. The beer was purchased primarily in pitchers measuring approximately twelve inches high by six to seven inches wide. Although plaintiff could not recall precisely the amount of beer he consumed during this 3-3½ hour period, he testified at trial to having drunk more than five glasses (Trial Transcript, hereinafter "Tr.", at p.571), while his roommate testified that he himself had consumed "a pitcher or two" (Tr. at 223). Other testimony established that plaintiff ate nothing from noon onwards that day. At approximately 6:00 P.M. the group decided to take up a collection among themselves and to purchase a 15½ gallon keg of beer, for consumption that evening. The keg was bought and set up at the Phi Delta Theta house and the small group, including plaintiff, at 7:00-7:30 P.M., resumed the drinking begun in the early afternoon at the Varsity Inn. At 8:30 P.M. plaintiff's girl friend, Nancy Lindberg, arrived at the party with her roommate, Susan Bowen. Miss Lindberg testified that, during the time whe was present, she observed plaintiff consume "four or five" twelve-ounce cups of beer. (Tr. 261, 277). The plaintiff testified that he could not recall the precise quantity he had consumed during the evening.

At approximately 11:30 P.M. either plaintiff or Parker suggested that they and the girls go to the Pike House, two blocks distant and the only fraternity on campus having a swimming pool, for a late night swim. Apparently, all intended to swim dressed in street clothes. (Tr. 231). The group departed for the Pike House, plaintiff carrying Miss Bowen draped over his shoulder, and Parker and another (one "Dennis") carrying Miss Lindberg between them, their hands and arms in chair-like fashion. The plaintiff and Miss Bowen arrived at the darkened pool area several minutes before the other three. Playfully, Boyce threatened to throw Miss Bowen into the pool, but protesting, she was able to persuade him to set her down. He placed her down, apparently with his back to the pool, and then he either dived or jumped into an empty pool, at a depth of four to five feet, landing on his back. On hitting the pool floor plaintiff instantaneously severed his spinal cord, causing virtual total paralysis from the shoulders down.

* * *

UNITED STATES v. MIRANDA
437 F.2d 1255, 1256 (2d Cir. 1971)

Before LUMBARD, Chief Judge, and MOORE and SMITH, Circuit Judges.

J. JOSEPH SMITH, Circuit Judge:

This is an appeal from an order entered in the United States District Court for the Southern District of New York, Inzer B. Wyatt, Judge, denying, without a hearing, a motion made pursuant to 28 U.S.C. § 2255 to set aside appellant's guilty plea and sentence for violations of the federal narcotics laws on the ground that he was mentally incompetent at the time he pleaded guilty. The appellant also contends that the district court erred in failing to order a mental examination at the time of the plea, pursuant to 18 U.S.C. § 4244.

Raymond Miranda was arrested on February 27, 1968 and charged with concealing 64.3 grams of heroin in violation of 21 U.S.C. §§ 173, 174. He was held at the West Street detention facility in lieu of $10,000 bail until March 21, 1968 when he was released to the custody of New York City police officials on an unrelated burglary charge. During this period when he was in federal custody, appellant suffered severe narcotic withdrawal and several drugs were administered to treat this illness. On one occasion while at West Street, Miranda attempted suicide. On April 4, 1968 Miranda appeared voluntarily in the district court and pleaded not guilty to the federal indictment. He was then released upon his own recognizance.

On August 12, 1968 appellant was again arrested, this time by New York City police officers on a narcotics offense. At the time of this arrest he was apparently using the alias of Joseph Ramos. Miranda again suffered severe withdrawal and was given medication from August 12 until at least August 19, 1968. On August 16th he again attempted to commit suicide. On August 22, 1968 Miranda pleaded guilty to the indictment, and on September 26, 1968 he was sentenced to a term of imprisonment of six years.

In his affidavit accompanying his motion, appellant averred that at the time of the guilty pleas he was held "in restraints" in the psychiatric ward at the Rikers Island prison hospital due to his attempted suicide and was under heavy narcotic medication; that he had previously attempted suicide; that he had been a drug addict since 1955; that he had been continuously under the influence of narçotics for some 16 months prior to his arrest on the federal charge in February, 1968; that he was "still under heavy narcotic sedation" when he was brought to this court and pleaded guilty and a month later when he was sentenced.

* * *

ISHAM v. PACIFIC FAR E. LINE, INC.
476 F.2d 835, 836 (9th Cir. 1973)

Before CHAMBERS, ELY and WALLACE, Circuit Judges.

CHAMBERS, Circuit Judge:

Martha Isham brought this personal injury action against Pacific Far East Line, Inc. (hereinafter Far East) in the District Court of Guam. Jurisdiction was based on diversity and the Organic Act of Guam, 48 U.S.C. § 1424(a).

Her husband was stationed on Guam while serving in the Navy. In the spring of 1968, Mrs. Isham purchased a passenger ticket to travel on the Far

East freighter, the *India Bear,* from San Francisco, California, to Guam. The *India Bear* made a stop at Honolulu to take on and discharge cargo.

On May 5, 1968, the *India Bear* put in at Wake Island. Wake does not have a deep water harbor. Ships lie at anchor offshore, and landing craft (LCM's) shuttle back and forth between ships and the docks. Wake is under the control of the Federal Aviation Administration (FAA). The FAA also operates the LCM's that shuttle between the docks and ships at anchor. Far East crew-members who have shore leave and passengers who wish to visit Wake also ride in the LCM's.

On the evening of May 5, several passengers from the *India Bear,* including Mrs. Isham, went ashore to visit Wake. Around 10:00 p.m., the passengers and several crew-members boarded the LCM for the return to the *India Bear.* The LCM was operated by Ichito Nagao, an FAA employee. Shortly after leaving the dock, the LCM struck a barge because of Nagao's carelessness. Mrs. Isham was thrown forward into the well of the ship. She broke both her wrists and injured her back. After receiving first aid at Wake, she was flown to Guam where she received care and recuperated in a U.S. Navy hospital. She continues to have some discomfort in her right wrist and occasional low back pains. Both ailments respond to aspirin.

A jury awarded her $90,000 for her injuries, a rather handsome amount considering the injuries. Far East has appealed the judgment against it.

* * *

Caveat

As an advocate, it is of the highest importance that you resist any temptation to distort the facts or ignore adverse facts. Your opponent will likely pounce on distortions or omissions, and destroy them. In doing so, your opponent will also likely place the remainder of your case in a bad light, because of the taint created by the revelation of your lack of candor.

Be very cautious when attempting to tone the facts in favor of your client. You are under a duty to the court to be truthful, and this means, among other things, that you must admit the facts which work against your client. Very few, if any, cases have facts that are perfect. Your side need not be perfect; it just must be better than the other side of the case. If possible, you should call adverse facts to the attention of the court before your opponent does, because your opponent can present them much more devastatingly than you would like for them to be presented.

* * *

To the same effect, compare the cases of *Dorrance's Estate,* 309 Pa. 151, 163 A. 303 (1932), including the dissenting opinions, and *In re Dorrance,* 115 N.J. Eq. 268, 170 A. 601 (Prerogative Ct. 1934).

11.
ARGUING THE LAW

"The prophecies of what the courts will do in fact, and nothing more pretentious, are what I mean by the law."

Holmes, *The Path of the Law,* 10 Harv. L. Rev. 457, 461 (1897).

What purpose is served by the argument of law?

We have talked about drafting a precise statement of the questions in a form which will suggest that the best answer to the question is the one which the advocate desires that the court accept. We have talked about stating the facts in the form of an accurate, candid, and persuasively-toned story which holds the court's interest, and on which the court will likely act in a way favorable to the advocate's client. The argument of law is designed to accomplish a similar purpose. It is the third leg on which the three-legged tower of effective advocacy rests.

The purpose of advocacy is to persuade the tribunal to render a decision in one of two or more possible ways. The judicial process is the choosing by the court from two or more good arguments the single argument which is not only good, but which in the court's opinion is the best.

In planning our argument of law, we must try to predict the reaction of a court composed of sensible, normally-emotional, legally-trained persons who have had individual lifetimes of pleasant and unpleasant experiences which have, at least in part, molded them, their attitudes, and their minds. It is mistaken for anyone to try to state a universal formula concerning the factors which influence a court in its process of deciding appeals. Do not try to determine how a court arrives at a decision on an appeal.

Always ask yourself, how will this particular court arrive at its particular decision in this particular case. Recognize that each and every case is composed of unique facts, some of which are peripheral and others of which will be selected by the court as material facts. As an advocate, you must be concerned with a particular court, a specific case, and a unique set of facts. Whatever we say on the subject of factors which influence decisions, it will be only a series of generalizations, and will be only a partial presentation. We do not know all of these factors, and we will probably never know them all.

In legal thought there is a large number of mutually-inconsistent rules and principles from which courts may often make choices when dealing with any particular case, *i.e.,* a group of facts. From time to time, persons talk about justice according to laws, and not according to men. While it is true that we have written laws in abundance, they are not self-executing. It is only through human beings that the written laws are executed and applied to concrete facts. Chief Justice Burger made this clear when, in *Walz v. Tax Comm'n,* 397 U.S. 664, 90 S.Ct. 1409, 25 L.Ed.2d 697 (1970), he said:

* * *

> The argument that making "fine distinctions" between what is and what is not absolute under the Constitution is to render us a government of men, not laws, gives too little weight to the fact that it is an essential part of adjudication to draw distinctions, including fine ones, in the process of interpreting the Constitution. We must frequently decide, for example, what are "reasonable" searches and seizures under the Fourth Amendment. Determining what acts of government tend to establish or interfere with religion falls well within what courts have long been called upon to do in sensitive areas.

* * *

The law is a plastic experience in life and therefore is subject to various applications and changes. It is dynamic, just as are other life experiences, and is therefore not altogether predictable. Why should we expect it to be wholly predictable? Benjamin Franklin said that in this world nothing is certain but death and taxes; our experience tells us that even the details of those assurances are often unpredictable.

I.

There are some identifiable factors in the appellate process which affect the decision of appellate cases. Perhaps a significant degree of predictability results from them. The outcome of each case that is briefed, argued, and decided will, to some extent, depend upon the interaction of these factors:

- The unique facts of the case.
- The sphere of influences acting upon the court which decides the case, *e.g.*, binding precedent from higher courts or an awareness that the decision about to be made will have far-reaching effect as a precedent.
- The individual judge or judges composing the court.
- The resourcefulness, ability, and expertise of the individual advocates in the case.

It is the last factor, the resourcefulness, ability, and expertise of the individual advocates, that can be a dominant influence.

Despite the fact that there is no identifiable, all-inclusive pattern which is the key to predicting court decisions, there are many stabilizing factors in the appellate process. It is true that courts and judges accept and reject arguments, and disagree with each other almost as often as attorneys and litigants themselves disagree. The entire life experience of each individual judge influences the concepts which a court or judge draws from the combined facts of a case, but the following matters militate to stabilize the court's decision-making operations:[1]

- A judge senses a responsibility for justice.

---

[1] *See generally* K. Llewellyn, *The Common Law Tradition* 19-51 (1960).

• A judge is a professional with external standards, the product of a professional experience which is in large part the same as that of other members of the bench and bar, from the time of entry into law school until the date of the decision.

• He or she is a legally-trained scholar.

• He or she must write and publish an opinion which will justify what he or she does.

• A judge has the benefit of adversary arguments of counsel; he or she may select those found appropriate and reject those found inappropriate.

• He or she is personally familiar with the legal literature and the arguments for and against the opinion which he or she finally accepts.

• He or she must face colleagues, and on appeal the decision is subject to review, modification, and a written and published opinion.

• After making a decision, the judge must face an electorate or an appointing or impeaching authority.

II.

Knowing as you do about the appellate process, what do you, as an advocate, do to accomplish your argument of law?

• Carefully analyze the facts of the problem case. There is no substitute for examining the facts one by one and determining the component parts of the unique case. The analysis of a problem case's component parts will probably result in their individually appearing more understandable than the collective facts appeared to be on first inspection.

A similar treatment of the legal issues and points of argument will result in the advocate having a better comprehension of an otherwise formidable set of issues and arguments, which theretofore were at best indistinct.

While it is important that the research and writing be accomplished exceptionally well and that they be of the highest quality, and it is true that these activities require a large amount of time and attention, it is equally important that a block of time be set aside for the purpose of thinking and reflecting about the case. In many instances advocates fail to allow a significant amount of time for thinking and reflecting, but instead spend virtually all of their allotted time researching and writing; this is a mistake.

• Transplant your careful analysis of the facts, the issues, and the arguments into the brief. Attempt to create in your reader's mind the same stimuli that caused you to reach the legal determinations that you have reached.

• Reasons, and principles based upon those reasons, are persuasive to a court, because it senses the responsibility for justice. When a court has independence within the sphere of the issues presented, *e.g.*, concerning Constitutional and federal questions in the United States Supreme Court, or concerning contract or tort questions in the highest courts of each of the 50 states, it is more free to weigh the reasons in the arguments, and less likely to follow precedent for the sake of *stare decisis*. Whether rules are strictly followed depends, to some extent, upon whether the rules are reasonable in the context of the facts of the problem case. Therefore, what one court considers proper, another court may consider improper; what may be acceptable in one century may be unacceptable in another century.

In contrast, in a court which lacks this independence, *e.g.*, an intermediate appellate court or a trial court considering a reviewable problem case, precedent and trends in the higher courts by which the problem case is likely to be reviewed are a major influence. It is useless, and a waste of the court's and counsel's time, to argue reasons to a trial court, when there is precedent from a court to which the trial court's decision is appealable holding opposite to your argument.

• Realize that courts have at their disposal a large number of mutually-inconsistent principles and cases, from which to make choices when dealing with any unique group of facts, and that many appellate cases can be decided in any of several ways and the judgment be wholly justified by a well-written and acceptable opinion. An advocate must demonstrate reasons why the principles and cases which he cites should apply to the problem case, in preference to the other principles and cases which his opponent cites. In this matter, the advocate must present his case positively and not merely deprecate the opponent's case.

• Legal literature in earlier times had a tendency to use foreign phrases and complicated sentence structure. Modern style is to the contrary. The judges to whom your briefs and arguments are directed are very busy; they may read 25,000 pages of briefs each year. They have no time, and equal inclination, to translate or look up the meanings of Latin words or maxims, or solve linguistic puzzles. Therefore, an advocate uses clear English and constructs his sentences with care, so that the points which he makes in his argument seem to have been reached with ease.

• An argument of law should beckon. If it invites acceptance, then the advocate's mission has had its path smoothed, because the judge is motivated to want to accept it. It will likely be useful to include with the argument of law a suggested rationale for the court's opinion in your client's favor.

• Dynamic and meaningful words, as distinguished from passive ones, are the order of the day when the advocate briefs or argues his case. The frequent use of a thesaurus and a dictionary will aid in the search for the best words to crystallize ideas into distinct and unmistakable expressions which make the intended point. Avoid adjectives and adverbs.

III.

In the argument of law, what should an advocate write about? There is no formula which will furnish an advocate a key to the desired decision. There are some things, though, that experience has shown to persuade the minds of courts. A partial list would include:

• Acceptance of the principle urged, or the application of the principle to similar facts, by a higher court, the court in which the case is pending, other courts, or legal writers. The relevance of the precedent cases to the problem case before the court must be demonstrated as concisely as possible by telling about the facts of the precedent case and its outcome, and thereby relating the precedent case to the problem case. Preferably, holdings of courts should be used, but dictum and other secondary authorities may be offered if holdings are not found.

• Demonstrate that the result urged is fair and right when applied to the unique facts of the problem case. If nonlegal disciplines such as accounting, economics, engineering, or medicine can add light to the argument, utilize those ideas in your argument.

• Offer good moral reasons.

• Describe the historical basis for the rule.

• Urge the adoption of principles which are in keeping with the court's image of justice.

IV.

The landmark civil-rights decision which signaled the death knell for racially-segregated public schools, *Brown v. Board of Education,* 347 U.S. 483 (1954), was the result of interaction between the court and appellate advocates. The outline of the successful parties' written argument in their brief before the United States Supreme Court, as shown by the following table of contents from which the page numbers have been deleted, furnishes illustrations of some of the advocate's skills previously mentioned. In the following verbatim reprint of that portion of the appellants' brief's table of contents, note particularly:

• the careful analysis of the problem;

• the suggestion of precedent which whittled down the earlier contrary doctrine of *Plessy v. Ferguson,* 163 U.S. 537 (1896);

• the invitation to change the older precedent in the light of new social findings;

• the precise selection of words;

• the moral basis for and fairness of the proposed outcome;

• the unfairness of a contrary holding;

• the historic background leading up to and surrounding the Constitutional Amendment and the principle of *Plessy v. Ferguson,* supra; and

• the allegation of later changes in society which lead naturally and inevitably to the proposed new principle.

[BROWN v. BOARD OF EDUCATION][2]

I. Normal exercise of the judicial function calls for a declaration that the state is without power to enforce distinctions based upon race or color in affording educational opportunities in the public schools.

---

[2] Brief for Appellants at ii-vi, Brown v. Board of Education, 347 U.S. 483 (1954). The page numbers have been deleted.

II. The statutory and constitutional provisions involved in these cases cannot be validated under any separate but equal concept.

A. Racial Segregation Cannot Be Squared With the Rationale of the Early Cases Interpreting the Reach of the Fourteenth Amendment.

B. The First Time the Question Came Before the Court, Racial Segregation In Transportation Was Specifically Disapproved.

C. The Separate But Equal Doctrine Marked An Unwarranted Departure From the Main Stream of Constitutional Development and Permits the Frustration of the Very Purposes of The Fourteenth Amendment As Defined by This Court.

D. The Separate But Equal Doctrine Was Conceived in Error.

1. The Dissenting Opinion of Justice Harlan in Plessy v. Ferguson.

2. Custom, Usage and Tradition Rooted in the Slave Tradition Cannot Be the Constitutional Yardstick for Measuring State Action Under the Fourteenth Amendment.

3. Preservation of Public Peace Cannot Justify Deprivation of Constitutional Rights.

4. The Separate but Equal Doctrine Deprives Negroes of That Protection Which the Fourteenth Amendment Accords Under the General Classification Test.

E. The Separate But Equal Doctrine Has Not Received Unqualified Approval in This Court.

F. The Necessary Consequence of the Sweatt and McLaurin Decisions is Repudiation of the Separate But Equal Doctrine.

III. Viewed in the light of history the separate but equal doctrine has been an instrumentality of defiant nullification of the Fourteenth Amendment.

A. The Status of the Negro, Slave and Free, Prior to the Civil War.

B. The Post War Struggle.

C. The Compromise of 1877 and the Abandonment of Reconstruction.

D. Consequences of the 1877 Compromise.

E. Nullification of the Rights Guaranteed by the Fourteenth Amendment and the Reestablishment of the Negro's Pre-Civil War Inferior Status Fully Realized.

Conclusion to Part I.

Part Two

I. The Fourteenth Amendment was intended to destroy all caste and color legislation in the United States, including racial segregation.

   A. The Era Prior to the Civil War Was Marked By Determined Efforts to Secure Recognition of the Principle of Complete and Real Equality For All Men Within the Existing Constitutional Framework of Our Government.

   Equality Under Law.

   B. The Movement For Complete Equality Reached Its Successful Culmination in the Civil War and the Fourteenth Amendment.

   C. The Principle of Absolute and Complete Equality Began to Be Translated Into Federal Law as Early as 1862.

   D. From the Beginning the Thirty-Ninth Congress Was Determined to Eliminate Race Distinctions From American Law.

   The Framers of the Fourteenth Amendment.

   E. The Fourteenth Amendment Was Intended to Write into the Organic Law of the United States the Principle of Absolute and Complete Equality in Broad Constitutional Language.

   F. The Republican Majority in the 39th Congress Was Determined to Prevent Future Congresses from Diminishing Federal Protection of These Rights.

   G. Congress Understood That While the Fourteenth Amendment Would Give Authority to Congress to Enforce Its Provisions, the Amendment in and of Itself Would Invalidate All Class Legislation by the States.

   Congress Intended to Destroy All Class Distinction In Law.

   H. The Treatment of Public Education or Segregation in Public Schools During the 39th Congress Must Be Considered in the Light of the Status of Public Education at That Time.

   I. During the Congressional Debates on Proposed Legislation Which Culminated in the Civil Rights Act of 1875 Veterans of the Thirty-Ninth Congress Adhered to Their Conviction That the Fourteenth Amendment Had Proscribed Segregation in Public Schools.

II. There is convincing evidence that the State Legislatures and conventions which ratified the Fourteenth Amendment contemplated and understood that it prohibited State legislation which would require racial segregation in public schools.

A. The Eleven States Seeking Readmission Understood that the Fourteenth Amendment Stripped Them of Power to Maintain Segregated Schools.

Arkansas.
North Carolina, South Carolina, Louisiana, Georgia, Alabama and Florida.
Texas.
Virginia.
Mississippi.
Tennessee.

B. The Majority of the Twenty-two Union States Ratifying the 14th Amendment Understood that it Forbade Compulsory Segregation in Public Schools.

West Virginia and Missouri.
The New England States.
The Middle Atlantic States.
The Western Reserve States.
The Western States.

C. The Non-Ratifying States Understood that the Fourteenth Amendment Forbade Enforced Segregation in Public Schools.

Delaware.
Maryland.
Kentucky.
California.

Conclusion to Part II.

PART THREE

I. This Court should declare invalid the constitutional and statutory provisions here involved requiring segregation in public schools. After careful consideration of all of the factors involved in transition from segregated school systems to unsegregated school systems, appellants know of no reasons or considerations which would warrant postponement of the enforcement of appellants' rights by this Court in the exercise of its equity powers.

A. The Fourteenth Amendment requires that a decree be entered directing that appellants be admitted forthwith to public schools without distinction as to race or color.

B. There is no equitable justification for postponement of appellants' enjoyment of their rights.

C. Appellants are unable in good faith to suggest terms for a decree which will secure effective gradual adjustment because no such decree will protect appellants' rights.

Conclusion.

Supplement.

V.

Some verbatim quotations from appellant's brief in *Brown v. Board of Educa-*

tion,[3] which are exemplary of effective arguments of law, are set forth below. When reading this material, be alert to observe:

- the argument's compelling invitation which the reader may accept;
- the precise choice of words;
- the attempt to take advantage of trends, principles, and earlier decisions which support appellant's position, but which are to some extent peripheral to it; and
- the unique argument, offered by resourceful counsel, that racial segregation in public schools produces a detrimental effect on the ability of a minority student to learn.

* * *

ARGUMENT

PART ONE

The question of judicial power to abolish segregated schools is basic to the issues involved in these cases and for that reason we have undertaken to analyze it at the outset before dealing with the other matters raised by the Court,

* * *

I

Normal exercise of the judicial function calls for a declaration that the state is without power to enforce distinctions based upon race or color in affording educational opportunities in the public schools.

This Court in a long line of decisions has made it plain that the Fourteenth Amendment prohibits a state from making racial distinctions in the exercise of governmental power. Time and again this Court has held that if a state's power has been exercised in such a way as to deprive a Negro of a right which he would have freely enjoyed if he had been white, then that state's action violated the Fourteenth Amendment.

In *Shelley v. Kraemer,* 334 U.S. 1, for example, a unanimous Court held that the State of Missouri and Michigan had violated the 14th Amendment when their courts ruled that a Negro could not own real property whose ownership it was admitted the state law would have protected him in, had he been white. This, despite the fact that the state court was doing no more than enforcing a private agreement running with the land. The sole basis for the decision, then, was that the Fourteenth Amendment compels the states to be color blind in exercising their power and authority.

---

[3] Brief for Appellants at 21-30, Brown v. Board of Education, 347 U.S. 483 (1954). The complete brief consists of 235 pages including a multitude of exhibits. The list of authorities cited in the brief is 26 pages long.

Buchanan v. Warley, 245 U.S. 60, was an earlier decision to the same effect. There, this Court invalidated a Louisville, Kentucky, ordinance which required racial residential segregation. Though it applied to Negro and white alike, the Court rightly recognized that the ordinance was an exercise of the state's power based on race and race alone. This, the court ruled, was a violation of the Fourteenth Amendment. To the same effect is *Barrows v. Jackson,* — U.S.—, 97 L. ed. Advance p. 961). And see *Oyama v. California,* 332 U.S. 633.

This court has applied the same rigorous requirement to the exercise of the state's power in providing public education. Beginning with *Missouri ex rel. Gaines v. Canada,* 305 U.S. 337, this Court has uniformly ruled that the Fourteenth Amendment prohibits a state from using race or color as the determinant of the quantum, quality or type of education and the place at which education is to be afforded. Most recently, this Court in *McLaurin v. Oklahoma State Regents,* 339 U.S 637, held that rules which made distinctions among students in the same school solely on the basis of color were forbidden by the Fourteenth Amendment. Thus, this Court has made it plain that no state may use color or race as the axis upon which the state's power turns, and the conduct of the public education system has not been excepted from this ban.

This judicial recognition that race is an irrational basis for governmental action under our Constitution has been manifested in many decisions and opinions of this Court. In *Yick Wo v. Hopkins,* 118 U.S. 356, this Court struck down local administrative action which differentiated between whites and Chinese. In *Hirabayashi v. United States,* 320 U.S. 81, 100, Chief Justice Stone, in a majority opinion, characterized racial distinctions as "odious to a free people". In *Korematsu v. United States,* 323 U.S. 214, 216, the Court viewed racial restrictions as "immediately suspect". Mr. Justice Jackson, concurring in *Edwards v. California,* 314 U.S. 180, 185, referred to race and color as "constitutionally an irrelevance". Mr. Justice Douglas, dissenting in *South v. Peters,* 339 U.S. 276, 278, considered discriminations based upon race, creed, or color "beyond the pale". In an unanimous opinion in *Henderson v. United States,* 339 U.S. 816, 825, the Court, while not reaching the constitutional question raised, described signs, partitions and curtains segregating Negros in railroad dining cars as emphasizing "the artificiality of a difference in treatment which serves only to call attention to a racial classification of passengers holding identical tickets and using the same public dining facility". Every member of the present Court has from time to time subscribed to this view of race as an irrational premise for government action.

The restrictions placed upon persons of Japanese origin on the West Coast during World War II were sustained in *Hirabayashi v. United States, supra,* and in *Korematsu v. United States, supra,* as emergency war measures taken by the national government in a dire national peril of the gravest nature. The military decision was upheld as within an implied war power, and the Court was unwilling to interfere with measures considered necessary to the safety of the nation by those primarily responsible for its security. Yet, in upholding these orders, the Court made some of the most sweeping condemnations of governmentally imposed racial and color distinctions ever announced by our judiciary. And while departure from accepted standards of governmental conduct was sustained in order to remove persons of Japanese origin from areas where sabotage and espionage might have worked havoc with the national war effort, once this removal was accomplished and individual loyalty determined, further restrictions based upon race or color could no longer be countenanced. *Ex Parte Endo,* 323 U.S 283.

Tunstall v. Brotherhood of Locomotive Firemen & Enginemen, 323 U.S. 210, and *Steele v. Louisville & Nashville R. R. Co.,* 323 U.S. 192, while not deciding the constitutional question, left no doubt that the Fifth Amendment had stripped the national government of power to enforce the racial discrimination assailed.

These decisions serve to underscore the constitutional prohibition against Congressional action grounded upon color except in so far as it may have temporary justification to meet an overwhelming national emergency such as that which led to decisions in the *Hirabayashi* and *Korematsu* cases.

The power of states is even more rigidly circumscribed. For there is grave doubt that their acts can be sustained under the exception made in the *Hirabayashi* and *Korematsu* cases with respect to the national government. See *Oyama v. California,* 332 U.S. 633. The Fourteenth Amendment has been defined as a broad prohibition against state enforcement of differentiations and discrimination based upon race or color. State action restricting the right of Negroes to vote has been struck down as a violation of the Fourteenth Amendment. *Nixon v. Condon,* 286 U.S. 73. Similarly, the Court has refused to sanction the systematic exclusion of Negroes from the petit or grand jury, *Hill v. Texas,* 316 U.S. 400; *Pierre v. Louisiana,* 306 U.S. 354; their representation on juries on a token or proportional basis, *Cassell v. Texas,* 339 U.S. 282; *Shepherd v. Florida,* 341 U.S. 50; or any method in the selection of juries susceptible of racial discrimination in practice. *Avery v. Georgia,* 345 U.S. 559.

Legislation depriving persons of particular races of an opportunity to pursue a gainful occupation has been held a denial of equal protection. *Truax v. Raich,* 239 U.S. 33; *Takahashi v. Fish and Games Commission,* 334 U.S 410. It is now well settled that a state may not make racial differences among its employees the basis for salary differentiations. *Alston v. School Board,* 112 F.2d 992 (CA 4th 1940), *cert. denied,* 311 U.S. 693.

Indeed, abhorrence of race as a premise for governmental action pervades a wide realm of judicial opinion dealing with other constitutional provisions. Sweeping decisions have enforced the right of Negroes to make effective use of the electoral process consistent with the requirements of the Fifteenth Amendment. *Guinn v. United States,* 238 U.S. 347; *Lane v. Wilson,* 307 U.S. 268; *Smith v. Allwright,* 321 U.S. 649; *Terry v. Adams,* 345 U.S. 461.

It should be added parenthetically that these decisions are not mere *pro forma* applications of the self-evidence requirements of the Fifteenth Amendment. On the contrary, the concept of state action has been utilized in a dynamic and expanding fashion as the Court has sought to reach any method or subterfuge with which the state has attempted to avoid its obligation under that constitutional amendment. *Smith v. Allwright, supra; Terry v. Adams, supra.* See *Rice v. Elmore,* 165 F.2d 387 (CA 4th 1947), *cert. denied,* 333 U.S. 875 and *Baskin v. Brown,* 174 F.2d 391 (CA 4th 1949), cases holding state non-action violative of the Fifteenth Amendment, the principle of which was expressly approved in *Terry v. Adams.*

State laws requiring racial segregation in interstate commerce have been declared an invalid invasion of commerce power reserved to the Congress. *Morgan v. Virginia,* 328 U.S. 373. But where a state sought to enforce against a carrier engaged in foreign commerce its local non-segregation policy, the state law was upheld. The Court considered it inconceivable that the Congress in the exercise of its plenary power over commerce would take any action in conflict with the local nondiscriminatory regulations imposed. *Bob-Lo Excursion Co. v. Michigan,* 333 U.S. 28. These two cases considered together strikingly exemplify this Court's position that fundamental national policy is offended by a requirement of segregation, but implemented by its prohibition.

The contention by a labor union that a state civil rights law which prohibited racial discrimination in union membership offended the Fourteenth Amendment was dismissed because such a position "would be a distortion of the policy manifested in that amendment which was adopted to prevent state legislation designed to perpetuate discrimination on the basis of race and color". *Railway Mail Association v. Corsi,* 326 U.S. 88, 94.

Thus, the Court has all but universally made short shrift of attempts to use governmental power to enforce racial distinctions. Yet, where such power has prohibited racial discrimination, it has been sustained even where it has been urged that the state is acting in derogation of other constitutional rights or protected interests.

At the graduate and professional school level, closest to the cases here, racial distinctions as applied have been struck down. *McLaurin v. Oklahoma State Regents,* 339 U.S. 637; *Sweatt v. Painter,* 339 U.S. 629. In those cases the educational process was viewed as a totality. The faculty of the school, the prestige of the institution, the fact that segregation deprived the Negro applicant of the benefits which he might secure in attending school with representatives of the state's dominant racial majority, the value judgment of the community with respect to the segregated school, and the impact of segregation on the individual were among the factors considered by the Court in determining that equal educational opportunities were not available. Those cases, we submit, control disposition of the cases here.

Since segregation was found to impair and inhibit an adult's ability to study in the *McLaurin* case, it seems clear that such segregation has even more far reaching adverse consequences on the mental development of the children involved here.

Sweatt's isolation from the dominant racial majority in a segregated law school was held to deprive him of an effective opportunity to learn the law. The basic function of the public school is to instruct each succeeding generation in the fundamental traditions of our democracy. The child can best come to believe in and respect these traditions by learning them in a setting in which they are in practical operation. But to be taught that our society is founded upon a concept of equality in a public school from which those racial groups are excluded which hold pre-eminence in every field in his community makes it all but impossible for such teachings to take root. Segregation here is detrimental to the Negro child in his effort to develop into a useful and productive citizen in a democracy.

The *Sweatt* and *McLaurin* cases teach that the Court will consider the educational process in its entirety, including, apart from the measurable physical facilities, whatever factors have been shown to have educational significance. This rule cannot be peculiar to any level of public education. Public elementary and high school education is no less a governmental function than graduate and professional education in state institutions. Moreover, just as Sweatt and McLaurin were denied certain benefits characteristic of graduate and professional education, it is apparent from the records of these cases that Negroes are denied educational benefits which the state itself asserts are the fundamental objectives of public elementary and high school education.

South Carolina, like the other states in this country, has accepted the obligation of furnishing the extensive benefits of public education. Article XI, section 5, of the Constitution of South Carolina, declares: "The General Assembly shall provide for a liberal system of free public schools for all children between the ages of six and twenty-one years". Some 410 pages of the Code of Laws of South Carolina deal with "education". Title 31, Chapters 122-23, S.C. Code, pp. 387-795 (1935). Provision is made for the entire state-supported system of public schools, its administration and organization, from the kindergarten through the university. Pupils and teachers, school buildings, minimum standards of school construction, and specifications requiring certain general courses of instruction are dealt with in detail. In addition to requiring that the three "R's" must be taught, the law compels instruction in "morals and good behaviour" and in the "principles" and "essentials of the United States Constitution, including the study of and devotion to American institutions". Title 31, Chapter 122, sections 5321, 5323, 5325, S.C. Code (1935). The other states involved here are attempting to promote the same objectives.

These states thus recognize the accepted broad purposes of general public education in a democratic society. There is no question that furnishing public education is now an accepted governmental function. There are compelling reasons for a democratic government's assuming the burden of educating its children, of increasing its citizens' usefulness, efficiency and ability to govern.

In a democracy citizens from every group, no matter what their social or economic status or their religious or ethnic origins, are expected to participate widely in the making of important public decisions. The public school, even more than the family, the church, business institutions, political and social groups and other institutions, has become an effective agency for giving to all people that broad background of attitudes and skills required to enable them to function effectively as participants in a democracy. Thus, "education" comprehends the entire process of developing and training the mental, physical and moral powers and capabilities of human beings. See *Weyl v. Comm. of Int. Rev.*, 48 F.2d 811, 812 (CA 2d 1931); *Jones v. Better Business Bureau,* 123 F.2d 767, 769 (CA 10th 1941).

The records in the instant cases emphasize the extent to which the state has deprived Negroes of these fundamental educational benefits by separating them from the rest of the school population. In the case of *Briggs v. Elliott* (No. 2), expert witnesses testified that compulsory racial segregation in elementary and high schools inflicts considerable personal injury on the Negro pupils which endures as long as these students remain in the segregated school. These witnesses testified that compulsory racial segregation in the public schools of South Carolina injures the Negro students by: (1) impairing their ability to learn (R. 140, 161); (2) deterring the development of their personalities (R. 86, 89); (3) depriving them of equal status in the school community (R. 89, 141, 145); (4) destroying their self-respect (R. 140, 148); (5) denying them full opportunity for democratic social development (R. 98, 99, 103); (6) subjecting them to the prejudices of others (R. 133) and stamping them with a badge of inferiority (R. 148).

Similar testimony was introduced in each of the other three cases here involved, and that testimony was undisputed in the case of *Briggs v. Elliott* (No. 2); *Brown v. Board of Education of Topeka, et al.* (No. 1); *Gebhart v. Belton* (No. 10). In *Davis v. County School Board* (No. 4), while witnesses for the appellees disputed portions of the testimony of appellants' expert witnesses, four of appellees' witnesses admitted that racial segregation has harmful effects and another recognized that such segregation could be injurious.

In the *Gebhart* case (No. 10) the Chancellor filed an opinion in which he set forth a finding of fact, based on the undisputed oral testimony of experts in education, sociology, psychology, psychiatry and anthropology (A. 340-341) that in "our Delaware society", segregation in education practiced by petitioners as agents of the state "itself results in the Negro children, as a class, receiving educational opportunities which are substantially inferior to those available to white children otherwise similarly situated''.

And the court below in the *Brown* case (No. 1) made the following Finding of Fact (R. 245-246):

> ''Segregation of white and colored children in public schools has a detrimental effect upon the colored children. The impact is greater when it has the sanction of the law; for the policy of separating the races is usually interpreted as denoting the inferiority of the negro group. A sense of inferiority affects the motivation of a child to learn. Segregation with the sanction of law, therefore, has a tendency to retard the educational and mental development of negro children and to deprive them of some of the benefits they would receive in a racially integrated school system.''

The testimony of the expert witnesses in the cases now under consideration, the Opinion of the Chancellor in the Delaware case and the Finding of Fact by the lower court in the Kansas case are amply supported by scientific studies of recognized experts. A compilation of these materials was assembled and filed as an Appendix to the briefs in these cases on the first hearing. The observation of Mr. Justice Jackson in *West Virginia State Board of Education v. Barnette,* 319 U.S. 624, 636 that public school children, being educated for citizenship, must be scrupulously protected in their constitutional rights, ''if we are not to strangle the free mind at its source and teach youth to discount important principles of our government as mere platitudes'', while made in somewhat different context, appropriately describes the high public interest which these cases involve.

In sum, the statutes and constitutional provisions assailed in these cases must fall because they are contrary to this Court's basic premise that, as a matter of law, race is not an allowable basis of differentiation in governmental action; they are inconsistent with the broad prohibition of the Fifth and Fourteenth Amendments as defined by this Court; they are clearly within that category of racism in state action specifically prohibited by the *McLaurin* and *Sweatt* decisions.

* * *

VI.
Winick, Gerver & Blumberg, *The Psychology of Judges,* LEGAL & CRIMINAL PSYCHOLOGY 121, 133-134 (H. Toch ed. 1961)[4]

[4] From ''The Psychology of Judges'' by Charles Winick, Israel Gerver, and Abraham Blumberg, in LEGAL AND CRIMINAL PSYCHOLOGY, edited by Hans Toch. Copyright © 1961 by Holt, Rinehart and Winston, Inc. Reprinted by permission of Holt, Rinehart and Winston, Inc.

* * *

One of the great American judges, who was an outstanding figure in the development of law in New York State, Chancellor James Kent, said well over a century ago, in explaining how he reached a decision: "I might once in a while be embarrassed by a technical rule, but I almost always found principles suited to my view of the case ..." (Frank, 1930). Even the famous legal philosopher, Justice Oliver Wendell Holmes, who is perhaps the classical exponent of the modern approach to law, has said that "a decision is the unconscious result of instinctive prejudices and inarticulate connections," and "even the prejudices which judges share with their fellow men have a good deal more to do than the syllogism in determining the rules by which men should be governed" (Holmes, 1881). Justice Cardozo stated that forces which judges "do not recognize and cannot name have been tugging at them ... and the result is an outlook on life ..." (Cardozo, 1921).

One federal judge, after years of service, concluded that he reached his decisions by hunch or feeling: "I ... give my imagination play, and brooding ... wait for the feeling, the hunch — that intuitive flash of understanding ..." (Hutcheson, 1929). Writing a few years later, a distinguished judge said that a judge reaches his decision "by a 'hunch' as to what is fair and just or wise or expedient ... the personality of the judge and the judicial hunch are not and cannot be described in terms of legal rules and principles" (Frank, 1932). Frank has pointed out that the "sentence" which the judge pronounces comes from the Latin verb *sentire,* which means "to feel," and that the judge experiences his decision on an emotional level. In a decision, he wrote that "much harm is done by the myth that merely by putting on a black robe, and taking the oath of office as a judge, a man ceases to be human ... If the judge did not form judgments of the actors in those courthouse dramas called trials, he could never render decisions" (Frank, 1946).

The English jurist Lord Macmillan also underscored that "the judge's mind remains a human instrument working as do other minds" (Macmillan, 1937).

A Supreme Court justice frankly stated: "I know that in this great mass of opinions by men of different temperaments and qualifications and viewpoints, writing at different times and under varying local influences, some printed judicial word may be found to support almost any plausible proposition" (Jackson, 1944). This suggests that the judge first reaches his decision and then may look for a precedent to document his "decision," in contrast to the usual view that the precedent search precedes the decision. Just how much of an opportunity a judge has to find the "judicial word" with which he is comfortable can be seen in Justice Stone's estimate that a good law library, as of 1923, would have about 18,500 volumes of reports and 5,500 volumes of statutes, with 350 new volumes of reports and 250 new volumes of statutes each year (Stone, 1924). He estimated that a good law library around A.D. 2023 would have 1,850,000 volumes of reports and 550,000 volumes of statutes. Judges have pointed out that the judge is a human being and does not "clink out" decisions as a computer does (Tate, 1958), but is practicing an art (Yankwich, 1957).

A number of judges have thus stated quite frankly that instead of following a formal logical scheme, they reach their decisions by a kind of intuitive Gestalt impression of the case and its issues. If there are many judges who do reach their decisions in this way, it is important to know this as well as to know how many judges do so. Its implications for juridical science are central: it is like the difference between explaining a particular learning phenomenon in Gestalt principles in contrast to the traditional theory that judges reach their decisions by a logical process akin to learning theory. Among the possible implications for the student of the bench is that the precedents and legal reasoning cited by the judge may not actually be the private rationale for some decisions.

* * *

REFERENCES, ID. 142-145

* * *

Cardozo, Benjamin N. *The nature of the judicial process.* New Haven: Yale Univer. Press, 1921.

Frank, Jerome. *Law and the modern mind.* New York: Brentano, 1930, pp. 104, 166.

Frank, Jerome. What courts do in fact. *Illinois Law Rev.*, 1932, 26, 762-776.

Frank, Jerome. In re J. P. Linenan and Company, 138 F(2d), 651-654, 1946.

Holmes, Oliver Wendell, Jr. *The common law.* Boston: Little, Brown, 1881, p. 35.

Hutcheson, Joseph C. The judgment intuitive: The function of the "hunch" in judicial decisions, *Cornell Law Quart.*, 1929, 14, 274-278.

Jackson, Robert. Decline of stare decisis is due to volume of opinion. *J. Amer. Judicature Soc.*, 1944, 28, 6-8.

Macmillan, Hugh P. *Law and other things.* Cambridge, England: Cambridge Univer. Press, 1937.

Stone, Harlan F. Some aspects of the problem of law simplification. In *Lectures on Legal Topics.* New York: Macmillan, 1924, p. 209.

Tate, Albert. The judge as a person. *Louisiana Law Rev.*, 1958, 19, 438-447.

Yankwich, Leon R. The art of being a judge. *Univer. of Penn. Law Rev.*, 1957, 105, 374-389.

See also, Van Koppen & Ten Kate, *Individual Differences in Judicial Behavior: Personal Characteristics and Private Law Decision-Making,* 18 Law & Soc'y Rev. 225-247 (1984).

12. PULLING IT ALL TOGETHER

The previous chapters concerning appellate briefs have dealt with (a) the statement of the issues, (b) the statement of the facts, and (c) the argument of law, in a disjointed fashion. For purposes of our detailed examination of the components of a brief, it is probably best to disjoin the brief as was done, but your ultimate goal is to pull the disjointed pieces together into a whole.

Tie Factual Claims to the Record

One of the very important things that has thus far only been alluded to is the necessity of tying factual claims in the statement of facts and the argument of law to the trial record. It is a significant failing to make and rely on factual claims without supporting them with a reference to the page(s) of the transcript of evidence or the trial court record where those facts were proven or admitted. As an example, if in an automobile wreck case the testimony of a bystander is that the road was wet, the north-south traffic light was green, and the defendant's vehicle was moving east at 40 m.p.h., state the facts somewhat in this fashion:

> According to the testimony of Mr. Gee, a bystander, the road was wet (Tr. p. 00). Mr. Aych's automobile was traveling east at 40 m.p.h. (Tr. p. 00) and the traffic light for north-south traffic showed green (Tr. p. 000).

The point to the foregoing example is that bold assertions in your brief of crucial facts are not effective; in order to make your statements of important facts credible, you must support them with specific references to the evidence in the record or transcript. Use such references frequently to back up your statements of the factual elements of your case, just as you cite precedent cases to support your claims of what the law is. If it is true that the statement of facts is, on many occasions, more important than the argument of law, then the references from your statement of facts and argument of law to the facts proven or admitted in the transcript or record are likely to be more important on those occasions than your citations of authorities.

Keep Long Quotations Out of the Brief

Often statutes play a major role in your argument of law. If your case tends to revolve around a statute, or several statutes, you may quote short statutes in your argument of law. If the statute is lengthy, set the statute out in a supplement which is appended at the back of your brief.

Similarly, if your case tends to center upon a written document which is a part of the facts, quote the pertinent provisions in your brief, if the pertinent provisions are concise. If the pertinent provisions are long, do not clutter your brief with a long quotation. Instead, paraphrase the provisions and set the longer quotation out in a supplement appended to the back of your brief.

When you rely on a supplement at the back of your brief, make appropriate references to the supplement from the statement of facts or the argument of law, as the case may be, so that your message is understandable. As an example, you could say:

> The appropriate statute relevant to disputes of this type is ——. See verbatim copy, Supplement, p. 00. Its application here is that . . . .

Furnish the Procedural Posture

Early in your brief, in a short portion in front of the statement of facts labeled *Statement of the Case,* give the court an answer to its ever-present question regarding each case that comes before it: "How did this case get here?" Succinctly describe the procedural posture of the case, in five or ten lines, indicating who initiated the lawsuit, which party is appealing, what kind of decision in the lower court is being appealed from, and giving enough other essential information that the court understands what relief is sought and what its purpose is in hearing the case.

The scope of review which you consider applicable to the appeal is an important part of your case. The court wants to know what you believe to be the grounds which it can apply to grant you the relief that you request, *e.g.,* prejudicial error, plain error, or abuse of discretion. Furnish this information in your *Statement of the Case.*

Spelling and Accuracy Count

Not infrequently a student will ask, "Does spelling count?" Of course spelling counts. Frequent misspelling, poor punctuation, errors in citations, and improper citation form tend to lessen the writer's credibility.

"What the brief writer actually meant will ordinarily shine through the obscurantism of possible ineptness, and the distraction is only mild. Yet, there is a gnawing feeling on occasion that the obviousness of the uncorrected errors indicates that the brief, having not been read for these errors, may be equally unreliable in its substantive reasoning or its analysis of authorities," says Judge Wilbur F. Pell, Jr., Judge of the United States Court of Appeals for the Seventh Circuit.[1]

There is a constant need for brief writers to closely proofread their intended final drafts. It is especially important that there be a final check of citations. If the citations are inaccurate they will raise doubts and cause the reader to be irritated. If you want the case which you cite to be read, furnish an accurate and complete citation so that your reader can find it easily; do not depend upon your reader to hunt for the correct citation, when you have not taken the trouble to verify it.[2]

Write Short and Simple Sentences

Lawyers, paralegals, and students are exposed to a lot of examples of poor writing. Much of the material in digests and *A.L.R.* is made up of unnecessarily long sentences that are difficult to comprehend. Lawyers, paralegals, and students may tend to emulate, paraphrase, or even quote the examples so provided. Some persons may believe that the use of long and complicated sentences is a hallmark of an educated writer.

A judicial research aide in an intermediate state court of appeals says that most of the briefs submitted are too long, too disorganized, and too poorly written. She says that they should be truly brief, to the point, well-written, organized, and devoid of irrelevant facts and legalese. A sentence longer than three lines is probably too long.[3]

A judge who has read many briefs says "tell it short and plain." "Tell it once — or twice at most," he says.[4] He also recommends Strunk & White as a guide to writing style.[5]

---

[1] Pell, *Read Before Signing,* 66 A.B.A. J. 977 (1980).

[2] For a collection of typographical errors, misnomers, and misstatements found in briefs, see Pell, *Id.*

[3] Daire, *From the Inside Looking Out to the Outside Looking In,* 58 Fla. B.J. 517-518 (1984).

[4] Godbold, *Twenty Pages and Twenty Minutes: Effective Advocacy on Appeal,* 30 Sw. L.J. 801, 811, 816 (1976).

[5] W. Strunk & E. White, *The Elements of Style* (3d ed. 1979). 92 p., Macmillan Pub. Co., N.Y.

Keep the Issues Few

There is an apparent consensus among judges and lawyers that you can damage your case by including too many issues. Most of them recommend three or less issues. Some say that if you include too many issues, you dilute your good issues with issues that are not good. Others say that when reading a brief with lots of issues, the reader receives the connotation that the writer is insecure or merely arguing hit-or-miss. One judge says that you should not obscure the crucial issues "by concealing them amid a thicket of minor or subsidiary claims."[6]

The Ethics of Advocacy

There are two codes of ethics for the legal profession which concern advocacy. The principal code, called the *Code of Professional Responsibility,* was adopted by the House of Delegates of the American Bar Association to be effective January 1, 1970; it has been adopted by and is presently in effect in nearly all of the state courts. The other code, called the *Model Rules of Professional Conduct,* was adopted by the House of Delegates of the American Bar Association on August 2, 1983; hearings are being held in various states concerning whether to adopt the *Model Rules* but few adoptions of it by the states have occurred so far.

CODE OF PROFESSIONAL RESPONSIBILITY [7]

(Selected portions; footnotes omitted).

CANON 7

A Lawyer Should Represent a Client Zealously
Within the Bounds of the Law

ETHICAL CONSIDERATIONS

EC 7-1 The duty of a lawyer, both to his client and to the legal system, is to represent his client zealously within the bounds of the law, which includes Disciplinary Rules and enforceable professional regulations. The professional responsibility of a lawyer derives from his membership in a profession which has the duty of assisting members of the public to secure and protect available legal rights and benefits. In our government of laws and not of men, each member of our society is entitled to have his conduct judged and regulated in accordance with the law, to seek any lawful objective through legally permissible means, and to present for adjudication any lawful claim, issue, or defense.

---

[6] Bright, *Appellate Briefwriting: Some "Golden" Rules,* 17 Creighton L. Rev. 1069 (1983-1984).

[7] Copyright 1971 by the American Bar Assocation.

EC 7-2 The bounds of the law in a given case are often difficult to ascertain. The language of legislative enactments and judicial opinions may be uncertain as applied to varying factual situations. The limits and specific meaning of apparently relevant law may be made doubtful by changing or developing constitutional interpretations, inadequately expressed statutes or judicial opinions, and changing public and judicial attitudes. Certainty of law ranges from well-settled rules through areas of conflicting authority to areas without precedent.

EC 7-3 Where the bounds of law are uncertain, the action of a lawyer may depend on whether he is serving as advocate or adviser. A lawyer may serve simultaneously as both advocate and adviser, but the two roles are essentially different. In asserting a position on behalf of his client, an advocate for the most part deals with past conduct and must take the facts as he finds them. By contrast, a lawyer serving as adviser primarily assists his client in determining the course of future conduct and relationships. While serving as advocate, a lawyer should resolve in favor of his client doubts as to the bounds of the law. In serving a client as adviser, a lawyer in appropriate circumstances should give his professional opinion as to what the ultimate decisions of the courts would likely be as to the applicable law.

Duty of the Lawyer to a Client

EC 7-4 The advocate may urge any permissible construction of the law favorable to his client, without regard to his professional opinion as to the likelihood that the construction will ultimately prevail. His conduct is within the bounds of the law, and therefore permissible, if the position taken is supported by the law or is supportable by a good faith argument for an extension, modification, or reversal of the law. However, a lawyer is not justified in asserting a position in litigation that is frivolous.

* * *

EC 7-10 The duty of a lawyer to represent his client with zeal does not militate against his concurrent obligation to treat with consideration all persons involved in the legal process and to avoid the infliction of needless harm.

* * *

EC 7-13 The responsibility of a public prosecutor differs from that of the usual advocate; his duty is to seek justice, not merely to convict. This special duty exists because: (1) the prosecutor represents the sovereign and therefore should use restraint in the discretionary exercise of governmental powers, such as in the selection of cases to prosecute; (2) during trial the prosecutor is not only an advocate but he also may make decisions normally made by an individual client, and those affecting the public interest should be fair to all; and (3) in our system of criminal justice the accused is to be given the benefit of all reasonable doubts. With respect to evidence and witnesses, the prosecutor has responsibilities different from those of a lawyer in private practice: the prosecutor should make timely disclosure to the defense of available evidence, known to him, that tends to negate the guilt of the accused, mitigate the degree of the offense, or reduce the punishment. Further, a prosecutor should not intentionally avoid pursuit of evidence merely because he believes it will damage the prosecutor's case or aid the accused.

EC 7-14 A government lawyer who has discretionary power relative to litigation should refrain from instituting or continuing litigation that is obviously unfair. A government lawyer not having such discretionary power who believes there is lack of merit in a controversy submitted to him should so advise his superiors and recommend the avoidance of unfair litigation. A government lawyer in a civil action or administrative proceeding has the responsibility to seek justice and to develop a full and fair record, and he should not use his position or the economic power of the government to harass parties or to bring about unjust settlements or results.

* * *

EC 7-23 The complexity of law often makes it difficult for a tribunal to be fully informed unless the pertinent law is presented by the lawyers in the cause. A tribunal that is fully informed on the applicable law is better able to make a fair and accurate determination of the matter before it. The adversary system contemplates that each lawyer will present and argue the existing law in the light most favorable to his client. Where a lawyer knows of legal authority in the controlling jurisdiction directly adverse to the position of his client, he should inform the tribunal of its existence unless his adversary has done so; but, having made such disclosure, he may challenge its soundness in whole or in part.

* * *

DISCIPLINARY RULES

DR 7-101 Representing a Client Zealously.

(A) A lawyer shall not intentionally:

(1) Fail to seek the lawful objectives of his client through reasonably available means permitted by law and the Disciplinary Rules, except as provided by DR 7-101(B). A lawyer does not violate this Disciplinary Rule, however, by acceding to reasonable requests of opposing counsel which do not prejudice the rights of his client, by being punctual in fulfilling all professional commitments, by avoiding offensive tactics, or by treating with courtesy and consideration all persons involved in the legal process.

(2) Fail to carry out a contract of employment entered into with a client for professional services, but he may withdraw as permitted under DR 2-110, DR 5-102, and DR 5-105.

(3) Prejudice or damage his client during the course of the professional relationship, except as required under DR 7-102(B).

(B) In his representation of a client, a lawyer may:

(1) Where permissible, exercise his professional judgment to waive or fail to assert a right or position of his client.

(2) Refuse to aid or participate in conduct that he believes to be unlawful, even though there is some support for an argument that the conduct is legal.

DR 7-102 Representing a Client Within the Bounds of the Law.

(A) In his representation of a client, a lawyer shall not:

(1) File a suit, assert a position, conduct a defense, delay a trial, or take other action on behalf of his client when he knows or when it is obvious that such action would serve merely to harass or maliciously injure another.

(2) Knowingly advance a claim or defense that is unwarranted under existing law, except that he may advance such claim or defense if it can be supported by good faith argument for an extension, modification, or reversal of existing law.

(3) Conceal or knowingly fail to disclose that which he is required by law to reveal.

(4) Knowingly use perjured testimony or false evidence.

(5) Knowingly make a false statement of law or fact.

(6) Participate in the creation or preservation of evidence when he knows or it is obvious that the evidence is false.

(7) Counsel or assist his client in conduct that the lawyer knows to be illegal or fraudulent.

(8) Knowingly engage in other illegal conduct or conduct contrary to a Disciplinary Rule.

(B) A lawyer who receives information clearly establishing that:

(1) His client has, in the course of the representation, perpetrated a fraud upon a person or tribunal shall promptly call upon his client to rectify the same, and if his client refuses or is unable to do so, he shall reveal the fraud to the affected person or tribunal.

(2) A person other than his client has perpetrated a fraud upon a tribunal shall promptly reveal the fraud to the tribunal.

DR 7-103 Performing the Duty of Public Prosecutor or Other Government Lawyer.

(A) A public prosecutor or other government lawyer shall not institute or cause to be instituted criminal charges when he knows or it is obvious that the charges are not supported by probable cause.

(B) A public prosecutor or other government lawyer in criminal litigation shall make timely disclosure to counsel for the defendant, or to the defendant if he has no counsel, of the existence of evidence, known to the prosecutor or other government lawyer, that tends to negate the guilt of the accused, mitigate the degree of the offense, or reduce the punishment.

* * *

DR 7-106 Trial Conduct.

(A) A lawyer shall not disregard or advise his client to disregard a standing rule of a tribunal or a ruling of a tribunal made in the course of a proceeding, but he may take appropriate steps in good faith to test the validity of such rule or ruling.

(B) In presenting a matter to a tribunal, a lawyer shall disclose:

(1) Legal authority in the controlling jurisdiction known to him to be directly adverse to the position of his client and which is not disclosed by opposing counsel.

(2) Unless privileged or irrelevant, the identities of the clients he represents and of the persons who employed him.

(C) In appearing in his professional capacity before a tribunal, a lawyer shall not:

(1) State or allude to any matter that he has no reasonable basis to believe is relevant to the case or that will not be supported by admissible evidence.

(2) Ask any question that he has no reasonable basis to believe is relevant to the case and that is intended to degrade a witness or other person.

(3) Assert his personal knowledge of the facts in issue, except when testifying as a witness.

(4) Assert his personal opinion as to the justness of a cause, as to the credibility of a witness, as to the culpability of a civil litigant, or as to the guilt or innocence of an accused, but he may argue, on his analysis of the evidence, for any position or conclusion with respect to the matters stated herein.

(5) Fail to comply with known local customs of courtesy or practice of the bar or a particular tribunal without giving to opposing counsel timely notice of his intent not to comply.

(6) Engage in undignified or discourteous conduct which is degrading to a tribunal.

(7) Intentionally or habitually violate any established rule of procedure or of evidence.

* * *

In an official footnote to DR 7-106(B)(1), the *Code of Professional Responsibility* says:

"In the brief summary in the 1947 edition of the Committee's decisions (p. 17), *Opinion 146* was thus summarized: *Opinion 146* — A lawyer should disclose to the court a decision directly adverse to his client's case that is unknown to his adversary.

. . . .

"We would not confine the Opinion to 'controlling authorities' — i.e., those decisive of the pending case — but, in accordance with the tests hereafter suggested, would apply it to a decision directly adverse to any proposition of law on which the lawyer expressly relies, which would reasonably be considered important by the judge sitting on the case.

. . . .

". . . The test in every case should be: Is the decision which opposing counsel has overlooked one which the court should clearly consider in deciding the case? Would a reasonable judge properly feel that a lawyer who advanced, as the law, a proposition adverse to the undisclosed decision, was lacking in candor and fairness to him? Might the judge consider himself misled by an implied representation that the lawyer know of no adverse authority?" *ABA Opinion* 280 (1949).

* * *

MODEL RULES OF PROFESSIONAL CONDUCT[8]

(Selected portions; Comments and Code Comparisons omitted).

* * *

CLIENT-LAWYER RELATIONSHIP

RULE 1.1 Competence

A lawyer shall provide competent representation to a client. Competent representation requires the legal knowledge, skill, thoroughness and preparation reasonably necessary for the representation.

RULE 1.2 Scope of Representation

(a) A lawyer shall abide by a client's decisions concerning the objectives of representation, subject to paragraphs (c), (d) and (e), and shall consult with the client as to the means by which they are to be pursued. A lawyer shall abide by a client's decision whether to accept an offer of settlement of a matter. In a criminal case, the lawyer shall abide by the client's decision, after consultation with the lawyer, as to a plea to be entered, whether to waive jury trial and whether the client will testify.

---

[8]Copyright 1983 by the American Bar Association.

(b) A lawyer's representation of a client, including representation by appointment, does not constitute an endorsement of the client's political, economic, social or moral views or activities.

(c) A lawyer may limit the objectives of the representation if the client consents after consultation.

(d) A lawyer shall not counsel a client to engage, or assist a client, in conduct that the lawyer knows is criminal or fraudulent, but a lawyer may discuss the legal consequences of any proposed course of conduct with a client and may counsel or assist a client to make a good faith effort to determine the validity, scope, meaning or application of the law.

(e) When a lawyer knows that a client expects assistance not permitted by the rules of professional conduct or other law, the lawyer shall consult with the client regarding the relevant limitations on the lawyer's conduct.

RULE 1.3 Diligence

A lawyer shall act with reasonable diligence and promptness in representing a client.

* * *

RULE 1.6 Confidentiality of Information

(a) A lawyer shall not reveal information relating to representation of a client unless the client consents after consultation, except for disclosures that are impliedly authorized in order to carry out the representation, and except as stated in paragraph (b).

(b) A lawyer may reveal such information to the extent the lawyer reasonably believes necessary:

(1) to prevent the client from commiting a criminal act that the lawyer believes is likely to result in imminent death or substantial bodily harm; or

(2) to establish a claim or defense on behalf of the lawyer in a controversy between the lawyer and the client, to establish a defense to a criminal charge or civil claim against the lawyer based upon conduct in which the client was involved, or to respond to allegations in any proceeding concerning the lawyer's representation of the client.

* * *

ADVOCATE

RULE 3.1 Meritorious Claims and Contentions

A lawyer shall not bring or defend a proceeding, or assert or controvert an issue therein, unless there is a basis for doing so that is not frivolous, which includes a good faith argument for an extension, modification or reversal of existing law. A lawyer for the defendent in a criminal proceeding, or the respondent in a proceeding that could result in incarceration, may nevertheless so defend the proceeding as to require that every element of the case be established.

RULE 3.2 Expediting Litigation

A lawyer shall make reasonable efforts to expedite litigation consistent with the interests of the client.

RULE 3.3 Candor Toward the Tribunal

(a) A lawyer shall not knowingly:

(1) make a false statement of material fact or law to a tribunal;

(2) fail to disclose a material fact to a tribunal when disclosure is necessary to avoid assisting a criminal or fraudulent act by the client;

(3) fail to disclose to the tribunal legal authority in the controlling jurisdiction known to the lawyer to be directly adverse to the position of the client and not disclosed by opposing counsel; or

(4) offer evidence that the lawyer knows to be false. If a lawyer has offered material evidence and comes to know of its falsity, the lawyer shall take reasonable remedial measures.

(b) The duties stated in paragraph (a) continue to the conclusion of the proceeding, and apply even if compliance requires disclosure of information otherwise protected by Rule 1.6.

(c) A lawyer may refuse to offer evidence that the lawyer reasonably believes is false.

(d) In an ex parte proceeding, a lawyer shall inform the tribunal of all material facts known to the lawyer which will enable the tribunal to make an informed decision, whether or not the facts are adverse.

RULE 3.4 Fairness to Opposing Party and Counsel

A lawyer shall not:

(a) unlawfully obstruct another party's access to evidence or unlawfully alter, destroy or conceal a document or other material having potential evidentiary value. A lawyer shall not counsel or assist another person to do any such act;

(b) falsify evidence, counsel or assist a witness to testify falsely, or offer an inducement to a witness that is prohibited by law;

(c) knowingly disobey an obligation under the rules of a tribunal except for an open refusal based on an assertion that no valid obligation exists;

(d) in pretrial procedure, make a frivolous discovery request or fail to make reasonably diligent effort to comply with a legally proper discovery request by an opposing party;

(e) in trial, allude to any matter that the lawyer does not reasonably believe is relevant or that will not be supported by admissible evidence, assert personal knowledge of facts in issue except when testifying as a witness, or state a personal opinion as to the justness of a cause, the credibility of a witness, the culpability of a civil litigant or the guilt or innocence of an accused; or

(f) request a person other than a client to refrain from voluntarily giving relevant information to another party unless:

(1) the person is a relative or an employee or other agent of a client; and

(2) the lawyer reasonably believes that the person's interests will not be adversely affected by refraining from giving such information.

RULE 3.5 Impartiality and Decorum of the Tribunal

A lawyer shall not:

(a) seek to influence a judge, juror, prospective juror or other official by means prohibited by law;

(b) communicate ex parte with such a person except as permitted by law; or

(c) engage in conduct intended to disrupt a tribunal.

* * *

RULE 3.8 Special Responsibilities of a Prosecutor

The prosecutor in a criminal case shall:

(a) refrain from prosecuting a charge that the prosecutor knows is not supported by probable cause;

(b) make reasonable efforts to assure that the accused has been advised of the right to, and the procedure for obtaining, counsel and has been given reasonable opportunity to obtain counsel;

(c) not seek to obtain from an unrepresented accused a waiver of important pretrial rights, such as the right to a preliminary hearing;

(d) make timely disclosure to the defense of all evidence or information known to the prosecutor that tends to negate the guilt of the accused or mitigates the offense, and, in connection with sentencing, disclose to the defense and to the tribunal all unprivileged mitigating information known to the prosecutor, except when the prosecutor is relieved of this responsibility by a protective order of the tribunal; and

(e) exercise reasonable care to prevent investigators, law enforcement personnel, employees or other persons assisting or associated with the prosecutor in a criminal case from making an extrajudicial statement that the prosecutor would be prohibited from making under Rule 3.6.

RULE 3.9 Advocate in Nonadjudicative Proceedings

A lawyer representing a client before a legislative or administrative tribunal in a nonadjudicative proceeding shall disclose that the appearance is in a representative capacity and shall conform to the provisions of Rules 3.3(a) through (c), 3.4(a) through (c), and 3.5.

*   *   *

OTHER THAN CLIENTS

RULE 4.1 Truthfulness in Statements to Others

In the course of representing a client a lawyer shall not knowingly:

(a) make a false statement of material fact or law to a third person; or

(b) fail to disclose a material fact to a third person when disclosure is necessary to avoid assisting a criminal or fraudulent act by a client, unless disclosure is prohibited by Rule 1.6.

*   *   *

RULE 4.4 Respect for Rights of Third Persons

In representing a client, a lawyer shall not use means that have no substantial purpose other than to embarrass, delay, or burden a third person, or use methods of obtaining evidence that violate the legal rights of such a person.

*   *   *

In the Comment to Rule 3.3, the *Model Rules of Professional Conduct* say:

*   *   *

Misleading Legal Argument

Legal argument based on a knowingly false representation of law constitutes dishonesty toward the tribunal. A lawyer is not required to make a disinterested exposition of the law, but must recognize the existence of pertinent legal authorities. Furthermore, as stated in paragraph (a)(3), an advocate has a duty to disclose directly adverse authority in the controlling jurisdiction which has not been disclosed by the opposing party. The underlying concept is that legal argument is a discussion seeking to determine the legal premises properly applicable to the case.

*   *   *

Cincinnati Chapter of the Federal Bar Association, Practitioner's Handbook for Appeals to the U.S. Court of Appeals for the Sixth Circuit 36-40 (J. Aug, H. Rosen & G. Ruehlman) (1971) [9]

[9]This useful *Handbook* has been revised three times and is in its fourth edition, published May, 1984. The 98-page, paperback fourth edition may be obtained for $1 per copy from the Office of the Clerk, U.S. Court of Appeals for the Sixth Circuit, Room 524 U.S. Post Office and Courthouse, Cincinnati, Ohio 45202.

WRITING A BRIEF

* * *

Importance of a Good Brief

It is the duty of the Court to do substantial justice in deciding the appeals before it. But the judges must necessarily rely on the opposing advocates to make them aware of the equities of the particular case, and to point out the facts of record and applicable rules of law that compel a just decision. Success in persuading the Court to decide in one's favor is more likely to follow from an effective and carefully prepared brief and argument than from a perfunctory presentation.

In writing the brief one must bear in mind that when it is read in advance of oral argument, as in the Sixth Circuit, it is the first step in persuasion. After argument it is a reminder of the points made orally and is capable of serving as the basis of an opinion.

In general, the appellant's brief should contain all that the judges will want to know, together with reference to whatever else they may need to consult in the record or in the precedents. Where the record is voluminous a supplement to the brief which indexes and digests the more important testimony may be of great help to the Court.

The appellee's brief should also contain all that the judges may need to know. While Fed. R. App. P. 28(b) provides that the appellee need not make any statement of the case unless he controverts that of the appellant, the appellee should give his own account except in those rare cases where there is no dispute on the facts and how they should be evaluated. A well-written statement of the facts is by itself the strongest argument of the law. There are, therefore, very few cases where the appellee can with safety leave this weapon solely to his adversary.

Essentials for an Effective Brief

To be effective, a brief should contain the following:

1. A succinct statement of how the case got to the Court, the basis of the Court's jurisdiction, what the court below did and who the judge was. This is a good place to orient the Court to the justice of your position by a terse preliminary indication of what was wrong below (if appellant) or why the lower court was right (if appellee).

2. Next, a statement of the question or questions upon which the appeal turns. This requires careful selection and choice of language. The main issue should be stressed and an effort made to present no more than two or three questions. The questions selected should be stated clearly and simply.

3. The brief should set forth the pertinent parts of such statutes as are involved with appropriate reference to the United States Code in the case of federal statutes. If these are voluminous they should be incorporated in a supplement to the brief. An increasing number of federal appeals depend in whole or in part on statutes and their interpretation.

4. There should be set forth a concise and objective account of the pertinent facts, with references to the appendix, or to the record, as the case may be to support each statement so that it may easily be verified. The statement should be a narrative chronological summary, rather than a digest of what each witness said. Relevant unfavorable facts should not be omitted or slighted. This factual statement is the most important part of the brief from the standpoint of the judges. Great care should be taken that the facts are well marshalled and stated. If this is done the facts themselves will develop the relevant and governing points of law. An effective statement summarizes the facts so that the reader is persuaded that justice and the precedents both require a decision for the avocate's client.

5. The factual statement, if more than a page or so in length, should be suitably broken up by appropriate headings which emphasize the flow and thrust of the statement. Nothing is more discouraging to the judicial eye than a great expanse of print with no guideposts and little paragraphing. Short paragraphs with topic sentences and frequent headings and subheadings assure that the Court will follow and understand the points that are being made.

6. Next follows the argument which should be suitably broken up into the main points. These points should have argumentative headings which relate the points of law to the facts of the case. Where necessary there should be argumentative subheadings. The body of the argument should consist of a reasoned discussion of the evidence and the relevant authorities. Several good cases in point, with a sufficient discussion of their facts to show how they are relevant, are much to be preferred over a profusion of citations. Quotations should be used sparingly and only if there is some explanation of the facts of the case which will show that the quotation is clearly in point. If a case is worth citing, it usually has a quote which will drive the point home, and one or two good cases are ordinarily sufficient. If the case cited does not have a good quote, a terse summary in a sentence or two will show the court that that is a case the court should read. A long discussion of the facts of the cases cited is usually not needed, except where there is a precedent so closely in point that it must be distinguished if the party is to prevail. What the Court wants to learn from the brief primarily are the facts of the case stated as succinctly and clearly as possible. If this is done, the rules of law desired to be applied may appear so obvious that extended discussion of the law is unnecessary.

* * *

Where precedents on a point are lacking or are uncertain, the brief must, of course, reason by analogy and in such cases references to and quotations from law reviews and legal writers are permissible and desirable.

Obviously the brief writer must select what is important and deal only with that: this requires that all that is not necessary should be ruthlessly discarded. Except in unusually complicated cases, a brief which treats more than three or four matters runs serious risk of becoming too diffused and giving the overall impression that no one claimed error can be very serious. Appellee's brief, in its turn, should squarely meet the appellant's points. The same care should be taken by the appellee to avoid diffusion and also present all substantial additional arguments available in support of the judgment below.

7. While the brief should be written with attention to style and interest, clarity and simplicity are the paramount considerations. Italics and footnotes should be used sparingly. Above all, accuracy is imperative in statements, record references, citations and quotations.

*　*　*

Instructor's Emphasis

Each Appellate Advocacy instructor is likely to differ in opinion concerning the proper amount of emphasis or weight to be placed on brief writing in relation to oral argument, and concerning the portions of a brief which should receive the most emphasis. Such a decision is, of course, a matter of professional opinion. The following represents your author's opinion regarding this matter, but each teacher is likely to make variations in it.

Not less than 60 per cent of the grade in the course should be based on the student's performance on the final draft of the written brief. The matters to be considered in evaluating each brief are as follows:

Statement of Issues

1. Stands Alone
2. Reasonable Length
3. Pertinent Facts
4. Persuasiveness
5. Makes the Point

Statement of the Case

Statement of Facts

1. Interesting
2. Accuracy and Candor
3. Reasonable Length
4. References to Record
5. Persuasiveness

Argument of Law

1. Headings and Subheadings
2. Use of Facts

3. Persuasiveness
4. Rational Arguments

Use of Precedent

1. Case Law as Primary Authority
2. Secondary Authority in Supporting Role
3. Distinguishing and Reconciliation

Form

1. Submitted on Time
2. Neatness
3. Uniform System of Citation

The entire purpose of your brief is to persuade the reader to accept the arguments advanced by you and to reject your opponent's arguments. Each brief must undertake to persuade the reader that its arguments are the best of two or more alternatives. It is only this characteristic that makes a brief a valuable working instrument.

General Rules Relating to Form of Briefs for Student Work[10]

1) Briefs need not contain a formal statement of jurisdiction.

2) Briefs should approximate a length of 20 pages, including the statement of the issues, the statement of the case, the statement of the facts and the argument of law, but excluding the cover, the table of points and authorities, and the supplement, if any.

3) Citations must conform to *A Uniform System of Citation. See* CHAPTER 2.

4) Briefs shall be typewritten, double-spaced, with black ribbon on 8½″ x 11″ unglazed, opaque, white paper. Right and left margins shall be 1½″. The brief must be assembled as one unit and bound on the left with staples or the equivalent. No special folders or binders should be used.

5) Order of assembly of briefs:

a) Cover
b) Table of Points and Authorities
c) Foreword (optional)
d) Statement of Issues

---

[10] These rules are especially drafted to help students know what is expected of them in their Appellate Advocacy course. They are mostly adopted from various official rules of court. Students who later encounter the official rules of the various appellate courts are likely to find those official rules reminiscent of these rules.

e) Statement of the Case
f) Statement of Facts
g) Argument of Law
h) Conclusion
i) Supplement (optional)

6) Each brief must contain a statement of the issues. Usually, the appellee or respondent will disagree with the statement of issues proposed by the appellant or petitioner, and will responsively reject it, submitting his or her own statement of the issues for consideration by the court. *See* CHAPTER 9.

7) The table of points and authorities should set forth in outline form with page references: (a) the main headings of the brief; (b) all subdivisions or subheadings thereof; and (c) under the main heading, "Argument," each separate point discussed with all authorities cited in support thereof subjoined with page references.

8) Each brief shall have a typewritten cover, stating thereon:

a) Court where the brief is filed, *e.g.,* "In the Supreme Court of ..."
b) Name of the case.
c) Whether the brief is filed for appellants or appellees, petitioners or respondents.
d) That the case is on: Certiorari to ...; or Appeal from ... (name of court below).
e) On lower right side: Name of counsel, course, section, date due, and designation of the party represented, *e.g.,* Counsel for Petitioner.
f) On lower left side: A signed statement of counsel that service upon opposing counsel has been made of a copy of the brief.[11]

9) The brief may contain any foreword or supplement, or both, which is appropriate to the argument.

10) The brief shall have a conclusion which in a few lines states what counsel wants the reviewing court to do.

11) The statement of the case should begin with the salutation, "May it please the Court:". The conclusion should end with "Respectfully submitted," immediately above the name of the writer.[12]

12) The statement of the case indicates briefly the nature of the lawsuit, the course of prior proceedings, the disposition of the lawsuit in the court below, and the scope of review. It should answer this question for the appellate judges: "How did this case get here?"

13) The statement of facts and argument of law should have appropriate references to the record. See CHAPTER 10: THE FACTS WIN THE CASE.

---

[11] This provision should be optional with the instructor. It is usually a requirement of court rules, however.

[12] These courtesies are a matter of style, not a mandate of rule or law. They are common in many courts and localities, and unknown in others.

14) The argument of law must contain the contentions of the party filing the brief with respect to the issues stated, the reasons therefor, and citations to the statutes, precedent cases, and other authorities. See CHAPTER 11: ARGUING THE LAW.

15) Counsel should avoid references to parties by such designations as "appellant" and "appellee." It promotes clarity to use descriptive terms such as "the employee," "the injured person," "the taxpayer," "the buyer," "the seller," or the actual names of parties.

The Evolution of a Brief

"Good legal writing is mostly rewriting." Bright, *Appellate Briefwriting: Some "Golden Rules,"* 17 Creighton L. Rev. 1069 (1983-1984).

The advocacy and appellate processes, like most other operations in the practice of law, require successive exercises of very good judgment. Good judgment does not come easily or quickly. If there is any one single point which is the most important in brief writing, it is this: Start early, allow the written work to age and mature, edit it, re-edit it, and continue to revise it.

One author in this field characterizes brief writing as an evolution.[13] An evolution is gradual. It takes time. In this context, evolution is synonymous with development, which likewise is a time-consuming process. In an advocate's quest for resourcefulness, he or she must remember that time is an innovator.

Ideas and inspiration often come from unexpected sources and on unanticipated occasions. A saturated familiarity with relevant precedent cases, treatises, and legal periodicals is imperative to stimulate resourcefulness. Scholarly social, economic, and other writings other than legal materials will occasionally be of assistance in this regard.

Unless the framework, and a lot of the building material of the brief are already in place, an advocate cannot perceive where the reinforcement, refinishing, and polishing are needed. He or she must allow ample time for the fog to lift[14] and for the evolution to reach a stage of excellence.

Persuasive Legal Material

The legal material that appears to be most persuasive to courts is primary material, *i.e.*, (a) reports of recent decisions from the court which is to make the decision or some court that is apt to review the decision, (b) the appropriate state or federal statutes, and (c) the rules of procedure applicable to the case. This is so despite the proliferation of secondary legal materials, *e.g.*, textbooks, treatises, and law review articles.

---

[13] H. Levy, *How to Handle an Appeal*, 727 (1968).

[14] *See* B. Cardozo, *The Paradoxes of Legal Science* 80-81 (1928).

The priorities which the courts seem to assign to the legal literature are as follows:[15]

(a) Higher court cases that appear to control the decision;
(b) Cases from the court where the case is pending;
(c) Out-of-the-jurisdiction cases;
(d) Lower court cases, with those from the same jurisdiction preferred;
(e) Law review discussions.

Opinions among judges vary concerning law review articles and other secondary materials, however. One judge says, "It is always useful and often persuasive to find counsel's position supported by an authoritative treatise or illuminated by law review commentaries and ALR annotations."[16] Another said that a careful judge will look to see whether the subject has been discussed, or the authorities collated and analyzed in a good law periodical; he also noted, however, that some other judges do not concur in this evaluation of law reviews.[17] It is important to remember that regardless of the judges' views concerning law review articles and other secondary material, at best they are only secondary material; they do not displace the precedent cases, statutes, or rules.

An inspection of the current reports of cases will show that there are at least two kinds of opinions. Particularly in the opinions of the United States courts, there is a tendency to cite a profusion of cases and an occasional secondary authority, and issue a long, exhaustive opinion. In other courts, especially state courts, there is a tendency to be succinct, cite a few primary authorities that support the point being made, and end the opinion via summary treatment. It is arguable that the complexity of the issues in the case affect this distinction. But nearly all judges and advocates caution against citing in a brief more than three good cases that support the point that the advocate wishes to make.

Modern cases are the principal authority relied upon by today's courts. It is probably fair to say that, in the main, the older the case the more it is suspect. As an example, a survey of twelve months of opinions in one state indicated that 134 cases cited reports of local state cases decided after 1951, and only twenty-three of the cases cited reports of the local state's cases decided in 1951 and before.[18] The ratio of use was nearly 6 to 1. Citations of out-of-state, state cases were only occasional.

In the decisions published by the courts, the role of secondary material is almost nonexistent by comparison. *American Jurisprudence 2d* is probably the most-frequently-relied-upon secondary source, and *Corpus Juris Secundum* is cited, too. As is stated previously, however, their best use is to find cases or

---

[15] Godbold, *Twenty Pages and Twenty Minutes: Effective Advocacy on Appeal,* 30 Sw. L.J. 801, 818 (1976).

[16] Tate, *The Art of Brief Writing: What a Judge Wants to Read,* 4 Litigation 11, 15 (No. 2, Winter 1978).

[17] Hughes, *Foreword,* 50 Yale L.J. 737 (1940-1941).

[18] Gilmer, *Decision-Making Literature,* 47 Ky. Bench & B. 45 (No. 3, July 1983).

obtain an overview of the law, not to cite them as authority. From there on, the role of secondary authority diminishes greatly. Local state practice books, *A.L.R.*, the *Restatements,* and nationally recognized treatises such as Corbin, McCormick, McQuillen, Prosser, and Wigmore receive a small bit of weight.

The indication from all of this is likely to be that primary authority such as constitutions, statutes, modern reports of cases, and the rules of procedure are the most persuasive. Do not conclude, however, that other legal literature is not useful. Merely recognize that it is not the material most likely to persuade a court to rule in your client's favor. Nearly all law books have their uses and are important in their proper place. Many law books and legal periodicals which are not mentioned in the opinions are important to find the cases that the courts want to know about, discover various new theories and arguments that you can use, and obtain an overview of new and unfamiliar topics.

Collateral Reference

Readers who wish to examine copies of briefs filed in the U.S. Supreme Court may consult *CIS Law Reprints,* published at Bethesda, Maryland, by Congressional Information Service.

Sample Portions of a Brief

The following portions of a brief are presented for the purpose of illustrating particular features. The remarks in the margins indicate the matters which are being illustrated.

* * *

Statement of Issues

Issue I

A lessee took possession of real property and allied personal property under two leases which did not limit the uses to which the property could be put, provided that the personal property might be abandoned if the lessee so chose, and provided that repairs, maintenance, alterations, additions, or improvements would be made by lessee, if they were made, except that lessor would be responsible for the exterior roof. The lessee elected to use the property for meat packing. After more than three years' occupancy and use of the property by lessee for meat packing purposes, government inspectors determined that if the lessee desired to continue to use that property for such purposes, substantial physical changes would have to be made in the property. The lessee elected not to make the changes, abandoned the property, and refused to pay the rent agreed to in the lease.

Succinctly state in the issues the crucial facts as viewed by your side. In this part of the issues, the pivotal portion of the lengthy written lease is paraphrased.

Other crucial facts in the case are condensed into the statement of the issue.

Is the lessee justified in abandoning the property and failing to pay the rent, which it obligated itself to do under the lease?

Issue II

Paraphrase the important facts in the written agreement, as viewed from your client's side of the dispute.

After the willful abandonment and breach of the leases by the lessee, the lessors elected to terminate the leases pursuant to the express provisions of the leases, which provided that the lessee could not avail itself of those provisions in order to avoid payment of the rental in the event of a willful breach.

Do the lessors' elections to terminate the leases preclude the lessors from recovering damages in full resulting from such a breach?

* * *

A salutation should precede the main portion of the brief immediatley before the Statement of the Facts.

May it please the Court:

Counterstatement of Facts

The two leases at issue here were both executed by Green Packing Company, as lessee. One was a lease of a tract of property fronting on the east side of South Second Street in Megalopolis, Kentucky, of which Brown Packing Company was lessor. The other was a lease of property contiguous to the above mentioned tract, of which Walter J. Brown was the lessor. In the first mentioned instrument, there were also leased some plant and refrigeration equipment, listed in the lease. In the second mentioned instrument, there were also leased some items of equipment called poultry-house property. Lessors and lessees also executed addenda to each lease.

Most notably, the following provisions, and lack of provisions, are characteristic of each lease:

(a) There are no restrictions upon the uses which lessee may choose to make of the leased property.

(b) There are no representations, warranties, or promises that the lessee will be able to obtain or retain any permit, license, or authorization to conduct any particular business on the property.

Support your factual claims with references to the transcript or record. The usual form is (Tr. p. 00, Q. 00).

(c) The lessee promised to repair, maintain, and "etc." the premises; the only similar duty on the lessors was to maintain the exterior roof (Paragraph 5 in each lease).

(d) Alterations, additions, and improvements were contemplated to be the responsibility of the lessee. The lessee agreed that before it undertook alterations, additions, or improvements, it would consult with the lessors, and obtain lessors' written agreements to them (Paragraph 7 in each lease).

Id.

(e) The personal property which was included in the leases was given minor, flexible, roles in these large transactions. Lessee could use it, buy it, replace it with his own, or set it aside and store it. (Paragraph 4, *a* and *b*, in each lease). If the lessee desired to replace any of the personal property and the parties were unable to agree upon the purchase price, lessor was permitted to sell it, retain the proceeds, and not replace it (Paragraph 1, each Addendum).

Id. See other similar examples below.

(f) The leases also had relevant provisions in them concerning damages to the lessors in the event of the breach of the leases. The lessors retained options to declare the leases void, if the lessee, therein called second party, failed to pay the rent as agreed. Lessors exercised those options. In the next sentence, each lease further provided:

"* * * However, the second party may not avail itself of this provision of this lease to avoid payment of the rental as provided herein and shall remain liable therefor in the event of such willful breach of the terms of this lease, subject to credit for such reasonable rental as the lessor may obtain during the remainder of the term. * * *" (Paragraph 2 of each lease).

Direct quotations are not ordinarily favored, but there may be times when it is almost imperative that a short quotation be used in order to make your point.

Plaintiffs allege willful breach by defendants, Green Packing Company, B. J. Green, and Abner East. (Complaint, Paragraph III).

The lessee accepted, and entered into possession of, the respective properties. It held, subleased, and operated them for over three years. A change in the governmental regulations applicable to the meat-packing business, which lessee had elected to conduct on the premises, made the premises unsuitable for the licensing of such a business in that location. Nothing made the premises unsuitable for various other uses to which they might reasonably be devoted, however.

The premises, in part, had been a super market or store in 1948 and for five or more years thereafter (Deposition of Walter J. Brown, p. 3-4, Q. 26-34). The property had also been used, in part, for rental deep-freeze storage (Id., p. 4, Q. 34-36). Two rooms in one of the buildings were rented to Black County, Kentucky, for several years, by both the owner, when he had possession, and by the lessee after it obtained possession of the property under the leases involved in this action. The County paid $150.00 per month to use the rooms to give away commodities and simultaneously store butter in the freezer of the other building. During the entire period that the lessee had possession of the premises which are at issue in this action, the lessee received $150.00 per month for this subletting. (Deposition of B. J. Green, p. 4, Q. 28-31 and p. 5-6, Q. 34-42). The same portion of the property had also been used as a garage and an office (Id., p. 3, Q. 20). There is no claim here that the property could not be reasonably and legally used for a large variety of purposes, including those mentioned above, despite the recent limitations on the unique uses to which lessee wanted to devote it.

With between six and seven years unexpired on its obligation to pay rent for its premises, lessee elected to abandon them after being unsuccessful in its efforts to persuade lessors to make changes in the premises, which the lessors had not obligated themselves to make, and which the lease instruments contemplated would be made by lessee if they were made. Those obligations are described in (c) and (d) above.

* * *

ARGUMENT

I.

THE LESSEE WAS NOT JUSTIFIED IN FAILING TO PAY THE RENT WHICH IT PROMISED TO PAY IN THE LEASE.

Subheadings must be topical and directional. The topic of this subheading is the failure to pay the rent. The direction is that the lessee was not justified in his failure to pay it.

(a) *The Premises are not Untenantable (Untenable).*

Topical and directional.

The lessee has selected the contingency provisions of the lease concerning rights and duties in the event that the premises become untenable, as its suggested release valve. One of the meanings of untenable is not able to be occupied. *Webster's Third New International Dictionary of the English Language* 2512 (P. Gove ed. 1966). In a case involving an earlier use of the term, untenable was viewed as a typographical error for untenantable. *Smith v. Gillen,* 245 S.W. 2d 596 (Ky. 1952). The word untenantable means incapable of being occupied or lived in, according to *Webster's Third New International Dictionary of the English Language* 2512 (P. Gove ed. 1966).

The argument concerning untenability or untenantability has no place in this dispute. In fact, the premises at issue in this case are capable of being occupied. The premises are not untenable or untenantable, because they can be occupied for a great many purposes, despite the government action. Premises which are leased for a specific purpose become untenantable when they cannot be used for the purposes for which they were leased. *Presbyterian Distribution Service v. Chicago Nat'l Bank,* 28 Ill. App. 2d 147, 171 N.E. 2d 86 (1960). If, however, as in this case, the premises were not rented for any specific purpose, and their use is unrestricted, untenantable means not fit to be rented or occupied by a tenant. *Reischmann v. L. N. Hartog Candy Co.,* 132 N.Y.S. 435 (Sup. Ct., App. Term 1911). It means a condition rendering premises unfit for occupation for any worthwhile purpose, J. Ballentine, *Ballentine's Law Dictionary* 1323 (3d ed. 1969). See also quotation, *Brief for Defendant,* bottom of p. 00. There are numerous worthwhile purposes for which the leased premises are fit, and the leases at issue here do not restrict the lessee in its choice of those purposes. Lessee's argument that the provision is ambiguous and that it therefore should be construed against the lessor is not demonstrated. There is no ambiguity. It means what it says, neither more nor less.

Tie the facts mentioned in the argument to the record, as you do in the statement of facts. See other similar examples below.

It is very important to write about the concrete facts of the problem case, as is done in this paragraph. Avoid abstract discussions of legal questions. Distinguish your case from the precedents cited by your opponent, by showing that the facts of the problem case are significantly different from the facts of the precedent.

The lessee's brief talks about precedent cases in which the lessee covenanted to repair, and attempts to demonstrate that the changes required here were more than repairs. Those precedents and arguments fall short of the facts of this case. This lessee made a great many other covenants in addition to a meager promise to repair, the most notable of which are lessee's undertakings to repair, maintain, "etc.", and to consult with lessors and obtain lessor's written agreement to any alterations, additions, or improvements that the lessee makes (Paragraph 5 and 7 in each lease). The lessee's argument in this regard overlooks two important factual features of this case: (a) The lessee's intention to assume the duty of making alterations and improvements, as revealed by the above-mentioned provisions in the leases; and (b) The alterations and improvements were required because of the use which the lessee made of the premises. Each of these features constitute material facts which, standing alone, take this case out of the principle on which lessee seeks to rely. Annot., 22 A.L.R. 3d 521, 537-538 (§ 7, b) and 539-540 (§ 8) (1968).

Lessors vigorously deny the following factual claim, quoted from lessee's brief, which is the core of the lessee's argument:

"Both parties in this action contemplated and intended that these premises would be used for meat packing only." (Brief for Defendant, p. 00).

The lease instruments scrupulously avoid such limitations. An effort to inject them into this case is an attempt to modify the express words of the written agreements. The lessee's own actions in subletting a portion of the premises to Black County, Kentucky, for the distribution of commodities in one building and refrigerated storage in another building for $150.00 per month during the entire period that the lessee held possession contradict that claim.

Vividly point out inaccurate factual claims in the opponent's brief.

The lessee's claim that the property became useless when the state authorities acted ignores the fact that the lessee elected to restrict its use of the property solely to the operations which the state authorities prohibited. Except for uses in connection with such operations, the property remains valuable and serviceable, and, among other uses, could have continued being used for the purposes for which Black County was using it.

(b) *The Facts of this Case Negate any Claim for Relief of Lessee on Account of the Governmental Action.*

Topical and directional.

Governmental activities and regulations have interfered with leases since the founding of this nation, and even before. The courts may have divided somewhat on the question of whether such regulations should relieve the lessees of their responsibilities, but Kentucky firmly holds that they do not excuse performance. In *Frazier v. Collins,* 300 Ky. 18, 187 S.W. 2d 816 (1945), a lessee sued his lessor to have his lease modified so as to provide for a smaller monthly rental, on account of newly imposed federal wartime restrictions on the sale of gasoline and tires. The Court did not view the economic effects of the federal restrictions as such a frustration as would justify the modification of the lease. The governmental acts did not make the obligation of the lease unlawful, prohibit its performance, or otherwise render performance impossible. It distinguished *Mid-Continent Petroleum Corp. v. Barrett,* 297 Ky. 709, 181 S.W. 2d 60 (1944), because there the lease expressly provided for economic contingencies, and the court construed the lease in that case to thereby grant relief to the lessee at its option, under the peculiar business conditions which the court found to exist. In deciding the latter case, the court explained that in the absence of a stipulation providing that the lessee may surrender or terminate the lease if he should be prevented form legally using the premises for the purposes contemplated, the lease is not invalidated by reason of a subsequent prohibitory or restrictive statute, ordinance, or administrative ruling, if the lessee may devote the property to other uses. Here, as contemplated in that statement of the Kentucky court, this lessee may devote, and in fact did devote, the property to uses other than those affected by the governmental action.

If the decisions are not uniformly in your client's favor, be candid and admit it. If you do not say so, the court will find it out anyway, probably from your opponent.

When relying heavily on precedent cases, tell about their facts and outcomes, so as to demonstrate to your reader how they bear on the problem case. This entire paragraph is directed toward that objective.

The American courts have recognized that the doctrine of frustration can be applicable to leases, but have indicated that there must be nearly total or absolute frustration. In nearly all of the decided cases, the courts have refused to release the lessee from his obligations under the lease, either because the restrictions involved did not sufficiently prevent him from doing business, or because the lease permitted him to engage in other business that was unrestricted. 1 *American Law of Property* § 3.104 (A. J. Casner ed. 1952, Supp). *Accord,* 51C C.J.S. *Landlord & Tenant* § 101 (1968). The court is reminded that the two leases at issue in this present case do not restrict or limit the uses to which the lessee may put the leased real property, and that the provisions concerning the personal property grant numerous options to the lessee, including setting the personal property aside and storing it. The leases, therefore, contemplate that the lessee may do whatever it will on the realty, and allow the lessee to put aside the personalty, if its selected uses for the real property are not compatible with the personalty. The real property at issue here is adaptable to numerous uses, including among other uses, super market, rental deep-freeze storage, commodities distribution, garage and office, for all of which purposes it has previously been used. (Deposition of Walter J. Brown, p. 3-4, Q. 26-36; Deposition of B. J. Green, p. 4, Q. 28-31, p. 5-6, Q. 34-42, p. 3, Q. 20).

Id.

Tie the facts mentioned in the argument to the record, as you do in the statement of facts.

Early in our nation's history, the United States Supreme Court considered a similar question in *Pollard v. Shaaffer,* 1 U.S. (1 Dall.) 210 (1787). A sugar house was leased in 1773 for 35 pounds per half year. In 1777, the British Army invaded the city and took possession of the premises, held them past the end of the term, and committed waste and destruction. The Court required the lessee to pay the rent because of his express covenant to pay it. The Court said that the lessee should run the hazard of casual losses because the lessee was to have the advantage of the casual profits. The lessee was excused from his covenant to repair, however, because the court divided the loss between the party with the term, the lessee, and the party with the reversion, the lessor. An even earlier case that held similarly centered about an invasion of England by Prince Rupert, whose army kept the lessee out of possession. *Paradine v. Jane,* Aleyn. 26, 82 Eng. Rep. 897 (K.B. 1647). The court said, "* * * he ought to pay his rent."

The historical development of the principle on which you rely can be persuasive, but it is probably better to use it in a supporting role. Therefore, this portion of the argument, I(b), opens with a statement of the current cases in the jurisdiction, moves to current secondary authority, and then supports that material with the older cases.

Similar to our problem case, *Lumiansky v., Tessler,* 213 Mass. 182, 99 N.E. 1051 (1912), concerned a collective lease of real property and furniture and fixtures. The lessee intended to use the property for a vaudeville and moving picture theatre. The lessee obligated himself to keep the premises, furniture, and fixtures in good and tenantable repair and condition. The lessor was to keep the outside in repair. In a suit by the tenant for a breach of covenants by the lessor, and a counterclaim by the lessor for breach of covenants and failure to pay rent, the pivotal issue was the significance of a state-police notification that certain additional interior changes must be made in the building. The notice suggested that if they were not made, the license would be revoked. The lessee knew of this, but made no effort to meet the requirements. The court held for the lessor. It pointed out that the lease contained no covenants on the part of the lessor that the license would be continued in force. In the present case, there is a similar lack of promise by lessor that the lessee's permit to use the premises for meat packing, or for any other purpose, would not be revoked. The repairs, changes, and alterations in the interior, for the lack of which the license was revoked, were the responsibility of the lessee. In the present case, lessee expressly promised to

It was fortunate that there were local-state cases in point. Nevertheless, it is worthwhile to tell about a precedent from another jurisdiction that applied the same principle and reached the same result in a case involving facts which were more similar to those of the problem case. The closer similarity of *Lumiansky* to the problem case lies in the fact that in both cases the leases were for real property and allied personal property, collectively, and that the personal property was repair, maintain, etc., and contemplated that it might also need to make alterations, additions, and improvements. (Paragraph 5 and 7 of each lease).

suitable to be used for only a fairly limited purpose. *Lumiansky* therefore serves to cement the Kentucky precedents, and other secondary authorities, to the problem case.

More recently, in *Friedman v. LeNoir,* 73 Ariz. 333, 241 P.2d 779 (1952), a lessee tried to recover from the lessor $1,133, which the lessee paid for work on the leased premises. The work had been required by a plumbing inspector under the authority of a city ordinance. The lease provided that the lessee was to maintain the entire premises and keep them in good repair, but that the lessee was not responsible for major structural alterations. The court held for the lessor although it did not classify the work as a repair. Seven or eight traps were installed on a sewer line and a decomposed ¾″ gas line was replaced with a 1½″ gas line. The court found this to be an alteration, but not structural, and not major. It relied on the written obligation of the lessee to maintain, which was in addition to the responsibility to repair. The court's attention is called to the broad undertaking of the lessee in the present lease. It agreed to repair and maintain, as in *Friedman v. LeNoir, id.*, and to do more, *i.e.*, "etc." Lessee also contemplated that it conceivably could be making alterations, additions, and improvements (Paragraph 5 and 7 in each lease). Those terms are not synonyms. They each have a distinctive meaning.

The purpose of this paragraph is similar to the purpose of the foregoing paragraph.

The intrinsic injustice of the lessee's argument should not be ignored. If lessee had found that this property which it leased was uniquely suited to some newly-discovered, highly-profitable business which it had not contemplated when it obtained its leases, it would have leaped to the opportunity to devote the property to that use. That privilege is a characteristic of these unrestricted leases, and the lessee would have been entitled to reap its benefits. Lessors could not have legally or fairly claimed that the lease should be cancelled so that they, instead of lessee, could enjoy those newly discovered profits. The seed of the difficulty here is that the transaction did not sweeten, as the lessee legitimately hoped would happen, but instead it soured, as the lessee reasonably should have realized might happen. Is it unjust that the lessee must pay in spite of the fortuitous event? It is not unjust, because the lessee received the leasehold interest, with its risks and its values. If unforeseen events had suddenly increased the value of the leasehold, the lessee would have profited thereby with no increase in the rent. It should also carry the risk of losses.

Policy arguments are very important because judges recognize their awesome responsibility to afford justice between the parties.

The lessee in this case is, in effect, asking the court to judicially rewrite the contract. This is distinguishable from the legitimate judicial function of construing it. The practice of making promises will lose much of its effectiveness, if promises are to be performed only when it suits the promisor's convenience. A promise which imposes no risk taking on the promisor is no promise at all, because such a promise would either be illusory, *e.g.*, "I will, if I want to," or it will be a prediction of some reasonably certain event, *e.g.*, "The sun will rise tomorrow." When parties with equal bargaining power, as the parties here appear to have been, finally agree upon precise words which they write into the instrument, the agreement is often the result of a hard-fought compromise. If they were to try to inject numerous imaginable catastrophes into the negotiations, the result would be irritation of the parties, doubt, and perhaps no agreement at all. After the fortuitous event which frustrates the agreement has occurred, to say that a party who has sustained damage and is suing to recover it would have graciously consented to insert some condition which the court is asked to create is to only conceal a value judgment under a cloud of unfounded, fictitious inference of fact.

Id.

II.

Topical and directional.

THE DAMAGE CLAUSES IN THE LEASES ENTITLE THE LESSORS TO RECOVER DAMAGES IN FULL FOR THE LESSEE'S WILLFUL BREACH OF THE LEASES.

If possible, support your arguments with the authorities which your opponent cites. Suggest that the facts of the problem case fit his authority, but in a way which he did not recognize, *e.g.*, that they indicate a decision in your client's favor, under his precedent. This is one of the ways in which you must use the facts of the problem case.

The lessee's brief only alludes to the facts which are the basis for the lessors' position here. The last two lines of the lessee's quotation from 49 Am. Jur. 2d *Landlord & Tenant* § 1054 (*Brief for Defendant,* top of p. 00) recognize that leases which have damage clauses are exceptions to the rule stated:

"... in the absence of a stipulation in the lease for his continued liability ..."

The facts of this dispute reveal the presence of such a stipulation, *i.e.*, a damage clause. Specifically, the leases at issue in this case not only provide for the lessors' (first parties') options to declare the leases null and void, as mentioned by defendants, but in the very next sentence, further promise:

Direct quotations are not ordinarily favored, but there may be times when it is almost imperative that a short quotation be used in order to make your point.

"However, the second party (lessee) may not avail itself of this provision of this lease to avoid payment of the rental as provided herein and shall remain liable therefor in the event of such wilful breach of the terms of this lease, subject to credit for such reasonable rental as the lessor may obtain during the remainder of the term." (Paragraph 2, both leases).

What could be more clear or definite? The leases provide that the lessee must pay damages in the event that the lessors exercise the options reserved to them. A tenant may continue to be liable to the landlord after the termination of the tenancy because of the inclusion in the lease of provisions imposing liability for rent, damages, or the deficiency arising in the case of the reletting. 52 C.J.S. *Landlord & Tenant* § 490 at 428 (1968); 36 C.J. *Landlord & Tenant* § 1142 at 336 (1941). Accord, 2 R. Powell, *The Law of Real Property* § 231(1) at 271-272 (1967 and Supp.).

A covenant that, on forfeiture, the lessor may relet the premises and hold the lessee for the difference between the rental provided for in the lease and the rent received from the reletting is valid. This is not an agreement to pay rent, but is a covenant of indemnity or provision for damages. 1 *American Law of Property* § 3.97 (A. J. Casner ed. 1952, Supp.). If such a lease is terminated, as lessors had every right to do here and as they did in fact do here, the lessor is entitled to rely on the damage clause in his lease for compensation for his actual loss. 1964 *Report, A.B.A. Section of Real Property, Probate & Trust Law,* Sec. II 105, 107-8. The lessors in this action accordingly rely on the damage clauses of their leases.

Normally, the early termination or expiration of a lease will conclude all rental obligations of the tenant. Therefore, one purpose of the damages clause is to preserve the tenant's liability beyond the premature termination date. This provision is also often designed to accelerate the time when damages are payable. 10 J. Rabkin & M. Johnson, *Current Legal Forms* 263 (1971).

Maybe there is a legitimate question here as to how lessors should proceed. Perhaps lessors can only recover a portion today, a portion next month, and another portion each month that the lease was designed to run. However, there is no question but that lessors are entitled to recover all of their damages for each and every month. To encourage a series of later suits only clogs the docket of the court and generates an unwelcome multiplicity of suits. This present, single action for damages can put an end to the dispute once and forever. An action to recover damages on account of the breach of a lease without waiting for the time of performance, as contradistinguished from an action for rent, invokes the doctrine of anticipatory breach. That doctrine permits an immediate action for damages without waiting for the time of performance. That doctrine is recognized in Kentucky, and may be applied to rental contracts. *Jordan v. Nickel,* 253 S.W.2d 237, 239 (Ky. 1952).

Be willing to admit that your case is not airtight, and that you do not have all of the answers. The court will discover it anyway. You can say so more gently than your opponent might say it.

Policy argument.

* * *

13.
TALKING WITH THE COURT

"I am a firm believer in the proposition that a poorly argued case, whether in the briefs or in oral argument, is apt to be a poorly decided case, ***"

Rehnquist, *Oral Advocacy: A Disappearing Art,* 35 Mercer L. Rev. 1015, 1020 (1984).[1]

"*** [T]he greatest barrier to an effective argument is boredom. It is imperative that the argument be vivid and striking."

Shapiro, *Oral Argument in the Supreme Court of the United States,* 33 Cath. U. L. Rev. 529, 539 (1984).

Participate in an Interesting Colloquy

The oral argument is your opportunity to talk with the court about your case, and in a limited sense participate in the court conference concerning it. It is not a talk to the court, but with the court. An oral argument is a dialogue, not a monologue. Each year the court hears large numbers of oral arguments, many of which are unremarkable. The court would like to have a refreshing experience when it hears yours. Judges become tired, bored, lose interest, and become distracted, but if your presentation is interesting and if you are a refreshing voice in the long day, you will have overcome a major obstacle in communicating with the court. Concerning this point, consider the following portions of a letter by a prominent American jurist to a close personal friend:

*   *   *

[1] Copyright 1984 by Supreme Court Justice William H. Rehnquist.

BOSTON, March 17, 1898

Dear Pollock:

As we don't shut up bores, one has to listen to discourses dragging slowly along after one has seen the point and made up one's mind. That is what is happening now and I take the chance to write as I sit with my brethren. I hope I shall be supposed to be taking notes.

* * *

Well goodbye. Other bores are talking now from those with whom I began, but it is another case which one makes up his mind on in 10 minutes & then is jawed to for an hour and a half. Remember me affectionately to Lady Pollock & the infants.

Yours Ever,
O. W. H.[2]

* * *

It is very important that as an oral advocate, you be yourself. Refrain from using words which are more suitable for a written page than for oral statements, or phrases that have come to your attention when reading an 18th- or 19th-century court opinion. An English jurist has this item of sound advice to offer us concerning our use of language in oral arguments:

A. Denning, The Road to Justice 51-53 (1955)

* * *

THE FIRST VIRTUE — COMMAND OF LANGUAGE

I have now done with the things which a lawyer must avoid. Let me come to the things which he must do. He must have a command of the English language so as to put his client's case clearly and strongly before the judge. I put this first because the very reason for employing an advocate is that he should present the case in the best possible light, and to do this he must have a command of the language in which he speaks. The key to the correct presentation of a case is at the outset to state the point at issue and then to recount the facts simply and in good order, keeping to what matters and omitting the rest. It is surprising how many advocates fail to observe those simple rules. Perhaps I may remind you of the famous rebuke which Mr. Justice Maule once made to counsel who was blundering along in haphazard fashion:

"Mr. Smith, but do you not think that by introducing a little order into your narrative, you might possibly render yourself a trifle more intelligi-

---

[2] Reprinted by permission of the publisher from 1 HOLMES-POLLOCK LETTERS 81-83, edited by Mark DeWolfe Howe, The Belknap Press of Harvard University Press, © 1941, 1961, 1969 by the President and Fellows of Harvard College.

ble? It may be my fault that I cannot follow you — I know that my brain is getting old and dilapidated; but I should like to stipulate for some sort of order. There are plenty of them. There is the chronological, the botanical, the metaphysical, the geographical, even the alphabetical order would be better than no order at all."[3]

The good advocate will therefore present his case simply and in good order, but he will attune his words to the tribunal before whom he appears. He will not expose himself to the kind of thing which is described by Mr. Justice Hilbery in his book on the *Duty and Art in Advocacy.* "A counsel, much given to emotional rhetoric, began to open a case before Mr. Justice Swift who was sitting alone. He had not gone far before he was giving full rein to his oratory. Mr. Justice Swift tapped on his desk 'Mr. Blank' he said 'there is no jury.' Then came the appropriate apology, and the counsel began again, and again was soon indulging in rolling periods and highly flowered declamation. For some time the judge suffered it, then there came again the tap of the pencil on the desk. 'Usher' he said, 'switch on the light over the jury box — Mr. Blank does not believe me.' That shows the danger of becoming too emotional and picturesque in language. I may remind you of the fate which befell Edmund Burke when he dramatically threw a dagger on the floor of the House of Commons. A cynical opponent arose at once and said 'the honourable Member has given us a knife, will he not produce the fork as well?' "

*   *   *

Do not read your argument. It is acceptable to use notes which will allow you to guide yourself through your argument, but you should refer to them no more than is absolutely necessary. Reading an argument raises an invisible screen between an advocate and the court, which results in a material reduction in an otherwise persuasive presentation. Many courts, by written rule, expressly disapprove of counsel reading their arguments.

The prospect of oral argument may appear foreboding, but for many persons oral argument is an enjoyable experience that aids in building their confidence. Some find it to be the most pleasant part of their activities.

The personalities of judges and opposing counsel should be so managed that they do not contribute unpleasantness to the experience. In this course all participants should refrain from brow-beating, belittling, and antagonizing their opponent. Hopefully, the pattern thus established will carry over into the professional life of each student who follows the vocation of advocate or judge, because impolite conduct has no proper place in the method of operation of court or counsel.

---

[3] Quoted in *Advocacy* by Lord Justice Birkett, p. 19.

The Argument to be Delivered by the Student

As is the case concerning the proper amount of emphasis or weight to be placed on brief writing, a decision as to the proper amount of weight or emphasis to be placed on oral argument is a matter of personal opinion. The following is your author's opinion in this regard, but each instructor is likely to make variations in it.

About 33 1/3 percent of the grade in the Appellate Advocacy course should be based upon performance in the final oral argument. Practice arguments should be had for the purpose of giving students the benefit of experience and constructive criticism before they present their final arguments.

The matters which should be considered in evaluating the final oral arguments are:

Salutation & Introduction of Counsel

Statement of Issues

1. Early
2. Well stated

Politeness toward Court, counsel, and parties

Speed of delivery

Appearance

Audibility

Extemporaneousness

1. Eye contact
2. Lack of reading
3. Gestures

Ability to communicate, using plain, understandable language

Statement of Facts

Argument of Law

1. Reasons
2. Use of case law and statutes
3. Familiarity with record

Composure & Response when Questioned

General Persuasiveness

A practitioners' handbook for one of the United States Courts of Appeals develops or restates many of these points. In numerous respects no one court can serve as a representative sample of all the American appellate courts because each court is made up of significantly different persons. If there were to be one court which could serve as a representative sample of the courts of the nation, perhaps this court would be as eligible as any other.

Cincinnati Chapter of the Federal Bar Association, Practitioners' Handbook for Appeals to the U.S. Court of Appeals for the Sixth Circuit 40-44 (J. Aug, H. Rosen & G. Ruehlman 1971)[4]

* * *

ORAL ARGUMENT

Having filed their briefs, the parties prepare for oral argument. Whoever is to argue the appeal must study the case afresh even though he has worked on the brief and tried the case in the court below, and it does not necessarily follow that counsel who tried the case below is best equipped to handle the appeal. Only counsel who will take the time thoroughly to familiarize himself with the record will be able to do justice to the argument.

The appellant's oral argument must catch the interest of the judges. Appellant's counsel must seek to persuade the judges that an injustice has been done and that it can be corrected in accordance with governing law and established precedents. The appellee, on the other hand, must convince the judges that the issues have been correctly and fairly handled by the court below or that in any event the ultimate determination below requires no alteration.

The oral argument is always of great importance. The Sixth Circuit does not encourage submissions without argument: the Court will listen to one side if the other submits his argument on briefs.

The importance of oral argument is emphasized by the fact that in a considerable majority of the arguments the case is finally decided in accordance with the impression which the judges have as they leave the bench. While it is quite true that the impression after oral argument derives from the reading of the briefs as well as from the argument, it is also true that the impression from reading the briefs may be changed or modified by the oral argument.

Although the oral argument and brief complement each other, each serves a different purpose. The oral argument should be something in the nature of a *tour de force* designed to persuade the judges that fair play and precedent support the position of the advocate. In contrast, the strength of the brief lies in its lucid, reasoned and documented statement of the facts, the reasons and the precedents in support of counsel's position. The brief should demonstrate the way in which the Court may arrive at the decision which the advocate has persuaded the Court is the right one.

---

[4]This useful *Handbook* has been revised three times and is in its fourth edition, published May, 1984. The 98-page, paperback fourth edition may be obtained for $1 per copy from the Office of the Clerk, U.S. Court of Appeals for the Sixth Circuit, Room 524 U.S. Post Office and Courthouse, Cincinnati, Ohio 45202.

Experience shows that the following guidelines should be observed in arguing an appeal:

1. Preparation for the Argument

If possible, counsel should become familiar with the Court by listening to arguments before his appeal is reached. He should know the names of the judges. Counsel's name should appear on the cover of the brief so that the judges can address him by name. In his imagination, counsel should change places with the Court, and he should ask himself what the judges will want to know and the order in which they will want to hear it.

2. The Opening Statement

If counsel fails to tell the Court in the first few words how he got there, what he complains about, why, and what he proposes the Court should do, he will probably be besieged by a multitude of questions at the outset. An effective opening statement is a prerequisite to an effective oral argument. Counsel must catch and hold the judges' attention in the first few minutes if he hopes properly to present his case. It is therefore of the utmost importance to first state the nature of the case and briefly recite its prior history. The appellant must isolate the critical issue on appeal immediately, thus acquainting the Court with the nature of the case, and then quickly move to a lucid and concise statement of the prior history of the action.

3. The Statement of Facts[5]

Because the judges already have read the briefs before oral argument, it is not necessary for counsel to state the facts in detail. His recital should cover facts which bear specifically upon the issues to be argued, and it should omit all extraneous and immaterial matter. Usually a chronological statement is easier for the Court to follow. The Court will seldom wish to hear a reading of any testimony unless counsel first explains the necessity for doing so. The facts should be fairly stated from the record and should include all important facts whether they be favorable or not.

4. The Argument

(a) *The applicable law.* Counsel should state the applicable rules of law relied upon. If any precedents are discussed, enough should be said about them so that the Court may see at once that they are in point. In general, however, these rules of law should be stated in general terms. A minute

---

[5] The practice of the United States Court of Appeals for the Sixth Circuit of reading the briefs and familiarizing itself with the case before oral argument is not a universal practice. Some courts will be unfamiliar with your case at the time that you initiate your oral argument.

dissection of case law should be avoided except where one or a few cases clearly would control the outcome or where cases, which on their face are against the position of the appellant, must be distinguished if he is to prevail. Quotations from cases should be kept to a minimum and citation of numerous cases is better left to the brief.

(b) *"Go for the jugular vein."* While the brief may cover several points for the sake of completeness, counsel in oral argument should limit himself to one or two points. At the same time counsel must be prepared to answer questions which may be asked about any point. By rehearsing the argument, counsel will learn how best to allocate his time among the points to be covered. Trivia and unnecessary complexity must be avoided. Through preparation and rehearsal of the argument, counsel will be better able to separate the important from the unimportant. Since the time allowed for oral argument is limited, counsel must emphasize only that which is significant to the determination of the issues.

(c) *Answering questions.* Counsel should answer questions as directly and categorically as possible, adding, where necessary, any qualifications or references to matters which are better developed later in the argument. It is usually best, however, not to postpone an answer until later in the argument. If counsel does not know the answer he should not hesitate to say "I don't know" with an offer to find out and advise the Court later. Where the questioning has been extensive, the Sixth Circuit may allow additional time upon request. On this point the presiding judge exercises his discretion case by case.

(d) *Delivery.* Read sparingly and only from necessity. On oral arguments points are more forcibly made in counsel's own words. Moreover, most judges prefer to read matter themselves. When counsel reads his argument, a veil is created between the Court and the advocate. The argument will lose all its spontaneity if read. Instead, the argument should be delivered from notes which remind counsel of the points he is to cover. In delivering the argument the techniques of good public speaking should be kept in mind. Counsel should speak clearly and make himself heard. He should avoid speaking in a monotone and should not race through the argument so rapidly as to make it unintelligible.

(e) *Avoid personalities.* Where personal reference is necessary, it should be made with an explanation which discloses the need, and it should be done in good temper.

(f) *Know the record.* Counsel should know the record from cover to cover. There are very few arguments which do not produce some question regarding the record. Yet all too often counsel does not know whether something is in the record or the appendix and where it may be found. Nothing wins the confidence of the Court more than an ability to answer accurately and immediately questions from the bench. It should be noted here that the judges may have to ask many questions because counsel have omitted relevant matter from the appendix.

(g) *Be flexible in argument.* A memorized argument tells the Court that counsel is not master of his case. No oral argument ever follows an exact prepared pattern; the advocate must be so well prepared that he can rework his argument according to the questions and the Court's interest, leaving off at any point and picking up the threads again according to the tides of battle.

(h) *Timing the argument.* Appellant should reserve a few minutes of the allotted time for rebuttal. The last word may be important. And if no such last word is needed, it is always an effective ending for counsel to be able to say that there is nothing which requires reply. When counsel has concluded his argument, he should sit down regardless of whether the allocated time has been used. Frequently appellant's counsel has not finished within his allowance because he has failed to calculate the time it will take for him to speak his piece, in which event the judge presiding will remind him that his time has run out.

(i) *Guidelines for the appellee.* The points enumerated, although applying to both the appellant and appellee, deal largely with the appellant's presentation. While appellant's counsel knows in advance what ground he must cover, the appellee's counsel can never be sure how much he will need to say in reply as he cannot foretell the Court's reaction to the appellant's argument. It happens not infrequently that a particular point, or even an entire appeal, is in such posture, by reason of the Court's questions and the attitudes of the judges, that appellee's counsel is well advised to say as little as possible. It may well be enough merely to say that in view of the argument he will rest on his brief unless the Court wishes to ask any questions.

Frequently the appellee must change the order of his response and meet at the outset points which have been raised in the Court's questions. If the judges have asked any questions to which the appellant has given answers at variance with the appellee's views, it may be advisable for the appellee to give his answers to those questions at the very outset.

As with the brief, there are few arguments where the appellee will be content with the appellant's version of the facts. The appellee must, moreover, be prepared to make his own statement without undue repetition of matters on which there is no disagreement. In many criminal appeals, for example, the appellant's counsel gives the Court only a very sketchy idea of the evidence.

Above all the appellee must be flexible with sufficient mastery of the case to know how much more or little to say and with the courage to say nothing at all when that seems best. This means that in some ways appellee's counsel has more difficult decisions at argument than does counsel for the appellant.

* * *

Purpose of Oral Argument

You cannot expect to cover your entire case in the few minutes that are allotted to you for oral argument. The best that you can hope for is to capsulate your client's view of the facts and the law, and offer reasons why your client should prevail. This means that with a lot of effort you must make a long story short and simultaneously accurate; it is not an easy task. This is, however, a hallmark of a capable and effective oral advocate.

Keep in mind this distinction between oral argument and your written brief. The function of oral argument is to make the court want to decide in your favor, and the function of the brief is to provide the court with the tools to do so.[6] For this reason, your oral argument should invite a rational decision based upon fairness, not a decision based upon the weight of precedent cases.

Is Oral Argument Worth the Trouble?

In order to make an effective oral argument that will last only fifteen minutes, a great deal of thinking, writing, practicing, and other time will be consumed. After all, the argument is fully written out in your brief, the judges have it, and why should you go to all of this extra work just for fifteen minutes in the courtroom?

The first part of the answer is that the oral argument is your only opportunity to meet with the judges who will decide your case, tell them face-to-face why your client should prevail, and allow them the opportunity to clear up unanswered questions about your case by speaking directly with you. Probably only twice will the judges who will decide your case meet together. Once in the conference following the oral argument, but first in the courtroom with you and opposing counsel to discuss the case. At the oral argument, you may create a lasting impression concerning your sincerity and the merits of your client's case; that will then carry over into the conference. It will give you the opportunity to clear up unclear matters of fact, and to dispel lingering doubts concerning the legal principles involved or the broader impact of a potential decision that you advocate.

The second part of the answer is that most judges and advocates agree that most of the time oral argument makes a difference. Empirical evidence concerning this point is scarce, and personal experiences contribute to the judges' and advocates' perceptions concerning oral argument's value. In one test period, however, oral argument changed one judge's mind in 31% of the cases, and changed another judge's mind in 17% of the cases. Both judges found oral argument helpful to them in about 80% of the cases.[7]

---

[6] Friedman, *Winning on Appeal,* 9 Litigation 15, 18 (No. 3, Spring, 1983).

[7] Bright & Arnold, *Oral Argument? It May Be Crucial!,* 70 A.B.A. J. 68-70 (September, 1984).

General Rules Relating to Students' Oral Arguments

1) Arguments are presented by counsel who dress in attire appropriate for serious occasions. Men wear suits, jackets, and ties. Counsel stand when they speak. Notes are placed on a lectern. A salutation to the Court precedes the argument. Examples of such a salutation include:

"May it Please the Court, ——"
"May it Please the Court and Counsel, ——"
"Your Honors ——"
"If Your Honors Please ——"

2) Following the salutation which you choose to give, tell the Court your name, the city or town where you live, the name of your client, and succinctly identify your client's position in the case.

3) Use ordinary conversational language. It is not helpful to call parties by procedural terms, *e.g.*, appellee, defendant, or petitioner, unless such a practice assists you in distinguishing the identities of the parties. It is usually better to call them by descriptive terms, *e.g.*, the buyer, the seller, the government, or the injured party, or by their names, *e.g.*, Mr. Green or Mrs. Smith. In instances where several parties or witnesses mentioned in the argument have the same last name, it is permissible to call them by their first names.

4) Each student should present a 15-minute oral argument, during which the Court asks questions of counsel.

5) Do not launch into a discussion of the case without telling the Court the case's procedural posture, *i.e,* how the case got to the present court, and what the litigation concerns generally. Does the case involve a prosecution for a crime, an automobile wreck, an airplane crash, the sale of goods, a secured transaction, the holder of a check, or a claimed violation of certain constitutional rights? Use any phrase which sets the scene and allows the Court to focus on the particular areas of law involved in the case.

6) Early in your argument concisely state the material facts. Keep in mind the other facts of the case, so that you may relate them if called upon by the court to do so. If you do not tell the Court about the facts, you are not telling the Court about your case. If the Court does not know the facts of your case, it will not know what it is deciding. The most helpful thing that you can do for the Court is to marshal the facts of the problem case. If you fail to marshal the facts early in your argument, you are likely to lose your lawsuit.

7) After counsel for the Appellant has stated his or her client's view of the facts and completed the argument, if counsel for the Appellee does not agree with the Appellant's statement of the facts, he or she should call the Court's attention to what the Appellee believes to be material facts not previously given, or what the Appellee believes to be facts claimed by the Appellant to be material but which the Appellee does not believe to be material, and state the reasons for such a claim. If the Appellee agrees with Appellant's statement of the facts, the

Appellee may so state and move on to something else, but complete agreement concerning the facts would be a rare occurrence.

8) During your argument of law, continue to emphasize and keep the Court's attention upon the facts of the problem case which you claim to be material.

9) *Appellants:* Tell the Court what happened below and indicate that you disagree, briefly stating your reasons for the disagreement. If this involves an attack on the reasons assigned by the lower Court, make your attack as firmly but politely as possible.

Appellees: Briefly state that you agree with the lower Court and why you agree.

At this stage both Appellants and Appellees are setting a catapult to launch themselves into an attack upon, or a defense of, the decision of the lower Court.

10) State your propositions of law. It is best to state all of them at once and then expand them each, one at a time. It is possible, and perhaps even likely, that you will not have time to deal with all of them again, because of the time that will be consumed by the Court's questions.

11) Present your strongest argument first. It is impossible to gauge your time accurately, and because your time is likely to run out before you have presented all of your intended arguments, make certain that you get your best arguments before the Court before the time runs out and you have to sit down. If you are so fortunate as to be able to present your entire argument before your time expires, the Court will not censure you for failing to use all of your allotted time; it may commend your ability.

12) Keep track of your time as best you can; perhaps you will want a watch in front of you. Many courtrooms will have a clock in view. Present your proposition No. 1, and after having presented it, move on to your proposition No. 2. In all events, stay flexible and composed. You must be prepared for the prospect of interruptions by the Court, inquiring into particular facts, principles of law, and authorities.

Preparing for the Oral Argument

In what is commonly a 15-minute oral argument, an advocate must try to convince the court that his client's view of the lawsuit is the better one. The 15 minutes is a relatively short period in which to do this, particularly when you consider all of the time that was previously put into the case from the interview stage, through the pleading, pretrial, trial, and brief-writing stages. All of the persuasion that can be mustered must be packed into the 15 minutes. Any words spoken which are not persuasive waste the valuable time of the bench and the advocates.

One good way to help make every word count is to take your oral argument through successive written and oral drafts. It is often wise to begin by writing out your oral argument and then revising it several times in its written form. Thereafter it is time to practice delivering the argument orally. Experienced appellate counsel strongly recommend that lawyers with appellate cases to present orally participate in a series of moot courts as preparation for their appearance in court.

At first you will want to stay close to the argument which you wrote, but soon you will be able, in large part, to abandon the written argument and present it without more than a minimum of notes, because through successive oral practices you will develop a comfortable familiarity with the message you want to deliver.

Speak your argument into a tape recorder and play it back. Listen for meaningless and untenable statements. Delete the meaningless and untenable; revise your oral argument based on what you hear on the tape recorder. Persuade a friend to act as a judge and question you about your argument as you practice delivering it. Insist that your friend be critical of both your statements of facts and your arguments of law. Insist that your friend interrupt you when he or she does not understand the facts which you relate or your argument of law, and require you to clarify them. This will sharpen your mental processes and improve your oral argument. It will prepare you to better articulate the facts and law of your client's case. Simultaneously, you will become accustomed to the interruptions of questions which characterize oral argument. This will help make your argument better and you more comfortable delivering it.

If you cannot find someone to listen to you practice, or if a tape recorder is not available, practice before a mirror or deliver your argument orally to your dog or cat. In any event, engage in a large number of practices.

Some persons can deliver their oral arguments without notes, and others can never get completely away from them. A topical outline is a good form of notes to use, because it takes up relatively little space on 4″ x 6″ index cards. Usually such an outline will suffice to refresh the speaker's recollection, and simultaneously it will aid the speaker to avoid reading the oral argument. Some persons find that, in addition to the topical outline, it is helpful to have one card whereon is written in full the advocate's first oral sentence. This helps "break the ice" without undue hesitation and discomfort. Some persons also like to have another card whereon is written the summary of the argument which the advocate wants to deliver at the close of the 15 minutes. This aids the speaker to finish the argument smoothly in the way that he or she planned.

* * *

One of the leading appellate advocates of the twentieth century was John W. Davis (1873-1955). Among his many notable accomplishments, he argued and won the 1952 case before the United States Supreme Court in which it was held that President Harry S. Truman exceeded his powers when he seized control of the nation's steel mills, *Youngstown Sheet & Tube Co. v. Sawyer,* 343 U.S. 579 (1952). He was one of the lead counsel who argued for the losing side in *Brown v. Board of Education,* 347 U.S. 483 (1954).

Mr. Davis' distinguished career is the subject of a biography, William H. Harbaugh, *Lawyer's Lawyer,* 1973, New York, Oxford University Press, xvi,

648 p. His oral argument in *Brown v. Board of Education,* and the oral arguments of the other counsel in that case, including Mr. Thurgood Marshall, who was one of the lead counsel for the winning side, are published in Leon Friedman, ed., *Argument,* 1969, New York, Chelsea House Publishers, *1,* 601 p. Both of these books are instructive for law students, and the latter one is particularly helpful to law students who desire to read a complete transcript of oral arguments in a case before the United States Supreme Court.

For our present purposes it is important to note that as a part of Mr. Davis' career, he was the author of what has become a classic article concerning appellate advocacy. That article is one of the most frequently cited writings concerning appellate advocacy and is reproduced below as a summary.

Davis, *The Argument of an Appeal,* 26 A.B.A. J. 895 (1940)[8]

If a lecture on the well-worn subject assigned to me is to be given in this series, no one knows better than the Chairman of your Committee on Post-Admission Legal Education that he and not I should be the person to give it. This is true in the first place because of the fact that in his lecture on summary judgment he has given the perfect example of what these lectures ought to be — informative, scholarly, helpful — and has set a standard which it is unfair to ask others to rival. And in the second place a discourse on the argument of an appeal would come with superior force from a judge who is in his judicial person the target and the trier of the argument than from a random archer like myself. Or, supposing fishes had the gift of speech, who would listen to a fisherman's weary discourse on flycasting, the shape and color of the fly, the size of the tackle, the length of the line, the merit of different rod makers and all the other tiresome stuff that fishermen talk about, if the fish himself could be induced to give his views on the most effective methods of approach. For after all it is the fish that the angler is after and all his recondite learning is but the hopeful means to that end.

I hope I may not be charged with levity or disrespect in adopting this piscatorial figure. I do not suggest any analogies between our reverend masters on the Bench and the finny tribe. God forbid! Let such conceits tempt the less respectful. Yet it is true, is it not, than in the argument of an appeal the advocate is angling, consciously and deliberately angling, for the judicial mind. Whatever tends to attract judicial favor to the advocate's claim is useful. Whatever repels it is useless or worse. The whole art of the

[8] Lecture delivered by John W. Davis before the Assocation of the Bar of the City of New York, October 22, 1940, under the auspices of the Committee on Post-Admission Legal Education; Mr. Justice Sheintag, Chairman of the Committee, presiding.

advocate consists in choosing the one and avoiding the other. Why otherwise have argument at all?

I pause for definition. Argument, of course, may be written as well as oral, and under our modern American practice written argument has certainly become the most extended if not always the weightier of the two. As our colleague Joseph H. Choate, Jr. recently remarked, "we have now reached the point where we file our arguments in writing and deliver our briefs orally". Yet it was not always so, and in certain jurisdictions it is not so today. In England, for instance, where many, perhaps most, cases are decided as soon as the argument is closed, counsel are not expected to speak with one strabismic eye upon the clock and the other on the court.

I recall that I once visited the chambers of the Privy Council in London hoping to hear a Canadian friend argue a Canadian appeal. When I arrived, his adversary had the floor and was laboriously reading to the Court from the open volumes, page by page and line by line, the reported cases on which he relied. Said I to the Clerk, "How long has he been speaking and when will So-and-So come on?" "He has now been speaking", said the Clerk, "for six consecutive days and I doubt if he concludes today." I picked up my hat and sadly departed, realizing into what an alien atmosphere I had wandered.

In the old days, when not only courts but lawyers and litigants are reputed to have had more time at their disposal, similar feats were performed at the American bar. It has been stated, for instance, that the arguments of Webster, Luther Martin and their colleagues in *McCulloch v. Maryland* consumed six days, while in the *Girard will case* Webster, Horace Binney and others, for ten whole days assailed the listening ears of the Court.

Those days have gone forever; and partly because of the increased tempo of our times, partly because of the increase of work in our appellate tribunals, the argument of an appeal, whether by voice or pen, is hedged about today by strict limitations of time and an increasing effort to provoke an economy of space. The rules of nearly every court give notice that there is a limit to what the judicial ear or the judicial eye is prepared to absorb. Sometimes the judges plead, sometimes they deplore, sometimes they command. The bar is continuously besought to speak with an eye on the clock and to write with a cramped pen.

Observing this duty of condensation and selection, I propose tonight to direct my remarks primarily to the oral argument. I begin after the briefs have all been filed; timely filed of course, for in this matter lawyers are never, hardly ever, belated. I shall assume that these briefs are models of brevity, are properly indexed, and march with orderly logic from point to point; not too little nor yet too much on any topic, even though in a painful last moment of proof-reading many an appealing paragraph has been offered as a reluctant sacrifice on the altar of condensation.

I assume also that the briefs are not overloaded with long quotations from the reported opinions, no matter how pat they seem; nor overcrowded with citations designed, it would seem, to certify to the industry of the brief-maker rather than to fortify the argument. A horrible example of this latter fault crossed my desk within the month in a brief which, in addition to many statutes and text-writers, cited by volume and page no less than 304 decided cases, a number calculated to discourage if not to disgust the most industrious judge.

I assume further that they are not defaced by *supras* or *infras* or by a multiplicity of footnotes which, save in the rare case where they are needed to elucidate the text, do nothing but distract the attention of the reader and interrupt the flow of reasoning. And I remark in passing that these are no more laudable in a judge's opinion than they are in a lawyer's brief.

I assume that there is not a pestilent "and/or" to be found in the brief from cover to cover; or if there is, that the court, jealous of our mother-tongue, will stamp upon the base intruder.

And finally I assume of course that there has been no cheap effort to use variety in type to supply the emphasis that well-constructed sentences should furnish for themselves. It may be taken as axiomatic that even judges, when they are so disposed, can read understandingly; and I should think that where the pages of a brief begin conversationally in small pica, nudge the reader's elbow with repeated italics, rise to a higher pitch with whole paragraphs of the text — not mere headings — in black letter, and finally shout in full capitals (and such have been observed), the judge might well consider that what was a well-intentioned effort to attract his attention was in reality a reflection on his intelligence.

So it is with our briefs brought to this state of approximate perfection that we approach our oral argument. Much has been said pro and con as to the utility of this particular exercise. The appellate court which I most frequently encountered in my early days at the bar made no secret of the fact that it regarded the time spent in hearing cases as a sheer waste; and the announcement "Submitted on briefs" always won an approving nod from the bench. Fortunately, I think, that was an idiosyncracy which has passed away even in that tribunal. There is much testimony, ancient and modern, for the contrary view.

Says Lord Coke, "No man alone with all his uttermost labors, nor all the actors in them, themselves by themselves out of a court of justice, can attain unto a right decision; nor in a court without solemn argument where I am persuaded Almighty God openeth and enlargeth the understanding of those desirous of justice and right". Agreeing with this pious sentiment, we lawyers sometimes think nevertheless that "God moves in a mysterious way, his wonders to perform". Judge Dillon in his lecture on the Laws and Jurisprudence of England and America, declares that as a judge he felt reasonably assured of his judgment where he had heard counsel and a very diminished faith where the cause had not been orally argued; for, says he, "Mistakes, errors, fallacies and flaws elude us in spite of ourselves unless the case is pounded and hammered at the bar". Chief Justice Hughes is on record to the effect that "The desirability of a full exposition by oral argument in the highest court is not to be gainsaid. It is a great saving of time of the court in the examination of extended records and briefs, to obtain the grasp of the case that is made possible by oral discussion and to be able more quickly to separate the wheat from the chaff". With all this, most judges I think, will agree always provided that the oral argument is inspired as it should be with a single and sincere desire to be helpful to the court.

Professing no special fitness for the task, I have ventured accordingly to frame a decalogue by which such arguments should be governed. There is no mystical significance in the number ten, although it has respectable precedent; and those who think the number short and who wish to add to the roll when I have finished, have my full permission to do so.

At the head of the list I place, where it belongs, the cardinal rule of all, namely: —

1) Change places, in your imagination of course, with the court.

Courts of appeal are not filled by demigods. Some members are learned, some less so. Some are keen and perspicacious, some have more plodding minds. In short, they are men and lawyers much like the rest of us. That they are honest, impartial, ready and eager to reach a correct conclusion must always be taken for granted. You may rightfully expect and you do expect nothing but fair treatment at their hands.

Yet those who sit in solemn array before you, whatever their merit, know nothing whatever of the controversy that brings you to them, and are not stimulated to interest in it by any feeling of friendship or dislike to anyone concerned. They are not moved as perhaps an advocate may be by any hope of reward or fear of punishment. They are simply being called upon for action in this appointed sphere. They are anxiously waiting to be supplied with what Mr. Justice Holmes called the "implements of decision". These by your presence you profess yourself ready to furnish. If the places were reversed and you sat where they do, think what it is you would want first to know about the case. How and in what order would you want the story told? How would you want the skein unravelled? What would make easier your approach to the true solution? These are questions the advocate must unsparingly put to himself. This is what I mean by changing places with the court.

If you happen to know the mental habits of any particular judge, so much the better. To adapt yourself to his methods of reasoning is not artful, it is simply elementary psychology; as is also the maxim not to tire or irritate the mind you are seeking to persuade. And may I say in passing that there is no surer way to irritate the mind of any listener than to speak in so low a voice or with such indistinct articulation or in so monotonous a tone as to make the mere effort at hearing an unnecessary burden.

I proceed to Rule 2 —

2) State first the nature of the case and briefly its prior history.

Every appellate court has passing before it a long procession of cases that come from manifold and diverse fields of the law and human experience. Why not tell the court at the outset to which of these fields its attention is about to be called? If the case involves the construction of a will, the settlement of a partnership, a constitutional question or whatever it may be, the judge is able as soon as the general topic is mentioned to call to his aid, consciously or unconsciously, his general knowledge and experience with that particular subject. It brings what is to follow into immediate focus. And then for the greater ease of the court in listening it is well to give at once the history of the case in so far as it bears on the court's jurisdiction. And sometimes there may be, I am not sure, a certain curiosity to know just whose judicial work it is that the court is called upon to review. For judges, like other men, judge each other as well as the law.

Next in order —

3) State the facts.

If I were disposed to violate the rule I have previously announced against emphasis by typography, I would certainly employ at this point the largest capital type. For it cannot be too often emphasized that in an appellate court the statement of the facts is not merely a part of the argument, it is more often than not the argument itself. A case well stated is a case far more than half argued. Yet how many advocates fail to realize that the ignorance of the court concerning the facts in the case is complete, even where their knowledge of the law may adequately satisfy the proverbial presumption. The court wants above all things to learn what are the facts which give rise to the call upon its energies; for in many, probably in most cases when the facts are clear there is no great trouble about the law. *Ex facto oritur jus,* and no court ever forgets it.

No more courteous judge ever sat on any bench than the late Chief Justice White, but I shall never forget a remark which he addressed to a distinguished lawyer, now dead, who was presenting an appeal from an order of the Interstate Commerce Commission. He had plunged headlong into a discussion of the powers of the Commission, and after he had talked for some twenty-five minutes, the Chief Justice leaned over and said in his blandest tone, "Now, Mr. So-and-So, won't you please tell us what this case is about. We could follow you so much better."

Of course there are statements and statements. No two men probably would adopt an identical method of approach. Uniformity is impossible, probably undesirable. Safe guides, however, are to be found in the three

C's — chronology, candor and clarity: Chronology, because that is the natural way of telling any story, stringing the events on the chain of time just as all human life itself proceeds; candor, the telling of the worst as well as the best, since the court has the right to expect it, and since any lack of candor, real or apparent, will wholly destroy the most careful argument; and clarity, because that is the supreme virtue in any effort to communicate thought from man to man. It admits of no substitute. There is a sentence of Daniel Webster's which should be written on the walls of every law school, court room and law office: "The power of clear statement," said he, "is the great power at the bar". Purple passages can never supply its absence. And of course I must add that no statement of the facts can be considered as complete unless it has been so framed and delivered as to show forth the essential merit, in justice and in right, of your client's cause.

4) State next the applicable rules of law on which you rely.

If the statement of facts has been properly done the mind of the court will already have sensed the legal questions at issue; indeed they may have hinted at as you proceed. These may be so elementary and well established that a mere allusion to them is sufficient. On the other hand, they may lie in the field of divided opinion where it is necessary to expound them at greater length and to dwell on the underlying reasons that support one or the other view. It may be that in these days of what is apparently waning health on the part of our old friend *Stare Decisis,* one can rely less than heretofore upon the assertion that the case at bar is governed by such-and-such a case, volume and page. Even the shadow of a long succession of governing cases may not be adequate shelter. In any event the advocate must be prepared to meet any challenge to the doctrine of the cases on which he relies and to support it by original reasoning. Barren citation is a broken reed. What virtue it retains can be left for the brief.

5) Always "go for the jugular vein".

I do not know from what source I quote that phrase but it is of course familiar. Rufus Choate's expression was "the hub of the case". More often than not there is in every case a cardinal point around which lesser points revolve like planets around the sun, or even as dead moons around a planet; a central fortress which if strongly held will make the loss of all the outworks immaterial. The temptation is always present to "let no guilty point escape" in the hope that if one hook breaks another may hold. Yielding to this temptation is pardonable perhaps in a brief, of which the court may read as much or as little as it chooses. There minor points can be inserted to form "a moat defensive to a wall". But there is no time and rarely any occasion in oral argument for such diversions.

I think in this connection of one of the greatest lawyers, and probably the greatest case winner of our day, the late John G. Johnson of Philadelphia. He was a man of commanding physical presence and of an intellect equally robust. Before appellate courts he addressed himself customarily to but a single point, often speaking for not more than twenty minutes but with compelling force. When he had concluded it was difficult for his adversary to persuade the court that there was anything else worthy to be considered. This is the quintessence of the advocate's art.

6) Rejoice when the court asks questions.

And again I say unto you, rejoice! If the question does nothing more it gives you assurance that the court is not comatose and that you have awakened at least a vestigial interest. Moreover a question affords you your only chance to penetrate the mind of the court, unless you are an expert in face reading, and to dispel a doubt as soon as it arises. This you should be able to do if you know your case and have a sound position. If the question warrants a negative answer, do not fence with it but respond with a bold *thwertutnay* — which for the benefit of the illiterate I may explain as a term used in ancient pleading to signify a downright No. While if the answer is in the affirmative or calls for a concession the court will be equally gratified to have the matter promptly disposed of. If you value your argumentative life do not evade or shuffle or postpone, no matter how embarrassing the question may be or how much it interrupts the thread of your argument. Nothing I should think would be more irritating to an inquiring court than to have refuge taken in the familiar evasion "I am coming to that" and then to have the argument end with the promise unfulfilled. If you are really coming to it indicate what your answer will be when it is reached and never, never sit down until it is made.

Do not get into your head the idea that there is a deliberate design on the part of any judge to embarrass counsel by questions. His mind is seeking help, that is all, although it may well be that he calls for help before he really needs it. You remember Bacon's admonition on the subject in his Essay on Judicature:

> "It is no grace to a judge", he says, "first to find that which he might have heard in due time from the bar, or to show quickness of conceit in cutting off evidence or counsel too short, or to prevent information by questions though pertinent."

On the other hand, Chief Justice Denison of the Supreme Court of Colorado puts the matter thus:

> "A perfect argument would need no interruption and a perfect Judge would never interrupt it; but we are not perfect. If the argument . . . discusses the truth of the first chapter of Genesis when the controlling issue is the constitutionality of a Tennessee statute it ought to be interrupted. . . . It is the function of the Court to decide the case and to decide it properly. . . . The Judge knows where his doubts lie, at which point he wishes to be enlightened; it is he whose mind at last must be made up, no one can do it for him, and he must

take his own course of thought to accomplish it. Then he must sometimes interrupt."

Judges are sometimes more annoyed by each others' questions than counsel, I have observed. I remember a former Justice of the Supreme Court much given to interrogation who engaged counsel in a long colloquy of question and answer at the very threshold of his argument. In a stage whisper audible within the bar Chief Justice White was heard to moan, "I want to hear the argument", "So do I, damn him," growled his neightbor, Justice Holmes. Yet questions fairly put and frankly answered give to oral argument a vitality and spice that nothing else will supply.

7) Read sparingly and only from necessity.

The eye is the window of the mind, and the speaker does not live who can long hold the attention of any audience without looking it in the face. There is something about a sheet of paper interposed between the speaker and listener that walls off the mind of the latter as if it were boiler-plate. It obstructs the passage of thought as the lead plate bars the X-rays. I realize that I am taking just this risk at present, but this is not a speech or an argument, only, God save the mark, a lecture.

Of course where the case turns upon the language of a statute or the terms of a written instrument it is necessary that it should be read, always, if possible, with a copy in the hands of the court so that the eye of the court may supplement its ear. But the reading of lengthy extracts from reported cases or long excerpts from the testimony can only be described as a sheer waste of time. With this every appellate court of my acquaintance agrees. A sentence here or a sentence there, perhaps, if sufficiently pertinent and pithy, but not I beg of you print by the paragraph or page.

There is a cognate fault of which most of us from time to time are guilty. This arises when we are seeking to cite or distinguish other cases bearing on our claims and are tempted into a tedious recital of the facts in the cited case, not uncommonly prefaced by the somewhat awkward phrase "That was a case where," etc. Now the human mind is a pawky thing and must be held to its work and it is little wonder after three or four or half a dozen such recitals that not only are the recited facts forgotten but those in the case at bar become blurred and confused. What the advocate needs most of all is that his facts and his alone should stand out stark, simple, unique, clear.

8) Avoid personalities.

This is a hard saying, especially when one's feelings are ruffled by a lower court or by opposing counsel, but none the less it is worthy of all acceptation, both in oral argument and in brief. I am not speaking merely of the laws of courtesy that must always govern an honorable profession, but rather of the sheer inutility of personalities as a method of argument in a judicial forum. Nor am I excluding proper comment on things that deserve reprobation. I am thinking psychologically again. It is all a question of keeping the mind of the court on the issues in hand without distraction from without.

One who criticizes unfairly or harshly the action of a lower court runs the risk of offending the quite understandable *esprit de corps* of the judicial body. Rhetorical denunciation of opposing litigants or witnesses may arouse a measure of sympathy for the person so denounced, while controversies between counsel impose on the court the wholly unnecessary burden and annoyance of preserving order and maintaining the decorum of its proceedings. Such things can irritate; they can never persuade.

9) Know your record from cover to cover.

This commandment might properly have headed the list for it is the *sine qua non* of all effective argument. You have now reached a point in the litigation where you can no longer hope to supply the want of preparation by lucky accidents or mental agility. You will encounter no more unexpected surprises. You have your last chance to win for your client. It is clear therefore that the field tactics of the trial table will no longer serve and the time has come for major strategy based upon an accurate knowledge of all that has occurred. At any moment you may be called on to correct some misstatement of your adversary and at any moment you may confront a question from the court which, if you are able to answer by an apt reference to the record or with a firm reliance on a well-furnished memory, will increase the confidence with which the court will listen to what else you may have to say. Many an argument otherwise admirable has been destroyed because of counsel's inability to make just such a response.

10) Sit down.

This is the tenth and last commandment. In preparing for argument you will no doubt have made an outline carefully measured by the time at your command. The notes of it which you should have jotted down lie before you on the reading desk. When you have run through this outline and are satisfied that the court has fully grasped your contentions, what else is there left for you do to? You must be vain indeed to hope that by further speaking you can dragoon the court into a prompt decision in your favor. The mere fact that you have an allotted time of one hour more or less does not constitute a contract with the court to listen for that length of time. On the contrary, when you round out your argument and sit down before your time has expired, a benevolent smile overspreads the faces on the bench and a sign of relief and gratification arises from your brethren at the bar who have been impatiently waiting for the moment when the angel might again trouble the waters of the healing pool and permit them to step in. Earn these exhibitions of gratitude therefore whenever you decently can, and leave the rest to Zeus and his colleagues, that is to say, to the judges on high Olympus.

Before I obey this admonition myself, may I say, Mr. Chairman, how painfully conscious I am that I have offered nothing new concerning the subject in hand. I have not even been able to cover old thoughts with new varnish. How I could have hoped to do so? The process of appeal from one tribunal to another is very old in the history of human justice. No matter in what form it is carried on the essentials of an appeal are always the same, and there is nothing very new to be said about it. The need for an appellate process arises from the innate realization of mankind that the human intellect and human justice are frail at their best. It is necessary therefore to measure one man's mind against another in order to purge the final result, so far as may be, of all passion, prejudice or infirmity. It is the effort to realize the maximum of justice in human relations; and to keep firm and stable the foundations on which all ordered society rests. There is no field of nobler usefulness for the lawyer, for him who in the splendid words of Chancellor D'Arguesseau, belongs to an order "as old as the magistracy, as noble as virtue, as necessary as justice".

14.

STUDYING MEDICINE ON YOUR OWN: A BIBLIOGRAPHIC ESSAY CONCERNING MEDICAL LITERATURE

If among practicing lawyers there is such a person as a representative lawyer, an average lawyer, or an ordinary lawyer, it is likely that upward to 80% of his or her problem cases will in some respect involve medical questions. Examples of this kind of case include civil commitment, drug abuse, drunken driving, environmental litigation, medical malpractice, paternity, personal injury claims, product liability, social security disability claims, workers' compensation claims, and wrongful death.

In some jurisdictions, medical literature may be used as direct evidence.[1] On various occasions, medical books may be used for purposes of cross-examination.[2] The occasional submission of a medical trial brief and the frequent compilation of copies of relevant medical-text material as preparation for personal-injury cases is recommended by knowledgeable and experienced trial attorneys.[3] Some times appellate courts will consider medical literature when reaching their decisions.[4]

Despite these realities of law practice, a relatively small amount of American legal or paralegal education is directed toward training in the medical aspects of law. There is a trend, however, toward devoting more time and effort to this subject, especially to training for competence in the medical facets of trials.

For many students, lawyers, and paralegals, depending upon the areas of law in which they find themselves studying or employed, an acquaintance with medical literature and medical knowledge will be a distinct advantage. Regardless of whether students learn about the medical aspects of law in school, or whether

---

[1] Annot., 84 A.L.R.2d 1338-1352 (1962); Annot., 17 A.L.R.3d 993-997 (1968). See also, Heilman v. Snyder, 520 S.W.2d 321 (Ky. 1975); Fed. R. Evid. 803(18).

[2] Annot., 60 A.L.R.2d 77-113 (1958); 12 N.A.C.C.A. L.J. 260-261 (1953); 5 N.A.C.C.A. L.J. 173 (1950).

[3] S. Schweitzer, *Cyclopedia of Trial Practice: Proof of Traumatic Injuries* § 533 (2d ed. 1972); 1 A. Averbach, *Handling Accident Cases* § 107 (Rev. ed. 1972).

[4] See, *e.g.*, Younger v. Webster, 9 Wash. App. 87, 510 P.2d 1182 (1973); Strunk v. Strunk, 445 S.W. 2d 145 (Ky. 1969).

they learn about them outside of school, they will of necessity teach themselves most of their medical knowledge by researching medical literature and reading and studying about the specific medical aspects of concrete problem cases. This chapter will survey and sample the medical literature, with the objective of assisting students, lawyers, and paralegals to understand where they may obtain credible medical information.[5]

It is unlikely that studying medical literature will do much more than help the student, lawyer, or paralegal to be knowledgeable concerning the testimony given in lawsuits by expert medical witnesses. The expert medical witness is, and will continue to be, essential for both sides in lawsuits involving medical questions. Frequently the lawyer will need the assistance of a medical consultant of some nature. Ideally, such a consultant would be a physician whose mission is to render medical advice to the lawyer. The consultant would, among other things, help the lawyer to evaluate the medical facets of the lawsuit, including telling the lawyer whether the determinations that he has reached from reading the medical literature are sound determinations in medical judgment; there is a certain amount of hazard when a nonphysician reaches a medical judgment solely from books, without the guidance of a medically trained person.[6]

OVERVIEW OF MEDICINE

Students, lawyers, and paralegals who believe that they will benefit from a succinct overview of medicine before embarking on a search of medical literature will find useful the Lawyers' Section in the front of *Stedman's Medical Dictionary,* 5th Unabridged Lawyers' Edition, 1982,[7] by William H. L. Dornette, who is both a physician and a lawyer. It discusses, among other things, the study of medicine and specialization, standard abbreviations of medical terms used in medical records, the nervous system, the skeletal system, the muscular system, mental illness, epilepsy, the introduction of hospital records as evidence, and disputed paternity.

The lawyers' section of *Stedman's* also contains copies of the National Interprofessional Code for Physicians and Attorneys, and portions of various medically-related uniform acts. It contains a roster of medical libraries in the United

[5] It is important that students, lawyers, and paralegals recognize the two distinct areas in which medical knowledge has a relationship to law practice, and the difference between them. When law influences medicine or the practice of medicine, the relationship is called, "Medical Jurisprudence." When medical knowledge is applied to help resolve legal disputes, *e.g.*, when medical science influences a lawsuit, the application is called "Forensic Medicine."

[6] See generally, Rein, *The Medical Expert — Two People: A New Concept,* 1975 Ins. L.J. 227.

[7] Cincinnati and Washington, Anderson Publishing Co. and Jefferson Law Book Co.

States and Canada, organized alphabetically by state or province, and by city within each state or province.

Dr. Dornette makes the following observation which should be useful to legal researchers dealing with medical problems:

> The lawyer approaches a medical problem differently from the physician. The physician is concerned with making a precise diagnosis in a timely fashion, in order that definitive therapy may be initiated in short order. He deals with simplicity only if the problem is an uncomplicated one. From the vantage point of the lawyer, however, medicine must be reduced to its simplest terms. It is his responsibility to become acquainted with medicine in these terms so that he may carry his message to the jurors and the bench, all of whom like the lawyer are laymen as far as medicine is concerned. Further, he generally has ample time to develop and understand the facts. In fact, the more time he is able to devote to a medical problem, the better his orientation and understanding will be.

OVERVIEW OF MEDICAL LITERATURE

Medical literature has many analogies to legal literature. Mainly, it consists of textbooks, treatises, and medical journals which tend to be classifiable according to medical specialties or scientific topics.

Medical textbooks and treatises serve purposes similar to the purposes of legal textbooks, legal treatises, and legal encyclopedias. Medical journals serve purposes similar to the purposes of law reviews, bar journals, and lawyers' reports of cases. *Excerpta Medica* performs a function similar to the function of a law digest, but it is not as frequently used as one might expect. *Index Medicus* and *Abridged Index Medicus* are common avenues to medical journal literature. Other indexes, listed in the following bibliography under "Finding Devices," aid in discovering medical journal literature.

Science Citation Index performs a function similar to *Shepard's Citations*.

Medical libraries do not contain counterparts to *American Jurisprudence 2d* and *Corpus Juris Secundum*. Physicians rely on various individual textbooks and treatises, each of which deals with a relatively narrow area of medicine.

Because of the rapid rate of progress of medical knowledge, the texts and treatises cannot always be relied upon as sources of the latest information concerning particular problems. Although occasional looseleaf books are found in medical libraries, pocket parts are seldom seen. If you want the latest information concerning a medical problem, you will likely have to look for it in the medical journals, via *Index Medicus, Abridged Index Medicus,* or one or more of the other periodical indexes.

Students studying the medical aspects of cases, and lawyers and paralegals whose employment involves medical questions, need to develop a working arrangement with a conveniently located medical library.[8] Of course, depending upon experience and the frequency of need, some medical books could be valuable additions to law libraries. Most, if not all, of the works listed in the following bibliography will be found in a large medical center library. Some of them can be found in libraries associated with bar associations, courts, dental schools, health departments, hospitals, law schools, medical schools, medical societies, nursing schools, pharmacy schools, public libraries, and universities.

MEDICAL JOURNALS

Medical journals are important storehouses of timely medical information. In order to take advantage of them, however, an independent index must ordinarily be used to analyze them.

The *Abridged Index Medicus,* which was designed for small medical libraries, indexes 117 medical journals. It is supplied in monthly advance parts with an annual cumulation and is economical to purchase. Some courts, law schools, and academic libraries subscribe to it or receive it as a federal depository.

The *Index Medicus,* which was designed for large medical libraries, is a giant finding device, indexing about 2,600 medical journals.

As is indicated by the following bibliography under "Finding Devices," there are other, more selective, indexes available for medical specialties and scientific topics. To a significant extent, you may find that one of these special indexes will best suit your needs when dealing with concrete problems, because of the peculiar nature of its coverage.

There are approximately 18,000 periodicals which relate to medicine. For the purpose of an overview of the medical journals, it is useful to observe that a large number of them are exclusively devoted to medical specialties or narrow scientific topics. For this reason, the following bibliography classifies some medical journals under the subject headings for which the textbooks and treatises are listed. Researchers should realize, however, that because of the large number of medical and scientific journals, they are likely to find references to journals which are not listed.

CLASSIFIED SUBJECT BIBLIOGRAPHY

The following bibliography of medical literature is classified primarily by subject. Some of the textbooks and treatises are short and others are long. Some

---

[8] For a roster of medical libraries in the United States and Canada, arranged alphabetically by states and provinces and by cities within each state and province, see *Stedman's Medical Dictionary,* 5th Unabridged Lawyers' Edition, 1982, Lawyers' Section L-6 to L-33.

of them are new and others are older. The particular works listed may or may not assist you, depending of course upon your specific needs. The works listed are intended to constitute significant beginning points for considerable research in medical literature. The reader should be constantly aware of the fact, however, that subsequent editions and completely new medical books frequently become available.

Like the author's treatment of the legal bibliography portion of this book, the list within each medical and scientific classification has been intentionally kept short and selective, so that this bibliography will be manageable.[9]

Allergy and Immunology

allergy (al′er-jĭ) [G. *allos,* other, + *ergon,* work ERG-]. 1. Acquired (induced) sensitivity; the immunologic state induced in a susceptible subject by an antigen (allergen), characterized by a marked change in the subject's reactivity.*** 2. That branch of medicine which embraces the study, diagnosis, and treatment of allergic manifestations. 3. An acquired hypersensitivity to certain drugs and biologic preparations.

immunology (im′u-nol′o-jĭ) [immuno- +G. *logos*, study]. The science concerned with the various phenomena of immunity, induced sensitivity, and allergy.

Textbooks & Treatises

Leo H. Criep, et al., *Dermatologic Allergy: Immunology, Diagnosis, Management,* 1967. Philadelphia, Saunders, xxvii, 605 p.

Elliott Middleton, Jr., Charles E. Reed & Elliot F. Ellis, eds., *Allergy: Principles and Practice,* 2d ed. 1983. St. Louis, C. V. Mosby Co., 2 v.

Roy Patterson, ed., *Allergic Diseases: Diagnosis and Management,* 2d ed. 1980. Philadelphia, Lippincott, xvi, 714 p.

Max Samter & David W. Talmage, *et al.*, eds., *Immunological Diseases,* 3d ed. 1978. Boston, Little, Brown, 2 v.

John M. Sheldon, Robert G. Lovell & Kenneth P. Matthews, *A Manual of Clinical Allergy,* 2d ed. 1967. Philadelphia, Saunders, xiii, 550 p.

Journals

Annals of Allergy, v. 1- , 1943- , Alexanderia, Va., American College of Allergists.

Journal of Allergy & Clinical Immunology, v. 1- , 1929- , St. Louis, Mosby.

---

[9] The definitions of the medical and scientific classifications published herein are from *Stedman's Medical Dictionary,* 5th Unabridged Lawyers' edition, 1982, and used by permission.

Anatomy

anatomy (ă-nat′o-mĭ) [G. *anatomē,* dissection, from *ana,* apart, + *tomē,* a cutting]. 1. The morphologic structure of an organism. 2. The science of the morphology or structure of organisms. 3. Dissection. 4. A work describing the form and structure of an organism and its various parts.

Barry J. Anson & Chester B. McVay, *Surgical Anatomy,* 6th ed. 1984. Philadelphia, Saunders, 2 v.

Henry Gray, *Anatomy of the Human Body,* 29th American Charles Mayo Goss ed. 1973. Philadelphia, Lea & Febiger, 1466 p.

Henry Gray, *Gray's Anatomy,* 36th Peter L. Williams, Roger Warwick, Mary Dyson, *et al.,* eds. 1980. Philadelphia, Saunders, xvii, 1578 p.

Johannes Sobotta, *Sobotta Atlas of Human Anatomy,* 10th English Helmut Ferner & Jochen Staubesand ed. 1983. Baltimore, Urban & Schwarzenberg, 2 v.

Anesthesiology

anesthesiology (an′es-the-zĭ-ol′o-jĭ) [anesthesia + G. *logos,* treatise]. The medical specialty concerned with the pharmacological, physiological, and clinical basis of anesthesia and related fields, including resuscitation, intensive respiratory care, and pain.

Textbooks & Treatises

Vincent J. Collins, *Principles of Anesthesiology,* 2d ed. 1976. Philadelphia, Lea & Febiger, xi, 1671 p.

William H. L. Dornette, *Anatomy for the Anesthesiologist: A Steroscopic Atlas,* 1963. Springfield, Ill., Thomas, 389 p. Anatomic structures, preparing and positioning patient, administering, mechanisms for complications.

Robert D. Dripps, James E. Eckenhoff & Leroy D. Vandam, *Introduction to Anesthesia: The Principles of Safe Practice,* 5th ed. 1977. Philadelphia, Saunders, xvi, 557 p. Basic. Techniques for safe anesthesia. Complications.

Ronald D. Miller, ed., *Anesthesia,* 1981. N.Y., Churchill Livingstone, 2 v.

Robert Moors Smith, *Anesthesia for Infants and Children,* 4th ed. 1980. St. Louis, Mosby, xii, 702 p.

William Derek Wylie & H. C. Churchill-Davidson, *A Practice of Anaesthesia,* 5th ed. 1984. London & Chicago, Lloyd-Luke & Year Book Medical Pubs., xvii, 1261 p.

Journals

Anesthesia and Analgesia, Current Researches, 1921-   , N.Y., Elsevier Science Pub. Co.

Anesthesiology, 1940- , Philadelphia, Lippincott. Research oriented.

Canadian Anaesthetists' Soc'y Journal, 1954- , Toronto, Douglas B. Craig, ed. Text and title in English and French.

Bacteriology

bacteriology (bak-tēr-ĭ-ol′o-jī) [bacterio- + G. *logos,* study]. The branch of science concerned with the study of bacteria.

bacterium, pl. **bacte′ria** (bak-tēr′ĭ-um, -ah) [Mod. L. fr. G. *baktērion,* dim. of *baktron,* a staff]. A prokaryotic microorganism that differs from blue-green bacteria (blue-green algae) primarily in that the blue-green bacteria perform photosynthesis accompanied by oxygen evolution and have a photosynthetic pigment system that includes chlorophyll *a* and *ß*-carotene.

Textbooks & Treatises

Robert Cruickshank, *et al.*, ed., *Medical Microbiology; A Guide to the Laboratory Diagnosis and Control of Infection,* 12th ed. 1973-1974, London, Churchill Livingstone, 2 v.

Edwin H. Lennette, *et al.*, eds., *Manual of Clinical Microbiology,* 3d ed. 1980. Washington, American Soc'y for Microbiology, xvii, 1044 p.

Graham S. Wilson, A. A. Miles & Elizabeth Asheshov, *Topley and Wilson's Principles of Bacteriology, Virology, and Immunology,* 6th ed. 1975. Baltimore, Williams & Wilkins, 2 v.

Journals

Journal of Applied Bacteriology, 1938- , Oxford, Eng., Blackwell Scientific Pubs.

Journal of Bacteriology, 1916- , Washington, American Soc'y for Microbiology.

Bibliographies

John B. Blake & Charles Roos, ed., *Medical Reference Works 1679-1966, 1967-* . Chicago, Medical Library Ass'n, viii, 343 p. and supps.

Boyd, *A Patient Care Survey: Are These Texts in Your Office Library?,* 18 Patient Care 100 (No. 20, November 30, 1984).

Brandon & Hill, *Selected List of Books and Journals for the Small Medical Library,* 73 Bull. Medical Lib. Ass'n 176 (April, 1985). 11th rev'd version.

Ehrhardt & Wheeler, *Sources of Medical Information,* 30 Fed'n of Ins. Couns. Q. 347 (1980).

Gilmer, *Lawyers in Medical Bookland,* 1970 U. Ill. L.F. 115, republished, 34 A.T.L. L.J. 97 (1972).

Sagall, *Attorney's Guide to Medical Literature,* 3 Am. J.L. & Med. 361 (1977).

Wender, Parrish, Holman, *et al., Primary Care Physician's Book List,* 71 Postgraduate Medicine 74 (No. 2, February, 1982).

Biochemistry — *See* "Toxicology & Biochemistry."

Cancer

cancer (CA) (kan′ser) [L. a crab, a cancer. CANC-]. A general term frequently used to indicate any of various types of malignant neoplasms, most of which invade surrounding tissues, may metastasize to several sites, and are likely to recur after attempted removal and to cause death of the patient unless adequately treated; especially any such carcinoma or sarcoma, but, in ordinary usage, especially the former.

ne′oplasm [neo- + G. *plasma,* thing formed]. New growth; tumor (2); an abnormal tissue that grows by cellular proliferation more rapidly than normal and continues to grow after the stimuli that initiated the new growth cease. N.'s show partial or complete lack of structural organization and functional coordination with the normal tissue, and usually form a distinct mass of tissue which may be either benign (benign *tumor*) or malignant (carcinoma).

Textbooks & Treatises

Lauren V. Ackerman, Juan A. Del Regato & Harlan J. Spjut, *et al., Cancer: Diagnosis, Treatment and Prognosis,* 6th ed. 1985. St. Louis, Mosby, xx, 1079 p.

American Cancer Soc'y, *Manual of Tumor Nomenclature and Coding,* 1968 ed., Washington, American Cancer Society, 74 p.

Martin J. Cline & Charles M. Haskell, *Cancer Chemotherapy,* 3d ed. 1980. Philadelphia, Saunders, vi, 397 p.

Vincent J. DeVita, Jr. Samuel Hellman & Steven A. Rosenberg, eds., *Cancer: Principles & Practice of Oncology,* 2d ed. 1985. Philadelphia, J. B. Lippincott Co., xlvii, 2 v., 2344 p.

James F. Holland & Emil Frei, III, *Cancer Medicine,* 2d ed. 1982. Philadelphia, Lea & Feibiger, xxiv, 2465 p.

Journals

Advances in Cancer Research, v. 1-   , 1953-   , N.Y. and London, Academic Press.

British Journal of Cancer, 1947-   , Basingstoke, Hampshire, Macmillan Press.

Cancer, 1948- , Philadelphia, Lippincott.

Yearbook of Cancer, 1956- , Chicago, Year Book Medical Pubs.

Cardiovascular System

car′diovas′cular [cardio- + L. *vasculum,* vessel]. Relating to the heart and the blood vessels or the circulation.

Textbooks & Treatises

Eugene Braunwald, ed., *Heart Disease: A Textbook of Cardiovascular Medicine,* 2d ed. 1984. Philadelphia, W. B. Saunders, xviii, 1844 p.

John F. Fairbairn, II, John L. Juergens & John A. Spittell, Jr., eds., *Peripheral Vascular Diseases,* 5th ed. 1980. Philadelphia, Saunders xiii, 981 p.

Henry Harold Friedman, *Diagnostic Electrocardiography and Vectorcardiography*, 3d ed. 1985. N.Y., McGraw-Hill, x, 668 p.

Mervin J. Goldman, *Principles of Clinical Electrocardiography,* 11th ed. 1982. Los Altos, Cal., Lange Med. Pubs., 437 p. 12th ed. 1985 forthcoming.

J. Willis Hurst & R. Bruce Logue, *et al.*, eds., *The Heart, Arteries and Veins,* 5th ed. 1982. N.Y., McGraw-Hill, xxvii, 1953, 60 p. 6th ed. 1985 forthcoming.

Henry J. Marriott, *Practical Electrocardiography,* 7th ed. 1983. Baltimore, Williams & Wilkins, xvii, 496 p.

N.Y. Heart Ass'n, Criteria Committee, *Nomenclature and Criteria for Diagnosis of Diseases of the Heart and Great Vessels,* 8th ed. 1979. Boston, Little, Brown, xiii, 349 p.

Earl N. Silver & Louis N. Katz, *Heart Disease,* 1975. N.Y., Macmillan Pub. Co., x, 1430 p. 2d 1985 ed. forthcoming.

Journals

American Heart Journal, 1925- , St. Louis, Mosby.

Blood, 1946- , Orlando, Fla., Grune & Stratton.

Circulation, 1950- , Dallas, American Heart Ass'n.

Dentistry

den′tistry. Odontology; odontonosology; the healing science and art concerned with the embryology, anatomy, physiology and pathology of the oral-facial complex, and with the prevention, diagnosis, and treatment of deformities, pathoses, and traumatic injuries thereof.

Textbooks & Treatises

Malcom A. Lynch, Vernon J. Brightman & Martin S. Greenberg, eds., *Burket's Oral Medicine: Diagnosis and Treatment,* 8th ed. 1984. Philadelphia, Lippincott, xviii, 958 p.

Donald A. Kerr, Major M. Ash, Jr., & H. Dean Millard, *Oral Diagnosis,* 6th ed. 1983. St. Louis, Mosby, viii, 383 p.

Gustav O. Kruger, ed., *Textbook of Oral and Maxillofacial Surgery,* 6th ed. 1984. St. Louis, Mosby, xvi, 782 p.

Journals

American Dental Association Journal, 1913- , Chicago, American Dental Ass'n.

Journal of Oral & Maxillofacial Surgery, 1943- , Philadelphia, Saunders.

Oral Surgery, Oral Medicine, Oral Pathology, 1948- , St. Louis, Mosby.

Dermatology

dermatology (der-mă-tol′o-jĭ) [dermato- + G. *logos,* study]. The branch of medicine concerned with the study of the skin, its chemistry, physiology, histopathology, cutaneous lesions, and the relationship of cutaneous lesions to systemic disease.

Textbooks & Treatises

Anthony N. Domonkos, Harry L. Arnold, Jr., & Richard B. Odom, *Andrews' Diseases of the Skin: Clinical Dermatology,* 7th ed., 1982. Philadelphia, Saunders, xi, 1108 p.

Thomas B. Fitzpatrick, *et al.*, eds., *Dermatology in General Medicine: Textbook and Atlas,* 2d ed. 1979. N.Y., McGraw-Hill, xvii, 1884 p. Supplemented by *Update: Dermatology in General Medicine,* 1983, same publisher, viii, 237 p. 3d 1985 ed. forthcoming.

Samuel L. Moschella, Harry J. Hurley, *et al., Dermatology,* 2d ed. 1985. Philadelphia, Saunders, 2 v.

Gordon C. Sauer, *Manual of Skin Diseases,* 4th ed. 1980. Philadelphia, Lippincott, xix, 371 p. 5th 1985 ed. forthcoming.

Journals

Archives of Dermatology, 1920- , Chicago, American Medical Ass'n.

British Journal of Dermatology, 1888- , Oxford, London & Edinburgh, Blackwell Scientific Pubs.

Diagnosis

diagnosis (di-ag-no′sis) [G. *diagnōsis,* a deciding. GNO-]. The determination of the nature of a disease.

Robert Stanley Blacklow, ed., *MacBryde's Signs & Symptoms: Applied Pathologic Physiology & Clinical Interpretation,* 6th ed. 1983. Philadelphia, Lippincott, xxiii, 935 p.

Mahlon H. Delp & Robert T. Manning, *Major's Physical Diagnosis: An Introduction to the Clinical Process,* 9th ed. 1981. Philadelphia, Saunders, xiv, 574 p.

Marcus A. Krupp, *et al., Physician's Handbook,* 21st ed. 1985. Los Altos, Cal., Lange Medical Pubs., 800 p.

Dictionaries

Blakiston's Gould Medical Dictionary, 4th ed. 1979. N.Y., McGraw-Hill, xxvi, 1632 p.

Dorland's Illustrated Medical Dictionary, 26th ed. 1981. Philadelphia, Saunders, xxix, 1485 p.

Dorland's Pocket Medical Dictionary, 23d ed. 1982. Philadelphia, Saunders, xxi, 754 p.

Arthur J. Finkel, *et al.,* eds. *Current Medical Information and Terminology,* 5th ed. 1981. Chicago, American Medical Ass'n, vi, 801 p.

Ffrangcon Roberts, *Medical Terms: Their Origin and Construction,* 5th ed. rev. 1971. London, Heinemann Medical Books, viii, 102 p.

J. E. Schmidt, *Paramedical Dictionary,* 1969. Springfield, Ill., Thomas, vi, 423 p.

J. E. Schmidt, *Reversicon: A Medical Word Finder,* 1958. Springfield, Ill., Thomas, xv, 440 p.

Stedman's Medical Dictionary, 5th Unabridged Lawyers' Edition, 1982. Cincinnati and Washington, Anderson Pub. Co. and Jefferson Law Book Co., xlvii, L-67, 1678 p. Includes the complete text of *Stedman's Medical Dictionary,* 24th ed. 1982, and a special 67 p. "Lawyer's Section" by William H. L. Dornette.

Taber's Cyclopedic Medical Dictionary, 15th ed. 1985. Philadelphia, Davis, xxx, 2170 p.

See also "Drugs" at Mary C. Griffiths.

Directories

Organizations

Stanley Alperin, Barbara Elizabeth Shaw, *et al.,* eds. *1985-86 Hospital Phone Book,* 1985. Miami, U.S. Directory Service, 248 p. paperback.

American College of Surgeons Yearbook. Geographical list of medical schools; alphabetical list of medical schools. Chicago, American College of Surgeons.

American Hospital Ass'n, *Guide to the Health Care Field,* 1984 ed. Tamara Schiller, Proj. Mgr. Chicago, American Hospital Ass'n, 1 v. various pagination, paperback, annual.

Anthony T. Kruzas, *et al.*, eds., *Health Services Directory,* 1981. Detroit, Gale Research Co., x, 620 p.

Persons

American Board of Medical Specialties, *Directory of Medical Specialists,* 21st ed. 1983-1984. Chicago, Marquis Who's Who, 2 v.

American College of Surgeons Yearbook. Geographical List of Fellows; Alphabetical List of Fellows. Chicago, American College of Surgeons.

American Medical Directory, 29th ed. 1985. Chicago, American Medical Association, 4 v.

American Men and Women of Science: Medical & Health Sciences 1977, 1977. N.Y., Bowker, xiii, 1720 p.

Drugs

drugs 1. A therapeutic agent; any substance, other than food, used in the prevention, diagnosis, alleviation, treatment, or cure of disease in man and animal. * * *.

Textbooks & Treatises

AMA Drug Evaluations, 5th ed. 1983. American Medical Ass'n Div. of Drugs, Chicago, American Medical Ass'n, xxii, 1884 p. Superseded *New Drugs, New and Nonofficial Drugs* and *New and Nonofficial Remedies* (1907-1967).

American Drug Index, annual, Philadelphia, J. B. Lippincott. 29th ed. 1985, Norman F. Billups & Shirley M. Billups, eds., ix, 725 p.

American Soc'y of Hospital Pharmacists, *American Hospital Formulary Service: Drug Information,* 1959- . Bethesda, Md., annual.

Drug Topics Red Book and cum. supp., 1 v. paperback. Oradell, N.J., Medical Economics, annual. Contains prices and descriptions of products.

Alfred Goodman Gilman, Louis S. Goodman, Alfred Gilman, *et al.*, eds., *Goodman & Gilman's The Pharmacological Basis of Therapeutics,* 6th ed. 1980. N.Y., Macmillan Co., xvi, 1843 p. 7th ed. 1985 forthcoming.

Mary C. Griffiths, *et al.*, eds., *USAN and the USP Dictionary of Drug Names,* 22d ed., 1984. Rockville, Md., U.S. Pharmacopeial Convention, 661 p., paperback, serial.

Bertram G. Katzung, ed., *Basic & Clinical Pharmacology,* 2d ed. 1984. Los Altos, Cal., Lange Medical Pubs., biennial serial.

Ruth R. Levine, *Pharmacology, Drug Actions and Reactions,* 3d ed. 1983. Boston, Little, Brown, xvi, 526 p.

E. E. J. Marler, comp., *Pharmacological and Chemical Synonyms,* 7th ed. 1983. Amsterdam, Excerpta Medica, 514 p. Published in English.

Walter Modell, ed., *Drugs of Choice 1984-1985,* 1984. St. Louis, C. V. Mosby Co., xv, 824 p., serial.

Physician's Desk Reference. Oradell, N.J., Medical Economics, 1 v., annual.

Physician's Desk Reference for Nonprescription Drugs. Oradell, N.J., Medical Economics, 1 v., annual.

Robert E. Rakel, ed., *Conn's Current Therapy: Latest Approved Methods of Treatment for the Practicing Physician,* 1985. Philadelphia, W. B. Saunders Co., xxxvi, 1020 p., serial.

Max Samter & Charles W. Parker, eds., *Hypersensitivity to Drugs,* 1972, N.Y., Pergamon Press, xi, 439 p. *International Encyclopedia of Pharmacology and Therapeutics,* Sec. 5, v. 1.

U.S. Pharmacopeial Convention, *The United States Pharmacopeia,* 21st rev., 1985. Rockville, Md., lvii, 1683 p. Includes *National Formulary,* 16th ed. 1985.

Journals

Advances in Drug Research, v. 1- , 1964- , N.Y. and London, Academic Press.

Clinical Pharmacology & Therapeutics, 1960- , St. Louis, Mosby.

Medical Letter on Drugs & Therapeutics, 1959- , New Rochelle, N.Y., Medical Letter. Biweekly.

Pharmacological Reviews, 1951- , Baltimore, Williams & Wilkins.

Side Effects of Drugs Annual, v. 1- , 1955- , Amsterdam, Elsevier Science Pubs.

Emergency Medicine

emergency (e-mer′jen-sĭ) [L. *e- mergo,* pp. *-mersus,* to rise up, emerge, fr. *mergo,* to plunge into, dip]. An unlooked-for contingency or happening; a sudden demand for action.

Harvey D. Cain, *Flint's Emergency Treatment & Management,* 7th ed. 1985. Philadelphia, Saunders, xi, 842 p.

John Mills, *et al.,* eds., *Current Emergency Diagnosis & Treatment,* 2d ed. 1985. Los Altos, Cal., Lange Medical Pubs., 864 p.

Peter Rosen, Frank J. Baker, II, *et al.,* eds., *Emergency Medicine: Concepts & Clinical Practice,* 1983. St. Louis, Mosby, 2 v.

Earle W. Wilkins, Jr., James J. Dineen, Ashby C. Moncure, *et al.,* eds., *MGH Textbook of Emergency Medicine: Emergency Care as Practiced at the Massachusetts General Hospital,* 1983. Baltimore, Williams & Wilkins, xix, 973 p.

Journal

Annals of Emergency Medicine, 1972- , Irving, Tex., American College of Emergency Physicians.

Family Practice

fam'ily [L. *familia*]. 1. A group of blood relatives, or, more strictly, the parents and their children. * * *

Cornelia Fleischer Mutel & Kelley J. Donham, *Medical Practice in Rural Communities,* 1983. N.Y., Springer-Verlag, xxi, 146 p.

Robert E. Rakel, ed., *Textbook of Family Practice,* 3d ed. 1984. Philadelphia, Saunders, xix, 1506 p.

Robert B. Taylor, John L. Buckingham, E. P. Donatelle, *et al.*, eds., *Family Medicine: Principles & Practice,* 2d ed. 1983. N.Y., Springer-Verlag, lii, 2020 p.

Journals

American Family Physician, 1970- , Kansas City, Mo., American Academy of Family Physicians.

Journal of Family Practice, 1974- , E. Norwalk, Conn., Appleton-Century-Crofts.

Finding Devices

Abridged Index Medicus, v. 1- , 1970- . Bethesda, Md., Nat'l Library of Medicine.

Biological Abstracts, v. 1- , 1926- . Philadelphia, Biosciences Info. Service.

Cancer Therapy Abstracts (Cancer Chemotherapy Abstracts), v. 1-20, 1960-1980. Franklin Institute Press.

Current Contents: Life Sciences, v. 1- , 1958- . Philadelphia, Institute for Scientific Information. Furnishes prompt information concerning medical journals, reproducing the tables of contents of journals currently being published and some in advance of publication date. Indexed by title-word and author. Weekly.

Dental Abstracts, v. 1- , 1956- . Chicago, American Dental Association.

Excerpta Medica, v. 1- , 1947- . Amsterdam, Excerpta Medica Foundation. Published in English. Organized by medical specialties, *e.g.*, arthritis and rheumatism, physiology, and surgery. Published in topical sections according to specialty and available in separate sections.

Index to Dental Literature (Index of the Periodical Dental Literature), 1839- Chicago, American Dental Association.

Index Medicus, v. 1- , 1960- . Washington, Nat'l Library of Medicine. Earlier series available.

Oral Research Abstracts, v. 1- , 1966- . Chicago, American Dental Association.

Psychological Abstracts, v. 1- , 1927- . Arlington, Va., American Psychological Assocation.

Science Citation Index, 1961- . Philadelphia, Institute for Scientific Information.

Forensic Medicine

See "Medical Law" at Chapter 5, Classified Bibliography.

Gastroenterology

gas'troenterol'ogy [gastro- + G. *enteron,* intestine, + *logos,* study]. The branch of medical science concerned with the function and disorders of the stomach and intestines.

J. Edward Berk, William S. Haubrich, *et al.*, eds., *Bockus Gastroenterology,* 4th ed. 1985. Philadelphia, Saunders, 7 v.

Richard T. Shackelford & George D. Zuidema, *Surgery of the Alimentary Tract,* 2d ed. 1978-1983. Philadelphia, Saunders, 4 v. v. 5 forthcoming 1985.

Howard M. Spiro, *Clinical Gastroenterology,* 3d ed. 1983, N.Y., Macmillan, xx, 1289 p. 1549 p.

Marvin H. Sleisenger & John S. Fordtran, eds., *Gastrointestinal Disease: Pathophysiology, Diagnosis, Management,* 3d ed. 1983. Philadelphia, Saunders, xxxi, 1850, lxii p.

Journals

Diseases of the Colon & Rectum, 1958- , Philadelphia, Lippincott.

Gastroenterology, 1943- , N.Y., Elsevier Science Pub. Co.

Geriatrics

geriatrics (Jĕr'ĭ-at'riks) [G. *gēras,* old age, + *iatrikos,* healing]. Presbytiatrics; the branch of medicine concerned with the medical problems and care of old people.

Reubin Andres, Edwin L. Bierman & William R. Hazzard, eds., *Principles of Geriatric Medicine,* 1985. N.Y., McGraw-Hill, xx, 992 p.

John C. Brocklehurst, ed., *Textbook of Geriatric Medicine and Gerontology,* 2d ed. 1978. Edinburgh and N.Y., Churchill Livingstone, viii, 838 p. 3d ed. forthcoming 1985.

Christine K. Cassel & John R. Walsh, eds., *Geriatric Medicine,* 1984, N.Y., Springer-Verlag, 2 v.

Isadore Rossman, ed., *Clinical Geriatrics,* 2d ed. 1979. Philadelphia, Lippincott, xxiii, 704 p. 3d ed forthcoming 1985.

Journals

Geriatrics, 1946- , Cleveland, Modern Medicine Pubs., Harcourt Brace Jovanovich Pubs.

Journal of the American Geriatrics Soc'y, 1953- , Philadelphia, Saunders.

Journal of Gerontology, 1946- , Washington, Gerontological Soc'y of America.

Gynecology — *See* "Obstetrics & Gynecology."

Heart — *See* "Cardiovascular System."

Hematology

hematology (he-mă-tol'o-jĭ, hem-ă-tol'o-jĭ) [hemato- + G. *logos,* study]. Hemology; the medical specialty that pertains to the anatomy, physiology, pathology, symptomatology, and therapeutics related to the blood and blood-forming tissues.

Textbooks & Treatises

Byrd Stuart Leavell & Oscar A. Thorup, Jr., *et al., Fundamentals of Clinical Hematology,* 4th ed. 1976. Philadelphia, Saunders, xiii, 755 p.

George A. McDonald, T. C. Dodds & Bruce Cruickshank, *Atlas of Haematology,* 4th ed. 1978. Edinburgh & N.Y., Churchill Livingstone, viii, 309 p.

Denis R. Miller, Robert L. Baehner, Campbell W. McMillan, *et al.*, eds., *Blood Diseases of Infancy and Childhood,* 5th ed. 1984. St. Louis, Mosby, xxv, 972 p.

William J. Williams, *et al.*, eds., *Hematology,* 3d ed. 1983. N.Y., McGraw-Hill, xxvi, 1728 p.

Maxwell M. Wintrobe, *et al., Clinical Hematology,* 8th ed. 1981. Philadelphia, Lea & Febiger, xxiii, 2021 p.

Journal

See "Cardiovascular System," Blood.

Hypnosis

hypnosis (hip-no'sis) [G. *hypnos,* sleep, + suffix *-osis,* condition]. 1. Hypnotic state or sleep; status hypnoticus; an artificially induced trance-like state resembling somnambalism in which the subject is highly susceptible to suggestion, oblivious to all else, and responds readily to the commands of the hypnotist.

Textbooks

Gordon J. Ambrose & George Newbold, *A Handbook of Medical Hypnosis,* 4th ed. 1980. London, Bailliere Tindall, ix, 213 p.

Jerome M. Schneck, ed., *Hypnosis in Modern Medicine,* 3d ed. 1963. Springfield, Ill., Thomas, 452 p.

William C. Wester II, Alexander H. Smith, Jr., *et al.*, eds., *Clinical Hypnosis: A Multidisciplinary Approach,* 1984. Philadelphia, Lippincott, xxv, 660 p.

Journal

American Journal of Clinical Hypnosis, 1958- , Des Plaines, Ill., American Soc'y of Clinical Hypnosis.

Infection — *See* "Bacteriology."

Internal Medicine

internal medicine, the branch of m. concerned with nonsurgical diseases of a constitutional nature in adults.

Textbooks & Treatises

A. McGehee Harvey, Richard J. Johns, Victor A. McKusick, *et al.,* eds., *The Principles and Practice of Medicine,* 21st ed. 1984. Norwalk, Conn., Appleton-Century-Crofts, xxiii, 1596 p.

Marcus A. Krupp, Milton J. Chatton & David Werdegar, eds., *Current Medical Diagnosis & Treatment,* 1985. Los Altos, Cal., Lange Medical Pubs., 1157 p., annual.

Robert G. Petersdorf, Raymond D. Adams, Eugene Braunwald, *et al.,* eds., *Harrison's Principles of Internal Medicine,* 10th ed. 1983. N.Y., McGraw-Hill, xxxii, 2212, 128 p.

James B. Wyngaarden & Lloyd H. Smith, Jr., eds., *Cecil Textbook of Medicine,* 17th ed. 1985. Philadelphia, Saunders, xxxi, 2341, xcv p.

Journals

British Medical Journal, 1832- , London, British Medical Ass'n.

Journal of American Medical Ass'n, 1848- , Chicago, American Medical Ass'n.

Lancet, 1823- , Boston, Little, Brown.

New England Journal of Medicine, 1812- , Boston, Mass. Medical Soc'y.

Kidney — *See* "Nephrology."

Medical Jurisprudence

See "Medical Law" at Chapter 5, Classified Bibliography.

Neoplasam — *See* "Cancer."

Nephrology

nephrology (nĕ-frol′o-jĭ) [nephro- + G. *logos,* study]. The branch of medical science concerned with the kidneys.

Textbooks & Treatises

Douglas A. K. Black & N. F. Jones, eds., *Renal Disease,* 4th ed. 1979. Oxford, Blackwell Scientific Pubs., xiv, 905 p.

Laurence E. Early & Carl W. Gottschalk, eds., *Strauss & Welt's Diseases of the Kidney,* 3d ed. 1979. Boston, Little, Brown, 2 v.

Solomon Papper, *Clinical Nephrology,* 2d ed. 1978. Boston, Little, Brown, xii, 633 p.

Journals

Kidney International, v. 1- , 1972- , N.Y., Springer-Verlag.

Nephron, v. 1- , 1964- , Basel, Switzerland, S. Karger AG. Published in English.

Neurology

neurology (nu-rol′o-jĭ) [neuro- + G. *logos,* study]. The branch of medical science concerned with the nervous system and its disorders.

Textbooks & Treatises

Raymond D. Adams & Maurice Victor, *Principles of Neurology,* 3d ed. 1985. N.Y., McGraw-Hill, x, 1186 p.

Joseph G. Chusid, *Correlative Neuroanatomy & Functional Neurology,* 18th ed. 1982. Los Altos, Cal., Lange Medical Pubs., 476 p. 19th ed. forthcoming 1985.

Mayo Clinic, *Clinical Examinations in Neurology,* 5th ed., 1981. Philadelphia, Saunders, xix, 384 p.

Lewis P. Rowland, ed., *Merritt's Textbook of Neurology,* 7th ed. 1984. Philadelphia, Lea & Febiger, xvi, 774 p.

Robert H. Wilkins & Setti S. Rengachary, eds., *Neurosurgery,* 1985. N.Y., McGraw-Hill, 3 v.

Journals

Archives of Neurology, v. 1- , 1959- , Chicago, American Medical Association.

Brain: A Journal of Neurology, 1878- , Oxford, Eng., Oxford Univ. Press, Clarendon Press.

See also "Psychiatry."

Obstetrics & Gynecology

gynecology (gi-nĕ-kol′o-jĭ, jin-ĕ-) [gyneco- + G. *logos,* study]. The branch of medicine which has to do with the diseases peculiar to women, primarily those of the genital tract, as well as female endocrinology and reproductive physiology.

obstet′rics [L. *obstetrix,* a midwife, fr. *ob- sto,* to stand before, denoting the position formerly taken by the midwife]. Tocology; the specialty of medicine concerned with the care of the pregnant woman during pregnancy, parturition, and the puerperium.

Textbooks & Treatises

Ralph C. Benson, ed., *Current Obstetric & Gynecologic Diagnosis & Treatment,* 5th ed. 1984. Los Altos, Cal., Lange Medical Pubs., 1082 p. paperback. Biennial.

Ralph C. Benson, *Handbook of Obstetrics & Gynecology,* 8th ed. 1983. Los Altos, Cal., Lange Medical Pubs., 804 p.

Howard W. Jones, Jr. & Georgeanna Seegar Jones, *Novak's Textbook of Gynecology,* 10th ed. 1981. Baltimore, Williams & Wilkins, xvi, 871 p.

Jack A. Pritchard, Paul C. MacDonald & Norman F. Gant, *Williams' Obstetrics,* 17th ed. 1985. Norwalk, Conn., Appleton-Century-Crofts, xi, 976 p.

J. Robert Willson, *Atlas of Obstetric Technic,* 2d ed. 1969. St. Louis, Mosby, vii, 313 p.

J. Robert Willson & Elsie Reid Carrington, *Obstetrics and Gynecology,* 7th ed. 1983. St. Louis, Mosby, viii, 737 p.

Journals

American Journal of Obstetrics & Gynecology, v. 1- , 1920- , St. Louis, Mosby.

Surgery, Gynecology & Obstetrics, v. 1- , 1905- , Chicago, Franklin H. Martin Memorial Fdn.

Ophthalmology

ophthalmology (of′thal-mol′o-jĭ) [ophthalmo- + G. *logos,* study]. The medical specialty concerned with the eye, its diseases, and refractive errors.

Textbooks & Treatises

William H. Havener, *Synopsis of Ophthalmology,* 6th ed. 1984. St. Louis, Mosby, xii, 460 p.

Frank W. Newell, *Ophthalmology Principles & Concepts,* 5th ed. 1982. St. Louis, Mosby, x, 559 p.

George L. Spaeth, ed., *Ophthalmic Surgery: Principles & Practice,* 1982. Philadelphia, Saunders, xiv, 775 p.

D. J. Spalton, R. A. Hitchings & P. A. Hunter, eds., *Atlas of Clinical Ophthalmology,* 1984. Philadelphia, Lippincott, 1 v., various pagination.

Daniel Vaughn & Taylor Asbury, *General Ophthalmology,* 10th ed. 1983. Los Altos, Cal., Lange Medical Pubs., 407 p.

Myron Yanoff & Ben S. Fine, *Ocular Pathology: A Text & Atlas,* 2d ed. 1982. Philadelphia, Harper & Row, xxiv, 916 p.

Journals

American Journal of Ophthalmology, v. 1- , 1884- , Chicago, Ophthalmic Pub. Co.

Archives of Ophthalmology, v. 1- , 1869- , Chicago, American Medical Ass'n.

Orthopaedics

orthopaedics, orthopedics (or-tho-pe′diks) [ortho- + G. *pais (paid-),* child]. The medical specialty concerned with the preservation, restoration, and development of form and function of the extremities, spine, and associated structures by medical, surgical, and physical methods.

Textbooks & Treatises

H. Robert Brashear, Jr. & R. Beverly Raney, *Shands' Handbook of Orthopaedic Surgery,* 9th ed. 1978. St. Louis, Mosby, xv, 548 p. 10th ed. forthcoming 1986.

John F. Connolly, ed., *DePalma's The Management of Fractures & Dislocations: An Atlas,* 3d ed. 1981. Philadelphia, Saunders, 2 v.

Allen S. Edmonson & A. H. Crenshaw, eds., *Campbell's Operative Orthopaedics,* 6th ed. 1980. St. Louis, Mosby, 2 v.

Albert B. Ferguson, Jr., *Orthopaedic Surgery in Infancy and Childhood,* 5th ed. 1981. Baltimore, Williams & Wilkins, xxiv, 935 p.

Journal

Journal of Bone & Joint Surgery, 1903- , London & Boston, Churchill Livingstone & Journal of Bone & Joint Surgery, Inc.

Otorhinolaryngology

otorhinolaryngology (o′to-ri′no-lăr-ing-gol′o-jĭ) [oto- + G. *rhis,* nose + *larynx,* larynx, + *logos,* study]. The combined specialties of diseases of the ear, nose, and larynx. * * *

John Jacob Ballenger, ed., *Diseases of the Nose, Throat, Ear, Head, and Neck,* 13th ed. 1985. Philadelphia, Lea & Febiger, xiii, 1432 p.

David Downs DeWeese & William H. Saunders, *Textbook of Otolaryngology,* 6th ed. 1982, St. Louis, Mosby, ix, 495 p.

William H. Saunders, Michael M. Paparella & Andrew W. Migletts, *Atlas of Ear Surgery,* 3d ed. 1980. St. Louis, Mosby, x, 435 p. 4th ed. forthcoming 1985.

Journal

Archives of Otolaryngology, 1919- , Chicago, American Medical Ass'n.

Pathology

pathology (pă-thol′o-jĭ) [patho- + G. *logos,* study, treatise]. The medical science, and specialty practice, concerned with all aspects of disease, but with special reference to the essential nature, causes, and development of abnormal conditions, as well as the structural and functional changes that result from the disease processes.

Textbooks & Treatises

James A. Halsted & Charles H. Halsted, eds., *The Laboratory in Clinica Medicine: Interpretation & Application,* 2d ed. 1981. Philadelphia Saunders, xxxv, 1083 p.

John Bernard Henry, ed., *Todd-Sanford-Davidsohn Clinical Diagnosis and Management by Laboratory Methods,* 17th ed. 1984. Philadelphia, Saunders, xx, 1502 p.

John M. Kissane, ed., *Anderson's Pathology,* 8th ed. 1985. St. Louis, Mosby, 2 v.

Stanley L. Robbins, Ramzi S. Cotran & Vinay Kumar, *Pathologic Basis of Disease,* 3d ed. 1984. Philadelphia, Saunders, x, 1467 p.

William A. Sodeman, Jr., & Thomas M. Sodeman, *Sodeman's Pathologic Physiology: Mechanisms of Disease,* 6th ed. 1979. Philadelphia, Saunders, xiv, 1145 p. 7th ed. forthcoming 1985.

Journals

American Journal of Clinical Pathology, 1931- , Philadelphia, Lippincott.

American Journal of Pathology, v. 1- , 1925- , Philadelphia, Harper & Row.

Pediatrics

pediatrics (pe′dĭ-at′riks) [G. *pais (paid-),* child + *iatreia,* medical treatment]. Pediatry; pedonosology; the branch of medical science concerned with children in regard to hygienic, physiologic, and pathologic conditions; the specialty concerned with the diseases of children.

Textbooks & Treatises

Mary Ellen Avery & H. William Taeusch, Jr., *Schaffer's Diseases of the Newborn,* 5th ed. 1984. Philadelphia, Saunders, xvi, 1012 p.

Richard E. Behrman & Victor C. Vaughan, III, *Nelson Textbook of Pediatrics,* 12th ed. 1983. Philadelphia, Saunders, xxix, 1899 p.

Edmund S. Crelin, *Anatomy of the Newborn: An Atlas,* 1969. Philadelphia, Lea & Febiger, xiii, 256 p.

Abraham M. Rudolph & Julien I. E. Hoffman, *Pediatrics,* 17th ed. 1982. Norwalk, Conn., Appleton-Century-Crofts, xxxvii, 1917 p.

Harry C. Shirkey, Heinz F. Eichenwald, *et al.*, eds., *Pediatric Therapy,* 6th ed. 1980. St. Louis, C. V. Mosby Co., xxvi, 1321 p.

See also "Surgery" at William T. Mustard, and "Radiology" at John P. Caffey.

Journals

American Journal of Diseases of Children, v. 1- , 1911- , Chicago, American Medical Ass'n.

Journal of Pediatrics, v. 1- , 1932- , St. Louis, Mosby.

Pediatric Clinics of North America, v. 1- , 1954- , Philadelphia, Saunders.

Pediatrics, 1948- , Elk Grove Village, Ill., American Academy of Pediatrics.

Physiology

physiology (fiz'ĭ-ol'o-jĭ) [L. or G. *physiologia,* fr. G. *physis,* nature, +*logos,* study]. The science concerned with living things, with the normal vital processes of animal and vegetable organisms.

Textbooks & Treatises

Arthur C. Guyton, *Textbook of Medical Physiology,* 6th ed. 1981. Philadelphia, Saunders, xxxiv, 1074 p.

Vernon B. Mountcastle, ed., *Medical Physiology,* 14th ed. 1980. St. Louis, Mosby, 2 v.

John B. West, ed., *Best & Taylor's Physiological Basis of Medical Practice,* 11th ed. 1984. Baltimore, Williams & Wilkins, xxvi, 1340 p.

Journals

American Journal of Physiology, v. 1- , 1898- , Bethesda, Md., American Physiological Soc'y.

Annual Review of Physiology, v. 1- , 1939- , Palo Alto, Cal., Annual Reviews, Inc.

Physiological Reviews, v. 1- , 1921- , Bethesda, Md., American Physiological Soc'y.

Proctology — *See* "Gastroenterology."

Psychiatry

psychiatry (si-ki'ă-trĭ) [psych- + G. *iatreia,* medical treatment]. Psychiatric medicine; psychiatrics. 1. The medical specialty dealing with mental disorders. 2. The diagnosis and treatment of mental diseases. ***

Textbooks & Treatises

Robert Jean Campbell, *Psychiatric Dictionary,* 5th ed. 1981. N.Y., Oxford Univ. Press, 693 p.

Howard H. Goldman, ed., *Review of General Psychiatry,* 1984. Los Altos, Cal., Lange Medical Pubs. 696 p.

Harold I. Kaplan & Benjamin J. Sadock, *Modern Synopsis of Comprehensive Textbook of Psychiatry/III,* 3d ed. 1981. Baltimore, Williams & Wilkins, xvii, 1034, xx p.

Harold I. Kaplan, Alfred M. Freedman & Benjamin J. Sadock, eds., *Comprehensive Textbook of Psychiatry/III,* 3d ed. 1980. Baltimore, Williams, & Wilkins, 3 v.

Lawrence C. Kolb & H. Keith H. Brodie, *Modern Clinical Psychiatry,* 10th ed. 1982. Philadelphia, Saunders, x, 900 p.

Journals

American Journal of Psychiatry, v. 1- , 1844- , Washington, American Psychiatric Ass'n.

American Journal of Psychotherapy, v. 1- , 1946- , N.Y., Ass'n for the Advancement of Psychotherapy.

Psychiatric Quarterly, v. 1- , 1927- , Albany, N.Y., State Department of Mental Health.

Psychosomatic Medicine, v. 1- , 1938- , N.Y., Elsevier Science Pub. Co.

See also "Neurology."

Public Health

Textbooks & Treatises

William Hobson, ed., *Theory and Practice of Public Health,* 5th ed., 1979. N.Y., Oxford Univ. Press, xiii, 785 p.

Walter W. Holland, Roger Detels, George Knox, *et al.*, eds., *Oxford Textbook of Public Health,* 1984-1985. N.Y., Oxford Univ. Press, 4 v.

John M. Last, ed., *Maxcy-Rosenau Public Health & Preventive Medicine,* 11th ed. 1980. N.Y., Appleton-Century-Crofts, xxv, 1926 p. 12th ed. forthcoming 1985.

N. Irving Sax, Benjamin Feiner, *et al.*, *Dangerous Properties of Industrial Materials,* 6th ed. 1984. N.Y., Van Nostrand Reinhold, xxiii, 3124 p.

Daniel M. Wilner, Rosabelle Price Walkley & Edward J. O'Neill, *Introduction to Public Health,* 7th ed. 1978. N.Y., Macmillan, x, 533 p. Earlier eds. by Harry S. Mustard.

Journals

American Journal of Public Health, v. 1- , 1911- , Washington, American Public Health Ass'n.

Archives of Environmental Health, v. 1- , 1950- , Washington, Heldref Pubs.

Radiology

radiology (ra-dĭ-ol´o-jĭ) [radio- + G. *logos,* study]. The science concerned with radiant energy, with the chemical and other actions of rays proceeding from luminous bodies (*e.g.*, radium and other radioactive substances, x-rays), and with the sources of these rays.

Sandra L. Hagen-Ansert, *Textbook of Diagnostic Ultrasonography,* 2d ed. 1983. St. Louis, Mosby, xvi, 683 p.

John H. Juhl, *Paul & Juhl's Essentials of Roentgen Interpretation,* 4th ed. 1981. Hagerstown, Md., Harper & Row, xii, 1213 p.

M. N. Maisey, K. E. Britton & D. L. Gilday, eds., *Clinical Nuclear Medicine,* 1983. Philadelphia, Saunders, xiv, 525 p.

Frederic N. Silverman, ed., *Caffey's Pediatric X-ray Diagnosis,* 8th ed. 1985. Chicago, Year Book Medical Pubs., 2 v.

Journal

Radiology, 1915- , Easton, Penna., Radiological Soc'y of N. America.

Sports Medicine

Richard B. Birrer, ed., *Sports Medicine for the Primary Care Physician,* 1984. Norwalk, Conn., Appleton-Century-Crofts, xv, 347 p.

Don H. O'Donoghue *et al., Treatment of Injuries to Athletes,* 4th ed. 1984. Philadelphia, Saunders, xxi, 714 p.

W. Norman Scott, Barton Nisonson & James A. Nicholas, eds., *Principles of Sports Medicine,* 1984. Baltimore, Williams & Wilkins, xiv, 433 p.

Journals

American Journal of Sports Medicine, 1973- , Baltimore, American Orthopaedic Soc'y for Sports Medicine.

Clinics in Sports Medicine, 1982- , Philadelphia, Saunders.

Surgery

surgery (sur'jĕ-rĭ) [L. *chiurgia;* G. *cheir,* hand, + *ergon,* work. CHIR-]. 1. The branch of medicine concerned with the treatment of disease, injury, and deformity by operation or manipulation. 2. The performance or procedures of an operation.

Textbooks & Treatises

American College of Surgeons, Committee on Pre and Postoperative Care, *Manual of Preoperative and Postoperative Care,* Stanley J. Dudrick, *et al.,* eds., 3d ed. 1983. Philadelphia, Saunders, xix, 822 p.

American College of Surgeons, Committee on Trauma, *Early Care of the Injured Patient,* Alexander J. Walt, Leonard F. Peltier, *et al.,* eds., 3d ed. 1982. Philadelphia, Saunders, xi, 443 p.

Henry Hollinshead, *Anatomy for Surgeons,* 2d ed. 1968-1971. N.Y. & London, Harper & Row and Hoeber, 3 v. 3d ed. 1982- forthcoming; v. 3 in print.

Earle E. Peacock, Jr., *Wound Repair,* 3d ed. 1984. Philadelphia, Saunders, xi, 526 p.

Mark M. Ravitch, Kenneth J. Welch, Clifford D. Benson, *et al.*, eds., *Pediatric Surgery,* 3d ed. 1979. Chicago, Year Book Medical Pubs., 2 v.

David C. Sabiston, Jr., ed., *Davis-Christopher Textbook of Surgery,* 12th ed. 1981. Philadelphia, Saunders, xxviii, 2481, lviii p.

Seymour I. Schwartz, G. Tom Shires, Frank C. Spencer, *et al.*, eds., *Principles of Surgery,* 4th ed. 1984. N.Y., McGraw-Hill, xiii, 2150, 75 p.

See also "Internal Medicine" at Robert H. Moser.

Journals

American Journal of Surgery, 1891- , N.Y., Technical Pub. Div. of Dun-Donnelly Pub. Corp.

Annals of Surgery, 1885- , Philadelphia, J. B. Lippincott Co.

Bulletin of the American College of Surgeons, 1916- , Chicago, American College of Surgeons.

Surgery, 1937- , St. Louis, Mosby.

Surgical Clinics of North America, , Philadelphia, Saunders.

Toxicology & Biochemistry

biochemistry (bi-o-kem′is-trĭ). Biological or physiological chemistry; the chemistry of living organisms and of the changes occurring therein.

toxicology (tok′sĭ-kol′o-jĭ) [toxico- + G. *logos,* study]. The science of poisons — their source, chemical composition, action, tests, and antidotes.

Textbooks & Treatises

Jay M. Arena, *Poisoning: Toxicology, Symptoms, Treatments,* 4th ed. 1979. Springfield, Ill, Thomas, xxix, 827 p. 5th ed. forthcoming 1985.

Thomas M. Devlin, ed., *Textbook of Biochemistry with Clinical Correlations,* 1982. N.Y., Wiley, xxxvi, 1265 p.

Robert H. Dreisbach, *Handbook of Poisoning: Prevention, Diagnosis, and Treatment,* 11th ed., 1983. Los Altos, Cal., Lange Medical Pubs., 632 p.

Robert E. Gosselin, Roger P. Smith, Harold C. Hodge, *et al., Clinical Toxicology of Commercial Products,* 5th ed. 1984. Baltimore, 1 v., various pagination.

Cyril J. Polson, M. A. Green & M. R. Lee, *Clinical Toxicology,* 3d ed. 1983. Philadelphia, Lippincott, x, 607 p.

See also "Pathology" at John Bernard Henry, "Public Health" at N. Irving Sax, and "Drugs."

Journal

Biochemical Journal, v. 1- , 1906- , London, Biochemical Soc'y.

Urology

urology (u-rol'o-jĭ) [uro- + G. *logos,* study]. The medical specialty concerned with the study, diagnosis, and treatment of diseases of the genitourinary tract, especially the urinary tract in both sexes and the genital organs in the male.

Textbooks & Treatises

James F. Glenn & William H. Boyce, eds., *Urologic Surgery,* 3d ed. 1983. Philadelphia, Lippincott, xxxii, 1118 p.

J. Hartwell Harrison, *et al.,* eds., *Campbell's Urology,* 4th ed. 1978. Philadelphia, Saunders, 3 v.

Robert H. Heptinstall, *Pathology of the Kidney,* 3d ed. 1983. Boston, Little, Brown, 3 v.

Donald R. Smith, *General Urology,* 11th ed. 1984. Los Altos, Cal., Lange Medical Pubs., 661 p.

See also "Nephrology."

Journals

British Journal of Urology, v. 1- , 1929- , Edinburgh, Churchill Livingstone.

Journal of Urology, v. 1- , 1917- , Baltimore, Williams & Wilkins.

A.
ILLUSTRATIONS

United States Statutes at Large.

62 Stat. 968, § 2283 (1948).

A copy of the original Act of Congress that was published in the official session laws of 1948, called *U.S. Statutes at Large*.

This was recompiled in the *United States Code* and is now known as 28 U.S.C. § 2283 (1982).

entered on the motion as from a final judgment on application for a writ of habeas corpus.

An application for a writ of habeas corpus in behalf of a prisoner who is authorized to apply for relief by motion pursuant to this section, shall not be entertained if it appears that the applicant has failed to apply for relief, by motion, to the court which sentenced him, or that such court has denied him relief, unless it also appears that the remedy by motion is inadequate or ineffective to test the legality of his detention.

CHAPTER 155—INJUNCTIONS; THREE-JUDGE COURTS

§ 2281. Injunction against enforcement of State statute; three-judge court required

An interlocutory or permanent injunction restraining the enforcement, operation or execution of any State statute by restraining the action of any officer of such State in the enforcement or execution of such statute or of an order made by an administrative board or commission acting under State statutes, shall not be granted by any district court or judge thereof upon the ground of the unconstitutionality of such statute unless the application therefor is heard and determined by a district court of three judges under section 2284 of this title.

Infra.

§ 2282. Injunction against enforcement of Federal statute; three-judge court required

An interlocutory or permanent injunction restraining the enforcement, operation or execution of any Act of Congress for repugnance to the Constitution of the United States shall not be granted by any district court or judge thereof unless the application therefor is heard and determined by a district court of three judges under section 2284 of this title.

§ 2283. Stay of State court proceedings

A court of the United States may not grant an injunction to stay proceedings in a State court except as expressly authorized by Act of Congress, or where necessary in aid of its jurisdiction, or to protect or effectuate its judgments.

§ 2284. Three-judge district court; composition; procedure

In any action or proceeding required by Act of Congress to be heard and determined by a district court of three judges the composition and procedure of the court, except as otherwise provided by law, shall be as follows:

(1) The district judge to whom the application for injunction or other relief is presented shall constitute one member of such court. On the filing of the application, he shall immediately notify the chief judge of the circuit, who shall designate two other judges, at least one of whom shall be a circuit judge. Such judges shall serve as members of the court to hear and determine the action or proceeding.

(2) If the action involves the enforcement, operation or execution of State statutes or State administrative orders, at least five days notice of the hearing shall be given to the governor and attorney general of the State.

If the action involves the enforcement, operation or execution of

United States Code.

28 U.S.C. § 2283 (1982).

The official, U.S. Government Printing Office edition of the *United States Code* wherein is codified 62 Stat. 968, § 2283 (1948).

This edition is seldom used by legal researchers because it is not published in a timely fashion and is not supplemented with editorial additions ("annotations").

§ 2283. Stay of State court proceedings

A court of the United States may not grant an injunction to stay proceedings in a State court except as expressly authorized by Act of Congress, or where necessary in aid of its jurisdiction, or to protect or effectuate its judgments.

(June 25, 1948, ch. 646, 62 Stat. 968.)

HISTORICAL AND REVISION NOTES

Based on title 28, U.S.C., 1940 ed., § 379 (Mar. 3, 1911, ch. 231, § 265, 36 Stat. 1162).

An exception as to acts of Congress relating to bankruptcy was omitted and the general exception substituted to cover all exceptions.

The phrase "in aid of its jurisdiction" was added to conform to section 1651 of this title and to make clear the recognized power of the Federal courts to stay proceedings in State cases removed to the district courts.

The exceptions specifically include the words "to protect or "effectuate its judgments," for lack of which the Supreme Court held that the Federal courts are without power to enjoin relitigation of cases and controversies fully adjudicated by such courts. (See *Toucey* v. *New York Life Insurance Co.*, 62 S.Ct. 139, 314 U.S. 118, 86 L.Ed. 100. A vigorous dissenting opinion (62 S.Ct. 148) notes that at the time of the 1911 revision of the Judicial Code, the power of the courts, of the United States to protect their judgments was unquestioned and that the revisers of that code noted no change and Congress intended no change).

Therefore the revised section restores the basic law as generally understood and interpreted prior to the Toucey decision.

Changes were made in phraseology.

§ 2284. Three-judge court; when required; composition; procedure

(a) A district court of three judges shall be convened when otherwise required by Act of Congress, or when an action is filed challenging the constitutionality of the apportionment of congressional districts or the apportionment of any statewide legislative body.

(b) In any action required to be heard and determined by a district court of three judges under subsection (a) of this section, the composition and procedure of the court shall be as follows:

(1) Upon the filing of a request for three judges, the judge to whom the request is presented shall, unless he determines that three judges are not required, immediately notify the chief judge of the circuit, who shall designate two other judges, at least one of whom shall be a circuit judge. The judges so designated, and the judge to whom the request was presented, shall serve as members of the court to hear and determine the action or proceeding.

(2) If the action is against a State, or officer or agency thereof, at least five days' notice of hearing of the action shall be given by registered or certified mail to the Governor and attorney general of the State. The hearing shall be given precedence and held at the earliest practicable day.

(3) A single judge may conduct all proceedings except the trial, and enter all orders permitted by the rules of civil procedure except as provided in this subsection. He may grant a temporary restraining order on a specific finding, based on evidence submitted, that specified irreparable damage will result if the order is not granted, which order, unless previously revoked by the district judge, shall remain in force only until the hearing and determination by the district court of three judges of an application for a preliminary injunction. A single judge shall not appoint a master, or order a reference, or hear and determine any application for a preliminary or permanent injunction or motion to vacate such an injunction, or enter judgment on the merits. Any action of a single judge may be reviewed by the full court at any time before final judgment.

(June 25, 1948, ch. 646, 62 Stat. 968; June 11, 1960, Pub. L. 86-507, § 1(19), 74 Stat. 201; Aug. 12, 1976, Pub. L. 94-381, § 3, 90 Stat. 1119.)

HISTORICAL AND REVISION NOTES

Based on title 28, U.S.C., 1940 ed., §§ 47, 47a, 380, 380a, and 792 (Mar. 3, 1911, ch. 231, §§ 210, 266, 36 Stat. 1150, 1162; Mar. 4, 1943, ch. 160, 37 Stat. 1013; Oct. 22, 1913, ch. 32, 38 Stat. 220; Feb. 13, 1925, ch. 229, § 1, 43 Stat. 938; Aug. 24, 1937, ch. 754, § 3, 50 Stat. 752; Apr. 6, 1942, ch. 210, § 3, 56 Stat. 199).

Provisions of sections 47, 47a, 380, and 380a of title 28, U.S.C., 1940 ed., relating to the Supreme Court's jurisdiction of direct appeals appear in section 1253 of this title.

Provisions of sections 47, 380, and 380a of title 28, U.S.C., 1940 ed., requiring applications for injunctions restraining the enforcement, operation or execution of Federal or State statutes or orders of the Interstate Commerce Commission to be heard and determined by three-judge district courts appear in sections 2281, 2282, and 2325 of this title.

The provision for notice to the United States attorney for the district where the action is pending was added because of the necessity of the United States attorney's preparation for hearing as soon as possible, to expedite such a case.

Provisions of sections 47, 47a, 380, and 380a of title 28, U.S.C., 1940 ed., respecting time for direct appeal appear in section 2101 of this title.

This revised section represents an effort to provide a uniform method of convoking three-judge district courts, and for procedure therein. It follows recommendations of a committee appointed by the Judicial Conference of the United States, composed of Circuit Judges Evan A. Evans, Kimbrough Stone, Orie L. Phillips, and Albert B. Maris.

The committee pointed out that section 380a of title 28, U.S.C., 1940 ed., is the latest and "most carefully drawn expression by Congress on the subject." Consequently, this section follows closely such section 380a and eliminates the discrepancies between sections 47, 47a, 380, and 380a of such title.

This section governs only the composition and procedure of three-judge district courts. The requirement that applications for injunctions be heard and determined by such courts will appear in other sections of this and other titles of the United States Code as Congress may enact from time to time. For example, see sections 2281, 2282, and 2325 of this title, sections 1213, 1215, 1255 of title 11, U.S.C., 1940 ed., Bankruptcy, section 28 of title 15, U.S.C., 1940 ed., Commerce and Trade, and section 44 of title 49, U.S.C., 1940 ed., Transportation.

United States District Judge W. Calvin Chestnut, has referred to the provisions relating to enforcement or setting aside or orders of the Interstate Commerce Commission as unfortunately lengthy and prolix. He has urged revision to insure uniform procedure in the several classes of so-called three-judge cases.

The provision that such notice shall be given by the clerk by registered mail, and shall be complete on the

United States Code Annotated.

28 U.S.C.A. § 2283 (1978).

Unofficial edition of *U.S.C.*, called *U.S.C.A.*, with history, cross-references, collateral references, and case notes ("annotations").

CHAPTER 155—INJUNCTIONS; THREE-JUDGE COURTS

[1] Does not conform to section catchline.

Historical Note

1976 Amendment. Pub.L. 94-381, § 4, Aug. 12, 1976, 90 Stat. 1119, substituted "Repealed" for "Injunction against enforcement of State statute; three-judge court required" in item 2281 and for "Injunction against enforcement of Federal statute; three-judge court required" in item 2282, and added "when required" following "district court" in item 2284.

§§ 2281, 2282. Repealed. Pub.L. 94-381, §§ 1, 2, Aug. 12, 1976, 90 Stat. 1119

Historical Note

Section 2281, Act June 25, 1948, c. 646, 62 Stat. 968, provided that an interlocutory or permanent injunction restraining the enforcement, operation or execution of a State statute on grounds of unconstitutionality should not be granted unless the application has been heard and determined by a three-judge district court.

Section 2282, Act June 25, 1948, c. 646, 62 Stat. 968, provided that an interlocutory or permanent injunction restraining the enforcement, operation or execution of any Act of Congress on grounds of unconstitutionality should not be granted unless the application therefor has been heard and determined by a three-judge district court.

Effective Date of Repeal. Repeal by Pub.L. 94-381 not applicable to any action commenced on or before Aug. 12, 1976, see section 7 of Pub.L. 94-381, set out as an Effective Date of 1976 Amendment note under section 2284 of this title.

§ 2283. Stay of State court proceedings

A court of the United States may not grant an injunction to stay proceedings in a State court except as expressly authorized by Act of Congress, or where necessary in aid of its jurisdiction, or to protect or effectuate its judgments.

June 25, 1948, c. 646, 62 Stat. 968.

Historical and Revision Notes

Reviser's Note. Based on Title 28, U.S.C., 1940 ed., § 379 (Mar. 3, 1911, c. 231, § 265, 36 Stat. 1162 [Derived from R.S. § 720]).

An exception as to Acts of Congress relating to bankruptcy was omitted and the general exception substituted to cover all exceptions.

The phrase "in aid of its jurisdiction" was added to conform to section 1651 of this title and to make clear the recognized power of the Federal courts to stay proceedings in State cases removed to the district courts.

The exceptions specifically include the words "to protect or effectuate its judgments," for lack of which the Supreme Court held that the Federal courts are without power to enjoin relitigation of cases and controversies fully adjudicated by such courts. (See Toucey v. New York Life Insurance Co., 62 S.Ct. 139, 314 U.S. 118, 86 L.Ed. 100. A vigorous dissenting opinion (62 S.Ct. 148) notes that at the time of the 1911 revision of the Judicial Code, the power of the courts of the United States to protect their judgments was unquestioned and that the revisers of that code noted no change and Congress intended no change).

Therefore the revised section restores the basic law as generally understood and interpreted prior to the Toucey decision.

Changes were made in phraseology.

Cross References

Bankruptcy proceeding, stay of actions pending determination, see section 29 of Title 11, Bankrutcy.
Interpleader, restraining institution of other proceedings, see section 2361 of this title.
State taxes, prohibiting district courts from enjoining assessment, levy or collection where there is adequate remedy in state courts, see section 1341 of this title.

Federal Rules of Civil Procedure

Injunctions, see rule 65, this title.

Library References

Courts ⚷508(1). C.J.S. Courts § 543.

West's Federal Forms

Interpleader actions, see § 3001 Comment.
Order, removal of case from state court, see § 1206.
Preliminary injunctions and temporary restraining orders, matters pertaining to, see § 5271 et seq.
Stays, Supreme Court procedures, see § 445 Comment.

Notes of Decisions

28 § 2283 INJUNCTIONS Part 6

Note 1

1. Prior law

Act Mar. 2, 1793, c. 23, § 5, 1 Stat. 335, from which was derived former section 379 of this title limited the general equity powers of federal courts and prevented them from granting relief by way of injunction in the cases included within its inhibitions. Toucey v. New York Life Ins. Co., Iowa & Mo.1941, 62 S.Ct. 139, 314 U.S. 118, 86 L.Ed. 100, 137 A.L.R. 967.

2. Construction

The frustration of superior federal interests by the general language of this section cannot reasonably be imputed. N. L. R. B. v. Nash-Finch Co., Neb.1971, 92 S.Ct. 373, 404 U.S. 138, 30 L.Ed.2d 328.

Exceptions to prohibition of this section against enjoining state court proceedings should not be enlarged by loose statutory construction. Atlantic Coast Line R. Co. v. Brotherhood of Locomotive Engineers, 1970, 90 S.Ct. 1739, 398 U.S. 281, 26 L.Ed.2d 234.

Any doubts as to propriety of a federal injunction against state court proceedings should be resolved in favor of permitting state courts to proceed in an orderly fashion to finally determine the controversy. Id.

This section is to be strictly applied, and unless one of the three exceptions listed in this section is evident, it constitutes an absolute ban upon a federal court injunction against a pending state court proceeding. Lektro-Vend Corp. v. Vendo Co., C.A.Ill.1976, 545 F.2d 1050, reversed on other grounds 97 S.Ct. 2881.

This section has been interpreted very strictly. Carter v. Ogden Corp., C.A.La. 1975, 524 F.2d 74.

Sensitive nature of federal interference with state court proceedings requires that this section be strictly construed. International Ass'n of Machinists and Aerospace Workers v. Nix, C.A.Ga.1975, 512 F.2d 125. See, also, Lamb Enterprises Inc. v. Kiroff, C.A.Ohio 1977, 549 F.2d 1052.

This section is entitled to a strict construction. Signal Properties, Inc. v. Farha, C.A.Tex.1973, 482 F.2d 1136.

This section must be applied liberally, to prevent needless friction between state and federal courts. Honey v. Goodman, C.A.Ky.1970, 432 F.2d 333.

Since disposition of United States Supreme Court has been toward strict construction of this section when United States is not directly involved as party, and danger of irritating conflict with state courts is great, court of appeals ought not lightly to undertake to relegate this section to meaninglessness. Baines v. City of Danville, Va., C.A.Va. 1964, 337 F.2d 579, certiorari denied 85 S. Ct. 1772, 381 U.S. 939, 14 L.Ed.2d 702, affirmed in part 357 F.2d 756, certiorari granted 86 S.Ct. 1915, 384 U.S. 890, 16 L. Ed.2d 996, rehearing denied 87 S.Ct. 12, 385 U.S. 890, 17 L.Ed.2d 121.

The hands-off doctrine expressed in this section is to be considered in light of function of said section as a pillar of federalism, and phrase "where necessary in aid of its jurisdiction" contained in said section should be interpreted narrowly, in direction of federal noninterference with orderly state proceedings. T. Smith & Son, Inc. v. Williams, C.A.La. 1960, 275 F.2d 397.

Former section 379 of this title should have been given such an interpretation as would effectuate its obvious purpose of preventing unseemly conflict between state and federal courts. Hyattsville Building Ass'n v. Bouic, 1916, 44 App.D.C. 408.

Language of this section limiting cases where federal court may issue injunction to stay proceedings in state court is clear and should be strictly construed. Eitel v. Faircloth, D.C.Fla.1970, 311 F.Supp. 1160, affirmed 436 F.2d 1080.

In view of their impact on delicate relationship between federal and state courts, exceptions to this section prohibiting federal courts from enjoining pending actions in state courts must be narrowly construed. Greater Continental Corp. v. Schechter, D.C.N.Y.1969, 304 F. Supp. 325, appeal dismissed 422 F.2d 1100.

3. Construction with other laws

Former section 379 of this title had to be construed in connection with former section 377 of this title, which authorized federal courts to issue all writs not specifically provided for by statute which were necessary for the exercise of their respective jurisdictions and agreeable to the practices and usages of law. Kline v. Burke Const. Co., Ark.1922, 43 S.Ct. 79, 260 U.S. 226, 67 L.Ed. 226. See, also, Canterbury v. Mandeville, C.C.A.Ill.1942, 130 F.2d 208, reversed on other grounds 63 S.Ct. 472, 318 U.S. 47, 87 L.Ed. 605; Western Fruit Growers v. U. S., C.C.A. 1941, 124 F.2d 381; Fenner v. Boykin, D. C.Ga.1925, 3 F.2d 674, affirmed 46 S.Ct. 492, 271 U.S. 240, 70 L.Ed. 927; U. S. v. Inaba, D.C.Wash.1923, 291 F. 416; Bowdoin College v. Merritt, C.C.Cal.1893, 59 F. 6; Sharon v. Terry, C.C.Cal.1888, 36 F.

United States Code Annotated — Pocket Part.

28 U.S.C.A. § 2283 (Supp. 1985).

Pocket part supplement for unofficial edition of *U.S.C.*, called *U.S.C.A.*, with additional annotations which update the 1978 bound volume.

TITLE 28

JUDICIARY AND JUDICIAL PROCEDURE

PART VI.—PARTICULAR PROCEEDINGS

CHAPTER 155—INJUNCTIONS; THREE-JUDGE COURTS

[§ 2281. Repealed. Pub.L. 94-381, § 1, Aug. 12, 1976, 90 Stat. 1119]

§ 2283. Stay of State court proceedings

Federal Practice and Procedure

Applicability to action brought under section 1983 of Title 42 seeking injunction of state proceedings, see Wright, Miller & Kane: Civil 2d § 2764.

Applicability to actions under rule pertaining to interpleader, see Wright & Miller: Civil §§ 1703, 1717.

Balancing of equities with respect to issuance of temporary restraining orders, see Wright & Miller: Civil § 2451.

Discussion of relitigation exception, see Wright, Miller & Cooper: Jurisdiction § 4405.

Federal injunctions against state proceedings, see Wright, Miller & Cooper: Jurisdiction § 4221 et seq.

Issuance of injunction by federal court to stay proceedings in state court, see Wright, Miller & Kane: Civil 2d § 2758; Wright, Miller & Cooper: Jurisdiction §§ 3523, 3573.

Permissibility of enjoining enforcement of state court judgment, see Wright, Miller & Cooper: Jurisdiction § 3530.

Relationship to rule pertaining to injunctions, see Wright & Miller: Civil §§ 2942, 2948.

Restraining state court proceedings, see Wright & Miller: Civil § 1418.

State injunctions against federal proceedings, see Wright, Miller & Cooper: Jurisdiction § 4212.

West's Federal Forms

Authority of courts to regulate custody of prisoners, see § 441 Comment.

Complaint, see § 1624 and Comment thereunder.

Interpleader actions, see § 3001 Comment.

Order, removal of case from state court, see § 1166.

Preliminary injunctions and temporary restraining orders, matters pertaining to, see § 5271 et seq.

Stays, Supreme Court procedures, see § 449 Comment.

West's Federal Practice Manual

Abstention, see § 7373 et seq.

Interpleader, see §§ 8958, 8964.

Notes of Decisions

1. Prior law

The exceptions to the antiinjunction statute should be narrowly construed and any doubts as to propriety of federal injunction against a state court proceeding should be resolved in favor of permitting the state court to proceed. Bluefield Community Hosp., Inc. v. Anziulewicz, C.A.W. Va.1984, 737 F.2d 405.

2. Construction

Lamb Enterprises, Inc. v. Kiroff, 549 F.2d 1052 [main volume] certiorari denied 97 S.Ct. 2927, 431 U.S. 968, 53 L.Ed.2d 1064.

Lektro-Vend Corp. v. Vendo Co., 545 F.2d 1050 [main volume] reversed on other grounds 97 S.Ct. 2881, 433 U.S. 623, 53 L.Ed.2d 1009, rehearing denied 98 S.Ct. 242, 434 U.S. 881, 54 L.Ed.2d 164, motion denied 98 S.Ct. 702, 434 U.S. 425, 54 L.Ed.2d 659, on remand 500 F.Supp. 332.

Import of this section is that federal court injunction of state litigation is to be exception, not the rule, and because of sensitive nature of federal interference with state court litigation, exceptions to rule against injunctions, including the third, which applies to relitigation of claims that threaten federal court's judgment, must be narrowly construed. Delta Air Lines, Inc. v. McCoy Restaurants, Inc., C.A.Fla.1983, 708 F.2d 582.

The "in aid of jurisdiction" exception to this section has been narrowly construed as a codification of a historical exception to this section and coexistent principles of comity and federalism for in rem actions in the context of which two courts would be vying for jurisdiction over the same res unless one of the judicial proceedings were stayed. Universal Business Computing Co. v. Comprehensive Accounting Corp., D.C.Ill.1982, 539 F.Supp. 1142.

This section authorizing federal court to enjoin state court proceedings should not be expanded by

United States Code Service.

28 U.S.C.S. § 2283 (1977).

Unofficial edition of *U.S.C.*, called *U.S.C.S.*, with history, collateral references, and case notes ("annotations").

CHAPTER 155. INJUNCTIONS; THREE-JUDGE COURTS

HISTORY; ANCILLARY LAWS AND DIRECTIVES

1976 Act Aug. 12, 1976, P. L. 94-381, § 4, 90 Stat. 1119, amended the analysis of this chapter by repealing items 2281 and 2282, and by inserting in item 2284 "when required;".

---

§§ 2281, 2282. [Repealed]

HISTORY; ANCILLARY LAWS AND DIRECTIVES

These sections (Act June 25, 1948, c. 646, § 1, 62 Stat. 968) were repealed by Act Aug. 12, 1976, P. L. 94-381, §§ 1, 2, 90 Stat. 1119. The sections provided for three-judge court for injunctions against enforcement of State and Federal statutes.

Other provisions:
Savings clause. Section 7 of Act Aug. 12, 1976, P. L. 94-381, 90 Stat. 1120, provided: "This Act [repeal of 28 USCS §§ 2281, 2282, and amendments to 28 USCS §§ 2284, 2403] shall not apply to any action commenced on or before the date of enactment [enacted Aug. 12, 1976]."

§ 2283. Stay of State court proceedings

A court of the United States may not grant an injunction to stay proceedings in a State court except as expressly authorized by Act of Congress, or where necessary in aid of its jurisdiction, or to protect or effectuate its judgments.
(June 25, 1948, c. 646, § 1, 62 Stat. 968.)

HISTORY; ANCILLARY LAWS AND DIRECTIVES

Prior law and revision:
This section is based on Act Mar. 3, 1911, c. 231, § 265, 36 Stat. 1162 (§ 379 of former Title 28).
An exception as to Acts of Congress relating to bankruptcy was omitted and the general exception substituted to cover all exceptions. The phrase "in aid of its jurisdiction" was added to conform to 28 USCS § 1651 and to make clear the recognized power of the Federal courts to stay proceedings in State cases removed to the district courts.

THREE-JUDGE COURT **28 USCS § 2283**

The exceptions specifically include the words "to protect or effectuate its judgments," for lack of which the Supreme Court held that the Federal courts are without power to enjoin relitigation of cases and controversies fully adjudicated by such courts. (See Toucey v New York Life Ins. Co. (1941) 314 US 118, 86 L Ed 100, 62 S Ct 139, 137 ALR 967, reh den 314 US 585, 86 L Ed 473, 62 S Ct 139. A vigorous dissenting opinion (62 S Ct 148) notes that at the time of the 1911 revision of the Judicial Code, the power of the courts of the United States to protect their judgments was unquestioned and that the revisers of that code noted no change and Congress intended no change.) Therefore the revised section restores the basic law as generally understood and interpreted prior to the Toucey decision.

CROSS REFERENCES

Bankruptcy Court's power to restrain proceedings in state court, 11 USCS § 11(a)(15).
Stay of suits against bankrupts until adjudication of petition, 11 USCS § 29.
Stay of proceedings for 3 years under agricultural composition in bankruptcy, 11 USCS § 203(s).
Stay of suits against debtor until final decree in bankruptcy, 11 USCS § 205(j).
Stay of proceeding to enforce state tax lien, 11 USCS § 403(c).
Stay of proceedings as part of corporate reorganization, 11 USCS §§ 513, 548.
Filing of bankruptcy petition as automatic stay of prior proceedings in state court, 11 USCS §§ 714, 907.
Stay of other proceedings until final decree in bankruptcy, 11 USCS § 814.
Bankruptcy petition as stay of proceedings to enforce lien, 11 USCS §§ 828, 1014.
Action resumed in state court after removal of case to federal court, 28 USCS § 1446(e).
Stays relating to interpleader actions, 28 USCS § 2361.
Injunction in Federal District Court, USCS Rules of Civil Procedure, Rule 65.
Filing of bankruptcy petition as automatic stay of actions against debtor and lien enforcement, USCS Rules of Bankruptcy, Rules 601, 8-501, 9-4, 10-601, 11-44, 12-43.

RESEARCH GUIDE

Am Jur:

9 Am Jur 2d, Bankruptcy § 289.
15 Am Jur 2d, Civil Rights §§ 16, 275.
20 Am Jur 2d, Courts §§ 12, 129.
30 Am Jur 2d, Executions § 677.
32 Am Jur 2d, Federal Practice and Procedure §§ 468, 514.
42 Am Jur 2d, Injunctions §§ 229, 230, 231, 232, 233, 234, 235.
45 Am Jur 2d, Interpleader § 47.
46 Am Jur 2d, Judgments § 798.

28 USCS § 2283 PARTICULAR PROCEEDINGS

Am Jur Trials:

Franchise Litigation, 21 Am Jur Trials, p. 453 (see § 68 on Federal Arbitration Act).

Forms:

20 Am Jur Pl & Pr Forms (Rev ed), Public Officers and Employees, Form 61.1.

21 Am Jur Pl & Pr Forms (Rev ed), Receivers, Forms 153, 154.

Annotations:

Supreme Court's rule, and exceptions to rule, against federal judicial intervention in pending or threatened state criminal proceedings. 44 L Ed 2d 692.

Propriety of federal injunction against use in state criminal trial of evidence unlawfully obtained. 27 L Ed 2d 984.

Power of federal District Court to enjoin state proceedings involving labor disputes. 98 L Ed 892; 99 L Ed 614.

Actionability under Federal Civil Rights Act with respect to proceedings to discipline attorney, to regulate admission to practice of law, or to restrain unauthorized practice of law. 9 ALR Fed 422 (see § 8[a] on effect of 28 USCS § 2283).

Anticipatory relief in federal courts against state criminal prosecutions growing out of civil rights activities. 8 ALR3d 301 (see § 10 on injunctions).

Injunction against exercise of power of eminent domain. 93 ALR2d 465 (see § 19 on effect of 28 USCS § 2283).

Bankruptcy Court's injunction against a mortgage or lien enforcement proceedings commenced before bankruptcy in another court. 40 ALR2d 663.

Law Review Articles:

Why Three-Judge District Courts? 25 Ala L Rev 371.

Exceptions to the Anti-Injunction Statute: The Power of Federal Courts to Enjoin Bad Faith Enforcement of Unconstitutional State Statutes Where a State Proceeding is Pending. 21 Am U L Rev 395.

Federal Jurisdiction in Procedure—Declaratory Judgment: A Federal Court May Issue a Declaratory Judgment Upon a Showing of Threatened Enforcement of a State Criminal Statute Challenged as Unconstitutional on its Face or as Applied. 41 Brooklyn L Rev 368.

Protecting Civil Liberties Through Federal Court Interventions in State Criminal Matters. 59 Calif L Rev 1549.

Appellate review of stay orders in the federal courts. 72 Columbia LR 518, Mar 1972.

Cannon, Federal Court Intervention in Juvenile Proceedings. 48 Denver LJ 503.

Federal Intervention in State Criminal Proceedings: Inadequate Remedies in Adequate Forums. 63 Geo LJ 1143.

Federal Courts—Intervention—A showing of Great and Immediate Irreparable Injury is not a Prerequisite to a Federal Declaratory

I. GENERAL CONSIDERATIONS

A. In General

1. Generally

United States Supreme Court cannot enjoin proceedings in subordinate court of state since there is no appellate relation between them. Slaughter-House Cases (1870) 77 US 273, 19 L Ed 915.

Predecessor to 28 USCS § 2283 did not deprive district court of jurisdiction otherwise conferred by federal statutes. Sovereign Camp Woodmen of World v O'Neill (1924) 266 US 292, 69 L Ed 293, 45 S Ct 49.

Predecessor to 28 USCS § 2283 is mere limitation upon general equity powers of United States courts and may be varied by Congress to meet requirements of federal litigation. Treinies v Sunshine Mining Co. (1939) 308 US 66, 84 L Ed 85, 60 S Ct 44, reh den 309 US 693, 84 L Ed 1034, 60 S Ct 464.

28 USCS § 2283 withholding, with specified exceptions, from federal courts jurisdiction to stay proceedings in state court, revised as well as codified law developed under § 265 of Judicial Code of 1911, earlier provision on same subject. Amalgamated Clothing Workers v Richman Bros. Co. (1955) 348 US 511, 99 L Ed 600, 75 S Ct 452, 56 Ohio Ops 249, 71 Ohio L Abs 177.

Any doubts as to propriety of a federal injunction against state proceedings should be resolved in favor of permitting state court to proceed in orderly fashion to finally determine the controversy. Atlantic C. L. R. Co. v Brotherhood of Locomotive Engineers (1970) 398 US 281, 26 L Ed 2d 234, 90 S Ct 1739.

Case should proceed promptly to state court trial where none of exceptions in 28 USCS § 2283 are applicable. Aaacon Auto Transport, Inc. v Eichler (1975, DC NY) 392 F Supp 926.

2. Purpose

Purpose of 28 USCS § 2283, which precludes federal courts from staying state court proceedings, is to avoid unseemly conflict between state and federal courts where litigants are private persons, not to hamstring Federal Government and its agencies in use of federal courts to protect federal rights. NLRB v Nash-Finch Co. (1971) 404 US 138, 30 L Ed 2d 328, 92 S Ct 373.

Basic purpose of federal anti-injunction statute (28 USCS § 2283) providing, subject to specified exceptions, that federal courts may not grant injunctions staying state court proceedings, is to prevent needless friction between state and federal courts. Mitchum v Foster (1972) 407 US 225, 32 L Ed 2d 705, 92 S Ct 2151.

Purpose of predecessor to 28 USCS § 2283 was to prevent federal courts, when exercising jurisdiction co-ordinate with state courts, from drawing to themselves right to determine adverse claims. Re Standard Gas & Electric Co. (1943, CA3 Del) 139 F2d 149, cert den 321 US 796, 88 L Ed 1085, 64 S Ct 848

Predecessor to 28 USCS § 2283 was originally enacted in 1793, with no recorded legislative history and for reasons which remain obscure; and modern courts have appeared to grope at its original purpose and function. Honey v Goodman (1970, CA6 Ky) 432 F2d 333.

Purpose of predecessor to 28 USCS § 2283 was to prevent clash of jurisdiction, and to preserve peaceful comity necessary between courts of two sovereignties. Pullen v Patton (1937, DC Tex) 19 F Supp 340; Union Cent. Life Ins. Co. v McAden (1937, DC Tex) 21 F Supp 110; United States v Cain (1947, DC Mich) 72 F Supp 897.

3. Comity and federalism

Explicit wording of 28 USCS § 2283, which contains general prohibition against federal injunctions staying state proceedings, implies that any doubts as to propriety of federal injunction against state court proceedings should be resolved in favor of permitting state courts to proceed in orderly fashion to finally determine controversy; and fundamental principle of dual system of courts leads inevitably to same conclusion. Atlantic C. L. R. Co. v Brotherhood of Locomotive Engineers (1970) 398 US 281, 26 L Ed 2d 234, 90 S Ct 1739.

United States Code Service — Pocket Part.

28 U.S.C.S. § 2283 (Supp. 1984).

Pocket part supplement for unofficial edition of *U.S.C.*, called *U.S.C.S.*, with additional annotations which update the 1977 bound volume.

(B) to testify; or

(C) to perform a duty imposed on such person under this title [28 USCS §§ 1 et seq.]; or

(2) ordering the release of a debtor in a case under title 11 [11 USCS §§ 1 et seq.] in custody under the judgment of a Federal or State court if—

(A) such debtor was arrested or imprisoned on process in any civil action;

(B) such process was issued for the collection of a debt—

(i) dischargeable under title 11 [11 USCS §§ 1 et seq.]; or

(ii) that is or will be provided for in a plan under chapter 11 or 13 of title 11 [11 USCS §§ 1101 et seq., 1301 et seq.]; and

(C) before the issuance of such writ, notice and a hearing have been afforded the adverse party of such debtor in custody to contest the issuance of such writ.

(Added Nov. 6, 1978, P. L. 95-598, Title II, § 250(a), Title III, § 314(j)(1), 92 Stat. 2672, 2677.)

HISTORY: ANCILLARY LAWS AND DIRECTIVES

Explanatory notes:

Former section 2256 (Act Oct. 28, 1977, P. L. 95-114, § 3, 91 Stat. 1220) was redesignated by Act Nov. 6, 1978, P. L. 95-598, Title III, § 314(j)(1), 92 Stat. 2677, (effective Nov. 6, 1978, as provided by § 402(d) of Act Nov. 6, 1978). It now appears at 18 USCS § 3244.

Effective date of section:

Act Nov. 6, 1978, P. L. 95-598, Title IV, § 402(b), 92 Stat. 2682, provided that this section "shall take effect on April 1, 1984.".

Applicability during transition period. Act Nov. 6, 1978, P. L. 95-598, Title IV, § 405(b), 92 Stat. 2685, provided: "During the transition period [commencing on Oct. 1, 1979, ending on Mar. 31, 1984], the amendments made by sections 241, 243, 250, and 252 of this Act [adding 28 USCS §§ 1471 et seq., amending 28 USCS §§ prec. 1, 1869(f), adding 28 USCS § 2256, amending 28 USCS prec § 2241, 28 USCS Appx., Rules of Evidence, Rule 1101] shall apply to the courts of bankruptcy continued by section 404(a) of this Act [11 USCS prec. § 101 note] the same as such amendments apply to the United States bankruptcy courts established under section 201 of this Act [adding 28 USCS §§ 151 et seq. amending 28 USCS prec. § 1].".

RESEARCH GUIDE

Federal Procedure L Ed:

5 Fed Proc, L Ed §§ 9:50, 9:284, 9:285.

Am Jur:

9 Am Jur 2d, Bankruptcy §§ 146, 422, 425.

Bankruptcy Service L Ed:

Bkr-L Ed, Summary §§ 6:11, 6:14.

Bkr-L Ed, Code Commentary and Analysis §§ 11:107, 11:110.

Bkr-L Ed, Related Statutes and Rules § 64:47.

Federal Regulation of Employment Service:

FRES, Job Safety and Health §§ 11:107, 11:110, 11:117.

CHAPTER 155. INJUNCTIONS; THREE-JUDGE COURTS

---

§ 2283. Stay of State court proceedings

RESEARCH GUIDE

Federal Procedure L Ed:

3 Fed Proc, L Ed § 4:21.

5 Fed Proc, L Ed § 9:397.

6 Fed Proc, L Ed §§ 11:59, 11:60, 11:61, 11:186, 12:5, 12:217.

10 Fed Proc, L Ed §§ 23:48, 28:8.

16 Fed Proc, L Ed § 40:625.

17 Fed Proc, L Ed § 42:326.

19 Fed Proc, L Ed §§ 47:96, 97, 98, [illegible], 102, [illegible] 109, 110, 111, 113, 114, 115, 117, [illegible]

Fed Proc, L Ed §§ 49 [illegible]

28 USCS § 2283 PARTICULAR PROCEEDINGS

Am Jur:
15 Am Jur 2d, Civil Rights §§ 16,275.
32B Am Jur 2d, Federal Practice and Procedure, §§ 1854, 2063.
42 Am Jur 2d, Injunctions § 232.
48 Am Jur 2d, Labor and Labor Relations § 1351.
61A Am Jur 2d, Pollution Control § 44.

Forms:
11 Federal Procedural Forms L Ed, Injunctions and Restraining Orders § 42:2.
11 Federal Procedural Forms L Ed, Interpleader §§ 44:4, 44:31.

Bankruptcy Service L Ed:
Bkr-L Ed, Summary §§ 2:17.9, 6:121.
Bkr-L Ed, Code Commentary and Analysis §§ 11:64, 11:76.

Federal Regulation of Employment Service:
FRES, NLRA Scope § 44:83.

Annotations:
Prohibition under anti-injunction statute (28 USCS § 2283) of federal court from granting injunction to stay proceedings in state court. 66 L Ed 2d 903.

Law Review Articles:
Berry, A federal forum for broad constitutional deprivation by property tax assessment. 65 Cal L Rev 828.
Williams, The new three-judge courts of reapportionment and continuing problems of three-judge court procedure. 65 Geo L Rev 971.
Bartels, Avoiding a Comity of Errors: A Model for Adjudicating Federal Civil Rights Suits that "Interfere" with State Civil Proceedings. 29 Stan L Rev 27.
Redish, The Anti-Injunction Statute Reconsidered. 44 U Chl L Rev 717.
Zeigler, An Accommodation of the Younger Doctrine and the Duty of the Federal Courts To Enforce Constitutional Safeguards in the State Criminal Process. 125 U Pa L Rev 266.
Sedler, Younger and Its Progeny: A Variation on the Theme of Equity, Comity and Federalism. 9 University of Toledo L Rev 681, Summer, 1978.
Degnan, Federalized Res Judicata. 85 Yale LJ 741.

INTERPRETIVE NOTES AND DECISIONS

4.5. Necessity of notice
14.5. Arbitration
38.5. Miscellaneous situations
67.5. Sex discrimination

1. Generally

Proceedings in state courts should normally be allowed to continue unimpaired by intervention of lower federal courts, with relief from error, if any, through state appellate courts and ultimately United States Supreme Court. Ferrer Delgado v Sylvia De Jesus (1976, DC Puerto Rico) 440 F Supp 979.

2. Purpose

General language of 28 USCS § 2283 was not intended to hamstring federal agencies in utilization of federal courts to protect federal rights. Marshall v Chase Manhattan Bank (Nat. Asso.) (1977, CA2 NY) 558 F2d 680.

Policies of avoiding litigation and promoting prompt resolution of disputes are not disserved by denying stay of state court proceeding where party requesting stay made no attempt to remove action to federal court at time suit was filed, but instead allowed state court proceedings to continue for many months, turning to federal court only after most issues had been resolved against it in state ligitation. Ultracashmere House, Ltd. v Meyer (1981, CA11 Ala) 664 F2d 1176.

Implicit purpose of 28 USCS § 2283 is to avoid conflict between different court judgments. Garrett v Hoffman (1977, DC Pa) 441 F Supp 1151.

28 USCS § 2283 is absolute prohibition against any injunction of anv state court proceedings, unless injunction falls within one of three specifically defined exceptions in Act; Act's purpose is to forestall inevitable friction between state and federal courts that ensues from injunction of state judicial proceedings by federal court. Studdert v Scanlon (1979, DC Mont) 468 F Supp 381.

3. Comity and federalism

Notions of comity require that federal court yield jurisdiction to state court where state court has previously acquired jurisdiction over all matters in dispute, substantive law governs, convenience of the parties is equally served and state court is capable of resolving dispute. Merrill Lynch, Pierce, Fenner & Smith, Inc. v Haydu (1982, CA11 Fla) 675 F2d 1169, CCH Fed Secur L Rep ¶ 98667.

Anti-Injunction Act (28 USCS § 2283) and exceptions therein are to be construed strictly in interest of comity and federalism. Alton Box Bd. Co. v Esprit de Corp. (1982, CA9 Cal) 682 F2d 1267, 1982-1 CCH Trade Cases ¶ 64711.

Even when Anti-injunction Act (28 USCS § 2283) does not prohibit stay of state court action, underlying policy of preserving independence of state's judicial system must be carefully weighed. Commodity Futures Trading Com. v Chilcott Portfolio Management, Inc. (1983, CA10 Colo) 713 F2d 1477.

This statute is intended to give effect to federal rule of comity and that rule is limited in its field of operation; it goes merely to question of equity in particular bill. Browning Debenture Holders' Committee v Dasa Corp. (1978, DC NY) 454 F Supp 88.

Kentucky Acts.

1958 Ky. Acts 325, ch. 77, § 4-403.

A copy of the original Act of the Kentucky General Assembly that was published in the official session laws of 1958, called *Kentucky Acts*.

This was recompiled in the two commercially-published, official editions of the *Kentucky Revised Statutes* and is now known as Ky. Rev. Stat. § 355.4-403. The different editions and their dates of publication are to be indicated in a parenthesis following the citation.

CHAPTER 77

damages are proximately caused by the wrongful dishonor is a question of fact to be determined in each case.

Section 4–403. *Customer's Right to Stop Payment; Burden of Proof of Loss.* (1) A customer may by order to his bank stop payment of any item payable for his account but the order must be received at such time and in such manner as to afford the bank a reasonable opportunity to act on it prior to any action by the bank with respect to the item described in section 4–303.

(2) An oral order is binding upon the bank only for fourteen calendar days unless confirmed in writing within that period. A written order is effective for only six months unless renewed in writing.

(3) The burden of establishing the fact and amount of loss resulting from the payment of an item contrary to a binding stop payment order is on the customer.

Section 4–404. *Bank Not Obligated to Pay Check More Than Six Months Old.* A bank is under no obligation to a customer having a checking account to pay a check, other than a certified check, which is presented more than six months after its date, but it may charge its customer's account for a payment made thereafter in good faith.

Section 4–405. *Death or Incompetence of Customer.* (1) A payor or collecting bank's authority to accept, pay or collect an item or to account for proceeds of its collection if otherwise effective is not rendered ineffective by incompetence of a customer of either bank existing at the time the item is issued or its collection is undertaken if the bank does not know of an adjudication of incompetence. Neither death nor incompetence of a customer revokes such authority to accept, pay, collect or account until the bank knows of the fact of death or of an adjudication of incompetence and has reasonable opportunity to act on it.

(2) Even with knowledge a bank may for ten days after the date of death pay or certify checks drawn on or prior to that date unless ordered to stop payment by a person claiming an interest in the account.

Section 4–406. *Customer's Duty to Discover and Report Unauthorized Signature or Alteration.* (1) When a bank sends

Banks-Baldwin Kentucky Revised Statutes.

Ky. Rev. Stat. Ann. § 355.4-403 (Baldwin 19).

Commercially-published, official edition of *Ky. Rev. Stat*. There is no state-published edition.

355.4–402 XXIX Commerce and Trade 134

BANKS-BALDWIN KENTUCKY REVISED STATUTES

Yet this presumption is not conclusive and the obligation growing out of the bill as between the drawer and acceptor will depend on the facts of the case and the nature of the contract between them. Turner v Browder, 5 Bush 216; Bailey v Wood, 114 Ky 27, 69 SW 1103, 24 KLR 801.

356.124

Certain checks were drawn and signed in lead pencil; in the blank spaces appropriate words and figures were inserted which did not completely fill these spaces. An unauthorized person raised the checks by inserting words and figures in portions of these spaces. The bank on which they were drawn paid the checks. In an action between it and the depositor, it was entitled to credits for the amounts of the checks as drawn and for nothing more. Commercial Bank of Grayson v Arden & Fraley, 177 Ky 520, 197 SW 951.

355.4–402 Bank's liability to customer for wrongful dishonor.

A payor bank is liable to its customers for damages proximately caused by the wrongful dishonor of an item. When the dishonor occurs through mistake liability is limited to actual damages proved. If so proximately caused and proved damages may include damages for an arrest or prosecution of the customer or other consequential damages. Whether any consequential damages are proximately caused by the wrongful dishonor is a question of fact to be determined in each case. (1958 c 77, § 4-402. Eff. 7-1-60.)

CROSS REFERENCES

See Kentucky Legal Forms, Text 301(22)(29)

AM JUR AND ALR ANNOTATIONS

Bank's liability for wrongful dishonor. 10 Am Jur 2d, Banks § 567 et seq.
Bank's liability for paying postdated check. 76 ALR2d 1301.

Comment: Accord, Berea Bank & Trust Co v Mokwa, 194 Ky 556, 239 SW 1044 (1922); Stanley, Banking Law of Kentucky, § 121.

See 48 Ky LJ 237.

Where the dishonor occurs through a mistake, damages cannot be assessed for hurt feelings, nerves or loss of time from work. Bank of Louisville Royal v Sims, 435 SW(2d) 57 (1968).

Annotations from former KRS 356.185

AM JUR AND ALR ANNOTATIONS

Priority as between checks simultaneously presented to drawee bank for payment. 61 ALR 960.

355.4–403 Customer's right to stop payment; burden of proof of loss.

(1) A customer may by order to his bank stop payment of any item payable for his account but the order must be received at such time and in such manner as to afford the bank a reasonable opportunity to act on it prior to any action by the bank with respect to the item described in KRS 355.4-303.
(1958 c 77, § 4-403. Eff. 7-1-60.)

(2) An oral order is binding upon the bank only for fourteen calendar days unless confirmed in writing within that period. A written order is effective for only six months unless renewed in writing.
(1958 c 77, § 4-403. Eff. 7-1-60.)

(3) The burden of establishing the fact and amount of loss resulting from the payment of an item contrary to a binding stop payment order is on the customer. (1958 c 77, § 4-403. Eff. 7-1-60.)

Former analogous law, KRS 287.405.

CROSS REFERENCES

See Kentucky Legal Forms, Text 301(30); Form 305.11

AM JUR AND ALR ANNOTATIONS

Customer's right to stop payment. 10 Am Jur 2d, Banks § 641 et seq.
Stipulation relieving bank from, or limiting its liability for disregard of, stop-payment order. 1 ALR2d 1155.
What conduct by drawee of check before receipt of stop payment order, renders order ineffectual. 10 ALR2d 428.
Bank's liability for payment of check drawn by one depositor after stop payment order by joint depositor. 55 ALR2d 975.

Comment: Accord generally: Stanley, Banking Law of Kentucky, § 128, and cases therein cited. Limitation as to the binding nature of oral order for period of 14 days is new.
See 48 Ky LJ 235, 236.

Annotations from former analogous section

AM JUR AND ALR ANNOTATIONS

356.187

Right to stop payment of certified check. 35 ALR 942.

356.189

Sufficiency, as regards mode of communication and content, of order to bank to stop payment of check. 88 ALR 741 to 744.
Right to countermand or stop payment on cashier's check or check or draft drawn by one bank upon another. 107 ALR 1463.
Stipulation relieving bank from or limiting its liability for disregard of stop-payment order. 1 ALR2d 1155.

355.4–404 Bank not obligated to pay check more than six months old.

A bank is under no obligation to a customer having a checking account to pay a check, other than a certified check, which is presented more than six months after its date, but it may charge its customer's account for a payment made thereafter in good faith. (1958 c 77, § 4-404. Eff. 7-1-60.)

CROSS REFERENCES

See Kentucky Legal Forms, Text 301(31)

AM JUR AND ALR ANNOTATIONS

Duty of bank to honor checks, generally. 10 Am Jur 2d, Banks § 267 et seq.

Comment: At present, in Kentucky, under the Negotiable Instruments Law, former KRS 356.186, checks must be presented within a "reasonable" time. See, Stanley, Banking Law of Kentucky, § 123.

355.4–405 Death or incompetence of customer.

(1) A payor or collecting bank's authority to accept, pay or collect an item or to account for proceeds of its collection if otherwise effective is not rendered ineffective by incompetence of a customer of either bank existing at the time the item is issued or its collection is undertaken if the bank does not know of an adjudication of incompetence. Neither death nor incompetence of a customer revokes such authority to accept, pay, collect or account until the bank knows of the fact of death or of an adjudication of incompetence and has reasonable opportunity to act on it.
(1958 c 77, § 4-405. Eff. 7-1-60.)

(2) Even with knowledge a bank may for ten days after the date of death pay or certify checks drawn on or prior to that date unless ordered to stop payment by

Editorial Additions
(“Annotations”)

The law as passed by
the General Assembly

Banks-Baldwin Kentucky Revised Statutes — Supplement.

Ky. Rev. Stat. Ann. § 355.4-403 (Baldwin Supp. 1984).

The supplement to this looseleaf, replaceable-chapter edition is not a pocket part; it is a pamphlet in the front of the post-binder volume.

Because this supplement has no entry where 355.4-403 should appear, you are assured that there is no additional information to update the principal material.

ARTICLE 3. COMMERCIAL PAPER

355.3-115 Incomplete instruments

659 SW(2d) 213 (Ky App 1983), Brooks v United Kentucky Bank. An agreement whereby one party guarantees to repay a loan if the principal should default and which does not specify a sum certain, is not payable at a particular time, and is made payable neither to order nor to bearer is not within the purview of this section.

355.3-403 Signature by authorized representative

660 SW(2d) 678 (Ky App 1983), Richardson v First National Bank of Louisville. Corporate officers who sign a promissory note without indicating that they are signing it in a representative capacity are personally liable for the debt.

355.3-605 Cancellation and renunciation

660 SW(2d) 678 (Ky App 1983), Richardson v First National Bank of Louisville. Where, through clerical error, a debtor was informed that his promissory note was paid in full, the indebtedness to the bank remained, since the bank lacked the requisite intent to cancel the instrument.

704 F(2d) 733 (1983), Hubbard v Realty Co, Inc v First National Bank of Pikeville. The intent of the parties determines whether a promissory note is discharged when the original note is surrendered by the bank to the debtor in conjunction with the creation of a renewal note that carries forward the terms of the surrendered note.

355.3-606 Impairment of recourse or of collateral

668 SW(2d) 564 (Ky App 1984), Kane v Citizens Fidelity Bank and Trust Co. Since KRS 355.3-606, which establishes suretyship defenses, applies only to negotiable instruments, it does not apply to a continuing guarantee agreement because such an agreement is not a negotiable instrument.

ARTICLE 4. BANK DEPOSITS AND COLLECTIONS

355.4-202 Responsibility for collection; when action seasonable

644 SW(2d) 649 (Ky App 1983), United Kentucky Bank v Eagle Machine Co, Inc. A bank that did not notify its customer that a check the customer had deposited was dishonored until forty-eight days after the bank had obtained the information has failed to use ordinary care and is liable for failure to give timely notice.

ARTICLE 9. SECURED TRANSACTIONS; SALES OF ACCOUNTS, CONTRACT RIGHTS AND CHATTEL PAPER

Bobbs-Merrill/Michie Kentucky Revised Statutes.

Ky. Rev. Stat. Ann. § 355.4-403 (Bobbs-Merrill 1972).

Commercially-published, official edition of *Ky. Rev. Stat*. There is no state-published edition.

173 UNIFORM COMMERCIAL CODE 355.4-404

3. —Improper Items.

Where the defendant bank dishonored two of the plaintiff's checks due to mistake and without malice, and due to the incident the plaintiff took a two weeks' leave of absence for her "nerves," she was not entitled to recover for her two weeks' lost time from work even if her mental state actually contributed to this loss. Bank of Louisville Royal v. Sims (1968), 435 S. W. (2d) 57.

Where the defendant bank dishonored two of the plaintiff's checks due to mistake and without malice, the plaintiff was not entitled to recover for her hurt feelings or for her "nerves." Bank of Louisville Royal v. Sims (1968), 435 S. W. (2d) 57.

4. —Consequential.

For "consequential" damages to be recovered, they must be proximately caused by the wrongful dishonor. Bank of Louisville Royal v. Sims (1968), 435 S. W. (2d) 57.

5. —Proximately Caused.

"Proximately caused" damages, whether direct or consequential, would be those which could be reasonably foreseeable by the parties as the natural and probable result of the breach. Bank of Louisville Royal v. Sims (1968), 435 S. W. (2d) 57.

The law as passed by the General Assembly

355.4-403. Customer's right to stop payment—Burden of proof of loss.—(1) A customer may by order to his bank stop payment of any item payable for his account but the order must be received at such time and in such manner as to afford the bank a reasonable opportunity to act on it prior to any action by the bank with respect to the item described in KRS 355.4-303.

(2) An oral order is binding upon the bank only for fourteen (14) calendar days unless confirmed in writing within that period. A written order is effective for only six (6) months unless renewed in writing.

(3) The burden of establishing the fact and amount of loss resulting from the payment of an item contrary to a binding stop payment order is on the customer. (Enact. Acts 1958, ch. 77, § 4-403, effective July 1, 1960.)

DECISIONS UNDER PRIOR LAW

ANALYSIS

1. Maker's liability for stop-payment.
2. Pleading.

1. Maker's Liability for Stop-Payment.

Holder of a check could maintain suit thereon against drawer, in case it was not paid due to stop-payment order. Thomson v. Peck (1927), 217 Ky. 766, 290 S. W. 722.

Where maker stopped payment on a check, he was liable for the amount thereon. Thomson v. Peck (1927), 217 Ky. 766, 290 S. W. 722.

2. Pleading.

Where it appeared that check was not honored because drawer countermanded payment, the petition was not bad on demurrer because of failure to allege that drawer was not injured by delay in presenting for payment. Hazard Bank & Trust Co. v. Morgan (1925), 211 Ky. 134, 277 S. W. 307.

Collateral Reference. 9 C. J. S., Banks and Banking, § 353.

Editorial Additions ("Annotations")

355.4-404. Bank not obligated to pay check more than six months old.—A bank is under no obligation to a customer having a checking account to pay a check, other than a certified check, which is presented more than six (6) months after its date, but it may charge its customer's account for a payment made thereafter in good faith. (Enact. Acts 1958, ch. 77, § 4-404, effective July 1, 1960.)

Kentucky Law Journal. Leary, Commercial Paper: Some Aspects of Article 3 of the Uniform Commercial Code, 48 Ky. L. J. 198 (1960).

Bobbs-Merrill/Michie Kentucky Revised Statutes — Supplement.

Ky. Rev. Stat. Ann. § 355.4-403 (Bobbs-Merrill Supp. 1984).

The supplement to this hardbound edition is a pocket part.

Because this supplement has no entry where 355.4-403 should appear, you are assured that there is no additional information to update the hardbound book.

or by a local clearinghouse, subdivision (1)(d) means that a payor bank is deemed to have made final payment of a check when it fails to revoke a provisional settlement by its midnight deadline. Blake v. Woodford Bank & Trust Co., 555 S.W.2d 589 (Ky. App. 1977).

2. Final Payment of Check.
Under subsection (2), final payment of a check "firms up" all of the provisional settlements made in the collection process. Blake v. Woodford Bank & Trust Co., 555 S.W.2d 589 (Ky. App. 1977).

Part 3. Collection of Items: Payor Banks

355.4-301. Deferred posting—Recovery of payment by return of items—Time of dishonor.

NOTES TO DECISIONS

ANALYSIS

1. Revocation of provisional settlement.
2. Midnight deadline.

1. Revocation of Provisional Settlement.
Where two checks, one of which had been dishonored and then again presented, were available to the payor bank for return and were not being held for protest, so that notice of dishonor was not available as a means of revoking the provisional settlement, the only way the bank could revoke such settlement was by returning the check before its midnight deadline and the provisions of KRS 355.3-511 excusing notice of dishonor were not applicable. Blake v. Woodford Bank & Trust Co., 555 S.W.2d 589 (Ky. App. 1977).

Under subsection (1), written notice of dishonor is a permitted method of revoking a provisional settlement only if the check is unavailable for return or it is being held for protest and, otherwise, the check itself must be returned. Blake v. Woodford Bank & Trust Co., 555 S.W.2d 589 (Ky. App. 1977).

2. Midnight Deadline.
Whether a payor bank has met its midnight deadline for return of an item is determined by this section, not by KRS 355.4-302. Blake v. Woodford Bank & Trust Co., 555 S.W.2d 589 (Ky. App. 1977).

355.4-302. Payor bank's responsibility for late return of item.

NOTES TO DECISIONS

3. Midnight Deadline.
Where a payor bank fails to return a check by its midnight deadline, it is liable for the face amount of the check because it is deemed to have paid the check and its liability does not rest on a failure to exercise ordinary care nor have any relationship to "damages" as such. Blake v. Woodford Bank & Trust Co., 555 S.W.2d 589 (Ky. App. 1977).

Whether a payor bank has met its midnight deadline for return of an item is not determined by this section, but by KRS 355.4-301. Blake v. Woodford Bank & Trust Co., 555 S.W.2d 589 (Ky. App. 1977).

Part 4. Relationship Between Payor Bank and Its Customer

355.4-402. Bank's liability to customer for wrongful dishonor.

NOTES TO DECISIONS

6. Suit for Wrongful Dishonor.
Where plaintiff-bank mistakenly transferred $30,000 to defendant bank for deposit to the account of a customer of the latter, then

notified defendant of the mistake requesting a retransfer, the defendant correctly refused to do so since it would have opened itself for suit for wrongful dishonor, under this section, had the customer sought to transfer the money so deposited. French Bank v. First Nat'l Bank, 585 S.W.2d 431 (Ky. App. 1979).

ARTICLE 6. BULK TRANSFERS

355.6-101. Short title.

NOTES TO DECISIONS

1. Application.

The provisions of the Uniform Commercial Code relating to bulk transfers do not apply to the sale of the assets of a restaurant-bar business. Kentucky Club, Inc. v. Fifth Third Bank, 590 S.W.2d 686 (Ky. 1979).

355.6-102. "Bulk transfer"—Transfers of equipment—Enterprises subject to this article—Bulk transfers subject to this article.

Kentucky Law Journal. Kentucky Law Survey, Peltier and Coleman, Commercial Law, 67 Ky. L.J. 523 (1978-1979).

355.6-103. Transfers excepted from this article.

Kentucky Law Journal. Kentucky Law Survey, Peltier and Coleman, Commercial Law, 67 Ky. L.J. 523 (1978-1979).

NOTES TO DECISIONS

1. Bulk Transfer Under Future Advances Clause.

Where a security agreement contained a future advances clause, an open account between the parties to the agreement came within the clause and was secured by the collateral named in the agreement so that a bulk transfer from the debtor to the secured party came within the exception of subdivision (3) of this section. Malone & Hyde, Inc. v. Maxwell, 557 S.W.2d 908 (Ky. App. 1977).

355.6-104. Schedule of property, list of creditors.—(1) Except as provided with respect to auction sales (KRS 355.6-108), a bulk transfer subject to this article is ineffective against any creditor of the transferor unless:

(a) The transferee requires the transferor to furnish a list of his existing creditors prepared as stated in this section; and

(b) The parties prepare a schedule of the property transferred sufficient to identify it; and

(c) The transferee preserves the list and schedule for six (6) months next following the transfer and permits inspection of either or both and copying therefrom at all reasonable hours by any creditor of the transferor, or files the list and schedule in the office of the county clerk.

(2) The list of creditors must be signed and sworn to or affirmed by the transferor or his agent. It must contain the names and business addresses of all creditors of the transferor, with the amounts when known, and also the

Uniform Laws Annotated, Uniform Commercial Code.

2A U.L.A. 170 (19).

Contains the nationally-recommended statutes which have been enacted in the various states, comments of the draftsmen, information concerning action in the jurisdictions which adopted it, collateral references to law review articles, and case notes.

§ 4–402 UNIFORM COMMERCIAL CODE
Note 11

Charge for a telephone call made by a customer as the result of bank's wrongful dishonor of two of her checks was a proper item of damages. Bank of Louisville Royal v. Sims, Ky.1968, 435 S.W.2d 57.

12. Estoppel

Facts that auctioneer had previously commingled personal funds with custodial account and that his personal checks could not be honored without withdrawal of funds from custodial account did not estop auctioneer from bringing action against bank which applied funds of custodial account to pay auctioneer's overdraft and dishonored checks payable to persons who consigned cattle to auction. Lumberton State Bank v. Fortenberry, Miss.1969, 222 So.2d 384.

13. Sufficiency of evidence

Although, in suit brought by Indian tribe for, inter alia, wrongful dishonor of its checks by bank, the complaint alleged that the tribe suffered injury to its commercial and financial reputation, and although the tribe's posttrial brief referred to damages flowing from its inability to account for federal grant moneys because of bank's setoffs against demand deposits, no evidence was offered from which the court could infer that any compensable damages were in fact sustained by the tribe. U. S. ex rel. Crow Creek Sioux Tribe v. Tri-County Bank of Chamberlain, S. D., D.C.S.D.1976, 415 F.Supp. 858.

In suit charging defendant bank with wrongfully paying out a savings account to individual defendants without authority to do so and for dishonoring check and charging individual defendants with conversion of $1,954.10 of plaintiff's money to their own use, evidence would support inferences in favor of plaintiff and trial court erred in granting judgment in favor of defendants at close of plaintiff's evidence. Indianapolis Saenger Chor, Inc. v. American Fletcher Nat. Bank & Trust Co., Ind.App.1971, 274 N.E.2d 728.

Where bank employee testified that resolution was altered after it was in bank's custody and testimony was uncontroverted and no reason appeared for doubting accuracy of observation or credibility of witness, statement should be accepted as true and was sufficient to create an inference as to bank's liability to plaintiff corporation which charged bank with wrongfully paying out savings account to individual defendants without authority to do so and with dishonoring check. Id.

In action by depositor based on alleged wrongful dishonor of two checks after bank had declared total obligation under retail installment contract due and had taken possession of depositor's account, where affidavit by bank officer in support of motion for summary judgment did not reflect, inter alia, date of or manner by which bank took possession of depositor's account and did not recite whether dishonored checks were presented for payment before balance was withdrawn through bank error by depositor or whether balance would have covered dishonored checks, allegations in affidavit were insufficient to establish that there was no material fact issue. Gustason v. Northeast Nat. Bank, Tex.Civ.App.1972, 486 S.W.2d 596.

§ 4–403. Customer's Right to Stop Payment; Burden of Proof of Loss

Nationally recommended statute which was enacted in Kentucky as KRS 355.4-403

(1) A customer may by order to his bank stop payment of any item payable for his account but the order must be received at such time and in such manner as to afford the bank a reasonable opportunity to act on it prior to any action by the bank with respect to the item described in Section 4–303.

(2) An oral order is binding upon the bank only for fourteen calendar days unless confirmed in writing within that period. A written order is effective for only six months unless renewed in writing.

(3) The burden of establishing the fact and amount of loss resulting from the payment of an item contrary to a binding stop payment order is on the customer.

Official Comment

Prior Uniform Statutory Provision: None.

Purposes:

1. This section is new. It is intended to replace separate statutes in twenty-nine states which regulate stop-payment orders.

2. The position taken by this section is that stopping payment is a service which depositors expect and are entitled to receive from banks notwithstanding its difficulty, inconvenience and expense. The inevitable occasional losses through failure to stop should be borne by the banks as a cost of the business of banking.

Nationally-recommended comments which were drawn up by the national drafters but were not enacted by Kentucky General Assembly

3. Subsection (1) follows the decisions holding that a payee or indorsee has no right to stop payment. This is consistent with the provision governing payment or satisfaction. See Section 3–603. The sole exception to this rule is found in Section 4–405 on payment after notice of death, by which any person claiming an interest in the account can stop payment.

4. Payment is commonly stopped only on checks; but the right to stop payment is not limited to checks, and extends to any item payable by any bank. Where the maker of a note payable at a bank is in a position analogous to that of a drawer (Section 3–121) he may stop payment of the note. By analogy the rule extends to drawees other than banks.

5. There is no right to stop payment after certification of a check or other acceptance of a draft, and this is true no matter who procures the certification. See Sections 3–411 and 4–303. The acceptance is the drawee's own engagement to pay, and he is not required to impair his credit by refusing payment for the convenience of the drawer.

6. Normally a direction to stop payment is first given by telephone. Notwithstanding statutes which require a written order, banks customarily accept such directions, and have been held to waive the writing. Subsection (2) is intended to protect both parties by making the oral direction effective for only a short time during which the drawer must confirm it in writing, and by eliminating thereafter any claim of waiver by acceptance of the oral direction.

7. The existing statutes all specify a time limit after which any direction to stop payment

§ 4-403 UNIFORM COMMERCIAL CODE

becomes ineffective unless it is renewed in writing; and the majority of them have specified six months. The purpose of the provision is, of course, to facilitate stopping payment by clearing the records of the drawee of accumulated unrevoked stop orders, as where the drawer has found a lost instrument or has settled his controversy with the payee, but has failed to notify the drawee. The last sentence of subsection (2), together with the second clause in Section 4-404, rejects the reasoning of such cases as Goldberg v. Manufacturers Trust Company, 199 Misc. 167, 102 N.Y.S.2d 144 (1951).

8. A payment in violation of an effective direction to stop payment is an improper payment, even though it is made by mistake or inadvertence. Any agreement to the contrary is invalid under Section 4-103(1) if in paying the item over the stop payment order the bank has failed to exercise ordinary care. The drawee is, however, entitled to subrogation to prevent unjust enrichment (Section 4-407); retains common-law defenses, e. g., that by conduct in recognizing the payment the customer has ratified the bank's action in paying over a stop payment order (Section 1-103); and retains common-law rights, e. g., to recover money paid under a mistake (Section 1-103) in cases where the payment is not made final by Section 3-418. It has sometimes been said that payment cannot be stopped against a holder in due course, but the statement is inaccurate. The payment can be stopped but the drawer remains liable on the instrument to the holder in due course (Sections 3-305, 3-413) and the drawee, if he pays, becomes subrogated to the rights of the holder in due course against the drawer. Section 4-407. Any defenses available against a holder in due course remain available to the drawer, but other defenses are cut off to the same extent as if the holder himself were bringing the action.

Cross References:

Point 3: Sections 3-603(1), 4-405.

Point 4: Section 3-121.

Point 5: Sections 3-411 and 4-303.

Point 8: Sections 3-305, 3-413, 3-418, 4-103 and 4-407.

Definitional Cross References:

"Account". Section 4-104.

"Bank". Section 1-201.

"Burden of establishing". Section 1-201.

"Customer". Section 4-104.

"Item". Section 4-104.

"Send". Section 1-201.

Action in Adopting Jurisdictions

Variations from Official Text.

California. Section reads:

"(1) A customer, or any customer if there is more than one, or any person authorized to sign checks or make withdrawals thereon may stop payment of any item payable, for or drawn against such customer's or customers' account but the bank may

Uniform Laws Annotated, Uniform Commercial Code — Supplement.

2A U.L.A. 17 § 4-403 (Supp. 19).

Pocket part supplement for *U.L.A.* with additional annotations which update the hardbound volume.

BANK DEPOSITS AND COLLECTIONS § 4-403

of check has no cause of action against bank; holder of check must look to drawer of check and only drawer of check can complain about bank's not honoring such check. Citizens Nat. Bank v. First Nat. Bank, Miss.1977, 347 So.2d 964.

2. Customers within section

Corporate president did not have a cause of action against bank for wrongfully dishonoring certain checks drawn on the corporation's account, as the account in question was that of the corporation, not its president, and as the record contained no support for the lower court's finding that the bank regarded the president, rather than the corporation, as its customer. Farmers Bank v. Sinwellan Corp., Del.1976, 367 A.2d 180.

3. Wrongful dishonor within section

Where bank stated in three letters that it agreed "to honor monthly drafts" drawn by equipment leasing company on the account of a corporate depositor for a period not to exceed 36 months and further stated "The only exception is for the lease to be paid in full earlier than the 36-month term," language of letters was unambiguous and constituted an unconditional guarantee agreement to honor the drafts; fact that depositor did not maintain sufficient funds in its account during a three-month period was not a sufficient excuse for the bank's refusal to honor drafts presented by the equipment leasing company. Baytown State Bank v. Don McMillian Leasing Co., Tex.Civ. App.1977, 551 S.W.2d 771

Where bank had entered into an unconditional agreement to honor monthly draft in certain amounts drawn on its corporate depositor's account and where bank thereafter dishonored the drafts for a three-month period, contending that such dishonor was not a breach of the agreement because the bank had intended to honor the drafts only if the depositor had sufficient funds to cover them, bank's conduct manifested a clear repudiation of the guarantee agreement. Id.

Where language of unconditional agreement to honor drafts drawn on depositor's account was clear and unambiguous, any mistake in interpreting language of agreement was unilateral on part of bank and did not preclude recovery for bank's anticipatory breach of the agreement. Id.

4. Mistaken dishonor

In view of volume of transactions which take place every business day and fact that wrongful dishonor might occur due to a simple accounting error, a bank's mere dishonor of drafts that it had agreed to honor would not in and of itself constitute a definite and unequivocal manifestation of an intention to repudiate the agreement to honor the drafts. Baytown State Bank v. Don McMillian Leasing Co., Tex.Civ.App. 1977, 551 S.W.2d 771.

5a. Joint accounts

Bank's obligation to plaintiff who drew two checks totaling $1,200 on joint checking account which had balance of $1,693.46 was extinguished by bank's payment on check drawn by plaintiff's joint depositor in the amount of $1,617.93. Andrews v. Citizens Bank, 1976, 229 S.E.2d 501, 139 Ga.App. 763.

Generally, in the absence of statute or an express agreement to the contrary, withdrawals from a joint deposit in a bank requires the authority of all the depositors. Id.

13. Sufficiency of evidence

In action against payor bank for damages for wrongful failure to pay checks, trial court was entitled to believe plaintiff's evidence that at time checks were presented to payor bank for payment plaintiff had no more than suspicion of possible "check-kiting" operation involving payor bank's customers, which evidence did not demonstrate bad faith of plaintiff in not informing payor bank of its suspicions. Community Bank v. U. S. Nat. Bank of Oregon, 1976, 555 P.2d 435, 276 Or. 471.

§ 4-403. Customer's Right to Stop Payment; Burden of Proof of Loss — Case note annotations

Notes of Decisions

Supplementary Index to Notes

Summary judgment 22

2. Generally

Liberal interpretation is intended for provision of Uniform Commercial Code providing that a customer may by order to his bank stop payment of any item payable for his account. Dziurak v. Chase Manhattan Bank, N.A., 1976, 388 N.Y.S.2d 496, 88 Misc.2d 641.

Once check had been acted upon by drawee bank, its drawer no longer had authority to stop payment. First Nat. Bank & Trust Co. of Augusta v. Georgia R. R. Bank & Trust Co., 1977, 235 S.E.2d 1, 238 Ga. 693.

Drawer of check has right to stop payment of it at any time before it has been certified or paid by drawee. Georgia R.R. Bank & Trust Co. v. First Nat. Bank & Trust Co. of Augusta, 1976, 229 S.E.2d 482, 139 Ga.App. 683.

4. Bank's right to stop payment

A check drawn by one bank on its account in another bank is a "bank check," and the drawer bank on such a check has the right to issue a stop payment to the drawee bank. Bruno v. Collective Federal Sav. and Loan Ass'n, 1977, 370 A.2d 874, 147 N.J. Super. 115.

5. Cashier's check

A "cashier's check" is a bill of exchange, accepted for payment as soon as it is issued, and a bank which issues a "cashier's check" cannot stop payment on it. Bruno v. Collective Federal Sav. and Loan Ass'n, 1977, 370 A.2d 874, 147 N.J.Super. 115.

With respect to issuing bank's ability to stop payment on cashier's check, analogies to customer's right to stop payment on ordinary check are inapposite and confusing; proper approach is to view issuing bank, acting in its dual role as drawer and drawee, as equivalent of maker of negotiable promissory note payable on demand. Laurel Bank & Trust Co. v. City Nat. Bank of Connecticut, 1976, 365 A.2d 1222, 33 Conn.Sup. 641.

Payment on cashier's check or "official bank check" issued by bank in fa-

United States Law Week.

The first place where a report of a U.S. Supreme Court case is published.
Brown v. Board of Education, 22 U.S.L.W. 4245 (U.S. May 18, 1954)

---

1. Date of publication is the date of the opinion. Mailed immediately.

2. Volume number; page number.

3. Date of opinion.

4. Official opinion.

5. Official footnotes.

1\. **5-18-54** ***The United States* LAW WEEK** **22 LW 4245** 2.

PAUL A. SWEENEY (ROBERT L. STERN, Acting Solicitor General, WARREN E. BURGER, Assistant Attorney General, and JOHN G. LAUGHLIN with him on the brief) for petitioner; WILLIAM C. WETHERBEE (PAUL J. SEDGWICK, ROLLAND LEE NUTT, and PARKER, STANBURY, REESE & McGEE with him on the brief) for respondent; RICHARD W. GALIHER, RICHARD L. WILLIAMS, and ROBERT G. BUTCHER filed brief for Fred L. Harrison as amicus curiae.

NOS. 1, 2, 4 AND 10.—OCTOBER TERM, 1953.

1	Oliver Brown, et al., Appellants, *v.* Board of Education of Topeka, Shawnee County, Kansas, et al.	On Appeal From the United States District Court for the District of Kansas.
2	Harry Briggs, Jr., et al., Appellants, *v.* R. W. Elliott, et al.	On Appeal From the United States District Court for the Eastern District of South Carolina.
4	Dorothy E. Davis, et al., Appellants, *v.* County School Board of Prince Edward County, Virginia, et al.	On Appeal From the United States District Court for the Eastern District of Virginia.
10	Francis B. Gebhart, et al., Petitioners, *v.* Ethel Louise Belton, et al.	On Writ of Certiorari to the Supreme Court of Delaware.

3\. [May 17, 1954.]

4\. MR. CHIEF JUSTICE WARREN delivered the opinion of the Court.

These cases come to us from the States of Kansas, South Carolina, Virginia, and Delaware. They are premised on different facts and different local conditions, but a common legal question justifies their consideration together in this consolidated opinion.[1]

In each of the cases, minors of the Negro race, through their legal representatives, seek the aid of the courts in obtaining admission to the public schools of their community on a nonsegregated basis. In each instance, they had been denied admission to schools attended by white children under laws requiring or permitting segre-

5\. [1] In the Kansas case, *Brown* v. *Board of Education*, the plaintiffs are Negro children of elementary school age residing in Topeka. They brought this action in the United States District Court for the District of Kansas to enjoin enforcement of a Kansas statute which permits, but does not require, cities of more than 15,000 population to maintain separate school facilities for Negro and white students. Kan. Gen. Stat. § 72-1724 (1949). Pursuant to that authority, the Topeka Board of Education elected to establish segregated elementary schools. Other public schools in the community, however, are operated on a nonsegregated basis. The three-judge District Court, convened under 28 U. S. C. §§ 2281 and 2284, found that segregation in public education has a detrimental effect upon Negro children, but denied relief on the ground that the Negro and white schools were substantially equal with respect to buildings, transportation, curricula, and educational qualifications of teachers. 98 F. Supp. 797. The case is here on direct appeal under 28 U. S. C. § 1253.

In the South Carolina case, *Briggs* v. *Elliott*, the plaintiffs are Negro children of both elementary and high school age residing in Clarendon County. They brought this action in the United States District Court for the Eastern District of South Carolina to enjoin enforcement of provisions in the state constitution and statutory code which require the segregation of Negroes and whites in public schools. S. C. Const., Art. XI, § 7; S. C. Code § 5377 (1942). The three-judge District Court, convened under 28 U. S. C. §§ 2281 and 2284, denied the requested relief. The court found that the Negro schools were inferior to the white schools and ordered the defendants to begin immediately to equalize the facilities. But the court sustained the validity of the contested provisions and denied the plaintiffs admission to the white schools during the equalization program. 98 F. Supp. 529. This Court vacated the District Court's judgment and remanded the case for the purpose of obtaining the court's views on a report filed by the defendants concerning the progress made in the equalization program. 342 U. S. 350. On remand, the District Court found that substantial equality had been achieved except for buildings and that the defendants were proceeding to rectify this inequality as well. 103 F. Supp. 920. The case is again here on direct appeal under 28 U. S. C. § 1253.

In the Virginia case, *Davis* v. *County School Board*, the plaintiffs are Negro children of high school age residing in Prince Edward County. They brought this action in the United States District Court for the Eastern District of Virginia to enjoin enforcement of provisions in the state constitution and statutory code which require the segregation of Negroes and whites in public schools. Va. Const., § 140; Va. Code § 22-221 (1950). The three-judge District Court, convened under 28 U. S. C. §§ 2281 and 2284, denied the requested relief. The court found the Negro school inferior in physical plant, curricula, and transportation, and ordered the defendants forthwith to provide substantially equal curricula and transportation and to "proceed with all reasonable diligence and dispatch to remove" the inequality in physical plant. But, as in the South Carolina case, the court sustained the validity of the contested provisions and denied the plaintiffs admission to the white schools during the equalization program. 103 F. Supp. 337. The case is here on direct appeal under 28 U. S. C. § 1253.

In the Delaware case, *Gebhart* v. *Belton*, the plaintiffs are Negro children of both elementary and high school age residing in New Castle County. They brought this action in the Delaware Court of Chancery to enjoin enforcement of provisions in the state constitution and statutory code which require the segregation of Negroes and whites in public schools. Del. Const., Art. X, § 2; Del. Rev. Code § 2631 (1935). The Chancellor gave judgment for the plaintiffs and ordered their immediate admission to schools previously attended only by white children, on the ground that the Negro schools were inferior with respect to teacher training, pupil-teacher ratio, extra-curricular activities, physical plant, and time and distance involved in travel. 87 A. 2d 862. The Chancellor also found that segregation itself results in an inferior education for Negro children (see note 10, *infra*), but did not rest his decision on that ground. *Id.*, at 865. The Chancellor's decree was affirmed by the Supreme Court of Delaware, which intimated, however, that the defendants might be able to obtain a modification of the decree after equalization of the Negro and white schools had been accomplished. 91 A. 2d 137, 152. The defendants, contending only that the Delaware courts had erred in ordering the immediate admission of the Negro plaintiffs to the white schools, applied to this Court for certiorari. The writ was

United States Reports.

The official, U.S. Government Printing Office edition of the reports of the U.S. Supreme Court. Publication of the advance parts and bound volumes is slow.

Brown v. Board of Education, 347 U.S. 483 (1954).

---

1. Page number 483 in v. 347.

2. Short title.

3. How the case got to the U.S. Supreme Court.

4. Date of opinion.

5. Official court reporter's headnotes (called syllabi if plural; syllabus if singular). These headnotes are not officially compiled in any digest. They do not constitute an official pronouncement of the court and are editorially supplied for the sole purpose of the reader's convenience.

BROWN *v.* BOARD OF EDUCATION. 483 **1.**

Syllabus.

BROWN ET AL. *v.* BOARD OF EDUCATION OF TOPEKA ET AL. **2.**

NO. 1. APPEAL FROM THE UNITED STATES DISTRICT COURT FOR THE DISTRICT OF KANSAS.* **3.**

Argued December 9, 1952.—Reargued December 8, 1953.—Decided May 17, 1954. **4.**

Segregation of white and Negro children in the public schools of a State solely on the basis of race, pursuant to state laws permitting or requiring such segregation, denies to Negro children the equal **5.** protection of the laws guaranteed by the Fourteenth Amendment—even though the physical facilities and other "tangible" factors of white and Negro schools may be equal. Pp. 486–496.

(a) The history of the Fourteenth Amendment is inconclusive as to its intended effect on public education. Pp. 489–490.

(b) The question presented in these cases must be determined, not on the basis of conditions existing when the Fourteenth Amendment was adopted, but in the light of the full development of public education and its present place in American life throughout the Nation. Pp. 492–493.

(c) Where a State has undertaken to provide an opportunity for an education in its public schools, such an opportunity is a right which must be made available to all on equal terms. P. 493.

(d) Segregation of children in public schools solely on the basis of race deprives children of the minority group of equal educational opportunities, even though the physical facilities and other "tangible" factors may be equal. Pp. 493–494.

(e) The "separate but equal" doctrine adopted in *Plessy* v. *Ferguson*, 163 U. S. 537, has no place in the field of public education. P. 495.

---

*Together with No. 2, *Briggs et al.* v. *Elliott et al.*, on appeal from the United States District Court for the Eastern District of South Carolina, argued December 9–10, 1952, reargued December 7–8, 1953; No. 4, *Davis et al.* v. *County School Board of Prince Edward County, Virginia, et al.*, on appeal from the United States District Court for the Eastern District of Virginia, argued December 10, 1952, reargued December 7–8, 1953; and No. 10, *Gebhart et al.* v. *Belton et al.*, on certiorari to the Supreme Court of Delaware, argued December 11, 1952, reargued December 9, 1953.

[The official opinion and official footnotes follow.]

Supreme Court Reporter.

One of two well-received, unofficial editions of the reports of the U.S. Supreme Court. Publication of advance parts is prompt. Bound volumes are published annually.

Brown v. Board of Education, 74 S.Ct. 686 (1954).

---

1. Page number 686 in v. 74.

2. Parallel volume in *United States Reports*.

3. Parallel official citation to *United States Reports*.

4. Style or name of cases. Use only name of first case mentioned.

5. Date of opinion.

6. West Publishing Company's editorial introduction or summary note.

7. Topic under which headnote and citation are found in West's digests; section number within the topic where headnote and citation are found.

8. Headnotes which are compiled in West's digests.

9. Page numbers of the material that follows, as found in the official *United States Reports*.

1. 686 74 SUPREME COURT REPORTER [347 U.S.] 2.

3. 347 U.S. 483

BROWN et al.

v.

BOARD OF EDUCATION OF TOPEKA, SHAWNEE COUNTY, KAN., et al.

4. **BRIGGS et al. v. ELLIOTT et al.**

DAVIS et al.

v.

COUNTY SCHOOL BOARD OF PRINCE EDWARD COUNTY, VA., et al.

GEBHART et al. v. BELTON et al.

Nos. 1, 2, 4, 10.

Reargued Dec. 7, 8, 9, 1953.

5. Decided May 17, 1954.

Class actions originating in the four
states of Kansas, South Carolina, Vir-
6. ginia, and Delaware, by which minor
Negro plaintiffs sought to obtain admission to public schools on a nonsegregated basis. On direct appeals by plaintiffs from adverse decisions in the United States District Courts, District of Kansas, 98 F.Supp. 797, Eastern District of South Carolina, 103 F.Supp. 920, and Eastern District of Virginia, 103 F.Supp. 337, and on grant of certiorari after decision favorable to plaintiffs in the Supreme Court of Delaware, 91 A.2d 137, the United States Supreme Court, Mr. Chief Justice Warren, held that segregation of children in public schools solely on the basis of race, even though the physical facilities and other tangible factors may be equal, deprives the children of the minority group of equal educational opportunities, in contravention of the Equal Protection Clause of the Fourteenth Amendment.

Cases ordered restored to docket for further argument regarding formulation of decrees.

7. **1. Constitutional Law ⇐47**

In resolving question whether segre-
8. gation of races in public schools constituted a denial of equal protection of the laws, even though the tangible facilities provided might be equal, court would consider public education in light of its full development and present status throughout the nation, and not in light of conditions prevailing at time of adoption of the amendment. U.S.C.A.Const. Amend. 14.

2. Constitutional Law ⇐220

The opportunity of an education, where the state has undertaken to provide it, is a right which must be made available to all on equal terms. U.S.C.A. Const. Amend. 14.

3. Constitutional Law ⇐220

The segregation of children in public schools solely on the basis of race, even though the physical facilities and other tangible factors may be equal, deprives the children of minority group of equal educational opportunities, and amounts to a deprivation of the equal protection of the laws guaranteed by the Fourteenth Amendment to the Federal Constitution. U.S.C.A.Const. Amend. 14.

4. Constitutional Law ⇐220

The doctrine of "separate but equal" has no place in the field of public education, since separate educational facilities are inherently unequal. U.S.C.A.Const. Amend. 14.

5. Appeal and Error ⇐819

In view of fact that actions raising question of constitutional validity of segregation of races in public schools were class actions, and because of the wide applicability of decision holding that segregation was denial of equal protection of laws, and the great variety of local conditions, the formation of decrees presented problems of considerable complexity, requiring that cases be restored to the docket so that court might have full assistance of parties in formulating appropriate decrees. U.S.C.A. Const. Amend. 14.

No. 1:

484 9.

Mr. Robert L. Carter, New York City, for appellants Brown and others.

Supreme Court Reporter — *Continued*

10. Names and addresses of lawyers in the case.

11. Official opinion.

12. Official footnotes.

Mr. Paul E. Wilson, Topeka, Kan., for appellees Board of Education of Topeka and others.

Nos. 2, 4:

0. Messrs. Spottswood Robinson III, Thurgood Marshall, New York City, for appellants Briggs and Davis and others.

Messrs. John W. Davis, T. Justin Moore, J. Lindsay Almond, Jr., Richmond, Va., for appellees Elliott and County School Board of Prince Edward County and others.

Asst. Atty. Gen. J. Lee Rankin for United States amicus curiae by special leave of Court.

No. 10:

485

Mr. H. Albert Young, Wilmington, Del., for petitioners Gebhart et al.

Mr. Jack Greenberg, Thurgood Marshall, New York City, for respondents Belton et al.

486

Mr. Chief Justice WARREN delivered the opinion of the Court. 11.

These cases come to us from the States of Kansas, South Carolina, Virginia, and Delaware. They are premised on different facts and different local conditions, but a common legal question justifies their consideration together in this consolidated opinion.[1]

2. 1. In the Kansas case, Brown v. Board of Education, the plaintiffs are Negro children of elementary school age residing in Topeka. They brought this action in the United States District Court for the District of Kansas to enjoin enforcement of a Kansas statute which permits, but does not require, cities of more than 15,000 population to maintain separate school facilities for Negro and white students. Kan.Gen.Stat.1949, § 72–1724. Pursuant to that authority, the Topeka Board of Education elected to establish segregated elementary schools. Other public schools in the community, however, are operated on a nonsegregated basis. The three-judge District Court, convened under 28 U.S.C. §§ 2281 and 2284, 28 U.S.C.A. §§ 2281, 2284, found that segregation in public education has a detrimental effect upon Negro children, but denied relief on the ground that the Negro and white schools were substantially equal with respect to buildings, transportation, curricula, and educational qualifications of teachers. 98 F.Supp. 797. The case is here on direct appeal under 28 U.S.C. § 1253, 28 U.S.C.A. § 1253.

In the South Carolina case, Briggs v. Elliott, the plaintiffs are Negro children of both elementary and high school age residing in Clarendon County. They brought this action in the United States District Court for the Eastern District of South Carolina to enjoin enforcement of provisions in the state constitution and statutory code which require the segregation of Negroes and whites in public schools. S.C.Const. Art. XI, § 7; S.C. Code 1942, § 5377. The three-judge District Court, convened under 28 U.S.C. §§ 2281 and 2284, 28 U.S.C.A. §§ 2281, 2284, denied the requested relief. The court found that the Negro schools were inferior to the white schools and ordered the defendants to begin immediately to equalize the facilities. But the court sustained the validity of the contested provisions and denied the plaintiffs admission to the white schools during the equalization program. 98 F.Supp. 529. This Court vacated the District Court's judgment and remanded the case for the purpose of obtaining the court's views on a report filed by the defendants concerning the progress made in the equalization program. 342 U.S. 350, 72 S.Ct. 327, 96 L.Ed. 392. On remand, the District Court found that substantial equality had been achieved except for buildings and that the defendants were proceeding to rectify this inequality as well. 103 F. Supp. 920. The case is again here on direct appeal under 28 U.S.C. § 1253, 28 U.S.C.A. § 1253.

In the Virginia case, Davis v. County School Board, the plaintiffs are Negro children of high school age residing in Prince Edward County. They brought this action in the United States District Court for the Eastern District of Virginia to enjoin enforcement of provisions in the state constitution and statutory code which require the segregation of Negroes and whites in public schools. Va.Const. § 140; Va.Code 1950, § 22–221. The three-judge District Court, convened under 28 U.S.C. §§ 2281 and 2284, 28 U.S.C.A. §§ 2281, 2284, denied the requested relief. The court found the Negro school inferior in physical plant, curricula, and transportation, and ordered the defendants

United States Supreme Court Reports, Lawyer's Edition.

One of two well-received, unofficial editions of the reports of the U.S. Supreme Court. Publication of advance parts is prompt. Bound volumes are published at intervals.

Brown v. Board of Education, 98 L.Ed. 873 (1954).

---

1. Parallel official citation to *United States Reports*.

2. Lawyers Co-Operative Publishing Company editorial introduciton or "summary" note, similar to the one in *A.L.R.2d*.

3. Cross-reference to an essay ("annotation") on the subject indicated.

4. Page number 873 in v. 98.

1953. BROWN v. BOARD OF EDUCATION OF TOPEKA 347 US 483 **1.**

*[483]

*OLIVER BROWN et al., Appellants,

v.

BOARD OF EDUCATION OF TOPEKA, Shawnee County, Kansas, et al. (No. 1.)

HARRY BRIGGS, Jr., et al., Appellants,

v.

R. W. ELLIOTT et al. (No. 2.)

DOROTHY E. DAVIS et al., Appellants,

v.

COUNTY SCHOOL BOARD OF PRINCE EDWARD COUNTY, Virginia, et al. (No. 4.)

FRANCIS B. GEBHART et al., Petitioners,

v.

ETHEL LOUISE BELTON et al. (No. 10.)

(347 US 483, 98 L ed 873, 74 S Ct 686, 38 ALR2d 1180)

SUMMARY OF DECISION

2. In each of the four cases involved the plaintiffs, Negro children, were denied admission to state public schools attended by white children under state laws requiring or permitting segregation according to race. There were findings below that the Negro and white schools involved had been equalized, or were being equalized, with respect to buildings, curricula, qualifications and salaries of teachers, and other tangible factors.

In an opinion by Warren, Ch. J., the Supreme Court unanimously held that the plaintiffs, by reason of the segregation complained of, were deprived of the equal protection of the laws guaranteed by the Fourteenth Amendment. The "separate but equal" doctrine announced in Plessy v. Ferguson, 163 US 537, 41 L ed 256, 16 S Ct 1138, involving equality in transportation facilities, under which equality of treatment is accorded by providing Negroes and whites substantially equal, though separate, facilities, was held to have no place in the field of public education.

In view of the complex problems presented by the formulation of the decrees, the cases were restored to the docket for argument by the parties.

SUBJECT OF ANNOTATION

3. Beginning on page 882

Race discrimination.

98 L ed 873 **4.**

United States Supreme Court Reports, Lawyers' Edition — *Continued*

5. Headnotes, similar to those in *A.L.R.2d,* which are compiled in Lawyers Co-Operative Publishing Company's *U.S. Supreme Court Digest Annotated.*

6. Caution: The titles and section numbers do not correspond with the *A.L.R. Digests'* titles and section numbers.

7. Date of opinion.

347 US SUPREME COURT OF THE UNITED STATES OCT. TERM,

HEADNOTES

Classified to U.S. Supreme Court Digest, Annotated

Supreme Court of the United States § 70 — consolidated opinion — racial segregation.

5. 1. Even though cases involving the validity of racial segregation laws are premised on different facts and different legal conditions, the common legal question justifies their consideration together in a consolidated opinion.

Constitutional Law § 17 — Fourteenth Amendment — construction — contemporary history.

2. The legislative history as to the adoption of the Fourteenth Amendment by Congress and its ratification by the states, the then existing practices in racial segregation, and the views of proponents and opponents of the Amendment, although casting some light, are not sufficient to resolve the question whether laws requiring or permitting segregation according to race in public schools violate the equal protection clause of the Amendment.

[*See annotation appended hereto, and annotation reference* 1.]

6. **Constitutional Law § 9; Courts § 775 — construction of Constitution — precedents — new conditions.**

3. In determining whether segregation in public schools deprives Negro students of the equal protection of laws guaranteed by the Fourteenth Amendment, the court must consider public education in the light of its full development and its present place in American life throughout the nation; the clock cannot be turned back to the time when the Amendment was adopted (1868) nor to the time when the Supreme Court announced the "separate but equal" doctrine (1896), under which equality of treatment is accorded by providing Negroes and whites substantially equal, though separate, facilities.

[*See annotation appended hereto.*]

Schools § 1 — equal opportunities.

4. Opportunity of education, where the state has undertaken to provide it, must be made available to all on equal terms.

[*See annotation references* 2, 3.]

Civil Rights § 6 — schools — racial segregation.

5. The equal protection clause of the Fourteenth Amendment prohibits the states from maintaining racially segregated public schools, even though the physical facilities and other tangible factors, such as curricula and qualifications and salaries of teachers, may be equal.

[*See annotation appended hereto, and annotation references* 2–5.]

Civil Rights § 6 — schools — separate but equal.

6. The "separate but equal" doctrine announced in Plessy v. Ferguson, 162 US 537, 41 L ed 256, 16 S Ct 1138, under which equality of treatment is accorded by providing Negroes and whites substantially equal, though separate, facilities, has no place in the field of public education

[*See annotation appended hereto, and annotation references* 2, 3, 5.]

[Nos. 1, 2, 4, and 10.]

Argued December 8–11, 1952. Restored to the docket for reargument June 8, 1953. Reargued December 7–9, 1953. Decided
7. May 17, 1954.

APPEAL by plaintiffs from a judgment of the United States District Court for the District of Kansas denying an injunction against enforce-

---

ANNOTATION REFERENCES

1. Resort to details of constitutional convention, committee reports, records, etc., as aid in construction of Constitution, 70 ALR 5.

2. Constitutional equality of school privileges as civil right, 44 L ed 262.

3. Equivalence of educational facilities extended by public school system to members of white and members of colored race, 103 ALR 713.

4. Compare 134 ALR 1276 on separation of pupils in recreational or social activities because of race, color, or religion.

5. Separate school for colored children as common or public school within contemplation of constitutional or statutory provision, 113 ALR 713.

98 L ed 874

[A reprint of the official opinion follows.]

American Law Reports, Annotated, Second Series.

A source of, among other things, editorially-selected reports of cases which illustrate the point concerning which an essay (''annotation'') is published. The publisher tends to select leading cases for this purpose.

Brown v. Board of Education, 38 A.L.R.2d 1180 (1954).

---

1. Page number 1180 in v. 38 A.L.R.2d.

2. Style or name of cases. Use only the name of the first case mentioned.

3. Date.

4. Parallel citations to *United States Reports, Lawyers' Edition, Supreme Court Reporter,* and this reporter.

5. Lawyers Co-Operative Publishing Company editorial introduction or ''summary'' note.

1. 1180 AMERICAN LAW REPORTS, ANNOTATED 38 ALR2d

[§ 11]

er, and the latter conducted the defense of the litigation on plaintiff's behalf in all its phases. At the conclusion of the trial, the complaint as against plaintiff was dismissed, and, the jury having disagreed at the conclusion of the entire case, there was a second trial, at which there was no claim against plaintiff, but in which he appeared to answer the cross complaint of the city and also to assert a cross complaint of his own against the plumbers who did the work. In this second trial, plaintiff was still represented by attorneys for defendant. As a result of the second trial, the injured person obtained a judgment against the city and the latter a judgment over against plaintiff for such part of the injured person's judgment as the city was required to pay. Defendant insurer having denied liability for the recovery by the city against plaintiff, the court held that the insurer, by defense of plaintiff in the first trial, had not estopped itself to deny liability for the city's judgment against plaintiff; in this connection it was noted that the injured person's claim against plaintiff was one which was within the coverage of the policy, and was properly defended by the insurer, and the insurer's further activity at the first trial in defending the cross complaint of the city would furnish no grounds for asserting an estoppel because it was manifestly impractical to defend the claim of the injured person without also undertaking the defense of the cross complaint. But the court ruled that, by virtue of its defense of plaintiff in the second trial, at which time there remained no claim against him except the one by the city, the insurer had estopped itself from asserting that it was not liable for the city's claim under the policy.

R. D. Hursh.

✦ Consult ALR2d SUPPLEMENT SERVICE for subsequent cases ✦

2. OLIVER BROWN et al., Appts.,

v.

BOARD OF EDUCATION OF TOPEKA, Shawnee County, Kansas, et al. (No. 1.)

HARRY BRIGGS, Jr., et al., Appts.,

v.

R. W. ELLIOTT et al. (No. 2.)

DOROTHY E. DAVIS et al., Appts.,

v.

COUNTY SCHOOL BOARD OF PRINCE EDWARD COUNTY, Virginia, et al. (No. 4.)

FRANCIS B. GEBHART et al., Petitioners,

v.

ETHEL LOUISE BELTON et al. (No. 10.)

United States Supreme Court — May 17, 1954 **3.**

4. (347 US 483, 98 L ed 873, 74 S Ct 686, 38 ALR2d 1180)

SUMMARY OF DECISION

5. In each of the four cases involved the plaintiffs, Negro children, were

American Law Reports, Annotated — *Continued*

6. Cross-reference to an essay ("annotation") on the subject indicated.

7. Title and section number under which headnote and citation of this case and other similar cases are found in *A.L.R.2d Digest*.

8. Headnotes which are compiled in *A.L.R. Digests*.

BROWN v. BOARD OF EDUCATION 1181
(347 US 483, 98 L ed 873, 74 S Ct 686, 38 ALR2d 1180)

denied admission to state public schools attended by white children under state laws requiring or permitting segregation according to race. There were findings below that the Negro and white schools involved had been equalized, or were being equalized, with respect to buildings, curricula, qualifications and salaries of teachers, and other tangible factors.

In an opinion by Warren, Ch. J., the Supreme Court unanimously held that the plaintiffs, by reason of the segregation complained of, were deprived of the equal protection of the laws guaranteed by the Fourteenth Amendment. The "separate but equal" doctrine announced in Plessy v. Ferguson, 163 US 537, 41 L ed 256, 16 S Ct 1138, involving equality in transportation facilities, under which equality of treatment is accorded by providing Negroes and whites substantially equal, though separate, facilities, was held to have no place in the field of public education.

In view of the complex problems presented by the formulation of the decrees, the cases were restored to the docket for argument by the parties.

---

6. **SUBJECT OF ANNOTATION**

Beginning on page 1188

Comment note.—Racial segregation.

HEADNOTES

Classified to ALR Digests

7. **Supreme Court of the United States § 1 — consolidated opinion — racial segregation.**

8. 1. Even though cases involving the validity of racial segregation laws are premised on different facts and different legal conditions, the common legal question justifies their consideration together in a consolidated opinion.

[See Am Jur, Courts §§ 131–135.]

Constitutional Law § 36 — Fourteenth Amendment — construction — contemporary history.

2. The legislative history as to the adoption of the Fourteenth Amendment by Congress and its ratification by the states, the then existing practices in racial segregation, and the views of proponents and opponents of the Amendment, although casting some light, are not sufficient to resolve the question whether laws requiring or permitting segregation according to race in public schools violate the equal protection clause of the Amendment.

[Annotated]

Constitutional Law § 31; Courts § 360 — construction of Constitution — precedents — new conditions.

3. In determining whether segregation in public schools deprives Negro students of the equal protection of laws guaranteed by the Fourteenth Amendment, the court must consider public education in the light of its full development and its present place in American life throughout the nation; the clock cannot be turned back to the time when the Amendment was adopted (1868) nor to the time when the Supreme Court announced the "separate but equal" doctrine (1896), under which equality of treatment is accorded by providing Negroes and whites substantially equal, though separate, facilities.

[Annotated]

Schools § 49 — equal opportunities.

4. Opportunity of education, where the state has undertaken to provide it, must be made available to all on equal terms.

[See Am Jur, Schools §§ 151–155.]

Civil Rights § 3; Schools § 52 — racial segregation — equivalence of facilities.

5. The equal protection clause of the Fourteenth Amendment prohibits the states from maintaining racially segregated public schools, even though the physical facilities and other tangible factors, such as curricula and qualifi-

[A reprint of the official opinion follows.]

American Jurisprudence, Second Series.

24 Am. Jur 2d *Divorce and Separation* (1983).

1. Scope note.
2. Cross-references.
3. Outline.
4. Detailed outline.

DIVORCE AND SEPARATION

by
W. A. Harrington, LL.B.
John W. Hopkins, LL.B.
Jack L. Litwin, LL.B.
Fred Luhman, J.D.
Irwin J. Schiffres, J.D.

Scope of Topic: This article is concerned with the dissolution by legal proceedings of the marriage relationship in whole or in part, the grounds for, and the general operation and effect of, such dissolution, and procedural matters pertaining to dissolution or divorce proceedings, with particular emphasis on the no-fault grounds for divorce. The article also discusses rights, duties, and liabilities respecting spousal support, the division of marital property, and the determination of property rights, including agreements pertaining to these matters and the equitable distribution by the court of marital property. The article also discusses the custody and support of the children of the parties, child visitation rights, the determination of the paternity or legitimacy of such children, and the operation and effect of foreign divorce and support or child custody judgments and decrees. **1.**

Treated elsewhere are adultery and fornication as criminal offenses (see 2 Am Jur 2d, Adultery and Fornication); the status and rights of, and presumptions as to, illegitimate children (see 10 Am Jur 2d, Bastards); criminal liability for abandonment, desertion or nonsupport of persons by other persons charged with such responsibility (see 23 Am Jur 2d, Desertion and Nonsupport); the domicil of husband and wife and of minor children (see 25 Am Jur 2d, Domicil §§ 48 et seq.); the capacities, disabilities, privileges, and liabilities of minor children (see 42 Am Jur 2d, Infants §§ 8 et seq.); ne exeat proceedings generally (see 57 Am Jur 2d, Ne Exeat); the rights, duties, and responsibilities as between parent and child (see 59 Am Jur 2d, Parent and Child); the effect of an invalid marriage on property rights (see 52 Am Jur 2d, Marriage §§ 109 et seq.); gifts to, or between, spouses (see 15A Am Jur 2d, Community Property §§ 68 et seq.; 38 Am Jur 2d, Gifts; 41 Am Jur 2d, Husband and Wife §§ 256 et seq.); agreements for the support of persons generally (see 73 Am Jur 2d, Support of Persons); the protection and custody of children (see 42 Am Jur 2d, Infants §§ 14 et seq.); adoption of children and the rights and duties pertaining to adopted children (see 2 Am Jur 2d, Adoption); the effect of divorce or separation on rights acquired by adverse possession (see 3 Am Jur 2d, Adverse Possession § 52); habeas corpus proceedings to determine or enforce the right to custody of a child (see 39 Am Jur 2d, Habeas Corpus); a spouse's right of action for alienation of affections or criminal conversation (see 41 Am Jur 2d, Husband and Wife §§ 463 et seq.); appeals in divorce and separation cases (see 4, 5 Am Jur 2d, Appeal and Error); the annulment of void or voidable marriages (see 4 Am Jur 2d, Annulment of Marriage); suits for spousal support, maintenance, or alimony without divorce (see 41 Am Jur 2d, Husband and Wife §§ 387 et seq.); the effect of divorce on the rights of the spouses in their community property (see 15A Am Jur 2d, Community Property §§ 101 et seq.); a spouse's right to dower or curtesy (see 25 Am Jur 2d, Dower and Curtesy); the homestead rights and exemptions of the spouses (see 40 Am Jur 2d, Homestead); the general rights and liabilities of husband and wife inter se and in regard to third persons (see 41 Am Jur 2d, Husband and Wife); and the nature, validity, and requisites of marriage (see 52 Am Jur 2d, Marriage). **2.**

Federal Aspects: This article discusses the general rules and principles under federal law in regard to jurisdiction in dissolution of marriage or divorce proceedings over members of the armed forces, awards of maintenance or alimony to a spouse, the division of certain types of property and property rights between the spouses, and the applicability of the full faith and credit clause of the United States Constitution to foreign divorce judgments and decrees. In addition, the article

DIVORCE AND SEPARATION 24 Am Jur 2d

discusses various federal statutes governing the effect of dissolution or divorce on certain retirement and other benefits, and whether the federal tax consequences of a distribution are to be considered by a state court in making an equitable distribution award. For the actual tax consequences of property divisions, see 33, 34, and 34A Am Jur 2d, FEDERAL TAXATION; for general regulations under ERISA, see Am Jur 2d New Topic Service, PENSION REFORM ACT.

Auto-Cite®:

Any case citation herein can be checked for form, parallel references, later history, and annotation references through the Auto-Cite computer research system.

★ Table of Parallel References see p ix. ★

3.

Outline

4.

24 Am Jur 2d DIVORCE AND SEPARATION

I. IN GENERAL

II. VALIDITY OF STATUTES; PUBLIC POLICY

A. IN GENERAL; VALIDITY

B. PUBLIC POLICY

III. GROUNDS

A. IN GENERAL

B. BREAKDOWN OF MARRIAGE; NO-FAULT DIVORCE

C. CRUELTY

1. IN GENERAL

Corpus Juris Secundum.

16 C.J.S. *Constitutional Law* (1984).

---

1. Analysis.
2. Sub-analysis.
3. Scope note.
4. Cross-references.

CORPUS JURIS SECUNDUM

CONSTITUTIONAL LAW

Analysis

See also descriptive word index in volume containing end of this Title

1.

2.

16 C. J. S. CONSTITUTIONAL LAW

Sub-Analysis

See also descriptive word index in volume containing end of this Title

§ 1 CONSTITUTIONAL LAW 16 C. J. S.

I. INTRODUCTION

3. **§ 1. Scope of Title**

In this title is discussed the fundamental organic law which regulates the structure and methods of administration of the government of the United States and the governments of the several states, and the relations between those governments and those persons and entities subject to them. Particular attention is given to law relating to written constitution and their establishment, adoption and amendment, as well as their construction, operation, effect, and enforcement.

This title also considers the law governing the distribution of powers and functions of government among different departments, officers and agencies, the police power which is inherent in governments and its exercise in general. In addition the declaration and protection by constitutions of life, liberty, and other civil and political rights of persons, rights of property and obligations of contracts are treated in this title.

4. Constitutional guaranties and protection with respect to citizenship are considered in C.J.S. Citizens, and the delegation of powers to municipal corporations and constitutional restrictions on them are discussed in C.J.S. Municipal Corporations. Other titles of this work which discuss constitutional provisions which relate to judicial remedies, both civil and criminal, include the titles Attachment, Habeas Corpus, Criminal Law, Arrest, Bail, Searches and Seizures, Indictments and Informations, and Juries.

Relations between the federal government and state governments and the effects of federal powers and state powers on each other are considered in C.J.S. States. Constitutional powers of other governmental entities are considered in appropriate titles of this treatise including, for example, Counties, Towns, and Schools and School Districts; and particular powers of governments and constitutional aspects of those powers in Eminent Domain, Internal Revenue, Taxation and other similar titles.

The operation of statutes passed in pursuance of constitutional provisions relating to specific topics is considered in many specific titles as in the case of civil rights,[1] anti-trust laws,[2] interstate commerce,[3] and intoxicating liquors.[4]

§ 2. Definitions

a. Constitution

b. Constitutional law

a. Constitution

A constitution is the original law by which a system of government is created and set up, and to which the branches of government must look for all their power and authority.

Library References

Constitutional Law 🔑 1.

A "constitution" may be defined as the original law by which a system of government is created and set up, and to which the branches of government must look for all their power and authority.[5] It is otherwise defined as that fundamental and organic law of a state which contains the principles on which government is founded, regulates the division of sovereign powers, and directs to what persons each of these powers is to be intrusted and the manner of its exercise.[6]

The term "constitution" is ordinarily employed

---

1. See C.J.S. Civil Rights.
2. See C.J.S. Monopolies.
3. See C.J.S. Commerce.
4. See C.J.S. Intoxicating Liquors.
5. Ga.—Wheeler v. Board of Trustees of Fargo Consol. School Dist., 37 S.E.2d 322, 327, 200 Ga. 323.
6. Mo.—State v. Roach, 130 S.W. 689, 230 Mo. 408, 139 Am.S.R. 639.

N.J.—Gulf Oil Corporation v. Board of Adjustment of City of Newark, 22 A.2d 570, 127 N.J.Law 327, affirmed 26 A.2d 246, 128 N.J.Law 376.

Other definitions

Me.—In re Opinion of the Justices, 107 A. 673, 118 Me. 544, 5 A.L.R. 1412.

Md.—Board of Sup'rs of Elections for Anne Arundel County v. Attorney General, 229 A.2d 388, 246 Md. 417.

Mass.—In re Opinion of the Justices, 9 N.E.2d 186, 297 Mass. 577—Anderson v. Secretary of Commonwealth, 151 N.E. 378, 255 Mass. 366—Loring v. Young, 132 N.E. 65, 239 Mass. 349.

N.Y.—Browne v. City of New York, 211 N.Y.S. 306, 213 App.Div. 206, affirmed 149 N.E. 211, 241 N.Y. 96.

Ohio.—Heald v. City of Cleveland, 19 Ohio N.P.N.S., 305.

Tex.—Texas Nat. Guard Armory Board v. McCraw, 126 S.W.2d 627, 132 Tex. 613.

Utah.—State v. Johnson, 114 P.2d 1034, 1036, 100 Utah 316.

Fundamental and organic laws

N.C.—State v. Godette, 125 S.E. 24, 188 N.C. 497.

U.S. Supreme Court Digest, Lawyers' Edition.

Vol. 2 (1984).

---

1. Scope note.

2. Cross-references.

3. Analysis.

DIGEST

OF THE

UNITED STATES SUPREME COURT REPORTS

ALIENS

1. **Scope of Topic:** This topic covers questions as to aliens generally; including the capacities, disabilities, and property rights of aliens; and matters as to immigration and the exclusion, deportation, and naturalization of aliens.

2. **Treated elsewhere** are alien enemies or the effect of war on the status, rights, and disabilities of aliens (see WAR); the right of aliens to inherit property (see DESCENT AND DISTRIBUTION); and the status, rights, and duties of nationals traveling through, or otherwise temporarily in, a foreign country, and the status of inhabitants on a cession, conquest, or other change of territory or government (see INTERNATIONAL LAW). Matters as to citizenship generally are treated in CITIZENSHIP. Matters as to nonresidents generally are treated in such topics as CONFLICT OF LAWS; CONSTITUTIONAL LAW; COURTS; DOMICIL; TAXES; WRIT AND PROCESS; etc.

[For fact-word approach see Word Index to this Digest]

VOLUME 1

3. I. IN GENERAL (VOL. 1)
§ 1 Generally.
§ 2 Who are aliens.

II. DISABILITIES, CAPACITIES, RIGHTS, DUTIES, AND LIABILITIES. (VOL. 1)
§ 3 Generally.
§ 4 As to patents.
§ 5 As to property generally.
§ 6 Grant or devise.
§ 7 Lease.
§ 8 Mining claims.
§ 9 State regulations.
§ 10 —Maryland.
§ 11 —Missouri.
§ 12 —Texas.
§ 13 —Vermont.
§ 14 —Virginia.
§ 15 Under laws of foreign countries.
§ 16 Effect of treaties.
§ 17 —with England.

Iowa Digest.

Vol. 18 (1985).

---

1. Scope note.

2. Cross-references.

3. Analysis.

4. Sub-analysis.

18 Iowa D—143

TRIAL

1. **SUBJECTS INCLUDED**

Judicial examination and determination of issues in civil cases, more particularly of issues of fact by courts sitting with or without a jury

Bringing cases to trial, notices of trial, notes of issue, and calendars and lists of causes for trial

Pretrial conference

Course and order of proceedings at trials in general

Reception of evidence and objections thereto

Arguments and conduct of counsel

Relative functions of court and jury

Instructions to juries in general

Custody and conduct of jury

Verdicts or other findings of juries

Findings and decisions by courts on trials without a jury

2. **SUBJECTS EXCLUDED AND COVERED BY OTHER TOPICS**

Adjournment or postponement of trial, see PRETRIAL PROCEDURE

Administrative hearings, see ADMINISTRATIVE LAW AND PROCEDURE, LABOR RELATIONS, and other specific topics

Arbitrators, umpires, etc., hearings by, see ARBITRATION, DEBTOR AND CREDITOR, LABOR RELATIONS

Bankrupt or insolvent acts, hearings and proceedings under, see BANKRUPTCY, DEBTOR AND CREDITOR

Courts of special or limited jurisdiction, hearings in, see ADMIRALTY, COURTS, EQUITY, and other specific topics

Criminal cases, trial in, see CRIMINAL LAW and specific topics relating to particular offenses

Evidence, rules of, see EVIDENCE, CRIMINAL LAW and specific topics covering relevancy and sufficiency of particular evidence

Federal Rules of Civil Procedure affecting trial, see FEDERAL CIVIL PROCEDURE

Instructions to jury, questions peculiar to particular subject matter, see AUTOMOBILES and other specific topics

Jury trial, constitutional right, and selection, impaneling and swearing jury, see JURY

Justices of the peace, trials before, see JUSTICES OF THE PEACE

Motions, demurrers and similar incidental proceedings, hearings on, see MOTIONS, PLEADING, PROCESS, and other specific topics

Particular causes or forms of action, or defenses or matters of fact, trials on issues and particularly questions of law or fact, see AUTOMOBILES and other specific topics

TRIAL 18 Iowa D—144

Place of trial, see VENUE

Pretrial conference, see PRETRIAL PROCEDURE

Referees, trials by, see REFERENCE

Submissions of controversies, hearings on, see SUBMISSION OF CONTROVERSY

Witnesses, attendance and examination, see WITNESSES

For detailed references to other topics, see Descriptive-Word Index

---

Analysis **3.**

I. NOTICE OF TRIAL AND PRELIMINARY PROCEEDINGS, 🔑1–8.

II. DOCKETS, LISTS, AND CALENDARS, 🔑9–17.

III. COURSE AND CONDUCT OF TRIAL IN GENERAL, 🔑18–31.

IV. RECEPTION OF EVIDENCE, 🔑32–105(6).

- (A) INTRODUCTION, OFFER, AND ADMISSION OF EVIDENCE IN GENERAL, 🔑32–58.
- (B) ORDER OF PROOF, REBUTTAL, AND REOPENING CASE, 🔑59–72.
- (C) OBJECTIONS, MOTIONS TO STRIKE OUT, AND EXCEPTIONS, 🔑73–105.

V. ARGUMENTS AND CONDUCT OF COUNSEL, 🔑106–133(6).

VI. TAKING CASE OR QUESTION FROM JURY, 🔑134–181.

- (A) QUESTIONS OF LAW OR OF FACT IN GENERAL, 🔑134–149.
- (B) DEMURRER TO EVIDENCE, 🔑150–158.
- (C) DISMISSAL OR NONSUIT, 🔑159–166.
- (D) DIRECTION OF VERDICT, 🔑167–181.

VII. INSTRUCTIONS TO JURY, 🔑182–296(13).

- (A) PROVINCE OF COURT AND JURY IN GENERAL, 🔑182–201.
- (B) NECESSITY AND SUBJECT-MATTER, 🔑202–219.
- (C) FORM, REQUISITES, AND SUFFICIENCY, 🔑220–247.
- (D) APPLICABILITY TO PLEADINGS AND EVIDENCE, 🔑248–254.
- (E) REQUESTS OR PRAYERS, 🔑255–269.
- (F) OBJECTIONS AND EXCEPTIONS, 🔑270–284.
- (G) CONSTRUCTION AND OPERATION, 🔑285–296.

VIII. CUSTODY, CONDUCT, AND DELIBERATIONS OF JURY, 🔑297–317.

IX. VERDICT, 🔑318–366.

- (A) GENERAL VERDICT, 🔑318–345.
- (B) SPECIAL INTERROGATORIES AND FINDINGS, 🔑346–366.

X. TRIAL BY COURT, 🔑367–405(3).

- (A) HEARING AND DETERMINATION OF CAUSE, 🔑367–387.
- (B) FINDINGS OF FACT AND CONCLUSIONS OF LAW, 🔑388–405.

XI. WAIVER AND CORRECTION OF IRREGULARITIES AND ERRORS, 🔑406–427.

4.

18 Iowa D—145 **TRIAL**

I. NOTICE OF TRIAL AND PRELIMINARY PROCEEDINGS.
- 🔑1. Condition of cause in general.
- 2. Trial of causes together.
- 3. Separate trials in same cause.
  - (1). In general.
  - (2). Discretion of court.
  - (3). Counterclaims and cross-claims.
  - (4). Particular parties, separate trial as to.
  - (5). Particular issues, separate trial of.
  - (6). —— Legal and equitable issues.
  - (7). Request or application.
- 4. Order of trial of separate issues.
- 5. Time or term of court for trial.
- 6. Notice of trial.
  - (1). In general.
  - (2). New notice after amendment.
  - (3). Effect of continuance or adjournment.
- 7. Note of issue.

II. DOCKETS, LISTS, AND CALENDARS.
- 🔑9. Trial dockets or calendars in general.
  - (1). In general.
  - (2). Notice of setting cause for trial.
- 10. Causes for particular dockets.
- 11. Transfer of causes.
  - (1). In general.
  - (2). Transfer from law to equity docket.
  - (3). Transfer from equity to law docket.
- 12. Short-cause calendars.
  - (1). In general.
  - (2). Striking cause from short-cause calendar.
- 13. Preferred causes.
- 13.1. —— Causes entitled to preference.
  - (1). In general; discretion of court.
  - (2). Nature of action.
  - (3). Nature or circumstances of parties.
  - (4). —— Age or disability; financial condition.
- 13.2. —— Causes over which preference may be had.
- 13.3. —— Proceedings to procure preference in general.
- 13.4. —— Time for application or notice and laches.
- 13.5. —— Notice.
- 14. Striking cause from docket.
- 15. Order of calling and hearing causes.
- 16. Holding or passing cause pending engagement of counsel.
- 17. Disposition of causes passed or continued.

III. COURSE AND CONDUCT OF TRIAL IN GENERAL.
- 🔑18. Regulation in general.
- 19. Presence of judge.
- 20. Publicity of proceedings.

18 Iowa Dig—6

West's New Jersey Digest 2d.

Vol. 6 (1985).
Covers cases since 1954.

---

1. Scope note.

2. Cross-references.

3. Analysis.

4. Sub-analysis.

CRIMINAL LAW

SUBJECTS INCLUDED

1.

Acts and omissions in violation of law punishable as offenses against the public

Nature and elements of crime in general

Capacity to commit crime, nature and extent of responsibility therefore in general, and responsibility of principals, accessories, etc.

Jurisdiction over and place of prosecution of crimes

Limitation of time for prosecution

Preliminary complaints, warrants, examination and commitment

Arraignment and pleas

Evidence in criminal proceedings

Trial, and acquittal or conviction

Motions in arrest of judgment and for new trial

Judgment or sentence and final commitment

Review on appeal, writ of error or certiorari

Prosecution and punishment of successive offenses or of habitual criminals

Modes of punishment and prevention of crime in general

SUBJECTS EXCLUDED AND COVERED BY OTHER TOPICS

2.

Arrest, see ARREST

Bail, see BAIL

Constitutional rights and privileges of accused not peculiar to matters within scope of this topic, see CONSTITUTIONAL LAW, INDICTMENT AND INFORMATION, JURY, SEARCHES AND SEIZURES, WITNESSES and other specific topics

Convicts, disabilities and regulation, see CONVICTS

Costs in criminal prosecutions, see COSTS

Extradition of fugitives, see EXTRADITION AND DETAINERS

Fines in general, see FINES

Grand juries and inquisitions by them, see GRAND JURY

Habeas corpus to obtain discharge from imprisonment, see HABEAS CORPUS

Included offenses, conviction under indictment for broader offense, see INDICTMENT AND INFORMATION

Indictments or other accusations, see INDICTMENT AND INFORMATION and specific topics relating to particular offenses

Injunction against commission of crime, see INJUNCTION

Judgment of acquittal, conviction or sentence, effect as adjudication, see JUDGMENT

CRIMINAL LAW

6 N J D 2d—2

Jury trial, right to and waiver, and qualifications and selection of jurors, see JURY

Juvenile offenders, special rules and proceedings, see INFANTS

Military offenses and court-martial prosecutions, see ARMED SERVICES, MILITARY JUSTICE

Pardon, commutation of sentence, and parole, see PARDON AND PAROLE

Particular classes of persons, criminal responsibility, see INFANTS, MENTAL HEALTH and other specific topics

Particular offenses, substantive and procedural questions peculiar to, see HOMICIDE, LARCENY and other specific topics

Pecuniary punishment and deprivation of property as punishment for violation of law, see FORFEITURES, PENALTIES, INTOXICATING LIQUORS and other specific topics

Prisons and reformatories, establishment and regulation, see PRISONS, REFORMATORIES

Prosecuting attorneys, see DISTRICT AND PROSECUTING ATTORNEYS

Searches and seizures, see ARREST, SEARCHES AND SEIZURES, INTOXICATING LIQUORS and other specific topics

Witnesses and their examination, see WITNESSES

For detailed references to other topics, see Descriptive-Word Index

---

3.

Analysis

CRIMINAL LAW 6 N J D 2d—4

XV. APPEAL AND ERROR, AND CERTIORARI,—Continued.

(B) PRESENTATION AND RESERVATION IN LOWER COURT OF GROUNDS OF REVIEW—Continued.

3. MOTIONS FOR NEW TRIAL OR IN ARREST; RESERVED OR CERTIFIED QUESTIONS, ⚩1063–1068.

(C) PROCEEDINGS FOR TRANSFER OF CAUSE, AND EFFECT THEREOF, ⚩1068½–1084.

(D) RECORD AND PROCEEDINGS NOT IN RECORD, ⚩1085–1128.

1. MATTERS TO BE SHOWN BY RECORD, ⚩1086.1–1087.3.
2. SCOPE AND CONTENTS OF RECORD, ⚩1088.1–1088.20.
3. BILL OF EXCEPTIONS, ⚩1090–1095.
4. CASE OR STATEMENT OF FACTS, ⚩1097–1102.
5. ABSTRACT OF RECORD, AND TRANSCRIPT OR RETURN, ⚩1103–1104(8).
6. AUTHENTICATION, TRANSMISSION, PRINTING, AND SERVICE OF COPIES, ⚩1105–1108.
7. DEFECTS, OBJECTIONS, AMENDMENT, AND CORRECTION, ⚩1109–1110(9).
8. CONCLUSIVENESS AND EFFECT; IMPEACHING AND CONTRADICTING, ⚩1111–1112.
9. QUESTIONS PRESENTED FOR REVIEW, AND MATTERS NOT APPARENT OF RECORD, ⚩1113–1128(4).

(E) ASSIGNMENT OF ERRORS AND BRIEFS, ⚩1129–1130.

(F) DISMISSAL, HEARING, AND REHEARING, ⚩1131–1133.

(G) REVIEW, ⚩1134–1180.

1. IN GENERAL, ⚩1134–1139.
2. PRESUMPTIONS, ⚩1141–1144.20.
3. DISCRETION OF LOWER COURT, ⚩1147–1156(5).
4. QUESTIONS OF FACT, VERDICTS, AND FINDINGS, ⚩1158–1160.
5. HARMLESS ERROR, ⚩1162–1177.
6. WAIVER OF ERROR; INTERMEDIATE COURTS; SUBSEQUENT APPEALS, ⚩1178–1180.

(H) DETERMINATION AND DISPOSITION OF CAUSE, ⚩1181–1193.

(I) LIABILITIES ON BONDS, ⚩1194–1199.

XVI. HABITUAL AND SECOND OFFENDERS, ⚩1200–1204.

(A) IN GENERAL, ⚩1200–1202.17.

(B) PROCEEDINGS, ⚩1203.1–1204.

XVII. PUNISHMENT AND PREVENTION OF CRIME, ⚩1205–1226.

---

4. **I. NATURE AND ELEMENTS OF CRIME AND DEFENSES IN GENERAL.**

⚩1. Nature of crime in general.
2. Power to define and punish crime.
3. —— In general.
4. —— United States.
5. —— States.
6. —— Territories.
7. —— Municipalities.
8. Application and operation of common law.
9. —— Adoption and abrogation.
10. —— Application in general.
11. —— Effect as to construction of statutes.
12. Statutory provisions.

Oklahoma Digest.

Vol. 8A (1984).

---

1. Scope note.

2. Cross-references.

3. Analysis.

4. Sub-analysis.

INSURANCE

1. **SUBJECTS INCLUDED**

Regulation and conduct of the business of insurance by individual underwriters or corporations, mutual or cooperative associations, and insurance agents or brokers

Organization, powers and liabilities of insurance companies and associations, and rights and liabilities of their members, officers, and agents

Contracts or policies of insurance and rights, liabilities, and remedies incident thereto

2. **SUBJECTS EXCLUDED AND COVERED BY OTHER TOPICS**

Associations for mutual benefit otherwise than by insurance, see BENEFICIAL ASSOCIATIONS

Burning property to defraud insurers, see ARSON, FIRES

Government war risk insurance, see ARMED SERVICES, SEAMEN, SHIPPING

Remedies of—

Declaratory judgment, see DECLARATORY JUDGMENT

Garnishment, see GARNISHMENT

Interpleader, see INTERPLEADER

Taxation of capital stock, property or income of insurance companies, see INTERNAL REVENUE, TAXATION

Workmen's compensation insurance, see WORKERS' COMPENSATION

For detailed references to other topics, see Descriptive-Word Index

---

3. *Analysis*

I. **NATURE, CONTROL, AND REGULATION,** ⚿1–31.

II. **INSURANCE ORGANIZATIONS,** ⚿31.1–72.13.

- (A) IN GENERAL, ⚿31.1–31.4.
- (B) STOCK COMPANIES, ⚿32–51.
- (C) MUTUAL COMPANIES, ⚿52–72.
- (D) REHABILITATION, INSOLVENCY, AND DISSOLUTION, ⚿72.1–72.13.

III. **INSURANCE AGENTS AND BROKERS,** ⚿73–113.

- (A) NATURE OF AGENCY, ⚿73–73.5.
- (B) AGENCY FOR INSURER, ⚿74–95.
- (C) AGENCY FOR APPLICANT OR INSURED, ⚿96–113.

IV. **INSURABLE INTEREST,** ⚿114–123.1.

8A Okl D—3 **INSURANCE**

XX. **MUTUAL BENEFIT INSURANCE, 🔑687–834.**
- (A) CORPORATIONS AND ASSOCIATIONS, 🔑687–710.
- (B) CONTRACT AND CERTIFICATE, 🔑711–730.2.
- (C) DUES AND ASSESSMENTS, 🔑731–743.
- (D) FORFEITURE OR SUSPENSION, 🔑744–765.1.
- (E) BENEFICIARIES AND BENEFITS, 🔑766–801.1.
- (F) ACTIONS FOR BENEFITS, 🔑802–834.

4.

I. **NATURE, CONTROL, AND REGULATION.**

🔑1. Right to insure in general.
2. What constitutes insurance.
3. Power to regulate.
3.1. Federal regulation.
4. Constitutional and statutory provisions.
4.1. —— Validity of statutes.
4.2. Administrative regulation in general; insurance department and officers.
4.3. Judicial supervision.
4.4. Construction and operation of regulations in general.
4.5. Business, persons, and corporations regulated.
5. Authority or license to do business.
6. Unauthorized insurance.
7. License fees and taxes.
8. Resources and securities; investments.
9. Reports, statements, and examination of books.
11. Conduct of business in general.
11.1. Contracts and policies; assigned risks.
11.2. Rate regulation.
11.3. —— Administrative establishment or adjustment of rates.
11.4. —— Factors considered in fixing rates.
11.5. —— Rating organizations and deviation.
11.6. —— Rate proceedings.
11.7. —— Judicial review.
11.8. —— Rebates.
12. Agents and brokers, regulation.
12.1. —— License in general.
12.2. —— Eligibility and right to license; issuance or refusal.
12.3. —— Renewal of license, revocation or suspension.
12.4. —— Judicial review of licensing action.
12.5. —— Compensation or commissions.
13.1. Government insurance.
15. Foreign companies.
16. —— What constitutes, "doing business."
17. —— Application of local laws.
18. —— Subjection to special requirements.
19. —— Retaliatory legislation.
20. —— Local authority or license and license fees or taxes.
21. —— Local funds and securities.

West's South Carolina Digest.

Vol. 6A (1985).

---

1. Scope note.

2. Cross-references.

3. Analysis.

4. Sub-analysis.

6A S C D—172

CONTEMPT

SUBJECTS INCLUDED 1.

Disobedience to the process, orders or rules of courts, and other acts or conduct in disregard of their authority or dignity, tending to impede or frustrate the administration of law

What constitutes such contempt, civil or criminal, in general

What persons are liable therefor

Power to punish contempt and proceedings therefor; and punishment of contempt

SUBJECTS EXCLUDED AND COVERED BY OTHER TOPICS 2.

Attorneys, summary jurisdiction of courts over, see ATTORNEY AND CLIENT

Other bodies, contempt of authority—

Administrative tribunals, see ADMINISTRATIVE LAW AND PROCEDURE and topics dealing with particular administrative tribunals

Congress, see UNITED STATES

State legislatures, see STATES

Particular writs, orders or other mandates of courts, disobedience to, see DIVORCE, EXECUTION, INJUNCTION, MANDAMUS, NUISANCE, WITNESSES and other specific topics

Receivers, interference with possession of, see RECEIVERS, CORPORATIONS

For detailed references to other topics, see Descriptive-Word Index

---

Analysis

I. ACTS OR CONDUCT CONSTITUTING CONTEMPT OF COURT, ⚷1–29. 3.

II. POWER TO PUNISH, AND PROCEEDINGS THEREFOR, ⚷30–69.

III. PUNISHMENT, ⚷70–82.

I. ACTS OR CONDUCT CONSTITUTING CONTEMPT OF COURT. 4.

⚷1. Nature and elements of contempt.
2. —— In general.
3. —— Criminal contempt.
4. —— Civil contempt.
5. Constitutional and statutory provisions.
6. Misconduct in presence of court.
7. Disturbance of proceedings of court.
8. Publications relating to court, jury, or officers.
9. Publications relating to pending proceedings.
10. Misconduct as officer of court.
11. Abuse of mandate or other proceeding.

Shepard's Citations.

Shepard's Kentucky Citations, 1969 Cases Volume.

Subject:
235 S.W.2d 767

1. Relates to citations of Kentucky cases in S.W.2d.

2. Volume 235 S.W.2d (the subject case, the cited case, or the older case).

3. Page 767 (the subject case, the cited case, or the older case).

4. Meaning:

Subject case is also reported in full at 314 Ky. 313.

Subject case is mentioned at 244 S.W.2d on page 770; the mention relates to headnote (syllabus) 1 of the subject case.

Subject case is mentioned at 289 S.W.2d on page 202; the mention relates to headnote (syllabus) 1 of the subject case.

Subject case is discussed at 63 Kentucky L.J. on page 303 and 70 Yale L.J. on page 551.

1.

SOUTHWESTERN REPORTER, 2d Series (Kentucky Cases)

3.

4.

Vol. 234
320SW[5]801
36A31042n

-974-
(314Ky291)
f314Ky296
f234SW977
243SW[6]61
d275SW[8]908
285SW[5]498
294SW[1]75
320SW[7]611
329SW[2]375
f333SW[1]754
382SW[8]855
382SW[9]855
382SW[5]857
42A2353n
79A2222n
79A2224n
79A2233n
79A2235n

-977-
(314Ky296)

2. Vol. 235

-62-
(314Ky333)
s239SW971

-66-
(314Ky419)
350SW[7]468

-437-
(314Ky339)
259SW[2]478
d265SW[1]776
d311SW[3]203
334SW[1]268
58KLJ461
16A23s
79A224n
79A232n
79A257n
79A275n
79A286n
12A3521n
12A3730n
18A3101n
18A3127n
18A3184n
18A3210n

-761-
(314Ky318)
305SW[4]324
d415SW[5]100
457SW[4]953
70KLJ472

-763-
(314Ky316)
399SW[2]314

-764-
(314Ky322)
251SW[2]879

-767-
(314Ky313)
244SW[1]770
289SW[1]202
63KLJ303
70YLJ551

-769-
Case 1
(314Ky882)

-769-
Case 2
(314Ky362)

-771-
(314Ky369)
375SW[6]826
47KLJ10

-774-
(314Ky365)
s255SW998

-775-
(314Ky367)

-776-
(314Ky359)
f246SW[3]592
303SW[3]547
337SW[1]729
337SW[2]730

-778-
(314Ky356)
531SW[3]509
44KLJ74

-779-
(314Ky883)

-780-
Case 1
(314Ky883)

-780-
Case 2
(314Ky344)
cc239SW959

-782-
Case 1
(314Ky883)

-782-
Case 2
(314Ky347)
255SW[5]499
Cir. 6
18BRW[11]129

-787-
(314Ky473)
f237SW[8]842
243SW[5]671
62KLJ966

-981-
(314Ky464)
cc259SW1
239SW[6]482
364SW[1]654
407SW[7]121
24A21250n
24A21272n

-986-
d340SW[3]461
394SW[1]941
451SW[6]424
29A2866n
82A2416n

-988-
(314Ky514)
254SW[5]933
261SW[9]664
d282SW[7]351
d339SW[7]472
575SW[5]485
Cir. 6
d198F2d[2]1015
d735F2d980
42KLJ287
50MnL831
69YLJ1132

-992-
(314Ky545)
16A23s
11A393n

-995-
(314Ky380)
655SW496
67KLJ109
17A379n

-998-
(314Ky384)
s310Ky446
s220SW971
s263SW133
262SW[7]380
300SW[2]228
38A2152n

-1000-
(314Ky394)

-1003-
(314Ky392)
d375SW[2]257

-1004-
(314Ky388)
252SW[1]423
264SW[2]873

-1007-
Case 1
(314Ky445)
387SW[1]13

-1007-
Case 2
(314Ky884)

-1008-
(314Ky399)
44KLJ69
1A3233n
1A3243n

-1009-
(314Ky446)
425SW[1]733

(314Ky436)
252SW[7]422
f301SW[1]589
Cir. 6
305F2d175
35A2293n
98A2972n

-1015-
(314Ky429)

-1017-
(314Ky441)
262SW[2]692
309SW[2]172
608SW[1]70

-1019-
(314Ky401)
675SW10

-1020-
(314Ky432)
258SW[3]457
263SW[5]129
555SW[2]612

Vol. 236

-259-
(314Ky453)
(27A2233)
391SW[1]370
467SW[1]332
Cir. 5
241F2d[1]220
Cir. 6
153FS[1]310

-261-
(314Ky450)
45MnL530
56A2186n
58A3255n

-262-
s309Ky637
s218SW659
258SW[1]697

-264-
(314Ky884)

-265-
(314Ky500)
613SW430

-266-
(314Ky457)
248SW[1]914
22A2856n
8A41275n

-268-
(314Ky507)
41KLJ327

-270-
Case 1
(314Ky884)

Case 2
(314Ky496)

-272-
(314Ky510)
(25A2250)
Cir. 6
308F2d[4]624

-275-
(314Ky503)
281SW[2]5
281SW[1]711

-277-
(314Ky461)

-279-
(314Ky459)
317SW[1]512
323SW[1]842

-454-
(314Ky558)
381SW[3]621
Cir. 6
407FS[3]1242

-455-
(314Ky595)
240SW[1]837
276SW[1]32
287SW[1]155
443SW[1]245

-457-
(314Ky535)
416SW[1]733
522SW[1]856

-460-
(314Ky591)
s252SW10
cc247SW496

-462-
(314Ky539)
o525SW[3]71
61KLJ902
19A21417n

-466-
(314Ky524)
s253SW382
394SW776
Cir. 6
716F2d[3]71
21A2385n
21A2405n

-469-
(314Ky531)
258SW[1]723
269SW[1]737
273SW[1]804
f277SW[1]7
c282SW622
291SW[1]546
350SW[1]142
44KLJ66
2A2307s
56A2137n
32A31238n
59A3194n

(314Ky564)
53A3686n

-474-
(314Ky560)
335SW[3]922
402SW[1]700
402SW[2]700
550SW[5]576
54KLJ60
31A2541n
31A2590n

-477-
(314Ky575)
44KLJ73
84A3503n

-478-
(314Ky552)
f243SW[3]483
243SW[3]661

-482-
(314Ky569)
60A2881n
60A2896n
83A3282n

-687-
(314Ky609)
f306SW[3]281
d432SW[3]441
453SW[4]20
655SW[8]502
56KLJ595
51A2267n
51A2288n
27A31040n

-690-
(314Ky634)
282SW[5]134
383SW[3]684
424SW[3]388
459SW[1]600
459SW[4]600
477SW[4]816
514SW[1]682
518SW[1]781
Cir. 6
d216F2d[1]106
411F2d[1]170
114FS[1]779

-692-
(314Ky577)
464SW[2]634
21A31180n
21A31393n
21A31398n
23A3785n
23A3798n
24A326n
24A335n

-695-
(314Ky581)
237SW[3]529
247SW[4]389
254SW[4]479
d264SW[6]672
q313SW[7]576
347SW[6]519
362SW[4]36

384SW[4]68
386SW[3]724
f397SW[6]156
421SW[4]823
d463SW[5]308
j539SW[3]310
42KLJ171
42KLJ337

-698-
(314Ky618)
254SW[2]715
273SW[2]361
291SW[1]48
299SW[2]786
303SW[5]268
306SW[1]302
346SW[1]724
412SW225
432SW[1]815
41KLJ325
1A3331n
1A3391n
1A3469n

-700-
(314Ky586)
s310Ky43
s219SW954

-703-
(314Ky631)
336SW[3]563
444SW[3]740
585SW[2]382
49A2985n
49A21006n

-705-
(314Ky600)
40KLJ331

-708-
(314Ky605)

-710-
(314Ky614)
286SW[3]522

-880-
(314Ky628)
383SW[1]692
472SW[1]510

-881-
(314Ky624)
267SW[2]527

-883-
(314Ky813)

-885-
(314Ky817)
255SW[1]50
261SW[1]641
266SW[1]328
317SW[1]885
386SW[1]952
437SW[1]743

-887-
(314Ky791)
302SW[2]112
310SW[2]517
45KLJ64
17A2754s
42A21417n
42A21426n

-893-
(314Ky641)
s301Ky472
s192SW366
239SW[10]250
252SW[9]431
265SW[9]777
268SW[10]395
291SW[10]13
64A21300n
64A21306n
64A21318n

-897-
(314Ky805)
(27A21341)
Cir. 6
d329F2d415
88A2944n
51A31177n
51A31215n

-901-
(314Ky885)

-902-
(314Ky802)
338SW[2]688

-904-
(314Ky622)

-905-
(314Ky639)
290SW[2]487
j344SW[2]388
700SW[2]394
42KLJ682
51KLJ9s
51KLJ97s

-906-
(314Ky664)
d550SW469
89A2888n

-910-
(314Ky647)
47KLJ283

-912-
(314Ky658)
cc284Ky698
cc145SW1055
305SW[3]541

-914-
Case 1
(314Ky627)

-914-
Case 2
(314Ky651)
d271SW[1]889
316SW[10]73

Continued

1724

BOOK ILLUSTRATIONS

Sources of federal statutes

State statutes

References to *Stat.* are to *United States Statutes at Large.* This is the first place where federal statutes, or acts of Congress, are officially published in a book after they are enacted into law. *U.S.C.* is *United States Code,* the place where the same statutes are officially reorganized and interfiled into the organizational plan of older federal statutes.

U.S.C.A. (United States Code Annotated) is a commercially edited version of the *U.S.C.* which supplies large amounts of additional references, most notably abstracts of reports of cases relevant to the statutes. *U.S.C.S. (United States Code Service)* replaced its predecessor, *F.C.A. (Federal Code Annotated). U.S.C.S.,* like *U.S.C.A.,* is a commercially edited version of the *U.S.C.,* but *U.S.C.S.* is notable for the fact that by offering fewer, selected references and case notes, it is often more manageable than *U.S.C.A. U.S.C.S.* is particularly valuable for its collateral references to *A.L.R., American Jurisprudence,* law review articles, and other books. *U.S.C.S.* is a good place to begin your research concerning federal statutes. If, after using *U.S.C.S.,* you feel that you need to research further, you can go to *U.S.C.A.*

United States Code Congressional and Administrative News, a commercial publication, fills a vacuum created by the slowness of official publishing of *Stat.* Monthly paperbacks, which are annually cumulated into bound volumes, furnish prompt copies of new statutes enacted by Congress, selected legislative histories, and other information relative to messages, proclamations and executive orders of the President, and new administrative regulations.

Analogous to the federal statutes, there are several places where the laws passed by the various state legislatures are found. When the laws are first enacted, they are officially published in various books, the generic name of which is "session laws." As an example, in Ohio the session laws are called *Laws of Ohio.* Commercial publishers often supply monthly looseleaf or pamphlet copies of the laws as and when they are enacted by the various legislatures while they are in session, *e.g., Baldwin's Laws of Ohio* and *Page's Ohio Revised Code Annotated Current Materials.*

After the legislatures' sessions end, the various new laws are blended with older laws which are still in effect into the titles and chapters of compilations of state laws, *e.g., Baldwin's Ohio Revised Code Annotated, Page's Ohio Revised Code Annotated, Arizona Revised Statutes Annotated, Purdon's Pennsylvania*

Annotations concerning various uniform laws

Sources of legal periodical articles

Consolidated Statutes Annotated, Code of Laws of South Carolina, and *Tennessee Code Annotated.*

Ordinarily, research concerning statutes is begun in the latter type of books, which reflect the status of the statute law as of some particular date. They are usually supplied with annotations similar to those in the commercial editions of the federal statutes. For laws subsequent to such date, the monthly looseleaf or pamphlet material mentioned above should be consulted. The evolutionary history of state statutes is usually obtained from the successive volumes of session laws, via notes in the compilations.

Large numbers of states have enacted various uniform laws. As an example, 49 states, the District of Columbia, and the Virgin Islands have enacted the Uniform Commercial Code, and the other state has enacted selected portions of it. As another example, more than 40 states, the District of Columbia, Guam, and the Virgin Islands have enacted the Uniform Partnership Act. Such unifications of state law result in precedent cases from one state concerning the various uniform acts being relevant to the law of the other states which adopted the same act.

Uniform Laws Annotated supplies case notes and legal periodical references which are pertinent to the various sections of uniform acts, regardless of the state or jurisdiction where they originated. It also supplies official comments of the draftsmen, which are frequently not published in the local-state statutes.

Uniform Commercial Code Reporting Service republishes precedent cases pertinent to the Uniform Commercial Code, regardless of the state or jurisdiction or their origin, and indexes them according to the section numbers of the Code to which they relate. It supplies parallel references to the official and unofficial reports in which the cases also appear. A *Digest* of the cases in *Uniform Commercial Code Reporting Service* is also available.

References to valuable legal periodical articles are obtainable via numerous indexes.

Very recent articles are indexed weekly in a service called *Current Index to Legal Periodicals.* The weekly classified pages of this service are collected in a binder. A monthly service called *Legal Contents* (formerly *Contents of Current Legal Periodicals*) furnishes similar advance information.

Current Law Index, consisting of monthly paperback issues and annual bound volumes, and the *Index to Legal Periodicals,* consisting of paperback advance parts and cumulated bound volumes, are regularly used for older legal periodical articles. The *Index to Legal Periodicals* omits references to certain short articles, however.

There are other, and sometimes better, indexes compiled by the editors of the

Legal encyclopedias

Access to A.L.R. annotations

periodicals to which they relate. If you can effectively use those other indexes for a particular reason, such as the narrow scope of your inquiry or your knowledge that the article which you seek was published in a particular periodical, then they are likely to better serve your purposes than the less-manageable general indexes, *e.g., Current Law Index* and *Index to Legal Periodicals*. For example, the articles in *The Journal of the American Trial Lawyers Association,* relating primarily to personal injury law, are better-indexed in *Anderson's Index to the A.T.L. (NACCA) Law Journal.*

Legal encyclopedias should not be indiscriminately accepted as authoritative statements of the law. At their best, they are only secondary authority; occasionally they are inaccurate. They are best used as devices for finding precedent cases, via their footnotes and pocket parts. Always read the precedent cases which they cite, if you desire to rely upon the statements in the legal encyclopedias, and cite the cases, not the encyclopedia.

Corpus Juris Secundum is supplemented with the footnotes in its predecessor, *Corpus Juris,* and with annual cumulative replacement pocket parts.

American Jurisprudence 2d is supplemented by *A.L.R.* and annual cumulative replacement pocket parts.

In a few states, there are legal encyclopedias which are oriented toward the case law of that individual state. They are also supplemented with annual cumulative replacement pocket parts.

Researchers may obtain access to *A.L.R.* annotations via the following avenues:

• *American Jurisprudence 2d.* As a by-product of your ordinary research in this legal encyclopedia, you will discover collateral references to the annotations in the *A.L.R.* series, by consulting the *American Jurisprudence 2d* footnotes and pocket parts.

• *Shepard's Citations.* If any precedent case which you have found is noted in any series of *A.L.R., Shepard's Citations* will signal that information as in the following examples:

5 AL^3 1276 n (noted in 3d series)

78 AL^2 104 s (noted in supplement to 2d series)

Updating A.L.R. first series

Updating A.L.R.2d, A.L.R.3d, A.L.R.4th, and A.L.R.Fed.

• *Quick Indexes. A.L.R.* (1st) and *A.L.R.2d* each have convenient, one-volume, topical indexes. They do not have supplements. *A.L.R. 3d* and *4th* share a separate, convenient, one-volume, topical index which has a pocket part in the front. A similar, three-volume *Federal Quick Index,* with a pocket part in front, organizes all federally related materials in all of the *A.L.R.* series, including *A.L.R. Fed.*, and various other works.

• *A.L.R. Digests. A.L.R.* first series and *A.L.R.2d* have their own separate digests which are interrelated by the use of common topic and section numbers; they are not supplemented. There is also a new *A.L.R. Digest* for *A.L.R.3d, 4th,* and *Federal.*

• *A.L.R. Word Index. A.L.R.* (1st) and *A.L.R.2d* have separate word indexes to annotations which are not supplemented.

The original 175-volume *A.L.R.* series was published in various years from 1919 through 1948. By the issuance of successive noncumulative bound and paperback supplements called *A.L.R. Blue Book(s),* which refer to the volume and page numbers in *A.L.R.*, additional references to later precedent cases, and superseding and supplementing annotations, relevant to the older annotations are provided. Because the *A.L.R. Blue Books* are not cumulative, a complete search requires that you examine each individual volume of the *A.L.R. Blue Books* published subsequent to the publication of the annotation, including the paperback supplement. It is best to examine the most recent *Blue Book* first and work backward.

A.L.R.2d, A.L.R.3d, A.L.R.4th, and *A.L.R.Fed.* have better supplementation than the original *A.L.R.* The annotations in those sets are continued in the supplements.

A.L.R.2d is updated via blue-bound supplements, called *A.L.R.2d Later Case Service,* which also contain pocket parts. Thus, you must look in two places to fully update *A.L.R.2d.*

A.L.R.3d, A.L.R.4th, and *A.L.R.Fed.* are directly updated via individual pocket parts in the bound volumes.

Digests

Abstracts of precedent cases and references to the reports in which they may be found are provided in the various digests. There are a great many different digests, mainly for the various states. One large publisher catalogs 59 different digests which it publishes. There are also other publishers of digests.

There is at least one digest for nearly every state, *e.g.*, *West's California Digest, Florida Digest, West's Indiana Digest, Missouri Digest, West's Ohio Digest, Vale Pennsylvania Digest,* and *West's Wisconsin Key Number Digest.* Some digests are divided by time periods, *e.g.*, *Federal Digest* (pre-1939), which is complemented by *Modern Federal Practice Digest* (1939-1961), *West's Federal Practice Digest 2d* (1961 to November, 1975), and *West's Federal Practice Digest 3d* (November, 1975, to date). Similarly, *Abbott New York Digest* [*1st*] and *2d* are divided at the various publication dates of the first edition and *West's New York Digest 3d* covers cases since 1961. Many other state digests are now being supplemented in the same way.

Although abstracts of the United States Supreme Court cases are a part of the contents of the federal digests mentioned, they are also separately organized in *U.S. Supreme Court Digest* and *U.S. Supreme Court Digest Lawyers' Edition.*

Martindale-Hubbell Law Directory, "Law Digests" volume, is an often overlooked and potentially very useful source of succinct legal information and beginning references. The "Law Digests" volume consists of the following parts:

1) Separate digests of the laws of each of the fifty states, the District of Columbia, Puerto Rico and the Virgin Islands. It includes information regarding state courts and United States District Courts sitting in those states under the topic "Courts."

2) A digest of the copyright, patent, and trademark laws of the United States.

3) Digests of the laws of the federal government of Canada and each of Canada's ten provinces.

4) Digests of the laws of many other foreign countries.

5) Information regarding the United States courts. Information concerning the United States District Courts is included in the topic "Courts" in the digests of state laws mentioned at 1 above.

6) Copies of Uniform Acts.

7) Selected international conventions.

8) American Bar Association directories and codes of conduct for lawyers and judges.

Bringing digests up to date

Missing and erroneous citations

Each digest has a time limit to its coverage. After certain volumes in the reports of cases, the digest does not organize the material.

When examining a digest, consult it methodically, by using all of the following items in the order listed: 1) bound volumes; 2) pocket parts; 3) paperback supplement; and 4) the individual bound volumes and advance sheets of reports of cases issued subsequent to the last pocket part or supplement. In bound reports of cases, the digest portion is usually in the back. In paperback advance sheets, the digest portion is usually in the front. On or near the back of the title page of each digest, pocket part, and supplement there is a chart which describes the limit of its coverage.

For various reasons you are apt to acquire references to precedent cases, the citations for which are missing, wrong, or incomplete. You can usually determine, however, the digest in which it should appear, by determing that, *e.g.*, it is a Kansas case or a Massachusetts case, it is a federal case decided before 1939, or it is a case decided in 1960 or 1981.

Use the "Table of Cases" in the appropriate digest to look up the citation by the case's name. Some digests also have a "Reverse Table of Cases" or a "Defendant Plaintiff Table" which indexes the cases in the reverse order of the parties, *i.e.*, the last party named is listed first.

When you know the state from which a state or federal case came, look for it in that state's digest.

When you know that it is a federal case, look for it in the appropriate federal digest.

When you know only the year, look for it in the appropriate *Decennial Digest*.

Sources of legal definitions

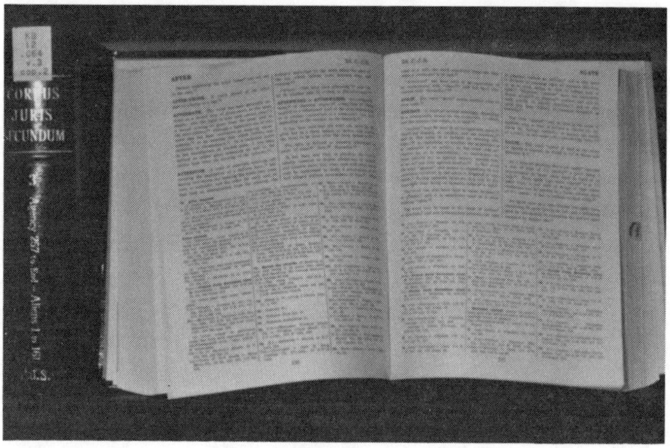

Shepard's Citations

When we need definitions of legal terms, it is easy to recall that the usual one-volume legal dictionaries, *e.g., Ballentine's Law Dictionary, Black's Law Dictionary,* and *The Law Dictionary,* can often satisfy our immediate needs.

It is important to remember, however, that there are other sources of legal definitions which on many occasions are more useful. *Corpus Juris Secundum (C.J.S.),* which we ordinarily think of as a source of long topical articles on law, is a useful source of definitions and references to the precedent cases from which the definitions were obtained. The definitions in *C.J.S.* are interfiled with the topical articles in alphabetical order.

Definitions may also be found in *American Jurisprudence 2d* by using the general index.

Words and Phrases is a large set of books which contains abstracts of definitions announced in precedent cases. In addition, each of the various state and federal digests contains a "Words and Phrases" volume or section near its end, which provides references to the precedent cases abstracted in that digest which contain various definitions.

There have been numerous editions of the *Bouvier's Law Dictionary,* the most recent of which were published in 1914 and 1934. The 1914 edition was reprinted in 1984. The *Bouvier's* dictionaries are useful to find definitions and collateral references concerning traditional legal concepts; they will frequently refer the researcher to the origins of various legal concepts.

Shepard's Citations is invaluable to determine the reception which a particular precedent case or statute has received in the subsequent legal literature. It is therefore very important that you know how to use it properly.

Be methodical. Before beginning your search, make certain that you have all of the volumes of the appropriate set of *Shepard's* in front of you. Always proceed from the oldest, through the newer, to the latest, according to the illustrations. Notice that in some states, *Shepard's* consists of several volumes, as in the Illinois illustration. *Shepard's Federal Citations* similarly consists of several volumes. In other instances *Shepard's* may be fewer volumes, as in the Hawaii example, and in the *Atlantic Reporter* example. In every *Shepard's* set there are both bound volumes and red or yellow, or both color, paperbacks which must always be consulted; that is where the latest information is. The spine of the bound volume ordinarily tells you the latest year covered in that particular volume. If the precedent case concerning which you are researching was decided in

Shepard's Special Citators

1981 and the spine of the volume says 1977, you will promptly recognize that the 1977 volume can be skipped. You can never skip volumes published after the date of your case, however, because at any time a former case may be commented upon in the legal literature, followed, criticized, or overruled.

When researching state cases, it is wise to use the state *Shepard's* instead of the National Reporter System *Shepard's,* because the state *Shepard's* will furnish more information than the national reporter system edition, particularly references to in-state law review comments concerning the precedent case. The National Reporter System *Shepard's* do not cover cases decided before the National Reporter System began.

There is also a handy *Shepard's* which gives you official names and citations for acts and cases identified only by a popular name.

Shepard's Citations principally offers various citators for the reports of cases and statutes of the 50 states, the federal courts and statutes, and the West Publishing Co. regional reporters.

There are other special *Shepard's* citators, however. Notable among them are:

Code of Federal Regulations Citations
Criminal Justice Citations
Ethics Citations
Federal Labor Law Citations
Law Review Citations
Patent and Trademark Citations
Restatement Citations
U.S. Administrative Citations

You may use these special citators to determine, among other things, the answers to such questions as:

- Are there cases or periodical articles explaining — C.F.R. § —?
- Have the Arkansas courts had occasion to apply the ABA Standards Relating to the Administration of Criminal Justice: Function of the Trial Judge number —?
- Has Code of Judicial Conduct Canon number — been applied in a reported Nebraska case?
- Has this law review article that I want to use been favorably or unfavorably commented upon by the courts or other law review articles?
- Have the Connecticut courts followed Restatement of Torts (Second) number —?

Restatement in the Courts

Advance sheets to reports of cases

The actions of the various state and federal courts concerning the *Restatements* can be discovered via the case notes in the bound and paperback noncumulative supplements to the *Restatements,* called *Restatement in the Courts.*

There are paperback advance parts for all units of the unofficial National Reporter System, *e.g., Federal Reporter 2d, Federal Supplement, Atlantic Reporter 2d,* and *Pacific Reporter 2d.*

Many official state reports have advance parts, too, e.g., the advance parts for *New York Reports 2d, Appellate Division Reports 2d,* and *Miscellaneous Reports 2d* are collectively published in the *Weekly Official Edition Law Reports and Session Laws State of New York.* Similarly, the advance parts for *Ohio State 3d, Ohio Appellate 3d* and *Ohio Miscellaneous 2d* are published weekly in the *Ohio Official Reports Advance Sheets,* and as an appendix to the Ohio State Bar Association publication, *Ohio Bar.*

Reports of cases of the United States Supreme Court

Officially, the reports of the cases decided by the United States Supreme Court are published in *United States Reports (U.S.).* The advance parts to the official reports are brown paperbacks.

Legal researchers often prefer to use one of the two commercial or unofficial editions, called *Supreme Court Reporter (S.Ct.)* and *U.S. Supreme Court Reports Lawyers' Edition (L.Ed.),* respectively. Both unofficial editions offer the following advantages over the official reports:

a) faster and more dependable service;

b) editorial additions.

The *Supreme Court Reporter* is integrated into the key number digest scheme of the *National Reporter System.* Its advance parts are gray, pink, or green paperbacks. *U.S. Supreme Court Reports Lawyers' Edition* is integrated into the *U.S. Supreme Court Digest* and is often supplied with auxiliary essays analogous to *A.L.R.* annotations. Its advance parts are ivory and green paperbacks.

Although the various volume and page numbers of *U.S., S.Ct.,* and *L.Ed.* are different, the bound volumes of *S.Ct.* and *L.Ed.* are supplied with star paging which ties the pages of the unofficial editions directly to the numbers of the volumes and pages in *U.S.* Note the parallel references to the official *U.S.* volume numbers on the spines of bound volumes of *S.Ct.* and *L.Ed.* Tables in the front of the bound volumes of *S.Ct.* and *L.Ed.* also correlate names of reported cases and official citations with the pages of the unofficial reports.

Local state practice books indispensable

Three places where the report of the same state case may be found

There is a high probability that in any one state there will be special books which judges, practicing lawyers, and paralegals frequently use and rely upon with reference to the local state problems before them. In many instances, such books are a legal researcher's first wave of attack on particular problems. Such books are concerned with details and how to accomplish particular objectives. They are indispensable to a legal researcher in that particular state. Civil procedure, criminal procedure, family law, jury instructions, legal forms, pleading and practice forms, real property, school law, and appellate practice are examples of the topics usually covered in such works.

Three places where the report of the same state case may be found: the official *Kentucky Reports,* the National Reporter System *South Western Reporter 2d,* and the reprint of the Kentucky cases in *South Western Reporter 2d* called *Kentucky Decisions*. This example is representative of the situation in a majority of the states.

Reports of cases of one state

Various states' statutes

Federal statutes ((*U.S.C.A.* and *U.S.C.S.*) and *United States Reports*

B. SAMPLE STATEMENTS OF THE CASE AND OPTIONAL FOREWORD

STATEMENT OF THE CASE

This is an appeal by the plaintiffs from the judgment of the United States District Court for the ——— District of ———, ——— Division, wherein damages were denied to the plaintiffs who were injured in a collision while they were passengers in a bus owned and operated by the defendants.

* * *

STATEMENT OF THE CASE

This is an appeal from a judgment of the ——— Circuit Court, which awarded damages for the wrongful death of an infant trespasser upon the property of the appellant.

* * *

STATEMENT OF THE CASE

The purpose of this action is to construe a will, and determine the limits within which the City of Springfield may use rent money collected from the renting of a parcel of ground left to the City under the will, which has been rented and will continue to be rented for several more years. The trial court decided against the use of the rent money proposed by the City, and the City appeals from that judgment.

* * *

COUNTERSTATEMENT OF THE CASE

This action was brought by Newtown Gas and Electric Company (hereafter called "N.G. & E."), against the Anonymous Insurance Company (hereafter called "Insurance Company"), for the recovery of proceeds under a fire and extended coverage insurance policy on account of a loss occasioned by damage to a large transformer. N.G. & E. alleged that the loss resulted from an "explosion" within the coverage of the policy, which allegation was denied by the Insurance Company. From a verdict and judgment of the trial court in favor of the Insurance Company, N.G. & E. has taken this appeal.

* * *

STATEMENT OF THE CASE

Sam Jones operated his pleasure boat down the Main River at nighttime, while carrying as passengers three other men and his wife, Sally. The boat struck a submerged obstruction consisting of an abandoned loading dock track, which extended from the shore line into the river a short distance under the surface of the water. As a result of the collision, Mr. Jones was killed and his wife Sally was seriously disabled. A Libel in Admiralty seeking damages for their injuries and for his death was instituted against the United States in the United States District Court for the ——— District of ———. The United States filed a Cross-Libel against Sam Jones' Estate for contribution of payment for whatever damages might be awarded to Sally Jones.

The matter was tried to the Court and resulted in a verdict in the primary action in favor of the United States, which had the effect of eliminating the contribution issue raised by the Cross-Libel. Sally Jones and Sam Jones' Estate appeal from the verdict.

The facts of the case were set forth in the Findings of Fact by Judge Smith. The first part of the findings was based on stipulations entered into between the parties, and the second part was based on evidentiary findings of the court.

SAMPLE OPTIONAL FOREWORD

FOREWORD

"* * * If legislative purpose is to be achieved, and if legislative action is to be fitted, as intended by the legislature, into the body of the law, adjustments, creative innovations and dynamic synthesis are required of the courts. * * *

"* * * It is folly to assume that in general, or that in most particulars, the legislature purports to provide complete direction. On the contrary, the legislative tradition in this country assumes and depends upon a dynamic and modernized common law system of law. * * *"

Breitel, *The Courts and Lawmaking,* LEGAL INSTITUTIONS TODAY AND TOMORROW 1, 36-37 (M. Paulsen ed. 1959).

C. SAMPLE STUDENT BRIEF

SAMPLE COVER PAGE

IN THE SUPREME COURT OF THE

STATE OF FRANKLIN

No. 0000

DR. HENRY HORN, Petitioner

vs.

HON. BENJAMIN CARDOZO JONES, JUDGE OF THE MODERN COUNTY

NISI PRIUS COURT, ET AL., Respondents

APPLICATION FOR WRIT OF PROHIBITION TO THE

MODERN COUNTY NISI PRIUS COURT

RESPONDENT'S BRIEF

BARBARA K. BARDEN
Cincinnati, Ohio
Counsel for Respondent
Robert W. Cleveland

This is to certify that a
copy of this brief has
been served on the adverse
parties.

____

SAMPLE TABLE OF POINTS AND AUTHORITIES

TABLE OF CONTENTS AND AUTHORITIES

i

ii

iii

Foreword, page 1, omitted. For sample foreword, *see* APPENDIX B.

SAMPLE STATEMENT OF ISSUES *See also* other samples at CHAPTER 7.

STATEMENT OF ISSUES

At the present level of medical knowledge, when a patient is stricken with progressively deteriorating kidney disease, the power of a committee to decide whether that patient is entitled to dialysis or kidney transplant is tantamount to the power to deprive that patient of life. The Constitution of the United States, through the fifth and fourteenth amendments, guarantees that no person shall be deprived of life without due process of law, and that no state shall deny persons within its jurisdiction the equal protection of the law. Three issues are to be decided here:

1. Does the acceptance of federal and state funds by a private hospital make a decision of a committee of that hospital the equivalent of state action, so that the courts can require the committee to guarantee due process of law to those over whom it exercises the power of life or death?

2. Does that committee, if it decides priorities for dialysis and kidney transplant for reasons such as the relative social worth of the candidate, or the dependency of other persons on the candidate for support, rather than basing its decision on the immediate need of a potential recipient for such equipment or organs in order to sustain his life, deprive that potential recipient of the equal protection of the law?

3. Should the courts require that a private hospital committee adhere to the full panoply of procedural safeguards inherent in a trial like evidentiary hearing, when it decides which patients are to receive life-saving treatment at that hospital?

2

SAMPLE STATEMENT OF THE CASE *See also* other samples at APPENDIX B.

STATEMENT OF THE CASE

This case is before the Court on the petition of Dr. Henry Horn for a writ of prohibition against the hearing of Mr. Robert W. Cleveland's suit by Judge Benjamin Cardozo Jones of the Modern County Nisi Prius Court of the State of Franklin.

3

SAMPLE STATEMENT OF FACTS

STATEMENT OF FACTS

May it please the Court:

In a tragedy too often re-enacted despite the giant achievements of modern medicine, Robert W. Cleveland has fallen victim to progressively deteriorating kidney disease, which doctors have told him can be corrected by the use of either dialysis machinery or kidney transplants. (Tr. p. 5, l. 1-5). Mr. Cleveland has applied for this life-saving treatment at Pleasant View Hospital, which is nominally a private institution, but which in fact receives both federal and state planning funds, Hill-Burton Hospital Construction Program funds, and Medicare and Medicaid funds. (Tr. p. 2, l. 3-6).

The scarcity of both dialysis equipment and organs for transplant requires that a system of priorities be set to govern their assignment to potential recipients. Mr. Cleveland alleges that in determining these priorities, Pleasant View Hospital and its Medical Director, Dr. Henry Horn, carry out anonymous committee decisions. The committee does not disclose the standards on which these decisions are reached. Applicants are not given an opportunity to appear before the committee to introduce evidence of their qualifications for treatment, and they are unable to confront and examine witnesses whose testimony the committee may consider in reaching its conslusions. (Tr. p. 2, l. 7-14). Mr. Cleveland charges that such a procedure is a violation of his rights under the fifth and fourteenth amendments to the Constitution of the United States, which guarantee him the equal

4

protection of the law and prohibit either the state or federal government from depriving him of life without due process of law. (Tr. p. 2, l. 8 and 14-16).

Mr. Cleveland is informed and believes, and therefore alleges, that four other persons, all older than he and heads of families, hold priorities higher than his on the list of potential recipients. (Tr. p. 3, l. 10-14). He has filed suit in the Modern County Nisi Prius Court, of the State of Franklin, asking that Pleasant View Hospital and Dr. Horn be required to disclose to him the basis for the hospital's decisions concerning allocation of dialysis and transplant priorities, to allow him to cross-examine and introduce witnesses at a hearing held to determine those priorities, and to disclose to him the names and addresses of the anonymous committee members. He also asks that the hospital be enjoined from making furture assignments of equipment and transplants without following these ordinary procedural safeguards, and that the court retain the action on its docket for further orders and relief. (Tr. p. 2, l. 16-26).

The other potential recipients, who are joined as defendants in the action, are Mrs. Florence Smith, a thirty-nine year old widowed mother of three (Tr. p. 3, l. 15-24); Eric Deutscher, married, age 62 (Tr. p. 3, l. 25-27; p. 4, l. 1-4); Sam Brown, age 41 and father of two teen-aged children (Tr. p. 4, l. 5-10);

5

and Jim Green, who is 32 and has four children. (Tr. p. 4, l. 11-26). Mr. Cleveland is 23 years old, and recently finished a distinguished undergraduate college career. He is engaged to be married, is independently wealthy, and plans to pursue graduate study in either medicine or law in order to devote the rest of his life to public service. (Tr. p. 2, l. 27-28; p. 3, l. 1-7).

6

SAMPLE ARGUMENT OF LAW

ARGUMENT OF LAW

I. The acceptance of Hill-Burton funds brings Pleasant View Hospital's action under the purview of the fifth and fourteenth amendment guarantees of due process and equal protection of the law.

A racial discrimination case established that a hospital receiving Hill-Burton funds is required to extend fifth and fourteenth amendment guarantees to physicians and patients. In Simkins v. Moses H. Cone Memorial Hospital, 323 F.2d 959, (4th Cir. 1963), Negro physicians, dentists and patients charged that they had been denied admission to hospitals because of race. In denying them declaratory and injunctive relief, the District Court had found that the hospitals had not been impressed with sufficient public interest to render them instrumentalities of the government and thus within reach of the fifth and fourteenth amendments. The Court of Appeals reversed, holding that the question was not whether an otherwise private body had actually been rendered an instrumentality of the government, but rather whether the state or federal government, or both, had become so involved in an otherwise private body that the hospital's activities had also become the activities of the governments, performed under their aegis. The most significant governmental contact of the hospitals was their participation in the Hill-Burton program, Hill-Burton Act, 42 U.S.C. §291 et seq. (1970), from which they received public funds paid by

7

the United States to the State of North Carolina. The Court of Appeals found the necessary state, including federal, action in the hospitals' participation in Hill-Burton to make the hospitals subject to the fifth and fourteenth amendments. Though the Hill-Burton Act required qualifying hospitals to meet requirements as to lack of discrimination on account of race, creed or color, it authorized the Surgeon General to make exceptions for states which provided separate but equal facilities; the racial discrimination there was thus affirmatively sanctioned, not compelled, by federal and state regulations. But the Fourth Circuit held that governmental action need not reach the level of compulsion to clothe otherwise private discrimination with state action.

The Simkins decision was explained in a later case in which doctors who had been denied admission to a hospital staff sought declaratory and injunctive relief on the grounds that such denial abridged their fourteenth amendment rights. The basis for denial was that the doctors did not maintain offices in the county from which the hospital required that all staff members be chosen. The hospital moved for dismissal on the grounds that the decision in Simkins was reached merely because of the presence of the element of racial discrimination. The court replied that the findings of state action in Simkins did not rest on finding that the plaintiffs were Negroes or that the discrimination had been

8

racial. State action was found merely because the hospitals had participated in the federally-endowed Hill-Burton program, which involves state supervision of hospital construction and maintenance. Sams v. Ohio Valley General Hospital Association, 257 F.Supp. 369 (N.D. W.Va. 1966). This case was later dismissed on its merits. On appeal, the Fourth Circuit reversed the dismissal on the grounds that restricting staff appointments to doctors with offices within a certain county constituted a classification without a rational basis and thus denied plaintiffs equal protection of the law. The opinion expressly approved that portion of the District Court opinion which said that receipt of Hill-Burton funds, in and of itself, made the hospital's action the equivalent of state action. Sams v. Ohio Valley Hospital Association, 413 F.2d 826 (4th Cir. 1969).

These cases establish that Pleasant View Hospital, in its receipt of Hill-Burton and other federal and state funds, must administer its treatment facilities in keeping with the fifth and fourteenth amendment guarantees of due process of law and equal protection of the law. It is the clear duty of the court to see that these guarantees are provided.

A. Due process requires that the committee grant potential recipients an evidentiary hearing.

Once the action of the hospital committee has been brought under the due process requirement, the court must decide what

9

constitutes due process in the committee hearing. Because the field of dialysis and transplant is relatively new, the law has not yet provided guidelines for allocation of treatment, and decisions regarding assignment of priorities have been left largely to the individual hospitals administering the treatment. With no specific law to guide us, we must look elsewhere to determine what limitations the courts should impose on hospitals which must decide priorities for treatment. The field of administrative law provides us with an analogous situation, if we liken the hospital committee to an administrative agency. In examining the procedural safeguards to which the courts require administrative agencies to adhere in administering statutorily granted rights, we can develop the procedures which the courts should require a hospital committee to observe in dealing with the far more important human right to life.

Whether a trial-type hearing, with cross-examination of witnesses, is required of an administrative agency, depends on whether adjudicative or legislative facts are at issue. A hearing of adjudicative facts, that is, those pertaining to a particular party, requires trial-like procedure; while legislative facts, or those which will help the tribunal decide questions of law, policy and discretion, may be decided without trial. K. DAVIS, ADMINISTRATIVE LAW TEXT, §7.03 (Third ed., 1972). Applying this principle to the hospital committee decision, we could

10

conclude that the committee would be free to set up criteria for allocating priorities, as long as these criteria were not unconstitutionally discriminatory, before individual applicants were heard. The courts then could require that the committee grant a full hearing to each applicant, giving him an opportunity to introduce and confront witnesses and to introduce evidence regarding his need for treatment, and allowing him to show how he meets these previously determined criteria.

DAVIS, Supra, §7.16, says that a trial-type hearing on disputed adjudicative facts should be given to one who has a sufficient interest or right at stake. This right to a hearing has been repeatedly upheld by the Supreme Court. In Willner v. Committee on Character and Fitness, 373 U.S. 96 (1963), the petitioner was an attorney who had been denied admission to the New York Bar by a committee which had not granted him a hearing and which relied on testimony of a witness whom the petitioner had not been allowed to confront. In reversing the lower court's denial of the petitioner's appeal for a de novo application, the Court held that procedural due process requires confrontation and cross-examination of those whose word deprives a person of his livelihood. The case for confrontation of witnesses by one such as Mr. Cleveland would be stronger still, because testimony of witnesses before the hospital committee could deprive him of his very life.

11

Greene v. McElroy, 360 U.S. 474 (1959), concerned an aeronautical engineer who was employed by a private manufacturer doing work for the government and who was denied a security clearance. When he was discharged for want of the security clearance, he was unable to find another job as an aeronautical engineer. The Court held that evidence used to prove the government's case, when governmental action seriously injures an individual, must be disclosed to that individual so that he may have a chance to show that the evidence is untrue. If we substitute the action of the hospital committee in the instant case for the government action in Greene, we see that Mr. Cleveland must be given the opportunity to prove how the committee's criteria for allocation apply to him. He most assuredly is in danger of being injured by the committee's action, should it decide against him, to an even greater degree than Greene was injured by denial of his security clearance.

Greene was relied on by the Court in its decision in Goldberg v. Kelly, 397 U.S. 254 (1970). The state of Illinois in that case had terminated welfare payments to a recipient without giving him an opportunity for an evidentiary hearing prior to the stoppage of payments. The Court held that this action denied the recipient due process in violation of the fourteenth amendment, and that conclusions as to a recipient's continued eligibility for welfare payments must rest solely on the legal rules and evidence adduced

12

at a hearing. If such a hearing is required prior to denial of a statutorily granted right like welfare, it is vastly more important to assure that a hearing will be held if the very right to life itself is to be denied.

The Supreme Court of Hawaii, in setting criteria for hearing by a hospital on a physician's application for staff privileges, said that a fair hearing would include timely notice, in order that the applicant could adequately prepare his application. Though the hospital board would have discretion as to whether the applicant would be entitled to counsel at the hearing, if the hospital's counsel were present the applicant's counsel should be also present. The decision should be based on substantial evidence produced at the hearing, and the board could not rely on ex parte communications not made known to the applicant. The board's decision should be written, to provide a record for judicial review. Silver v. Castle Memorial Hospital, 497 P.2d 564 (Hawaii 1972).

The Fifth Circuit described due process in administrative hearings as comprising an opportunity for parties to know the claims of opposing parties, to present evidence to support their contentions, and to cross-examine witnesses for the other side. Though common law rules of evidence need not strictly be adhered to, the findings must conform to the evidence adduced at the hearing. Hornsby v. Allen, 326 F.2d 605 (5th Cir. 1964). In Goldberg v.

13

Kelly, supra, it was held that impartiality of the decision maker was an essential element of due process. This element can be guaranteed to Mr. Cleveland only by disclosing the names of the committee members; for to determine whether the decision makers are impartial, the reviewing court must know who they are and what interests they might possibly represent. The remaining due process elements, as set out in Hornsby v. Allen, supra, are identical to the guarantees for which Mr. Cleveland has asked the court.

B. Equal protection of the law requires that selection be either rationally based or determined by lot.

A far more complicated problem than assuring due process in the hearing stage is that of assuring equal protection to potential dialysis and transplant recipients in determining the criteria on which priorities will be based. Selection must of course begin with the medical qualifications of candidates, with younger persons regarded as better risks for dialysis than older ones; the healthier a candidate generally, the better chance he has for selection. Sanders & Dukeminier, Medical Advance and Legal Lag: Hemodialysis and Kidney Transplantation, 15 U.C.L.A. L. Rev. 357 (1968). A committee will look to the candidate's rehabilitation potential, that is, his ability and desire to continue in active life, despite constant fluctuations of bodily state; and because the physical restrictions of hemodialysis

14

often require that one undergoing such treatment change jobs, the committee will consider the candidate's ability to adapt to other work. Other things being equal, the committee will choose candidates with dependents, and some committees base their choice on what they consider the individual's relative social worth. Ibid.

It has been suggested that while selection alone does not deny the equality of human life, in basing this selection on social worth, society is saying that one person's life is more worthy of preservation than another's. When the arguably small return society gains from social-worth determinations is balanced against the infringement on equality of life which such determinations inflict, there results no such compelling societal interest in these determinations as will justify denying equal protection to candidates for treatment. Patient Selection for Artificial and Transplanted Organs, 82 HARV. L. REV. 1322 (1969). There are areas in which there would seem to be a compelling societal interest in the selection process. One of these is the candidate's ability to pay for treatment, which in the case of hemodialysis can be long and costly. Even though wealth may be a suspect classification for equal protection purposes, it has been suggested that providing this treatment at public expense might tie up public funds to the detriment of other important medical research areas. Another societal interest in selection

15

centers on the candidate's occupation; priorities could be awarded to those persons with essential skills. Society's interest in preserving the family would call for giving priority to parents. Basing selection on the committee's view of worthy religious and moral standards would appear to be a violation of the establishment clause of the Constitution. Ibid.

Use of these criteria, whatever the procedural safeguards observed in administering them, still threatens to deny equal protection of the law to candidates for treatment. Who is to say, in the final analysis, which human being is more worthy of survival than another, and for what reason? Freund, Ethical Problems in Human Experimentation, 273 N. ENG. J. MED. 687 (1965):

> "The governing principle is not the merit or need or value of the victim but equality of worth as a human being. The governing principle, it might be said, is that men shall not play God with human lives."

To set a standard for allocation of priorities without thus playing God with human lives, we can look for authority to a familiar case in American jurisprudence, U.S. v. Holmes, 26 F.Cas. 360 (No. 15,383) (C.C. E.D. Pa. 1842). This was the manslaughter trial of a seaman who was one of 41 persons crowded into a long boat after their ship, the "William Brown", had struck an iceberg and capsized. Because there was insufficient room in the boat for all, fourteen male passengers were thrown overboard to lighten the load. Judge Baldwin, instructing the Holmes jury, said that if there was any time to foresee impending disaster, lots should have been drawn to decide who was to be sacrificed. He likened the situation to one in which food aboard ship has run out, and sacrifice of one person is necessary to appease the hunger of the others; and he observed that all writers agreed that the rule in such a case should be to decide the victim by drawing lots.

Despite the many years intervening between the case of the overloaded lifeboat and the present short supply of dialysis equipment and organs available for transplant, the two situations are strikingly similar. Both present us with persons dependent for life itself on something of which there is not ample supply for all. That which was suggested as a solution in the first instance, drawing of lots, may well be the only way the second instance may be handled and still provide equal protection to the persons involved. After it has been decided that applicants are medically qualified for dialysis or transplant, all those who apply for treatment at the same time could simply draw lots to determine priority. This method would assure equality of protection for all, and would avoid the element of playing God which is necessarily introduced into the selection process when selection is based on social-worth criteria.

II. The writ of prohibition should be denied.

In asking for a writ of prohibition against Judge Benjamin Cardozo Jones, Dr. Horn and Pleasant View Hospital imply that in

17

hearing Mr. Cleveland's complaint Judge Jones will be exercising jurisdiction which his court does not possess over the decisions of a committee of a private hospital which should be free to exercise its own discretion in assignment of priorities for dialysis and kidney transplant for whatever medical and social reasons it deems best.

Granting this writ would place the hospital's need for protection of its administrative discretion and privacy above Mr. Cleveland's basic right to life. Denying the writ would, at most, subject the hospital to the relatively minor inconvenience of an alteration of its committee procedure. If the court should exceed its jurisdiction in imposing guidelines on the committee, the hospital will have recourse to appellate tribunals to establish that the court should have interfered. If the hospital succeeds in this appellate process, it will then be free to reinstate its original methods of assignment of dialysis and transplant priorities.

On the other hand, if the court is prohibited from acting here, it is very likely that Mr. Cleveland will have no recourse whatever, because his very life depends on receiving treatment as soon as possible. If revelation of the standards by which recipients are chosen, or disclosure of his place on the priority list, should indicate that he will not soon be treated at Pleasant View, Mr. Cleveland can well afford to seek treatment elsewhere.

18

Keeping the standards and decisions secret makes it impossible for him to make an informed, rational decision on this matter.

In Ex Parte Fahey, 332 U.S. 258 (1947), the Supreme Court described a writ of prohibition as an extraordinary remedy which should be resorted to only where appeal is a clearly inadequate remedy. The Ohio Supreme Court has held that prohibition is an extraordinary judicial writ issuing out of a court of superior jurisdiction to prevent an inferior tribunal from usurping jurisdiction with which the inferior court is not legally vested, and may not be substituted for the usual orderly process of appeal. State ex rel. Schumacher v. Victor, 171 Ohio St. 189, 168 N.E.2d 398 (1960). Similarly, the New York court has held that the writ of prohibition is an extraordinary remedy which does not issue where the grievance can be redressed by ordinary proceedings at law or in equity, or merely to prevent error which may be readily corrected on appeal. Lee v. County Court of Erie Co., 27 N.Y.2d 432, 267 N.E.2d 452, 318 N.Y.S.2d 705, (1971), cert. denied 404 U.S. 823 (1972).

If Mr. Cleveland were asking the court to enjoin the hospital entirely from proceeding with all hemodialysis or renal transplants until his complaint could be decided, such an extraordinary remedy as prohibition might be justified, because the injunction would deny treatment to others as much in need as

19

Mr. Cleveland. However, this is not the case. Mr. Cleveland has asked only that the hospital be enjoined from making further assignments without complying with the procedural guarantees for which he asks the court. If Judge Jones is allowed to hear this case, and if he grants the injunction as Mr. Cleveland asks, the hospital will not be prevented from treating victims of kidney disease, but will only be required to guarantee them due process and equal protection in determining whether to treat them. If this action exceeds the court's jurisdiction, the hospital has an adequate remedy through appeal, without having to interrupt its primary function of care of the ill. Consideration of the competing interests involved here, administrative convenience on one side, and the right to life itself on the other, makes it clear that this is simply not one of those extraordinary situations in which the extraordinary remedy of prohibition is justified.

III. <u>The hospital is a quasi-public institution, subject to judicial supervision</u>.

There has been a recent trend away from allowing private hospitals freedom from judicial control of their actions. The groundwork was laid in this area by <u>Falcone v. Middlesex Co. Medical Society</u>, 34 N.J. 582, 170 A.2d 791 (1961). In this action to compel the county medical society to admit Dr. Falcone to membership, the court held that the society acted in an arbitrary,

20

unreasonable and illegal manner in applying an unwritten requirement of four years' attendance at an AMA-approved medical college to deny membership to a duly-licensed physician. Membership in the society was necessary to be admitted to hospital staffs. The court pointed out that the society is not the kind of voluntary membership association with which the public has little or no concern, because it engages in activities vitally affecting the health and welfare of the people. Its power should be viewed as a fiduciary power to be exercised in a reasonable and lawful manner for the advancement of the interests of the medical profession and the public generally. When its action runs counter to the public policy of the state and the true interests of justice, such action can and will be stricken down. In explaining its interference with the activities of a private society, the court said:

> "Public policy is the dominant factor in the moulding and remoulding of common law principles to the high end that they may soundly serve the public welfare and the true interests of justice."

The Falcone decision was relied on by the same court when it reviewed the denial of an osteopath's hospital staff privileges in Greisman v. Newcomb Hospital, 40 N.J. 389, 192 A.2d 817 (1963). The hospital claimed that because it was a private institution it might in its discretion exclude doctors from its staff, and that no legal ground existed for judicial interference with the hospital's refusal to consider the plaintiff's application.

21

The court pointed out that in the development of the law, activities much less public in nature than those of a hospital had been subjected to judicial supervision and control to the extent necessary to satisfy the felt need of the times. Judges have often applied the common law to regulate private businesses for the public good, e.g., the duty of serving all comers on reasonable terms imposed by the common law on innkeepers, carriers, farriers and the like. Though hospital officials are vested with large amounts of managing discretion, they must never lose sight of the fact that hospitals are operated not for private ends, but for the benefit of the public. The Supreme Court of Hawaii recently echoed this view of the public nature of a private hospital in granting judicial review of the denial of private hospital staff privileges. Silver v. Castle Memorial Hospital, 497 P.2d 564 (Hawaii 1972).

Another case granting judicial review of the denial of hospital staff privileges was Davidson v. Youngstown Hospital, 19 Ohio App.2d 246, 250 N.E.2d 892 (1969). The court said that a private, non-profit hospital that receives part of its funds from public sources and receives tax benefits because of its non-profit and non-private aspects may be private in the sense that it is nongovernmental, but is in no position to claim immunity from public supervision and control because of its private nature. Its power to pass on staff memberships is a

22

fiduciary power, to be exercised reasonably and for the public good.

Courts which are willing to supervise the activity of private hospitals in the area of staff admissions should find no difficulty in extending the scope of their review to the reasonableness of the standards and procedures used by hospital committees to make life and death decisions affecting members of the public. The need for establishing criteria for assignment of hemodialysis and transplant priorities would seem to be just the sort of felt need of the times to which the Greisman court referred, and the courts should not shrink from the challenge of meeting that need.

CONCLUSION

The courts, as guardians of the right to life which our Constitution guarantees us, should be free to set up the guidelines by which this basic human right shall be administered, even in the absence of specific statutory authority to do so. The state and federal governments may not deprive anyone of life without due process of law. When the power to deny life is being exercised by a committee of private citizens, justice demands that such a committee be required to observe the same standards to which governments are restricted.

23

The writ of prohibition should be denied, and Judge Jones should be allowed to proceed with his determination of the merits. The court should supervise the action of the hospital allocation committee to ensure that all potential dialysis and transplant recipients receive an evidentiary hearing before impartial decision makers regarding their qualifications and need for treatment, that priorities are based on the evidence produced at such hearing, and that the hearing is conducted with all the procedural safeguards guaranteed by the fifth and fourteenth amendments to the Constitution of the United States, including notice, confrontation and cross-examination of witnesses, and an opportunity to produce witnesses and evidence. To ensure that potential recipients are guaranteed equal protection of the law, the criteria on which selection is made should have a rational basis of overriding societal interest in the survival of some individuals in preference to others. The fairest selection would be by lot.

Respectfully submitted,
BARBARA K. BARDEN
Cincinnati, Ohio
Counsel for Respondent
Robert W. Cleveland

24

D.
SAMPLE STUDENT ORAL ARGUMENTS

The following is a transcript of oral arguments made by first year law students in the hypothetical case of *Ann Austin as Executrix of Bill Austin v. F. & C. Railroad Co.*, pending before the hypothetical United States Court of Appeals for the Fourteenth Circuit. The lawsuit is a diversity of citizenship case. Therefore the United States Court of Appeals will apply the law of the State of Kanawha, a hypothetical state of the United States.

* * *

COUNSEL FOR APPELLANT

PRESIDING JUDGE: State the case for the appellant, please.

COUNSEL: May it please the Court. My name is Victoria Daiker. I am counsel for appellant, Ann Austin. This cause originated as a wrongful death action against F. & C. Railroad Co. in the United States District Court for the Northern District of Kanawha, Western Division. Summary judgment in favor of defendant was entered by that court. We come here to ask that summary judgment be set aside, primarily because questions of fact exist in this case that require determination by a jury.

Certain facts are settled. On the morning of July 19, 1971, a misty, drizzly morning about one half hour after daybreak, Bill Austin, the decedent, attempted to drive southward on Pike Street up the grade and across the double set of railroad tracks at the Pike Street crossing in Southwood, Kanawha, but an F. & C. train, traveling westward at about 45 miles per hour, struck Austin's car and killed Austin and his passenger, Charles Dawson.

Issues of negligence are not ordinarily accepted for summary judgment; rather, the function of summary adjudication, as the court said in a 1956 decision, is solely to determine whether there is a question of fact to be tried. In a 1965 interpretation of Rule 56(c) of the Federal Rules of Civil Procedure, this Court again held that summary judgment should only be granted when the moving party can establish the utter nonexistence of any genuine issue of fact. Another 13th Circuit case, using Kanawha law, went still further to say that, even though basic facts are not in dispute, parties in good faith may, nevertheless, disagree about inferences, and those inferences, too, should be resolved by a jury. This rule has also been applied by this court in railroad-car collision cases. Central to our appeal today are the contentions that this case, Austin v. F. & C. Railroad Co., is riddled with questions of fact, that those questions of fact relate directly to two issues: Number one, was F. & C. guilty of wanton misconduct; Number two, were the actions of Austin, appellant's decedent, negligent so as to bar recovery by his widow and children?

The first issue, the railroad's wanton misconduct, is dependent upon exactly how we define the railroad's role in Bill Austin's death. We submit that enough evidence exists for reasonable minds to find, number one, that the Pike Street crossing was extrahazardous, and, number two, that F. & C. failed to provide an adequate warning system for this particular crossing.

JUDGE NO. 1: Mrs. Daiker, can you tell us why it was extrahazardous, please?

COUNSEL: Why it was extrahazardous. In Kanawha, the scope of the railroad's duty to warn motorists crossing its tracks depends on the sign. The minimum warning for a public crossing is a crossbuck sign, the traditional sort of sign. The F. & C. crossing had such a sign, but even where a railroad has fulfilled this minimum requirement of the Kanawha legislature, a jury can find it negligent in failing to provide more protection for a particular crossing. The Pike Street crossing was extrahazardous, I think. The Southwood City Commission thought so, too. It had requested additional signals for the crossing because the accident record indicated what the Commisson described as an emergency situation. For three years, the Commission had made formal requests for automatic gates and signals that are tripped by the approach of a train on the tracks, and it would prevent automobiles from moving into a train's path.

The crossbuck signs can indicate that the tracks are there. What the sort of automatic gates and signals do is indicate that there is a train on the track. This is what the Pike Street crossing didn't have. Austin and Dawson were the 4th and 5th fatalities recorded by the police at Pike Street since 1948. This is the 15th accident, and the 11th accident involving the collision of a railroad train and a car at that crossing.

JUDGE NO. 1: Mrs. Daiker, excuse me — doesn't the motorist have an obligation, though, as far as crossing the tracks?

COUNSEL: The motorist has an obligation to look and listen before he moves onto the track, but that obligation isn't absolute. There are many factual questions posed by this particular case, primarily because the driver and his passenger are both dead and can give us no information. The only witnesses are the three crewmen of the train, and what they say about what Austin could see, why he moved onto the tracks, why he didn't get off the tracks, why he didn't get out of the car, has to be speculative. They can only guess, really. It is important not only what he could see, did he see the train?

Lawson, the fireman, thinks that he did, thinks that he saw the train, but Sharp, who was the pilot engineer, isn't so sure about that, doesn't think so, according to his testimony.

Did the car stall? Is that why Austin continued across the tracks? Lawson thinks the car stalled — he's sure of it — thinks he saw Austin moving the key, but Sharp — who had almost the same position of observation — isn't sure about that at all. He thinks that it's even possible that Austin was looking in the other direction, toward the other train coming from the opposite direction, that he could, perhaps, see and hear. Where the question is plaintiff's contributory negligence, a jury must measure the relationship of his actions with his injury. Recent cases in Kanawha — all 13th Circuit cases in the past 10 years — indicate that questions of contributory negligence are for the jury to decide. We think that the record here is not adequate for the court to come to a conclusion to render a summary judgment on this issue. There are the sort of questions of fact: what did Bill see, why did he move onto the track, that a jury should decide.

PRESIDING JUDGE: Mrs. Daiker, I am aware that Ecksmobile Corporation is not a party to this appeal, but I am also aware that the record indicates that there was some claim made against Ecksmobile as to a defect in the car. Do you attach any significance relative to this appeal to the claim that there was a defect in the car in relation to the starting?

COUNSEL: Well, I think that whether there was a defect in the car was not, does not make any difference about the obligation of the railroad. First of all to —

PRESIDING JUDGE: Pardon me, how about the negligence of the decedent?

COUNSEL: About the negligence of the decedent, well, the only thing it seems to me that the defect in the car might have caused was the stalling of the car with respect to the second set of tracks. It isn't that the car stopped on the tracks. This is not the basis of any question about decedent's negligence. It is why he went on to the tracks to begin with, why he went on to the second set of tracks, so it really doesn't seem to be important. It might be useful for us to know exactly what happened and why the car stopped. Lawson said it sort of leaped forward. I am curious to know what went wrong with the car, but I don't think it really makes any difference in determining the negligence of the decedent or determining the railroad's wanton misconduct.

PRESIDING JUDGE: In view of the fact that there has been no resolution of that claim against Ecksmobile, concerning the automobile, might it not be a good idea to send this back to be tried with that claim in order to determine precisely what, if any, part in this Ecksmobile played?

COUNSEL: It might be useful to try the two causes together. I think it would be useful to try the F. & C. cause even by itself because I do think there is a question here of F. & C.'s misconduct, whatever was wrong with the car, or was not wrong with the car. F. & C.'s crew saw Austin on the tracks, he was discovered by them. They saw him on the tracks, and, at the time did not even move into emergency.

They were moving toward the crossing at 50 miles an hour. There is a statute, excuse me, an ordinance, in Southwood that calls for a much, much less speed. Even if that ordinance was not ordinarily enforced, it constitutes concern by the city as does their request about the various crossings within the city. The railroad negligently moved very fast through the city and the crew did not try to immediately move into emergency when they saw Austin. Frankly, there is a —

JUDGE NO. 1: Excuse me — did the crew give any kind of warning to the decedent at all?

COUNSEL: The crew says — the three members of the crew say that it sounded the whistle and bell — that is the minimum requirement when moving toward a crossing in Kanawha — sounding the whistle and bell. They had been doing that, anyway, supposedly, as they came toward the crossing. When they saw the car, they sounded the whistle and bell.

I think most of us can recognize from a practical point of view that if you are stuck on a track, sounding the whistle and bell is not going to help you. I think most of us can recognize that if there are trains coming from both directions at you, and they are both, perhaps, sounding the whistle and bell, it is difficult to tell which one of them is closer, how much time you have, how far away the object that is coming toward you is. I think there are many issues of fact.

JUDGE NO. 1: Let me ask you this, then should he even have been on the track, or was there enough visibility that he could have seen both trains from before the tracks and when did he first stop to look?

COUNSEL: I think that this is another question, whether he stopped; one and only one crewman, really, says that he does not think that the car stopped first. One way or the other, the Kanawha cases have indicated that the important thing for a car to do when it's stopped at a crossing is look and listen — to stop where it's looking and listening will be effective. It's possible, considering the history of this particular crossing, that the only place — the crossing was on a grade — you had to go up an incline and down an incline to get to it — there were bushes on the side and a ditch — it is quite possible that the only place he could truly see anything was up on the first set of tracks, and that he actually moved up on to the tracks in order to see, and that he, perhaps, — again all these things are conjecture, we do not know — there is nothing that really tells us this in the record, and we don't have Austin to tell us. That's one of the reasons we think this should be decided by a jury. But, anyway, perhaps he moved upon the tracks to see, and then was surprised to discover a train coming toward him.

JUDGE NO. 2: Did he know the crossing? Is there any evidence in the record?

COUNSEL: Yes, he did travel across the crossing before. I don't think that the question is whether Bill Austin knew the tracks were there. The question is whether there was a train on the tracks and at this point, there was. If there had been automatic signals, he would have been warned of this in time, and, in fact, if there'd been a gate, he wouldn't have been able to move onto the tracks while a train was close enough to be dangerous. That was the reason that the City Commission wanted gates and automatic signals for these tracks.

From the time the City Commission asked for the gates and signals, it took approximately three years for the railroad to agree to set them up, and, even after they agreed — the final agreement was the August before Austin's accident — it took 11 months for the railroad to get the men out to begin the construction of the gates and signals. During that time, it does not seem, at least from what the crewmen tell us, that they gave any indication that they should be especially cautious near this crossing, that they should go slow, that they should do anything that was different. They let them go along with business as usual, in spite of the dangerousness of the crossing. For this reason, among others, we think that the railroad was guilty of wanton misconduct with regard to all motorists at this crossing, and particularly with regard to Bill Austin in this particular situation.

PRESIDING JUDGE: You have two minutes.

COUNSEL: To sum up. Thank you. Summary judgment should be reserved for those cases with no questions of fact. Austin v. F. & C. Railroad Co. is not such a case. Only a jury can decide, number 1) if the crossing was extrahazardous, as we have said; 2) whether, because of this, the railroad had a duty to provide more than the minimum crossbuck signs; 3) whether the speed of the train was wantonly reckless and a danger to motorists, especially in the light of the history of that crossing; 4) whether the trainmen violated their last clear chance duty by not going into emergency when they saw Bill on the track; 5) whether Bill's actions contributed materially to his death.

There is ample case law to support our contention that the combination of high speed and an extrahazardous crossing is evidence of wanton misconduct on the part of the railroad. More importantly, there is much recent case law to support our other contention that questions about the misconduct of this defendant and about the negligence of the decedent should be submitted to a jury. For these compelling reasons, we ask that the court set aside the summary judgment and leave the case of Austin v. F. & C. Railroad Co. to the jury, where it rightly belongs.

PRESIDING JUDGE: Thank you, Mrs. Daiker. Mr. Heldman, will you state the case for the appellee, please?

COUNSEL FOR APPELLEE

COUNSEL: May it please the court. My name is Paul Heldman and I represent the appellee, F. & C. Railroad Co. My opponent has given you all the relevant facts of this case, and there are no material disputes about these facts.

First, it was Mr. Austin's negligence which caused his death on July 19, 1971. The weather that morning, as the record shows, was drizzly, but the weather was not adversely affected. There were no obstructions at the crossing, as the testimony of the police officer, Officer Kirkland, shows, and the photos taken at the scene by George Salude show, and it is interesting to note that, even if there were obstructions, Kanawha case law requires a greater degree of care of motorists approaching the crossing. Mr. Austin drove up to the crossing when the train was 850 to 900 feet from the crossing, and rather than stop before the crossing — he is not obligated to do that — he chose to halt on the first set of tracks, the north tracks. Nevertheless, he was safely out of the train's path.

Mrs. Daiker says that there's a dispute as to whether he looked at the train, whether he saw the train coming. But he has a duty to look, and if we interpret the facts in their best light for the plaintiff, as we must, he did look and he did listen, so Kanawha case law then asks the question: what did the motorist see, or what should he have seen and what should he have heard? Here, there is ample evidence to show that he must have seen the massive locomotive, and he must have seen its bright headlight. He must have heard the thunder of that locomotive and the bell and the loud horn which was testified by all three crewmen as operating.

Mr. Austin's response to this ample warning was to go ahead anyway to attempt to cross the tracks, and it was that ill-considered response that resulted in his tragic death.

PRESIDING JUDGE: Now, Mr. Heldman, it seems to me that everything you say may be correct, but don't we have this element of the failure, or the possible failure, of the Ecksmobile car to operate?

COUNSEL: It is possible that the car stalled on the second set of tracks for one of two reasons, either a human failure or a mechanical failure. In either case, it was not the conduct of F. & C. which caused the accident.

PRESIDING JUDGE: I understand, but it may be that it would have been wise to let a jury hear all this evidence and decide whether —

COUNSEL: Yes, Your Honor, that matter will be litigated, as the record shows, between the Ecksmobile Corporation and Mrs. Austin.

PRESIDING JUDGE: But F. & C. has a judgment now that says that the deceased was negligent. It could well be that after the Ecksmobile Corporation case is decided, it may be found that this man was not negligent after all, that he did all he could.

COUNSEL: That is possible, Your Honor. If that is true, however, it is the Ecksmobile Corporation's fault which caused the accident, and no conduct of the F. & C. Therefore, to litigate this case with F. & C. as a party is pointless.

PRESIDING JUDGE: Mr. Heldman, there is no holding that F. & C., in fact, was not negligent. There is a holding here that F. & C., in fact, was not wantonly and willfully negligent, but the lower degree has not been resolved, which prompts me to suggest that we send this case back, try them both together, and then see whether, after all the facts are out, F. & C. might still prevail.

COUNSEL: From F. & C.'s point of view, the worst that could possibly happen in such a trial is: 1) a finding that F. & C. is negligent, which I will show they were not; and 2) that the Ecksmobile Corporation was negligent because it is obvious now from the record that either the Ecksmobile Corporation or Mr. Austin was negligent in causing the accident. In either case, F. & C. will not be liable for the death of Mr. Austin. Therefore, it is pointless to litigate the point.

It was Mr. Austin's fault. It was Mr. Austin's response to the warning of the train to cross the tracks, and, under Kanawha case law, the case of Lurch v. K. & O. Railroad, this failure to respond to the imminent warning of a train is contributory negligence as a matter of law. I might point out that whether it was mechanical failure or human failure, he never should have started in the first place. It was this mistake in judgment which caused the accident.

PRESIDING JUDGE: Are you suggesting he was racing the train? Is that what you say the evidence shows?

COUNSEL: No, the evidence shows that he made a mistake in judgment, that he was safely out of the train's path before he started to cross the tracks. Had he not started across the tracks, he never would have been killed. He did cross the tracks, and there was some dispute about whether he might have made it if the car had not stopped, or whether he would have been hit, anyway.

JUDGE NO. 2: Mr. Heldman, wasn't there some evidence about a train coming from the other direction?

COUNSEL: There was a train coming from the other direction, and its headlight was visible to the crewmen in F. & C.'s train. However, that train was too far away. That train was two miles away and no reason in the world for him to have any concern about that train. That train was proceeding at a maximum speed of 30 miles per hour, and we know from the record that there was an area west of Pike Street where such speed was required, so that it would have taken at least four minutes for that train to reach the Pike Street crossing. Mr. Austin was in no danger from that train.

Since Mr. Austin was not in danger, the appellant must show that F. & C. exhibited willful and wanton misconduct. The Kanawha Supreme Court defines such conduct as that which manifests a disposition to perversity. This phrase is indicative of the stringent standards that this state requires to show such conduct.

Nothing in the F. & C.'s conduct could be characterized in this way. Appellant contends the speed of its train manifested willful or wanton misconduct. There was a 6 mile per hour ordinance, which was passed in 1910 by the City of Southwood. That ordinance was not applicable.

PRESIDING JUDGE: Why?

COUNSEL: First, because, as Kanawha case law shows, it was unreasonable and it was arbitrary. There have been cases that hold that 12 miles per hour ordinances in urban areas are unreasonable and, therefore, invalid.

PRESIDING JUDGE: But we have no facts here on which to base this unreasonableness judgment.

COUNSEL: This was an urban-rural-residential area. But, more important, I think the record shows in seven places that the city had notice of the speed at which trains used this crossing, which was anywhere from 30 to 63 miles per hour. Indeed, there is one report in the record in which it says plainly that the train was traveling at 63 miles per hour. No citations were issued.

F. & C., or any railroad, was never warned, never cited for the speed of its trains. The city had full notice, and I think the only logical inference from that is that the city knew that its speeds were reasonable.

Appellant also contends that the maintenance of the crossing — the condition of the crossing, itself, manifested willful and wanton misconduct. Kanawha law requires first, that a railroad company place a large crossbuck sign at each crossing, which F. & C. did, and, beyond that, nothing more is required unless the Utilities Commission of Kanawha declares the crossing dangerous, which, of course, did not happen here. There is correspondence in the record between the City of Southwood and F. & C., which shows an agreement between the city and the railroad, whereby the city would pay 90% of the new equipment to be erected at the crossing. This equipment was in the process of being constructed at the time of the accident. F. & C. was in full compliance with the agreement and was working on schedule. There have been instances in which a crossing might be so extraordinarily dangerous that extra care or extra activity is required of the railroad. It is not the case here. In those cases where an extrastatutory duty has been found, the plaintiff must show something especially deceptive, something to separate that crossing from other crossings. Such is not the case here.

An example of an extra dangerous crossing occurred in the Clear v. B. & G. case. There, an accident occurred at night, and the crossing was located in such a way that it was next to an interstate highway, so that when a motorist approached at night, it would be impossible to distinguish the headlights of a train from the headlights of the cars. There was something deceptive about that crossing, something such that a motorist exercising reasonable care might have been unable to detect a train, and, therefore, unable to avoid an accident.

JUDGE NO. 1: Excuse me, counsellor, what is the safety record of this particular crossing in this case?

COUNSEL: There were accidents which occurred at the crossing. I think there were something like 14 accidents since 1948. Several of those accidents were, as much as we can tell, caused by drunken driving, several of those accidents had nothing whatsoever to do with the train, but I think, as Judge Jones, the trial judge, noted, those accidents standing alone should not be considered, because there is no evidence that this is in any way unusual for any railroad crossing. And again, standing alone, those accidents showed nothing.

JUDGE NO. 2: Something you said earlier troubles me. To say that the speed is not unreasonable because the city has never cited the railroad before for its speed, do you contend that because the city has never imposed a criminal liability against the railroad a civil liability will not be made to stick?

COUNSEL: No, no I don't mean to say that at all. We don't know exactly what the crossing looks like. We have a good idea, but I'm showing that we can glean from the record that the speed was reasonable because, first, looking at the photographs, there were no obstructions and from the few remarks made, we know that it was a residential rural area, and because the city has had full notice for 20 years that trains were using these crossings at these rates of speeds. In fact, the speed of F. & C.'s train was slightly less than some of the speeds used by other trains at the crossing, and the city, nevertheless, never cited any of these railroads. The city knew about the speeds and they must have known that the speeds were reasonable.

PRESIDING JUDGE: Mr. Heldman, all of these things that you tell me are very persuasive on the subject of speed. I wasn't convinced when you covered the subject of speed a few minutes ago, and I still am not convinced that these things should not go to a jury, rather than to a judge. The jury might decide just like the judge did, but, then again, the jury might not. Can you address yourself to the question of whether a judge should be resolving this on a motion for summary judgment, or whether a jury should resolve it in the normal way?

COUNSEL: Yes, Your Honor. There are no disputes about the facts, which appear in the record. As a matter of law, the Lurch case shows the duty of the motorist, and there is another case, Pickle, which said that speed, of itself, is not negligence, that, if a train has issued its required warnings, as was the case here, or, if there are no obstructions so that the motorist can see the train, which is also the case here, then in either case, speed is not a question for the jury. This was a Kanawha Supreme Court case, and, I'm sorry, I don't have the cite with me here.

PRESIDING JUDGE: It's undoubtedly in your brief.

COUNSEL: Yes, it is.

PRESIDING JUDGE: Mr. Heldman, you have one and one-half minutes to finish.

COUNSEL: All right, I will try to sum up. First, there was no dispute about any material fact. Second, Mr. Austin's negligence caused the accident. He pulled onto the track when he knew full well that a train was approaching and, nevertheless, decided to cross the tracks. Third, there was no conduct of F. & C. which could be characterized as willful or wanton. The record shows that the train was traveling at a reasonable speed, and that the crossing was unobstructed. Thank you.

PRESIDING JUDGE: Thank you.

E.
APPENDIX OF ABBREVIATIONS

EXPLANATIONS OF ABBREVIATIONS AND REFERENCES TO REPORTS OF CASES AND OTHER LEGAL PUBLICATIONS

There are a great many sources of legal abbreviations, one of the most commonly used of which is *A Uniform System of Citation,* fourteenth edition, 1986, published by the Harvard Law Review Association. *A Uniform System of Citation* has received wide acceptance, but many publishers refuse to observe its rules, and instead use their own abbreviations. Such publishers often decipher their abbreviations in a legend near the front of their books. Many courts prescribe their own forms of abbreviation for use in briefs and opinions in those courts. Writers have used various abbreviations over the years. The abbreviations established by *A Uniform System of Citation* have changed in the various editions. These facts cause some abbreviations for the same reference to vary from one publication to another. Those variations are, to a significant extent, included herein.

A. Atlantic Reporter; Association.

A.2d Atlantic Reporter, Second Series.

A. & E. Adolphus and Ellis, Queen's Bench, Eng., 1834-41.

A. & E. (N.S.). Adolphus and Ellis, Queen's Bench, Eng., New Series, 1841-52.

A. & E. Cas. American and English Annotated Cases, 1906-12.

A. & E. Ency. American and English Encyclopedia of Law.

A.B.A. American Bar Association.

A.B.A.J. American Bar Association Journal.

A.B.A. Rep. American Bar Association Reports.

A.B.F. American Bar Foundation.

A.C. Court of Appeal in Chancery, Eng.; Appellate Court; Appeal Court, Chancery.

A.D., A.D.2d New York Appellate Division Reports, since 1896.

ADEA Age Discrimination in Employment Act of 1967.

A.F.T.R. American Federal Tax Reports.

A.F. JAG L. Rev. Air Force JAG Law Review.

A.G. Attorney General.

A.K. Marsh. A.K. Marshall, Kentucky Court of Appeals, 1817-21.

A.L.I. American Law Institute.

ALJ or **A.L.J.** Administrative Law Judge.

A.L.R. American Law Reports [First Series].

A.L.R.2d American Law Reports, Second Series.

A.L.R.3d American Law Reports, Third Series.

A.L.R.4th American Law Reports, Fourth Series.

A.L.R. Fed. American Law Reports, Federal.

A.M.A. American Medical Association.

A.M.C. American Maritime Cases.

APA Administrative Procedures Act.

A.T.L. L.J. Journal of the American Trial Lawyers Association.

Abb. Adm. Abbott's Admiralty, U.S. District Court, Southern District of New York, 1847-50.

Abb. App. or **Abb. App. Dec.** Abbott's New York Court of Appeals Decisions.

Abb. Dec. Abbott's Decisions, New York.

Abb. N.C. Abbott's New Cases, Practice, New York, 1874-1894.

Abb. Pr. Abbott's Practice Cases, New York Courts, 1854-1865.

Abb. Pr. (N.S.) Abbott's Practice Cases, New Series, New York, 1863-1875.

Abb. U.S. Abbott, U.S. Circuit and District Courts, 1865-1871.

Abr. Abridged; Abridgment.

Abr. Ca. Eq. Abridgment of Cases in Equity, Eng.

Act. Acton's Prize Causes, Privy Council, Eng., 1809-1811.

Act. Can. Acta Cancellaria, Reports and Entries in Chancery, Monro, Eng., 1545-1625.

Act. Reg. Acta Regia. Royal Acts.

Ad. Administrative.

Ad. & E. See A. & E.

Ad. L. Bull. Administrative Law Bulletin.

Ad. L. Rev. Administrative Law Review.

Add. Addison, Pennsylvania County Courts and Court of Errors, 1791-1799.

Add. E.R. Addams' Ecclesiastical Reports, Eng., 1822-1826.

Adm. Admiralty.

Adv. Adversus; Against. Used to cross-index; indicates that the names of the parties in a case have been reversed.

Aik. Aikens, Vermont Supreme Court, 1825-1827.

Al. Aleyn, King's Bench, Eng., 1646-1648.

Ala. Alabama Reports, Supreme Court, 1840-1976. For earlier reports, see Minor, Stew., Stew. & P., and Port.

Ala. App. Alabama Appellate Court Reports, 1910-1976.

Ala. L.J. Alabama Law Journal, Montgomery, 1882-1884.

Ala. L. Rev. Alabama Law Review.

Ala. Sel. Cas. Alabama Select Cases, Supreme Court, 1861-1863.

Alas. Alaska Reports, 1900-1959 (nonstandard).

Alb. L.J. Albany Law Journal, Albany, N.Y., since 1870.

Alb. L. Rev. Albany Law Review.

Alc. & N. Alcock and Napier, King's Bench, Ireland, 1831-1833.

Alc. R. Cas. Alcock's Registry Cases, Ireland, 1832-1837.

Ald. or Alden Alden's Condensed Reports, Pennsylvania.

Allen. Massachusetts Supreme Court, vols. 83-96, 1861-1867.

Allen (N.B.) New Brunswick Reports, 1848-1866.

Am. American.

Am. & E. Corp. Cas. American and English Corporation Cases (excepting Railway), Northport, N.Y.

Am. & E. Ry. Cas. American and English Railway Cases, Northport, N.Y.

Am. & Eng. Ann. Cas. American and English Annotated Cases, 1906-1912.

Am. Bankr. L.J. American Bankruptcy Law Journal.

Am Bankr. R. American Bankruptcy Reports.

Am. Bankr. Rev. American Bankruptcy Review.

Am. B.A. American Bar Association Annual Reports.

Am. Cor. Cas. American Corporation Cases, Chicago.

Am. Cr. Rep. American Criminal Reports, Chicago.

Am. Dec. American Decisions, from earliest period to 1869, San Francisco.

Am. Fed. Tax R. American Federal Tax Reports.

Am. Hist. Rev. American Historical Review.

Am. J. Comp. L. American Journal of Comparative Law.

Am. J. Int'l L. American Journal of International Law.

Am. J. Legal Hist. American Journal of Legal History.

Am. Jur. American Jurist, Boston, 1829-1843; American Jurisprudence, [First Edition].

Am. Jur. 2d. American Jurisprudence, Second Edition.

Am. Lab. Leg. Rev. American Labor Legislation Review.

Am. L.C. American Leading Cases, Hare and Wallace.

Am. L.J. American Law Journal, Philadelphia, 1808-1810, 1813-1814, 1817; New Series, 1848-1852. Another periodical of same name, Columbus, Ohio, 1884-1885.

Am. L. Mag. American Law Magazine, Philadelphia, 1843-1846.

Am. L. Rec. American Law Record, Cincinnati.

Am. L. Reg. American Law Register, Philadelphia.

Am. L. Reg. (N.S.) American Law Register, New Series.

Am. L. Rev. American Law Review.

Am. L.T. American Law Times, Washington, 1868-1877.

Am. Prob. Rep. American Probate Reports, New York.

Am. R. or **Am. Rep.** American Reports, Albany, N.Y., 1871-1888.

Am. Ry. Cas. American Railway Cases, Boston, 1854-1856.

Am. Ry. Rep. American Railway Reports, New York, 1873-1881.

Am. St. R. or **Am. St. Rep.** American State Reports, San Francisco, 1888-1911.

Am. Tr. M. Cas. American Trade Mark Cases, Cincinnati, from earliest period to 1871.

Am. U.L. Rev. American University Law Review.

Amb. Ambler Chancery, Eng., 1737-1783 (some earlier cases in an appendix).

Ames, Cas. B. & N. Ames, Cases on Bills and Notes, Boston, 1881.

And. Anderson Common Pleas, Eng., 1534-1604.

Andr. Andrews, King's Bench, Eng., 1737-1738.

Ann. Annual; Annaly, King's Bench, Eng., 1733-1738. See Lee, t.H.

Annals Annals of the American Academy of Political and Social Science.

Anno. Cas. American and English Annotated Cases.

Annot. Annotation.

Anst. Anstruther, Exchequer, Eng., 1792-1797.

Anth. Anthon, New York Supreme Court, Nisi Prius Cases, 1807-1851.

Ap. C. Appeal Cases, Law Reports.

App. Appendix; Appleton (Me.); Appellate Reports.

App. D.C. Appeal Cases, District of Columbia, 1893-1941.

App. Div., App. Div. 2d, Appellate Division, New York Supreme Court (nonstandard).

App. & S. Appleton and Shepley (Me.).

Arb. J. Arbitration Journal.

Arch. Court of Arches, England.

Arch. P.L. Cas. Archbold, Poor Law Cases, England, 1842-1858.

Ariz. Arizona Reports, Supreme Court, since 1866.

Ariz. App. Arizona Appeals Reports, 1965-1976.

Ariz. L. Rev. Arizona Law Review.

Ariz. St. L.J. Arizona State Law Journal.

Ark. Arkansas Reports, Supreme Court, since 1837.

Ark. L. Rev. Arkansas Law Review.

Arkley Judiciary Reports, Scotland, 1846-1848.

Arm. M. & O. Armstrong, Macartney and Ogle, Nisi Prius, Ireland, 1840-1842.

Arn. Arnold, Common Pleas, Eng., 1838-1839.

Arn. & H. Arnold and Hodges, Queen's Bench, Eng., 1840-1841.

Ash. Ashmead, Pennsylvania, various courts, 1808-1841.

Asp. Aspects; Aspinall, Maritime Cases, New Series, Eng., 1870-1878.

Ass. Liber Assisarum, Book of Assizes, Queen's Bench, Eng., 1327-1377.

Ass'n Association.

Atk. Atkyns, Chancery, Eng., 1736-1754.

Atl. Atlantic Reporter.

Att'y Gen. Attorney General.

Austr. L.J. Australian Law Journal.

Av. Cas. Aviation Cases.

B. Bar; Bench; Boston.

B. & A. Barnewall and Alderson, King's Bench, Eng., 1817-1822.

B. & Ad. Barnewall and Adolphus, King's Bench, Eng., 1830-1834.

B. & B. Broderip and Bingham, Common Pleas, Eng., 1819-1822.

B. & C. Barnewall and Cresswell, King's Bench, Eng., 1822-1830.

B. & L. Browning and Lushington, Admiralty, Eng., 1863-1866.

B. & P. Bosanquet and Puller, Common Pleas, Eng., 1796-1804.

B. & P. (N.R.) Bosanquet and Puller, New Reports, Common Pleas, Eng., 1804-1807.

B. & S. Best and Smith, Queen's Bench, Eng.

B.C. Bail Court, Eng.

B.C.C. Bail Court Cases, Eng., Lowndes and Maxwell, 1852-1854.

B.C. Ind. & Com. L. Rev. Boston College Industrial and Commercial Law Review.

B.C.L. Rev. Boston College Law Review.

B.C.R. Bail Court Reports, Eng., Saunders and Cole, 1842-1848.

B.J. Bar Journal.

B. Mon. Ben Monroe, Kentucky Court of Appeals, 1840-1857.

B.R. Bancus Regis; King's Bench, Eng., Bankruptcy Reports; Bankruptcy Reporter, since 1979 (nonstandard).

B.R. or **B. Reg.** National Bankruptcy Register, United States Courts, 1867-1879.

B.T.A. Board of Tax Appeals Reports (U.S.) 1924-1942.

B.U.L. Rev. Boston University Law Review.

B.Y.U. L. Rev. Brigham Young University Law Review.

Bac. Abr. Bacon's Abridgment.

Bail. Bailey, South Carolina, Superior Courts and Court of Appeals, 1828-1832.

Bail. Eq. Bailey, South Carolina, Equity Cases, 1830-1831.

Bald. or **Bald. C.C.** Baldwin, U.S. Circuit Court, Third Circuit, 1827-1833.

Ball & B. Ball and Beatty, Chancery, Ireland, 1807-1814.

Balt. L.T. Baltimore Law Transcript, 1868-1870.

Ban. & A. Banning and Arden, Patent Cases, U.S. Courts.

Bank. Bankruptcy (nonstandard).

Bank. C.T. Rep. Bankrupt Court Reporter, New York, 1867-1868.

Bank. & Ins. Bankruptcy and Insolvency Reports, English Courts, 1853-1855.

Bankr. Bankruptcy Reporter, since 1979; Bankruptcy.

Bar. & Arn. Barron and Arnold, Election Cases, Eng., 1843-1846.

Bar. & Aust. Barron and Austin, Election Cases, Eng., 1842.

Barb. Barbour, New York Supreme Court, 1847-1877.

Barb. Ch. Barbour, New York Chancery Cases, 1845-1848.

Barn. Barnardiston, King's Bench, Eng., 1726-1734.

Barn. Ch. Barnardiston, Chancery, Eng., 1740-1741.

Barnes Notes of Cases, Common Pleas, Eng., 1732-1756.

Barr Pennsylvania State Reports, vols. 1-10.

Batty King's Bench, Ireland, 1825-1826.

Baxt. Baxter, Tennessee Supreme Court, 1871-1878.

Bay South Carolina Superior Courts, 1783-1804.

Beasl. Beasley, New Jersey Equity, vols. 12-13, 1858-1861.

Beat. Beatty, Chancery, Ireland, 1813-1830.

Beav. Beavan, Roll's Court, Eng., 1838-1866.

Beav. & W. Beavan and Walford, Parliamentary Cases, 1846.

Bee Admiralty Cases, U.S. District Courts, 1792-1808. (An appendix contains some earlier decisions. See Hopk. Adm.)

Bel. Bellewe, King's Bench, Eng., 1378-1400.

Bell. App. Scotch Appeals, House of Lords, 1842-1850.

Bell, C.C. Crown Cases, Reserved, Eng., 1858-1860.

Bell, Com. Commentaries on the Laws of Scotland.

Bell, Dec. Decisions, Court of Session, Scotland, 1794-1795.

Bell, Dict. of Dec. Bell's Dictionary of Decisions, Court of Sessions, Scotland, 1808-1833.

Bell, Sess. Cas. Bell, Session Cases, Scotland, 1790-1792.

Belt Supplement to Vesey, Sr., Chancery, Eng., 1845-1855.

Ben. Benedict, U.S. District Court, Southern Dist. of N.Y., 1865-1879.

Ben. Benloes, Bendloes, or Benlowes. Different spellings appear in different places in the same volume, called "New Benloes." King's Bench, Eng., 1530-1627.

Bench and Bar Law Periodical, Chicago, 1869-1874.

Benl. & D. Benloe or Bendloe, called "Old Benloe," and Dalison, separate reports bound together. Com. Pleas, Eng., 1512-1579. Four cases, 1357-1512, inserted.

Benn. Bennett (California).

Benn. F.I. Cas. Bennett, Fire Insurance Cases, New York, 1872-1877.

Benn. & H. Bennett and Heard, Leading Criminal Cases, Boston, 1869.

Bent. Bentley, Chancery, Ireland, 1831.

Bert. Berton, New Brunswick, 1835-1839.

Best & S. See B. & S.

Bibb Kentucky Court of Appeals, 1808-1817.

Big. Cas. Bigelow's Cases, King's Bench, Eng., 1066-1195.

Big. Cas. B. & N. Bigelow's Leading Cases, Bills and Notes, Boston, 1880.

Big. Cas. Torts Bigelow's Cases in Torts, Boston, 1875.

Big. L. & A. Ins. Cas. Bigelow's Life and Accident Insurance Cases, New York, 1872-1877.

Bing. Bingham, Common Pleas, Eng., 1822-1834.

Bing, N.C. Bingham, New Cases, Common Pleas, Eng., 1834-1840.

Binn. Binney, Pennsylvania Supreme Court, 1799-1814.

Biss. Bissell, U.S. Circuit Court, Seventh Circuit, 1851-1883.

Bitt. Pr. Cas. Bittleston, Practice Cases, Eng., 1875-1876.

Bitt. W. & P. Bittleston, Wise and Parnell, New Magistrate's Cases, Eng., 1844-1850.

Bkcy. Bankruptcy (nonstandard).

Bkcy. & Ins. R. Bankruptcy and Insolvency Reports, Eng., 1853-1855.

Bkg. L.J. Banking Law Journal (nonstandard).

Bl. C.C. Blatchford's Circuit Court Reports.

Bl. Com. Blackstone, Commentaries on the Laws of England.

Bl. H. Henry Blackstone, Common Pleas, Eng., 1788-1796.

Bl. R., or **Bl. W.** Sir William Blackstone, King's Bench, 1746-1779.

Black U.S. Supreme Court, vols. 66-67.

Black., D. & O. Blackham, Dundas and Osborne, Nisi Prius, Ireland, 1846-1848.

Black., W. Sir Wm. Blackstone's Reports, K.B.

Blackf. Blackford, Indiana Supreme Court, 1817-1847.

Bland Maryland High Court of Chancery, 1797-1832.

Blatch. Blatchford, U.S. Circuit Court, Second Circuit.

Blatch. & H. Blatchford and Howland, U.S. District Court, Southern Dist. of N.Y., 1827-1837.

Blatch. Pr. Blatchford, Prize Cases, U.S. Courts, Southern Dist. of N.Y., 1861-1865.

Bli. Bligh, House of Lords, Eng., 1819-1821.

Bli. (N.S.) Bligh, House of Lords, Eng., New Series, 1827-1837.

Bond U.S. Courts, Southern Dist. of Ohio, 1856-1871.

Bos. & Pul. Bosanquet and Puller's Reports, C.P.

Bos. & P.N.R. Bosanquet and Puller's New Reports, C.P.

Bosw. Bosworth, New York City Superior Court, vols. 14-23, 1856-1863.

Bott. Poor Law Cases, Eng., 1768-1827.

Boyce Boyce's Report, Delaware.

Br. & F. Brodrick and Fremantle, Ecclesiastical Cases, Eng., 1695-1864.

Br. & G. Brownlow and Goldesborough, Common Pleas, Eng., 1558-1625.

Br. & Mac. Browne and Macnamara, Railway and Canal Cases, Eng.

Br. N.C. Brooke, New Cases, King's Bench and Chancery, Eng., 1515-1558.

Br. N.C. Brooke's New Cases, K.B.

Brac. Bracton De Legibus et Consuetudinibus Angliae.

Bradf. Bradford, New York Surrogate's Court, 1849-1857.

Bradw. Bradwell, Illinois Appellate Courts, 1877-1886.

Brain. Leg. Pr. Brainard's Legal Precedents, Land and Mining Cases, Washington.

Branch Branch (Florida).

Brayt. Brayton, Vermont Supreme Court, 1815-1819.

Breese Illinois Supreme Court, vol. 1.

Brev. Brevard, South Carolina Constitutional and District Court, 1793-1816.

Brews. Brewster, Pennsylvania, various courts, 1856-1873.

Bridg. Sir J. Bridgman, King's Bench, Eng., 1613-1633.

Bridg. O. Orlando Bridgman, Common Pleas, Eng., 1660-1667.

Bright. Brightly, Court of Nisi Prius, at Philadelphia, and Pennsylvania Supreme Court, 1809-1851.

Brod. & B. Broderip and Bingham's Reports, C.P.

Bro. Ch. Brown (William), Chancery Cases, Eng., 1778-1794.

Bro. P.C. Brown, House of Lords (Parliamentary) Cases, Eng., 1702-1778.

Bro. P.C. Brown, Parliament Cases.

Bro. Sup. Brown's Supplement to Morison's Dictionary of Decisions, Scotland, 1620-1768.

Bro. Syn. Brown's Synopsis of Decisions, Court of Session.

Brock. Brockenbrough, U.S. Circuit Court, Fourth Circuit, 1802-1836. See Va. Cas.

Brock. & H. Brockenbrough and Holmes, Virginia General Court, 1789-1826.

Broun Justiciary Cases, Scotland, 1842-1845.

Brown, Adm. Admiralty, U.S. Courts, Western Districts.

Brown, N.P. Nisi Prius Cases, Michigan.

Browne Pennsylvania Common Pleas, First Judicial District, 1801-1814.

Brownl. Brownlow and Goldesborough's Reports, C.P.

Bruce Court of Session, Scotland, 1714-1715.

Brunner Collected Cases, U.S. Courts, 1791-1880.

Buck Reports in Bankruptcy, Eng., 1816-1820.

Bull. Bulletin; Weekly Law Bulletin, Ohio.

Bulst. Bulstrode, King's Bench, Eng., 1609-1638.

Bunb. Bunbury, Exchequer, Eng., 1713-1741.

Burn. Burnett, Wisconsin Territory, Supreme Court, 1842.

Burr. Burrow, King's Bench, Eng., 1756-1772.

Burr. S.C. Burrow, Settlement Cases, King's Bench, Eng., 1732-1776.

Bus. Law. Business Lawyer.

Busb. Busbee, North Carolina Supreme Court, 1852-1853.

Busb. Eq. Busbee, North Carolina Cases in Equity, 1852-1853.

Bush Kentucky Court of Appeals, 1866-1879.

C. Cases; Chancellor; Chancery; Chapter; Codex (Juris Civilis) Justinian; College; Common; Court. See also, Cow.

C.A. Court of Appeals; California Appellate Reports (nonstandard).

C.A.A. Civil Aeronautics Authority Reports.

C.A.B. Civil Aeronautics Board Reports.

C. & E. Cababe and Ellis, Queen's Bench, Eng., 1882-1885.

C. & J. Crompton and Jervis, Exchequer, Eng., 1830-1832.

C. & K. Carrington and Kirwan, Nisi Prius, Eng., 1843-1853.

C. & L.C.C. Cave and Leigh, Crown Cases, Eng.

C. & M. Crompton and Meeson, Exchequer, 1832-1834.

C. & P. Carrington and Payne, Nisi Prius, Eng., 1823-1841.

C.B. Chief Baron of the Exchequer; Common Bench; Common Bench Reports, Eng., 1845-1856.

C.B. (N.S.) Common Bench Reports, New Series, Eng., 1856-1865.

C.C. Chancery Cases; Circuit Court; County Court; Crown (or Criminal) Cases.

C.C.A. Circuit Court of Appeals; County Court Appeals.

CCH Commerce Clearing House.

C.C. (N.S.) Circuit Court Reports, New Series.

C.C.P. Court of Common Pleas.

C.C.P.A. Court of Customs and Patent Appeals.

C.C.R. Crown Cases Reserved.

C.E. Canada East.

CETA Comprehensive Employment and Training Act.

C.F.R. Code of Federal Regulations.

C.J. Chief Judge; Chief Justice; Corpus Juris.

C.J.B. Chief Judge in Bankruptcy.

C.J.C. Cowper's Justiciary Cases.

C.J.S. Corpus Juris Secundum.

C.L. Mag. Criminal Law Magazine and Reporter, Jersey City, N.J.

C.L.P. Act Common Law Procedure Act, 1871, Eng.

C.L.R. Common Law Reports, 1853-1855; California Law Review (nonstandard); Columbia Law Review (nonstandard).

C.M.A. United States Court of Military Appeals Reports, 1951-1975.

C.M.R. United States Court-Martial Reports, 1951-1977.

C.M. & R. Crompton, Meeson and Roscoe, Exchequer, Eng., 1834-1835.

C.P. Common Pleas.

C.P.D. Common Pleas Division, Law Reports, Eng.

C.R. Carolous Rex; King Charles I.

C.S. Court of Session, Scotland; Custos Rotulorum; Keeper of the Rolls.

C.S.C.A. Court of Session Cases, Scotland, 1821-1875.

C.S.C.R. Cincinnati Superior Court Reporter, 1870-1873.

C.W. Canada West.

Ca. or **Cas.** Cases t. (tempore) F., in time of Finch; t. Holt, in time of Holt; t. H., in time of Hardwicke; t. K., in time of King; t. N., in time of Northington; t. Talb., in time of Talbot; B.R., or t. Wm. III., in time of William III. (12 Mod.).

Cai. Caines, New York Supreme Court, 1803-1805.

Cai. Cas. Caines' Cases, New York Court of Errors, 1796-1805.

Caines Caines, New York.

Caines' Cas. See, Cai. Cas.

Cal. Calfornia Reports, Supreme Court, since 1850.

Cal. App. California Appellate Reports, since 1905.

Cal. App. Supp. California Appellate Reports Supplement, since 1929.

Cal. L.J. California Law Journal, San Francisco, 1862-1863.

Cal. L.R. California Legal Record, San Francisco, 1878-1879.

Cal. L. Rev. California Law Review (nonstandard).

Cal. Rptr. California Reporter, since 1959.

Cal. St. B.J. California State Bar Journal.

Cal. Unrep. California Unreported Cases, 1855-1910.

Cal. W. L. Rev. California Western Law Review.

Cald. Caldecott, Settlement Cases and Justice of the Peace, Eng., 1776-1785.

Calif. L. Rev. California Law Review.

Call Call's Reports, Virginia Court of Appeals, 1796-1818; U.S. Circuit Court, 1793-1825.

Calth. Calthrop, King's Bench, Eng., 1609-1618.

Cam. & N. Cameron and Norwood, North Carolina Court of Conference, 1800-1804.

Cam. Scacc. Camera, Scaccarii, Exchequer Chamber.

Camb. L.J. Cambridge Law Journal.

Campb. Campbell, Nisi Prius, Eng., 1807-1816.

Can. Canada Supreme Court Reports.

Can. B. Rev. Canadian Bar Review.

Can. L.J. Canada Law Journal, 1855-1864.

Can. L.J. (N.S.) Canada Law Journal, New Series.

Can. L.T. Canadian Law Times.

Cap. U. L. Rev. Capital University Law Review.

Car. & K. See C. & K.

Car. & M. Carrington and Marshman, Nisi Prius, Eng., 1841-1842.

Car. & P. See C. & P.

Car. H. & A. Carrow, Hamerton and Allen, Magistrate's Courts, 1844-1847. See New Sess. Cas.

Car. L.R. or **Car. L. Rep.** Carolina Law Repository, N.C., 1811-1816.

Carp. Carpmael, Patent Cases, Eng., 1602-1842.

Carr. & Kir. Carrington and Kirwan's Reports, N.P.

Carr. & P. Carrington and Payne's Reports, N.P.

Cart. Carter, Common Pleas, Eng., 1664-1675.

Carth. Carthew, King's Bench, Eng., 1686-1700.

Cary Chancery, Eng., 1557-1604.

Cas. Casualty; Cases.

Cas. B.R. Cases in King's Bench t. Wm. III. (12 Mod.).

Cas. C.L. Cases in Crown Law.

Cas. C.R. Cases temp. Wm. III. (12 Mod.).

Cas. Eq. Abr. Abridgment of Cases in Equity, Eng.

Cas. L. & Eq. Cases in Law and Equity (10 Mod.).

Cas. P. Cases in Parliament.

Cas. Pr. C.P. Cases of Practice, Common Pleas, Eng., 1706-1740; with rules and orders, 1457-1741.

Cas. Pr. K.B. Cases of Practice, King's Bench, Eng., 1732-1760.

Case & Com. Case and Comment.

Case W. Res. L. Rev. Case Western Reserve Law Review.

Casey Pennsylvania State Supreme Court, vols. 25-36.

Cath. U.L. Rev. Catholic University of America Law Review.

Cent. Central.

Cent. Dig. Century Digest.

Cent. L.J. Central Law Journal.

Cent. Rep. Central Reporter, Rochester.

Ch. Chancery.

Ch. C.R. Chancery Chambers Reports, Canada, 1858-1872.

Ch. Cas. Chancery Cases, Eng., 1660-1688.

Ch. Cas. Ch. Choyce Cases in Chancery, Eng., 1557-1606.

Ch. Cas. Sp. Special Cases in Chancery, Eng., 1669-1693.

Ch. Pre. Precedents in Chancery, Eng., 1689-1723.

Ch. R. Reports in Chancery, Eng., 1625-1710.

Chand. Chandler, Wisconsin Supreme Court, 1849-1852; Chandler New Hampshire Reports.

Chap. Chapter.

Charlt. Charlton, T.U.P., Georgia Superior Courts, 1805-1810.

Charlt. Charlton, R.M., Georgia Superior Courts, 1811-1837.

Chas. Charles I., Eng.

Chase's Dec. Chase's Decisions, U.S. Circuit Court, Fourth Circuit, 1865-1869.

Chem. Chemical.

Chest. Co. R. Chester County (Pa.) Reports, 1866-1885.

Cheves South Carolina Court of Appeals, at Law, 1839-1840.

Cheves, Ch. or **Eq.** South Carolina Court of Appeals, in Equity, 1839-1840.

Chi.-Kent L. Rev. Chicago-Kent Law Review.

Chi. L.J. Chicago Law Journal, 1878-1879.

Chi. L.N. Chicago Legal News.

Chi. L. Rec. Chicago Law Record.

Chip. D. D. Chipman, Vermont Supreme Court, 1789-1824.

Chip. N. N. Chipman, Vermont Supreme Court, 1789-1791.

Chip. (N.B.) Chipman, New Brunswick Supreme Court, 1825-1827.

Chit. Chitty, Bail Court Reports, Eng., 1819, 1770-1882.

Cin. L.B. Cincinnati Law Bulletin.

Cin. L. Rev. University of Cincinnati Law Review (nonstandard).

Cin. Super. Ct. or **Cin. Superior Ct.** Superior Court of Cincinnati.

Cir. Ct. Circuit Court.

City Ct. R. City Court Reports, New York.

City H. Rec. City Hall Recorder, New York, Criminal, 1816-1821.

Civ. App. Court of Civil Appeals.

Civ. Lib. Rev. Civil Liberties Review.

Civ. Pro. Rep. Civil Procedure Reports, New York, various courts.

Cl. & F. Clark and Finnelly, House of Lords, Eng., 1831-1846.

Clark Clark, Ala. and Pa.

Clarke Ch. New York Court of Chancery, 1839-1841.

Clarke (Ia.) Iowa Supreme Court, vols. 1-8.

Clarke & H. Clarke and Hall, Contested Election Cases, in Congress, 1789-1834.

Clay. Clayton, York Assize, Nisi Prius, Eng., 1631-1650.

Clev. B.J. Cleveland Bar Association Journal.

Clev. L. Rec. Cleveland Law Record, 1855-1856.

Clev. L. Rep. Cleveland Law Reporter, 1878-1879.

Clev.-Mar. L. Rev. Cleveland-Marshall Law Review.

Clev. St. L. Rev. Cleveland State Law Review.

Cliff. Clifford, U.S. Circuit Court, First Circuit, 1858-1878.

Cliff. & S. Clifford and Stephens, Referee's Court in Parliament, Eng., 1867-1872.

Co. County; Coke, King's Bench and other courts, Eng., 1572-1616.

Co. Ct. Cas. County Court Cases, Eng., 1844-1846.

Co. Ct. Chr. County Courts Chronicle, London, 1847-1884.

Co. Ct. Rep. County Courts Reports, London, 1860-1880.

Co. Inst. Coke's Institutes, 1, 2, 3, and 4.

Co. Lit. Coke on Littleton.

Co. M.C. Coke's Magna Charta.

Co. on Court. Coke's 4th Inst.

Co. P.C. Coke's Pleas of the Crown (3rd Inst.).

Coch. Cochran, Nova Scotia Law Reports (N.S.), 1859.

Cock. & R. Cockburne and Rove, Election Cases, Eng., 1833.

Cod. Jur. Civ. Codex Juris Civilis.

Code Rep. The Code Reporter, New York, various courts, 1848-1851.

Code R. (N.S.) Code Reports, New Series, New York, various courts, 1850-1852.

Col. & C. Coleman and Caines' Cases, New York Supreme Court, 1794-1805.

Col. Cas. Coleman's Cases, New York Supreme Court, 1793-1800.

Col. C.C. Collyer's Chancery Cases, 1844-1846.

Col. J. Columbian Jurist, New York, 1885-1886.

Cold. Coldwell, Tennessee Supreme Court, 1860-1870.

Coll. Colles, Cases in Parliament, House of Lords, Eng., 1697-1713.

Colo. Colorado Reports, Supreme Court, since 1864.

Colo. App. Colorado Court of Appeals Reports, since 1891.

Colo. L.R. Colorado Law Reporter, Denver, 1880-1884.

Colo. Law. Colorado Lawyer.

Colt. Coltman, Registration Cases, Eng.

Colum. J.L. & Soc. Probs. Columbia Journal of Law & Social Problems.

Colum. J. Transnat'l L. Columbia Journal of Transnational Law.
Colum. L. Rev. Columbia Law Review.
Com. Comment; Commerce; Commercial; Common; Commentaries; Communication.
Com. L.J. Commercial Law Journal.
Comb. Comberbach, King's Bench, Eng., 1685-1698.
Comm. Committee.
Comm'n Commission.
Comm'r Commissioner.
Comp. Comparative.
Comst. Comstock, New York Court of Appeals, vols. 1-4.
Comyn King's Bench, Eng., 1695-1739.
Con. & L. Conner and Lawson, Chancery, Ireland, 1841-1843.
Con. Sur. Connoly, New York Surrogate's Courts.
Conf. Conference.
Cong. Congress; Congressional.
Cong. Dig. Congressional Digest.
Conn. Connecticut Reports, Supreme Court of Errors, since 1814. See Kirby, Root, and Day.
Conn. B.J. Connecticut Bar Journal.
Conn. Cir. Ct. Connecticut Circuit Court Reports, 1961-1974.
Conn. L. Rev. Connecticut Law Review.
Conn. Supp. Connecticut Supplement, since 1935.
Consist. Consistory Reports, Haggard.
Consol. Consolidated.
Const. Constitution; Constitutional.
Const. (S.C.) Treadway's S.C. Constitutional Reports.
Const. N.S. (S.C.) Mills' S.C. Constitutional Reports.
Constr. Construction.
Cont. Contract, Contracts.
Contemp. Contemporary.
Conv. (n.s.) Conveyance & Property Lawyer.
Cooke Tennessee, various courts, 1811-1814.
Cooke & A. Cooke and Alcock, King's Bench, Ireland, 1833-1834.
Cooke, Pr. Ca. Practice Cases in Common Pleas Court, Eng., 1706-1747.
Coop. Pr. C. Cooper's Practice Cases in Chancery, Eng., 1837-1838; miscellaneous cases, 1820-1838.
Coop. Ch. Cooper, Tennessee, Court of Chancery, 1872-1878.
Coop. t. Br. Cooper, Cases in Chancery t. Lord Brougham, 1833-1834.
Coop. t. Cott. Cooper, Cases in Chancery, t. Lord Cottenham, 1846-1847; miscellaneous cases, 1557-1847.
Coop t. Eld. Cooper, Cases in Chancery t. Lord Eldon, 1792-1815.
Corb. & D. Corbett and Daniell, Election Cases, Eng., 1819.
Corp. J. Corporation Journal.
Cosm. Cosmetic.
Coup. (S.C.) Couper, Scotch Justiciary, 1868-1885.
Cow. Cowen, New York Supreme Court and Court of Errors, 1821-1829.
Cow. Cr. Rep. Cowen's Criminal Reports, State Courts and U.S. Supreme Court, 1860-1874.
Cowp. Cowper, King's Bench, Eng., 1774-1778.
Cox, C.C. Cox's Criminal Cases, Eng.
Cox, Ch. Chancery, Eng., 1783-1796.

Cox, M. & H. Cox, Macrae and Hertslet, County Courts, Eng., 1847-1852.

Cox, Mag. Cas. Cox's Magistrate Cases, 1859-1882.

Coxe New Jersey Law, vol. 1, 1790-1795.

Cr. & Ph. Craig and Phillips, Chancery, Eng., 1840-1841.

Cr. & St. Craigie and Stewart, Scotch Appeals, House of Lords, 1726-1821. Last three vols. by Paton. See Pat. App.

Crabbe Crabbe's Reports, U.S. District Court, Eastern District of Pennsylvania, 1836-1846.

Cranch Cranch's U.S. Supreme Court Reports, vols. 5-13, 1801-1815.

Cranch, C.C. Cranch, U.S. Circuit Court for District of Columbia, 1801-1840.

Cranch Pat. Dec. Cranch's Patent Decisions (N.S.).

Craw. & D. Crawford and Dix, Circuit Cases, Ireland, 1839-1846.

Craw. & D., Ab. C. Crawford and Dix, Abridged Cases, Ireland, 1837-1838.

Crim. Criminal.

Crim. App. Court of Criminal Appeals.

Crim. Def. Criminal Defenses, Select American Cases, St. Louis.

Crim. L. Mag. Criminal Law Magazine, Jersey City, N.J.

Crim. L. Rep. or **Crim. L. Rptr.** Criminal Law Reporter.

Cripps Ecclesiastical Courts, Eng., 1846-1849.

Cro. Croke, Queen's Bench and King's Bench, Eng., 1582-1641; occasionally, Keilwey's Reports, published by Serjeant Croke.

Cromp. Crompton's Courts.

Cromp. & J. Crompton and Jervis' Reports, Ex.

Cromp. & M. Crompton and Meeson's Reports, Ex.

Ct. Cl. U.S. Court of Claims.

Ct. Cust. App. U.S. Court of Customs Appeals.

Ct. Mil. App. U.S. Court of Military Appeals.

Ct. of Cl. See Ct. Cl.

Cum. Bull. Cumulative Bulletin, U.S. Treasury Department.

Cum. L. Rev. Cumberland Law Review.

Cum.-Sam. L. Rev. Cumberland-Samford Law Review.

Cunn. Cunningham, King's Bench, Eng., 1734-1835.

Cur. Com. Current Comment and Legal Miscellany, Philadelphia.

Current Med. Current Medicine for Attorneys.

Curt. Curtis, U.S. Circuit Court, First Circuit, 1851-1856.

Curt. E.R. Curteis, Ecclesiastical Reports, Eng., 1834-1844.

Cush. Cushing, Massachusetts Supreme Court, vols. 55-66, 1848-1853.

Cushm. Cushman, Mississippi High Court of Errors and Appeals, vols. 23-29.

Cust. Ct. Customs Court Reports.

Cyc. Cyclopedia of Law and Procedure.

D. U.S. District Court; Davis; Defendant; Digest (Juris Civilis); District; Division; Disney.

D. & C. Deacon and Chitty, Bankruptcy, Eng., 1832-1835; Pennsylvania District and County Reports (nonstandard).

D. & C. 2d, D. & C. 3d, Pennsylvania District and County Reports, Second Series and Third Series (nonstandard).

D. & L. Dowling and Lowndes, various courts, Eng., 1843-1849.

D. & M. Davison and Merivale, Queen's Bench, Eng., 1843-1844.

D. & R. Dowling and Ryland, King's Bench, Eng., 1822-1827.

D. & R. Mag. Cas. Dowling and Ryland, Magistrates' Cases, Eng., 1822-1827.

D. & R. (N.P.C.) Dowling and Ryland, Nisi Prius Cases, Eng., 1822-1823.

D.C. District Court; District of Columbia; District of Columbia Reports, 1801-1893. See also, MacArth.

DEA Drug Enforcement Administration.

D.L.R. Dominion Law Reports, Can.

D.L.R.2d Dominion Law Reports, Second Series, Can.

D.L.R.3d Dominion Law Reports, Third Series, Can.

D.P. Domus Procerum; House of Lords.

D.P.R. Decisiones de Puerto Rico, since 1899.

D.T., or **Dak.** Dakota Territory Supreme Court.

Dakota Dakota Reports, Supreme Court of Dakota, 1867-1889.

Dal. Dalison, Common Pleas, Eng., 1546-1574.

Dall. Dallas, U.S. Courts and Courts of Pennsylvania, 1754-1806.

Dall. (Tex.) Dallam, Supreme Court of Texas, before annexation, 1840-1844.

Dallas Dallas Styles, Scotland.

Dalr. Dalrymple's Decisions, Court of Session, Scotland, 1698-1720.

Daly New York Court of Common Pleas.

Dan. Daniell, Exchequer, Equity, Eng., 1817-1820.

Dana Kentucky Court of Appeals, 1833-1840.

Dan. & Ll. Danson and Lloyd's Mercantile Cases, King's Bench, Eng., 1828-1829.

Dav. Davies, Common Law Reports, Ireland, 1604-1612. See also, Daveis.

Daveis U.S. District Court, Maine, 1839-1849 (cited as 2 Ware).

Day Connecticut Supreme Court of Errors, 1802-1813.

Dea. Deane, Admiralty and Ecclesiastical Courts, Eng., 1855-1857.

Dea. & Sw. Deane and Swabey, Probate and Divorce, Eng., 1855-1857.

Deac. Deacon, Bankruptcy, Eng., 1835-1840.

Deac. & Chit. Deacon and Chitty, Bankruptcy, Eng., 1832-1835.

Deady U.S. Courts, Oregon and California, 1861-1869.

Dears. & B. Dearsley and Bell, Crown Cases Reserved, Eng., 1856-1858.

Dears. C.C. Dearsley, Crown Cases, Eng., 1852-1856.

Deas & A. Deas and Anderson, Court of Session, Scotland, 1829-1832.

D. Chip. D. Chipman (Vermont).

Dec. Dig. Decennial Digest.

De G. De Gex, Bankruptcy, Eng., 1844-1848; 1839-1850.

De G. & J. De Gex and Jones, Chancery and Bankruptcy Appeals, 1857-1859.

De G. & Sm. De Gex and Smale, Chancery and Bankruptcy Appeals, 1846-1852.

De G., F. & J. De Gex, Fisher and Jones, Chancery and Bankruptcy Appeals, 1859-1862.

De G., J. & S. De Gex, Jones and Smith, Chancery and Bankruptcy Appeals, 1862-1865.

De G., M. & G. De Gex, Macnaghten and Gordon, Chancery and Bankruptcy Appeals, 1851-1857.

Dec. Eng. J.J. Decisions of English Judges, Court of Session, Scotland, during the usurpation, 1655-1661.

Def. Defense.

Del. Delaware Reports, Supreme Court, 1832-1966. See also, Har. and Houst.; Delane, Election Cases, Eng., 1832-1835.

Del. Cas. Delaware Cases, 1792-1830.

Del. Ch. Delaware Chancery Reports, 1814-1968.

Del. Co. R. Delaware County (Pa.) Reports.

Delinq. Delinquency.

Dem. Demarest, Surrogate's Court, N.Y., 1882-1888.

Den. L.J. Denver Law Journal.

Den. C.C. Denison, Crown Cases, Eng., 1844-1852.

Denio New York Supreme Court and Court of Errors, 1845-1848.

Dep. or **Dep't** Department.

Dep't State Bull. U.S. Department of State Bulletin.

Desau. Desaussure, South Carolina Court of Chancery and Court of Appeals, 1784-1817.

Det. C.L. Rev. Detroit College Law Review.

Dev. Development; Devereux, North Carolina Supreme Court, at Law, 1826-1834.

Dev. & B. Devereux and Battle, North Carolina Supreme Court, at Law, 1834-1839.

Dev. & B. Eq. Devereux and Battle, North Carolina Supreme Court, in Equity, 1834-1839.

Dev. Ct. Cl. Devereux, U.S. Court of Claims, 1856.

Dev. Eq. Devereux, North Carolina Supreme Court, in Equity, 1826-1834.

Dick. Dickens, Chancery, Eng., 1559-1797.

Dick. Dickinson (N.J.).

Dick. L. Rev. Dickinson Law Review.

Dict. Dictionary.

Dict. of Dec. Dictionary of Decisions, Court of Session, Scotland (Morison and others), from beginning to 1822.

Dig. Digest.

Dill. Dillon, U.S. Circuit Court, Eighth Circuit, 1870-1880.

Dipl. Diplomacy.

Dirl. Dirleton, Court of Session, Scotland, 1665-1677.

Dis. or **Disney** Disney's Cincinnati Superior Court Reports, 1854-1859.

Dist. District.

Distrib. Distributor or Distributing.

Div. Division.

Dod. Dodson, Admiralty, Eng., 1811-1822.

Dom. Proc. Domus Procerum; House of Lords, Eng.

Don. Ch. Donnelly, Chancery, Eng., 1836-1837.

Don. Ir. L. Cas. Donnell, Irish Land Cases, 1871-1876.

Doug. Douglas, King's Bench, Eng., 1778-1785.

Doug, E.C. Douglas, Election Cases, Eng., 1775-1776.

Doug. (Mich.) Douglass, Michigan Supreme Court, 1843-1847.

Dow House of Lords, Eng., 1812-1818.

Dow & C. Dow and Clark, House of Lords, Eng., 1827-1832.

Dow. & Ry. N.P. Dowling and Ryland's K.B. Reports; Dowling and Ryland's Nisi Prius.

Dowl. Dowling's Practice Cases, various courts, Eng., 1830-1841.

Dowl. (N.S.) Dowling's Practice Cases, various courts, Eng., New Series, 1841-1843.

Drap. Draper, King's Bench, Upper Canada, 1829-1831.

Drew. Drewry, Chancery, Eng., 1852-1859.

Drew. & Sm. Drewry and Smale, Chancery, Eng., 1859-1865.

Drink. Drinkwater, Common Pleas, Eng., 1840-1841.

Dru. Drury, Chancery, Ireland, t. Ld. Sugden, 1843-1844.

Dru. t. Nap. Drury, Chancery, Ireland t. Ld. Napier, 1858-1859.

Dru. & Wal. Drury and Walsh, Chancery, Ireland, 1837-1840.

Dru. & War. Drury and Warren, Chancery, Ireland, 1841-1843.

Dru. Sel. Cas. Drury, Select Cases in Chancery, Ireland, 1858-1859. Same as Dru. t. Nap.

Dud. (Ga.) Dudley, Georgia Superior Courts, 1830-1833.

Dud. (S.C.) Dudley, South Carolina Court of Appeals, at Law, 1837-1838.

Dud. Eq. Dudley, South Carolina Court of Appeals, in Equity, 1837-1838.

Duer New York City Superior Court, 1852-1857.

Dunl., B. & M. Dunlop, Bell and Murray, Court of Session, Scotland, 1838-1862.

Duq. L. Rev. Duquesne Law Review.

Durie (also called Dury), Court of Session, Scotland, 1621-1642.

Durn. & E. Durnford and East, Term Reports, King's Bench, Eng., 1785-1800.

Dury See Durie.

Dutch. Dutcher, New Jersey Law Reports, vols. 25-29, 1855-1862.

Duv. Duvall, Kentucky Court of Appeals, 1863-1866.

Duv. (Can.) Duval, Canada Supreme Court.

Dy. Dyer, King's Bench, Eng., 1513-1582.

E. East; Eastern.

E. & A. Ecclesiastical and Admiralty Division, Law Reports.

E. & Ir. App. Cas. English and Irish Appeal Cases, House of Lords, Eng.

EAJA Equal Access to Justice Act.

E.D. Eastern District.

EEOC Equal Employment Opportunity Commission.

ERISA Employee Retirement Income Security Act of 1974, as amended.

E. Rep. Eastern Reporter, Albany, N.Y.

Eag. & Y. Eagle and Younge, Tithe Cases, Exchequer, Eng., 1204-1825.

East King's Bench, Eng., 1800-1812.

Ecc. or **Eccl.** Ecclesiastical.

Ecc. or **Eccl. & Adm.** See E. & A.

Ecc. & Mar. Ecclesiastical and Maritime Cases, Eng., 1841-1850.

Econ. Economic, Economics or Economy.

Ed. Edition; Editor; Edward.

Eden Chancery, Eng., 1757-1766.

Edg. Edgar, Court of Session, Scotland, 1724-1725.

Edin. L.J. Edinburgh Law Journal, 1832-1833.

Edm. Edmond's Select Cases, New York Courts, 1834-1848.

Educ. Education or Educational.

Edw. Edward I. of England.

Edw. Admr. Edwards, Admiralty, Eng., 1808-1812.

Edw. Ch. Edwards, New York Vice-Chancellor's and Supreme Court, 1831-1850.

El. & B. Ellis and Blackburn, Queen's Bench, Eng., 1852-1858.

El. & E. Ellis and Ellis, Queen's Bench, Eng., 1858-1861.

El., B. & E. Ellis, Blackburn and Ellis, Queen's Bench, Eng., 1858-1860.

El., B. & S. Ellis, Best and Smith's Reports, Q.B.

Elchies Faculty Collection, Court of Session, Scotland, 1733-1754.

Elec. Electric; Electrical; Electricity.

Em. Ct. App. Emergency Court of Appeals.

Eng. England; English; English's Reports (Arkansas).

Eng. Ch. English Chancery Reports, American Reprint, 1821-1865.

Eng. Com. L. English Common Law Reports, American Reprint, 1813-1865.

Eng. Ex. English Exchequer Reports, American Reprint, 1853-1869.

Eng. J.J. See Dec. Eng. J.J.

Eng. Rep. English Reports—Full Reprint.

Env't Environment.

Envtl. or **Envt'l** Environmental.

Eq. Equity; Equity Division, Law Reports and Law Journal.

Eq. Ca. Abr. Equity Cases Abridged, Anonymous, Eng., 1732-1769.

Eq. R. Equity Reports, Eng., 1853-1855.

Equip. Equipment.

Er. Error.

Esp. Espinasse, Nisi Prius, Eng., 1793-1810.

Est. Estate or Estates.

Et al. (Et alii, aliae, alios) And others.

Et. seq. (Et sequentes, sequentia) And the following.

Et ux., or **Et uxor.** And wife.

Et vir. And husband.

Ex. Exchequer; Exchequer Reports by Welsby, Hurlstone and Gordon, Eng., 1847-1856.

Ex. Ch. Exchequer Chamber.

Ex. D. Exchequer Division, High Court of Justice, Eng.

Exch. Exchange.

Exr. or **Ex'r** Executor.

Ex rel. Ex relatione; at the instance of; on behalf of; on relation of.

Exrx. Executrix.

Ex'x Executrix.

F. Federal Reporter, since 1880; Forum.

F.2d Federal Reporter, Second Series.

F. & F. Foster and Finlayson, Nisi Prius, Eng., 1856-1867.

F.C.A. Federal Code Annotated.

F. Cas. Federal Cases, 1789-1880.

FOIA Freedom of Information Act.

F.R.D. Federal Rules Decisions, since 1938.

F. Supp. Federal Supplement, since 1932.

F.T.C. Federal Trade Commission Decisions; Federal Trade Commission.

Fac. Dec. fo. Faculty Decisions, Court of Session, Scotland, folio edition, 1752-1825.

Fac. Dec. 8vo. Faculty Decisions, Court of Session, Scotland, 8vo. edition, 1825-1841.

Fairf. Fairfield, Maine Supreme Court, vols. 10-12, 1833-1835.

Falc. Falconer, Court of Session, Scotland, 1681-1686, (Pt.2nd. of Gilmour and Falconer).

Falc. & F. Falconer and Fitzherbert, Election Cases, 1835-1838.

Falc. D. David Falconer, Court of Session, Scotland, 1744-1751.

Fam. Family.

Far. Farresley, King's Bench, Eng. (7 Modern Reports), 1702-1703, with additions in Leach's Edition, 1733-1744.

Fed. Federal; Federal Reporter (non-standard).

Fed. B.J. Federal Bar Journal.
Fed. Com. B.J. Federal Communications Bar Journal.
Fed. Cas. Federal Cases (non-standard).
Fed. R. App. P. Federal Rules of Appellate Procedure.
Fed. R. Civ. P. Federal Rules of Civil Procedure.
Fed. R. Crim. P. Federal Rules of Criminal Procedure.
Fed. R. Evid. Federal Rules of Evidence.
Fed. Reg. Federal Register.
Fed'n Federation.
Ferg. Ferguson, Consistorial Court, Scotland, 1811-1817.
Fiduc. or **Fiduciary** Pennsylvania Fiduciary Reporter, since 1951.
Fin. Finance.
Finch, H. Chancery, Eng., 1673-1680.
Finch, T. Chancery, Eng., 1689-1722. See Prec. Ch.
Fish. Fisher's Patent Cases, U.S. Circuit and Supreme Courts, 1848-1873.
Fish. Dig. Fisher's Digest, all courts, Eng.
Fish. Pat. Rep. Fisher's Patent Reports (U.S.).
Fish. Pr. Fisher, Prize Cases, U.S. Courts, 1812-1813.
Fish. (W.H.) Wm. H. Fisher, Patent Reports, 1821-1851.
Fitz G. Fitz Gibbons, King's Bench and other courts, Eng., 1728-1732.
Fla. Florida Reports, Supreme Court, 1846-1948.
Fla. St. U.L.Rev. Florida State University Law Review.
Fla. Supp. Florida Supplement, since 1948.
Flan. & K. Flanagan and Kelly, Rolls Court, Ireland, 1840-1842.
Flippin U.S. Circuit Court, Sixth Circuit, 1859-1880.
Fo. or **Fol. Dict.** Folio Dictionary of Decisions, Court of Session, Scotland, 1540-1808. See also, Kames & W.
Fogg New Hampshire Supreme Court, vols. 32-37.
Foley Poor Law Cases, Eng., 1601-1730.
Fonbl. Fonblanque, Bankruptcy, Eng., 1849-1852.
Food Drug Cosm. L.J. Food Drug Cosmetic Law Journal.
Forb. Forbes, Court of Session, Scotland, 1705-1713.
For. Forensic; Forrester, Cases, time of Talbot, Eng., 1734-1738.
Forrest Exchequer, Eng., 1800-1801.
Forst. Forster, Crown Cases, Ireland, 1767.
Fort. Fortnightly; Fortescue, various courts, Eng., 1695-1736.
Forum The Forum, Law Review, Baltimore, 1874-1875.
Fost. Foster, Crown Cases, Eng., 1708-1760.
Fost. (N.H.) Foster, New Hampshire Supreme Court, vols. 21-31.
Found. Foundation or Foundations.
Fount. Fountainhall, Court of Session, Scotland, 1678-1712.
Fox & S. Fox and Smith, King's Bench, Ireland, 1822-1824.
Fras. Fraser, Election Cases, Eng., 1790-1792.
Freem. Freeman, King's Bench, Eng., 1670-1704.
Freem. Ch. Freeman, Chancery, Eng., 1660-1706.
Freem. (Ill.) Freeman, Illinois.
Freem. (Miss. Ch.) Freeman, Mississippi Superior Court of Chancery, 1839-1843.

G. & D. Gale and Davison, Exchequer, Eng., 1841-1843.

G. & J. Glyn and Jameson, Bankruptcy, Eng., 1815-1828.

Ga. Georgia Reports, Supreme Court, since 1846. See Charlt., Charlt. R.M., Dud., and Ga. Dec.

Ga. App. Georgia Appeals Reports, since 1907.

Ga. Dec. Georgia Decisions, Superior Courts, 1842-1843.

Ga. L.R. Georgia Law Reporter, Atlanta, 1885-1886.

Ga. L. Rev. Georgia Law Review.

Gaii Institutionum Commentarii, IV.

Gal. & Dav. Gale and Davidson's Reports, K.B.

Gale Exchequer, Eng., 1835-1836.

Gall. Gallison, U.S. Circuit Court, First Circuit, 1812-1815.

Gaz. Weekly Law Gazette.

Gaz. Bkcy. Gazette of Bankruptcy, Eng., 1862-1863.

Gen. General.

Geo. George; Georgetown; King George, Eng.

Geo. L.J. Georgetown Law Journal.

Geo. Wash. L. Rev. George Washington Law Review.

George Mississippi Supreme Courts, vols. 30-39.

Gibbs Michigan Supreme Court, vols. 2-4.

Giff. Giffard, Chancery, Eng., 1854-1865.

Giff. & H. Giffard and Hemming, Chancery, Eng., 1731-1736.

Gil. Gilfillan (Minn.).

Gilb. Gilbert, Chancery and Exchequer, Eng., 1706-1725.

Gilb. Q.B. Gilbert, Queen's Bench, Eng., 1713-1714.

Gill Maryland Court of Appeals, 1843-1851.

Gill & J. Gill and Johnson, Maryland Court of Appeals, 1829-1842.

Gilm. Gilmour, Court of Session, Scotland, 1661-1666.

Gilm. (Ill.) Gilman, Illinois Supreme Court, vols. 6-10.

Gilm. (Va.) Gilmer, Virginia Court of Appeals, 1820-1821.

Gilp. Gilpin, U.S. District Court, Pennsylvania, 1828-1836.

Glanv. Glanville, Tractatus De Legibus et Consuetudinibus Regni Angliae.

Glanv. P.C. Glanville, Parliamentary Cases, Eng., 1623-1624.

Glasg. Reg. Glasgow Registration Appeal Court, 1835-1843.

Glass. Glasscock, all courts, Ireland, 1831-1832.

Glyn & J. Glyn and Jameson, Bankruptcy, Eng., 1815-1828.

Godb. Godbolt, King's Bench, Eng., 1575-1638.

Godol. Godolphin, King's Bench, Eng.

Gonz. L. Rev. Gonzaga Law Review.

Gosf. Gosford, Court of Session, Scotland.

Goulds. Gouldsborough, all courts, Eng., 1585-1601.

Gov. Governor.

Gov't Government.

Gow Nisi Prius, Eng., 1818-1820.

Grant Cas. Grant's Cases, Pennsylvania Supreme Court, 1814-1863.

Grant, (U.C.) Upper Canada Error and Appeal Reports, 1846-1866.

Grant, (U.C.) Ch. Grant, Chancery, Upper Canada, 1849-1882.

Gratt. Grattan, Virginia Court of Appeals, 1844-1880.

Gray Massachusetts Supreme Court, Vols. 67-82, 1854-1860.

Green New Jersey Law Reports, vols. 13-15, 1831-1836.

Green, Ch. New Jersey Court of Chancery, vols. 2-4.

Green, C.E. New Jersey Chancery Reports, vols. 16-27.

Green Bag Law Magazine, Boston.

Green, Cr. Law R. Green, Criminal Law Reports, N.Y.

Green, J.S. Green, J.S., N.J.

Green, Tr. Green's Trials for High Treason, Scotland, 1820.

Greene Iowa Supreme Court, 1847-1854.

Greenh. P.P. Greenhood's Public Policy.

Greenl. Greenleaf, Maine Supreme Court, vols. 1-9.

Guar. Guaranty.

Guild Prac. Guild Practitioner.

Guthrie Sheriff Court Cases, Scotland, 1854-1878.

Gwil. Gwillim, Tithe Cases, Eng., 1224-1824.

H. Handy's Reports (Ohio).

H. & C. Hurlstone and Coltman, Exchequer, Eng., 1862-1866.

H. & G. Hurlstone and Gordon, Exchequer, Eng., 1854-1857.

H. & H. Horn and Hurlstone, Exchequer, Eng., 1838-1839.

H. & N. Hurlstone and Norman, Exchequer, Eng., 1856-1862.

H. & P. Hopwood and Philbrick, Election Cases, Eng., 1863-1867.

H. & R. Harrison and Rutherford, Common Pleas, Eng., 1866-1868.

H. & T. Hall and Twells, Ld. Chancellor and Appeal, Eng., 1849-1850.

H. & W. Hurlstone and Walmsley, Exchequer, Eng., 1840-1841.

H.Bl. Henry Blackstone, Common Pleas, Eng., 1788-1796.

H.L. House of Lords, Eng.

H.L.C. House of Lords Cases, Clark and Finnelly, Eng., 1847-1866.

H.L.R. House of Lords Reports, New Series, Eng.

H.R. House of Representatives; House of Representatives bill.

H.R. Rep. House of Representatives Report.

Had. Earl of Haddington, Court of Session, Scotland, 1592-1624.

Hagg. Adm. Haggard, Admiralty, Eng., 1822-1838.

Hagg. Con. Haggard, Consistory, Eng., 1752-1821.

Hagg. Eccl. Haggard, Ecclesiastical, Eng., 1827-1833.

Hailes Court of Session, Scotland, 1766-1791.

Hall New York City Superior Court, 1828-1829.

Hall & T. Hall and Twells, Chancery, Eng., 1849-1850.

Hall's J. of Jur. The Journal of Jurisprudence, Philadelphia, 1821.

Halst. Halstead, New Jersey Law, vols. 6-12, 1821-1831.

Halst. Ch. Halstead, New Jersey Chancery, vols. 5-8, 1845-1853.

Ham. Hammond, Ohio Reports, vols. 1-9.

Han. (N.B.) Hannay, New Brunswick Supreme Court, 1867-1871.

Hand Hand (N.Y.).

Handy Handy's Cincinnati Superior Court Reports, 1854-1856.

Hanm. Hanmer's Lord Kenyon's Notes, K. B.

Har. (Del.) Harrington, Delaware Superior Court, 1832-1854.

Har. (Mich.) Harrington, Michigan Court of Chancery, 1836-1842.

Har. (N.J.) Harrison, New Jersey Law, vols. 16-19, 1837-1842.

Har. & G. Harris and Gill, Maryland Court of Appeals, 1826-1829.

Har. & H. Harrison and Hodgin, Municipal Courts, Upper Canada, 1845-1851.

Har. & J. Harris and Johnson, Maryland Court of Appeals, 1800-1826.

Har. & McH. Harris and McHenry, Maryland Provincial Court and Court of Appeals, 1658-1799.

Har. & R. Harrison and Rutherford, Common Pleas, Eng., 1865-1866.

Har. & W. Harrison and Wollaston, King's Bench, Eng., 1835-1836.

Harc. Harcarse, Court of Session, Scotland, 1681-1691.

Hard. Hardres, Exchequer, Eng., 1655-1669.

Hardin Kentucky Court of Appeals, 1805-1808.

Hare Chancery, Eng., 1841-1853.

Harp. Harper, South Carolina Constitutional Court, 1823-1824.

Harp. Eq. Harper, South Carolina Court of Appeals, in Equity, 1824.

Harris Pennsylvania State Supreme Court, vols. 13-24.

Hart, Pat. Dec. Hart's Patent Decisions Digest.

Harv. C.R.-C.L. L. Rev. Harvard Civil Rights-Civil Liberties Law Review.

Harv. Int'l L.J. Harvard International Law Journal.

Harv. J. on Legis. Harvard Journal on Legislation.

Harv. L. Rev. Harvard Law Review.

Harv. Women's L.J. Harvard Women's Law Journal.

Hask. Haskell (U.S.).

Hastings L.J. Hastings Law Journal.

Haw. Hawaii Reports, Supreme Court, since 1847 (nonstandard).

Hawk. P.C. Hawkin's Pleas of the Crown.

Hawks North Carolina Supreme Court, 1820-1826.

Hay. & Haz. Hayward & Hazelton (D.C.), 1841-1862.

Hayes Exchequer, Ireland, 1830-1832.

Hayes & J. Hayes and Jones, Exchequer, Ireland, 1832-1834.

Hayw. (N.C.) Haywood, North Carolina Superior Courts, 1789-1806.

Hayw. (Tenn.) Haywood, Tennessee Court of Errors and Appeals, 1816-1818; 1813-1818 in appendix.

Head Tennessee Supreme Court, 1858-1859.

Heisk. Heiskell, Tennessee Supreme Court, 1870-1874.

Hem. & M. Hemming and Miller, Chancery, Eng., 1862-1865.

Hemp. Hempstead, U.S. Courts, Ninth Circuit, 1820-1855.

Hen. & M. Hening and Munford, Virginia Court of Appeals and Superior Court of Chancery, 1806-1810.

Het. Hetley, Common Pleas, Eng., 1627-1631.

Hill (N.Y.) New York Supreme Court and Court of Appeals, 1841-1845.

Hill (S.C.) South Carolina Court of Appeals, 1833-1837.

Hill (S.C.) Ch. South Carolina Court of Appeals in Chancery, 1833-1837.

Hill & D. Hill and Denio (Lalor's Supplement), New York Supreme Court, etc., 1842-1844.

Hilly. Hillyer (Cal.).

Hilt. Hilton, New York Court of Common Pleas, 1855-1860.

Hist. Historical; History.

Hob. Hobart, King's Bench, Eng., 1603-1625.

Hodges Common Pleas, Eng., 1835-1837.

Hoff. Ch. Hoffman, New York Assistant Vice-Chancellor's Court, 1839-1840.

Hoff. L.C. Hoffman's Land Cases, U.S. District Court, Cal., 1853-1858.

Hog. Hogan, Rolls Court, Ireland, 1816-1834.

Holmes U.S. Circuit Court, First Circuit, 1870-1875.

Holt, Adm. Admiralty Court Cases, Eng., 1863-1867.

Holt, Eq. Holt's Equity Reports, Eng., 1845.

Holt (K.B.) Sir John Holt, King's Bench, Eng., 1688-1710.

Holt (N.P.) Holt's Nisi Prius Reports, Eng., 1815-1817.

Home Court of Session, Scotland, 1735-1744. See Kames.

Home, Dict. of Dec. Home, Dictionary of Decisions, Court of Session, Scotland, 1540-1791.

Hop. & C. Hopwood and Coltman, Registration Cases, Eng., 1868-1878.

Hope Court of Session, Scotland.

Hopk. Hopkins, New York Court of Chancery, 1823-1826.

Hopk. Adm. Hopkinson, Admiralty Decisions, 1779-1805. Published also as an appendix to Bee.

Hosp. Hospital.

Hous. L.Rev. Houston Law Review.

Houst. Houston; Houston, Delaware Superior Court, 1855-1879.

Houst. C.C. Houston, Delaware Criminal Cases, 1856-1879.

How. Howard, U.S. Supreme Court, vols. 42-65, 1843-1860.

How. App. Cas. Howard's Court of Appeals Cases, N.Y., 1847-1848.

How. L.J. Howard Law Journal.

How. Miss. Howard, Mississippi Supreme Court, vols. 2-8, 1834-1843.

How. Pr. Howard, Practice Reports, New York Courts, 1844-1884.

How. Pr. (N.S.) Howard, Practice Reports, New York Courts, New Series.

Hud. & B. Hudson and Brooke, Irish Common Law Reports, 1827-1831.

Hugh. C.C. Hughes, U. S. Circuit Court, Fourth Circuit, 1792-1883.

Hughes Kentucky Court of Appeals, 1785-1801.

Hum. Human.

Hume Court of Session, Scotland, 1781-1822.

Humph. Humphreys, Tennessee Supreme Court, 1839-1851.

Hun New York Supreme Court.

Hut. Hutton, Common Pleas, Eng., 1584-1638.

I. & N. Dec. Immigration and Nationality Decisions.

I.C.C. Interstate Commerce Commission Reports.

ICC Prac. J. ICC Practitioners' Journal.

Ia. Iowa Reports, Supreme Court, 1855-1968 (nonstandard).

Ib. or **Ibid.** Ibidem; In the same place, volume, or case.

Id. Idem; The same.

Ida. Idaho Reports, since 1866 (nonstandard).

Ill. Illinois Reports, Supreme Court, since 1819. See also, Breese, Scam., and Gilm.

Ill. App. Illinois Appellate Court Reports, since 1877.

Ill. B.J. Illinois Bar Journal.

Ill. Ct. Cl. Illinois Court of Claims Reports, since 1889.

Ill. L.F. University of Illinois Law Forum.

Ill. L. Rev. Illinois Law Review.

Ind. Indiana Reports, Supreme Court, since 1848. See also, Blackf., Smith.

Ind. App. Indiana Court of Appeals Reports; Indiana Appellate Court Reports; since 1891.

Ind. L.J. Indiana Law Journal.

Ind. L.M. Indiana Law Magazine, Indianapolis, 1883-1885.

Ind. L. Rev. Indiana Law Review.

Indem. Indemnity.

Indian Terr. Indian Territory Reports (Oklahoma), 1896-1907.

Indus. Industrial; Industries; Industry.

Ins. Insurance.

Ins. Counsel J. Insurance Counsel Journal.

Ins. L.J. Insurance Law Journal.

Inst. Institute; Institutes, Coke's or Justinian's.

Int. Com. Interstate Commerce Commission Reports (nonstandard).

Int. Rev. Bull. Internal Revenue Bulletin.

Int. Rev. Rec. Internal Revenue Record, New York.

Int'l International.

Int'l Aff. International Affairs.

Int'l & Comp. L. Q. International and Comparative Law Quarterly.

Intra. Intramural.

Inv. Investment.

Ir. Ireland; Irish.

Ir. App. Cas. Irish Appeal Cases, House of Lords, Eng., 1726-1740.

Ir. C.L.R. Irish Common Law Reports, 1850-1866.

Ir. Ch. Irish Chancery Reports, 1850-1866.

Ir. Eq. Irish Equity Reports, 1838-1851.

Ir. J. Irish Jurist, 1849-1866.

Ir. L. Rec. Irish Law Recorder, 1827-1831; New Series, 1833-1838.

Ir. L. Rep. Irish Law Reports, Dublin, 1838-1850.

Ir. L.T. Irish Law Times and Solicitors' Journal.

Ir. R. (C.L.) Irish Reports, Common Law, 1867-1878.

Ir. R. (Eq.) Irish Reports, Equity, 1867-1878.

Ired. Iredell, North Carolina Supreme Court at Law, 1840-1852.

Ired. Eq. Iredell, North Carolina Supreme Court, in Equity, 1840-1852.

Irv. Irvine's Justiciary Cases, Scotland, 1852-1867.

J. Journal; Judge; Justice.

J. & W. Jacob and Walker, Chancery, Eng., 1819-1821.

J.A. Judge Advocate.

JAG J. JAG [Judge Advocate General] Journal.

J.A.M.A. Journal of the American Medical Association.

J. Air L. & Com. Journal of Air Law and Commerce.

J. Am. Jud. Soc'y Journal of American Judicature Society.

J. Am. Soc'y C.L.U. Journal of American Society of Chartered Life Underwriters.

J. Bus. L. Journal of Business Law.

J. Crim. L.C. & P.S. Journal of Criminal Law, Criminology and Police Science.

J. Fam. L. Journal of Family Law.

J. For. Sci. Journal of Forensic Sciences.

J.J. Marsh. J.J. Marshall, Kentucky Court of Appeals, 1829-1832.

J. Law & Econ. Journal of Law and Economics.

J. Legal Ed. or **J. Legal Educ.** Journal of Legal Education (**Ed.** nonstandard).

J. Mar. J. Prac. & Proc. John Marshall Journal of Practice and Procedure.

J.P. Justice of the Peace; The Justice of the Peace, and County, Borough, Poor Law Union, and Parish Law Recorder, London.

J.P. Ct. Justice of the Peace's Court.

J. Pat. Off. Soc'y Journal of Patent Office Society.

J. Plan. L. Journal of Planning Law.

J. Pub. L. Journal of Public Law.

J. Tax. or **J. Tax'n** Journal of Taxation.

Jac. Jacob, Chancery, Eng., 1821-1822.

James Nova Scotia Law Reports, 1853-1855.

Jebb & B. Jebb and Bourke, King's Bench, Ireland, 1841-1842.

Jebb & S. Jebb and Symes, King's Bench, Ireland, 1838-1841.

Jebb, C.C. Jebb's Crown Cases, Reserved, Ireland, 1822-1840.

Jeff. Jefferson, Virginia General Court, 1730-1740, 1768-1772.

Jenk. Jenkins, Exchequer, Eng., 1220-1623.

Johns. Johnson, Chancery, Eng., 1858-1860.

Johns. Johnson, New York Supreme Court, etc., 1806-1823.

Johns. & H. Johnson and Hemming, Chancery, Eng., 1860-1862.

Johns. Cas. Johnson's Cases, New York Supreme Court, etc., 1794-1803.

Johns. Ch. Johnson, New York Court of Chancery, 1814-1823.

Jones Jones (Pa.)

Jones (Ir.) Exchequer, Ireland, 1834-1838.

Jones (N.C.) North Carolina Supreme Court, at Law, 1853-1862.

Jones (N.C.) Eq. North Carolina Supreme Court, in Equity, 1853-1863.

Jones & C. Jones and Cary, Exchequer, Ireland, 1838-1839.

Jones & L. Jones and Latouche, Chancery, Ireland, 1844-1846.

Jones & McMurtie Jones and McMurtie (Pa.).

Jones & S. Jones and Spencer, New York City Superior Court, vols. 33-41.

Jones, T. King's Bench, Eng., 1667-1685.

Jones, W. King's Bench, Eng., 1620-1640.

Jour. of Jur. Journal of Jurisprudence and Scottish Law Magazine, Edinburgh.

Jour. of L. Journal of Law, Philadelphia, 1830-1831.

Jud. Judicature; Judicial.

Jur. Juridical; Jurist; The Jurist, Reports all courts, Eng., 1837-1854.

Jur. (N.S.) The Jurist, New Series, all courts, Eng., 1855-1866.

Jur. Sc. The Scottish Jurist, Court of Session, 1829-1873.

Jur. St. Judicial Styles, Scotland.

Jurid. Juridical.

Jurid. Rev. Juridicial Review.

Juris. Jurisprudence.

Just. Justice; Justinian Institutes.

Just. Cas. Justiciary Cases, Scotland.

Just. P. Justice of the Peace and Local Government Review.

Juv. Juvenile.

L. & C.C.C. Leigh and Cave, Crown Cases Reserved, Eng., 1861-1865.

L. & C.P. Law and Contemporary Problems (nonstandard).

L. & M. Lowndes and Maxwell, Bail Court, Eng., 1852-1854.

L.A. Los Angeles.

L.C. Library of Congress; Lord Chancellor; Lower Canada.

L.C. Adm. Lower Canada Admiralty Courts, 1873-1884.

L.C. Jur. Lower Canada Jurist.

L.C.L.J. Lower Canada Law Journal, Montreal, 1865-1868.

L.C.R. Lower Canada Reports, 1850-1867.

L. Cent. The Law Central, Washington, D.C., 1881.

L. Ct. Law Court.

L. Div. Law Division.

L. Ed. Lawyer's Edition, United States Supreme Court Reports, 1754-1956.

L. Ed. 2d Lawyers' Edition, United States Supreme Court Reports, Second Series, since 1956.

L.I.L. Lincoln's Inn Library.

L. Inst. J. Law Institute Journal.

L.J. Law Journal; Lord Justice.

L.J. Notes of Cas. Law Journal Notes of Cases, London.

L.J. (N.S.) Law Journal (New Series), Eng., Reports of all courts.

L. Lib. J. or **L. Libr. J.** or **L. Library J.** Law Library Journal (nonstandard).

L.M. & P. Lowndes, Maxwell and Pollock, Bail Court, Eng., 1850-1851.

L. Mag. The Law Magazine, London, Eng., 1828-1856.

L. Mag. & R. The Law Magazine and Review, London, Eng.

L.Q. Law Quarterly.

L.Q.R. or **L.Q. Rev.** Law Quarterly Review (nonstandard).

L.R. Law Reports, all courts, London, Eng.

L.R.A. Lawyers' Reports Annotated.

L.R. & Q.J. Law Review and Quarterly Journal, London, 1844-1856.

L.R. (Ir.) Law Reports, Ireland.

L.S. Mag. The Law Students' Magazine, London, 1844-1853.

L. Rep. The Law Reporter, Boston, 1838-1866; The Law Reporter, all courts, Eng.

L. Rev. Law Review.

L.T. The Law Times, all courts, Eng.

L.T. (N.S.) The Law Times (New Series), all courts, Eng.

La. Louisiana Reports, Supreme Court, 1830-1841, 1900-1972. See also, Mart., Rob.

La. Ann. Louisiana Annual Reports, Supreme Court, 1846-1900.

La. App. Louisiana Courts of Appeal Reports, 1924-1932.

La. L.J. Louisiana Law Journal, New Orleans, 1841-1842, 1876-1878.

La. L. Rev. Louisiana Law Review.

La Them. La Themis, Law Periodical, Lower Canada.

Lab. L.J. Labor Law Journal.

Lalor Supplement to Hill and Denio, New York Supreme Court, 1842-1844.

Lanc. Bar The Lancaster (Pa.) Bar, Law Periodical.

Land Econ. Land Economics.

Lane Exchequer, Eng., 1605-1612.

Lang. & T. Langfield and Townsend, Exchequer, Ireland, 1841-1842.

Lang. Con. Langdell's Select Cases on Contracts.

Lang. Sales Langdell's Select Cases on Sales of Personal Property.

Lans. Lansing, New York Supreme Court, 1869-1873.

Lans. Ch. Lansing's Chancery (N.Y.).

K. King.
K.B. Court of King's Bench.
K.C. King's Counsel.
K. & G. Keane and Grant, Registration Appeal Cases, Eng., 1854-1862.
K.C.R. Reports in time of King, Chancellor, 1724-1734.
K.L.S. Kentucky Law Summary (nonstandard).
Kames Court of Session, Scotland, 1716-1768.
Kames & W. Kames and Woodhouslee, Dictionary of Decisions, Court of Session, Scotland, 1540-1804.
Kames, R.D. Kames' Remarkable Decisions, Court of Session, Scotland, 1716-1752.
Kames, S.D. Kames' Select Decisions, Court of Session, Scotland, 1752-1768.
Kan. Kansas Reports, Supreme Court, since 1862. See also McCa.
Kan. App. Kansas Court of Appeals Reports, 1895-1901.
Kan. App. 2d Kansas Court of Appeals Reports, Since 1977.
Kan. L.J. Kansas Law Journal, Topeka.
Kan. L. Rev. University of Kansas Law Review (nonstandard).
Kay Chancery, Eng. (V.C. Wood), 1853-1854.
Kay & J. Kay and Johnson, Chancery, Eng. (V.C. Wood), 1854-1858.
Keb. Keble, King's Bench, Eng., 1661-1678.
Keen Rolls Court, Eng. 1836-1838.
Keilw. Keilwey, King's Bench, 1496-1530.
Kel. Sir John Kelyng, King's Bench, Eng., 1662-1669.
Kel. 1, 2 Wm. Kelynge's Reports, Eng., two parts—Chancery, 1730-1732; King's Bench, 1731-1734.
Kelly Georgia Supreme Court.
Ken. Kenyon, Notes of Cases, King's Bench and Chancery, Eng., 1753-1759.
Kent Kent's Commentaries on American Law.
Kern. Kernan, New York Court of Appeals, vols. 11-14.
Kerr New Brunswick, 1840-1848.
Keyes New York Court of Appeals, 1863-1868.
Kilk. Kilkerran, Court of Session, Scotland, 1738-1752.
Kirby Connecticut Superior Court, 1785-1788.
Kn. Knapp, Privy Council, Eng., 1829-1836.
Kn. & O. Knapp and Ombler, Election Cases, Eng., 1834-1837.
Kulp Kulp (Pa.)
Ky. Kentucky Reports, Court of Appeals, 1785-1951. See also, Hughes, Sneed, Hardin, Bibb, A.K. Marsh., Litt., T.B. Mon., B. Mon., J.J. Marsh., Dana, Met., Duv., and Bush.
Ky. Ct. App. Kentucky Court of Appeals, since 1976.
Ky. L.J. Kentucky Law Journal.
Ky. L.R. or **Ky. L.Rep.** or **Ky. L. Rptr.** Kentucky Law Reporter, 1880-1908 (Ky. L.R. & Ky. L.Rep. nonstandard).
Ky. Op. Kentucky Opinions, 1864-1886.
Ky. St. B.J. Kentucky State Bar Journal.

L. Law; Lord.
L. 5, (Long quinto.) One of the parts of the Year Books.
L. & A. Ins. Cas. Life and Accident Insurance Cases, New York, 1872-1877.
L. & Bk. Bull. Law and Bank Bulletin, Cincinnati, 1857-1858.

Latch King's Bench, Eng., 1625-1628.

Law. Lawyer; Lawyers; Lawyers'; Lawyer's.

Law. & Banker Lawyer and Banker and Central Law Journal.

Law & Contemp. Prob. or **Probs.** Law and Contemporary Problems (Prob. nonstandard).

Law & Eq. Rep. Law and Equity Reporter, New York, 1876-1877 (merged in The Reporter).

Law Chr. The Law Chronicle, or Journal of Jurisprudence, Edinburgh, 1829-1832; The Law Chronicle, London, 1833-1835.

Law Dig. The Law Digest, London, 1845-1856.

Law. Guild Rev. Lawyers' Guild Review.

Law Int. The Law Intelligencer, Providence, 1829-1831.

Law L. The Law List, London.

Law Lib. J. Law Library Journal (nonstandard).

Law Libr. J. Law Library Journal.

Law Q. Rev. Law Quarterly Review.

Law Rec. The Law Recorder, all courts, Ireland, 1827-1836.

Law Rep. Law Reporter (Mass.); Law Repository, North Carolina Supreme Court, 1811-1816.

Law Rep. News Law Report News.

Law, The Monthly Law Journal, London, 1874-1875.

Lawy. Rep. Lawyers' Reports, all cases of general interest in State and U.S. courts, Rochester.

Lea Lea (Tenn.).

Leach, C.C. Leach, Crown Cases, Eng., 1730-1814.

Lee Ecclesiastical Courts, Eng., 1752-1758; Lee (Cal.).

Lee, t. H. Lee's Reports in time of Hardwicke, King's Bench, Eng., 1733-1738.

Leg. Adv. The Legal Adviser, Chicago.

Leg. Chr. Legal Chronicle, Pottsville, Pa.

Leg. Exam. The Legal Examiner, and Law Chronicle, London, 1831-1833, 1869-1872.

Leg. Gaz. Legal Gazette, Philadelphia, various courts, 1869-1876.

Leg. & Ins. Rep. Legal and Insurance Reporter.

Leg. Int. Legal Intelligencer, Philadelphia.

Leg. N. Legal News, Montreal.

Leg. Obs. Legal Observer, Eng., 1830-1857.

Leg. Rep. The Legal Reporter, Dublin, 1840-1841.

Legal Intell. Legal Intelligencer.

Legis. Legislation.

Lehigh Va. Law Rep. Lehigh Valley Law Reporter.

Leigh Virginia Court of Appeals and General Court, 1829-1842.

Leon. Leonard, King's Bench, Eng., 1582-1615.

Lev. Levinz, King's Bench, and other courts, Eng., 1660-1696.

Lew. C.C. Lewin's Crown Cases, Eng., 1822-1838.

Ley King's Bench, Eng., 1608-1629.

Lib. Liberties; Library (nonstandard).

Lib. Ass. Liber Assissarum; Book of Assizes, King's Bench, 1327-1377. Year Book, pt. 5.

Libr. Library; Librarian.

Lilly Nisi Prius Reports, Eng., 1688-1693.

Lit. Littleton, Common Pleas and Exchequer, Eng., 1626-1631.

Litt. Littell, Kentucky Court of Appeals, 1822-1824.

Litt. Sel. Cas. Littell's Select Cases, Kentucky Court of Appeals, vol. 16 Kentucky Reports, 1795-1821.

Liv. L. Mag. Livingston's Law Magazine, New York, 1853-1856.

Liv. L. Reg. Livingston's Law Register, New York, 1849-1868.

Ll. & G. Lloyd and Goold, Chancery, Ireland, 1834-1839.

Ll. & W. Lloyd and Welsby, Queen's Bench, Eng., 1829-1830.

Lock. R.C. Lockwood's Reversed Cases, New York Court of Errors, 1799-1847.

Lofft King's Bench, Eng., 1772-1774.

Longf. & T. Longfield and Townsend, Exchequer, Ireland, 1841-1842.

Low. Lowell, U.S. Circuit Court, District of Massachusetts, 1865-1877.

Loy. L. Rev. Loyola of New Orleans Law Review.

Loy. L.A. L. Rev. Loyola of Los Angeles Law Review.

Loy. U. Chi. L.J. Loyola University of Chicago Law Journal.

Lud. Luders, Election Cases, Eng., 1784-1787.

Lum. Lumley's Poor Law Cases, various courts, Eng., 1834-1842.

Lush. Lushington, Admiralty, Eng., 1860-1863.

Lutw. Lutwyche, Common Pleas, Eng., 1682-1704.

Lutw. R.C. Lutwyche, Registration Cases, Eng., 1843-1853.

Luz. L. Obs. Luzerne Legal Observer, Carbondale (Pa.), 1860-1864.

Luz. L.R. Luzerne Legal Register, Wilkesbarre (Pa.), 1872-1888.

M. & C. Mylne and Craig, Chancery, Eng., 1835-1841.

M. & G. Manning and Granger, Common Pleas, Eng., 1840-1845.

M. & M. Moody and Malkin, Nisi Prius, Eng., 1826-1830.

M. & P. Moore and Payne, Common Pleas, Eng., 1827-1831.

M. & R. Manning and Ryland, King's Bench, Eng., 1827-1830.

M. & R. Mag. Cas. Manning and Ryland, Magistrate's Cases, Eng., 1827-1830.

M. & Rob. Moody and Robinson, Nisi Prius, Eng., 1830-1844.

M. & S. Maule and Selwyn, King's Bench, Eng., 1813-1817.

M. & Scott Moore and Scott, Common Pleas, Eng., 1831-1834.

M. & W. Meeson and Welsby, Exchequer, Eng., 1836-1847.

M.C. Magistrates' Cases; Master Commissioner; Member of Congress; Municipal Court (nonstandard).

M.C.C. Moody's Crown Cases, Eng., 1824-1844.

M.J. Military Justice Reporter, since 1975.

M.R. Master of the Rolls, Eng.

Mac. & G. Macnaghten and Gordon, Chancery, Eng., 1849-1852.

Mac. & H. Macrae and Hertslet, Insolvency Cases, Eng., 1840-1852.

MacArth. MacArthur, District of Columbia, Supreme Court, 1873-1879.

MacArthur & M. MacArthur and Mackey (D.C.).

MacArthur's Pat. Cas. MacArthur's Patent Cases, U.S.

Mac F. Mac Farland, Jury Courts, Scotland, 1838-1839.

Mac. P.C. Macrory's Patent Cases, 1841-1856.

Mac. Mackey, District of Columbia Supreme Court.

Mach. Machine; Machinery.

Macl. & R. Maclean and Robinson, Scotch Appeals, House of Lords, 1839.

Macl. R. Cas. Maclaurin, Remarkable Criminal Cases, Scotland, 1670-1773.

Macph. Macpherson and others, Court of Session, Scotland, 1862-1873

Macq. Macqueen, Scotch Appeals, House of Lords, 1849-1865.

Macq. L.C. Macqueen, Leading Cases of Parliamentary Divorce, Eng., 1669-1842.

Madd. Maddock, Chancery, Eng., 1815-1822.

Madd. & G. Maddock and Geddart, Chancery, Eng., 1821; Maddock and Geldart, Chancery, Eng., 1821.

Mag. Magistrate.

Magis. Ct. Magistrate's Court.

Man. Manhattan; Manitoba Reports, 1875-1883; Manning (Mich.).

Man. L.J. Manitoba Law Journal, 1884-1885.

Man. L.R. Manitoba Law Reports.

Man. Unrep. Cas. Manning's Unreported Cases (La.).

Manson Manson English Reports.

Mar. Marine; Maritime.

Mar. L.C. (N.S.) Maritime Law Cases, New Series, Eng.

Mar. L.R. Maritime Law Reports, Admiralty, Eng., 1860-1871.

March King's Bench, Eng., 1639-1642.

Marq. L. Rev. Marquette Law Review.

Marr. Marriage; Marriott, Admiralty, Eng., 1776-1779.

Marsh. Marshall, Common Pleas, Eng., 1813-1816.

Marsh. A.K. Marshall, A.K., Kentucky Court of Appeals, 1817-1821.

Marsh. Dec. Chief Justice Marshall's Decisions, by Brockenbrough, 1802-1836.

Marsh. J.J. Marshall, J. J., Kentucky Court of Appeals, 1829-1832.

Mart. (La.) Martin, Louisiana Supreme Court, 1809-1823.

Mart. (La. N.S.) Martin, Louisiana Supreme Court, New Series, 1823-1830.

Mart. (N.C.) Martin, various courts, North Carolina, 1778-1797.

Mart. & Y. Martin and Yerger, Tennessee Supreme Court, 1825-1828.

Marvel Marvel (Del.).

Mas. Mason, U. S. Circuit Court, First Circuit, 1815-1830.

Mass. Massachusetts Reports, Supreme Judicial Court, since 1804. See Quin., Wms., Tyng, Pick., Met., Cush., Gray, Allen.

Mass. App. Ct. Massachusetts Appeals Court Reports, since 1967.

Mass. App. Dec. Massachusetts Appellate Decisions, since 1941.

Mass. App. Div. Massachusetts Appellate Division Reports, 1936-1950.

Mass. L. Rev. Massachusetts Law Review.

Mat. Matrimonial and Divorce Division, Eng.

McAll. McAllister, U. S. District Court, California, 1855-1859.

McCa. McCahon, U.S. Courts, Kansas, 1858-1868 (nonstandard).

McCart. McCarter, New Jersey Equity, vols. 14, 15, 1861-1862.

McCl. McCleland, Exchequer, Eng., 1824.

McCl. & Yo. McCleland and Younge, Exchequer, Eng., 1824-1825.

McCord South Carolina Constitutional Court and Court of Appeals, 1821-1828.

McCord, Ch. South Carolina Court of Appeals, in Chancery, 1825-1827.

McCra. McCrary, U.S. Circuit Court, Eighth Circuit, 1874-1883.

McGloin Louisiana Courts of Appeal, 1880.

McLean U. S. Circuit Court, Seventh Circuit, 1829-1855.

McMull. McMullan, South Carolina Court of Appeals, at Law, 1835-1842.

McMull. Eq. McMullan, South Carolina Court of Appeals, in Equity, 1840-1842, 1827-1837.

Md. Maryland Reports, Court of Appeals, since 1851. See Har. & McH., Har. & J., Gill. & J., Gill., Bland.

Md. App. Maryland Appellate Reports, since 1967.

Md. Ch. Maryland High Court of Chancery Reports, 1847-1854.

Md. L. Rec. Maryland Law Record, Baltimore.

Md. L. Rep. Maryland Law Reporter, Baltimore, 1871-1872.

Md. L. Rev. Maryland Law Review.

Me. Maine Reports, Supreme Court, 1820-1965.

Me. L. Rev. Maine Law Review.

Med. Media (nonstandard); Medical; Medicine.

Med. L.J. Medico-Legal Journal, New York. 1884-1886.

Med. Trial Tech. Q. Medical Trial Technique Quarterly.

Megone Cases under the Companies Acts, Eng., 1888-1890.

Meigs Tennessee Supreme Court, 1838-1839.

Melb. Melbourne.

Mem. Memorandum; Memoranda; Memphis.

Mem. L.J. Memphis Law Journal, 1878-1879.

Mem. St. U.L. Rev. Memphis State University Law Review.

Mer. Merivale, Chancery, Eng., 1815-1817.

Met. Metcalf, Massachusetts Supreme Court, vols. 42-54, 1840-1847.

Met. (Ky.) Metcalfe, Kentucky Court of Appeals, 1858-1863.

Mfg. Manufacturing.

Mfr. Manufacturer.

Mich. Michigan Reports, Supreme Court, since 1847. See Doug., Har., and Walk.

Mich. App. Michigan Appeals Reports, since 1965.

Mich. Ct. Cl. Michigan Court of Claims Reports, 1938-1942.

Mich. L.J. Michigan Law Journal.

Mich. L. Rev. Michigan Law Review.

Mich. N.P. Michigan Nisi Prius Reports, Circuit Courts, 1869-1871.

Mil. L. Rev. Military Law Review.

Miles Philadelphia District Court, 1835-1842.

Miller Miller (La.).

Miller's Dec. Miller's Decisions, U.S. 8th Circuit Ct.

Mills South Carolina Constitutional Court, 1817-1818.

Milw. Milward, Ecclesiastical, Ireland, 1819-1843.

Min. Mineral.

Min. Rep. Mining Reports, State and U.S. Courts, Chicago.

Minn. Minnesota Reports, Supreme Court, 1851-1977.

Minn. L. Rev. Minnesota Law Review.

Minor Alabama Supreme Court, 1820-1826.

Misc. or **Misc. Rep.** N.Y. Miscellaneous Reports.

Misc. 2d N.Y. Miscellaneous Reports, Second Series.

Miss. Mississippi Reports, 1818-1966. See also, Walk., How., Sm. & N., Freem.

Miss. L.J. Mississippi Law Journal.

Mkt. Market.

Mkts. Markets.

Mo. Missouri Reports, Supreme Court, 1821-1956.

Mo. App. Missouri Appeal Reports, 1876-1951.

Mo. Jur. Monthly Jurist, Bloomington, Ill., 1877-1878.

Mo. L. Mag. Monthly Law Magazine, London, 1838-1841.

Mo. L. Rev. Missouri Law Review.

Mo. W.J. Monthly Western Jurist, Bloomington, Ill., 1875-1877.

Moak English Reports, American reprint of all cases of value in the U.S.

Mod. Modern; Modern Reports, King's Bench, Eng., 1663-1732.

Mod. C.L. & Eq. Modern Cases in Law in Equity.

Mod. L. Rev. Modern Law Review, London.

Mol. Molloy, Chancery, Ireland, 1807-1832.

Mon. Monroe, T. B., Kentucky Court of Appeals, 1824-1828.

Mon. B. B. Monroe, Kentucky Court of Appeals, 1840-1857.

Monag. Monaghan (Pa.).

Mont. Montana Reports, Supreme Court, since 1868.

Mont. & A. Montagu and Ayrton, Bankruptcy, Eng., 1833-1838.

Mont. & B. Montagu and Bligh, Bankruptcy, Eng., 1832-1833.

Mont. & Ch. Montagu and Chitty, Bankruptcy, Eng., 1838-1840.

Mont. & Mac. Montagu and MacArthur, Bankruptcy, Eng., 1828-1830.

Mont. Bkcy. Montagu, Bankruptcy Reports, Eng., 1830-1832.

Mont. Co. Law Repr. or **Rptr.** Montgomery County (Pa.) Law Reporter.

Mont. D. & D. Montagu, Deacon & De Gex, Bankruptcy, Eng., 1840-1844.

Mont. L.R. Montreal Law Reports, (Q.B.) Queen's Bench, (S.C.) Supreme Court.

Mont. L. Rev. Montana Law Review.

Month. Law. Bul. Monthly Law Bulletin, N.Y.

Moo. & R. Moody and Robinson's Reports, N. P.

Moo. & S. Moore and Scott's Reports, C. P.

Moody Crown Cases Reserved, Eng., 1824-1844.

Moore J. B. Moore, Common Pleas, Eng., 1817-1827.

Moore, Sir F. Queen's Bench, Eng., 1512-1621.

Moore, Ind. Ap. Moore's Indian Appeals, Privy Council, 1836-1872.

Moore, P.C.C. Moore's Privy Council Cases, 1836-1862.

Moore, P.C.C.(N.S.) Moore's Privy Council Cases (New Series), 1862-1873.

Mor. Dict. of **Dec.** Morison, Dictionary of Decisions, Court of Session, Scotland, 1540-1808.

Mor. Syn. Morison, Synopsis of Decisions, Court of Session, Scotland, 1808-1816.

Morr. Morris, Iowa Supreme Court, 1839-1846.

Morr. Bkcy. Morrell, Reports of Cases under English Bankruptcy Act of 1883, 1884-1890.

Morr. Min. R. Morrison's Mining Reports.

Mos. Mosley, Chancery, Eng., 1726-1730.

Mun. Municipal.

Mun. Ct. Municipal Court.

Munic. L.J. Municipal Law Journal (nonstandard).

Munf. Munford, Virginia Court of Appeals, 1810-1820.

Mur. & H. Murphy and Hurlstone, Exchequer, Eng., 1837.

Murph. Murphey, North Carolina Supreme Court, 1804-1819.

Murr. Murray, Jury Courts, Scotland, 1815-1830.

Mut. Mutual.

My. Fed. Dec., Myer, Federal Decisions, all U.S. Courts, from organization to 1882, arranged by subjects.

Myl. & C. Mylne and Craig, Chancery, Eng., 1835-1841.

Myl. & K. Mylne and Keen, Chancery, Eng., 1832-1835.

Myrick Probate Court Reports, San Francisco, 1872-1879.

N. North; Northern.

N.A. North America.

NACCA L.J. National Association of Claimant's Counsel of America Law Journal.

N. & M. Neville and Manning, King's Bench, Eng., 1832-1836.

N. & P. Neville and Perry, Queen's Bench, Eng., 1836-1838.

N.B. New Brunswick Reports. See also, Chip., Bert., Kerr, Allen, Han., Pugs., Pugs. & B.

N.B.R. National Bankruptcy Register, 1867-1879

N. Benl. New Benloe, King's Bench, Eng., 1509-1625.

N.C. North Carolina Reports, Supreme Court. See also, Mart. Hayw., Tayl., Conf., Cam. & N., Murph., Car. L. R., N.C.T.R., Hawks, Dev., Dev. & B., Ired., Busb., Jones, Winst., Phil.

N.C. App. North Carolina Court of Appeals Reports, since 1968.

N.C.C.A. Negligence & Compensation Cases Annotated (nonstandard).

NCCUSL National Conference of Commissioners on Uniform State Laws.

N.C.L.Rev. North Carolina Law Review.

N.C.T.R. North Carolina Term Reports, 1816-1818.

N.D. North Dakota Reports, Supreme Court, 1890-1953; Northern District.

N.D.L.Rev. North Dakota Law Review.

N.E. North Eastern Reporter.

N.E.2d North Eastern Reporter, Second Series.

NEPA National Environmental Policy Act of 1969.

N.Eng. Rep. New England Reporter, Rochester.

N.F. Newfoundland.

N.H. New Hampshire Reports, Supreme Court, since 1816. See also, Smith.

N.Ir.L.Q. Northern Ireland Legal Quarterly.

N., H. & C. Nichol, Hare and Carrow, English Railway Cases, 1835-1855.

N.J. New Jersey Reports, Supreme Court, since 1948.

N.J. Eq. New Jersey Equity Reports, Court of Chancery and Supreme Court in Equity, since 1830. See also, Sax., Green, Halst., Stock., Beas., McCart., Greene, C.E., Stew.

N.J.L. New Jersey Law Reports, Supreme Court and Court of Errors and Appeals, Cases at Law, 1790-1948. See also, Coxe, Pen.,

South., Halst., Green, Har., Spen., Zab., Dutch., Vroom.

N.J.L.J. New Jersey Law Journal.

N.J. Misc. New Jersey Miscellaneous Reports, 1923-1949.

N.J. Super. New Jersey Superior Court Reports, since 1948.

N.L. Nelson's Lutwyche Reports, C.P.

N.M. New Mexico Reports, Supreme Court and Court of Appeals, since 1890.

N.M. L.Rev. New Mexico Law Review.

N.P. Nisi Prius; Ohio Nisi Prius Reports (nonstandard).

N.R. New Reports (Bosanquet and Puller), Common Pleas, Eng., 1804-1807; New Reports, all courts, Eng., 1862-1865.

N.R. (N.S.) New Reports (New Series), Queen's Bench, Eng., 1862-1873.

N.S. or **n.s.** New Style; New Series; N.S. Nova Scotia Law Reports.

N.S. Dec. Nova Scotia Decisions, Supreme Court, 1866-1875.

N.S. Eq. Nova Scotia Equity Reports, 1873-1882.

N.W. North Western Reporter.

N.W. 2d North Western Reporter, Second Series.

N.Y. New York Reports, Court of Appeals, since 1847. See also, Comst., Seld., Kern.

N.Y. Ann. Cas. New York Annotated Cases.

N.Y.C. Rep. or **Rptr.** New York Code Reporter, 1848-1851.

N.Y. Civ. Pro. R. New York Civil Procedure Reports.

N.Y. Cr. R. New York Criminal Reports, Albany.

N.Y.L.F. New York Law Forum.

N.Y.L.J. New York Law Journal.

N.Y.L. Sch. L. Rev. New York Law School Law Review.

N.Y. Leg. N. New York Legal News.

N.Y. Leg. Obs. New York Legal Observer, 1842-1854.

N.Y. Mo. L.B. New York Monthly Law Bulletin.

N.Y.S. New York Supplement, since 1938.

N.Y.S.2d New York Supplement, Second Series.

N.Y. St. R. New York State Reporter, Albany.

N.Y. Sup. Ct. New York Supreme Court Reports, 1873-1896.

N.Y. Super. New York City Superior Court. See also, Hall, Sandf., Duer, Bosw., Rob., and Sweeney.

N.Y. Supp. New York Supplement (nonstandard).

N.Y. Supr. New York Supreme Court Reports, 1873-1896. See also, Barb., Lans., Hun., Thomps. & C.

N.Y. Tr. New York Transcript.

N.Y. Tr. (N.S.) New York Transcript, New Series.

N.Y.U.L.Q.Rev. New York University Law Quarterly Review.

N.Y.U.L.Rev. New York University Law Review.

N.Y.W.Dig. The New York Weekly Digest.

Nat. Natural; National (nonstandard).

Nat'l or **Natl.** National.

Nat'l B.J. National Bar Journal.

Nat'l Bk. Cas. National Bank Cases, Albany and San Francisco, 1864-1889.

Nat'l B.R. National Bankruptcy Register, New York, 1867-1879.

Nat'l Corp. Rep. National Corporation Reporter.

Nat'l Munic. Rev. National Municipal Review (nonstandard).

Nat'l Tax J. National Tax Journal.

Neb. Nebraska Reports, Supreme Court, since 1860. Some Territorial cases added.

Neb. L.J. Nebraska Law Journal.

Neb. L. Rev. Nebraska Law Review.

Negl. & Comp. Cas. Ann. Negligence & Compensation Cases Annotated.

Negl. & Comp. Cas. Ann. (n.s.). Negligence & Compensation Cases Annotated, New Series.

Negl. & Comp. Cas. Ann. 3d Negligence & Compensation Cases Annotated, Third Series.

Negl. & Comp. Cas. Ann. 4th Negligence & Compensation Cases Annotated, Fourth Series.

Nels. Nelson, Chancery, Eng., 1625-1695.

Nev. Nevada Reports, Supreme Court, since 1865.

New Benl. New Benloe, King's Bench, Eng., 1509-1625.

New Eng. New England.

New L.J. New Law Journal.

New Mag. Cas. New Magistrates' Cases, Eng., Brittleston, Wise and Parnell, 1844-1850.

New Ses. Cas. New Session Cases, Carron, Hamerton and Allen, and others, all courts, Eng., 1844-1851.

New T.R. New Term Reports, all courts, Eng., 1835-1841.

Newb. Adm. Newberry, U.S. District Courts in Admiralty, 1842-1857.

1983 42 U.S.C. §1983, concerning civil actions for deprivation of rights.

Nolan King's Bench, Magistrates' Cases, Eng., 1791-1792.

North. Northington, Chancery (by Eden), Eng., 1757-1766.

Northam. Law Rep. or **Rptr.** Northampton Law Reporter.

Notre Dame Law. Notre Dame Lawyer.

Nott & H. Nott and Huntington, U.S. Court of Claims, vols. 1-7.

Nott & McC. Nott and McCord, South Carolina Constitutional Court, 1817-1820.

Noy King's Bench, Eng., time of Elizabeth, James and Charles.

Nw. U. L. Rev. Northwestern University Law Review.

O. Ohio Reports, Supreme Court, 1821-1851 (nonstandard).

O.A.G. Opinions of the Attorney General (nonstandard).

O.Benl. Old Benloe, Common Pleas, Eng., 1486-1580.

O.C.C. Ohio Circuit Court Reports (nonstandard).

O.C.D. Ohio Circuit Decisions (nonstandard).

O.D. Ohio Decisions (nonstandard).

O.G. or **O.G. Pat. Off.** Official Gazette, U.S. Patent Office.

O.L.A. Ohio Law Abstract (nonstandard.).

O.L.D. Ohio Lower Court Decisions (nonstandard).

O.L.J. Ohio Law Journal, Columbus, 1880-1884 (nonstandard).

O.L.R. Ohio Law Reporter (nonstandard).

O.O. Ohio Opinions (nonstandard).

O.R. Ohio Reports, Supreme Court, 1821-1851 (nonstandard).

O.S. Ohio State Reports, Supreme Court, since 1852 (nonstandard).

OSHA Occupational Safety and Health Act of 1970, as amended.

O.S.L.J. Ohio St. L.J. (nonstandard).

O. Supp. Ohio Supplement (non-standard).

Off. Office.

Ohio. App. Ohio Appellate Reports.

Ohio App.2d, 3d Ohio Appellate Reports, Second Series and Third Series.

Ohio C.C., Ohio C.C.(n.s.) Ohio Circuit Court Reports, 1885-1917.

Ohio C.C.R. Ohio Circuit Court Reports, 1885-1901.

Ohio C. Dec. Ohio Circuit Decisions, 1885-1901.

Ohio Dec. Ohio Decisions.

Ohio L. Abs. Ohio Law Abstract.

Ohio L.Bull. Ohio Law Bulletin.

Ohio Leg. N. Ohio Legal News.

Ohio Misc. Ohio Miscellaneous Reports, since 1965.

Ohio Misc. 2d Ohio Miscellaneous Reports, Second Series.

Ohio N.P., Ohio N.P. (n.s.), Ohio Nisi Prius Reports, 1894-1934.

Ohio N.U.L.Rev. Ohio Northern University Law Review.

Ohio Op. Ohio Opinions.

Ohio Op.2d, 3d Ohio Opinions, Second Series and Third Series.

Ohio S. & C.P. Dec. Ohio Superior and Common Pleas Decisions.

Ohio St. Ohio State Reports, Supreme Court, since 1852.

Ohio St. 2d, 3d Ohio State Reports, Second Series and Third Series.

Ohio St. L. J. Ohio State Law Journal.

Oil & Gas Tax Q. Oil and Gas Tax Quarterly.

Okla. Oklahoma Reports, Supreme Court, 1890-1953.

Okla. B.J. Journal of the Oklahoma Bar Association.

Okla. Crim. Oklahoma Criminal Reports, 1908-1953.

Okla. L. Rev. Oklahoma Law Review.

Olc. Adm. Olcott, Admiralty, U.S. District Court, Southern District of New York, 1843-1847.

Old. Oldright, Nova Scotia Law Reports, 1860-1866.

Old Ben. See O. Benl. and Benl. & D.

O'm. & H. O'Malley and Hardcastle, Election Cases, 1869-1880.

Ont. Ontario High Court of Justice.

Ont. App. Ontario Appeal Reports.

Ont. Pr. Ontario Practice Reports.

Op. Att'y Gen. Opinions, U.S. Attorney General, since 1791. For state Attorney General Opinions, add in parenthesis the abbreviation for the state, *e.g.*, Op. Att'y Gen. (Ky.).

Ord. Order.

Or. Oregon Reports, Supreme Court, since 1853.

Or. App. Oregon Reports, Court of Appeals, since 1969.

Or. T.R. Oregon Tax Reporter, since 1962.

Or. L. Rev. or **Ore. L. Rev.** Oregon Law Review.

Otto U.S. Supreme Court, vols. 91-107.

Outerbridge Outerbridge (Pa.).

Over. Overton, Tennessee, various courts, 1791-1817.

Owen King's Bench, Eng., 1556-1615.

Oxley Young's Admiralty Decisions, Canada, 1865-1880.

P. Pacific Reporter; Plaintiff; Probate Division, Law Reports, Eng.; Parliament; Pleas.

P.2d Pacific Reporter, Second Series.

P. & D. Perry and Davison, Queen's Bench, Eng., 1838-1841.

P. & K. Perry and Knapp, Election Cases, Eng., 1833.

P.C. Privy Council, Law Reports, Eng.; Pleas of the Crown; Probate Court.

P.C.C. Penal and Correctional Code (Model Penal Code).

P. Ct. Probate Court.

P-H Prentice-Hall.

P.J. Presiding Judge or Presiding Justice.

P.L. Mag. Poor Law Magazine, Glasgow and Edinburgh.

P.R.R. Puerto Rico Reports, 1899-1972.

P.U.R. Public Utilities Reports Annotated.

P.U.R. (n.s.) Public Utilities Reports, New Series.

P.U.R. 3d, 4th Public Utilities Reports, Third Series or Fourth Series.

P.W. or **P. Wms.** Peer Williams, Chancery, Eng., 1695-1735.

Pa. Pennsylvania Reports, Supreme Court, 1829-1832; Pennsylvania State Reports, since 1845. See also, Da., Add., Yeates, Bin., Bright., Serg. & R., Rawle, Pen. & W., Pa. R., Watts, Whart., Watts & S., Grant, Cas., Barr, Jones, Harris, Casey, Wright, Smith.

Pa. C., Pa. Co. Ct. or **Pa. County Ct.** Pennsylvania County Court Reports, 1885-1921.

Pa. Commw. Pennsylvania Commonwealth Court Reports, since 1970.

Pa. D. Pennsylvania District Reports, 1892-1921.

Pa. D. & C. Pennsylvania District and County Reports, since 1921.

Pa. D. & C.2d, 3d Pennsylvania District and County Reports, Second Series or Third Series.

Pa. Dist. R. Pennsylvania District Reports, 1892-1921.

Pa. Fiduc. Pennsylvania Fiduciary Reporter, since 1951.

Pa. L.J. Pennsylvania Law Journal, 1842-1848.

Pa. L.J. Rep. Pennsylvania Law Journal Reports, Clarke, 1842-1861.

Pa. L. Rec. Pennsylvania Law Record, Philadelphia, 1879-1880.

Pa. St. Pennsylvania State Supreme Court, since 1845 (nonstandard).

Pa. Super. or **Pa. Super. Ct.** Pennsylvania Superior Court Reports, since 1895.

Pac. Pacific; Pacific Reporter.

Pac. C. L.J. Pacific Coast Law Journal, San Francisco, 1878-1882.

Pac. L. Mag. Pacific Law Magazine, San Francisco, 1867.

Pac. L.R. or **L. Rptr.** Pacific Law Reporter, San Francisco, 1870-1878.

Pagin Pagin's Federal Precedents and Forms.

Paige New York Court of Chancery, 1828-1845.

Paine U.S. Circuit Court, Second Circuit, 1810-1840.

Palm. Palmer, King's Bench, Eng., 1619-1629.

Park. Parker, Exchequer, Eng., 1743-1766.

Park. C.C. Parker, Criminal Cases, various courts of New York, 1823-1868.

Pars. Eq. Cas. Parsons' Equity Cases, First Judicial District, Pennsylvania, 1841-1851.

Pat. Patent.

Pat. App. Patterson, Scotch Appeals, House of Lords, 1851-1873.

Pat. & H. Patton, Jr., and Heath, Virginia Special Court of Appeals, 1855-1857.

Pat. & T.M. Rev. Patent and Trade Mark Review.

Pag. L. Ann. Patent Law Annual.

Pat. Off. Ga. Official Gazette, U.S. Patent Office.

Paton Scotch Appeals, House of Lords, Eng., 1753-1821.

Pea. Peake's Reports, K.B., Eng.

Peake Nisi Prius, Eng., 1790-1812.

Peake Add. Cas. Peake's Additional Cases, Nisi Prius, Eng., 1795-1812. (Cited as 2nd Peake).

Pears. Pearson's Decisions, Twelfth Judicial District, Pennsylvania, 1851-1880.

Peck Tennessee Supreme Court, 1821-1824.

Peck (Ill.) Illinois Supreme Court, vols. 11-30.

Peckw. Peckwell, Election Cases, Eng., 1802-1806.

Pen. Pennington, New Jersey Laws, vols. 2 and 3, 1806-1813.

Pen. & W. Penrose and Watts, Pennsylvania Supreme Court, 1829-1832.

Pennewill Pennewill (Del.).

Pennyp. Pennypacker, Pennsylvania Supreme Court, cases omitted from regular reports, 1881-1884.

Pers. Personal.

Pet. Peters, U.S. Supreme Court, vols. 26-41, 1828-1842.

Pet. Adm. Peters' Admiralty Decisions, U.S. District Court, Eastern District of Pennsylvania, 1780-1807.

Pet. C.C. Peters, U.S. Circuit Court, 1803-1818.

Phil. Ch. Phillips, Chancery, Eng., 1841-1849.

Phil. E.C. Phillips, Election Cases, Eng., 1780-1781.

Phil. Ecc. Phillimore Ecclesiastical Courts, Eng., 1809-1821.

Phil. (N.C.) Phillips, North Carolina Supreme Court, at Law, 1866-1868.

Phil. (N.C.) Eq. Phillips, North Carolina Supreme Court, in Equity, 1866-1868.

Phil. L.J. Philippine Law Journal.

Phil. R. Ecc. Robert Phillimore, Ecclesiastical Judgments, Eng., 1867-1875.

Phila. Reports of various courts in Philadelphia.

Pick. Pickering, Massachusetts Supreme Court, vols. 18-41, 1822-1840.

Pickle Pickle's Reports (Tenn.).

Pig. & R. Piggott and Rodwell, Election Cases, Eng., 1843-1845.

Pike Arkansas Supreme Court, vols. 1-5.

Pinn. Pinney, Wisconsin Supreme Court, 1839-1852.

Pitc. Pitcairn, Criminal Trials, Scotland, 1488-1624.

Pitt. Pittsburgh.

Pitts. Various courts, Pittsburgh, Pa., 1853-1873.

Pitts. L.J. Pittsburgh Legal Journal.

Pl. Pleas.

Plan. Planning.

Plow. Plowden, various courts, Eng., 1550-1579.

Pol. Political; Politics; Pollexfen, King's Bench, Eng., 1669-1684.

Pol. Sci. Q. Political Science Quarterly (nonstandard).

Police J. Ct. Police Justice's Court.

Pol'y Policy.

Poph. Popham, King's Bench, Eng., 1592-1627.

Port. Porter, Alabama Supreme Court, 1834-1839.

Port. Ind. Porter, Indiana.

Pow., R. & D. Power, Rodwell and Dew, Election Cases, Eng., 1848-1856.

Pr. Ed. Prince Edward's Island Reports, 1850-1882.

Pr. R. Practice Reports, Upper Canada.

Prac. Practical; Practice; Practitioners.

Prac. Law. Practical Lawyer.

Pratt Contraband Cases in High Court of Admiralty, Eng., 1740-1751. Appendix of Treaties, 1604-1827.

Pratt P.L. Cas. Bott's Poor Law Cases edited by Pratt, Eng., 1768-1827.

Prec. Ch. Precedents in Chancery, Eng., 1689-1722 (edited by T. Finch).

Price Exchequer, Eng., 1814-1824.

Price Pr. Cas. Price, Notes of Practice Cases, Exchequer, Eng., 1830-1831.

Pro., or **Prob.** Probate Division, Law Reports, Eng.

Prob. Probate; Problems (nonstandard).

Probs. Problems.

Proc. Procedures; Proceedings.

Prod. Product; Production.

Prop. Property.

Psych. Psychiatry; Psychology.

Pub. Public.

Pub. Doc. Public Documents.

Pub. L. Public Law.

Pugs. Pugsley, New Brunswick, Supreme Court, 1872-1876.

Pugs. & B. Pugsley and Burbidge, New Brunswick Supreme Court, 1877-1881.

Pyke Quebec, King's Bench, 1809-1810.

Q. Quarterly; Queen; Quebec (nonstandard).

Q.B. Queen's Bench.

Q.B. (N.S.) Adolphus and Ellis, Queen's Bench, New Series, 1841-1852.

Q.B. Div. Queen's Bench Division, Law Reports, Eng.

Q.L.J. Quarterly Law Journal, Richmond, Va., 1856-1859.

Q.L.R. Quebec Law Reports.

Que. Quebec.

Queb. Q.B. Quebec Queen's Bench Reports.

Quin. Quincy, Massachusetts, various courts, 1761-1772.

R. Reports; Reporter; Review; Rex; Regina; King; Rolls Court.

R. & M. Ryan and Moody, Nisi Prius, Eng., 1823-1826.

R. & R.C.C. Russell and Ryan's Crown Cases, Eng., 1800-1823.

R.C.L. Ruling Case Law.

RESPA Real Estate Settlement Procedures Act.

R.I. Rhode Island Reports, Supreme Court, since 1828.

RICO Racketeer Influenced and Corrupt Organizations Act.

R.M. Charlt. R.M. Charlton, Georgia.

R.R. Railroad.

Railw. Cas. Railway Cases, Eng., by Nicholl, Hare, Oliver, Beavan, etc., all courts, 1835-1854.

Rand. Randolph, Virginia Court of Appeals, 1821-1828.

Rawle Pennsylvania Supreme Court, 1828-1835.

Raym. Lord Raymond, King's Bench and Common Pleas, Eng., 1694-1732.

Raym., T. T. Raymond, various courts, Eng., 1660-1682.

Rayner Tithe Cases, Eng., 1575-1782.

Real Pr. Cas. Real Property Cases, all courts, Eng., 1842-1847.

Rec. Record.

Rec. A.B. City N.Y. Record of the Association of the Bar of the City of New York.

Record of N.Y.C.B.A. Record of the Association of the Bar of the City of New York (nonstandard).

Redf. Redfield, New York Surrogate's Court, 1846-1882.

Redf. & B. Redfield and Bigelow, Leading Cases on Bills and Notes.

Reev. E.L. Reeve's English Law.

Ref. Referee; Referees; Referee's; Refining; Reform.

Ref. J. Referees' Journal; Journal of the National Association of Referees in Bankruptcy.

Reg. Register; Regulation.

Rel. Relations.

Reorg. Reorganizations.

Rep. Reporter (nonstandard for reports of cases); Reports; Representative; Coke's Reports; The Reporter, Boston.

Rep. Ch. Reports in Chancery, Eng., 1625-1710.

Res. Reserve.

Rev. Review; Revised.

Rev. Leg. Revue Legale, Montreal.

Rice South Carolina Court of Appeals and Errors, at Law, 1838-1839.

Rice Ch. South Carolina Court of Appeals and Errors, in Equity, 1838-1839.

Rich. Richmond; Richardson, South Carolina Court of Appeals and Errors, at Law, 1844-1868.

Rich. Cas. Richardson Cases, South Carolina Court of Appeals and Errors, 1831-1832; 1828-1834.

Rich. Eq. Richardson, South Carolina Court of Appeals and Errors, in Equity, 1844-1868.

Rich. & W. Richardson and Woodbury (N.H.).

Ridg. App. Ridgeway's Irish Appeals, 1784-1796.

Ridg., L. & S. Ridgeway, Lapp and Schoales, Ireland, 1793-1795.

Ridg. t. Hard. Ridgeway, King's Bench, Eng., 1733-1736; Chancery, in time of Hardwicke, 1744-1745.

Riley South Carolina Court of Appeals, etc., at Law, 1836-1837.

Riley Ch. South Carolina Court of Appeals, etc., in Equity, 1836-1837.

Ritchie Equity Decisions, Nova Scotia, 1873-1882.

Rob. Adm. Robinson, High Court of Admiralty, Eng., 1798-1808.

Rob. Eccl. Dr. Robertson, Ecclesiastical Courts, Eng., 1844-1853.

Rob. (La.) Robinson, Louisiana Supreme Court, 1841-1846.

Rob. (N.Y.) Robertson, New York City Superior Court, vols. 24-30, 1863-1868.

Rob. (Va.) Robinson, Virginia General Court and Court of Appeals, 1842-1844.

Rob., W. Dr. W. Robinson, Admiralty, Eng., 1838-1852.

Robb Pat. Cas. Robb's Patent Cases, U.S. Courts, 1789-1850.

Robert. Sc. App. Robertson, Scotch Appeals, House of Lords, Eng., 1707-1727.

Robin. Sc. App. Robinson, Scotch Appeals, House of Lords, Eng., 1840-1841.

Robt. Robertson, New York City Superior Court.

Rocky Mt., or **Mtn., L. Rev.** Rocky Mountain Law Review (**Mt.** nonstandard).

Rog. Rec. Rogers, New York City Hall Recorder.

Rolle King's Bench, Eng., 1614-1624.

Rom. Cas. Romilly, Notes of Cases, Eng., 1767-1787.

Root Connecticut Supreme Court, 1764-1797.

Rose Bankruptcy, Eng., 1810-1816.

Rot. Cur. Rep. Rotuli Curiae Regis. Rolls of the King's Bench, Eng., 1194-1199.

Rowe Law Courts, England and Ireland, 1798-1810.

Rptr. Reporter (reports of cases).

Russ. Russell, Chancery, Eng., 1823-1829.

Russ. & M. Russell and Mylne, Chancery, Eng., 1829-1833.

Rut.-Cam. L. Rev. Rutgers-Camden Law Review.

Rut., or **Rutgers, L. Rev.** Rutgers Law Review (**Rut.** nonstandard).

Ry. Railway.

Ry. & Can. Cas. Railway and Canal Cases, Eng., Neville and Macnamara; Brown and Macnamara.

Ry. & Cor. L.J. Railway and Corporation Law Journal, New York.

S. Section; Series; South; Southern.

S. & D. Shaw and Dunlop, Court of Session, Scotland, 1800-1862.

S. & R. See Serg. & R.

S. & S. Simon and Stewart, Chancery, Eng., 1822-1826.

S. & Sm. Searle and Smith, Probate and Divorce, Eng.

S. & T. Swabey and Tristram, Probate and Divorce, Eng.

S.C. South Carolina Reports, since 1868. For prior reports, see also, Bay, Brev., De Sau., Const., Nott & McC., McCord, Harp., Bail., Hill, Riley, Dud., Rice, Cheves, McMul., Speers, Strob., Rich.

S.C. Eq. South Carolina Equity Reports, 1784-1868.

S.C.L. South Carolina Law Reports, 1783-1868.

S.C.L.Q. South Carolina Law Quarterly.

S.C. L. Rev. South Carolina Law Review.

S. Cal. L. Rev. Southern California Law Review.

S. Ct. Supreme Court Reporter, since 1882.

S.D. South Dakota Reports, Supreme Court, 1890-1976; Southern District.

S.D. L. Rev. South Dakota Law Review.

S.E. South Eastern Reporter.

S.E.2d South Eastern Reporter, Second Series.

S.F. San Francisco.

SIPA Securities Investor Protection Act of 1970.

S.L.T. Southern Law Times, Chattanooga, Tenn.

S. Tex. L.J. South Texas Law Journal.

S.W. South Western Reporter.

S.W.2d South Western Reporter, Second Series.

S.W.L.J. Southwestern Law Journal and Reporter, Nashville, 1844. See also, Sw. L.J.

Sadler Sadler, Penn.

Salk. Salkeld, King's Bench, Eng., 1689-1712.

San Fern. V. L. Rev. San Fernando Valley Law Review.

Sandars' Just. Sandars, Justinian.

Sandf. Sandford, New York City Superior Court, vols. 3-7, 1847-1852.

Sandf. Ch. Sandford, New York Court of Chancery, 1843-1847.

Saund. Saunders, King's Bench, Eng., 1666-1672.
Saund. & C. Saunders and Cole, Bail Court, Eng., 1846-1848.
Saus. & Sc. Sausse and Scully, Chancery, Ireland, 1835-1840.
Sav. Savile, Common Pleas, Eng., 1580-1594.
Saw. Sawyer, U.S. Courts, Ninth Circuit.
Sax. Ch. Saxton, New Jersey Court of Chancery, 1830-1832.
Say. Sayer, King's Bench, Eng., 1751-1756.
Sc. Scotch.
Sc. Jur. The Scottish Jurist, Court of Sessions, 1829-1873.
Sc. L.J. Scottish Law Journal, Glasgow, 1858-1861.
Sc. L.M. Scottish Law Magazine, Edinburg, 1862-1867.
Sc. L.R. Scottish Law Reporter.
Scam. Scammon, Illinois Supreme Court, vols. 2-5.
Sch. School.
Sch. & L. Schoaler and Lefroy, Chancery, Ireland, 1802,1809.
Sci. Science; Sciences; Scientific.
Sco. Scott, Common Pleas, Eng., 1834-1840.
Sco. (N.R.) Scott's New Reports, Common Pleas, Eng., 1840-1845, 1859-1860.
Scot. Scotland.
Scot. L. Rev. Scottish Law Review and Sheriff Court Reports.
Scots L.T. Scots Law Times.
Sec. Section; Securities.
Sel. Cas. Select Cases t. King; cases published anonymously under this title, Chancery, Eng., 1724-1733.
Seld. Selden, New York Court of Appeals, vols. 5-10.
Seld. Notes. Selden's Notes, N.Y.
Sen. Senator.
Ser. Series.
Serg. & R. Sergeant and Rawle, Pennsylvania Supreme Court, 1814-1828.
Serv. Service.
Ses. Cas. Sessions Cases, King's Bench, Eng., 1710-1846. See New Ses. Cas.
Ses. Cas. Sc. Court of Session Cases, Scotland.
Shaw Court of Session, Scotland, 1821-1838.
Shaw & D. Shaw and Dunlop, Court of Session, Scotland, 1800-1862.
Shaw & McL. Shaw and McLean, Scotch Appeals, House of Lords, 1835-1838.
Shaw, J. Justiciary Cases, Scotland, 1848-1852.
Shaw, P. Justiciary Cases, Scotland, 1819-1831.
Shaw, T. Court of Teinds, Scotland, 1821-1831.
Shaw App. Shaw's Scotch Appeals, House of Lords, 1821-1824.
Shep. (Me.) Shepley, Maine Supreme Court, vols. 13-30, 1836-1849.
Shep. Sel. Cas. Shepherd's Select Cases, Alabama Supreme Court, 1861-1863.
Shep. Touch. Sheppard's Touchstone.
Show. Shower, King's Bench, Eng., 1678-1694.
Show. P.C. Shower's Parliamentary Cases, Eng., 1694-1698.
Sid. Siderfin, King's Bench and Exchequer, Eng., 1657-1670.
Silv. Silvernail, N.Y. Supreme Court.
Sim. Simons, Chancery, Eng., 1826-1852.
Sim. (N.S.) Simons, Chancery, Eng., New Series, 1850-1852.
Sim. & St. Simons and Stuart, Chancery, Eng., 1822-1826.

Skin. Skinner, King's Bench, Eng., 1681-1697.

Sm. Eq. Manual Smith's (Jos. W.) Manual of Equity.

Sm. & G. Smale and Gifford, Chancery, Eng., 1852-1858.

Sm. & M. Smedes and Marshall, Mississippi High Court of Errors and Appeals, 1843-1850.

Sm. & M. (Ch.) Smedes and Marshall, Mississippi Superior Court of Chancery, 1840-1853.

Smith King's Bench and Chancery, Eng., 1803-1806.

Smith & B. Smith and Batty, King's Bench, Ireland, 1824-1825.

Smith, E.D. New York Common Pleas, 1850-1858.

Smith (Ind.) Indiana Supreme Court, 1848-1849.

Smith, L.C. Smith's Leading Cases (Hare and Wallace).

Smith (N.H.) Superior and Supreme Courts, New Hampshire, 1796-1816.

Smith (Pa.) Pennsylvania State Supreme Court, vols. 51-81.

Smythe Common Pleas and Exchequer, Ireland, 1839-1840.

Sneed (Ky.) Printed Decisions, Kentucky Court of Appeals, 1801-1805.

Sneed (Tenn.) Tennessee Supreme Court, 1853-1858.

So. Southern Reporter.

So.2d Southern Reporter, Second Series.

Soc. Social; Sociological; Sociology.

Soc'y Society.

Sol. Solicitor (nonstandard).

Sol. J. Solicitors' Journal (nonstandard).

Sol. J. & R. Solicitors' Journal and Reporter, London.

Solic. Solicitors; Solicitors'; Solicitor's

Sou. L.J. Southern Law Journal, Tuscaloosa, Ala., 1878-1879.

Sou. L.J. & R. Southern Law Journal and Reporter, Nashville, 1879-1882.

Sou. L.R. Southern Law Review, Nashville, 1872-1874.

Sou. L.R. (N.S.) Southern Law Review, New Series.

South. Southard, New Jersey Law, vols. 4 and 5, 1816-1820.

Speers South Carolina Court of Appeals, etc., at Law, 1842-1844.

Speers Eq. South Carolina Court of Appeals, etc., in Equity, 1842-1844.

Spenc. Spencer, New Jersey Law, vol. 20, 1842-1846.

Spinks Ecclesiastical and Admiralty, Eng., 1853-1855.

Spinks Pr. Cas. Spinks Prize Cases, Eng., 1854-1856.

Spot. Spottiswoode, Court of Session, Scotland.

Spr. Sprague (U.S.)

Sprague Admiralty Decisions, U.S. District Court, Massachusetts, 1841-1864.

St. Saint; State; Street.

St. Tr. State Trial, Eng., 1163-1820.

St. Tr. (N.S.) State Trial, New Series, Eng., 1820-1831.

Stair Court of Session, Scotland, 1661-1681.

Stan. L. Rev. Stanford Law Review.

Stark. Starkie, Nisi Prius, Eng., 1814-1822.

Starr & Curtis Starr and Curtis' Illinois Statutes.

Stat. United States Statutes at Large; Statute; Statutes.

Staunf. St. P.C. & Pr. Staunforde Pleas and Prerogative.

Stew. Stewart, Alabama Supreme Court, 1827-1831.

Stew. & P. Stewart and Porter, Alabama Supreme Court, 1831-1834.

Stew. Adm. Stewart, Vice-Admiralty Reports, Nova Scotia, 1803-1813.

Stew. (N.J.) Stewart, New Jersey Equity, vols. 28-45, 1877-1889.

Stiles Stiles (Iowa).

Stockt. Stockton, New Jersey Equity, vols. 9-11, 1853-1858.

Story U.S. Circuit Court, First Circuit, 1839-1845.

Stra. Strange, all courts, Eng., 1715-1747.

Strobh. Strobhart, South Carolina Court of Appeals, etc., at Law, 1843-1850.

Strobh. Eq. Strobhart, South Carolina Court of Appeals, etc., in Equity, 1846-1850.

Stu. Stuart, King's Bench, Lower Canada, 1810-1835.

Stu. Adm. Stuart, Vice-Admiralty Reports, Lower Canada, 1836-1874.

Stu., M. & P. Stuart, Milne and Peddie, Court of Session, etc., Scotland, 1851-1853.

Stud. Studies.

Sty. Style, King's Bench, Eng., 1645-1655.

Sumn. Sumner, U.S. Circuit Court, First Circuit, 1829-1839.

Sup. Ct. Supreme Court (state).

Sup. Jud. Ct. Supreme Judicial Court.

Super. Ct. Superior Court.

Supra. Above; Before.

Sur. Surety.

Sur. Ct. Surrogate's Court.

Sw. L.J. Southwestern Law Journal.

Swa. Adm. Swabey, Admiralty, Eng., 1855-1859.

Swa. & Tr. Swabey & Tristram, Probate and Divorce, Eng., 1858-1865.

Swan Tennessee Supreme Court, 1851-1853.

Swans. Swanston, Chancery, Eng., 1818-1819.

Sweeney New York City Superior Court, vols. 31 and 32, 1869-1870.

Swin. Swinton, Justiciary Court, Scotland, 1835-1841.

Swin. Reg. Swinton, Registration Appeals, Scotland, 1835-1843.

Syme Justiciary Court, Scotland, 1826-1829.

Symp. Symposium.

Sys. System.

T. Territory; Term; **t.** during the time of.

T.B. Mon. T.B. Monroe, Kentucky Court of Appeals, 1824-1828.

T. & M. Temple and Mew, Criminal Appeal, Eng., 1848-1851.

T.C. Tax Court of U.S. since 1942.

T.D. Treasury Decisions.

T.L.R. The Times Law Reports, London.

T.M. Trademark.

T.R. Term Reports (Durnford and East), King's Bench, Eng., 1785-1800.

Tam. Tamlyn, Rolls Court, Eng., 1829-1830.

Taney U.S. Circuit Court, Fourth Circuit, 1836-1861.

Tanner Tanner (Ind.).

Tapp. Tappan, Ohio Common Pleas, Fifth Circuit, 1816-1819.

Taunt. Taunton, Common Pleas, Eng., 1807-1819.

Tax. or **Tax'n** Taxation.

Taxes Taxes: The Tax Magazine.

Tayl. (N.C.) Taylor, North Carolina Superior Courts, 1798-1802.

Tayl. (N.C.T.R.) Taylor, North Carolina Term Reports, Supreme Court, 1816-1818.

Tayl. (U.C.) Taylor, King's Bench, Upper Canada, 1823-1827.

Tchrs. Teachers.

Tech. Technical; Technique; Technology.

Tel. Telegraph; Telephone.

Temp. L.Q. Temple Law Quarterly.

Tenn. Tennessee Reports, Supreme Court, 1791-1971. See also, Over., Cooke, Hayw., Peck, Mart. & Y., Yerg., Meigs, Humph., Swan, Sneed, Head, Cold., Baxt., Heisk., and Lea.

Tenn. App. Tennessee Appeals Reports, 1925-1971.

Tenn. Cas. Tennessee Cases (Shannon).

Tenn. Ch. Tennessee Chancery Reports, 1872-1878. See Coop.

Tenn. Crim. App. Tennessee Criminal Appeals Reports, 1967-1971.

Tenn. L. Rev. Tennessee Law Review.

Tex. Texas Reports, Supreme Court, 1846-1962. See also, Dall.

Tex. App. Texas Appeals Reports, 1873-1892.

Tex. Civ. App. Texas Civil Appeals Reports, 1892-1911.

Tex. Civ. Cas. Texas Court of Appeals Decisions, Civil Cases, 1876-1892.

Tex. Cr. R. or **Tex. Crim.** Texas Criminal Reports, 1876-1963. (**Cr. R.** nonstandard).

Tex. L.J. Texas Law Journal, Tyler, 1877-1882.

Tex. L.R. Texas Law Review, Austin, 1883-1886. Cf. **Tex. L. Rev.** Texas Law Review, University of Texas, School of Law, Austin.

Tex. Supp. Texas Supplement.

Tex. Tech L. Rev. Texas Tech Law Review.

Thac. Thacher, Criminal Cases, Boston Municipal Court, 1823-1843.

Thomp. & C. Thompson and Cook; New York Supreme Court, 1874-1875.

Thomp. Tenn. Cas. Thompson's Unreported Tennessee Cases.

Thoms. Thomson, Nova Scotia Decisions, 1834-1851; 1856-1859.

Tiffany Tiffany (N.Y.).

Tinw. Tinwald, Court of Session, Scotland.

Tit. Title.

Tol. Toledo.

Toth. Tothill, Chancery, Eng., 1559-1646.

Tr. Trust; Trusts.

Transnat'l Transnational.

Transp. Transport; Transportation.

Tread. Treadway, South Carolina Constitutional Court, 1810-1816.

Tuck. Tucker, New York Surrogate's Court, 1862-1869.

Tuck. S.C. Tucker's Select Cases, Newfoundland.

Tud. L.C. Tudor's Leading Cases.

Tul. L. Rev. Tulane Law Review.

Turn. Turner (Ark.).

Turn. & R. Turner and Russell, Chancery, Eng., 1822-1824.

Tyler Vermont Supreme Court, 1800-1803.

Tyng Tyng's Reports, Massachusetts Supreme Court, vols. 1-17, 1806-1822.

Tyr. Tyrwhitt, Exchequer, Eng., 1830-1835.

Tyr. & G. Tyrwhitt and Granger, Exchequer, Eng., 1835-1836.

U. University(ies).

U. Balt. L. Rev. University of Baltimore Law Review.

U.C. Upper Canada.

UCC or **U.C.C.** Uniform Commercial Code.

U.C.C.C. Uniform Consumer Credit Code.

U.C.(C.P.) Upper Canada, Common Pleas.

U.C.C. L.J. Uniform Commercial Code Law Journal.

UCCRS or **UCC Rep. Serv.** Uniform Commercial Code Reporting Service.

U.C.D.L.Rev. University of California-Davis Law Review.

U.C.E. & A. Upper Canada, Error and Appeals, 1846-1866.

U.C. Jur. Upper Canada Jurist, 1844-1848.

U.C.(K.B.) Upper Canada, King's Bench, 1823-1830.

U.C.L.A. Law Review University of California at Los Angeles Law Review.

U.C.L.J. Upper Canada, Law Journal, Toronto, 1855-1864. See Can. L.J.

U.C.M.J. Uniform Code of Military Justice.

U.C.(Q.B.) Upper Canada, Queen's Bench, 1832-1843.

U.C.(Q.B.N.S.) Upper Canada, Queen's Bench, New Series.

U. Chi. L. Rev. University of Chicago Law Review.

U. Cin. L. Rev. University of Cincinnati Law Review.

U. Colo. L. Rev. University of Colorado Law Review.

U. Det. J. Urb. L. University of Detroit Journal of Urban Law.

U. Det. L.J. University of Detroit Law Journal.

U. Fla. L. Rev. University of Florida Law Review.

U. Ill. L. F. University of Illinois Law Forum.

U. Kan. City L. Rev. University of Kansas City Law Review.

U. Kan. L. Rev. University of Kansas Law Review.

UMKC L. Rev. University of Missouri at Kansas City Law Review.

U. Mich. J.L.Ref. University of Michigan Journal of Law Reform.

U. Mo. Bull. L. Ser. University of Missouri Bulletin Law Series.

U.N. United Nations.

U.P.A. Uniform Partnership Act.

U.P.C. Uniform Probate Code.

U. Pa. L. Rev. University of Pennsylvania Law Review.

U. Pitt. L. Rev. University of Pittsburgh Law Review.

URESA Uniform Reciprocal Enforcement of Support Act.

U. Rich. L. Rev. University of Richmond Law Review.

U. Tol. L. Rev. University of Toledo Law Review.

U. West L.A. L. Rev. University of West Los Angeles Law Review.

U.S. United States; United States Reports, since 1790. See also, Dal., Cranch., Wheat., Pet., How., Black., Wal., and Otto.

U.S. App. D.C. United States Court of Appeals Reports, District of Columbia, since 1941.

U.S.C. United States Code.

U.S.C.A. United States Code Annotated.

U.S.C.C. United States Circuit Court.

U.S.C.C.A. United States Circuit Court of Appeals.

U.S.C.M.A. United States Court of Military Appeals Reports (nonstandard).

U.S.C.S. United States Code Service.

U.S.D.C. United States District Court (nonstandard).

U.S.F. L. Rev. University of San Francisco Law Review.

U.S. Jur. United States Jurist, Washington, 1871-1873.

U.S.L.J. United States Law Journal, New York and New Haven, 1822-1826.

U.S.L. Mag. United States Law Magazine, New York, 1850-1852.

U.S.L. Rev. United States Law Review.

U.S.L.W. United States Law Week, since 1933.

U.S.P.Q. United States Patent Quarterly.

U.S.R.S. United States Revised Statutes.

Univ. University (nonstandard).

Urb. Urban.

Utah Utah Reports, Supreme Court, 1855-1974.

Util. Utilities; Utility.

v. Versus; Volume.

V.C. Vice-Chancellor.

V.I. Virgin Island Reports, since 1917.

V.P. Vice-President.

Va. Virginia Reports, Supreme Court and Supreme Court of Appeals, since 1790. See also, Jeff., Wash., Call, Hen. & M., Hunf., Gilm., Ran., Leigh, Rob., Gratt.

Va. Cas. Virginia Cases, General Court, 1789-1826.

Va. J. Int'l L. Virginia Journal of International Law.

Va. L.J. Virginia Law Journal, Richmond.

Va. L. Reg. (n.s.) Virginia Law Register, New Series.

Va. L. Rev. Virginia Law Review.

Val. U. L. Rev. Valparaiso University Law Review.

Van Ness Prize Cases, U.S. District Court, New York, 1814.

Vand. L. Rev. Vanderbilt Law Review.

Vaugh. Vaughan, Common Pleas, Eng., 1666-1674.

Vent. Ventris, King's Bench, Eng., 1668-1691.

Vern. Vernon, Chancery, Eng., 1680-1719.

Vern. & S. Vernon and Scriven, King's Bench, Ireland, 1786-1788.

Ves. Vesey, Chancery, Eng., 1746-1755.

Ves. Jr. Vesey, Jr., Chancery, Eng., 1789-1817.

Ves. & B. Vesey and Beames, Chancery, Eng., 1812-1814.

Ves. Sr. See Ves.

Vict. Victoria.

Vill. L. Rev. Villanova Law Review.

Vin. Abr. Viner's Abridgment, English Law.

Vroom New Jersey Law, vol. 30-85.

Vt. Vermont Reports, Supreme Court, since 1826. See also, Chip., N., Chip., D., Tyler, Brayt., and Aik.

W. West; Western; Wright (Ohio) (nonstandard).

W. & S. Wilson and Shaw, Scotch Appeals, House of Lords, 1825-1834.

W. & T. White and Tudor's Leading Cases, Equity.

W. Bl. Sir Wm. Blackstone, various courts, Eng., 1746-1779.

W.C.R. West Coast Reporter, San Francisco.

W.D. Western District.

W., H. & G. Welsby, Hurlstone and Gordon, Exchequer, 1847-1856.

W.L.B. Weekly Law Bulletin, Cincinnati.

W.L.G. Weekly Law Gazette, Cincinnati, 1857-1860.

W.L.J. Western Law Journal, Cincinnati, 1843-1853.

W.L.M. Western Law Monthly, Cleveland, 1859-1863.

W.N. Weekly Notes, all courts, Eng.

W.N. Cas. Weekly Notes of Cases, all courts, Pennsylvania, Philadelphia.

W.P.C. Wollaston's Practice Cases, all courts, Eng., 1840-1841.

W.R. Weekly Reporter, all courts, Eng.

W. Res. L. Rev. Western Reserve Law Review.

W. Va. West Virginia Reports, Supreme Court of Appeals, 1863-1973.

W. Va. L. Rev. West Virginia Law Review.

W., W. & D. Willmore, Wollaston and Davison, Queen's Bench, Eng., 1837.

W., W. & H. Willmore, Wollaston and Hodges, Queen's Bench, Eng., 1838-1839.

Wal. See Wall.

Wal. C.C. Wallace, U.S. Circuit Court, Third Circuit, 1801.

Wal., Jr. Wallace, Jr., U.S. Circuit Court, Third Circuit, 1842-1862.

Walk. Ch. Walker, Michigan Court of Chancery, 1842-1845.

Walk. (Miss.) Walker, Supreme Court of Mississippi, 1818-1832.

Walk. (Pa.) Walker, Pennsylvania Supreme Court, cases omitted from regular reports, 1853-1884.

Wall. Wallace, U.S. Supreme Court, vols. 68-90, 1863-1874.

Wallis Chancery, Ireland, 1766-1791.

Ware U.S. District Court, Maine, 1822-1866. Includes Daveis.

Wash. Washington; Washington Reports, Supreme Court, since 1889.

Wash. App. Washington Appellate Reports, since 1969.

Wash. C.C. Washington, U.S. Circuit Court, Third Circuit, 1803-1827.

Wash. (Va.) Washington, Virginia Court of Appeals, 1790-1796.

Wash. & Lee L. Rev. Washington and Lee Law Review.

Wash. L. Rev. Washington Law Review, Seattle.

Wash. Terr. Washington Territory Reports, 1854-1888.

Wash. U. L.Q. Washington University Law Quarterly, St. Louis.

Watts Pennsylvania Supreme Court, 1832-1840.

Watts & S. Watts and Sergeant, Pennsylvania Supreme Court, 1841-1845.

Web. P.C. Webster's Patent Cases, Eng., 1601-1855.

Welsh Registry Cases, Ireland, 1832-1840.

Wend. Wendell, New York Supreme Court and Court of Errors, 1828-1841.

Went. Off. Exor. Wentworth's Office of Executor.

West House of Lords, Eng., 1839-1841.

West t. H. West's Reports, time of Hardwicke Chancery, 1736-1739.

West. Jur. Western Jurist, Des Moines, 1867-1883.

Western Res. L. Rev. Western Reserve Law Review (nonstandard).

Whart. Wharton, Pennsylvania Supreme Court, 1835-1841.

Whart. St. Tr. Wharton's State Trials, U.S.

Wheat. Wheaton, U.S. Supreme Court, vols. 14-25, 1816-1827.

Wheel. C.C. Wheeler's Criminal Cases, New York Courts, 1791-1824.

Whit. Pat. Cas. Whitman, Patent Cases, U.S., 1810-1874.

White Justiciary Cases, Scotland, 1885-1888.

Wight. Wightwick, Exchequer, Eng., 1810-1811.

Willes Various courts, Eng., 1737-1758.

Williams Williams (Vt.).

Wilm. Wilmot's Notes and Opinions, King's Bench, Eng., 1757-1770.

Wils. Wilson, King's Bench and Common Pleas, Eng., 1742-1774.

Wils. & S. Wilson and Shaw, Scotch Appeals, House of Lords, 1825-1834.

Wils. Ch. Wilson, Chancery, Eng., 1818-1819.

Wils. Ex. Wilson, Exchequer, Eng., 1805-1817.

Wils. Super. or **Sup. Ct.** Wilson, Superior Court of Marion County, Indiana, 1871-1874.

Winch Common Pleas, Eng., 1622-1625.

Winst. Winston, North Carolina Supreme Court at Law, 1863-1864.

Winst. Eq. Winston, North Carolina Supreme Court, in Equity, 1863-1864.

Wis. Wisconsin; Wisconsin Reports, Supreme Court, since 1853; Court of Appeals since 1978. See Burn., Chand., and Pinn.

Wis. L.N. Wisconsin Legal News, Milwaukee, 1878-1882.

Wis. L. Rev. Wisconsin Law Review.

Withr. Withrow (Iowa).

Wm. & Mary L. Rev. William & Mary Law Review.

Wm. Mitchell L. Rev. William Mitchell Law Review.

Wms. Peere Williams, Chancery, Eng., 1695-1735.

Wms. (Mass.) Williams, Massachusetts Supreme Court, vol. 1, 1804-1805.

Wol. Pr. Wollaston, Practice Cases, Eng., 1840-1841.

Wolf. & B. Wolferstan and Bristowe, Election Cases, Eng., 1859-1864.

Wolf. & D. Wolferstan and Dew, Election Cases, Eng., 1857-1858.

Wood T. Cas. Wood, Tithe Cases, Eng., 1650-1798.

Wood. & M. Woodbury and Minot, U.S. Circuit Court, First Circuit, 1845-1847.

Woods U.S. Circuit Court, Fifth Circuit, 1867-1883.

Woodw. Dec. Woodward's Decisions (Pa.).

Woolw. Woolworth, U.S. Circuit Court, Eighth Circuit, 1863-1869.

Wright Ohio Supreme Court, 1831-1834, 1 vol.

Wright (Pa.) Pennsylvania State Supreme Court, vols. 37-50.

Wyo. Wyoming Reports, Supreme Court, 1870-1959.

Wyo. L.J. Wyoming Law Journal.

Wythe Virginia High Court of Chancery, 1788-1799.

Y. & C. Younge and Collyer, Exchequer, Eng., 1834-1840.

Y. & C. Ch. Younge and Collyer, New Chancery Cases, Eng., 1841-1843.

Y. & J. Younge and Jervis, Exchequer, Eng., 1826-1830.

Y.B. Yearbook; Year Books, King's Bench, Eng., 1307-1537.

Y.B. Ed. I. Year Books, King's Bench, Eng., during reign of Edward I., 1272-1307.

Yates Select Cases, New York Courts, 1811.

Yeates Pennsylvania, various courts, 1791-1808.

Yel. Yelverton, King's Bench, Eng., 1602-1612.

Yerg. Yerger, Tennessee Supreme Court, 1818-1837.

You. Younge Reports, Exchequer.

Young Admiralty Decisions, Nova Scotia, 1865-1880.

Younge Exchequer, Equity, Eng., 1830-1832.

Zab. Zabriskie, New Jersey Law, vols. 21-24, 1845-1855.

INDEX

References are to page numbers. Entries in italic type are titles of books or periodicals.